WATERPROOF BOOKS™

Miracle-Gro

Container Gardens

Simple steps for creating easy-care gardens

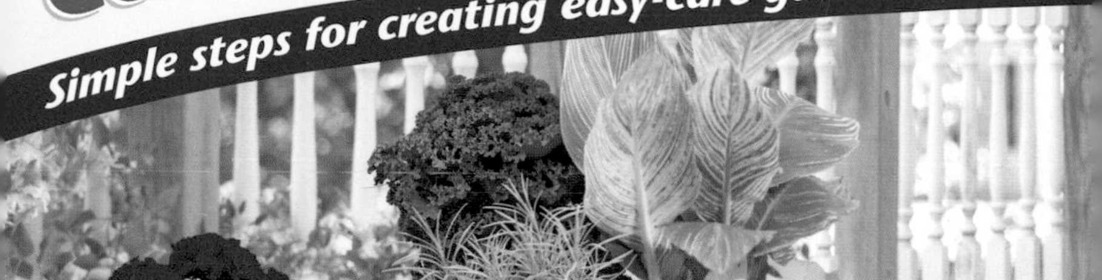

SELECT

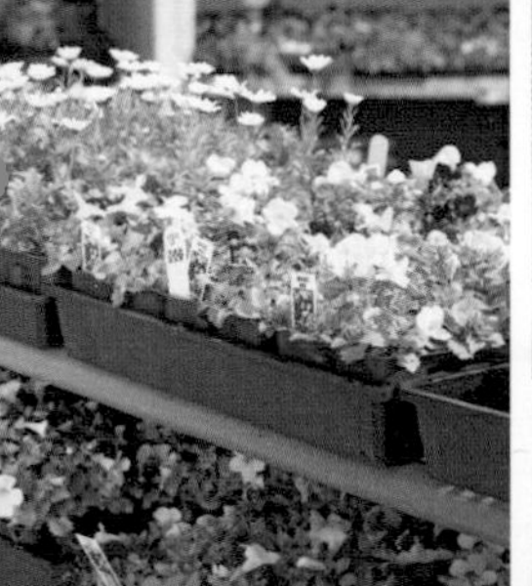

PLANT

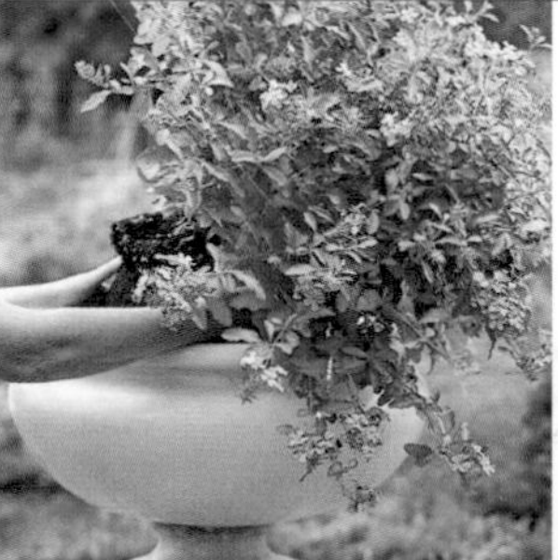

CARE

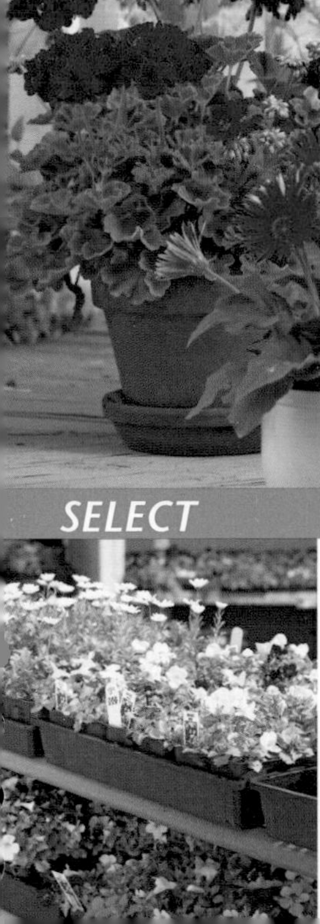

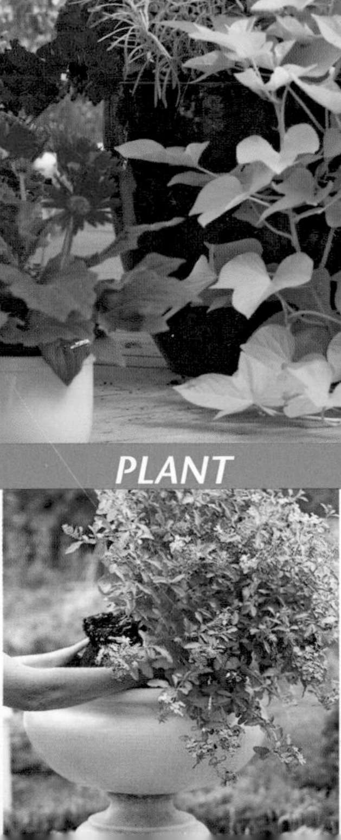

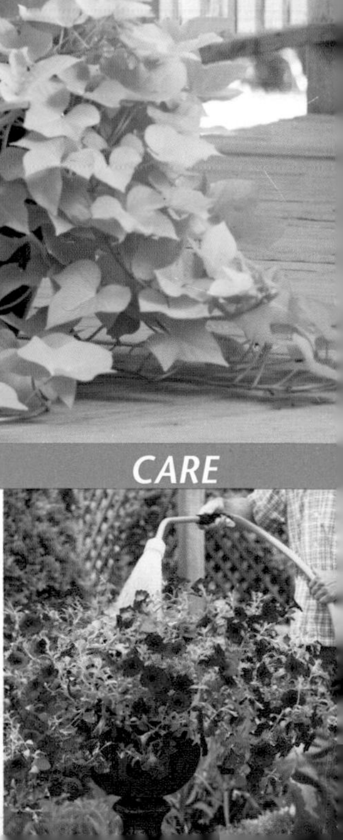

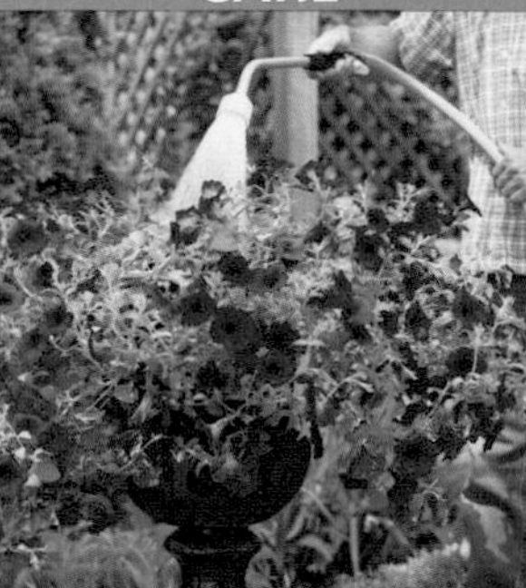

Miracle-Gro®
Container Gardens
Simple steps for creating easy-care gardens
Table of Contents

Meredith® Books
Des Moines, Iowa

Miracle-Gro® Container Gardens
Editor: Marilyn Rogers
Contributing Writer: Megan McConnell Hughes
Contributing Designer: Studio G Design
Copy Chief: Terri Fredrickson
Publishing Operations Manager: Karen Schirm
Senior Editor, Asset & Information Management: Phillip Morgan
Edit and Design Production Coordinator: Mary Lee Gavin
Editorial Assistant: Kathleen Stevens
Book Production Managers: Pam Kvitne, Marjorie J. Schenkelberg, Rick von Holdt, Mark Weaver
Contributing Copy Editor: Linda Armstrong
Contributing Proofreaders: Pegi Bevins, Susan Brown, Terri Krueger
Contributing Illustrator: Lori Gould
Contributing Indexer: Kathleen Poole
Contributing Photo Researcher: Susan K. Ferguson
Contributing Inputter: Janet Anderson

Meredith® Books
Executive Director, Editorial: Gregory H. Kayko
Executive Director, Design: Matt Strelecki
Managing Editor: Amy Tincher-Durik
Executive Editor: Benjamin W. Allen
Senior Editor/Group Manager: Michael McKinley
Senior Associate Design Director: Ken Carlson
Marketing Product Manager: Brent Wiersma

Publisher and Editor in Chief: James D. Blume
Editorial Director: Linda Raglan Cunningham
Executive Director, Marketing: Steve Malone
Executive Director, New Business Development: Todd M. Davis
Executive Director, Sales: Ken Zagor
Director, Operations: George A. Susral
Director, Production: Douglas M. Johnston
Director, Marketing: Amy Nichols
Business Director: Jim Leonard

Vice President and General Manager: Douglas J. Guendel

Meredith Publishing Group
President: Jack Griffin
Senior Vice President: Karla Jeffries

Meredith Corporation
Chairman: William T. Kerr
President and Chief Executive Officer: Stephen M. Lacy

In Memoriam: E.T. Meredith III (1933–2003)

Library of Congress Control Number: 2006930015
ISBN-13: 978-0-696-23203-9

If you would like more information on other Miracle-Gro products, call 800/225-2883 or visit us at: www.miraclegro.com

All of us at Meredith® Books are dedicated to providing you with information and ideas to enhance your home and garden. We welcome your comments and suggestions. Write to us at: Meredith Books, Garden Editorial Department, 1716 Locust St., Des Moines, IA 50309-3023.

Color your world

Containers are the ultimate garden accessory. Brimming with color from spring until frost, their flowers and fragrances enliven your outdoor oasis. Tuck in a few plants favored by birds and butterflies and you will enjoy the antics of these creatures from your patio. Or pack a large pot with your favorite summer veggies and enjoy an easy-care garden buffet right outside your door. Quick and inexpensive to create, containers are a cinch to customize to your outdoor decor and require just a few minutes of care a day to look their best. You'll find step-by-step instructions, inspirational container plantings, and a roundup of the best plants for containers on the following pages. Happy planting!

HOW TO USE THIS BOOK

You'll find the fundamentals of container gardening—from selecting a pot to fertilizing—in Container Basics, the first section of this book. Following on page 21 are ideas for creating themed containers complete with planting pointers and care tips. Turn to Recipes for Success on page 45 for easy-to-follow instructions for planting 21 containers. Finally explore the best plants for containers in the Plant Gallery beginning on page 67.

Informative plant lists throughout the book highlight the best plants for unique containers and gardening situations.

Gather great planting ideas from color-rich photos!

Step-by-step instructions show you how to design, plant, and care for your containers.

In the Container Gardens section, beginning on page 21, you'll find many inspiring photos, along with tips and techniques for creating specific types of containers ranging from windowboxes to hanging baskets.

Container Basics

Container Considerations

With a little ingenuity, you can turn almost anything into a home for a potted garden. If a vessel will hold soil and allow water to freely drain through, it will make an excellent container. In addition to the containers available at garden centers, many found treasures make nifty planting pots. Take a look around your garage or garden shed. Give a leaky watering can or a holey work boot a new lease on life by planting it with your favorite blossoms. The following guidelines will help you select the right container for your needs, whether you're buying or finding.

1

Good drainage

Waterlogged soil is a surefire way to kill a container garden. Having enough drainage holes in the bottom of the container and using good potting soil are key to avoiding problems. Although most containers sold at garden centers have at least one drainage hole, large pots may need more.

Be prepared to add drainage holes to any container. It is best to err on the side of too much drainage than too little. ❶ Drill one ½-inch-diameter hole per square foot of surface area in the bottom of the container. (Use a masonry bit if drilling into terra-cotta.)

Also test any found object you hope to use as a container before you plant it. Fill the object with water. If the water runs through freely, the object should be OK to use. Otherwise drill several holes in it.

Size and portability

Plants have the amazing ability to adapt to a multitude of growing conditions—small growing spaces being one of them. However, most perform better if their roots have adequate room. Most annual and vegetable plants thrive in containers that are 10 to 12 inches deep and at least as wide. Perennials and woody plants require even more space.

Container size becomes an important issue

if you plan to move them from place to place. If you want to move your containers around your yard, choose small pots or ones made of lightweight material, such as plastic or fiberglass. You can also place your containers on a wheeled saucer or use a dolly to cart them around. If you opt for small containers, group several together for a more impressive display.

Materials

Terra-cotta, wood, and ceramic are popular container materials. Advances in technology have made it hard to distinguish a plastic or fiberglass pot from a classic concrete or terra-cotta creation. Container construction material not only affects the look of the pot, but also influences the weight, ability to withstand weather extremes, and cost. See the table below for comparison. Don't forget to consider unique objects as potential plant pots. A leaky bucket makes a fun and inexpensive planting container when you provide adequate drainage.

Container Material	Cost	Weight	Sunproof	Winterproof
Terra-cotta and ceramic	Low to moderate	Moderate	Yes	No
Wood	Low to moderate	Moderate to heavy	Yes	Yes
Concrete	Low to high	Heavy	Yes	Often but not always
Plastic, fiberglass, foam	Low to moderate	Light	No, unless specifically treated by the manufacturer	No, unless specifically treated by the manufacturer
Metal	Low	Light to moderate	Yes	Yes

Selecting Plants

A springtime trip to your local greenhouse can be invigorating and overwhelming at the same time. The riot of color is likely to send you into a buying frenzy, as well as present a creative quandary for even the most advanced gardeners. Follow these tips and you'll come away with the perfect ingredients for an attractive container garden.

Good planting partners

In general, all plants will grow in a container as long as you meet their growing needs. Plants have specific water and sunlight requirements that must be fulfilled in order for them to thrive. For example, hosta needs a shaded location and regular watering. If grown in sun and rarely watered, it will languish and eventually die. Conversely many plants grow with abandon in hot, sunny locations.

In order for a container garden of mixed plants to remain lush and beautiful all summer, all of the plants must have similar growing requirements. Before visiting the greenhouse, assess the light conditions where you will place your containers. Pair shade-loving plants with other shade-lovers. Group plants together that thrive with little moisture and so on. Learn about a plant's preferred growing conditions on the plant tag that accompanies it.

Once you know which plants will work together, you can start planning good-looking combinations.

COLOR Combine your favorite colors with abandon in mixed plantings. If the combination is pleasing to you, then it is perfect. A few design techniques, however, will help you get more from your container garden.

First let color set the tone. For a bold, attention-grabbing planting, call on warm hues such as red, yellow, and orange. To create a serene environment, choose plants with foliage and flowers in cool colors of blue, green, or purple. Next think about how close you'll usually be when viewing the container garden. Warm colors shine from a distance. Cool colors have more impact up close.

TEXTURE Texture adds interest to a planting. A plant's foliage and the shape and size of its flowers contribute to the texture of a plant. Combine several textures in a container for a natural look. Foliage plants offer contrast with flowering plants, and ornamental grasses and trailing plants, such as ivy, also lend a texture boost.

PROPORTION Finally proportion determines whether a container garden looks balanced. ❶ As a general rule, the plant portion of a container garden should be twice the height of the container. Plants grow, so this relationship will change; base your selection on the size of the plants at maturity. You'll find this information on the plant tag.

Annuals: What to Buy

Healthy plants hit the garden running. Follow these tips for selecting ready-to-go plants.

1. KEEP AN EYE OUT FOR DISEASE. If you spot a sickly plant in a cell pack, as on the lower leaves of this flower, don't buy any seedlings from that flat, lest you take the disease home. If your choice is limited, choose packs located as far from the diseased plant as possible.

2. LOOK FOR HEALTHY ROOTS. Slip seedlings out of their cells to examine roots. A large mass of roots with little soil is a sign that the seedlings have been in their cell packs too long. Look for a balance between the amount of healthy, white roots and the amount of soil.

3. CHOOSE SHORT AND STOCKY. Leave behind stretched out leggy, plants, such as these celosia. Tall seedlings have most likely been in cell packs too long. If stems are stocky and have healthy foliage from top to bottom, they're a safer bet.

Potting Mixes

The best soil for your containers is a commercial growing mix that contains no native soil. Soil from your garden—even the best topsoil—does not work in containers. It compacts too readily and is too dense and heavy for optimum growth in the limited confines of a container. Generic garden soil can also be contaminated with weed seeds and disease-producing organisms. For the greatest success, look for potting mix with the following qualities.

ABILITY TO ABSORB WATER AND DRAIN FREELY Potting soil needs to be porous so that water readily flows into and out of them and so that they don't pack down tightly. Potting soils also need the ability to hold moisture and nutrients. While you don't want the soil to be waterlogged, it does need to hold enough water to keep roots from drying out. Ingredients such as sphagnum peat moss, coir pith (processed coconut husk), and composted pine bark add porosity as well as water- and nutrient-holding ability. Perlite, the white particles in a potting soil, aids in drainage.

APPROPRIATE DENSITY For most container gardening, light- and medium-weight mixes are best because they have high porosity, are easy to handle, yet are rigid enough to anchor roots. They are also usually heavy enough to prevent pots from being knocked over. You won't find the density of the potting mix listed on the label, but it will be apparent when you feel the soil. Use light- to medium-weight mixes in hanging baskets and window boxes, where weight is an important concern. These mixes are also preferred for container gardens of succulent plants. Heavier mixes help to anchor tall plants, which are apt to topple over in wind. However, they may be too dense for good growth; placing a brick in the bottom of the container to add weight is a better solution.

GOOD WETABILITY Organic materials often contain naturally occurring oils and waxes, which can cause them to shed water and be difficult to rewet when they dry out. Good potting mixes will include a wetting agent that prevents this problem and increases the ability of the mix to absorb water quickly. Some potting soils, such as Miracle-Gro Moisture Control Potting Mix, also have special components that allow them to absorb excess water and then release it to the plant as needed. Moisture

Control Potting Mix is especially useful for containers that are regularly located in hot, windy spots or if you often forget to water.

SUFFICIENT NUTRIENTS Container plants rely on supplemental nutrients to produce their summer-long flower and foliage show. Good potting mixes include a wide array of fertilizers (as many as five kinds in one mix) that combine controlled-release pellets with fast-acting, water-soluble nutrients to promote optimum growth. All Miracle-Gro potting mixes contain these two types of growth-promoting nutrients. Avoid potting mixes that contain few or no nutrients; fertilizers must be mixed into these soils before planting. The potting mix packaging is your source of information for quantity and quality of nutrients.

ABSENCE OF WEED SEEDS, INSECTS, AND DISEASE ORGANISMS The sphagnum peat moss, coir pith, and perlite used in the best potting mixes are inherently low in contaminants. If compost is included, it should be processed by the manufacturer to kill weed seeds, insects, and disease organisms without killing beneficial fungi and bacteria.

Pots, Planters, Hanging Baskets	Bag Size
8"	8 qt.–10 qt.
12"	16 qt.
16"	1 cu. ft–32 qt.
20"	2 cu. ft.
24"	2.5 cu. ft.–55 qt.
Flower Boxes	**Bag Size**
24×6×6"	16 qt.
36×6×6"	1 cu. ft–32 qt.

Planting

You can plant a container garden at any time, but in early spring when a frost or freeze is possible, be prepared to shelter tender plants from the elements. Begin your garden by collecting plants, potting mix, and containers. If the container is lightweight, you can work on a potting bench or table. Or plant in place if the container will be too heavy to move when filled. Proceed with these simple step-by-step potting instructions.

1

1 MOISTEN POTTING MIX. Open the bag of potting mix; if it is dry, pour in warm water, fold over the bag, and knead the mix. Allow it to absorb the water, which can take up to an hour. The goal is to create a moist, but not soggy, mix that clumps together so that it is easy to plant in. If you need to moisten a large batch of soil, pour the mix onto a tarpaulin or into a wheelbarrow then add water.

2

2 COVER DRAINAGE HOLES. You may have heard that you should place broken pot shards or gravel in the bottom of a pot to aid drainage and prevent soil from leaking out. Research has proven that this practice is actually detrimental to plants; it slows drainage instead of improving it. If a container's drainage holes are large, laying pieces of old window screen over them will prevent soil from spilling out without harm.

3

3 PARTIALLY FILL THE CONTAINER WITH SOIL. Fill the container half full of potting mix if you are planting larger plants, or to within a few inches of the rim if plants are small. Set the potted plants into the container to get an idea of how your planned arrangement will look.

4 UNPOT PLANTS. Pop small plants out of their plastic cell packs or pots by pushing on the bottom of the pot while supporting the

plant and covering the soil surface with the fingers of your other hand. To remove a plant from a large pot, lay the pot on its side and push firmly against one side. Repeat on the other side, then turn the pot upside down and try to slide the root ball out of the pot. If it resists, use utility shears to cut off the bottom of the pot and free the roots.

You may find that the roots are tightly wound around the soil. Gently loosen them with your fingers, or use a knife to make shallow vertical slices through the root ball in two or three places.

5 PLANT. Set large plants on the layer of potting mix in your containers. Check that the tops of their root balls sit 1 to 3 inches below the rim of the pot. Pour potting mix around their roots, tamping it gently to fill all empty spaces. Make sure you don't plant too deep. The final tamped-down potting mix should be level with the top of the root ball.

Next add smaller plants. The tops of their roots should sit about 2 inches from the tops of the containers. Scoop out a hole in the mix for each root ball. Tuck in each plant and gently pat down the mix around it.

Always be sure to allow 1 to 2 inches at the top of the container to create a reservoir for watering. Fill the pot to the rim loosely with potting soil, and after the initial watering the soil will settle to about 2 inches below the rim.

6 WATER WELL. When you are finished planting, water with a slow, gentle spray. Fill pots to the top, letting the water sink in until it flows from the drainage holes. Add more soil if necessary and water again.

Unless the containers are too heavy to move, place them in a shady area out of the wind. Water lightly whenever the surface feels dry. Move the pots to their final location in a couple of days, after plants have recovered from the initial shock of transplanting.

Container Care: Watering

You'll be surprised how fast the soil in a container dries out—especially on warm and windy days. So plan on dedicating a few minutes a day to watering your container garden. Plants will reward regular, deep watering with healthy foliage and abundant blooms.

1

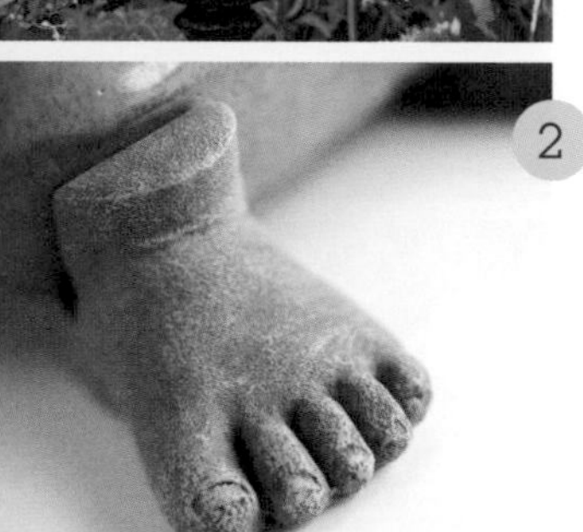

2

3

When to water

Some plants, such as succulents, prefer a semidry soil; others, such as impatiens, wilt even when soil is still slightly moist. The best way to tell whether your pots need water is to poke your finger into the soil and feel it. If it feels dry to the touch about 1 inch below the surface, it's time to water. Water succulents when the soil about 2 inches below the surface is dry. You may need to check small containers or containers in hot, sunny, or windy spots two or three times a day. Large pots or containers in shady conditions will need water less often.

Water in the morning when less water is lost to evaporation and the sun quickly dries leaves, preventing disease problems.

How much to water

Your container has received enough moisture when water freely drains out the bottom. Fill the container to the rim and allow the water to soak into the soil and flow out the drainage holes. If no water drains within a few minutes, fill the pot with water again.

Try to water regularly, because all soilless mixes are difficult to rewet once they have dried out. Should your container get too dry, the soil will pull away from the sides of the pot. Water will run off immediately without being absorbed, fooling you into thinking that your potting mix has been moistened when in fact it is swiftly shedding water.

To solve the problem, soak the pot for one hour in a large container filled with water. If it is impractical to move the pot, plug the drainage holes with corks or strips of duct tape. Then fill the container to the brim and let the soil soak up the moisture. Repeat. After water is absorbed, remove the plugs.

Watering tools

❶ Watering cans and water wands with hoses are some of the most popular container watering tools. Since they are not automatic, they ensure you see and touch your plants daily to make certain they have adequate water. Another benefit is you'll often catch pest or culture problems early while there is plenty of time to remedy the situation.

❷ To protect decks, patios, or other surfaces under your pots from stains or mildew, set the container on pot feet. These small risers lift pots off the ground, allowing air to freely circulate underneath and preventing water spots.

Several innovations can take the daily chore out of watering. ❸ Self-watering containers have built-in reservoirs. Capillary action draws the moisture from the reservoir into the soil above. Some self-watering containers reduce watering chores to once a month.

❹ Finally, drip irrigation completely eliminates the daily chore of hand-watering your container garden. Drip systems are ideal for forgetful gardeners or for those interested in saving time and labor, especially if you combine them on an automatic timer. ❺ A system of thin, flexible tubes carries water to plants according to a schedule set on the timer. Installing drip irrigation in your containers is much easier than it looks, thanks to kits and specialized parts. A bit of planning and an afternoon of installation will give you months of freedom from watering chores.

While you are away

Remember your potted plants when you plan your summer vacation. To help them survive while you're away, move them to a place protected from direct sun and wind. Water the plants thoroughly before you leave.

If you will be gone for more than a week, set the pots on top of bricks or stones inside large saucers or tubs. Pour 2 inches of water into this reservoir, or until the water reaches the bottoms of the pots. If you have only a few containers, ask a neighbor to check them and water as necessary.

Container Care: Feeding

Container gardens rely on you for all of their nutritional needs. Confined to the limited space of the pot, the plants will quickly become stressed if their need for nutrients is not met. Regular feedings assure the best blooms and healthiest foliage in your container garden.

All plants need essential nutrients such as nitrogen, phosphorus, and potassium to thrive, but container plants have special needs. Potting soil is relatively infertile, and with each watering nutrients leach out of the container. For that reason container plants need frequent feedings.

Using a high-quality potting mix that contains plant food to get plants off to a quick, healthy start is a great way to begin feeding your container plants. Miracle-Gro Moisture Control Potting Mix, Miracle-Gro Potting Mix, and Miracle-Gro Organic Choice Potting Mix all contain a continuous-release plant food. If your potting mix does not include plant food, give it a boost before planting by incorporating a continuous-release product, such as Osmocote, which will feed plants continuously for up to four months.

Feed as you water

Supplement the nutrients in the potting soil with a weekly dose of quick-release plant food to meet your plants' immediate needs. ❶ Mix a water-soluble plant food such as Miracle-Gro Water Soluble All Purpose Plant Food in a watering can according to package directions, then water as usual.

❷ If you are caring for a lot of container plants, Miracle-Gro LiquaFeed Ready-To-Use Plant Feeding system makes quick work of the chore. Simply attach the feeder to a garden hose and apply. Feed a 12- to 14-inch-diameter container by spraying it with the balanced plant food solution for about 15 seconds.

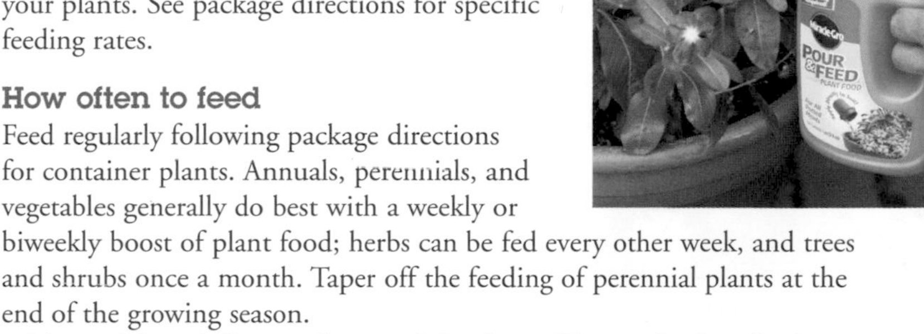

It is not necessary to feed plants only when you water; it is merely convenient. ❸ Feed your plants anytime with Miracle-Gro Pour & Feed Liquid Plant Food. Simply apply this pre-mixed solution to the soil surrounding your plants. See package directions for specific feeding rates.

How often to feed

Feed regularly following package directions for container plants. Annuals, perennials, and vegetables generally do best with a weekly or biweekly boost of plant food; herbs can be fed every other week, and trees and shrubs once a month. Taper off the feeding of perennial plants at the end of the growing season.

It's possible to kill your plants with kindness. Too much plant food will cause stunted growth and edges of leaves to curl and turn yellow or brown. Excessive plant food applications are also harmful to the environment. Always follow label directions for amount and frequency of plant food applications.

Feed Smart

- Use a potting mix that contains plant food.
- Supplement the potting mix with an application of water-soluble plant food, such as Miracle-Gro Water Soluble All Purpose Plant Food, on a regular basis as per package directions.
- Always follow package directions when applying plant food.

Container Care: Quick Tips for Good Looks

It's the details that count in a container garden—healthy foliage, fresh flowers, and an attractive soil surface. A few minutes a day is all that's needed to keep your container gardens looking nursery-fresh. Follow these swift, easy maintenance steps.

❶ DEADHEAD. Remove flowers as soon as they begin to wilt or fade. Your fingers are good tools for pinching off blossoms past their prime; shears work well too.

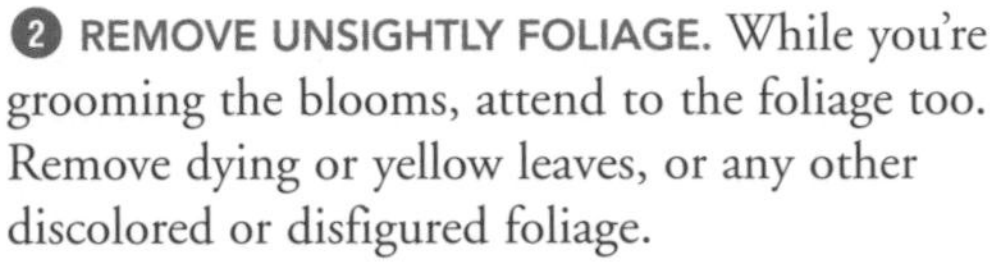

❷ REMOVE UNSIGHTLY FOLIAGE. While you're grooming the blooms, attend to the foliage too. Remove dying or yellow leaves, or any other discolored or disfigured foliage.

❸ PINCH FOR COMPACT GROWTH. Prevent the lax and leggy look by pinching off the growing tip and first pair or two of leaves on each plant stem. This will encourage new side shoots to sprout, forming a denser plant.

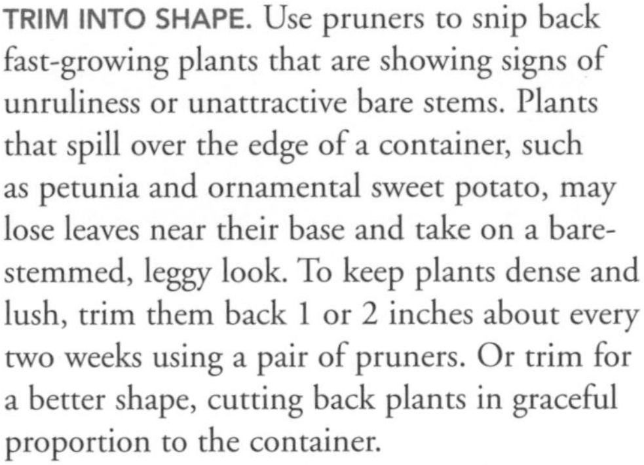

TRIM INTO SHAPE. Use pruners to snip back fast-growing plants that are showing signs of unruliness or unattractive bare stems. Plants that spill over the edge of a container, such as petunia and ornamental sweet potato, may lose leaves near their base and take on a bare-stemmed, leggy look. To keep plants dense and lush, trim them back 1 or 2 inches about every two weeks using a pair of pruners. Or trim for a better shape, cutting back plants in graceful proportion to the container.

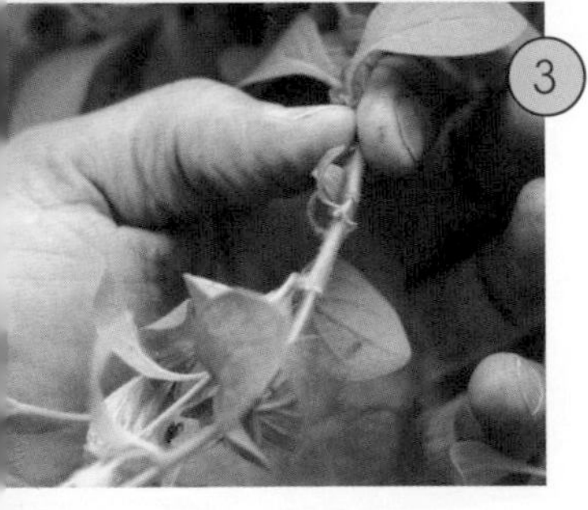

PRUNE WOODY PLANTS. Keep woody plants such as roses, shrubs, and trees in shape with selective pruning. Remove errant branches and dead wood. Thin fruit trees or flowering shrubs for better bud production.

4 SLIP IN SUBSTITUTES. When flowering plants are past their peak, or when you just want a change, use a hand trowel to lift out the tired plant and insert a replacement for a fresh, new look.

REPOT. The roots of shrubs and trees can soon become overcrowded in a container, so that the plants are frequently water stressed. When you notice that a plant needs frequent watering, move it to a bigger pot or trim the roots to keep the plant producing attractive foliage, flowers, or fruit. If you don't want to use a large pot, rein in the plant by pruning the roots to keep the top growth and roots in balance. Remove the plant from the pot, then using pruners or a knife, slice off an inch or two of roots from the bottom and sides of the root ball. Replant using fresh potting mix in the bottom of the pot and around the plant.

5 MULCH. To conserve water and add a handsome touch to containers that are not densely planted, cover the soil with attractive mulch—such as compost, finely shredded bark, sandstone pebbles, or river rock.

KEEP AN EYE OUT FOR PESTS. With the close attention you give containers, you're bound to quickly notice any signs of pest or disease problems, such as disfigured or discolored foliage or visible pests. Remove and discard affected plant parts, handpick insects, and use insect or disease controls if necessary. In some cases it may be best to discard a severely infested plant. The *Ortho Home Gardener's Problem Solver* is an excellent resource for diagnosing and treating plant problems.

WEED. Weeds are a rarity in container gardens, but be alert for strays and give them the heave-ho at once.

Container Care: Overwintering Containers

When freezing winter weather moves in, plants and pots suffer the effects. Porous containers made of clay, plastic, metal, or concrete may chip, crack, or break apart during repeated freezes. Empty containers and store them out of the weather. Move tender plants that you want to save indoors for the winter (be sure they are free of insects). Some tender plants tolerate the relatively low light levels, dry air, and warmth of indoor rooms quite well. Others are best left on a sunny enclosed porch that remains cool but never freezes. For plants that will stay outdoors, follow these cold-weather tips.

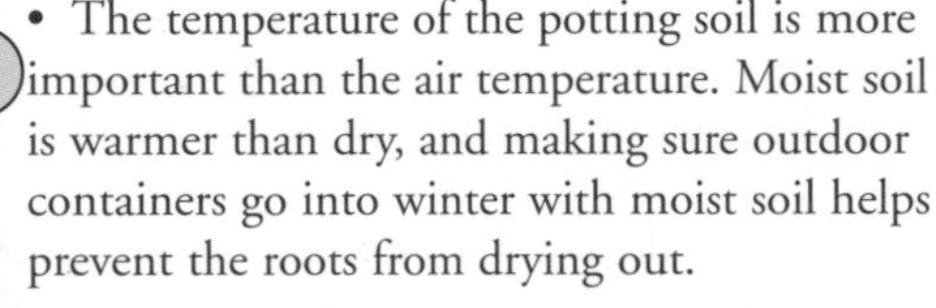

• The temperature of the potting soil is more important than the air temperature. Moist soil is warmer than dry, and making sure outdoor containers go into winter with moist soil helps prevent the roots from drying out.

• Save difficult-to-overwinter perennial plants, such as roses, by planting them in the ground in late summer or early fall. Buy new plants for your containers the next spring.

• Move perennials, trees, shrubs, and vines in containers from a raised deck to a protected ground-level site. Bare ground radiates heat and helps insulate plants from chilling winds. You could also sink the container into the ground and cover its top with a layer of mulch. Beware, though, this method can stain the outside of the container. Borderline hardy plants do better with this method.

• You can also protect your plants by insulating them. For example, wrap the sides and tops of large containers with several layers of bubble wrap. ❶ Wrap a weatherproof tarp around this layer, then wrap everything with a layer of burlap, which will look better than the tarp. Another option for an exposed large pot is to set a cylinder of chicken wire over the pot. Make the cylinder about 12 inches taller and 6 inches or more larger in diameter than the container. Fill the space between the container walls and the wire with fallen leaves or straw, ensuring that the surface is covered.

Container Gardens

Mixed Pots

The next several pages profile ten different container themes. You'll find growing advice specific to window boxes, potted herb gardens, hanging baskets, and other types of container gardens. Care tips, design ideas, and plant lists unique to each theme will help you create an easy-care container garden that looks stellar from spring until frost.

One of the most popular container themes is a mixed container. Medleys of favorite flowers and foliage, mixed container gardens are as unique as the gardener who creates them. Customize a mixed container to your home and landscape. Choose a color palette that complements your home and buy plants with blossoms and leaves in those shades. Or set the mood with a theme suggested by the plants. For example, tropical plants, such as cannas, caladium, and begonias, warm up the chilliest of locales. Grasslike plants and small shrubs add a natural feel to your container creations.

Most important, have fun creating your mixed container. There is just one rule—all the plants must have similar growing requirements. Pair plants that grow in full sun with others that thrive in sun. Water-loving plants should grow alongside other water-lovers for easy care.

DESIGN TIP Choosing a handful of plants from a greenhouse brimming with bloom-laden treasures is a daunting task. When you are overcome by the plethora of pretty choices, keep this container design strategy in mind: ❶ ❷ For a classic, eye-pleasing planting, combine a plant that has an upright or spiky outline with a plant that has a mounding shape and one that trails. For quick reference this concept is often called "spiky, mounding, trailing."

❸ The upright-growing plant forms the focal point of the container. The mounding plant creates a cushion of color around the pot rim, and the trailing plant spills over the edge. See the plant lists on page 24 for a roundup of spiky, mounding, and trailing plants for mixed containers.

CARE Cluster pots that thrive with frequent, deep watering together to help remind you to give them all a long drink. By grouping mixed containers, you'll not only create an impressive display, but you'll also cut down on time spent hauling a hose or watering can from place to place. ❹ Entryways, patios, porches, and decks are all perfect hosts for a cluster of three or more containers.

1
2
3
4

Containers for Shade

While shade is often viewed as a limiting factor when it comes to gardening, it is a wonderful asset in the world of container gardening. Shade cast by a building or overhead trees will keep plants cooler than those growing in the blazing sun. Shade will also reduce evaporation—occasionally allowing soil to stay moist for days at a time. There are hundreds of container-friendly plants that thrive in shade. Mix and match your favorites and step back to watch your shaded nook blossom!

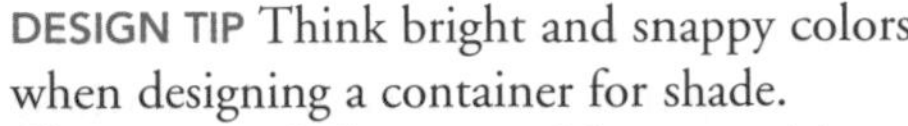

DESIGN TIP Think bright and snappy colors when designing a container for shade. ❶ Plants with flowers or foliage in white, yellow, or pink are like small lamps in shade—they highlight nearby plants and structures and brighten their surroundings. Silver foliage and white flowers create a similar effect.

❷ Plants with variegated foliage, such as caladium, are a great choice as they add both highlights and texture. ❸ Texture alone can create a dramatic composition for shady spots.

As with all good plantings, you'll want to choose plants that will thrive in the amount of light available and that complement their surroundings. For example, the hart's tongue fern *(Asplenium* spp.) in ❸ offers an elegant touch that matches the french doors leading to the patio.

CARE There are varying degrees of shade. Most shaded areas are not dark all day long. As the sun moves through the sky, occasional shafts or patches of sunlight will illuminate various areas. If this is the case in your chosen site, place plants that prefer partial shade, such as bellflower, in the areas that get the most light. Partial shade, which means an hour or two of direct sun or several hours of dappled sunlight, greatly expands the number of plant choices for a shade garden. See plant tags to determine if a plant prefers partial shade or full shade.

Plants for shade containers

The following shade-loving plants do well in containers. Annuals and perennials that have colorful foliage do a nice job of supplementing the flower show.

Foliage

BEGONIAS, BERGENIA, COLEUS, CORAL BELLS, ENGLISH IVY, HOSTAS, LUNGWORT, SWEET POTATO

Flowers

ASTILBE, BEGONIA, CAMELLIA, FUCHSIA, HELLEBORE, IMPATIENS, LILY-OF-THE-VALLEY, PANSY

PROJECT: Light up a shady patio

Add a glow to a shaded patio or porch with this simple planting project. Depending on the time of day and your mood, this festive container garden can serve as a birdbath or as lighting for a party.

❹ Collect four containers: a tall pot for the base, a large bowl for planting, a small pot to serve as the base for a saucer, and a small glazed saucer. We used terra-cotta pots, but you can use containers made of any material.

❺ Place the tall pot upside down as a base for the large bowl. Then place the small pot upside down in the bowl and set the saucer on it. Plant the bowl with a selection of shade annuals or perennials. The plants here are tricolor st. johnswort *(Hypericum ×moseranum* 'Tricolor'), 'Beedham's White' dead nettles *(Lamium* hybrid), and purple lobelia.

❻ Finish the centerpiece by adding polished stones to the saucer and filling it almost to the rim with water. If you're having a party, replace the water with several votive candles.

Window Boxes

Window boxes are jewelry for your home. Bedeck your windows with these blooming treasure troves and enjoy their color and fragrance both inside the house and out. Keep in mind that window boxes are not restricted to windows; they are equally effective at embellishing porch and deck railings. Hardware available at any home center or hardware store makes it simple to hang window boxes from any location.

1

DESIGN TIP Maintain an unobstructed view out a window by selecting low-growing or airy plants for a window box. ❶ Plants with a low-mounding habit and those that spill over the edge of the box are especially effective. You will see the planting every time you glance out the window, so it is especially important to select plants that contribute good foliage to the composition even when they are not in bloom.

2

CARE Properly position and mount a window box with these tips.

• Window box plantings are most appealing when plants reach the glass. ❷ Place your window box so that its top edge is just below the window frame. Avoid the temptation to use the windowsill as a support; it is not designed to bear such a burden.

3

• A filled window box is heavy; you will need sturdy hardware to hold it securely in place. ❸ Attach the window box to the wall with brackets (L-shape metal strips are a popular choice) or use a shelf to support it.

• A box placed tightly against the house can cause moisture damage to the window frame and siding. Prevent problems by mounting the brackets so that the box is held 2 to 3 inches away from the wall to allow air circulation.

Plants for window boxes

A good window box plant is low-growing—so it does not impede your view out the window—and long-blooming. Here's a listing of a few favorites.

BEGONIA, CALIBRACHOA, EDGING LOBELIA, FLOWERING TOBACCO, GERANIUM, IMPATIENS, IVY GERANIUM, LANTANA, PETUNIA, VERBENA HYBRIDS

PLANTING: Window box basics

❹ Begin by selecting mounding and trailing plants with a variety of flower and foliage characteristics for interest. Fill the window box three-fourths full with a high-quality potting mix. Attaching the box to the window before planting makes the job easier.

❺ Set still-potted plants on top of the soil; rearrange them until you like the design. Arrange the plants so that the tallest ones are toward the back of the window box and either in the center or on the ends. Fill in with shorter plants. Place trailing plants in front to drape over the edge.

❻ Unpot plants, loosen their roots, and set them in the soil at the same depth as their nursery pots.

Water thoroughly. To keep the garden neat, pinch off or deadhead spent blooms and remove yellowed and dead leaves as needed. In midsummer, cut back straggly and nonflowering plants, reducing their size by about one-third. This will promote reblooming through the cooler days of autumn.

Hanging Baskets

Hanging baskets provide a quick splash of color in areas where an in-ground garden would be impossible—on the deck, on the porch, and next to the front door. Build your own hanging basket and enjoy a custom arrangement that accents the color of your house, puts fragrance at nose height, and makes your sitting spaces as inviting as your garden.

DESIGN TIP ❶ The hook or bracket that holds your hanging garden can be inconspicuous or a decorative asset. Visit a home supply store, garden center, or nursery to find hangers in myriad styles, colors, and materials. Antique shops and flea markets can also have just the right hook. Select hardware that complements the style of your house: a white gingerbread bracket for a Victorian home, a sleek angled hanger for a modern ranch. Make sure the bracket is sturdy enough to hold the heavy weight of the freshly watered container. Attach the bracket to a wall, post, or other support with screws instead of nails, which can pull out under the weight of the basket.

CARE ❷ Plan to water your hanging basket daily. Because of the height of hanging containers, you'll want a system that delivers water in a slow but steady stream to allow the potting mix to soak it up without excessive runoff. A watering wand attached to the end of your garden hose makes the chore easier by extending your reach and eliminating the need to fill and lift a sprinkling can. Self-watering pots are a boon to busy gardeners, and they also protect plants in sunny sites from suffering when you're not home to water. Drip irrigation emitters are a permanent labor-saving solution, but the tubing that runs from the faucet to the plant can be challenging to camouflage. Disguise it by tucking it in eaves or on top of an arbor above the hanging basket.

Plants for hanging baskets

An eye-pleasing hanging basket includes both mounding and trailing plants. Tuck the trailing plants along the edge of the container to mask the sides, and situate the mounding plants in the center.

Terrific trailers

BACOPA, BROWALLIA, FAN FLOWER, LICORICE PLANT, IVY GERANIUM, PROSTRATE ROSEMARY, SWEDISH IVY

3

4

PLANTING: Basket basics

Standing water in a pot can cause roots to drown, so make sure your hanging container or basket has good drainage. Most containers come with drainage holes in place, but if yours doesn't, you'll want to create some. ❸ For plastic-lined baskets such as this one, snip 8 to 10 holes in the bottom of the liner. Loosely woven baskets have ample drainage—sometimes too much. Line them with a 1- to 2-inch layer of moist sphagnum moss or a preformed coconut fiber liner to keep the soil from washing away.

❹ Get plants off to a quick start by gently loosening circling roots to encourage them to grow outward.

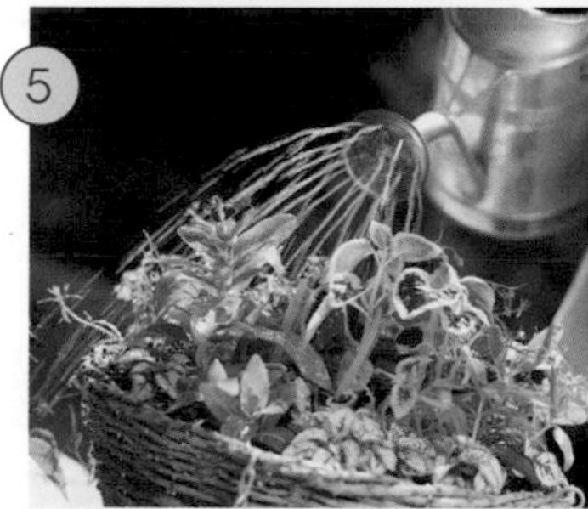
5

After planting, water your new basket. ❺ Use a gentle stream of water so as not to dislodge the plants. In a couple of weeks when the plants have taken root, watering will be less likely to uproot them.

6

❻ Feed and water regularly, and your plants will grow with gusto. Cut back cascading plants, removing several inches of each stem's length as soon as plants show signs of legginess. They'll quickly regrow lush stems.

Herb Gardens

Herbs flourish in containers, and their combined textures meld into a collection that's pretty as well as practical. With herbs just steps away from the kitchen, it takes only seconds to gather a handful of fresh basil leaves or a few sprigs of flavorful rosemary to infuse your meals with flavor. Not only are the stems and leaves of many herbs edible, but so are the flowers, which add color to your dishes. Herbs thrive in full sun, growing best when they receive at least 6 hours of sunlight a day.

DESIGN TIP As when designing all containers, employ the concept of combining spiky, mounding, and trailing herbs for a balanced look. ❶ Also use the herbs' textures to create a pleasing arrangement. Herbs are primarily green, so intensify the color of a planting by pairing light- and dark-leafed plants, for example, herbs with chartreuse foliage and ones with dark green leaves. For added contrast work in plants with variegated foliage.

❷ Introduce dinner guests to the flavor of fresh herbs with a snip-and-eat herb centerpiece. Fill a pretty terra-cotta bowl with herbs and give guests pairs of scissors so they can snip bits of the herbs' leaves and flowers to sprinkle on their food.

For a savory combination include one plant each of basil, chives, marjoram, oregano, rosemary, sage, and thyme. For sweet flavors, offer pansy, lavender, peppermint, orange mint, stevia, and vanilla grass.

CARE Wire baskets, like the one used in the Hanging Herb Garden project, work especially well because they promote the proper drainage that herbs require. Allow the plants to grow for a month before you start harvesting the stem tips. Some herbs, such as mint and oregano, grow quickly, becoming leggy in a few weeks. Snip them back a few inches to clean up their appearance and promote dense growth.

Herbs and edible flowers for container gardens

BORAGE, CALENDULA, CHIVES, DAYLILIES, LAVENDER, LEMON BALM, MINTS, NASTURTIUM, OREGANO, PANSY, PARSLEY ROSEMARY, SAGE, SWEET BASIL, THYME,

3

Remove flowers from herbs such as basil by pinching or snipping with scissors to ensure they continue producing flavorful foliage.

4

PROJECT: A hanging herb garden

Filled with herbs, this eye-level planting provides greenery that looks and tastes great. Gather one three-tier wire-mesh hanging basket from a kitchen store, one bag of long-strand sphagnum moss, one bag of Miracle-Gro Moisture Control potting mix, a bucket of water, and approximately seven herb plants.

5

❸ Soak the sphagnum moss in a pail of water for about an hour. Next, wring out handfuls of moss and press them into the wire mesh of all three baskets. Snip off extra-long strands of moss hanging outside the mesh, then fill the inside cavity with potting mix.

❹ Remove the herbs from their pots and snuggle the root ball of each plant into the potting mix. Water well, drain, and hang.

❺ This basket is planted with sun-loving herbs. Pineapple mint is in the bottom tier, silver marjoram fills the middle basket, and golden marjoram is at the top.

Vegetable Delights

Whether your edible garden is perched on a balcony or next to in-ground plants, container gardening gives you growing space for fresh vegetables, offering a satisfying harvest without the work of weeding.

The key when growing vegetables is to plant them in large containers so that their roots have ample room. When possible use containers that are at least 20 inches in diameter and 12 inches deep to provide room for dense root growth, which is important for producing large fruit. Additionally the large amount of potting mix they hold insulates roots from heat.

1

DESIGN TIP Maximize containers' confined growing space by planting a succession of crops that will be ready for harvest in spring, summer, and fall. For example, in early spring plant lettuce and spinach. When the chance of frost has passed, remove some of the lettuce and spinach and tuck a patio tomato plant into the empty space. By early summer the lettuce and spinach will cease producing succulent foliage. Replace them with your favorite variety of peppers, which will grow alongside the tomatoes for harvest into fall.

CARE ❶ Most vegetables thrive in full sun. Flowers and foliage are more forgiving than food plants when it comes to maintenance. Forget to water your tomatoes, and it may take them quite a while to recover from your neglect. Water at least once a day in summer. Mulch the soil surface with dried grass clippings or other organic material to help conserve moisture and prevent the sun's heat from stressing plants.

Use potting mix enriched with continuous-release plant food. Frequently augment it with a plant food that is immediately available to plants, such as Miracle-Gro Water Soluble All Purpose Plant Food.

Vegetables that do well in pots

Dwarf, patio, and pixie varieties have been specifically bred for container gardening. They are smaller plants, but their fruit and leaves may be the same-size as or smaller than standard selections. Try these for starters:

BASIL: 'GREEN BOUQUET' OR 'SPICY GLOBE'
BEET: 'LITTLE BALL' OR 'LITTLE CHICAGO'
BUSH BEAN: 'RED SEED' OR 'ROYALTY PURPLE'
CARROT: 'PARMEX BABY BALL', 'LITTLE FINGER', OR 'TINY SWEET'
CUCUMBER: 'BUSH CHAMPION'
② LETTUCE: 'GREEN ICE', 'LITTLE GEM', 'RED RIDING HOOD', 'RED SAILS', OR 'TOM THUMB'
MELON: 'HONEY BUN' CANTALOUPE; 'BABY FUN' WATERMELON
PEPPER: 'BABY BELL' OR 'JINGLE BELL'
SQUASH: 'MINI PAK' OR 'ZUCCHINI SILVER'
TOMATO: 'HUSKY CHERRY RED', 'PATIO', 'SMALL FRY', OR 'SWEET BABY GIRL'

2

3

4

PLANTING: Trellised vegetables

Vining and trailing vegetable plants can grow like Jack's beanstalk, so make sure to offer support that hoists them up instead of out in your container garden. Train vines of squash, cucumbers, and pole beans along a railing or fence behind the container or ③ provide a tepee, trellis, or stakes for them to climb.

④ Install the supports when you plant the container, even though they will tower over the young plants. This avoids possible root damage from poking poles into the soil around a mature plant.

As plants grow, gently and loosely tie them to the supports with short pieces of twine or cloth.

Container Water Gardens

Add the soothing sound or sight of water to your container garden. When perched on a patio or balcony, the water feature will beckon winged visitors for up-close viewing, and if the container houses a fountain, the soothing trickling of water will mask obtrusive sounds from the world beyond.

A container-size water garden is inexpensive to create and simple to maintain. Water features without fountains are often easier to create. All you need is a water-tight pot and a few water-loving plants. Gardens with fountains usually require a nearby electrical outlet. Although they are a little more work to set up, the water music they provide is worth the effort.

DESIGN TIP ❶ Any container that holds water—or can be made to hold water—can be the start of a small, serene water feature. Finding a container that holds water is easy. Home decor stores are filled with all kinds of possibilities, from kitchen mixing bowls to painted Chinese fishbowls. Antique shops are another good place to seek out an unusual container for your water feature.

Depth is important especially if plants are not free-floating but in pots. ❷ Select a container that is at least 6 inches deep for small plants. Large plants such as pickerel weed and cattails, need a container that is 6 inches deeper than the length of the plant's roots.

❸ Fountains are a nice addition to container water gardens, adding soothing sounds to their surroundings. Some plants, such as water lilies, however, do not appreciate water splashing on their leaves.

CARE A container water garden can be a year-round asset in mild regions and a temporary beauty in colder areas. In cold areas, overwinter plants indoors in a dishpan or plastic tub of water placed in a sunny spot. Or buy new plants each year. Disassemble the fountain and store the pump, fountain, and pot in a garage,

Plants for container water gardens
The following plants are at home floating in a shallow-bowl water garden.

FAIRY MOSS, MINIATURE WATER LILY, WATER HYACINTH, WATER LETTUCE, SALVINIA

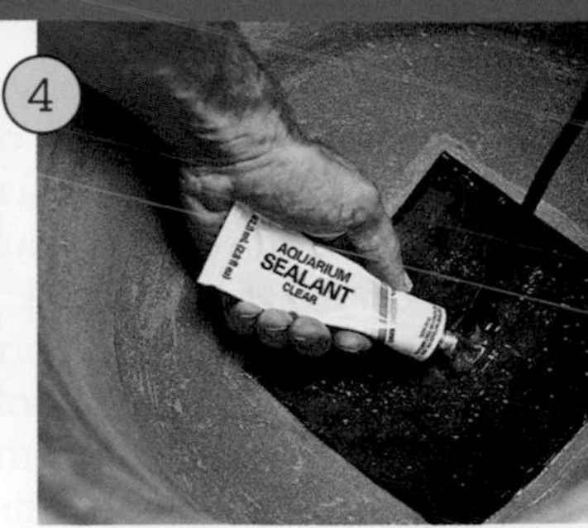

basement, or other spot where the temperature stays above freezing.

PROJECT: A bubbling urn

Turn a simple urn into a container water garden. You'll need one watertight urn, one small submersible pump, one 8- to 12-inch piece of PVC pipe—see the pump specifications for the diameter of the pipe—one 6- by 6-inch rubber patch, and a tube of clear silicone aquarium sealant.

❹ In the bottom of the urn, drill a hole wide enough to accommodate the pump's plug and cord. Cut an X in the center of the rubber patch, push the plug through the X, then through the hole. Pull down on the cord until 6 inches of cord remains inside the urn.

Cover the bottom of the rubber patch with sealant and apply the patch over the hole. Seal the X around the cord. Allow the sealant to dry for several hours. Or simply hook the cord over the edge of the pot and mask it with shrubs or tall perennials growing behind the urn.

❺ Place bricks in the bottom of the urn. Set the pump on the bricks. Add a PVC pipe extension to the pump to raise the height of the outflow so that it is level with the water surface.

❻ Fill the urn with water and plug in the pump. Periodically top off the water as it evaporates or splashes out of the urn.

Cutting Gardens

Enjoy the bounty of your garden inside and out when you plant a container garden of flowers you grow to supply your indoor bouquets. Although it may seem counter-intuitive that a container garden for cutting could also be a lovely accent, careful planning can make it so. Stock the pot with flowers of various shapes and sizes, including vining plants to trail over the edge of the pot. A successful container of cut flowers will bloom all summer long. In fact, cutting the blooms of many plant species promotes rebloom, providing a long-lasting supply of blossoms for bouquets.

1

2

3

DESIGN TIP Plant three or more containers of flowers for cutting to ensure you have ample blossoms for both bouquets and the garden. ❶ When grouped, cut-flower container gardens are especially striking; clustering them together also makes harvesting a cinch.

CARE Most cutting flowers thrive in full sun. Place your cut flower container garden where it will receive six to eight hours of direct sunlight a day. Regular feeding is also important. Fuel these fast-growing plants with a controlled-release plant food mixed into the potting soil at planting time or use a Miracle-Gro potting mix, which has the plant food mixed in. Supplement these nutrients with a readily available water-soluble plant food, such as Miracle-Gro All Purpose Plant Food, every two weeks.

Careful plant selection will keep your cut-flower container garden looking lovely outside while providing bouquets for enjoyment inside the house. ❷ For example, zinnias are in constant bloom. Snip fresh blooms every few days and be sure to clip off spent flowers.

❸ Pair flowers for cutting with trailing plants to mask the edge of the container, giving the pot a lush appearance. Verbena, fan flower, and vinca are good choices for trailing plants.

Flowers for cut-flower container gardens

Valued for their ability to rebloom freely after flowers are cut, these favorites thrive in pots.

BLACK-EYED SUSAN, BUTTERFLY BUSH, CALENDULA, COCKSCOMB, COSMOS, DAHLIA, GLOBE AMARANTH, HELIOTROPE, LARKSPUR, SALVIA, SNAPDRAGON, STOCK, SWEET PEA, ZINNIA

PROJECT: A bouquet from seed

It's easy and inexpensive to grow flowers for cutting from seed, especially when you grow annuals such as zinnia. Sow the seeds and nurture them in a sunny place. When they have filled out and start blooming, then you can move them into public view and start cutting the flowers for bouquets. You need only a container with adequate drainage, high-quality potting mix, all-purpose plant food, and seeds.

Fill pots with potting mix to about 1 inch from the top. Tamp down lightly. Scatter the seeds over the soil surface. Cover with about ¼ inch of potting mix and again, tamp down lightly. Water well. Set the seeded pots in a sunny, warm place. Keep the soil evenly moist. The seedlings will soon sprout.

❹ In a few weeks when the seedlings have two or three sets of leaves, thin the planting. ❺ Using scissors or pruners, cut out seedlings, leaving about eight of the strongest seedlings, spaced 3 to 4 inches apart.

Move the pots of plants into full sun in a spot where air circulates freely. Water well when the surface soil feels dry. Feed plants with an all-purpose water-soluble plant food according to label directions. ❻ You'll have blooms in a few short weeks.

Containers for All Seasons

Take cues from Mother Nature and update your containers as the seasons change. Celebrate the first warm days of spring with cool-weather-loving annuals, perennials, and bulbs. When spring turns to summer, stock your container garden with plants that thrive in the heat. And in fall freshen up the combination with plants that will carry the garden to the first frost in style.

1

2

3

DESIGN TIP Make a container garden look fresh in every season by combining permanent plants with a few changing players. By anchoring a container with permanent plants, you create a structure similar to a garden that features shrubs and perennials. The hallmark of a permanent plant is that it adds interest to the pot in every growing season. Excellent permanent plants include agave, blue fescue, boxwood, heavenly bamboo, maiden grass, and New Zealand flax.

Seasonal Plants

These ideas are only a beginning; your local garden centers and nurseries offer hundreds of possibilities.

Spring

BLEEDING HEART, FORGET-ME-NOT, PANSY, LUNGWORT, SPRING BULBS (tulips, hyacinths, and daffodils)

Summer

CALIBRACHOA, GERBERA DAISY, OSTEOSPERMUM, SALVIA, SWEET ALYSSUM

Fall

ASTER, CHRYSANTHEMUM, ORANGE POT MARIGOLD, PANSY

CARE Make the seasonal task of changing out accent plants simple by sinking place-holding pots in between the permanent plants to prevent their roots from filling the empty spaces in the design. For example, when you plant the container garden, put an empty 4- to 6-inch pot in the center. ❶ In spring, it can hold daffodils. ❷ The daffodils are replaced by lilies in summer and ❸ then chrysanthemums in fall. Simply slip the seasonal potted plant into the place-holding pot. There is no need to remove the seasonal plant from its pot.

PROJECT: Chilling bulbs

Bulbs are a sweet way to greet spring in a seasonal container garden. Most spring-blooming bulbs need 10 to 15 weeks of cold between 35° and 50°F in order to bloom well. This chilling period is easy to accomplish in the garden and can be duplicated with the following method in which you start the bulbs in small pots in fall, then move them to your container garden just before they bloom in spring.

Note: Not all bulbs require chilling. If you're not sure if a bulb variety requires winter chill, ask at the garden center when you buy them.

❹ In early winter plant the bulbs in 6-inch plastic pots. Insert a plant label that lists the variety and date of planting in each pot. Protect the bulbs by placing them in an unheated garage or other spot where temperatures are cool but not freezing. Water as needed to keep the pots moist throughout winter. After the bulbs have chilled for the recommended amount of time, move them to a window that receives indirect light until they begin to sprout.

❺ After the bulbs sprout, transplant them into a container garden along with other spring-flowering plants such as pink English daisies and purple and white violas.

Unique Containers

Gardening, whether in the ground or in containers, should be fun. Finding unusual accent pieces to decorate your garden beds and borders adds to the sometimes childlike wonder of growing plants. Container options are endless and readily available. Poke around your garage and you're likely to turn up two or three possibilities.

Think about your old tools that no longer work properly or are too rusted to fix. For a movable garden, plant directly in a wood or metal containers, such as wagons or wheelbarrows, or use either to hold pots. Kids' toys, the ubiquitous leaky boot ❶, the odd piece of furniture (chair or TV cabinet), an old sink, watering cans ❷, or even a bicycle ❸ offer plantable possibilities for garden art.

1

2

3

DESIGN TIP Flea markets and antique shows are great places to turn up unusual container candidates. Keep your eye out for kitchen bowls and pots that are past their prime—a few holes here and there will save you the trouble of adding drainage holes before planting. From colanders to egg baskets, kitchen tools present many planting possibilities.

CARE Unique containers often do not contain adequate drainage. Remedy the situation by drilling one or more holes in the bottom of your container. It's easy to drill through clay, ceramic, resin, fiberglass, and wood planters. Use a drill with an appropriate bit made for masonry or wood, and wear protective goggles. Place a cross of masking tape over the spot where you plan to drill to prevent the pot from cracking as you drill.

To punch drainage holes in the bottom of metal containers, use a large nail and a hammer. Hardware store staff can also help you find an appropriate bit for drilling through the metal.

Also consider weatherproofing when selecting a unique container. Many practical-objects-turned-planting-pots are not able to stand up to the rigors of the outdoors year after year. Extend the life of wooden items with a coat of wood preservative or paint. Be sure to use a wood preservative that does not contain pentachlorophenol, such as Thompson's Water Seal or Cuprinol.

No matter what type of material a container is made of, you can increase its longevity by storing it in a cool, dry place, such as a garage or dry basement, in winter.

PLANT SELECTION Look to the pot for plant inspiration when designing a unique container. For example, consider these three notable pairings of unique pots and plants. ❹ A hollowed-out, dried gourd lends itself to a fall-inspired planting of ornamental grasses. ❺ A simple hanging basket calls for plants that will bloom happily in the sometimes dry confines of the airy basket. ❻ And finally not many plants will thrive in the tiny growing space along the brim of an old hat, but succulent plants such as hen-and-chicks readily step up to the challenge.

4

5

6

Sweet-scented plants

While anything goes when it comes to choosing plants for unique containers, consider adding some of the fragrant bloomers below. That way, you can enjoy the sweet scents of nature every time you water, tend to, or simply brush against these longtime favorites.

ANGEL'S TRUMPET, FLOWERING TOBACCO, HELIOTROPE, JASMINE, MADAGASCAR, JASMINE, ORIENTAL LILY, PETUNIA, STOCK, SWEET ALYSSUM, TUBEROSE

1

2

3

PROJECT: Wall art

Used up all your gardening space? Not a problem! Turn an old wooden soft drink case into an instant living sculpture—a vertical garden on a wall. Succulents (water-storing plants) have a dramatic texture and an undemanding nature. They thrive in dry situations, although they need watering from time to time. Choose from among dozens of groups of succulents. This planting combines ghost plants *(Graptopetalum paraguayense),* rosettes, and burro's tail *(Sedum morganianum).*

For this project you need a wooden case divided into sections, one bag of long-strand sphagnum moss, a bucket of water, and enough succulent plants to fill the openings in the case.

Soak the moss in a bucket of water for at least one hour. Grab a handful of moss and squeeze out the excess water. ❶ Place a handful of wet moss in the bottom of each of the box's compartments.

❷ Remove a plant from its nursery pot and shake any extraneous potting mix off the roots. Wrap the roots in a small handful of wet sphagnum moss. Stuff the moss-wrapped root mass into a compartment. Tuck in additional wet moss to secure the plant in place.

Let the box settle for two weeks before hanging it up for display. This allows the plants to begin rooting in place. ❸ Water the planting at least once a week. Feed two or three times in summer, using an all-purpose water-soluble plant food at the rate of ¼ teaspoon per gallon of water. Unless you live in a warm climate, move the box to a sunny place indoors for the winter.

Recipes for Success

Star Power

Here bright-eyed anemones are tucked into a silver compote. Once a serving dish, this planter filled with a combination of plants is a fitting centerpiece for a summer soiree. If you don't have a compote, any shallow bowl or pot with adequate drainage will work well.

- Light: Part shade.
- Water: Water as needed to maintain evenly moist soil. Be sure to drill a drainage hole in the compote before planting.
- Care tips: This combination thrives in cool weather. When spring turns to summer replace the anemones with African daisies and substitute your favorite trailing plant for the bacopa, if it does not stand up to the heat. Trim the bacopa back by half if it becomes leggy. In summer, deadhead the African daisies to promote new blooms. Feed plants with Miracle-Gro Water Soluble All Purpose Plant Food.

STAR POWER

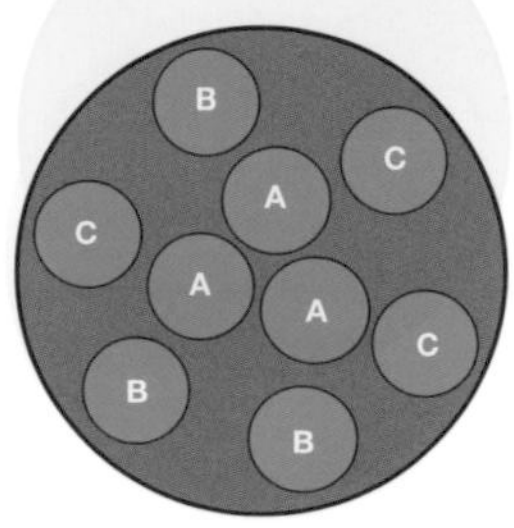

Plant list:

FOR A 12"-DIAMETER POT

A. 'CHARMER' GRECIAN WINDFLOWER (3 PLANTS)

B. BACOPA (3 PLANTS)

C. CURRY PLANT (3 PLANTS)

Spread the Cheer

Give your outdoor space an energizing boost with this vibrant collection of yellow-hued annual sun worshippers.

•Light: Full sun.
•Water: Water daily to maintain an evenly moist soil.
•Care tips: Help the sometimes floppy sunflowers stand tall by loosely tying them to a green garden stake, which will blend into the foliage. After sunflowers fade in late summer, replace them with 'Karl Forester' ornamental grass for fall interest. Encourage the snapdragons, marigolds, and celosia to spend up new blooms by deadheading them regularly. Trim back the sweet potato vine if it becomes leggy.

Feed plants with Miracle-Gro Water Soluble All Purpose Plant Food every two weeks.

SPREAD THE CHEER

Plant list:

FOR AN 18"-DIAMETER POT
A. YELLOW PLUME CELOSIA (3 PLANTS)
B. LOOSESTRIFE (3 PLANTS)
C. MARIGOLD (3 PLANTS)
D. YELLOW SNAPDRAGON (3 PLANTS)
E. 'TEDDY BEAR' SUNFLOWER (3 PLANTS)
F. 'TRICOLOR' SWEET POTATO VINE (3 PLANTS)

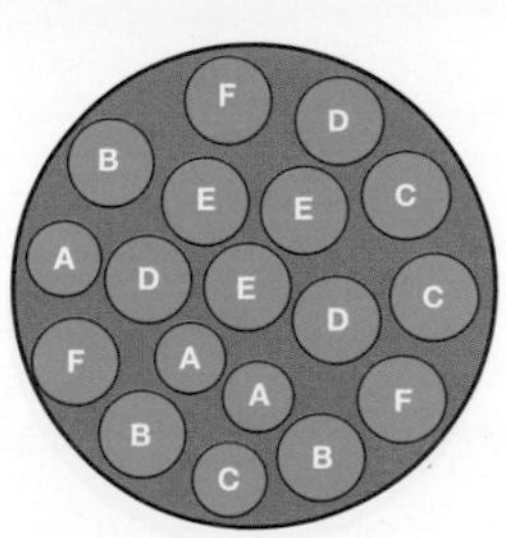

TERRIFIC TEXTURE

Terrific Texture

An intriguing mix of leaf shapes elevates this combination of cool purple- and violet-hue plants from ordinary to extraordinary. Count on this combination to bloom from spring until frost.

•Light: Full sun.
•Water: Water daily to maintain evenly moist soil.
•Care tips: Pinch the bloom spikes off coleus to promote bushy growth. Deadhead globe amaranth and heliotrope to encourage repeat blooms.

Globe amaranth is easy to dry for a lasting bouquet. Simply harvest flowers shortly after they open. Hang them to dry in bundles of 10 or less in a dry, dark place for 2 weeks. Feed plants every two weeks with Miracle-Gro Water Soluble All Purpose Plant Food.

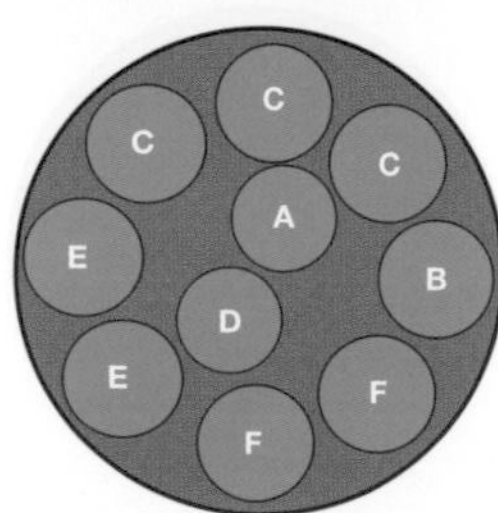

Plant list:

FOR A 14"-DIAMETER POT
A. CABBAGE PALM (1 PLANT)
B. 'MARS' COLEUS (1 PLANT)
C. GLOBE AMARANTH (3 PLANTS)
D. HELIOTROPE (1 PLANT)
E. ANY RED VARIEGATED COLEUS (2 PLANTS)
F. CAPE PRIMROSE (2 PLANTS)

Nectar Feast

Stocked with nectar-rich hibiscus, impatiens, and salvia, this red-hot container beckons hummingbirds and butterflies all summer.

•Light: Full sun.
•Water: Water daily to maintain evenly moist soil.
•Care tips: Encourage the hibiscus to bloom all summer long with regular deadheading. Miracle-Gro Water Soluble All Purpose Plant Food will also promote the formation of new blooms. Watch for spider mites on the hibiscus; dislodge them with a strong spray of water.

Overwinter the hibiscus in a cool, sunny window. Except for the Japanese blood grass the other plants in the container are annuals. Pull them from the planter before bringing the hibiscus inside. Replant with annuals in spring and move container outside after all chance for frost has passed.

NECTAR FEAST

Plant list:

FOR AN 18"-DIAMETER POT
A. HIBISCUS (1 PLANT)
B. JAPANESE BLOOD GRASS (4 PLANTS)
C. SCARLET SAGE (6 PLANTS)
D. NEW GUINEA IMPATIENS (6 PLANTS)

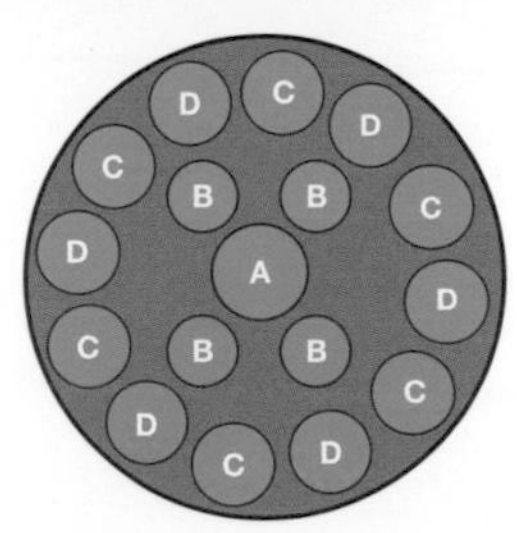

SHRUB SENSATION

Shrub Sensation

Dark orange buttercups complement the chartreuse foliage of a dwarf cypress in this sensational container.

- •Light: Full sun.
- •Water: Water every other day; daily during periods of hot weather.
- •Care tips: Buttercups thrive in cool weather and fade in summer's heat. Grow this combination all winter in mild climates and in spring in cold climates. Replace the buttercups with orange marigolds, zinnias, or African daisies in summer.

In cold climates, overwinter the false cypress by transplanting it into the garden in early fall. Prune the shrub in spring to maintain a pleasing shape.

Using pruning shears, trim back the lotus vine if it becomes leggy.

Feed plants every other week with Miracle-Gro Water Soluble All Purpose Plant Food.

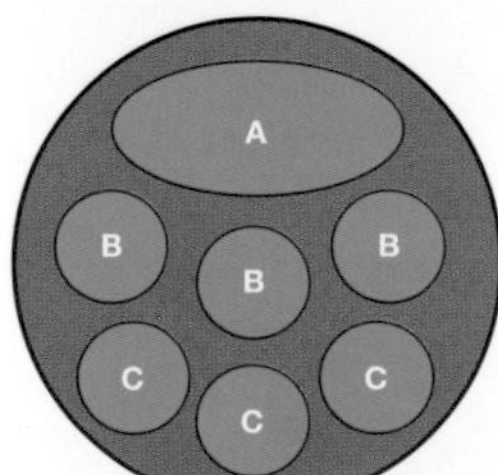

Plant list:

FOR A 14"-DIAMETER POT

A. 'ELLWOODII' FALSE CYPRESS (1 PLANT)

B. 'AMAZON SUNSET' LOTUS (3 PLANTS)

C. ORANGE PERSIAN BUTTERCUP (3 PLANTS)

Eye-Catching Combo

Use a container to enliven a lackluster section of the garden. This bold-hue combination draws the eyes of passersby from spring through fall. This pedestal is made from pressure-treated lattice and 1×2s. You can use a pedestal of any sort, such as an old wooden chair or a tree stump, to elevate the pot.

•Light: Full sun.
•Water: Water daily to maintain evenly moist soil.
•Care tips: Sweet potato is likely to skim the ground by midsummer. If it gets too rangy for your taste, simply give it a haircut.

'Kong Rose' coleus is prized for its massive leaves. Promote large leaves and bushy growth by pinching off flower spikes as soon as they develop.

This combo is a heavy feeder. Feed the plants every other week with Miracle-Gro Water Soluble All Purpose Plant Food.

EYE-CATCHING COMBO

Plant list:

FOR AN 18"-DIAMETER POT
A. 'KONG ROSE' COLEUS (1 PLANT)
B. 'MARGARITA' SWEET POTATO (1 PLANT)
C. PINK VINCA (5 PLANTS)

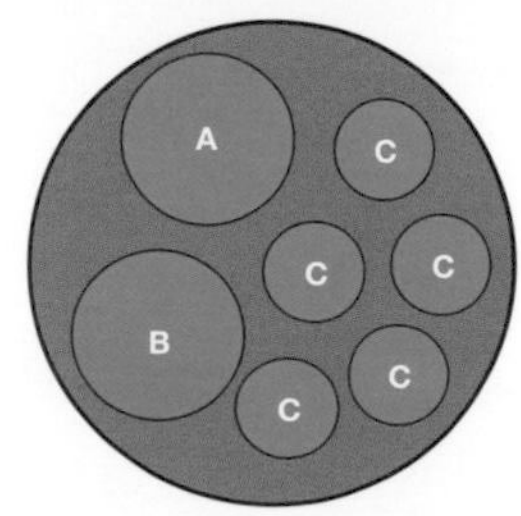

COLOR ON HIGH

Color on High

Think outside the patio, porch, or deck for your next blooming container garden. This planting basket also serves as a garden focal point. If you are not able to find a stand like the one pictured here, suspend the planted basket from a shepherd's hook, available at garden centers.

•Light: Full sun.
•Water: Water daily to maintain evenly moist soil. Coconut fiber-lined baskets like this one dry out quickly in hot, windy conditions. Regular watering is a must; you may need to water in the morning and evening in order to maintain adequate soil moisture.
•Care tips: Trim back petunia by half if it becomes leggy. Strawflowers make great cut flowers and they also dry well. Cut them just after they open. Feed plants every two weeks with Miracle-Gro Water Soluble All Purpose Plant Food.

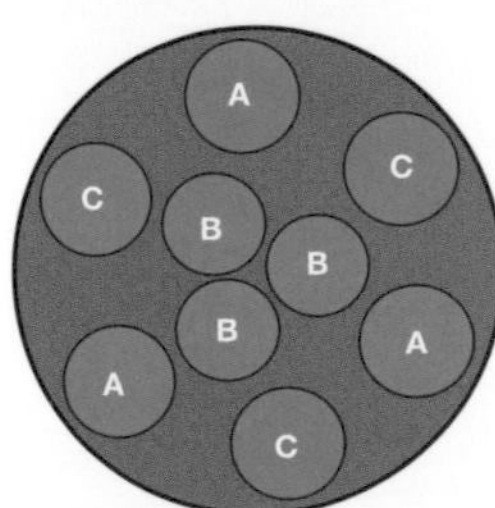

Plant list:

FOR A 14"-DIAMETER POT

A. 'RAMBLIN' VIOLET' WAVE PETUNIA (3 PLANTS)

B. STRAWFLOWER (3 PLANTS)

C. 'CUZCO YELLOW' CREEPING ZINNIA (3 PLANTS)

Grow Cardoon

Similar to a globe artichoke, cardoon has leaves like a thistle that can spread 6 feet out. Their impressive texture and size create a unique focal point in a container garden. Coleus and diascia provide a striking color and texture contrast to the thistlelike leaves of cardoon.

- Light: Full sun.
- Water: Water daily to maintain evenly moist soil.
- Care tips: Cardoon requires high temperatures to produce full-size leaves. Its growth habit is more refined in areas with cool summers.

Give it a boost by feeding it every other week with Miracle-Gro Water Soluble All Purpose Plant Food. Also, begin with the largest cardoon transplant you can find in spring. Search speciality nurseries and garden centers for a large plant. If you are not able to find cardoon in your area, New Zealand flax is a good texture-rich substitute.

GROW CARDOON

Plant list:

FOR A 14"-DIAMETER POT
A. CARDOON (1 PLANT)
B. 'ROSE QUEEN' COLEUS (3 PLANTS)
C. 'SUN CHIMES RED' DIASCIA (3 PLANTS)

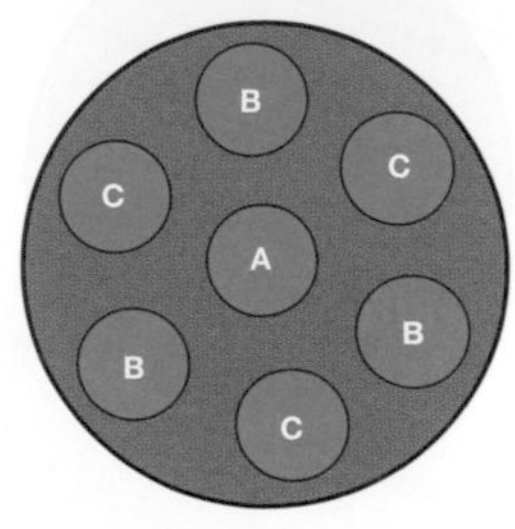

Containers for Shade

FUN WITH FOLIAGE

Fun with Foliage

Hot fun in a terra-cotta pot combines the bright mixed colors of coleus with a fancy-leaf geranium. A versatile plant, many varieties of coleus happily grow in sun or shade. When selecting a coleus at the garden center, read the plant tag to learn if it grows best in sun or shade.

•Light: Part shade or full sun.
•Water: Water daily to maintain evenly moist soil.
•Care tips: Pinch flower spikes off coleus to promote a bushy plant. The growth tips can also be pinched back by about one inch to encourage dense growth.

Deadhead the geranium when most of the florets are bloomed out. If the loosestrife takes on a gangly appearance, trim it back to half of its size.

Feed plants every two weeks with Miracle-Gro Water Soluble All Purpose Plant Food.

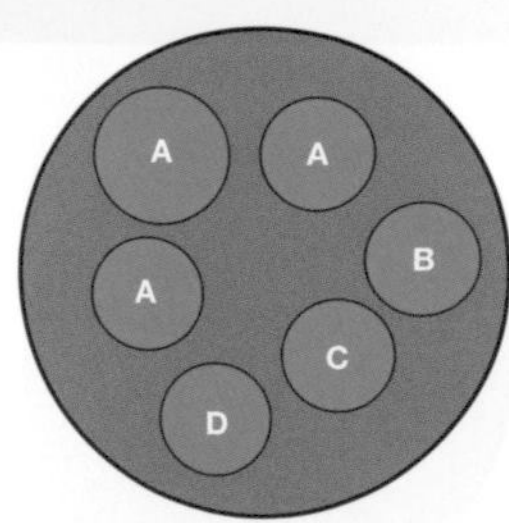

Plant list:

FOR A 14"-DIAMETER POT

A. RED COLEUS, INCLUDING YELLOW-EDGED, WIZARD SERIES, AND A LARGE RED-LEAFED VARIETY (3 PLANTS)
B. 'AMBER WAVES' CORAL BELLS (1 PLANT)
C. 'OUTBACK SUNSET' LOOSESTRIFE (1 PLANT)
D. 'VANCOUVER CENTENNIAL' GERANIUM (1 PLANT)

Shade Solution

Wake up dense shade with this planting combination. The purple-blue leaves of Persian shield complement the blue ceramic container while begonias and wishbone flower bloom from spring through fall. Begonias and wishbone flower are available in several colors. Choose your hues for this shade-loving container combination.

This low-growing combination is most pleasing in a shallow dish container like the one used here. Look for a container that is 6 to 8 inches deep.

•Light: Part shade.
•Water: Water daily to maintain evenly moist soil.
•Care tips: This combo requires almost no maintenance. Simply feed plants every two weeks with Miracle-Gro Water Soluble All Purpose Plant Food and pinch stem tips of Persian shield to promote a dense habit. Wax begonias and wishbone flowers are "self cleaning." They need no deadheading.

SHADE SOLUTION

Plant list:

FOR A 12"-DIAMETER POT
A. WHITE WAX BEGONIA (3 PLANTS)
B. PERSIAN SHIELD (2 PLANTS)
C. WISHBONE FLOWER (5 PLANTS)

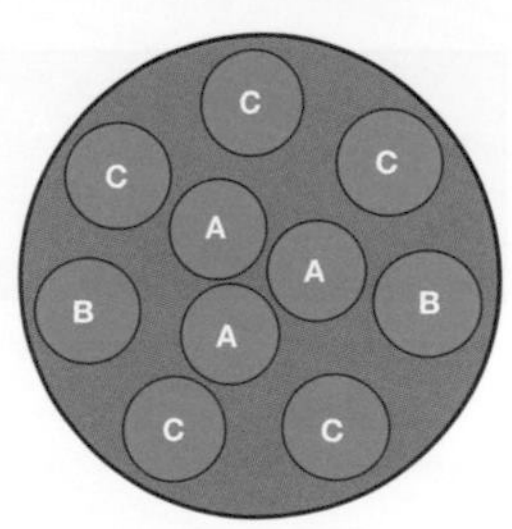

MAKE A SPLASH

Make a Splash

Lighten a shady locale with pink foliage. The white box these shade-loving plants are nestled in highlights the flowers and interesting texture of the foliage. A coat of spray paint will quickly transform any window box.

Although window boxes are made for placing beneath your favorite window, they are also great ornaments for a deck or patio. Add a flounce of flowers to your deck railing by attaching window boxes using "L" brackets or outline your patio with a ring of lushly planted boxes.

•Light: Full shade or part shade.
•Water: Water daily to maintain evenly moist soil.
•Care tips: Pinch flower spikes off coleus to promote a bushy plant. Keep caladium looking neat by trimming dead or diseased leaves off at the soil level. Feed plants every two weeks with Miracle-Gro Water Soluble All Purpose Plant Food.

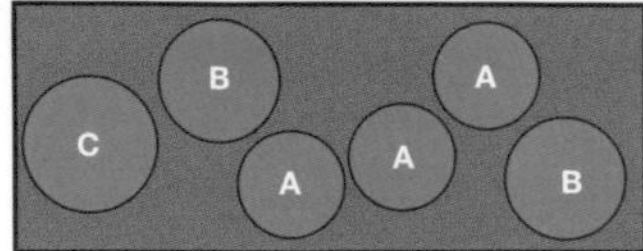

Plant list:

FOR A 6"-WIDE AND 12"-LONG BOX

A. 'MARIBEL PINK SHADES' BEGONIA (3 PLANTS)

B. PINK CALADIUM (2 PLANTS)

C. 'BLACK DRAGON' COLEUS (1 PLANT)

Pretty in Pink

A window on the north side of your house is the perfect perch for this shade-loving combination of plants. Although the box shown here sits on a window ledge, it is best to secure window boxes to your house with "L" brackets. Visit your local garden center or hardware store to find sturdy "L" brackets or other hardware designed for anchoring a window box to a structure.

•Light: Full shade or part shade.
•Water: Water daily to maintain evenly moist soil.
•Care tips: Cut back the ivy if it grows out of bounds. Pinch flower spikes off the coleus to create dense plants. The impatiens are self-cleaning.

Feed plants every two weeks with Miracle-Gro Water Soluble All Purpose Plant Food.

PRETTY IN PINK

Plant list:

FOR A 6"-WIDE AND 18"-LONG BOX

A. 'DUCKFOOT' COLEUS (3 PLANTS)
B. PINK IMPATIENS (3 PLANTS)
C. PALE PINK DARK-EYED IMPATIENS (3 PLANTS)
D. ANY ENGLISH OR ALGERIAN IVY (2 PLANTS)

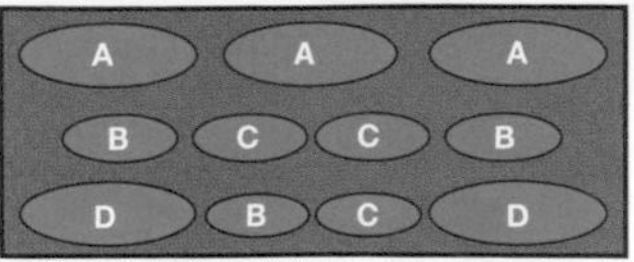

PLANT SPHERE

Plant Sphere

Add color and interest to the bottom of your basket by using a moss-lined wire-mesh basket like this one. The wide openings of the mesh allow you to plant trailing annuals and vines into the sides and bottom of the basket.

•Light: Part shade.
•Water: Water daily to maintain evenly moist soil. Moss-lined baskets dry out quickly and in particularly hot, windy, sunny locations you may need to water in the morning and early evening to maintain adequate soil moisture. A watering wand attached to a garden hose will make easy work of watering this basket.
•Care tips: See page 33 for directions on planting a wire-mesh basket. In midsummer trim back the verbena if it becomes scraggly. Make sure this combo receives plenty of nutrients. Feed the planting every other week with Miracle-Gro Water Soluble All Purpose Plant Food.

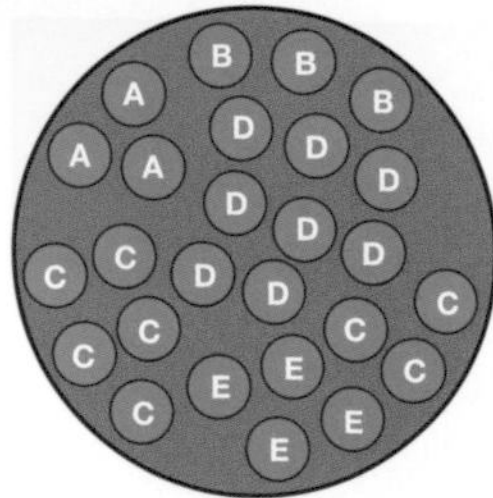

Plant list:

FOR A 14"-DIAMETER BASKET

A. 'PURPLE KNIGHT' ALTERNANTHERA (3 PLANTS)
B. PINK ANNUAL VERBENA (3 PLANTS)
C. WHITE, PINK, AND RED IMPATIENS (8 PLANTS)
D. WISHBONE FLOWER (8 PLANTS)
E. RED WAX BEGONIA (4 PLANTS)

Bells of Color

Ring in summer with long-blooming, bell-shape flowers such as calibrachoa and petunia. These plants will flower from spring until the first frost when watered and fed regularly.

•Light: Full sun or part shade.
•Water: Water daily to maintain evenly moist soil.
•Care tips: Before planting, line wicker baskets like this one with thick plastic to lessen soil moisture evaporation. Cut several drain holes in the plastic. Shear back trailing plants if they become gangly. Support these fast-growing plants with an application of Miracle-Gro Water Soluble All Purpose Plant Food every two weeks.

BELLS OF COLOR

Plant list:

FOR A 16"-DIAMETER BASKET

A. 'SUPERBELLS TEQUILA SUNRISE' CALIBRACHOA (4 PLANTS)
B. 'FLYING COLORS CORAL' DIASCIA (4 PLANTS)
C. 'COMPACT INNOCENCE' NEMESIA (3 PLANTS)
D. 'SUPERTUNIA PRISCILLA' PETUNIA (6 PLANTS)

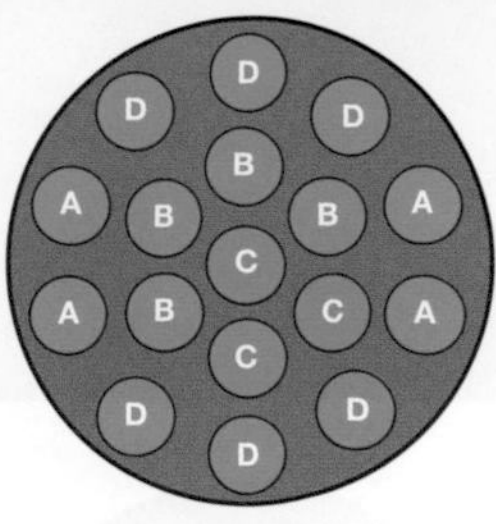

SPRING PINK

Spring Pink

When the dullness of late winter strikes, plant up a pretty pink combo like this one. Dramatically textured and colorful foliage fills a simple gray-painted pot.

•Light: Full shade or part shade.
•Water: Water daily to maintain evenly moist soil.
•Care tips: If you are not able to find a cyclamen plant at your local garden center, check a floral shop. They often stock cyclamen in many different colors.

When the threat of frost has passed, place the container garden outside. In the meantime it will be happy indoors in a partly sunny window. When spring turns to summer, replace cool-weather-loving cyclamen with pink wishbone flower and enjoy blooms through fall.

Encourage the geranium to rebloom by pinching off spent blossoms. Feed plants every two weeks with Miracle-Gro Water Soluble All Purpose Plant Food.

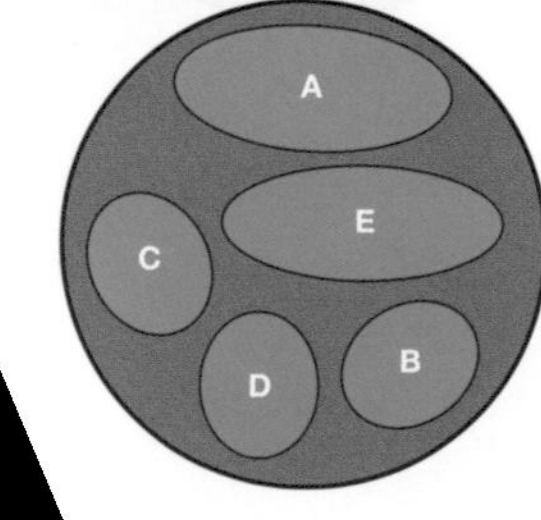

Plant list:

FOR A 14"-DIAMETER POT

A. 'ROYAL PICTA' PEACOCK PLANT (1 PLANT)
B. 'CENTER STAGE' REX BEGONIA (1 PLANT)
C. BUTTON FERN (1 PLANT)
D. 'SILVERADO PURPLE FLAME' CYCLAMEN (1 PLANT)
E. 'MARTHA WASHINGTON' GERANIUM (1 PLANT)

The Heart of Spring

Old-fashioned bleeding heart, a perennial, is the centerpiece of this spring container. The pink, heart-shaped flowers standout when paired with bright pink impatiens. Snip a few bleeding heart blossoms and enjoy them in a vase indoors.

•Light: Full shade or part shade.
•Water: Water daily to maintain evenly moist soil.
•Care tips: Trim creeping charlie regularly to keep it from touching the ground, where it will root and spread. Cut bacopa back by half in midsummer for lush, new growth. After the bleeding heart flowers fade, transplant it into the garden and substitute a fancy-leaf begonia or other shade plant. Bleeding heart is a perennial, hardy to Zone 4. It will wither to the ground in midsummer but will send up new shoots the following spring and bloom for weeks.

THE HEART OF SPRING

Plant list:

FOR A 14"-DIAMETER POT
A. BACOPA (2 PLANTS)
B. BLEEDING HEART (1 PLANT)
C. DOUBLE PINK IMPATIENS (5 PLANTS)
D. SINGLE PINK IMPATIENS (3 PLANTS)
E. VARIEGATED SWEDISH IVY (1 PLANT)

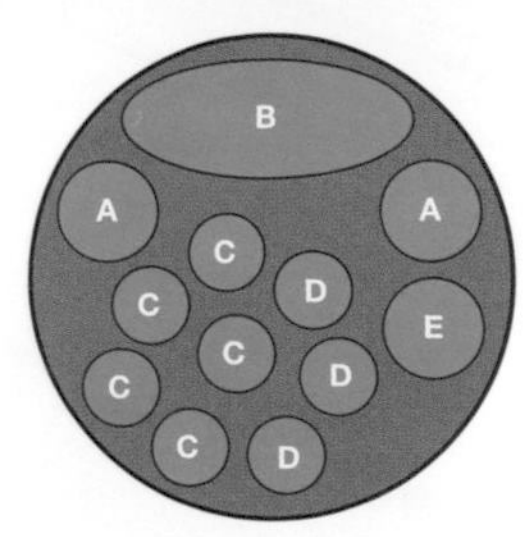

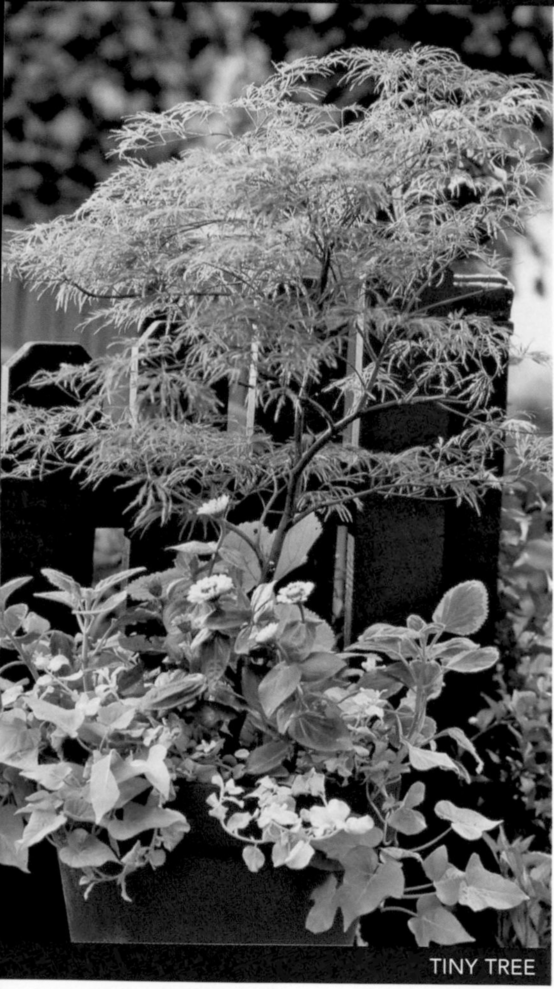

TINY TREE

Tiny Tree

Dwarf Japanese maples are ideal pot plants that offer a choice of dozens of leaf shapes, leaf colors, and growth habits. Look for unique Japanese maples at garden centers that specialize in offering unique trees and shrubs.

•Light: Part shade.
•Water: Water daily to maintain evenly moist soil.
•Care tips: Woody plants, such as the Japanese maple in this combination thrive in deep pots. For best growth plant it in a pot that is at least 12 inches deep. Overwinter a Japanese maple by moving it to an unheated building, such as a garage, after the leaves fall.

Deadhead zinnia to promote rebloom. Pinch back the growing tips of sweet potato vine and licorice plant to encourage compact growth. Feed plants once a month with Miracle-Gro Water Soluble All Purpose Plant Food.

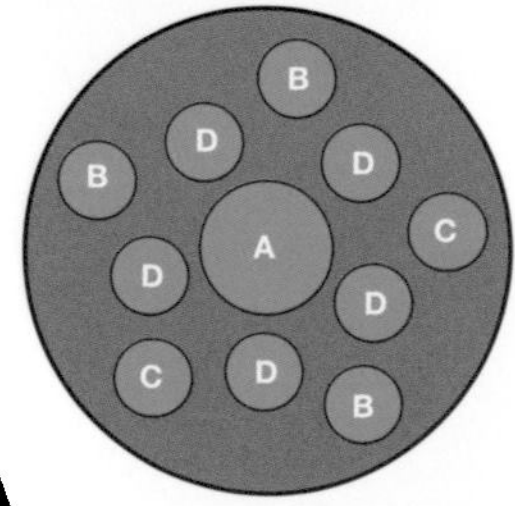

Plant list:

FOR AN 18"-DIAMETER POT
A. DWARF JAPANESE MAPLE (1 PLANT)
B. 'AUREA' LICORICE PLANT (3 PLANTS)
C. 'MARGARITA' SWEET POTATO (2 PLANTS)
D. 'GREEN ENVY' ZINNIA (5 PLANTS)

Fall Foliage

Mimic the striking hues of fall on your porch or patio with this mixed planting.

Increasingly popular New Zealand flax is the star of this combination. Its strap-like leaves are a striking element in any container garden and add instant height. New Zealand flax is available in several different hues of purple or green and multiple degrees of variegation.

•Light: Part shade.
•Water: Water as needed to maintain evenly moist soil; this combination can handle occasional drought.
•Care tips: Nearly maintenance-free, the only requirement of this container is a regular feeding. Use a balanced plant food such as Miracle-Gro Water Soluble All Purpose Plant Food every other week.

FALL FOLIAGE

Plant list:

FOR A 14"-DIAMETER POT
A. DWARF KALANCHOE (1 PLANT)
B. GOLDEN PLECTRANTHUS (1 PLANT)
C. JEWEL ORCHID (1 PLANT)
D. SNAKE PLANT (1 PLANT)
E. SOCIETY GARLIC (1 PLANT)
F. NEW ZEALAND FLAX (1 PLANT)
G. 'PRINCE OF ORANGE' PHILODENDRON (1 PLANT)
H. LICORICE PLANT (1 PLANT)

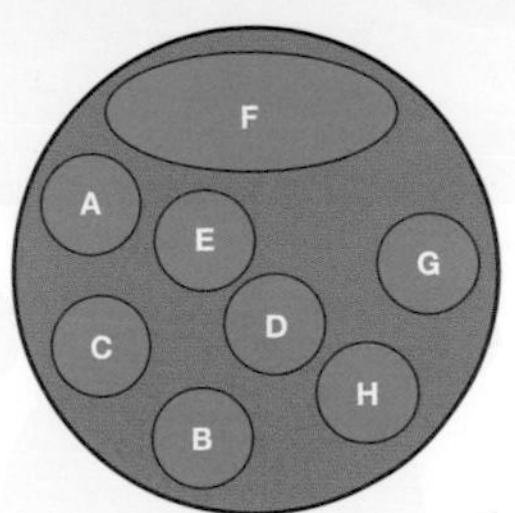

Container Crop

Turn an inexpensive birdbath into a planter by drilling drainage holes into the bottom of its bowl. With the base in place, you'll have easy, no-bend/no-stoop access to your herbs.

- Light: Full sun.
- Water: Water daily to maintain evenly moist soil.
- Care tips: If a birdbath is not available, substitute any large pot. Sow lettuce seed in spring and plant starts of basil and parsley after the chance of frost has passed. Begin harvesting lettuce when it is 2 inches tall. Harvest basil and parsley anytime after planting. Pinch flower spikes off of basil plants to encourage bushy growth.

The lettuce will fizzle when temperatures rise. Replace it with your favorite culinary herbs and add fresh-from-the-garden flavor to summer meals.

For nonstop flavor, feed plants every two weeks with MIracle-Gro Water Soluble All Purpose Plant food.

CONTAINER CROP

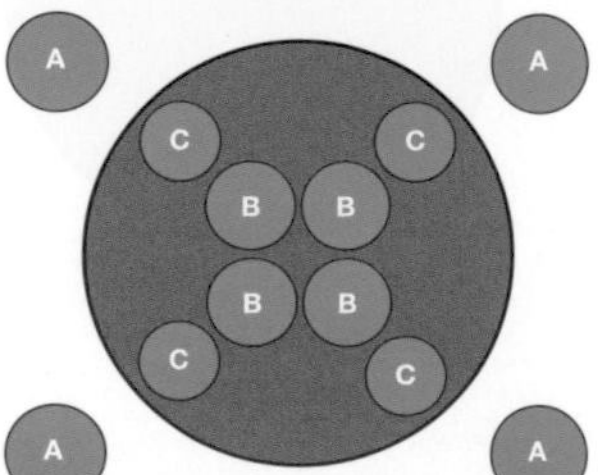

Plant list:

FOR A 14" DIAMETER POT

A. BASIL (4 PLANTS)

B. LETTUCE (4 PLANTS)

C. PARSLEY (4 PLANTS)

Plant Gallery

AFRICAN DAISY

African daisy *(Osteospermum ecklonis)*

FULL SUN • 8"–24" TALL AND WIDE • MOUNDING • BLOOMS SPRING TO FALL

AFRICAN DAISY is a cool-season annual that blooms in lavender, purple, white, or orange. Some have flat petals; those of others are rolled. Recent plant breeding efforts have resulted in a plethora of varieties that stand up to the heat of summer. Once planted exclusively in spring and fall, these hybrid osteospermum color containers throughout the growing season. Deadhead plants to promote bloom and water diligently; do not allow plants to wilt. **'LEMON SYMPHONY'** has yellow flowers with purple centers.

AGERATUM

Ageratum *(Ageratum houstonianum)*

FULL SUN • 6"–12" TALL AND WIDE; SOME VARIETIES UP TO 24" • TIDY MOUNDS • BLOOMS SPRING TO FALL

AGERATUM'S fuzzy clusters of flowers in shades of blue, purple, or white decorate containers all summer. Plants are exceptionally easy to grow and have good drought tolerance. Put ageratum along the edge of a container or behind trailing plants. If it becomes leggy in midsummer, shear it back by half. Long-blooming purple and blue varieties include **'ARTIST ALTO BLUE'**, **'ARTIST BLUE'**, and **'ARTIST PURPLE'**.

ANGELONIA

Angelonia *(Angelonia augustifolia)*

FULL SUN • 24"–36" TALL AND 12" WIDE • UPRIGHT • BLOOMS SPRING TO FALL

Also known as summer snapdragon, **ANGELONIA** has wands of blue, purple, white, pink, or pairs of these colors. Its impressive height and tolerance of extended periods of high temperatures make it a great plant for anchoring the center of a container planting. It grows best in slightly moist soil. **'ANGELFACE BLUE BICOLOR'** has dainty blue-and-white striped petals.

Bacopa *(Sutera hybrids)*

SUN TO SHADE • 4"–12" TALL AND WIDE • TRAILING • BLOOMS SPRING TO FALL

The small, delicate flowers of **BACOPA** cascade over the edge of a container shortly after planting. Its vigorous growth gives containers and hanging baskets a lush appearance. It can easily trail 3 feet in just one season. Heat and drought will take a toll on bacopa. Water regularly to help plants thrive. White is the most common color, but pink, purple, and lavender varieties are also available. Try the prolific white-blooming cultivars **'GIANT SNOWFLAKE'** and **'SNOWSTORM'**.

BACOPA

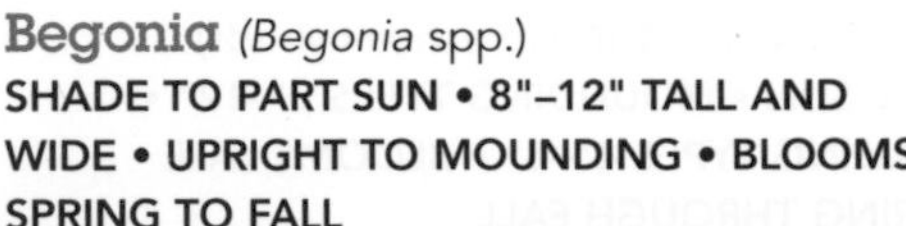

Begonia *(Begonia spp.)*

SHADE TO PART SUN • 8"–12" TALL AND WIDE • UPRIGHT TO MOUNDING • BLOOMS SPRING TO FALL

With its luminous leaves and nonstop flowers, begonias of all types are favorites for container gardens in shade. **WAX BEGONIAS** bear small flowers in red, pink, or white. Foliage is shiny green or flushed red. **TUBEROUS BEGONIAS** bloom in spectacular hues of yellow, red, orange, white, and pink. **REX BEGONIAS** offer foliage with interesting textures and colors. Keep begonias consistently moist and feed them every two weeks. Overwinter begonias by bringing them inside to a sunny window in fall.

BEGONIA

Black-eyed susan *(Rudbeckia hirta)*

FULL SUN • 12"–36" TALL AND 12"–18" WIDE • UPRIGHT MOUNDS • BLOOMS SUMMER AND FALL

In a container garden, grow **BLACK-EYED SUSAN** as an annual. Its yellow daisies draw attention as well as complement other flower and foliage colors. Deadhead black-eyed susan to encourage repeat flushes of bloom. It is an excellent cutting flower. **'IRISH EYES'** has yellow flowers with green centers. **'GOLDILOCKS'** has double to semi-double golden-orange flowers.

BLACK-EYED SUSAN

BLACK-EYED SUSAN VINE

Black-eyed susan vine

(Thunbergia alata)

FULL SUN • CLIMBS TO 8' TALL • TRAILING OR CLIMBING • BLOOMS SUMMER AND FALL

BLACK-EYED SUSAN VINE quickly scrambles up any sturdy structure, cloaking it in soft green foliage and trumpet-shaped yellow, white, or orange flowers. Plant it alone to add height to a group of container gardens. Or let it trail over the pot in a mixed pot. Regular watering is key to vigorous growth; don't let the vine wilt. Feed regularly with Miracle-Gro All Purpose Plant Food and trim wayward stems. **'SUNNY'** is a vigorous grower with yellow flowers.

CALIBRACHOA

Calibrachoa *(Calibrachoa* hybrids)

FULL SUN • MOUNDING TYPES 8"–12" • TRAILING TYPES 4"–6" • BLOOMS LATE SPRING THROUGH FALL

Blanketed with flowers resembling petite petunias, **CALIBRACHOA** is a popular new annual. Some varieties form tidy mounds while others trail and spill over the edges of containers. Check the plant tag to be sure you purchase the growth habit you desire. Calibrachoa is available in many colors including pink, white, red, purple, yellow, and orange. Feed plants every two weeks and water daily. Deadheading is not needed.

CELOSIA

Celosia *(Celosia argentea plumosa)*

FULL SUN • 8"–24" • UPRIGHT • BLOOMS SUMMER THROUGH FALL

CELOSIA shows off dense, brightly hued plumes in yellow, orange, red, and pink. Encourage abundant flower production by deadheading spent flowers as they fade. The plant will send up a new flush of blooms in a couple of weeks. Celosia grows best when watered and fed regularly. **'FLAMINGO FEATHER'** has light pink flowers atop 24-inch-tall stems.

Chrysanthemum

(Chrysanthemum ×grandiflorum)

SUN TO PARTIAL SHADE • 8"–24" TALL AND WIDE • MOUNDING • BLOOMS IN FALL

CHRYSANTHEMUM offers flowers that open in vivid hues of white, yellow, pink, bronze, burgundy, or red. These easy-to-grow plants, which are a short-lived perennial in the garden, appear at garden centers in late summer to early fall, just as their flowers are beginning to open. Let them perk up a pot of summer-blooming annuals by replacing plants that no longer look their best. Regular watering will prolong the chrysanthemum's colorful blooms.

CHRYSANTHEMUM

Coleus *(Solenostemon scutellarioides)*

SHADE TO PART SUN • 12"–24" TALL AND 12" WIDE • UPRIGHT • DISPLAYS SPECTACULAR FOLIAGE SPRING THROUGH FALL

Colorful, mottled foliage is the calling card of **COLEUS**. The leaves of this shade-loving plant can be solid or variegated in hues of yellow, chartreuse, green, pink, red, violet, burgundy, or nearly black. Pinch stem tips and remove flower spikes to increase bushiness. Feed plants regularly with Miracle-Gro All Purpose Plant Food. Hundreds of varieties are available.

COLEUS

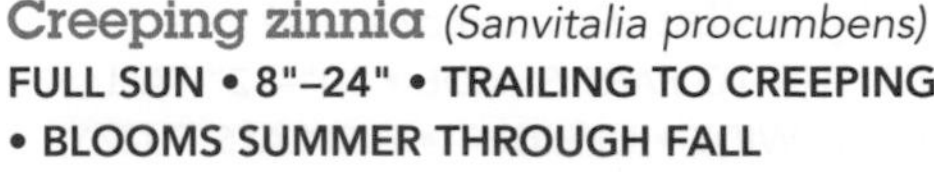

Creeping zinnia *(Sanvitalia procumbens)*

FULL SUN • 8"–24" • TRAILING TO CREEPING • BLOOMS SUMMER THROUGH FALL

CREEPING ZINNIA displays small, round yellow daisies on a low-spreading mound of foliage. It thrives in heat and its stems spill like a waterfall down the side of a pot. It is a great choice for hanging baskets and window boxes as well as for pots. Avoid overwatering; creeping zinnia does best when kept on the dry side. Pinch stems if they trail too long. Shear off spent flowers if they become unsightly. Feed plants with a continuous-release plant food. **'SUNBINI'** is a prolific bloomer in golden-yellow.

CREEPING ZINNIA

DAHLBERG DAISY

Dahlberg daisy *(Thymophylla tenuiloba)*

FULL SUN • 12" TALL AND WIDE • MOUNDING • BLOOMS SPRING THROUGH SUMMER

Bright-eyed **DAHLBERG DAISY** is a sunny addition to spring and summer container gardens. Its lacy foliage and mounding habit add valuable texture and shape to a planting. Dahlberg daisy is drought tolerant and does especially well in moss-lined hanging baskets, which tend to dry out quickly. Deadhead plants by shearing off spent blooms. Feed plants with a continuous-release plant food.

DIANTHUS

Dianthus *(Dianthus* spp.)

FULL SUN • 8"–18" TALL AND WIDE • MOUNDING • BLOOMS SPRING THROUGH FALL

Also called carnation or pink, **DIANTHUS** offers petite ruffled flowers, some with a spicy scent, and tidy blue-green foliage. Perennials as well as annuals are available and do well in containers. Some varieties grow upright, while others start upright, then cascade when their flowers open. Most dianthus grow best in regions with cool summers; they perform poorly in Zone 9 and higher. After plants finish blooming, remove spent flowers. A new flush will follow in a few weeks. Water daily and feed monthly.

DUSTY MILLER

Dusty miller *(Senecio cineraria)*

FULL SUN TO PART SHADE • 10"–12" TALL AND 6" WIDE • UPRIGHT • DISPLAYS FUZZY, SILVER FOLIAGE FROM SPRING THROUGH FALL

DUSTY MILLER is a container workhorse. Its nearly white velvety foliage adds eye-catching color and texture to a mixed container and stands tall through heat and occasional periods of drought. For best growth water every other day and feed plants monthly. Snip off flower spikes to encourage bushy growth. **'SILVERDUST'** has lacy leaves; those of **'CIRRUS'** are broad and finely toothed.

Fan flower *(Scaevola aemula)*

FULL SUN • 8"–12" TALL • CASCADING • BLOOMS SPRING THROUGH FALL

Called **FAN FLOWER** because of its fans of flowers, this annual is a relative newcomer to the container gardening world. Use it at the edge of containers to take advantage of its trailing habit. Keep soil evenly moist and feed plants once a week. Fan flower needs no deadheading, but you may need to cut back leggy stems to encourage branching. **'NEW WONDER'** has purple flowers and a vigorous habit. **'WHITE CHARM'** has white flowers that measure an inch across.

FAN FLOWER

Flowering tobacco *(Nicotiana alata)*

FULL SUN TO PART SHADE • 8"–16" TALL AND 8" WIDE • UPRIGHT • BLOOMS SPRING THROUGH FALL

Favorites of hummingbirds, the white, pink, red, yellow, or lavender trumpets of flowering tobacco rise above the plant's trouble-free foliage on tall stems. Keep plants neat and tidy by deadheading spent flower stems. Water regularly, especially in hot weather. Feed monthly. Plants in the **DOMINO SERIES** have large, upward-facing flowers.

FLOWERING TOBACCO

Fuchsia *(Fuchsia* hybrids)

SHADE TO PART SUN • 12"–24" TALL AND WIDE • UPRIGHT OR TRAILING • BLOOMS SPRING THROUGH FALL

FUCHSIA'S trailing stems and pendulous flowers form a lush display by early summer that continues until the first frost. Look for cultivars with variegated foliage and single or double flowers. Keep soil moist and feed plants lightly every two weeks with an acidifying plant food. Pinch stem tips in early summer to encourage bushiness. Deadhead plants to keep the flowers coming regularly. Grow fuchsia as a perennial in Zones 9 and 10.

FUCHSIA

GERANIUM

Geranium *(Pelargonium* spp.)

FULL SUN TO PART SHADE • 12"–24" TALL AND WIDE • MOUNDING • BLOOMS SPRING THROUGH FALL

Drought-tolerant, easy-to-grow **GERANIUMS** send up wand after wand of brightly hued flowers in shades of pink, red, lavender, and white. Pinch stem tips to encourage branching. Water moderately and fertilize twice a month. Deadhead regularly to encourage new flowers.

GERBERA DAISY

Gerbera daisy *(Gerbera jamesonii)*

FULL SUN • 8"–16" TALL AND 12" WIDE • BLOOMS SPRING THROUGH FALL

Sturdy stems hold the spectacular flowers of **GERBERA DAISY** several inches above the plant's foliage. These bright-eyed flowers are available in a rainbow of hues and are excellent as cut flowers. The plants will bloom throughout the summer as long as you feed them every two weeks and water daily. Deadhead to redirect plant resources into developing new flowers. Plants in the **FESTIVAL SERIES** grow 10 inches tall and have 3-inch-wide flowers.

GLOBE AMARANTH

Globe amaranth *(Gomphrena globosa)*

FULL SUN • 12"–24" TALL AND 12" WIDE • MOUNDING SHAPE WITH FLOWERS ON TALL STALKS• BLOOMS SUMMER THROUGH FALL

GLOBE AMARANTH shines in summer's heat. It is blanketed with round clusters of flowers in hues of white, pink, purple, or red. Use the flowers fresh or harvest and dry them for an everlasting bouquet. Globe amaranth is drought-tolerant but does best when watered every other day. Pinch stem tips to promote bushiness, and deadhead spent flowers. Feed every two weeks. **'STRAWBERRY FIELDS'** is a vigorous red-flowering variety.

Impatiens *(Impatiens walleriana)*

SHADE • 8"–12" TALL AND 10" WIDE • MOUNDING • BLOOMS SPRING TO FALL

A popular component of shade gardens, **IMPATIENS** thrive in containers. Their vivid flowers bloom in shades of white, pink, purple, orange, and red. Regular watering is essential because plants wilt rapidly in hot, dry conditions. Keep soil moist but not wet. Feed twice a month. Pinch stem tips after planting for bushy growth. Cut back leggy plants in midsummer. **'VICTORIAN ROSE'** flowers look like miniature pink roses. **NEW GUINEA HYBRIDS** are robust, perform well in sun, and often have variegated or red leaves.

IMPATIENS

Lantana *(Lantana camara)*

FULL SUN • 10"–40" TALL AND 20" WIDE • CASCADING • BLOOMS SUMMER THROUGH FALL • HARDY IN WARM REGIONS

Available in many colors of white, purple, red, yellow, orange, and pink and a variety of forms—from trailing to upright to mounded—**LANTANA** is a valuable container plant. Use it as a focal point or call on it to cascade over the edge. Lantana tolerates hot, dry conditions but blooms most profusely when fed lightly and watered daily. Pinch stem tips to encourage branching. Some varieties are fragrant. Note: Lantana seeds are poisonous.

LANTANA

Licorice plant *(Helichrysum petiolare)*

FULL SUN TO PART SHADE • 6"–12" TALL AND WIDE • GROWN FOR ITS FOLIAGE

LICORICE PLANT'S velvety-soft silver leaves cascade over the edge of pots, window boxes, and hanging baskets. Plants grow rapidly and can quickly overtake its companions in the container. If plants get out of control, shear them. Water regularly. Feed licorice plant once a month. Prune as needed to direct growth. **'LIMELIGHT'** has soft lemon-yellow foliage.

LICORICE PLANT

MARGUERITE DAISY

Marguerite daisy

(Argyranthemum frutescens)

FULL SUN • 12"–20" TALL AND WIDE • MOUNDING • BLOOMS SPRING THROUGH FALL

MARGUERITE DAISY, with its upright habit and months-long bloom time, is a great choice to anchor a container. It blooms in shades of yellow, white, pink, and lavender. Grow in a 10-inch pot with good drainage. Water regularly and feed lightly. Deadhead regularly and cut back often to keep fresh blooms coming and plants bushy. **'FIRST BLUSH'** has light pink, double flowers. **'BUTTERFLY'** is a popular yellow bloomer.

NEMESIA

Nemesia *(Nemesia fruticans)*

FULL SUN • 10"–16" TALL AND 10" WIDE • BLOOMS SPRING THROUGH FALL

This charming plant bears delicate clusters of pleasantly fragrant blossoms. It is perfect for planting at the base of taller plants or for anchoring the center of a hanging basket. Purple, pink, and white varieties are available. Many **NEMESIA** reseed; you'll find plants popping up in your garden next spring if you don't deadhead diligently. Water daily and feed every two weeks. **'AROMATICA TRUE BLUE'** is a fragrant purple and yellow variety.

ORNAMENTAL CABBAGE

Ornamental cabbage *(Brassica oleracea)*

FULL SUN TO PART SHADE • 12"–18" TALL AND WIDE • MOUNDING • GROWN FOR COLORFUL FOLIAGE

ORNAMENTAL CABBAGE leaves may be green, bluish-green, pink, white, or purple. They are sometimes ruffled and sometimes lacy and grow in a tight rosette shape. Plants do best in the cool temperatures of spring and fall. Water every other day and feed once a month. Good companions include pansies, stock, chrysanthemums, and asters. **'PEACOCK SERIES'** cultivars have feathery, finely toothed, red, white, and green leaves.

Ornamental sage *(Salvia spp.)*

FULL SUN • 12"–18" TALL AND 12" WIDE • UPRIGHT TO MOUNDING • BLOOMS SUMMER THROUGH FALL

SAGES are popular container garden annuals thanks to their long-lasting wands of colorful blooms. They bloom in purple, red, pink, and white blossoms. Some have variegated foliage. Keep soil moist and feed lightly each week. Cut spent flower stems to encourage blooms. **'VICTORIA BLUE' BLUE SALVIA** *(S. farinacea)* is an annual variety with intense blue-purple flowers. **SCARLET SAGE** *(S. splendens)* blooms in bright red.

ORNAMENTAL SAGE

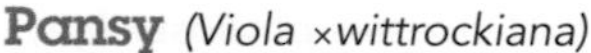

Pansy *(Viola ×wittrockiana)*

SUN OR PART SHADE • 6"–8" TALL AND WIDE • MOUNDING • BLOOMS SPRING AND FALL

PANSIES bloom with abandon in cool temperatures; in areas with mild winters and cool summers, they bloom nearly all year. Grow them with bulbs and other spring-bloomers or with fall-blooming favorites such as mums and asters. Keep soil moist and feed lightly every two weeks. Deadheading promotes bloom but is not necessary for a beautiful plant. **'CRYSTAL BOWL HYBRIDS'** are particularly heat-tolerant. **JOHNNY-JUMP-UP** *(V. tricolor)* has smaller flowers and a dense, mounding habit. It has similar cultural requirements to pansies.

PANSY

Perilla *(Perilla frutescens)*

FULL SUN TO SHADE • 24"–36" TALL AND 12" WIDE • UPRIGHT • GROWN FOR FOLIAGE

PERILLA has strikingly attractive dark purple foliage similar to that of basil. This upright plant is perfect for the center of a pot. Its small flowers are insignificant. Group two or three plants together in a large pot for an eye-catching statement. Perilla thrives in heat but requires regular watering and feeding. It tolerates both sun and shade. Encourage perilla to branch by pinching its stem tips. **'MAGILLA'** has dark leaves with creamy pink streaks down the center.

'MAGILLA' PERILLA

PETUNIA

Petunia (*Petunia ×hybrida*)

FULL SUN • 6"–12" TALL AND WIDE • MOUNDING OR TRAILING • BLOOMS SPRING THROUGH FALL

Trailing **PETUNIAS** are perfect for cloaking the side of your container with vibrant color. Simply plant them along the edge of your pot to cascade toward the ground. Use mounding petunias to hide the stems of taller plants. Petunias are vigorous growers and require regular watering. Feed them lightly every two weeks. Cut stems back by half when plants become leggy. **WAVE SERIES** petunias are especially floriferous trailing plants.

POLKA-DOT PLANT

Polka-dot plant (*Hypoestes phyllostachya*)

SHADE TO PART SUN • 10"–12" TALL AND 9" WIDE • MOUNDING • GROW FOR MOTTLED FOLIAGE

As its name implies, **POLKA-DOT PLANT** leaves are splashed with creamy-white speckles. Polka-dot plant tolerates drought and thrives in the cramped growing conditions of a container garden. Water plants every other day and feed plants monthly. Encourage polka-dot plant to branch by pinching the stem tips and removing flower spikes. **'CARMINA'** has bright red foliage. **'PURPURIANA'** has purple leaves.

POLYANTHUS PRIMROSE

Polyanthus primrose

(Primula ×polyantha)

SHADE TO PART SUN • 6" TALL AND 8" WIDE • MOUNDING • BLOOMS IN SPRING AND FALL

These cheerful plants boast white, yellow, pink, red, lavender, or blue-violet flowers. They thrive in cool temperatures and combine well with spring bulbs and other springtime favorites. **POLYANTHUS PRIMROSE** grows best in slightly moist soil and requires feeding every two weeks while in bloom to thrive. In mild-winter areas, plants will bloom all winter and into spring. Where winters are cold, plant them in containers in spring.

Snapdragon *(Antirrhinum majus)*

FULL SUN • 12"–18" TALL AND 8"–10" WIDE • UPRIGHT • BLOOMS SPRING THROUGH FALL

SNAPDRAGONS' upright habit is useful in the middle of containers. Tall varieties make focal points in a pot; shorter varieties are handy for covering the lower portions of leggy plants. They bloom in a rainbow of hues. Easy-to-grow snapdragons grow best in moist soil and benefit from regular feeding. Deadhead to promote rebloom. **'TAHITI SERIES'** snapdragons are dwarf plants with red, orange, pink, or white flowers. **'ROCKET SERIES'** cultivars grow 36 to 48 inches tall.

SNAPDRAGON

Stock *(Matthiola incana)*

FULL SUN TO PART SHADE • 12"–32" TALL AND 18" WIDE • UPRIGHT • BLOOMS IN SPRING AND FALL

A couple of **STOCK** plants in a container will perfume a patio or deck with a pleasing sweet fragrance. Stock is a cool-season annual. Plant it as soon as the chance of frost has passed and enjoy its white, pink, purple, red, or yellow blooms until the beginning of summer. Deadhead spent flower stalks to encourage repeat bloom. Water daily and feed every two weeks. **'CINDERELLA SERIES'** plants bear double flowers on 8- to 10-inch-tall stems.

STOCK

Strawflower *(Helichrysum bracteatum)*

FULL SUN • 10"–18" TALL AND 12" WIDE • MOUNDING; SOME VARIETIES CASCADE • BLOOMS SPRING THROUGH FALL

STRAWFLOWERS are grown for their summer-long good looks. The plants' papery, strawlike flowers last for weeks and quickly repeat blooming if you deadhead them. Lustrous dark green leaves form a nice backdrop for the other plants in the pot. Strawflowers bloom in shades of yellow, pink, and white. Avoid overwatering; plants like dry soil. The **'SUNDAZE SERIES'** has large yellow, pink, or white flowers on 10-inch-tall plants.

STRAWFLOWER

SWEET ALYSSUM

Sweet alyssum *(Lobularia maritima)*

FULL SUN • 4" TALL AND 10" WIDE • SPRAWLING MOUND • BLOOMS SPRING THROUGH FALL

SWEET ALYSSUM'S narrow leaves are all but hidden by its mass of white, pink, rose, or purple blooms. Plant it at the edge of a pot to take advantage of its habit, which will cascade over the rim of a pot. Sweet alyssum is also a good choice to insert into the side of a moss-lined hanging basket. After the first flush of bloom, cut plants back by half to encourage rebloom. Keep soil moist. Plants will decline in hot weather. Trim them back, and they often will return with cool temperatures.

SWEET POTATO

Sweet potato *(Ipomoea batatas)*

FULL SUN OR PART SHADE • 6" TALL AND 12"–36" LONG • CASCADING • GROW FOR VIGOROUS COLORFUL FOLIAGE

SWEET POTATO plants have a vigorous growth habit, quickly cloaking the sides of a pot, with foliage scrambling across the ground below. Ideal for hanging baskets, sweet potato should be snipped back to be kept in bounds and to discourage legginess. Keep plants moist and feed them once a month. Grasshoppers and other insects chew holes in the leaves. Cut off tattered foliage. **'MARGARITA'** has bright chartreuse leaves; **'BLACKIE'** boasts dark purple, almost black, foliage.

TWINSPUR

Twinspur *(Diascia* hybrids)

FULL SUN • 8"–16" TALL AND WIDE • MOUNDING TO UPRIGHT • BLOOMS SPRING TO FALL

Cover the edges of your containers with the delicate flowers of **TWINSPUR**. Available in shades of pink and red, twinspur get their name from the unique shape of their flowers. Plants do best in cool weather. Water daily and feed every two weeks. Twinspur will quickly drop flowers if allowed to dry out. **'TRAILING RED'** has vibrant deep red flowers, and **'APPLEBLOSSOM'** has lovely pink-and-white blooms.

Verbena *(Verbena ×hybrida)*

FULL SUN TO PART SHADE • 4"–14" TALL • TRAILING • BLOOMS SPRING THROUGH FALL

VERBENA'S long stems tumble over the sides of the pot, spilling flowers in nearly every hue but yellow. Use it in hanging pots, window boxes, and mixed pots. Feed every two weeks and provide moderate water. When stems finish blooming, pinch them back to the nearest flower bud or lightly shear stems to encourage another flush of bloom. **'TEMARI HYBRIDS'** are more bushy. **'TAPIEN HYBRIDS'** are only 3 to 7 inches tall.

VERBENA

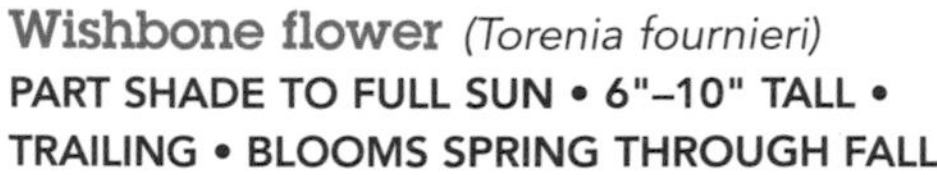

Wishbone flower *(Torenia fournieri)*

PART SHADE TO FULL SUN • 6"–10" TALL • TRAILING • BLOOMS SPRING THROUGH FALL

Low-growing **WISHBONE FLOWER** is perfect for the edges of containers. It will form a tidy mound, and its pale lavender flowers gently spill over the side of a pot as the plant grows. Wishbone flower thrives in partial shade but will tolerate sun, especially in northern regions. Keep plants moist. **'SUMMER WAVE HYBRIDS'** are stockier plants with larger flowers in more intense shades of purple and pink.

WISHBONE FLOWER

Zinnia *(Zinnia elegans)*

FULL SUN • 6"–24" TALL AND 12" WIDE • UPRIGHT • BLOOMS SUMMER AND FALL

ZINNIAS are a diverse group of plants. They bloom in every color but black and range in height from ground-hugging 6-inchers to lofty 3-foot-tall plants. Short, bushy types, such as **'PETER PAN HYBRIDS'** and **'DREAMLAND HYBRIDS'** (both 12 inches tall), are best for containers. Sizes and shapes vary too. Zinnias tolerate heat but must be watered regularly. Because they are highly susceptible to powdery mildew, direct the water to the plant base to keep foliage dry. Fertilize monthly. Deadhead regularly to keep plants in bloom.

ZINNIA

FOUNTAIN GRASS

Annual fountain grass

(Pennisetum setaceum)

FULL SUN • 24"–48" TALL AND 18" WIDE • BLOOMS IN SUMMER

Perhaps the most popular ornamental grass for container gardens, **FOUNTAIN GRASS** offers season-long good looks. Purple fountain grass (*P. s.* 'Rubrum') has beautiful burgundy leaves and plumes that range from purple to pink and creamy white. Fertilize container plants every two weeks. Water generously, never letting soil dry out. **'DWARF RUBRUM'**, **'RED RIDING HOOD'**, and **'EATON CANYON'** are popular, purple selections that grow 30 inches tall.

HAKONE GRASS

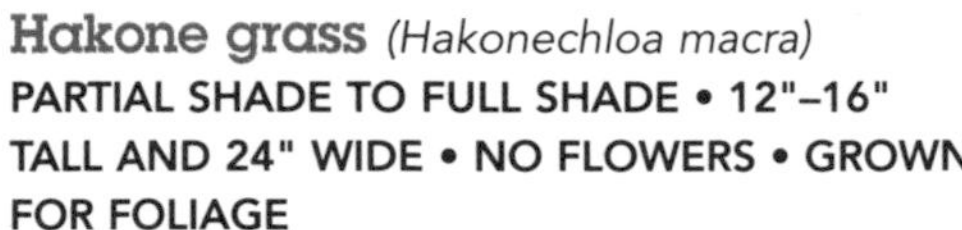

Hakone grass *(Hakonechloa macra)*

PARTIAL SHADE TO FULL SHADE • 12"–16" TALL AND 24" WIDE • NO FLOWERS • GROWN FOR FOLIAGE

Unlike the many popular upright growing grasses, **HAKONE GRASS** has a mounding or weeping habit. Plant it at the edge of a container to drape over the side. Hakone grass is hardy to Zone 5 and can be transplanted into the garden in early fall. Water every other day and feed plant monthly. The leaves of **GOLDEN HAKONE GRASS** (*H. m.* 'Aureola') are chartreuse striped with green.

MAIDEN GRASS

Maiden grass

(Miscanthus sinensis 'Gracillimus')

FULL SUN • 48" TALL AND 24" WIDE • BLOOMS LATE SUMMER THROUGH WINTER

MAIDEN GRASS is a large, stately grass best suited for large containers. It has narrow green leaves with white veins down their centers. The foliage turns bronze in fall and bleaches to nearly white in winter. Fluffy plumes appear in late summer and persist through winter. It is hardy in Zones 4 through 9 and can be planted in the garden in early fall. Maiden grass is drought tolerant but does best when watered every other day. Feed monthly.

Mexican feather grass

(Stipa tenuissima)

FULL SUN • 12"–18" TALL AND WIDE • BLOOMS IN SUMMER

This perennial grass (hardy to Zone 7) has needle-thin leaves and airy flower heads. Its neat and tidy habit makes it an excellent focal point for a container garden. Both its seedheads and foliage turn light gold by late summer. Allow **MEXICAN FEATHER GRASS** to remain in the container through winter so you can enjoy the buff stems and plumes until spring. It does best in moderately fertile potting soil that you let dry between waterings.

MEXICAN FEATHER GRASS

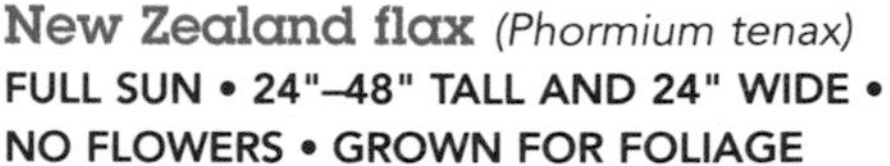

New Zealand flax *(Phormium tenax)*

FULL SUN • 24"–48" TALL AND 24" WIDE • NO FLOWERS • GROWN FOR FOLIAGE

NEW ZEALAND FLAX is a striking architectural plant. Its straplike leaves are often variegated with shades of green, white, red, or yellow. It is an excellent plant for the center of a large planter where you want height, color, and texture. While it is small, this slow-growing plant should be combined with small mounding or cascading plants so that it is not outgrown over the summer. Water amply and fertilize weekly until late summer. Overwinter New Zealand flax in a cool (50°F) spot out of direct sunlight; keep it on the dry side.

NEW ZEALAND FLAX

Sedge *(Carex spp.)*

FULL SUN TO PART SHADE • 10"–16" TALL AND 10" WIDE • NO FLOWERS • GROW FOR FOLIAGE

SEDGES are graceful plants with thin leaves. Some, such as **WEEPING BROWN SEDGE** *(C. flagellifera),* have a pleasing cascading habit while others grow upright. Sedges combine well with perennials such as coral bells, dead nettle, and asters. **LEATHERLEAF SEDGE** (*C. buchananii)* has bronze-colored leaves. Sedges have excellent drought tolerance. Water every other day and feed monthly.

SEDGE

CORAL BELLS

Coral bells *(Heuchera* spp.)

PART SHADE • 8"–30" TALL AND 12" WIDE • MOUNDING • BLOOMS SPRING AND EARLY TO MID SUMMER

CORAL BELLS is grown for its colorful mounds of foliage and sprays of bright flowers. (New hybrids may have less showy white flowers.) Purple-leaved hybrids contrast nicely with green, silvery, or chartreuse foliage and pastel flowers. Keep plants moist and fertilize monthly. Remove spent flower stems to encourage longer bloom. Transplant coral bells into the garden in early fall. Zones 3–8.

DEAD NETTLE

Dead nettle *(Lamium* spp.)

SHADE TO SUN • 6"–12" TALL AND 24" WIDE • TRAILING TO MOUNDED • BLOOMS SPRING AND EARLY SUMMER

DEAD NETTLE is one of the few plants that offers attractively variegated foliage and pleasing flowers. Flowers are available in shades of white and pink. The green foliage is splashed with white, silver, or yellow. Plant dead nettle near the edges of pots or window boxes. It will drape over the edge of the container as it grows. Water daily and feed monthly. **'GOLDEN ANNIVERSARY'** has pink flowers and gold, variegated foliage. Zones 3–7.

FERNS

Ferns (many species)

SHADE • 6"–48" TALL AND 6"–24" WIDE, DEPENDING ON SPECIES • UPRIGHT OR MOUNDING • GROW FOR FOLIAGE

A **FERN'S** lacy fronds fill the spaces around more colorful plants in a container garden. Some are upright; others drape. Moderately fertile potting mix that is high in organic matter ensures healthy growth. Keep soil moist and fertilize monthly. **BUTTON FERN** (*Pellaea rotundifolia*) grows 6 to 8 inches tall and wide and has pleasing round leaflets. **JAPANESE PAINTED FERN** (*Athyrium nipponicum* 'Pictum') has maroon stems and gray-green leaves. Hardiness varies among the species.

White gaura *(Gaura lindheimeri)*

FULL SUN OR PART SHADE • 10"–36" TALL AND 12" WIDE • UPRIGHT AND AIRY • BLOOMS IN SUMMER

GAURA is a popular perennial with a graceful, airy habit and tolerance of a variety of growing conditions. Its delicate flowers rise like tiny butterflies above the green foliage below. Deadhead spent flowers to encourage continuous blooming. Gaura is drought-tolerant; allow the soil to dry slightly between waterings. Feed monthly. **'PERKY PINK'** grows no more than 12 inches tall and has pink flowers on long stems. Zones 5–9.

WHITE GAURA

Hosta *(Hosta* spp.)

SHADE TO PART SUN • 6"–24" TALL AND 6"–36" WIDE • MOUNDING • BLOOMS IN SUMMER • GROW MAINLY FOR FOLIAGE

HOSTAS are grown for their bold heart-shape leaves, which vary from blue-green to yellow-green, often variegated or roughly textured. Plants may be as little as 6 inches to several feet tall and wide. Grow large hostas alone or in mixed pots. Yellow-green types need part sun for best color; blue-green ones do best in shade. Keep plants watered and feed lightly every month. Overwinter hostas in their containers in an unheated garage or sink the pot into a bed and mulch it. Zones 3–8.

Yarrow *(Achillea* spp.)

SUN • 24" TALL AND WIDE • MOUNDING TO UPRIGHT • BLOOMS IN SUMMER

YARROW has fragrant fernlike foliage that adds great texture to a planting combination. Its sulfur yellow, white, pink, or red flowers open in early summer and then fade to a muted hue as they mature. This drought-tolerant plant is a great choice for containers. Water every other day or so. Feed plants once a month during the growing season. **'CORONATION GOLD'** has long-lasting yellow flowers. **'CERISE QUEEN'** has medium pink flowers that fade to cream-pink in late summer. Zones 3–9.

YARROW

TULIPS

Spring-flowering bulbs

FULL SUN TO PART SHADE • 6"–24" TALL AND 3"–12" WIDE • BLOOMS IN SPRING

Enjoy harbingers of spring in your container garden weeks before traditional container planting time with the help of spring-flowering bulbs. When planted and chilled properly spring-flowering bulbs will poke up through the soil in your containers at about the same time they emerge in the landscape. For more on preparing spring bulbs for container gardens, see page 41.

Bulbs recommended for forcing

CROCUSES
'FLOWER RECORD'—purple
'JEANNE D'ARC'—white
'MAMMOTH YELLOW'—yellow

DAFFODILS
'BRIDAL CROWN'—double, white flower with an orange center
'CARLTON'—golden yellow
'GERANIUM'—white flower with an orange center
'TETE A TETE'—yellow miniature

GRAPE HYACINTH
'BLUE SPIKE'—double, blue flower
'EARLY GIANT'—deep blue

HYACINTHS
'AMETHYST'—lilac purple
'CARNEGIE'—white
'JAN BOS'—pinkish red
'YELLOW QUEEN'—yellow

PAPERWHITE NARCISSUS (No chilling required)
'BETHLEHEM'—creamy white
'GALILEE'— pure white
'GRAND SOLEIL D'OR'—yellow flower with an orange center

TULIPS
'ANGELIQUE'—double, pink
'APRICOT BEAUTY'—apricot
'CHRISTMAS MARVEL'—cherry pink
'MONTE CARLO'—double, yellow
'PAUL RICHTER'—scarlet red
'SHIRLEY'—white-edged purple

Caladium (*Caladium bicolor*)

SHADE • 24" TALL AND WIDE • NO FLOWERS • GROWN FOR FOLIAGE

CALADIUM has large, heart-shape leaves marked with white, pink, or red, or a combination of all three colors that offer an exotic, tropical look. Caladium needs ample water and monthly feeding to thrive. It is usually grown as an annual, but the tubers can be overwintered indoors and moved outside when temperatures stay above 60°F. **'FREIDA HEMPLE'** and **'POSTMAN JOYNER'** have a green edge and a red center. **'FIRE CHIEF'**, **'ROSEBUD'**, and **'WHITE QUEEN'** all tolerate partial sun.

Canna (*Canna* cultivars)

FULL SUN OR PART SHADE • 3'–7' TALL AND 2'–3' WIDE • BLOOMS IN SUMMER • ALSO GROWN FOR ATTRACTIVE FOLIAGE

CANNA

CANNA'S bold texture and color brings a touch of the tropics. Start tubers indoors in midwinter (they'll take three weeks to send up shoots) or plant pre-sprouted tubers from the garden center in early summer. Canna is easy-to-grow; it thrives with daily watering and feeding every two weeks. **'PRETORIA'** has orange flowers and yellow-and-green striped leaves. **'PRESIDENT'** has scarlet flowers and glossy green foliage.

Dahlia (*Dahlia* hybrids)

FULL SUN OR PART SHADE • 1'–4' TALL AND WIDE • FLOWERS IN SUMMER

DAHLIA

DAHLIA is grown for its petal-packed flowers. This excellent cutting flower comes in shades of pink, white, red, yellow, orange, and purple. Plant the dormant tuber directly into a container in late spring or begin with a sprouted plant. Dahlias are heavy feeders. Feed plants every two weeks with Miracle-Gro All Purpose Plant Food. Clip off spent blooms as soon as they fade, and the plant will quickly send up more flowers. **'ESTHER'** grows 1 to 2 feet tall and has yellow-orange flowers. **'ARABIAN NIGHT'** has wine-red, ball-shape flowers; it grows 1 to 2 feet tall.

Trees and shrubs

BOXWOOD

DAPHNE

DWARF BUTTERFLY BUSH

Plant most trees and shrubs in their own large containers. Trees suitable for planters grow slowly; even dwarf forms rarely attain more than a couple of inches of new growth a year.

In cold areas, overwinter containers of trees and shrubs by enclosing them within a cylinder of chicken wire filled with dried leaves or straw. Alternatively wrap pots with burlap for insulation. Nestle these pots against the east or north side of your house to keep them sheltered and warmer than they would be in an open location.

Protect broadleaf and needled evergreens from moisture loss by spraying them with an antitranspirant. Use the product before daytime temperatures regularly sink below 45°F.

Bay laurel *(Laurus nobilis)*
FULL SUN TO PART SHADE • 6' TALL AND 4' WIDE • HARDY IN ZONES 8–10
Use this large, broadleaf evergreen as a background or screen plant in a container garden. Keep soil moderately moist and feed lightly from spring to midsummer. Pinch stem tips to shape plants and encourage branching.

Bird's nest spruce *(Picea abies* 'Nidiformis')
FULL SUN • 3' TALL AND WIDE • HARDY IN ZONES 4–9
Spray bird's nest spruce with an antitranspirant in winter to prevent the needles from turning brown. Feed with a controlled-release plant food and water as needed to keep soil moist.

Boxwood *(Buxus* spp.)
PART SHADE • 24" TALL AND 18" WIDE • HARDY IN ZONES 5–8
This broad-leaf evergreen can be pruned into geometric shapes. Grow in a protected spot out of the wind. Keep soil moist and fertilize monthly. Prune to shape in spring.

Daphne *(Daphne ×burkwoodii)*
PART SHADE • 36" TALL AND WIDE • HARDY IN ZONES 4–8
Fragrant flowers decorate this broad-leaf evergreen in spring. Feed with a controlled-release plant food and allow plants to dry out slightly between waterings.

Butterfly bush *(Buddleia davidii)*

FULL SUN • 3'–5' TALL AND 3' WIDE • HARDY IN ZONES 5–8

Pink, purple, white, and yellow summer flowers attract butterflies. Encourage a bushy plant by pinching off bloom spikes shortly after planting. Allow flowers to develop after the shrub fills out. Water daily and feed every two weeks.

PLUM

Holly *(Ilex crenata* and *I. opaca)*

SUN TO PART SHADE • 36" TALL AND WIDE • HARDY IN ZONES 5–9

You'll need a male and female plant of this broadleaf evergreen to produce red berries. Fertilize in late winter. Keep soil moist during the growing season and barely moist in winter. Prune in winter before new growth begins.

RHODODENDRON AND AZALEA

Japanese maple

(Acer palmatum dissectum)

PART SHADE • 6' TALL AND WIDE • HARDY IN ZONES 6–9

Choose from varieties with leaves in shades of green, red, and yellow. Prune lightly in early summer. Water as needed to maintain moist soil and feed with a controlled-release plant food.

Lemon *(Citrus limon)*

FULL SUN • 10' TALL AND WIDE • HARDY IN ZONES 9–11

Provide ample water and plant food. Lemons need no pruning, but you may want to prune to shape plants. Overwinter this fruiting plant in an enclosed porch or sunroom where it will receive medium light.

Purpleleaf plum *(Prunus ×cistena)*

FULL SUN • 6' TALL AND 5' WIDE • HARDY IN ZONES 2–8

Purple foliage, fragrant spring flowers, dark purple fruit in early summer are the hallmarks of purpleleaf plum. Feed plants monthly throughout the growing season beginning in spring when leaves reach full size. Water as need to keep soil moist.

Rhododendron and azalea *(Rhododendron* spp.)

PART TO FULL SHADE • 24" TALL AND WIDE • HARDY IN ZONES 6–8

Colorful spring flowers decorate these broadleaf evergreens. Use an acidifying plant food, following package directions. Deadhead faded blooms. Prune lightly to shape plants.

LETTUCE

STRAWBERRY

SWEET PEPPER

Vegetables

Bush and pole beans

8 PLANTS PER 24-INCH POT • WARM SEASON
Containers should have a minimum depth of 10 inches. Sow seeds 1½ to 2 inches apart. Thin seedlings to 4 inches apart for bush beans and 6 inches apart for pole beans. Bush beans require no stakes; pole beans require a 6-foot-tall trellis for support. Pick regularly to keep plants bearing.

Carrot

9 PLANTS PER 12-INCH POT • COOL SEASON
Use a 6- to 9-inch-deep pot for short carrots and 12- to 16-inch-deep pot for long varieties. Sow seeds ½ inch apart and deep. Thin to 3 inches apart.

Cucumber

1 PLANT PER 12-INCH POT • WARM SEASON
Sow seeds 3 inches apart and 1 inch deep in a 12- to 18-inch-deep container. Thin seedlings to 8 inches apart. Set up a sturdy trellis in the pot at planting and twine vines up it as they grow. Pick regularly or plants will stop bearing.

Lettuce

4 PLANTS PER 12-INCH POT • COOL SEASON
Sow seeds 1 inch apart and ¼ inch deep in a 12-inch-deep pot. Thin seedlings to 8 inches apart. Harvest a few outer leaves at a time or cut the whole plant. Discard plants when they become bitter.

Onion

9 BULBS PER 12-INCH POT • COOL SEASON
Plant onion sets (small bulbs) 1 to 2 inches apart and 3 inches deep in an 8- to 10-inch-deep container. Plant onions every two weeks for a continuous supply.

Radish

12 PLANTS PER 12-INCH POT • WARM SEASON
Use a 6- to 12-inch-deep container depending on whether you are growing long or round radishes. Sow seeds ½ inch deep and 1 inch apart. Pair radishes, a spring crop, with tomatoes and peppers, which mature in summer.

Strawberry

5 PLANTS PER 16-INCH POT • PERENNIAL

Plant strawberries in containers that are at least 8 inches deep. Feed plants every two weeks while they are growing and blooming. Everbearing strawberries produce fruit all summer. Check with your local extension service to learn which varieties do best in your area. Hardy in Zones 4–10.

Sweet and hot peppers

1 PLANT PER 14-INCH POT • WARM SEASON

Transplant seedlings to pots that are at least 15 inches deep. Harvest peppers while they are green. Where summers are long, you can let them ripen to red or yellow.

TOMATO

Swiss chard

4 PLANTS PER 12-INCH POT

Sow seeds 1 to 2 inches apart and 1 inch deep in a 10- to 12-inch-deep container. Thin seedlings to 10 inches apart. Begin harvesting outer leaves when plants are 4 inches tall.

Tomato

1 PLANT PER 24-INCH POT • WARM SEASON

Transplant seedlings into a 24-inch-deep pot for indeterminate tomatoes (those that set fruit all summer), an 18-inch-deep pot for determinate varieties (those that have just one crop), and an 8- to 10-inch-deep pot for patio tomatoes. Both indeterminate and determinate varieties will need staking.

BASIL

Herbs

Basil

24" TALL AND 12" WIDE • ANNUAL

Plant basil in spring in a 9-inch-deep pot. You can grow it from seed or transplant seedlings. Keep soil moist and fertilize regularly. Basil does best in warm weather. Pinch off flowers to promote foliage growth.

Chives

SUN TO PART SHADE • 12" TALL AND 18" WIDE • PERENNIAL

Chives require moist soil and plentiful plant food. The container should be at least 9 inches deep. Hardy in Zones 3 to 11. Harvest leaves throughout the growing season.

LAVENDER

OREGANO

PARSLEY

Cilantro

24" TALL AND 10" WIDE • ANNUAL

Cilantro is a popular ingredient in Mexican dishes. Grow it in a 9-inch-deep pot in sun to part sun. Keep soil moist and fertilize regularly. Remove flowers that form in midsummer to encourage continued leaf production.

Lavender

SUN • 18" TALL AND 24" WIDE • PERENNIAL

Grow lavender in full sun in a pot that is at least 12 inches deep. Keep soil moderately moist; take care not to overwater. Lavender needs little plant food. Harvest and dry the fragrant foliage and flowers. Hardy in Zones 5–9.

Mint

24" TALL AND 36" WIDE • PERENNIAL

Grow mint in sun or part shade and provide good moisture and ample fertilizer. Choose a pot that is at least 9 inches deep. Mint is a vigorous grower; do not plant it in the garden, as it will quickly take over nearby plants. Hardy in Zones 5–10.

Oregano

24" TALL AND WIDE • PERENNIAL

Transplant oregano seedlings into a 9-inch-deep container. Grow them in a sunny spot. Water when the top inch of soil is dry and fertilize once a month. Harvest oregano by snipping the tender stems. Overwinter plants indoors. Hardy in Zones 5–9.

Parsley

12" TALL AND WIDE • ANNUAL

Grow parsley in a 9-inch-deep pot in sun to part sun. Keep soil moist and fertilize regularly. Remove flowers that form in midsummer to encourage continued leaf production.

Rosemary

24" TALL AND WIDE • PERENNIAL

Transplant rosemary seedlings or cuttings into a 9- to 12-inch-deep container. Grow it in full sun. Water when soil is dry. Feed plants monthly or every other month. Where rosemary is not hardy, overwinter it indoors in a sunny window. Hardy in Zones 8–10.

INDEX

Index

Hardiness Zone Map

This map of climate zones helps you select plants for your garden that will survive a typical winter in your region. The United States Department of Agriculture (USDA) developed the map, basing the zones on the lowest recorded temperatures across North America. Zone 1 is the coldest area and Zone 11 is the warmest.

Plants are classified by the coldest temperature and zone they can endure. For example, plants hardy to Zone 6 survive where winter temperatures drop to –10° F. Those hardy to Zone 8 die long before it's that cold. These plants may grow in colder regions but must be replaced each year. Plants rated for a range of hardiness zones can usually survive winter in the coldest region as well as tolerate the summer heat of the warmest one.

To find your hardiness zone, note the approximate location of your community on the map, then match the color band marking that area to the key.

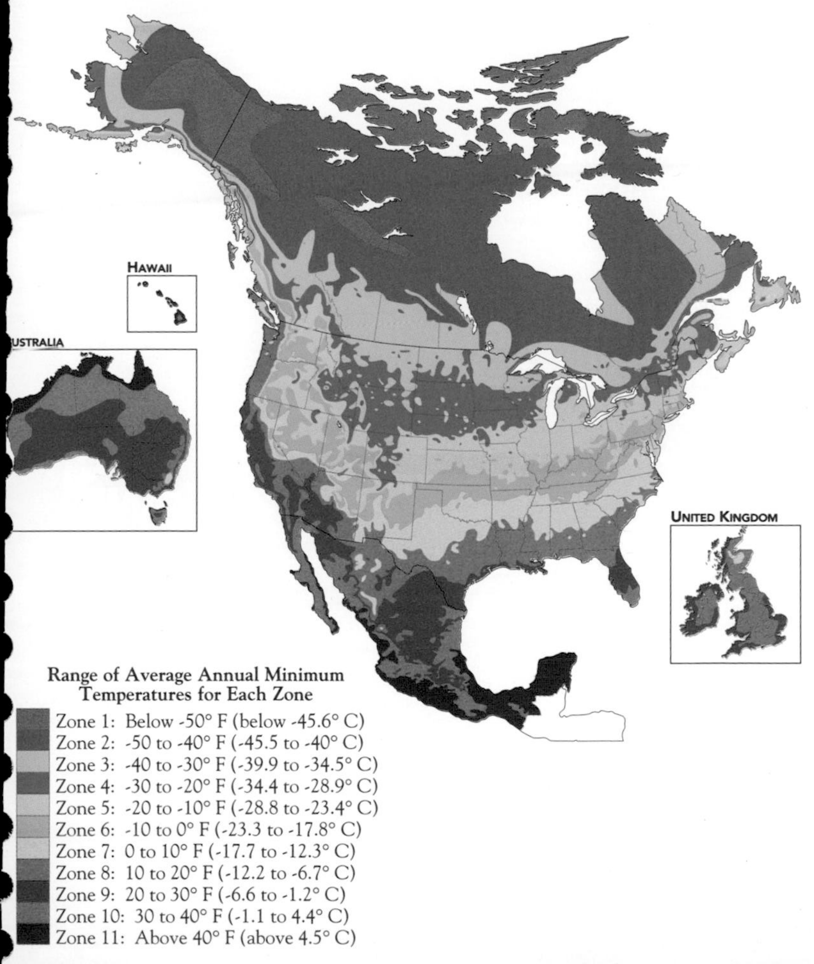

Take Them Outdoors!

WATERPROOF BOOKS™

New For Spring 2007
- Scotts Sprinklers and Watering Systems
- Miracle-Gro Container Gardens
- Ortho Lawn Problem Solver

Other Great Waterproof Titles
- Scotts Lawns
- Miracle-Gro Water Gardens
- Miracle-Gro Vegetables
- Miracle-Gro Roses
- Miracle-Gro Perennials
- Ortho Flower Problem Solver

All Your Garden Tools Should Be This Rugged.

Pocket-Size • Cleanable • Durable • Tear-Resistant • Lightweight

Container Gardens

Miracle-Gro Container Gardens shows you how to garden even when you have no garden space. Create potted gardens spilling over with colorful flowers, luscious vegetables, or long-lasting perennials. It's all you need to know in a compact package. Best of all, it's printed on waterproof paper.

- **STEP-BY-STEP PHOTOS** walk you through the process of creating beautiful container gardens.
- **RECIPES** provide complete planting and care advice for 21 gardens.
- **SELECTION GUIDE** features the best plants for container gardens.

THIS BOOK IS WATERPROOF

- Use it in the garden.
- Lay it flat for easy reference.
- Wipe pages clean of spills and dirt.
- Make notes on it for later reference.

$9.95
$12.95 in Canada
Visit us at meredithbooks.com

ISBN 978-0-696-23203-9

Acknowledging the diversity of practice in different laboratories, the authors of the chapters in this volume have been left free from editorial interference, to speak authentically with "their own voices" on the details of the procedures they describe. Consequently, it is not surprising that minor differences can readily be found by readers comparing, for instance, SDS-PAGE recipes between chapters, notwithstanding that the same source (Laemmli, 1970) is cited by all the authors concerned. The frequency with which some basic methodological motifs (for example, overlay blotting and the use of GST fusion proteins) recur in several chapters is a measure of the strength and importance of these techniques. A guiding editorial principle throughout the *Methods in Molecular Biology* series is that each chapter should constitute a self-contained description—these repetitions are therefore not only inevitable but essential in the service of this objective. The accumulated experience and "know-how" from 20 independent laboratories is distilled into the protocols featured in this volume. In many cases, the methods and applications described have originated or been developed in the laboratories of the contributing authors, and in all cases these laboratories are actively (and often eminently) engaged in research in the area(s) of their contribution(s). It is a rapidly growing field, one in which technical innovation continues to open up new and exciting possibilities: the areas of surface plasmon resonance and two-hybrid analysis are cases in point. It is hoped that the protocols gathered together here will serve as a firm methodological foundation for laboratories newly entering into this area and as a trusty reference work for those already well-established in it.

Acknowledgments

The editor gratefully acknowledges the cooperation and collaboration of the 34 authors contributing to this volume and the encouragement of the Series Editor, John Walker, and production team at Humana Press, headed by Tom Lanigan. Colleagues at the Hannah Research Institute, and the institute's director, have helped and advised me in many different ways and I am pleased for this opportunity to acknowledge their support in bringing this project to fruition; special thanks must go to Eileen D'Agostino for her secretarial and organizational backup. The Hannah Research Institute is funded by the Scottish Office Agricultural, Environment, and Fisheries Department.

Roger A. Clegg

Contents

Contributors

NEIL G. ANDERSON • *Hannah Research Institute, Ayr, Scotland, UK; Present Address: School of Biological Sciences, University of Manchester, UK*

JAMES BEATTIE • *Hannah Research Institute, Ayr, Scotland, UK*

GRAEME B. BOLGER • *Veterans Affairs Medical Center; Departments of Medicine (Hematology/Oncology) and Oncologic Science, Huntsman Cancer Institute, University of Utah, Salt Lake City, UT*

KEVIN P. CAMPBELL • *Howard Hughes Medical Institute, Department of Physiology and Biophysics, University of Iowa College of Medicine, Iowa City, IA*

ERIC CHANAT • *Laboratoire de Biologie Cellulaire et Moléculaire, Institut National de la Recherche Agronomique, Jouy-en-Josas, France*

VINCENT M. COGHLAN • *Vollum Institute, Oregon Health Sciences University, Portland, OR*

ALAN COOPER • *Chemistry Department, Glasgow University, Glasgow, Scotland, UK*

MICHAEL CSUKAI • *Department of Molecular Pharmacology, Stanford University Medical Center, Stanford, CA*

ANDREA S. DITTIÉ • *Secretory Pathways Laboratory, Imperial Cancer Research Fund, London, UK*

ROBERT A. ERDMAN • *Geisinger Clinic, Sigfried and Janet Wein Center for Research, Danville, PA*

MAREE C. FAUX • *Vollum Institute, Oregon Health Sciences University, Portland, OR*

MATTHIAS FRECH • *Friedrich Miescher Institute, Basel, Switzerland*

MORAG A. GRASSIE • *Department of Biochemistry, University of Glasgow, Scotland, UK*

CHRISTINA A. GURNETT • *Howard Hughes Medical Institute, Department of Physiology and Biophysics, University of Iowa College of Medicine, Iowa City, IA*

MARK HARRIS • *MRC Retrovirus Research Laboratory, Department of Veterinary Pathology, University of Glasgow, UK; Present Address: Department of Microbiology, University of Leeds, UK*

ZACHARY E. HAUSKEN • *Vollum Institute, Oregon Health Sciences University, Portland, OR*

BRIAN A. HEMMINGS • *Friedrich Miescher Institute, Basel, Switzerland*

MILES D. HOUSLAY • *Division of Biochemistry and Molecular Biology, University of Glasgow, Scotland, UK*

WILLIAM A. MALTESE • *Geisinger Clinic, Sigfried and Janet Wein Center for Research, Danville, PA*

R. A. JEFFREY MCILHINNEY • *MRC Anatomical Pharmacology Unit, Oxford, UK*

FRAUKE MELCHIOR • *Department of Cell Biology, Scripps Research Institute, La Jolla, CA*

GRAEME MILLIGAN • *Department of Biochemistry, University of Glasgow, Scotland, UK*

DARIA MOCHLY-ROSEN • *Department of Molecular Pharmacology, Stanford University Medical Center, Stanford, CA*

JEAN H. OVERMEYER • *Geisinger Clinic, Sigfried and Janet Wein Center for Research, Danville, PA*

GEORGE PANAYOTOU • *Ludwig Institute for Cancer Research, London, UK*

ALAIN PAULOIN • *Laboratoire de Biologie Cellulaire et Moléculaire, Centre de Recherche de Jouy, Jouy-en-Josas, France*

JAMES G. PRYDE • *Respiratory Medicine Unit, Rayne Laboratory, Department of Medicine (RIE), University of Edinburgh Medical School, Edinburgh, UK*

MICHAEL F. G. SCHMIDT • *Institute for Immunology and Molecular Biology, Berlin, Germany*

GRANT SCOTLAND • *Division of Biochemistry and Molecular Biology, University of Glasgow, Scotland, UK*

JOHN D. SCOTT • *Vollum Institute, Oregon Health Sciences University, Portland, OR*

VICTORIA E. S. SCOTT • *Howard Hughes Medical Institute, Department of Physiology and Biophysics, University of Iowa College of Medicine, Iowa City, IA*

ROB STEIN • *Ludwig Institute for Cancer Research and Department of Oncology, University College London Medical School, London, UK*

SHARON A. TOOZE • *Secretory Pathways Laboratory, Imperial Cancer Research Fund, London, UK; Present Address: Institute for Immunology and Molecular Biology, Berlin, Germany*

MICHAEL VEIT • *Cell Biochemistry and Biophysics Program, Rockefeller Research Labs, Sloan-Kettering Institute, New York*

1

Surface Plasmon Resonance

Measuring Protein Interactions in Real Time

George Panayotou

1. Introduction

Interactions between macromolecules play a central role in most biological processes. Their analysis in vitro can shed light on their role in the intact cell by providing valuable information on specificity, affinity, and structure–function relationships. Significant progress in this respect has come with the advent, in the last few years, of commercially available biosensor technology ***(1)***. This has allowed the study of macromolecular interactions in real timc, providing a wealth of high-quality binding data that can be used for kinetic analysis, affinity measurements, competition studies, and so on. A major advantage of biosensor analysis is that there is no requirement for labeling one of the interacting components and then separating bound from free molecules—a fact that simplifies experimental procedures and provides more accurate measurements.

The most successful and widely used procedure for biosensor analysis is based on the phenomenon of surface plasmon resonance (SPR), which occurs upon the interaction of monochromatic light with a gold surface, under conditions of total internal reflection ***(2,3)***. As a result of SPR, a component of the incoming light (called the evanescent wave) penetrates the gold layer, resulting in a dip in the intensity of the reflected light. This occurs only at a certain angle of the incoming light, and the value of this angle depends on the refractive index of the medium in contact with the gold surface. The latter is coated with a hydrophilic dextran layer on which one of the interacting components is immobilized. The binding partner is injected over this surface and, as binding occurs, the refractive index of the medium is increased and the resulting change in the angle at which the intensity dip occurs is recorded ***(4)***. This response is

From: *Methods in Molecular Biology, Vol. 88: Protein Targeting Protocols*
Edited by: R. A. Clegg Humana Press Inc., Totowa, NJ

converted to arbitrary resonance units (RU). Within certain limits, there is a linear relationship between the mass of macromolecule bound on the surface and the response obtained. Therefore, in order to have a detectable response, the molecular size of the bound macromolecule is also important. The sensitivity of commercially available instruments varies. For the more widely used BIAcore™ and BIAlite™ instruments *(5)*, a mol-wt detection limit of 2 kDa is specified, although good quality data for reliable kinetic analysis usually requires molecules with mol wt greater than 10 kDa. With the more recently available BIAcore 2000™ instrument, sensitivity is improved by as much as 10-fold.

The applications of biosensor technology are too numerous to list all here. Because of the large size of antibody molecules, very good results can be obtained with SPR instruments when characterizing antibody affinities, as well as in epitope mapping *(6)*. Signal transduction pathways involve a large number of protein–protein interactions; they have also been analyzed successfully, for example, in growth factor binding to receptors and the subsequent interaction with signaling proteins *(7,8)*. The latter often contain small modular parts, such as SH2, SH3, and PH domains, which mediate and regulate signaling interactions. Therefore, instead of using full-size proteins, many studies have employed recombinant domains, which are easier to obtain and retain the binding characteristics of the intact proteins. SPR analysis is not restricted to protein–protein interactions; any macromolecule with a suitable size will change the refractive index of the medium in contact with the biosensor surface and therefore give a signal. Studies have been done with protein–DNA interactions, as well as with protein–lipid interactions *(9,10)*. Moreover, intact viruses, and even cells, can also be injected over the biosensor surface, in order to analyze their binding to receptors, lectins, and so on.

This chapter is aimed at the researcher who has access to a BIAcore instrument and has undertaken basic training in its operation. Given the wide range of potential applications, the emphasis here is on providing a general guide for the optimization of the methodology, which the researcher should modify for each particular application.

2. Materials

2.1. Equipment

1. BIAcore instrument (Biacore AB, Uppsala).
2. Sensor chips.
3. Disposable desalting columns.
4. 0.2-µm Disposable filters.
5. Degassing apparatus (pump or helium gas cylinder).

2.2. Reagents

1. *N*-Hydroxysuccinimide (NHS).
2. *N*-Ethyl-*N*'-(3-dimethylaminopropyl)-carbodiimide (EDC).
3. Acetate buffer, pH range 4.0–4.8.
4. 1*M* Ethanolamine, pH 8.5.
5. Goat anti–glutathione-*S*-transferase (GST) antibody (Biacore).
6. Rabbit antimouse IgG.
7. Avidin 1 mg/mL in water.
8. Standard running buffer: 20 m*M* HEPES, pH 7.5, 150 m*M* NaCl, 3.4 m*M* EDTA, 0.005% Tween-20.

3. Methods

3.1. Preparation of Running Buffer

A variety of different buffers can be used, depending on the application, but several considerations of pH, ionic strength, and use of detergents need to be taken into account (*see* **Notes 1–3**).

1. Prepare the running buffer fresh on each day of use.
2. Filter the buffer through a bottle-top 0.2-μm filter.
3. Degas thoroughly under vacuum (at least 20 min), or by bubbling helium gas for about 10 min.
4. Keep a small amount in a separate bottle for preparing dilutions for injections, and so on (*see* **Note 4**).
5. Insert the two tubes in the bottle, using small filter units at each end. These should be changed regularly and with every different buffer (*see* **Note 5**).

3.2. Use and Care of Biosensor Chips

1. BIAcore chips are guaranteed for continuous use of up to 3 d, but their useful life can be extended to months if treated properly. One very important factor is not to allow buffer to dry in the flow cells (*see* **Note 6**).
2. Redocking of used chips is possible, but it cannot be guaranteed that optimal performance will be restored. After undocking, the chip should be removed from its protective cover, placed immediately in a 50-mL tube containing running buffer, and kept at 4°C. For redocking, rinse the chip in distilled water and dry very carefully, using a stream of compressed air or lint-free paper. Then insert the chip in its cover (which should be kept free of dust) and perform as soon as possible the standard docking procedure, followed by the RINSE command (*see* **Note 7**).

3.3. Immobilizing One of the Interacting Molecules

This is probably the most crucial step for a successful biosensor analysis *(11)*. There are two major considerations when deciding which one of the two macromolecules whose interaction is studied will be immobilized on the surface and which will be injected in solution: size and stability. Since the signal depends on the size of the injected macromolecule, it is preferred that the smallest of the two components be immobilized. Moreover, the most stable of the two partners should be immobilized because it will have to withstand the regeneration procedure that is included at the end of each interaction in order to strip away any bound material and prepare the immobilized compound for the next injection. In many cases, this is not possible and an indirect method of attaching one component to the chip has to be followed (*see* **Subheadings 3.3.2.–3.3.3.**). The same is true if the immobilization procedure itself affects the binding, for example, by masking the interaction site.

3.3.1. Covalent Immobilization

This is the method of choice for stable macromolecules, such as many antibodies or small peptides. Two procedures are available: one for free amino groups (such as the N-terminus or lysine residues of a protein) and one for cysteine residues. All necessary reagents are available as kits from Biacore. The amino group method is the most widely used and, if the reagents are purchased separately, the following procedure should be used.

1. Mix equal volumes of 11.5 mg/mL NHS and 75 mg/mL EDC immediately before use (*see* **Note 8**).
2. Activate the surface by injecting 20–40 µL of the mix (the amount depending on the desired level of immobilized protein).
3. Inject the protein in acetate buffer (*see* **Note 9**).
4. More protein can be injected if the immobilization level required has not been attained.
5. Block all unreacted sites on the matrix with a 40-µL injection of a 1*M* ethanolamine solution.
6. If the regeneration agent that will be used later is known, it should be included in order to remove any noncovalently attached molecules.

3.3.2. Immobilization via Avidin or Streptavidin

This is the method used for biotinylated ligands, such as a peptide, protein, or an oligonucleotide. This is particularly advantageous for small ligands, because, when bound to avidin, they are better exposed at the dextran surface. The biotin can also act as a flexible spacer arm, thus preventing possible steric hindrance.

1. Immobilize streptavidin or avidin using the method described above and acetate buffer at pH 4.0. A level of 3000 to 6000 RU should be suitable for most applications (*see* **Note 10**).
2. Ensure that no free biotin is found in the preparation of the biotinylated material, using extensive dialysis, desalting columns or purification on a chromatography

system (for example, reversed-phase high-pressure liquid chromatography can be used for small peptides).

3. Inject the biotinylated material in small pulses of dilute solutions, until a suitable level of binding of the interaction partner is achieved (*see* **Note 11**).

3.3.3. Immobilization via Anti-GST or Other Antibodies

In cases in which direct covalent immobilization is problematic, indirect coupling via antibodies may be used. The main disadvantages are the possible involvement of antibody epitopes in the binding reaction and the constant dissociation of antigen from low-affinity antibodies, which will affect any affinity evaluation and the reproducibility of binding. Widespread use of GST-fusion proteins has led to the development of specific anti-GST antibodies as capturing molecules (a kit is commercially available from Biacore). Some small domains that are important in mediating signaling interactions, such as SH2 and PH domains, appear to be sensitive to direct immobilization and this procedure can be used for their GST-fusion form. Since the antibodies are directed against GST, there is little chance that they will interfere with binding, which could be the case with antibodies against the domains themselves.

1. Since a ternary complex will be formed, it is important that a substantial amount of antibody (approx 15,000 RU) be immobilized (*see* **Note 12**).
2. After the antigen is captured, allow dissociation to occur until a relatively stable baseline is reached (*see* **Note 13**).

3.4. Regeneration

The regeneration procedure needs to be considered carefully, so that, ideally, all bound material is removed and the covalently immobilized macromolecule retains its binding properties and can be used for repetitive injections. Because the conditions for regeneration generally tend to be rather harsh, the time of contact of the regeneration solution with the immobilized macromolecule should be kept to a minimum. One or two 4-µL pulses are usually sufficient.

1. Small peptides that are not expected to have a defined secondary structure are usually quite stable. For example, SH2- and SH3-domain ligands (tyrosine-phosphorylated and proline-rich sequences, respectively) can be regenerated with one 4-µL pulse of 0.05% sodium dodecyl sulfate (SDS), whether they are immobilized directly or via a biotin–avidin interaction.
2. Monoclonal antibodies vary greatly in their stability to regeneration agents. A starting point would be a pulse of 10 m*M* HCl (*see* **Note 14**).
3. The anti-GST antibodies mentioned above can be regenerated with 0.2*M* Glycine, pH 2.2 (*see* **Note 15**).

3.5. Preparation of Proteins

1. If a protein or peptide is to be immobilized directly, it is essential that no primary amines be present in the buffer, because they will couple to the matrix. Dialyze or pass the protein through a desalting column in order to exchange the buffer.
2. In the case of proteins that will be injected over the surface, it is advisable that they be transferred into running buffer in order to avoid sudden changes in the refractive index at the beginning and end of the injection. Small disposable buffer-exchange columns are usually the best choice, since they are much faster than dialysis (*see* **Note 16**).
3. For a detailed kinetic analysis, it is advisable that the injected protein be as pure as possible, so that its concentration can be accurately determined, and also to avoid nonspecific interactions of the contaminants. For a qualitative analysis, purity is less important, provided that a control surface is also used.
4. Cell lysates, conditioned media, or fractions from purification steps can also be used (*see* **Note 17**). Depending on the active concentration of the studied analyte, it may be necessary to concentrate the lysate or conditioned medium, using, for example, centrifugal filtration units with pore sizes of a defined mol-wt cutoff. Since many other components are present, it is essential to use a control surface in order to correct for nonspecific binding.

3.6. Optimization of Kinetic Analysis

Apart from the general considerations discussed above, special care is required to obtain data that are suitable for determination of association and dissociation rate constants.

1. The most commonly encountered problem is that of mass-transport limited interactions. They usually occur when all the incoming protein binds to the surface, and therefore the rate of binding is determined by the rate of transport of the protein to the ligand. Although this could be overcome by increasing the flow rate, this is not always practical, because it will also reduce substantially the interaction time (*see* **Note 18**). Mass-transport problems are evident when the data are plotted as log(dRU/dt) vs time. For an interaction obeying a simple one-to-one binding model, a linear, downward slope is obtained during the "on" phase. When mass-transport problems occur, the plot is then parallel to the time axis at least for the initial phase of the interaction and may start going downward later. These data cannot be used for reliable kinetic analysis. The best way to eliminate this problem is to reduce the number of binding sites on the surface. This should be optimized during the immobilization procedure. As a general guide, a response of 100–500 RU should be sufficient to obtain reliable data.
2. For an accurate estimation of the dissociation rate constant, it is important that dissociating material not be allowed to rebind to the surface. This is particularly true for interactions that are characterized by fast "on" and fast "off" kinetics. The problem is more evident later than earlier in the dissociation phase, because relatively more sites are available for rebinding. Increasing the flow rate during

dissociation may reduce the problem, but the best solution is to inject an excess of a competing substance that will interact with the dissociating protein and thus prevent its rebinding to the surface. Use the CO-INJECT command to inject the competitor immediately after the end of the protein injection so that the whole of the dissociation phase can be studied (*see* **Note 19**).

3.7. Equilibrium Binding Studies

Although the affinity of an interaction can be calculated from the kinetic constants, the latter are often not determined accurately, either because simple kinetic models do not fit the data or because of the experimental limitations described above. In this case, the affinity can be estimated from equilibrium binding data.

1. Prepare a series of dilutions of the protein, so that an approx 1000-fold range of concentrations is obtained.
2. Inject over the immobilized ligand and record the response obtained at equilibrium. Depending on the signal, repeat with more concentrations until a sigmoidal curve is obtained when plotting the response versus the log10 of the concentration of the injected protein (*see* **Note 20**).
3. In order to correct for bulk effects, inject the same range of concentrations over a control surface and subtract the response from that obtained with the specific ligand.
4. Estimate the affinity constant from the binding curve. This can be done with software supplied with the instrument, or by Scatchard analysis.

3.8. Competition Assays

A similar approach can be used to determine the potency of the inhibitor of an interaction. In this case, an IC50 value can be obtained, so that different inhibitors can be compared.

1. Ensure that a response of approx 300–600 RU is obtained for a typical protein interaction, and that equilibrium is reached.
2. Prepare a series of dilutions of the inhibitor (over a range of at least 1000-fold) and mix with the same amount of protein.
3. Inject over the immobilized ligand and record the response at equilibrium.
4. Plot the percent of specific binding vs the log10 of the inhibitor concentration and calculate the IC50 as the concentration that will reduce the binding obtained in the absence of inhibitor by half.

4. Notes

1. Preferably the pH of the running buffer should be above 7.0. This is because the dextran layer on which the interactions occur is carboxymethylated, and, at acidic pH values, the proteins might interact electrostatically with the matrix, giving high nonspecific binding. As a starting point, a HEPES buffer at pH 7.5 should be tried.

2. For the same reason, it is important that the ionic strength of the running buffer be adjusted. If possible, use 150 m*M* NaCl. Below 50 m*M* nonspecific interactions with the dextran layer may occur.
3. A low amount (0.005%) of the detergent Tween-20 (available as P20 in a highly purified 10% solution by Biacore) can help reduce nonspecific binding of hydrophobic proteins and will also prevent adsorption of molecules on the tubing, flow cells, and so on. However, it is not essential and can be left out, if it interferes with the interaction.
4. It is good practice to use the same buffer, because small variations between different preparations may result in sudden jumps of the signal at the beginning and end of each injection.
5. If the instrument is to be used at a temperature over 25°C, it is advisable to place the bottle in a heated water bath and to pass a slow stream of helium through the buffer for the duration of the experiments. This is to prevent the formation of bubbles during injection, which can distort the sensorgrams.
6. It is recommended that a continuous flow of 5 μL/min be appended to each programmed sequence of injections ("Continue" command from the "Users working tools" menu), especially if the instrument will not be used for several hours or overnight.
7. Always perform a dip check after docking to ensure that a proper signal is obtained for all flow cells.
8. Stock solutions of the two reagents should be kept at –20°C.
9. The pH of this solution is very important, since immobilization depends on the initial electrostatic interaction of the protein with the matrix. The lower the pH, the stronger this binding will be, but the likelihood of amino groups being protonated (and therefore unable to couple efficiently) will increase. It is advisable that various concentrations of a protein are made up in solutions of pH varying between 4.0 and 4.8 and are then injected over a surface that has not been treated with the NHS/EDC mix, so that only the electrostatic interaction will be observed. The highest pH at which a strong signal is obtained should be used subsequently. In this way, the amount of immobilized material can be fine-tuned.
10. Streptavidin coated chips are available commercially, but if the level of immobilized material needs to be optimized, avidin or streptavidin can be immobilized directly on a normal chip using the standard NHS/EDC procedure.
11. Because of the high affinity of the biotin–avidin interaction, there is usually no detectable dissociation of biotinylated material from the surface, even after more than 100 rounds of binding and regeneration.
12. As a rough guide the antibody should be able to capture approx 2000–3000 RU of a GST-fusion protein (or other antigen).
13. Injection of a short pulse of detergent (1% Tween-20 or 25 m*M* octyl-glucoside) or 0.5*M* NaCl may help to elute loosely associated antigen and to stabilize the baseline.
14. If the antibody is affected adversely by the regeneration, then an indirect method of coupling should be considered, such as via a secondary polyclonal antiserum.

The latter are usually stable and can be regenerated in some cases with a pulse of 100 m*M* HCl.

15. In some cases, removal of the bound GST-fusion protein is not complete, and a pulse of 0.05% SDS can be tried.
16. If differences in the buffers cannot be avoided, then inject the same protein over a control, nonbinding surface and use the instrument software to subtract the resulting sensorgram.
17. Many detergents will give high bulk signals and may also interact with the matrix. However, Tween-20 can be used up to a concentration of 5% without significant problems.
18. In the BIAcore instrument, a maximum of 50 μL can be injected at a time; however, up to 750 μL can be used with the BIAcore 2000.
19. The concentration of competitor required to completely prevent rebinding depends on the affinity of the interaction and should be determined empirically by trying a series of dilutions.
20. The amount of ligand immobilized, as well as the flow rate and volume injected, has again to be optimized, so that equilibrium is indeed reached during the course of the interaction.

References

1. Grifiths, D. G. and Hall, G. (1993) Biosensors—what real progress is being made? *Trends Biotech.* **11,** 122–130.
2. Fisher, R. J. and Fivash, M. (1994) Surface plasmon resonance based methods for measuring the kinetics and binding affinities of biomolecular interactions. *Curr. Opin. Biotech.* **5,** 389–395.
3. Panayotou, G., Waterfield, M. D., and End, P. (1993) Riding the evanescent wave. *Curr. Biol.* **3,** 913–915.
4. Malmqvist, M. (1993) Biospecific interaction analysis using biosensor technology. *Nature* **361,** 186–187.
5. Jönsson, U. and Malmqvist, M. (1992) Real time biospecific interaction analysis. The integration of Surface Plasmon Resonance detection, general biospecific interface chemistry and microfluidics into one analytical system. *Adv. Biosensors* **2,** 291–336.
6. Malmqvist, M. (1993) Surface Plasmon Resonance for detection and measurement of antibody-antigen affinity and kinetics. *Curr. Opin. Immunol.* **5,** 282–286.
7. Zhou, M., Felder, S., Rubinstein, M., Hurwitz, D. R., Ullrich, A., Lax, I., and Schlessinger, J. (1993) Real-time measurements of kinetics of EGF binding to soluble EGF receptor monomers and dimers support the dimerisation model for receptor activation. *Biochemistry* **32,** 8193–8198.
8. Panayotou, G., Gish, G., End, P., Truong, O., Gout, I., Dhand, R., Fry, M. J., Hiles, I., Pawson, T., and Waterfield, M. D. (1993) Interactions between SH2 domains and tyrosine-phosphorylated PDGF β-receptor sequences: analysis of kinetic parameters using a novel biosensor-based approach. *Mol. Cell. Biol.* **13,** 3567–3576.

9. Bondeson, K., Frostell-Karlsson, Å, Fägerstam, L., and Magnusson, G. (1993) Lactose repressor–operator DNA interactions: kinetic analysis by a Surface Plasmon Resonance biosensor. *Anal. Biochem.* **214,** 245–251.
10. Masson, L., Mazza, A., and Brousseau, R. (1994) Stable immobilisation of lipid vesicles for kinetic studies using Surface Plasmon Resonance. *Anal. Biochem.* **218,** 405–412.
11. O'Shannessy, D. J., Brigham-Burke, M., and Peck, K. (1992) Immobilisation chemistries suitable for use in the BIAcore Surface Plasmon Resonance detector. *Anal. Biochem.* **205,** 132–136.

2

Microcalorimetry of Protein–Protein Interactions

Alan Cooper

1. Introduction

Microcalorimetry can be used to determine directly the energetics and stoichiometry of macromolecular interactions by detecting the heat energy changes that, in most circumstances, accompany association or dissociation processes. These heat effects are small, but commercial instrumentation suitable for biological work is readily available and relatively easy to use. The fundamentals of modern microcalorimetry techniques have been covered earlier in this series and elsewhere ***(1–7)***, and some recent examples of its use for protein–protein and other interaction studies may be found in **refs. *8–13***. The two kinds of calorimetry most commonly used for investigating biomolecular systems are differential scanning calorimetry (DSC), in which changes brought about by increasing (or decreasing) temperature may be detected; and isothermal titration calorimetry (ITC), in which heat-energy changes during mixing of two solutions are measured. Both techniques can be used to examine protein–protein and other macromolecular interactions, though ITC is usually the more versatile and more readily interpretable technique.

1.1. Theory

Only the barest outlines are given here. The theory of complex equilibria is treated in some considerable detail in various standard texts (e.g., **refs. *14–19***).

1.1.1. ITC

The reversible, co-operative association between two dissimilar proteins or subunits, P and Q, may in general be described by the equilibrium:

$$mP + nQ \rightleftharpoons P_mQ_n \;;\; \Delta H_{ass}$$

From: *Methods in Molecular Biology, Vol. 88: Protein Targeting Protocols*
Edited by: R. A. Clegg Humana Press Inc., Totowa, NJ

with equilibrium constant, or association constant: $K_{ass} = [P_MQ_N]/[P]^M[Q]^N$ where the square brackets ([ ]) indicate molar concentrations of each species present at equilibrium, not total concentrations (*see* **Note 1**).

Other schemes might involve multiple, sequential binding steps; for example:

$$P + Q \rightleftharpoons PQ;\ \Delta H_1;\ K_1 = [PQ]/[P][Q]$$
$$PQ + Q \rightleftharpoons PQ_2;\ \Delta H_2;\ K_2 = [PQ_2]/[PQ][Q]$$
$$PQ_{i-1} + Q \rightleftharpoons PQ_i;\ \Delta H_i;\ K_i = [PQ_i]/[PQ_{i-1}][Q]$$

and so on.

But rarely do we have sufficiently detailed experimental information to analyze such complex situations, and much simpler models are usually assumed adequate.

For interactions between dissimilar molecules (heteromolecular associations), conventional ITC experiments are useful. Titration of one protein (P) in a calorimeter cell, with sequential additions of the second protein (Q), gives a series of heat pulses, each of which is proportional to the differential increase in complex concentration for each injection, until, when complexation is complete, heat pulses fall to control levels (*see* **Fig. 1** for example). Both the magnitude of the individual heat pulses and the shape of the differential thermal titration curve depend on the heat (enthalpy) of association (ΔH_{ass}), the stoichiometric ratio *(n/m)*, and the association constant(s), K_{ass}. For very tight binding situations, the break in the thermal titration curve at binding equivalence can be quite sharp, giving very good indication of the *n/m* of the complex. Nonlinear regression analysis is generally used to estimate other binding parameters, following standard procedures, typically using Origin software supplied with Microcal instruments (Northampton, MA).

For homomolecular interactions, involving dimer or higher oligomer formation of identical proteins or subunits, a different ITC procedure is adopted. High concentrations of oligomeric protein (P) are diluted by injection into buffer, and any dissociation of oligomers gives a heat pulse (usually, but not necessarily, endothermic) proportional to the extent of dissociation. For a sequence of such injections, as the protein concentration gradually increases in the calorimeter cell, progressively less dissociation occurs and heat pulses diminish with each injection (*see* **Fig. 2** for example). Again, the magnitude and shape of the dilution thermogram can be used to give estimates of ΔH and K (*see* **Subheading 1.1.4.**).

1.1.2. DSC

The thermal unfolding/denaturation of a protein will be affected by ligand binding or complex formation, and the energetics of this can be followed by DSC experiments and may be used, at least in principle, to explore protein–protein interactions. Such interactions between proteins or subunits in their

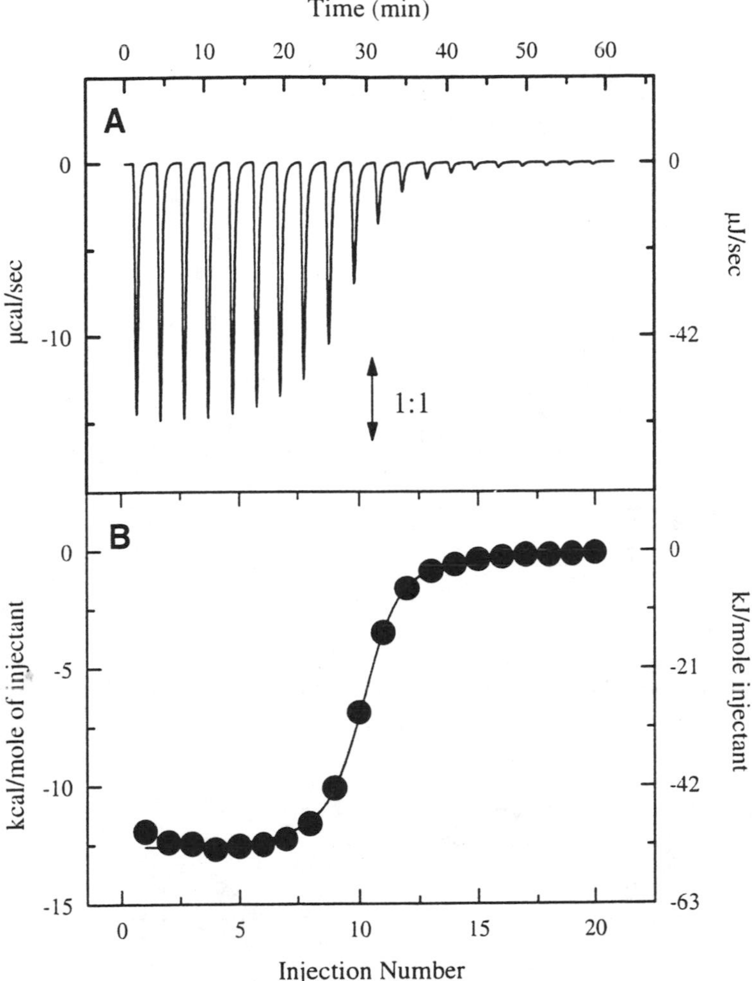

Fig. 1. Typical calorimetric titration data for heteromolecular association: **(A)** Raw data showing exothermic heat pulses for 20 × 5-μL injections of a peptide ligand (7.43 m*M* *N*-acetyl-Lys-D-Ala-D-Ala) into vancomycin solution (0.29 m*M*, calorimeter cell volume 1.4 mL), at 25°C, pH 7.0; **(B)** Integrated heat data, corrected for dilution controls and fit (solid line) to a simple 1:1 binding isotherm with $K_{ass} \approx 600{,}000M^{-1}$ and ΔH_{ass} = –53 kJ mol^{-1} (–12.7 kcal mol^{-1}). **Note:** the deviation of experimental points from the theoretical curve at low injection number is a real indication of nonideal aggregation behavior in this system (*see* **ref. *10***).

native state will inevitably stabilize the protein(s) against thermal denaturation. This will affect both the shape and position of the unfolding transition in the DSC thermogram ***(20,21)***.

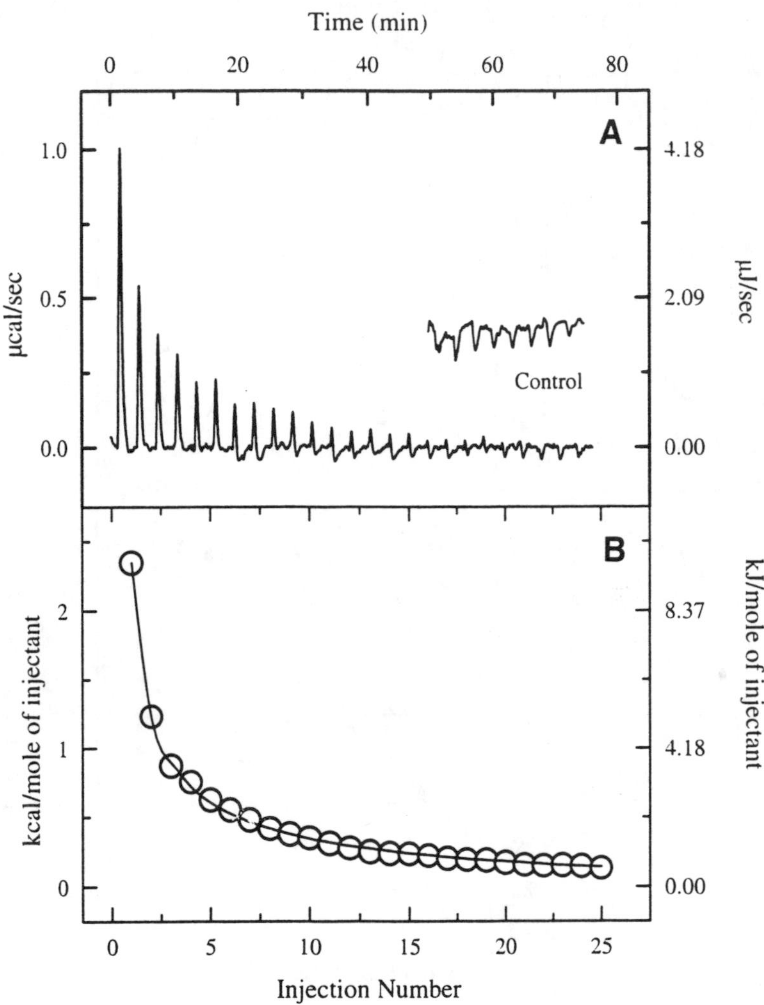

Fig. 2. Calorimetric data for the endothermic dissociation of insulin dimers at pH 2.5. **(A)** Raw data for injection of insulin, 8.8 mg/mL, 25 × 10-μL injections, into buffer at 25°C, with control data showing the calorimetric response for blank buffer injections on this very sensitive scale. **(B)** Integrated injection heats, corrected for control heats and fit (solid line) to a dimer dissociation model (*see* **Subheading 1.1.4.**) with estimated $K_{ass} \approx 78{,}000M^{-1}$ and $\Delta H_{ass} = -44$ kJ mol^{-1} (–10.5 kcal mol^{-1}).

If the interactions between proteins are very strong, such that, for example, thermal dissociation and unfolding occur simultaneously:

$$P_n \rightleftharpoons nU$$

where U denotes the unfolded polypeptide monomer, then the thermal transition is highly cooperative and the DSC thermogram much sharper than would be expected for the monomeric protein. In such cases the ratio of van't Hoff enthalpy to calorimetric enthalpy ($\Delta H_{VH}/\Delta H_{cal}$) gives an estimate of the size of the cooperative unit, which in ideal cases is equal to *n* (*see* **refs.** ***2*** and ***5*** for details). More detailed analysis in tight-binding situations involving different molecules or subunits can give estimates of binding constants of $10^{40} M^{-1}$ or more in favorable cases ***(21)***.

1.1.3. General Thermodynamics

Standard thermodynamic expressions for relating K_{ass} and ΔH_{ass} to standard Gibbs free energy ($\Delta G°_{ass}$) and standard entropy of complexation ($\Delta S°_{ass}$) are as follows:

$$\Delta G°_{ass} = -RT.\ln(K_{ass}) = \Delta H°_{ass} - T.\Delta S°_{ass}$$

where R is the gas constant (8.314 J K^{-1} mol^{-1}) and T the absolute temperature (in °K). It is conventional to assume (with little error) that the (hypothetical) standard-state enthalpy ($\Delta H°_{ass}$) is identical to that measured experimentally (ΔH_{ass}).

When experiments have been done over a range of temperatures, the variation in association enthalpy with temperature gives the differential heat capacity (at constant pressure) for the process (*see* **Note 2**):

$$\Delta C_p = d(\Delta H_{ass})/dT$$

Note that equilibrium association constants (K_{ass}) may also frequently be expressed as dissociation constants (K_{diss}), which are just the inverse of Kass. For example, for a simple 1:1 complex:

$$P + Q \rightleftharpoons PQ$$

$$K_{ass} = [PQ]/[P][Q]$$

and

$$K_{diss} = 1/K_{ass} = [P][Q]/[PQ]$$

i.e., it is the equilibrium for the reverse, dissociation reaction. For simple processes such as this, the dissociation constant has the units of concentration, and may be visualized as the concentration of free ligand (protein) required to give 50% complexation (i.e., for example, K_{diss} = [Q] when [P] = [PQ]).

1.1.4. Dimer Dissociation Heats (Theory)

Heats of dilution data for a simple monomer–dimer system may be analyzed as follows. If only monomer or dimer states of protein P are possible:

$$P + P \rightleftharpoons P_2; (H_{ass}; K_{ass} = [P_2]/[P]^2$$

the equilibrium concentration of monomers is given by:

$$[P] = \{(1 + 8.K_{ass}.C)^{1/2} - 1\}/4.K_{ass} \quad (1)$$

where C is the total protein concentration, expressed as monomer:

$$C = [P] + 2[P_2] \quad (2)$$

Now, in an ITC dilution experiment we measure the heat change (δq) when a small volume (δV) of concentrated protein solution (concentration C_0) is injected into the calorimeter cell (volume V_0) containing initially buffer, but, for later injections, more dilute protein solution. The heat arises from dimers present in the higher concentration solution that dissociate upon entering the lower concentration environment.

For the *i*th injection of a series, the observed heat is given by:

$$\delta q_i = \Delta H_{ass}\{V_0([P_2]_i - [P_2]_{i-1}) - \delta V([P_2]_0 - [P_2]_{i-1})\} \quad (3)$$

where $[P_2]_0$, $[P_2]_i$, and $[P_2]_{i-1}$ are the dimer concentrations in the original (syringe) solution and in the calorimeter cell after the *i*th and (i - 1) th injections: total concentrations C_0, C_i, and C_{i-1}, respectively. (The last term in this expression is a small correction factor to allow for the quantity of solution displaced from the constant-volume calorimeter cell during each δV addition.)

Equations 1–3 may be used in standard nonlinear regression (least-squares) procedures to fit experimental dilution data and obtain estimates of K_{ass} and ΔH_{ass}. Similar, though more algebraically complex, expressions may be derived for dissociation processes involving higher oligomers or other mechanisms. Such mechanisms frequently give sigmoidal dilution thermograms, in contrast to the hyperbolic shapes for the dimer dissociation shown here; this might give empirical indications that the process under investigation is more complex than simple dimers can model.

Equation 1 is algebraically identical (apart from a factor 2) to that giving free monomer concentrations in a simple infinite-polymerization model ***(22)***. Consequently, calorimetric dilution data alone might be insufficient to discriminate between dimer and polymer interaction models, and other experimental approaches might be needed to resolve possible ambiguities.

2. Materials

2.1. Instrumentation

Although a range of DSC equipment is commercially available, relatively few such instruments are suitable for use with the reasonably dilute protein solutions required here. Choice is even more limited for ITC equipment, and most current workers use Microcal instruments, whose sensitivity and rapid response are ideal for such measurements (*see* **refs.** ***3*** and ***6*** for details). Microcal also supplies comprehensive software (Origin) for data collection and analysis, though this does not (yet) include facility for analyzing dilution/dissociation data of the kind obtained here. Isothermal titration is also possible with TAM instruments (ThermoMetric, Northwich, Cheshire, UK), among others, and a new generation of DSC equipment is promised (**ref.** ***22***; CSC, Provo, UT) based on improvements to the original Privalov DASM.

The ITC experiments described here were done in a Microcal OMEGA instrument: standard operating procedures at 25°C, using a 250-μL injection syringe with 400 rpm stirring. Program the instrument to give a series of 10- to 20-μL injections at 3 to 4-min intervals, 10–20 s per injection (*see* **Note 3**).

2.2. Buffers and Proteins

Choice of reagents and buffers will depend on the system of interest (*see* **Note 4**). Examples here are for the insulin dissociation trial experiments described in **Subheading 3.2.**

1. Insulin buffer: 0.1*M* glycine, adjusted to pH 2.5 with conc HCl. This may be stored cold (preferably after sterile filtering), but should be allowed to warm to room temperature and should be gently degassed prior to use.
2. Insulin solution: Bovine Zn-insulin (Sigma, I-5500; monomer mw 5734). Solutions in glycine/HCl buffer should be prepared fresh daily and microcentrifuged before use, to remove particulate matter. 1–2 mL is adequate for a series of experiments, with concentrations of about 10 mg/mL (*see* **Notes 5–7**).

3. Methods

Experimental details for calorimetric experiments on any particular protein–protein interaction will depend very much on the specific properties of the system of interest, and only general guidelines can be given here. Different procedures are adopted, depending on whether the interactions are hetero- or homomolecular.

3.1. Titration Calorimetry (Heterocomplexes)

Typical experiments usually involve injection of small portions (5–20 μL) of one protein ("protein Q") from the ITC injection syringe into the calorimeter cell (approx 1.5 mL) containing the second protein component ("protein P"). Concentrations should usually be such as to exceed anticipated stoichiometric binding during the complete injection series. Particular care must be taken to ensure that extraneous heat effects from buffer mismatch or dilution effects are minimized. The general procedure (using Microcal ITC equipment) might be as follows (*see* **Note 8** and **Fig. 1** for example).

1. Equilibrate both proteins against the same buffer, preferably by extensive dialysis of the two samples in the same pot, and use the final dialysis buffer for any subsequent dilutions or control experiments.
2. Determine protein concentrations. The protein (P) in the calorimeter cell should normally be at a concentration of at least 10 μ*M* to give measurable signals (*see* **Note 9**).
3. Gently degas protein P and buffer solutions to eliminate generation of air bubbles, which give erratic and noisy baselines during stirring in the calorimeter cell (*see* **Note 10**).
4. Load degassed protein P into the ITC cell, and protein Q into the syringe, equilibrate, and program a sequence of injections, following standard instrumental procedures. Up to 25 × 10-μL injections might be normal.
5. Perform control experiments under identical conditions for injection of protein Q into buffer, buffer into protein P, and buffer into buffer (the latter are usually quite small). These control heat effects must be subtracted from experimental data before analysis.
6. Analyze using standard (Microcal Origin) or other software to give K, ΔH, and n (or n/m) (*see* **Note 11**).

3.2. Dilution Calorimetry (Homocomplexes)

The energetics of dissociation of protein dimers or higher aggregates can be estimated from heats of dilution measurements *(11,23)*. An example based on insulin dissociation follows (**Fig. 2**).

3.2.1. ITC of Insulin Dissociation—A Trial Experiment

Insulin forms dimers or hexamers in solution under various conditions *(25)*, and the dissociation of these oligomers provides a useful practice exercise for ITC techniques. Dilution of insulin solution into buffer results in partial dissociation of oligomers, with an endothermic heat uptake that can be detected relatively easily by ITC *(24)*. At neutral pH the effects are quite small, since oligomerization is strong under physiological conditions. Dimer dissociation is much greater at lower pH (*see* **Note 4**), and the following procedure illustrates many of the standard features. Details are for a Microcal OMEGA instrument (*see* **Subheading 2.1.**), but may be readily modified for other titration microcalorimeters.

1. Load the ITC cell and injection syringe with degassed insulin buffer, preferably as close to the working temperature (25°C) as possible, to minimize equilibration times.
2. Program the ITC for a sequence of injections (25 × 10 μL) and run, once suitably equilibrated. This gives control mixing heats, which should be relatively small (<1 μcal per injection) (*see* **Note 12**).
3. Reload the injection syringe with insulin solution and repeat the above injection sequence. This should give a series of progressively decreasing endothermic heat

pulses in the 1–2 μcal/s range caused by dissociation of insulin dimers (*see* **Fig. 2** for example).

4. Integrate injection heat data (Microcal Origin or other software), correct for control mixing heats, and analyze according to theoretical models described elsewhere here (*see* **Subheading 1.1.4.** and **Note 13**).

3.3. Differential Scanning Calorimetry

Practical details covering DSC of proteins, applicable also to protein complexes, are given elsewhere in this series ***(2)***. Unfortunately, the thermal unfolding of many proteins of interest tends to be irreversible and marred by precipitation of the denatured protein. This distorts the DSC thermogram and makes detailed interpretation unreliable. Nevertheless, some useful indication of protein–protein interaction may be given by shifts in T_m, even when full thermodynamic analysis is not feasible.

4. Notes

1. Strictly, the molar concentrations indicated by [ ] should be thermodynamic activities, but, at the low concentrations usually encountered, activity corrections are rarely justified.
2. Interpretation of the signs and magnitudes of thermodynamic parameters associated with protein–protein interaction is complex and controversial ***(26,27)***. Enthalpies (heats) of binding may be exothermic or endothermic, frequently vary with temperature, and may be zero in some circumstances ***(12)***. Negative ΔC_p values (ΔH_{ass} decreasing with increasing temperature) are usually taken as a sign of significant hydrophobic contribution to the interaction. Empirical rules relating experimental parameters to buried surface area at the protein–protein interface have been described ***(28,29)***.
3. Kinetics: Most macromolecular association/dissociation processes are fast on the calorimetric time-scale ($t_{1/2} \approx 30$ s), but occasionally experimental ITC heat pulses appear broader than expected, and this can give order-of-magnitude estimates for the rates of the process. In such cases, the interval between injections in an ITC experiment may need to be increased to allow proper return to baseline and accurate integration of total heat effects.
4. Association processes that depend strongly on pH will necessarily involve protonation (H^+ ion) changes that may give rise to additional and unexpected heat effects ***(1)***. Such situations may be clarified by use of a range of different buffers.
5. Accurate insulin concentrations may be determined from UV spectra of suitably diluted portions, assuming a molar extinction coefficient (ε_{280}) of $5734M^{-1}$, equivalent to $A_{280}{}^{1\%} = 10.0$ in a 1-cm path-length cuvet ***(30,31)***.
6. Normally, protein solutions should be dialyzed against buffer before use in ITC experiments to minimize artifacts arising from heats of dilution of extraneous salts or slight mismatch in buffer compositions. This is not usually necessary here for the relatively pure, commercially available insulin samples, at least for practice purposes.

7. Apparent stoichiometries and other parameters will depend critically on the purity of the protein preparations and the accuracy of the concentrations assumed. Although, in principle, calorimetric measurements are unaffected by inert protein or other impurities, their presence may interfere with concentration measurements and affect the quantitative validity of any results.
8. Though not strictly protein–protein interaction, a suitable and convenient practice system might be the peptide antibiotic complexation between vancomycin and *N*-acetyl-Lys-D-Ala-D-Ala, as described in **ref. *10***.
9. The optimal concentration in the injection syringe (protein Q) depends on anticipated stoichiometry of the complex and the total volume to be injected, but might typically be 5–10 times greater than P, assuming 1:1 complexation and using a 250-μL syringe. This can sometimes lead to difficulties caused by poor solubility of one of the components, in which case, try reversing P and Q. Protein concentrations should also be chosen, wherever possible, to optimize the titration for binding constant determination. A rough rule of thumb is that ($K \times$ protein concentration $\times$ stoichiometry) should be in the region of 5–500, though useful work can be done outside this range when circumstances, such as low solubility or scarcity of sample, dictate.
10. Degassing is best done with gentle stirring under modest vacuum (e.g., water aspirator), with the sample at room temperature: 2–3 min is usually sufficient, long enough to degas (small bubbles), but avoid boiling (large bubbles). Degassing of protein Q, in the syringe, is not usually required.
11. For very weak binding the stoichiometry *(n)* may be poorly defined, and nonlinear regression analyses may not converge sensibly or uniquely. In such cases, fix n (if known from other sources) and fit to just K and ΔH. For very tight binding ($K > 10^8$), K will not normally be well defined, but good estimates of n and ΔH should be obtained. Note that the apparent stoichiometry will depend on the units and mol wt used to express the protein or subunit concentrations.
12. 1 cal = 4.184 J; Microcal instruments are still calibrated in non-SI units (calories) rather than joules.
13. Data should be consistent with dimer dissociation with $K_{diss} \approx 10\ \mu M$ and $\Delta H_{diss} \approx 40$ kJ mol^{-1}. For small heat effects such as these, careful measurement and correction for control heats is essential for accurate estimates of K_{diss} and ΔH_{diss}.

Acknowledgments

Thanks to Margaret Nutley, Michelle Lovatt, and Deborah McPhail for collaboration in some of the experimental work mentioned here. The biological microcalorimetry facilities in Glasgow are funded by grants from the Biotechnology and Biological Sciences Research Council and the Engineering and Physical Sciences Research Council.

References

1. Cooper, A. and Johnson, C. M. (1994) Introduction to microcalorimetry and biomolecular energetics, in *Methods in Molecular Biology*, vol. 22: *Microscopy,*

Optical Spectroscopy, and Macroscopic Techniques (Jones, C., Mulloy, B., and Thomas, A. H., eds.), Humana, Totowa, N. J., 109–124.

2. Cooper, A. and Johnson, C. M. (1994) Differential scanning calorimetry, in *Methods in Molecular Biology*, vol. 22: *Microscopy, Optical Spectroscopy, and Macroscopic Techniques* (Jones, C., Mulloy, B., and Thomas, A. H., eds.), Humana, Totowa, NJ, pp. 125–136.
3. Cooper, A. and Johnson, C. M. (1994) Isothermal titration microcalorimetry, in *Methods in Molecular Biology*, vol. 22: *Microscopy, Optical Spectroscopy, and Macroscopic Techniques* (Jones, C., Mulloy, B., and Thomas, A. H., eds.), Humana, Totowa, NJ, pp. 137–150.
4. Privalov, P. L. and Potekhin, S. A. (1986) Scanning calorimetry in studying temperature-induced changes in proteins. *Methods Enzymol.* **131,** 4–51.
5. Sturtevant, J. M. (1987) Biochemical applications of differential scanning calorimetry. *Ann. Rev. Phys. Chem.* **38,** 463–488.
6. Wiseman T., Williston, S., Brandts, J. F., and Lin, L.-N. (1989) Rapid measurement of binding constants and heats of binding using a new titration calorimeter. *Anal. Biochem.* **179,** 131–137.
7. Bundle, D. R. and Sigurskjold, B. W. (1994) Determination of accurate thermodynamics of binding by titration microcalorimetry. *Methods Enzymol.* **247,** 288–305.
8. Cooper, A., McAlpine, A., and Stockley, P. G. (1994) Calorimetric studies of the energetics of protein-DNA interactions in the *E. coli* methionine repressor (MetJ) system. *FEBS Lett.* **348,** 41–45.
9. McAuley-Hecht, K. E. and Cooper, A. (1993) Microcalorimetry of enzyme-substrate binding: yeast phosphoglycerate kinase. *J. Chem. Soc. Faraday Trans.* **89,** 2693–2699.
10. Cooper, A. and McAuley-Hecht, K. E. (1993) Microcalorimetry and the molecular recognition of peptides and proteins. *Phil. Trans. R. Soc. Lond. A* **345,** 23–35.
11. Burrows, S. D., Doyle, M. L., Murphy, K. P., Franklin, S. G., White, J. R., Brooks, I., McNulty, D. E., Scott, M. O., Knutson, J. R., Porter, D., Young, P. R., and Hensley, P. (1994) Determination of the monomer-dimer equilibrium of interleukin-8 reveals it is a monomer at physiological concentrations. *Biochemistry* **33,** 12,741–12,745.
12. Bowden, S. J., Cooper, A., Kalia, Y. N., and Perham, R. N. (1997) Entropy-driven protein-protein interactions in the assembly of the pyruvate dehydrogenase multienzyme complex from *Bacillus stearothermophilus*, submitted.
13. Evans, L. J. A., Cooper, A., and Lakey, J. H. (1996) Direct measurement of the association of a protein with a family of membrane receptors. *J. Mol. Biol.* **255,** 559–563.
14. Edsall, J. T. and Gutfreund, H. (1983) *Biothermodynamics: the Study of Biochemical Processes at Equilibrium.* Wiley, Chichester.
15. Weber, G. (1975) Energetics of ligand binding to proteins. *Adv. Protein Chem.* **29,** 1–83.
16. Wyman, J. (1964) Linked functions and reciprocal effects in hemoglobin: a second look. *Adv. Protein Chem.* **19,** 223–286.

17. Cantor, W. R. and Schimmel, P. R. (1980) *Biophysical Chemistry, Part III: the Behavior of Biological Macromolecules.* Freeman, W. H., San Francisco.
18. Edsall, J. T. and Wyman, J. (1958) *Biophysical Chemistry*, vol. 1. Academic, NY.
19. Wyman, J. and Gill, S. J. (1990) *Binding and Linkage: Functional Chemistry of Biological Macromolecules.* University Science Books, Mid Valley, CA.
20. Fukada, H., Sturtevant, J. M., and Quiocho, F. A. (1983) Thermodynamics of the binding of L-arabinose and of D-galactose to the L-arabinose-binding protein of *Escherichia coli. J. Biol. Chem.* **258,** 13,193–13,198.
21. Brandts, J. F. and Lin, L.-N. (1990) Study of strong to ultratight protein interactions using differential scanning calorimetry. *Biochemistry* **29,** 6927–6940.
22. Stoesser, P. R. and Gill, S. J. (1967) Calorimetric study of self-association of 6-methylpurine in water. *J. Phys. Chem.* **71,** 564–567.
23. Privalov, G., Kavina, V., Freire, E., and Privalov, P. L. (1995) Precise scanning calorimeter for studying thermal properties of biological macromolecules in dilute solution. *Anal. Biochem.* **232,** 79–85.
24. Lovatt, M., Cooper, A., and Camilleri, P. (1996) Energetics of cyclodextrin-induced dissociation of insulin oligomers. *Eur. Biophys. J.* **24,** 354–357.
25. Blundell, T. L., Dodson, G., Hodgson, D., and Mercola, D. (1972) Insulin: The structure in the crystal and its reflection in chemistry and biology. *Adv. Protein Chem.* **26,** 279–402.
26. Weber, G. (1993) Thermodynamics of the association and the pressure dissociation of oligomeric proteins. *J. Phys. Chem.* **97,** 7108–7115.
27. Weber, G. (1995) van't Hoff revisited: enthalpy of association of protein subunits. *J. Phys. Chem.* **99,** 1052–1059.
28. Chothia, C. and Janin, J. (1975) Principles of protein–protein recognition. *Nature* **256,** 705–708.
29. Spolar, R. and Record, M. T. (1994) Coupling of local folding to site-specific binding of proteins to DNA. *Science* **263,** 777–784.
30. Gill, S. C. and von Hippel, P. H. (1989) Calculation of protein extinction coefficients from amino acid sequence data. *Anal. Biochem.* **182,** 319–326.
31 Pace, C. N., Vajdos, F., Fee, L., Grimsley, G., and Gray, T. (1995) How to measure and predict the molar absorption coefficient of a protein. *Protein Sci.* **4,** 2411–2423.

3

Partitioning of Proteins in Triton X-114

James G. Pryde

1. Introduction

Cultured mammalian cells and tissues can be solubilized by the nonionic detergent Triton X-114 (octylphenoxy polyethoxyethanol). This detergent, when in solution above its critical micelle concentration, increases its micelle weight when warmed from 0 to 20°C and in the process decreases its critical micelle concentration. This induces intermicellar interactions, which lead to turbidity (the cloud point) and phase separation of the detergent at 20°C. A simple low-speed centrifugation step recovers the detergent-enriched phase as an oily pellet. Following solubilization and warming to 20°C, integral membrane proteins partition into the detergent-enriched phase, and peripheral and cytosolic proteins are recovered from the detergent-depleted aqueous phase.

This method of separation in Triton X-114 has established itself as one of the most powerful tools for preparing membrane proteins for analysis. In its beautiful simplicity, this technique, introduced by Bordier in 1981 ***(1)***, has proven to be reproducible and has found many applications. With particular reference to protein targeting, the technique has been utilized to assess the requirement of the N-terminal domain of the cyclic AMP-specific phosphodiesterase RD1, whose removal prevents plasma membrane association ***(2)***. The properties and many of the applications of Triton X-114 have already been reviewed ***(3–5)***. Here, are described a few simple protocols that use Triton X-114 as a tool for enriching membrane proteins for analysis and for fractionating membrane components.

2. Materials

2.1. Precondensation of Triton X-114

1. Triton X-114 from Boehringer Mannheim, East Sussex, UK. Cat. no. 1 033 441. Store this solution at 4°C.

From: *Methods in Molecular Biology, Vol. 88: Protein Targeting Protocols*
Edited by: R. A. Clegg Humana Press Inc., Totowa, NJ

2. Butylated hydroxytoluene used to scavenge free radicals.
3. 10X Tris–salt buffer, pH 7.6: 100 m*M* Tris-HCl, pH 7.6, 1.5*M* NaCl. Store this solution at 20°C.

2.2. Reagents for Colorimetric Estimation of Triton X-114

1. Standard Triton X-114 solution: Weigh out 2 g of 100% Triton X-114 and dissolve it in 50% ethanol to a volume of 1 L.
2. Ammonium cobaltothiocyanate reagent: Dissolve 17.8 g of ammonium thiocyanate and 2.8 g of cobalt nitrate hexahydrate in 100 mL of water.
3. Dichloromethane is used to extract the blue precipitate that forms.

2.3. Solubilization of Proteins From Mammalian Cells

1. 10X Tris–salt buffer pH 7.6: 100 m*M* Tris-HCl, pH 7.6, 1.5*M* NaCl.
2. Protease inhibitor cocktail 1000-fold concentrated: antipain, pepstatin, leupeptin, and aprotinin, 1 mg/mL each, and phenylmethylsulfonyl fluoride and benzamidine at 40 mg/mL (Sigma, Poole, Dorset, UK), all dissolved in dimethylsulphoxide. Store at –20°C in a glass vial.
3. 1% Triton X-114 in Tris–salt buffer, pH 7.6, used for solubilizing cells.
4. 0.06% Triton X-114 in Tris–salt buffer, pH 7.6. This solution is used to wash detergent pellets. The small amount of detergent is present at 3–4 times the critical micelle concentration, to prevent loss of the detergent in the pellet to the wash buffer.

2.4. Immunoprecipitation of Chandipura Virus G Protein

1. Chinese hamster ovary cells are grown on a 60-mm culture dish in α-(MEM) growth medium containing 10% fetal calf serum (FCS) and 100 μg/mL each of penicillin and streptomycin.
2. Labeling medium: RPMI-1640 minus L-methionine and L-cysteine, 1% (v/v) FCS (dialyzed against 2 × 100 volumes of PBS), 50 μCi/mL [^{35}S]TransLabel (ICN, Oxfordshire, UK). For labeling times greater than 3 h, add L-methionine to 2.5 μg/mL.
3. Chase medium: growth medium containing 1.5 mg/mL L-methionine and 10 μg/mL cycloheximide to arrest the translation of mRNA into protein. Cycloheximide is stored at –20°C as a 20 mg/mL stock in ethanol.
4. Immunoprecipitation buffer: 50 m*M* Tris-HCl, pH 8.0, 0.4*M* NaCl, 1% (w/v) deoxycholate, 1% (w/v) Nonidet® P40, 5 m*M* EDTA.
5. Suspension of 10% (w/v) *Staphylococcus aureus* cells (Pansorbin® Cells, Calbiochem-Novabiochem, Nottingham, UK), washed three times with the immunoprecipitation buffer.

2.5. Isolation of Chromaffin Granules

1. A stock solution of 2.0*M* sucrose is used to make the homogenization buffer and the gradient steps. Check the concentration of sucrose on a refractometer.
2. 1.0*M* HEPES NaOH, the pH adjusted to 7.4 with 4*M* NaOH (the final pH after a 50 dilution is 7.2).

3. Methods

3.1. Precondensation Of Triton X-114

Before Triton X-114 can be used, it needs to be purified by successive rounds of precondensation ***(1)***. This procedure reduces the concentration of more hydrophilic detergent molecules, which partition into the detergent-depleted phase to a final concentration of 0.04–0.06% and minimizes the anomalous appearance of integral membrane proteins in the detergent-depleted phase ***(3, 7)***.

3.1.1. Precondensation Procedure

1. Weigh out 20 g of Triton X-114 into a 1-L glass separating funnel.
2. Add 980 mL of 10 m*M* Tris HCl, pH 7.6, 150 m*M* NaCl (Tris–salt buffer) and 16 mg of butylated hydroxytoluene dissolved in 200 μL of ethanol. Disperse the detergent at 0°C.
3. After dissolution of the detergent, place the mixture in an incubator at 30°C for 18 h. The mixture will cloud and the detergent micelles will sediment.
4. Draw off the sedimented detergent phase and discard the upper detergent-depleted phase.
5. Repeat the precondensation procedure a further two times by making the condensed detergent solution back up to 1 L with ice-cold Tris–salt buffer, pH 7.6. The third of the condensed phases has a Triton X-114 concentration of about 10% (w/v).
6. Store the detergent in 20-mL aliquots at –20°C in glass bottles.

3.2. Estimation of Triton Concentration

3.2.1. Spectrophotometric Method

The final Triton X-114 concentration is estimated by assuming a molecular mass of 537 and a molar absorption of 1.46×10^3 at pH 8.0 and 20°C in the presence of 1% SDS at 275 nm *(8)*. A 19-m*M* solution of Triton X-114 is therefore 1% (w/v).

3.2.2. Colorimetric Method

A colorimetric method can be used to estimate the concentration of Triton ***(9)***. This procedure uses ammonium cobaltothiocyanate to react with the ethylene oxide groups of Triton X-114 to form a blue precipitate, which is extracted into a solvent.

1. To standards (0–400 μg) and samples of Triton X-114 solution in a final volume of 300 μL of 50% ethanol, add 400 μL of ammonium cobaltothiocyanate reagent.
2. Leave the tubes for 5 min at 20°C.
3. Add dichloromethane and vortex the tubes for 2 min.
4. Centrifuge the tubes for 2 min at 1000 rpm, then remove the lower phase of dichloromethane with a Pasteur pipet and record its spectrum from 580 to 700 nm on a spectrophotometer. The difference in absorbance at 622 and 687 nm is proportional to the amount of Triton present.

3.3. Separation of Mammalian Cell Proteins Using Chandipura Virus G Protein as a Model Integral Membrane Protein

3.3.1. Procedure

1. Harvest cells (2.5×10^6) from plastic culture dish by scraping or by releasing the cells with 0.05% trypsin/0.02% EDTA. Sediment the cells at 14,000 rpm for 10 s in an Eppendorf microcentrifuge 5415C.
2. Wash the cells three times with 1 mL of ice-cold Tris–salt buffer, pH 7.6.
3. To the cell pellet, add 250 µL of 1% Triton X-114 in Tris–salt buffer pH 7.6, containing 1:1000 diluted protease inhibitor cocktail (*see* **Subheading 2.3.**).
4. Sediment nuclei and insoluble material at 14,000 rpm for 10 min at 4°C in an Eppendorf microcentrifuge. Remove the supernatant to a clean 1.5-mL microcentrifuge tube and discard the pellet.
5. Warm the solubilized protein mixture at 30°C for 3 min.
6. Centrifuge the cloudy sample for 3 min at 5000 rpm at 20°C in an Eppendorf microcentrifuge. The detergent phase containing integral membrane proteins forms an oily 25-µL pellet. The soluble proteins remain in the upper detergent-depleted phase.
7. Carefully remove and discard the detergent-depleted phase without disturbing the detergent pellet. Add 225 µL of ice-cold Tris–salt buffer, pH 7.6, supplemented with 0.06% TX-114, to the detergent-enriched pellet, and mix well. Leave the sample on ice until it clears of detergent micelles.
8. Repeat the phase separation up to three times as necessary, discarding the detergent-depleted phase each time. The proteins enriched in the detergent phase can now be separated by sodium dodecyl sulfate-polyacrylamide gel electrophoresis (SDS-PAGE) or subjected to further purification, for example, by immunoprecipitation, which is described in **Subheading 3.4.2.**

3.3.2. Preparation of Samples for PAGE

1. Add an equal volume of twofold concentrated SDS gel sample buffer (0.25*M* Tris-HCl, pH 6.5, 20% [w/v] glycerol, 8% SDS, 0.01% bromophenol blue) to the detergent pellet containing the integral membrane proteins.
2. If reduction of the proteins is required, add 1 m*M* dithiothreitol, then heat at 100°C for 3 min.
3. Cool the samples and centrifuge them at 14,000 rpm in an Eppendorf microcentrifuge for 2 min to collect the water that condenses on the lid of the tube.
4. Treat the sample with 10 m*M* iodoacetamide for 30 min at 20°C.
5. Finally, centrifuge the sample at 14,000 rpm for 2 min and transfer to a clean microcentrifuge tube, leaving behind any insoluble pellet. The sample can now be loaded onto the gel.

3.3.3. Analysis of Proteins in the Aqueous Phase

1. To analyze the proteins in the detergent-depleted phase, precipitate the proteins with trichloroacetic acid at a final concentration of 10%. Collect the pellet by low-speed centrifugation at 5000 rpm for 10 min (*see* **Note 1**).

2. Wash the pellet once with 1 mL of ice-cold ethanol and centrifuge at 5000 rpm for 10 min (*see* **Note 2**).
3. Wash the pellet once with ethanol/ether (1:1) and centrifuge at 5000 rpm.
4. Finally, wash the pellet once with ether and then centrifuge it at 5000 rpm, and then dry it with nitrogen.
5. Solubilize the pellet in 25–50 µL of 1X SDS gel sample buffer.

3.4. Immunoprecipitation of Chandipura Virus G Protein

Immunoprecipitation of proteins on fixed *Staphylococcus aureus* cells from a complex mixture of radiolabeled proteins, using a specific antibody, normally involves creating stringency conditions to prevent the nonspecific precipitation of proteins with the specific antibody antigen complex. Enriching proteins in the detergent phase of Triton X-114 before immunoprecipitation provides a convenient method for removing soluble proteins prone to adhere to immunoprecipitates. The following procedure has been designed for the immunoprecipitation of the coat protein (G protein) of Chandipura virus with a polyclonal antibody, from infected Chinese hamster ovary cells pulse-labeled with [^{35}S]methionine, but is generally applicable.

3.4.1. Labeling Cells

1. Wash Chandipura virus infected Chinese hamster ovary cells (2.5 × 10^6) twice with 5 mL of PBS and once with 5 mL of RPMI-1640 minus L-methionine without added radiolabel (*see* **Note 3**).
2. Incubate the cells at 37°C for 30 min in 2 mL of RPMI-1640 minus L-methionine without added radiolabel.
3. Add 1 mL of labeling medium containing 50 µCi/mL [^{35}S]methionine to the cells (*see* **Subheading 2.4., item 2**).
4. At the end of the pulse period, aspirate the medium, and add 5 mL of chase medium (*see* **Subheading 2.4., item 3**), which has been warming at 37°C.
5. To stop the chase place the dishes on ice, aspirate the medium, and wash 3X with 5 mL of ice-cold PBS.

3.4.2. Immunoprecipitation

1. Solubilize the cells in Triton X-114 and phase-separate the proteins, as described in **Subheading 3.3.1.**
2. Add 500 µL of immunoprecipitation buffer to the detergent pellet, and mix.
3. Add antibody, for example, 5 µL of anti-G-protein polyclonal antibody. Incubate at 37°C for 1 h or at 4°C for 18–24 h. Centrifuge at 14,000 rpm in a microcentrifuge at 4°C to remove any precipitate, then add 25 µL of *Staphylococcus aureus* cells for 1 h at 37°C.
4. Pellet the *Staphylococcus aureus* cells by centrifuging at 5000 rpm in a microcentrifuge for 10 min and discard the supernatant. Wash the cells 3X with immunoprecipitation buffer.
5. Wash the cells with 500 µL of water and pellet them.

6. Recover the immunoprecipitate by resuspending the cells in 25 μL of water (this prevents the formation of sticky pellets, which cannot be resuspended efficiently when simply placed in sample buffer), and then add an equal volume of 2X concentrated SDS sample buffer, to recover protein, and process as described in **Subheading 3.3.3.**

3.5. Fractionation of Membrane-Associated Proteins After Solubilization in Triton X-114

Triton X-114 has been used to solubilize and fractionate the proteins of the lipid-rich membrane of bovine adrenal medullary chromaffin granules. A phase separation protocol was developed that separated soluble and integral membrane proteins ***(1)*** and identified two families of chromaffin granule integral membrane proteins, in addition to those found in the detergent-enriched phase and found anomalously in the detergent-depleted phase ***(6)***. The method was generally applicable to membrane fractions (*see* **Note 4**); an example using chromaffin granule membranes is shown in **Fig. 1**.

3.5.1. Preparation of Chromaffin Granule Membranes

Chromaffin granule membranes were isolated as described by Pryde and Phillips ***(6)*** and a brief description is given here.

1. Homogenize bovine adrenal medulla in 0.3*M* sucrose containing 20 m*M* HEPES NaOH, pH 7.0, and 0.2 m*M* PMSF at 0°C (buffered sucrose).
2. Centrifuge the homogenate at 1500g_{av} for 5 min and retain the supernatant.
3. Centrifuge the supernatant at 19,000g_{av} for 30 min and keep the pellet for the preparation of chromaffin granules.
4. Resuspend the pink granule pellets in buffered sucrose and layer them over buffered 18*M* sucrose, and centrifuge at 161,000g_{av} for 1 h.
5. Lyse the pellet of granules in 20 m*M* HEPES NaOH, pH 7.0, and recover the membranes by centrifugation at 161,000g_{av} for 20 min.
6. To further purify the granule membranes layer them over a step gradient of buffered 1.0*M* sucrose and recover the pure membranes from the 1.0*M* sucrose interface.
7. Finally, wash the membranes in 20 m*M* HEPES NaOH, pH 7.0, 1 m*M* DTT, 1 m*M* EDTA by resuspending them by homogenization and recover them by centrifugation at 161,000g_{av} for 20 min; store them at –20°C.

3.5.2. Solubilization

Wash chromaffin granule membranes in Tris–salt buffer, pH 7.6, sediment them by centrifugation at 161,000g_{av} for 20 min, and resuspend them by homogenization. Add ice-cold Triton X-114, so that the final detergent-to-protein ratio is 5:1.

3.5.3. Lipid-Enriched Fraction

One minute after full solubilization of the membranes on ice, a white precipitate will form. This precipitate is only evident with membranes that have a

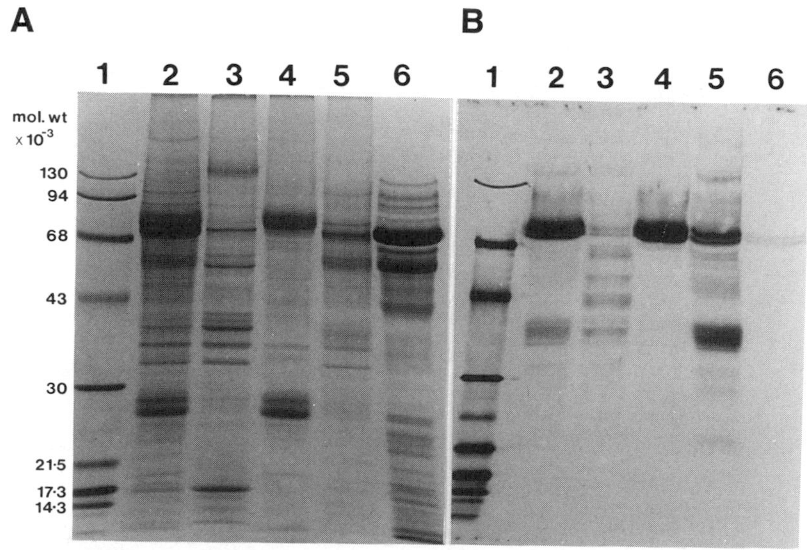

Fig. 1. Phase separation of chromaffin-granule membrane proteins. Proteins were phase-separated in Triton X-114 and analyzed under reducing conditions on an 8–15%-polyacrylamide gel. Track 1, standard proteins: β-galactosidase (M_r 130,000); phosphorylase (M_r 94,000); bovine serum albumin (M_r 68,000); ovalbumin (M_r 43,000); carbonic anhydrase (M_r 30,000); trypsin inhibitor (M_r 21,500); myoglobin (M_r 17,200); lysozyme (M_r 14,300). Track 2, complete chromaffin-granule membranes. Track 3, phospholipid-enriched phase, which contains the subunits of the proton-translocating ATPase and the dicyclohexlcarbodiimide-reactive protein (M_r 17,000). Track 4, detergent-enriched phase containing dopamine β-hydroxylase (M_r 75,000) and cytochrome b561 (M_r 27,000). Track 5, Detergent-depleted phase containing chromogranin A (M_r 70,000), the major protein of the chromaffin granule lysate, which is shown in Track 6. Track 6, chromaffin granule lysate (matrix proteins); the major band is chromogranin A (M_r 70,000). **(B)** A Western blot of **(A)** decorated with [^{125}I]lentil lectin. The major lentil lectin-binding protein is the membrane form of dopamine β-hydroxylase, which partitions into the detergent-enriched phase (Track 4). The soluble form of dopamine β-hydroxylase partitions into the detergent-depleted phase (Track 5). The only other major lentil lectin-binding protein is glycoprotein III, an integral membrane protein (M_r 37,000) that partitions anomalously into the detergent-depleted phase (Track 5). (Reproduced with permission from **ref.** ***2***.)

high lipid content, and is not formed, for example, after mitochondrial membranes are solubilized (*see* **Note 4**). Recover the precipitate by centrifugation at 58,000g_{av}. Wash the pellet once in ice-cold Tris–salt buffer, pH 7.6, containing 2% Triton X-114, and once in Tris–salt buffer, pH 7.6 alone. The proteins in this lipid pellet can then be solubilized with 18 mg/mL *n*-octyl β-glucoside ***(10)***.

3.5.4. Phase Separation

To recover integral membrane proteins that partition into the detergent phase, warm the mixture to 30°C for 3 min. The detergent phase can then be recovered as an oily pellet after centrifugation at $2500g_{av}$ for 5 min at 20°C. This separation can be carried out over a 0.25*M* sucrose cushion to separate the detergent pellet from the detergent-depleted phase, but, in practice, there is little advantage in doing this. It is as effective to simply remove the upper detergent-depleted phase, being careful not to disturb the detergent-enriched pellet, which, in the case of chromaffin granule membranes, is colored red by cytochrome b_{561}. Any proteins carried over from the detergent-depleted phase into the detergent-enriched phase are washed away by resuspending the pellet in Tris–salt buffer, containing 0.06% Triton X-114 to the volume used during the solubilization and repeating the phase separation three times.

3.5.5. Detergent-Depleted Phase

Make the detergent-depleted phase 2% in Triton X-114 and place on ice for dissolution of the detergent. Warm the mixture at 30°C again, then centrifuge and discard the detergent pellet. The supernatant contains soluble proteins from the cytosol, luminal proteins from organelles, peripheral membrane proteins, and some integral membrane proteins.

3.5.6. Dialysis of the Detergent-Depleted Phase

The detergent-depleted phase contains 0.06% (w/v) residual detergent; this is sufficient to allow the anomalous partitioning of some integral membrane proteins containing bulky hydrophilic domains into the detergent-depleted phase *(3)*. This detergent can be removed by dialysis for 1–2 d against Tris–salt buffer, pH 7.6, containing Amberlite XAD-2, which binds detergent. A group of integral membrane proteins precipitate and can be recovered by centrifugation for 2 h at $165{,}000g_{av}$. In some cases, homologous association between hydrophobic domains on solubilized membrane proteins, to remove them from the aqueous environment, will retain some integral membrane proteins in solution; examples of this include, the Thy-1 antigen on lymphocytes and cytochrome b_5 (*see* **ref. *3*** for other examples).

3.5.7. Preparation of Samples for Electrophoresis

Before the proteins in the Triton X-114 fractions obtained from the lipid-rich chromaffin granule membranes can be separated by PAGE, they require removal of lipid and detergent with ice-cold acetone/ethanol (1:1) in glass tubes.

1. Resuspend the detergent-enriched phase in 10 vol of ice-cold acetone/ethanol. Once the protein has precipitated, recover it by centrifugation at 2500*g* for 5 min. The lipid-enriched fraction will require up to 75 vol to remove all the lipid.

   Caution: Do not carry this procedure out in –20°C freezer or a refrigerator, because acetone and ethanol vapor present an explosion hazard.
2. Dry the pellets under a stream of nitrogen and then solubilize the protein in SDS-gel sample buffer, as described in **Subheading 3.3.2.** Using this procedure, no lipid will be present to cause distortion of the dye front on the polyacrylamide gel, which becomes a problem when low mol wt proteins, such as the dicyclohexyl-carbodiimide-reactive protein, are to be resolved (*see* **Fig. 1A**).

3.5.8. Controls for Phase Partitioning

Integral membrane proteins generally partition exclusively into the detergent-enriched phase. However, there are a number of membrane proteins shown by other criteria to be integral, which partition anomalously into the detergent-depleted phase *(3, 7)*. Therefore, when investigating the partitioning of a complex mixture of proteins, it is necessary to formally demonstrate that phase partitioning has progressed efficiently. If an integral membrane protein is present in the detergent-depleted phase, then it is possible that the partitioning procedure is at fault. To eliminate this possibility, samples can be spiked with an integral membrane protein that has been demonstrated to partition solely into the detergent-enriched phase, and with a soluble protein that partitions into the detergent-depleted phase. For example, the G protein of Chandipura virus, which is an integral membrane protein, and human transferrin a soluble protein, have been used to demonstrate that under conditions in which these partition, respectively, into the detergent-enriched and detergent-depleted phases, an integral membrane protein of the rat liver Golgi complex partitions into the detergent-depleted phase *(11)*. With antibodies to both these proteins, simply Western-blot samples of fractions and show that uncharacterized proteins partitions with one of the characterized proteins as is shown in **Fig. 2**.

4. Notes

1. High g-values produce compact pellets that are difficult to solubilize in SDS-gel sample buffer.
2. Detergent is precipitated by trichloroacetic acid, but this is removed by the organic solvents.
3. If subcellular fractions are to be produced (*see* **ref. 2**), avoid the use of PBS for cell washing. Washing cells in PBS prior to breaking them in a glass Dounce homogenizer renders them more difficult to break. These washes are best carried out in a HEPES-based homogenization buffer such as 50 m*M* KCl, 50 m*M* HEPES KOH, pH 7.4, 10 m*M* EGTA, 2 m*M* $MgCl_2$ (KHEM).
4. The method described here for fractionating membrane proteins, following their solubilization in Triton X-114, appears to be generally applicable *(1)*. It is only

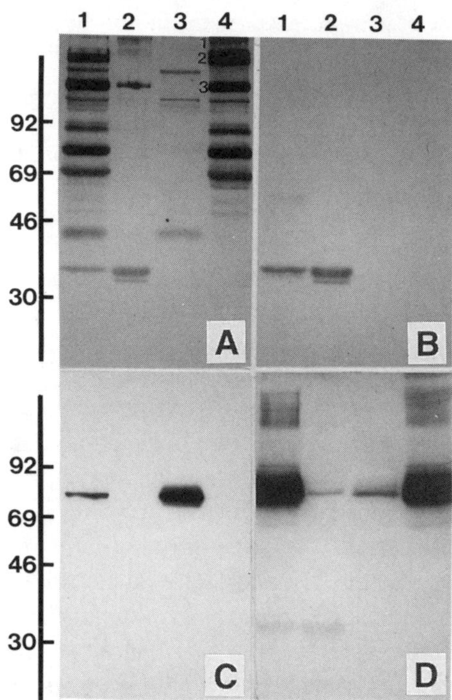

Fig. 2. Solubilization and phase-separation of rat liver Golgi membranes in Triton X-114. Golgi membranes were solubilized and phase separated in 1% Triton X-114 and the proteins separated on 10% polyacrylamide gels and transferred to nitrocellulose for immunoblotting analysis. **(A–D)** Lane 1, Golgi membranes spiked with purified Chandipura virus and human transferrin; lane 2, material not solubilized at 0°C; lane 3, detergent-enriched phase; lane 4, detergent-depleted phase. These blots were probed with: (A) antiserum raised to Golgi membranes (JPR3); (B) preimmune rabbit serum; (C) monoclonal antibody to Chandipura virus G protein; (D) antihuman transferrin antibody. The numbers 1, 2, and 3 refer, respectively, to Golgi membrane proteins of M_r 500, 200, and 100 kDa, the affinity purified antibodies of which stain the Golgi complex by immunofluorescence microscopy. (Reproduced with permission from **ref. *10***.)

lipid-rich membranes, such as those from chromaffin granule membranes, that produce the lipid-enriched precipitate following solubilization ***(6)***. The membrane lipids of other organelles remain in solution when solubilized by Triton X-114, but there is some detergent-insoluble material that must be removed by high-speed centrifugation. It is clear that no two membrane fractions behave in the same way when solubilized. Mitochondrial membranes solubilized in Triton X-114 are either enriched in the detergent-enriched phase, or are present in the detergent-depleted phase, and there is no appreciable insoluble material. Bordier ***(1)*** found a similar distribution with human erythrocyte membranes and similar results were found with platelets ***(12)*** and granulocytes ***(13)***.

References

1. Bordier, C. (1981) Phase separation of integral membrane proteins in Triton X-114 solution. *J. Biol. Chem.* **256,** 1604–1607.
2. Pryde, J. G. (1986) Triton X-114: a detergent that has come in from the cold. *Trends Biochem. Sci.* **11,** 160–163.
3. Brusca, J. S. and Radolf, J. D. (1994) Isolation of integral membrane proteins by phase partitioning with Triton X-114. *Methods Enzymol.* **228,** 182–193.
4. Sanchez-Ferrer, A., Bru, R., and Garcia-Carmona, F. (1994) Phase separation of biomolecules in polyoxyethylene glycol nonionic detergents. *Crit. Rev. Biochem. Mol. Biol.* **29,** 275–313.
5. Pryde, J. G. and Phillips, J. H. (1986) Fractionation of membrane proteins by temperature-induced phase separation in Triton X-114. *Biochem. J.* **233,** 525–533.
6. Maher, P. A. and Singer, S. J. (1985) Anomalous interaction of the acetylcholine receptor protein with the nonionic detergent Triton X-114. *Proc. Natl. Acad. Sci.* **82,** 958–962.
7. Alcaraz, G., Kinet, J-P., Kumar, N., Wank, S. A., and Metzger, H. (1984) Phase separation of the receptor for immunoglobulin E and its subunits in Triton X-114. *J. Biol. Chem.* **259,** 14,922–14,927.
8. Garewal, H. S. (1973) A procedure for the estimation of microgram quantities of Triton X-100. *Anal. Biochem.* **54,** 319–324.
9. Perez-Castineira, J. R. and Apps, D. K. (1990) Vacuolar H^+-ATPase of adrenal secretory granules. *Biochem. J.* **271,** 127–131.
10. Pryde, J. G. (1994) A group of integral membrane proteins of the rat liver Golgi contains a conserved protein of 100 kDa. *J. Cell Sci.* **107,** 3425–3436.
11. Shakur, Y., Pryde, J. G., and Houslay, M. D. (1993) Engineered deletion of the unique N-terminal domain of the cyclic AMP-specific phosphodiesterase RD1 prevents plasma membrane association and the attainment of enhanced thermostability without altering its sensitivity to inhibition by rolipram. *Biochem. J.* **292,** 677–686.
12. Clemetson, K. J., Bienz, D., Zahno, M.-L., and Luscher, E. F. (1984) Distribution of platelet glycoproteins and phosphoproteins in hydrophobic and hydrophilic phases in Triton X-114 phase partition. *Biochem. Biophys. Acta* . **778,** 463–469.
13. Pember, S. O., Heyl, B. L., Kinkade, J. M., and Lambeth, J. D. (1984) Cytochrome b_{558} from (bovine) granulocytes. *J. Biol. Chem.* **259,** 10,590–10,595.

4

Co-Immunoprecipitation

Identification of Interacting Proteins

Neil G. Anderson

1. Introduction

1.1. Background

The targeting of proteins, via precise protein–protein interactions, to specific intracellular locations, is a recurring theme in cell biology. This has become particularly evident from the explosion of recent studies in the general area of signal transduction. Over the past 5–10 yr great strides have been made in understanding the intracellular signaling processes that regulate proliferative, metabolic, and other cellular responses. These mechanisms are complex and usually involve the participation of many signaling molecules linked by a series of catalytic and noncatalytic interactions. The physical association of two or more proteins in a signaling pathway is necessary in order to attain efficiency of signaling and to maintain specificity of response. A number of categories of protein–protein interaction are known to occur. These include the interaction between enzyme and substrate, the interaction between *src* homology 2 (SH2) domains and phosphotyrosyl residues within specific peptide sequences, and the binding of SH3 domains to polyprolyl sequences ***(1)***. The development of techniques that can provide evidence for the interaction of two or more proteins in the intact cell has been instrumental in establishing the existence of many signaling pathways. This chapter aims to describe one such technique, that of co-immunoprecipitation.

1.2. Principle of Co-Immunoprecipitation

Immunoprecipitation involves the precipitation of a molecule, usually a protein, from a crude mixture of other proteins and biological molecules, often a

From: *Methods in Molecular Biology, Vol. 88: Protein Targeting Protocols*
Edited by: R. A. Clegg Humana Press Inc., Totowa, NJ

cell or tissue homogenate, using an antibody to the protein of interest and a means of precipitating the complex to allow its separation from the initial mixture. The refinement of techniques for the production of high titer and exquisitely selective antibodies has made this method the one of choice for the analysis of protein function and modification in intact cells and tissues. Changes in catalytic or binding activity or in phosphorylation state can readily be analyzed by immunoprecipitation techniques. An obvious corollary arising from the use of this method is the ability to coprecipitate proteins interacting with the protein that the antibody recognizes. Thus, if protein X forms a stable complex with protein Y in the cell, immunoprecipitation of X may result in coprecipitation of Y. Two basic strategies are available for such co-immunoprecipitation experiments. The first involves testing the hypothesis that two or more known proteins interact. In this case immunological probes must be available for each protein. The second strategy involves a search for unknown cellular proteins capable of interacting with a known protein. In this case, cellular proteins are first radioactively labeled with either [^{32}S]methionine (to screen for interactions with cellular proteins) or [^{32}P]phosphate (to screen for interactions with phosphoproteins), proteins that interact with the known protein are identified initially by gel electrophoresis and autoradiography. The method detailed herein concentrates on the immunoprecipitation aspects of the technique. For detailed methodology concerning the metabolic labeling of cells, the reader is referred to **refs.** ***2*** and ***3***, and to Chapters 3 and 18 of this volume.

2. Materials

2.1. Equipment

1. End-over-end mixer (Stuart Scientific, Redhill, Surrey, UK).
2. Refrigerated microcentrifuge (Camlab, Cambridge, UK).
3. Vertical gel electrophoresis system (Bio-Rad, Hemel Hempstead, UK).
4. Western blotting apparatus (Pharmacia, St. Albans, UK).
5. Gel dryer (Pharmacia).

2.2. Buffers and Solutions

1. Lysis buffer: 25 m*M* HEPES, pH 7.5 (4°C), 5 m*M* EDTA, 5 m*M* EGTA, 50 m*M* NaCl, 50 m*M* NaF, 30 m*M* Na pyrophosphate, 10% (v/v) glycerol, and 1% (v/v) Triton X-100. Store at 4°C for up to 2 wk. Add the following from concentrated stock solutions fresh on the day of the experiment: 2 m*M* Na orthovanadate (final concentration), 1 m*M* phenylmethylsulfonyl fluoride, 2 μg/mL leupeptin, 2 μg/mL aprotinin, and 2 μg/mL pepstatin A.
2. High-Salt Wash Buffer: 100 m*M* Tris-HCl, pH 8.0, 500 m*M* LiCl.
3. Sodium dodecyl sulfate (SDS)-sample buffer (X2): 125 m*M* Tris-HCl, pH 6.7, 5% 2-mercaptoethanol, 25% (v/v) glycerol, 2.5% (w/v) SDS, 0.01% (w/v) phenol red.

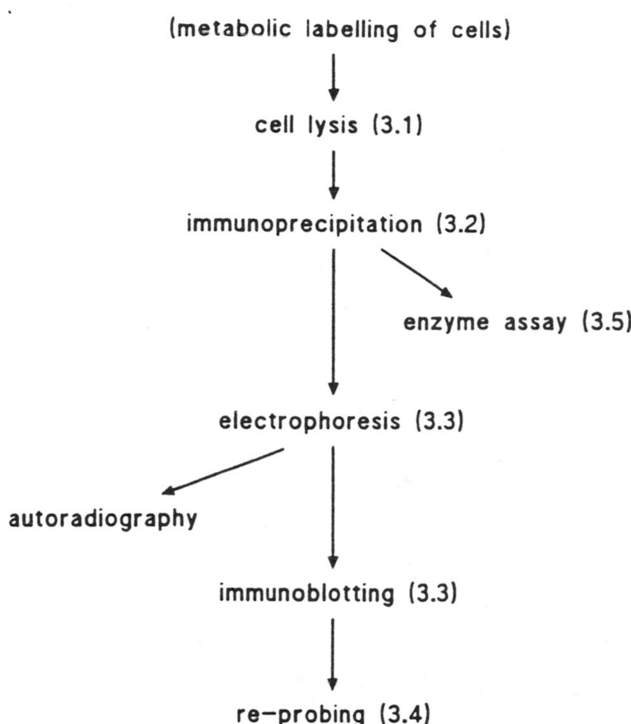

Fig. 1. Strategy for co-immunoprecipitation of proteins from cultured cells.

4. Tween–TBS: 10 m*M* Tris-HCl, pH 7.4, 137 m*M* NaCl, 0.1% (v/v) Tween-20.
5. Stripping buffer: 100 m*M* Tris-HCl, pH 6.7, 100 m*M* 2-mercaptoethanol, 2% (w/v) SDS.

3. Methods

The method describes a detailed standard procedure for immunoprecipitation of proteins from growth factor-stimulated Swiss 3T3 fibroblast cells grown on 100-mm plastic dishes. The same principle applies to nonadherent cell lines, primary cell cultures, or whole tissues, although in each case the initial extraction procedure will be different. Clearly, if handling samples prepared from cells metabolically labeled with either ^{35}S or ^{32}P, thought must be given to adequate shielding of samples during the procedure and to the safe disposal of waste materials. The basic strategy is outlined in **Fig 1**.

3.1. Cell Lysis

The first question to consider is the amount of cellular material that will be required. Obviously, this depends primarily on the abundance of the protein of interest, but, as a general starting point, 1–2 mg of cellular protein should be sufficient for most immunoprecipitation experiments.

1. Starve confluent cultures of Swiss 3T3 cells by switching to serum-free culture medium for several hours (usually overnight). Inclusion of 25 m*M* HEPES in this medium prevents large fluctuations in pH when handling the cells.
2. Remove cells from the incubator and add a concentrated solution of the appropriate growth factor to each plate. Control plates of cells should be removed from the incubator at the same time and receive the requisite quantity of diluent.
3. At the end of the stimulation period, transport the cells immediately to a tray of ice (preferably in a 4°C room). At this point, it is vital that cells are rapidly cooled to preserve growth factor-induced modifications to cellular proteins. Therefore, if several plates are to be processed, two persons should work together.
4. Remove the medium with an aspirator and immediately add 10 mL of ice-cold phosphate buffered saline (PBS) to the cell monolayer.
5. Remove the PBS by aspiration, then add 1 mL of lysis buffer to the washed cells (*see* **Subheading 2.2.** and **Notes 1** and **2**). All subsequent steps should be carried out at 4°C.
6. Gently scrape the cells into the lysis buffer using a plastic stirring rod (Nalgene, Hereford, UK). If cells from more than one plate are to be combined, the scraped material from plate 1 is applied to plate 2, and so on.
7. Transfer the combined cell suspensions to a microcentrifuge tube on ice. Rotate the tube on an end-over-end mixer for 20 min and then centrifuge at $12{,}000g_{max}$ in a refrigerated microcentrifuge for 10 min.
8. Transfer the supernatant, containing the extracted cellular protein, into fresh tubes, and discard the insoluble material. At this stage, remove a sample of the lysate for determination of protein content. Because of the presence of detergent in the lysis buffer, the sample should be diluted prior to assay. We routinely use the Bradford assay ***(4)***, having diluted samples 20–100 times. Remove a second sample of the lysate (50–100 μL) and denature by adding an equal volume of 2X SDS sample buffer (*see* **Subheading 2.2.**), followed by boiling for 5 min. This sample will be run on the gel alongside the immunoprecipitated samples (*see* **Subheading 3.3.**).

3.2. Immunoprecipitation

1. Place the remainder of the lysate prepared in **Subheading 3.1.** on an end-over-end mixer for 1 h, with 50 μL of a 50% slurry of either protein A- or protein G-agarose (Pierce-Warriner, Chester, UK), depending on which will be used for antibody precipitation later (*see* **Note 3**).
2. Following the preclearing step, pellet the agarose beads by centrifugation in a microcentrifuge for 5 s.
3. Transfer equal quantities (in terms of cellular protein) of the cleared cell lysate to screw-cap microcentrifuge tubes containing the primary immunoprecipitating antibody (*see* **Note 4**). The amount of lysate and antibody used must be determined by experiment, but, as a starting point, 5–10 μL of crude antiserum or 5–10 μg purified antibody should be added to a cell lysate containing 1 mg of protein.

4. Incubate the samples for 3 h (*see* **Note 5**).
5. To precipitate the antibody–antigen complexes, add 50 µL of 50% slurry of washed protein A-agarose or protein G-agarose and rotate the samples for a further 1 h.
6. Wash the agarose beads three times, using 0.75 mL of lysis buffer for each wash, followed by two washes with high-salt buffer (*see* **Subheading 2.2.**) and a final wash with 10 m*M* Tris (pH 7.4) (*see* **Note 6**). Finally, carefully remove all traces of buffer from the beads, using a fine needle or pipet.
7. To elute proteins from the beads, add 50 µL of 2X SDS sample buffer and heat the samples to 95°C for 5 min. Pellet the beads in a microcentrifuge and carefully transfer the supernatant containing the eluted proteins to fresh tubes. Rinse the beads with 25 µL of 1X SDS sample buffer, spin down, and combine the supernatant with the initial eluate (*see* **Note 7**).

3.3. Electrophoresis and Western Blotting

1. Run the samples on standard discontinuous SDS-PAGE gels (7–12% acrylamide in the separating gel, depending on the molecular masses of the proteins under analysis). For the analysis of radioactive samples, gels are fixed following electrophoresis, then dried and exposed to X-ray film. If the gel is to be transferred to nitrocellulose for immunoblotting, a sample of the original lysate (approx 50 µg; **Subheading 3.1., step 5**) or, ideally, a purified sample of the protein of interest (if available), should be run on the gel alongside the test samples, as a positive control.
2. Following electrophoresis, electrophoretically transfer the proteins to nitrocellulose (*see* **Note 8**).
3. Place the nitrocellulose in a plastic box and stain with Ponceau S solution (1% [w/v] in 1% acetic acid) for 2 min to assess transfer efficiency. This should also reveal the presence of a heavily stained protein band, of M_r around 50,000, in the immunoprecipitate samples, representing the IgG heavy chain of the immunoprecipitating antibody. Equal staining of this band between samples confirms that similar amounts of immunoprecipitate sample have been transferred (*see* **Subheading 3.6.2.**). Remove the Ponceau S by rinsing the nitrocellulose several times in distilled water.
4. Block the nitrocellulose in a solution of 3% (w/v) BSA for 1 h (37°C) or 3 h (25°C). This and subsequent steps should be carried out on a variable-speed shaking platform.
5. Rinse the nitrocellulose for 15 min with Tween–TBS (*see* **Subheading 2.2.**).
6. Add the primary detecting antibody diluted in a solution of Tween–TBS containing 1% BSA and 0.05% thimerosal (*see* **Note 9**) for 1–3 h at room temperature.
7. Rinse the nitrocellulose four times for a total of 30 min with Tween–TBS.
8. Add a solution of secondary antibody diluted in Tween–TBS containing 1% BSA for 30 min to 1 h (*see* **Note 9**).
9. Repeat **step 7**.
10. Immerse the nitrocellulose in fresh ECL reagent for 1 min. Drain off excess fluid, but do not blot dry. Carefully wrap the nitrocellulose in plastic film and expose to X-ray film for an appropriate time.

3.4. Reprobing of Immunoblots

Following immunoblotting, it should be possible to probe for other putative coprecipitating proteins. Reprobing immunoblots depends on the complete removal of the original detection reagents. It is vital that the nitrocellulose does not dry out prior to the reprobing. Wrapping the nitrocellulose in plastic film with storage at 4°C will prevent this.

1. To strip the immunoblot, immerse the nitrocellulose in 50 mL of stripping buffer (*see* **Subheading 2.2.**) and incubate in a shaking water bath for 30 min at a temperature of 50–70°C (the optimal temperature varies and must be determined by prior experiment [*see* **Note 10**]).
2. Rinse the nitrocellulose several times in Tween–TBS. At this stage re-exposure of the immunoblot to ECL reagents will determine whether the original reagents have been completely removed.
3. Reblock the nitrocellulose in 3% BSA solution and then probe with the appropriate antibody, as described in **Subheading 3.3.**

3.5. Coprecipitation of Enzymatic Activity

In addition to probing immunoprecipitates with an antibody to detect the presence of a particular protein, if one suspects that putative coprecipitating proteins possess catalytic activity, this activity may be assayed directly in the immunoprecipitates. For example, immunoprecipitation of IRS-1 from insulin-stimulated cells results in the coprecipitation of PI 3-kinase. Assay of the IRS-1 immunoprecipitates with an appropriate substrate shows a concomitant increase in associated PI 3-kinase activity ***(6)***. Failure to detect a particular activity, on the other hand, cannot be taken as evidence that the protein is not present, since conformational changes induced by antibody binding could inhibit enzyme activity.

3.6. Analysis of Results

Results from a typical co-immunoprecipitation experiment are illustrated schematically in **Fig. 2**. In **Fig. 2A**, protein X has been immunoprecipitated from [^{32}P]-labeled cells. In addition to X itself, a number of other labeled protein bands are present. Some occur in both unstimulated (–) and stimulated (+) samples, and may represent proteins constitutively associated with the immunoprecipitated protein or proteins precipitated nonspecifically. The intensities of two other bands (arrowed) are increased and may represent proteins that associate with X as a result of cell stimulation. Another possibility, however, is that these proteins are constitutively associated with the immunoprecipitated protein and undergo increased phosphorylation as a result of cell stimulation. Repeating the experiment under conditions in which cellular proteins have been labeled with [^{32}S]methionine should distinguish between these two possibilities.

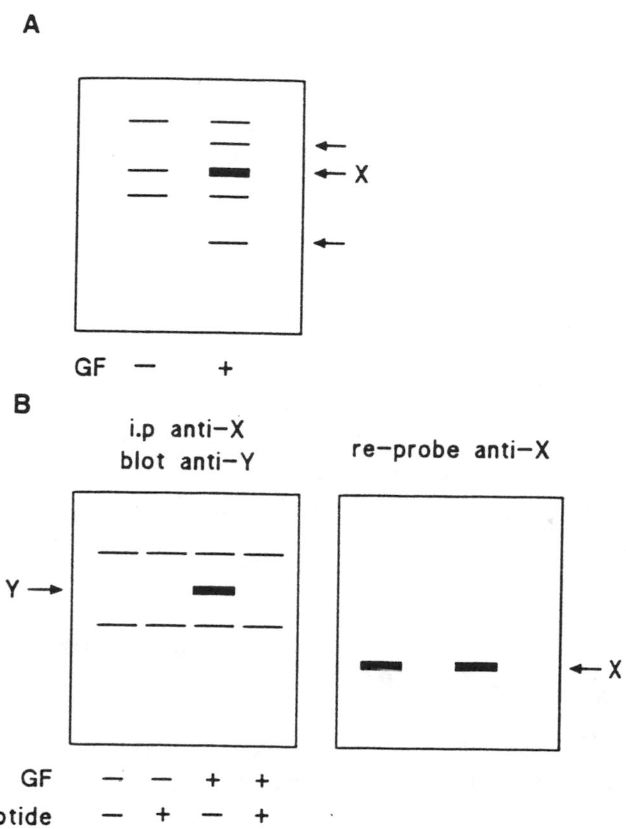

Fig. 2. Schematic representation of results from coimmunoprecipitation studies. **(A)** Representation of an autoradiogram. Protein X was immunoprecipitated from [^{32}P]-labeled control (–) and growth factor (GF) stimulated (+) cells. Protein bands exhibiting increased labeling caused by growth factor stimulation are indicated by arrows to the right of the figure. **(B)** Nonlabeled cells. Left panel: Immunoblotting with antibody to protein Y of samples immunoprecipitated with antibody to protein X, in the presence (lanes 2 and 4) or absence (lanes 1 and 3) of X competing peptide, from control (–) or growth factor (GF) stimulated (+) cells. Right panel: The immunoblot shown in the left panel has been reprobed with antibody to protein X. Results are discussed in the text.

In **Fig. 2B** (left panel), proteins immunoprecipitated from nonlabeled cells with antibody to X have been immunoblotted with an antibody to protein Y. Y is detected only in the sample prepared from stimulated cells; the obvious conclusion is that X and Y associate following stimulation. A number of nonspecific bands occur in all lanes. In the presence of an excess of competing peptide (containing the sequence epitope recognized by the antibody; *see* **Note 11**), protein X is not immunoprecipitated (lanes 2 and 4; *see* **Subheading 3.6.1.**). In **Fig. 2B** (right panel), the immunoblot on the left has been reprobed with the antibody to X. As anticipated, X is detected in equal amounts in lanes 1 and 3.

Results similar to those illustrated schematically in **Fig. 2** provide good evidence for protein–protein interactions. However, a number of questions must first be asked before concluding that a particular protein band detected on a gel or immunoblot represents a protein that genuinely associates with the immunoprecipitated protein directly. These questions fall generally into those of specificity and quantification (*see also* **Note 12**).

3.6.1. Specificity

One important question is this: Do the coprecipitating proteins directly associate with the primary protein, or are they precipitated nonspecifically during the execution of the experiment? The following tests should answer this question.

3.6.1.1. Is Coprecipitation Growth Factor-Dependent?

In most cases the experimenter is looking for a putative protein association event as a result of cell stimulation. Therefore, the appearance of associated proteins only in the sample from stimulated cells is a good indicator of a specific interaction. Of course, in some cases dissociation of preformed protein complexes may occur in response to cell stimulation.

3.6.1.2. Antibody Checks

The appearance of coprecipitating proteins should be solely dependent on the presence of the primary precipitating antibody. Control experiments using nonimmune (or, preferably, preimmune) serum, secondary antibody alone, or protein A/G-agarose alone should produce negative results. In addition, if the primary antibody was raised to a synthetic peptide sequence, addition of this peptide prior to immunoprecipitation should compete both direct and coprecipitating protein interactions (*see* **Fig. 2B**).

3.6.2. Quantification

When comparing two samples, for example, from control and stimulated cells, it is important to ascertain that equal quantities of protein have been immunoprecipitated. Using the same amount of starting material is obviously crucial. Equal staining of immunoblots with Ponceau S has already been referred to (*see* **Subheading 3.3.**). A third and definitive check involves probing the immunoprecipitates with an antibody that recognizes the protein originally immunoprecipitated. Generally, since one would have first used another antibody to probe for coprecipitating proteins, this procedure involves stripping the immunoblot of bound detection reagents (*see* **Subheading 3.4.**), followed by reprobing with the immunoprecipitating antibody. A schematic representation of a reprobing experiment is shown in **Fig. 2B** (right panel).

4. Notes

1. Preserving the association of proteins following cell breakage necessitates taking steps to minimize postlysis protein modification by agents such as proteases and phosphatases. For example, many interactions (such as those between phosphotyrosyl residues and SH2 domains) depend on the phosphorylation of one of the interacting proteins ***(1)***. Carrying out the procedure at 4°C is crucial to reduce the activities of proteases and phosphatases. In the procedure outlined above, the lysis buffer (*see* **Subheading 2.1.**) contains a range of agents that severely inhibit the activities of most proteases and phosphatases. However, it may be necessary in certain situations to include a wider range of inhibitors, or to increase the concentration of one or more of the existing inhibitors.
2. The type and concentration of detergent, necessary for the efficient solubilization of cellular proteins, may influence the outcome of the experiment. High concentrations of detergent may destroy some protein–protein interactions. In addition, the species of detergent used may influence the strength of a particular association. Reduction of detergent concentration or the use of other nonionic detergents, such as Brij ***(7)*** may allow detection of some interactions that would otherwise be destroyed.
3. The use of either protein A or protein G depends on the species in which the immunoprecipitating antibody was raised. Protein G binds strongly to the IgG of most species, but Protein A has a more limited selectivity. The protein A or G agarose generally is supplied as a slurry containing ethanol or other preservatives. The beads should therefore be washed twice in lysis buffer prior to use. Washing involves a 5 s spin in a microcentrifuge, removal of supernatant and resuspension of beads in lysis buffer. Prior to immunoprecipitation it is best to preclear the sample by adding a suspension of protein A or G beads. This allows nonspecific interactions between sample proteins and the protein A or G, or with the agarose itself, to be removed prior to immunoprecipitation with the specific antibody.
4. If the antibody used for immunoprecipitation recognizes an epitope at or near a site of potential protein interaction it is unlikely that such an interaction will be detected. The use of a range of antibodies raised to different peptide sequences on the protein should be considered.
5. The time used for the immunoprecipitation step is a compromise between maximizing the amount of protein precipitated and minimizing potential proteolytic or dephosphorylation events. Generally, precipitation at 4°C is efficient and there is little to be gained by prolonged incubation times greater than 3 h. The efficiency of immunoprecipitation of any protein can easily be checked by immunoblotting of lysate samples before and after immunoprecipitation.

6. The washing of immunoprecipitate complexes (*see* **Subheading 3.2.**) is necessary to remove nonspecific interactions, but should not be so harsh as to destroy true protein–protein interactions. For example, some weak interactions may be destroyed by high-salt buffers. Various washing procedures should therefore be tested.
7. Problems may arise if antibody used for both immunoprecipitation and immunoblotting was raised in the same species. For example, if samples contain rabbit IgG heavy chain from the immunoprecipitating antibody, and another rabbit antibody is used for immunoblotting, then the secondary detection antibody will strongly react with the heavy-chain protein band. This is especially problematical if putative coprecipitating proteins have a similar molecular mass as the IgG heavy chain, i.e., approx 50,000. If antibodies from different species are available, then these should be used. Alternatively, prior crosslinking of the antibody to the protein A or G *(7)* will permit the elution of antigen only.
8. Conditions for electrophoretic transfer depend on the protein being analyzed and should be varied until optimized (*see* **ref. 5**). For the analysis of proteins in the low molecular mass range (<60,000) we transfer for 3 h at a constant current of 400 mA. For the analysis of proteins with a molecular mass range (>60,000), we transfer gels for 16–18 h at 125 mA.
9. The optimal dilution of the antibody used for immunoblotting must be determined by experiment. Detection of small amounts of protein may require a relatively high concentration of antibody, but this may lead to nonspecific binding. There are many methods available for the detection of immunoreactive proteins on Western blots, but our laboratory has recently employed the enhanced chemiluminescence (ECL) system (Amersham, Little Chalfont, Buckinghamshire, UK), which offers a high degree of sensitivity without the need to use radioactively labeled reagents. Horseradish peroxidase-linked secondary antibodies are used for detection of immunoreactive bands. Again dilutions depend on various parameters, such as the concentration of primary antibody used and the amount of antigen available for detection.
10. The stripping of immunoblots may result in >50% losses of antigen from the nitrocellulose; these losses must be taken into account when considering the sequence of probing and reprobing. For example, nonabundant cellular proteins should be probed for first. Similarly, low-titer antibodies should be used in the initial detection, rather than after stripping.
11. Peptide competitor strategies are only applicable if the antibody used is either an antipeptide antibody or a monoclonal with a mapped continuous epitope. For other antibodies, the entire protein antigen may be used as a competitor.
12. The technique of co-immunoprecipitation is a widely used and powerful technique for the initial demonstration of protein–protein interaction. This method has been instrumental in piecing together many signaling pathways, particularly those mediating the mitogenic responses of cells to growth factors. Clearly, the procedure has its limitations. It may not be able to detect very weak interactions, or, if the proteins are of low abundance, the immunological probes may not be of

sufficient sensitivity. A major limitation is the inability of the method to unequivocally prove that two or more coimmunoprecipitated proteins actually interact in the intact cell. Despite the range of possible control experiments, the possibility of postlysis artifactual interactions occurring can never be ruled out. The method must therefore be seen as a starting point that indicates possible interactions. Other molecular techniques using purified proteins or immunocytochemistry may subsequently provide the necessary corroborating evidence that two proteins colocalize *in situ*.

References

1. Cohen, G. B., Ren, R., and Baltimore, D. (1995) Modular binding domains in signal transduction proteins. *Cell* **80,** 237–248.
2. Garrison, J. C. (1993) Study of protein phosphorylation in intact cells, in *Protein Phosphorylation: A Practical Approach* (Hardie, D. G., ed.), Oxford University Press, Oxford, UK, pp. 1–30.
3. Feuerstein, N., Huang, D., and Prystowsky, M. B. (1995) Rapamycin selectively blocks interleukin-2-induced proliferating cell nuclear antigen gene expression. *J. Biol. Chem.* **270,** 9454–9458.
4. Bradford, M. M. (1976) A rapid and sensitive method for the quantitation of microgram quantities of protein utilizing the principle of protein-dye binding. *Anal. Biochem.* **72,** 248–254.
5. Towbin, H., Staehelin, T., and Gordon, J. (1979) Electrophoretic transfer of proteins from polyacrylamide gels to nitrocellulose sheets: procedure and some applications. *Proc. Natl. Acad. Sci. USA* **76,** 4350–4355.
6. Backer, J. M., Myers, M. G., Shoelson, S. E., Chin, D. J., Sun, X. J., Miralpeix, M., Hu, P., Margolis, B., Skolnik, E. Y., Schlessinger, J., and White, M. F. (1992) Phosphatidylinositol 3' kinase is activated by association with IRS-1 during insulin stimulation *EMBO J.* **11,** 3469–3479.
7. He, T.-C., Jiang, N., Zhuang, H., and Wojchowski, D. M. (1995) Erythropoietin induced recruitment of Shc via a receptor phosphotyrosine-independent, JAK-2-associated pathway. *J. Biol. Chem.* **270,** 11,055–11,061.

5

Overlay, Ligand Blotting, and Band-Shift Techniques to Study Kinase Anchoring

Zachary E. Hausken, Vincent M. Coghlan, and John D. Scott

1. Introduction

One common theme in protein–protein interactions is that binding often occurs through relatively small domains. This is particularly true in the area of signal transduction, in which numerous studies have demonstrated that the subcellular location of protein kinases and phosphatases is regulated through association with structural proteins or cellular organelles *(1,2)*. This has led to the proposal by Hubbard and Cohen of a targeting hypothesis, in which both classes of enzyme are maintained in close proximity to specific substrates by targeting domains *(3)*. Kinase and phosphatase targeting not only facilitates the rapid and preferential phosphorylation of substrates, but optimally positions these enzymes at sites where they can be efficiently activated in response to the appropriate signals *(3)*.

Evidence supporting this model has shown that protein tyrosine kinases and phosphatases couple to downstream cytoplasmic enzymes through modular adapter proteins that contain Src homology (SH2 and SH3) domains *(4)*. Both of these peptide-binding domains are conserved secondary structures that specifically recognize linear sequence motifs on their recipient proteins *(5,6)*. Serine and threonine kinases and phosphatases use variations on this theme to achieve their correct subcellular targeting *(2)*. Phosphatases type I and 2A (PP-1 and PP-2A) are localized by a growing family of targeting subunits *(7,8)*, and phosphatase 2B, calcineurin, is targeted to the postsynaptic densities of neurons *(9)*. Compartmentalization of protein kinase C (PKC) occurs through interaction with substrate-binding proteins, sometimes called receptors for

From: *Methods in Molecular Biology, Vol. 88: Protein Targeting Protocols*
Edited by: R. A. Clegg Humana Press Inc., Totowa, NJ

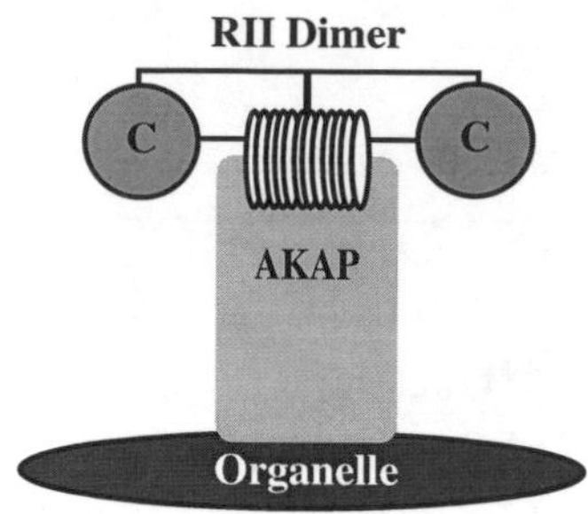

Fig. 1. Models for RII–AKAP interaction. A schematic diagram depicting possible topologies of RII–AKAP interaction.

activated c-kinases (RACKs) ***(10,11)***. Subcellular targeting of the cAMP-dependent protein kinase (PKA) occurs through its association with A-kinase anchoring proteins (AKAPs) ***(12,13)***. Work on PKA anchoring has been facilitated by the development of several in vitro binding techniques, such as the solid-phase overlay, interaction cloning strategies and band-shift analysis, which exploit the properties of PKA–AKAP interaction ***(14)***. The goal of this chapter is to use PKA anchoring as a model system to describe these techniques and outline their use for investigating protein/protein interactions. Special emphasis has been placed on providing the reader with the precise protocols, presented in a step by step approach, that highlight the advantages and pitfalls of each procedure.

1.1. PKA–AKAP Interaction

PKA anchoring is directed through the association of the regulatory (R) subunit dimer with an amphipathic helix on the anchoring protein **(Fig. 1)**. Although there have been a few isolated reports of PKA anchoring directed through the type I R subunit (RI) ***(15)***, it is generally accepted that the type II R subunit (RII) is the principle targeting subunit ***(16,17)***. Mapping of the AKAP-binding site on RII has demonstrated that dimerization is required for anchoring ***(18)***. Deletion analysis has suggested that the localization and dimerization domains are contained within distinct but overlapping regions within the first 30 residues of each RII protomer ***(19)***. In addition, mutagenesis studies have identified two isoleucine side chains on each RII protomer as principle sites of contact with the anchoring protein **(Fig. 1)**, but other studies have demonstrated that additional hydrophobic contacts occur in regions downstream of these isoleucines ***(19,20)***.

In contrast, the RII-binding site on the AKAP seems to involve a region of secondary structure that is confined to a short stretch of amino acids. Deletion analysis and mutagenesis studies have demonstrated regions of 14–24 residues on several AKAPs that exhibit a high probability of amphipathic α-helix formation are essential for anchoring ***(21–24)***. In fact, peptides corresponding to these helical regions specifically bind RII or the type II PKA holoenzyme with a high affinity (K_d ~4 n*M*) ***(25)***. Recently, these peptides have been used as potent anchoring inhibitors to disrupt the localization of PKA in vivo ***(26,27)***. The AKAPs' compact binding domain makes RII–AKAP interactions particularly amenable to analysis by the binding techniques described in this chapter. The following sections provide detailed protocols for in vitro binding techniques, such as solid-phase overlay assays (*see* **Subheading 3.1.**), overlay-based cloning strategies (*see* **Subheading 3.2.**), peptide overlays (*see* **Subheading 3.3.**), and band-shift analysis (*see* **Subheading 3.4.**).

2. Materials

2.1. Protein Overlay Techniques

2.1.1. Radioactive (^{32}P) RII Overlay

1. Sodium dodecyl sulfate-polyacryamide gel electrophoresis (SDS-PAGE).
2. Immobilon or nitrocellulose.
3. Immobilon stain: 46% Methanol, 9% acetic acid, 0.05% Coomassie blue; or Ponceau stain: 0.2% Ponceau in 1% acetic acid.
4. Immobilon destain: 46% methanol, 9% acetic acid.
5. BLOTTO: Tris-buffered saline, pH 7.0 (TBS), 5% dry milk, 1% bovine serum albumin (BSA).
6. RII (2 μg).
7. PKA catalytic subunit (0.1 μg) and [γ-^{32}P] ATP (50 μCi).
8. PKA reaction buffer: 50 m*M* MOPS, pH 6.8, 50 m*M* NaCl, 2 m*M* $MgCl_2$, 1 m*M* DTT, 0.1 mg/mL BSA.
9. TBS/0.05% Tween-20 (TTBS).
10. 3MM paper.
11. 2X sample buffer: 100 m*M* DTT, 2% SDS, 80 m*M* Tris-HCl, pH 6.8, 10% glycerol, and 0.0012% bromophenol blue.
12. Vertical electrophoresis apparatus and gel solutions.
13. Gel transfer apparatus.

2.1.2. Nonradioactive RII Overlay

1. 0.5 μg/mL of BLOTTO.
2. TTBS.
3. Anti-RII antibodies (1:20,000).
4. HRP-conjugated secondary antibody (1:10,000).
5. Chemiluminescence kit.
6. SDS-PAGE.
7. Immobilon or nitrocellulose.

8. Immobilon stain: 46% Methanol, 9% acetic acid, 0.05% Coomassie blue, or Ponceau stain: 0.2% Ponceau in 1% acetic acid.
9. Immobilon destain: 46% methanol, 9% acetic acid.
10. RII (2 μg).
11. 3MM paper.
12. 2X sample buffer: 100 m*M* DTT, 2% SDS, 80 m*M* Tris-HCl, pH 6.8, 10% glycerol, and 0.0012% bromophenol blue.
13. Vertical electrophoresis apparatus and gel solutions.
14. Gel transfer apparatus.

2.1.3. Slot-Blot Overlay

1. Nitrocellulose filter.
2. Target protein ~2 mg.
3. Slot-blot manifold.
4. BLOTTO: TBS, pH 7.0, 5% dry milk, 1% BSA.
5. Bait protein (^{32}P-labeled or antibait protein antibodies).

2.2. Interaction Screening

2.2.1. Radioactive RII Interaction Screening

1. PKA catalytic subunit (0.1 μg) and γ^{32}P ATP (50 μCi).
2. PKA reaction buffer: 50 m*M* MOPs, pH 6.8, 50 m*M* NaCl, 2 m*M* $MgCl_2$, 1 m*M* DTT, 0.1 mg/mL BSA.
3. Bacteriophage λ (e.g., λgt11 or λZap) cDNA expression library.
4. IPTG-soaked nitrocellulose filters.
5. BLOTTO: TBS, pH 7.0, 5% dry milk, 1% BSA.
6. Bait protein.
7. TBS/0.05% Tween-20 (TTBS).
8. Plastic wrap.
9. Autoradiography film.

2.2.2. Nonradioactive RII Interaction Screening

1. Bacteriophage λ (e.g. λgt11 or λZap) cDNA expression library.
2. BLOTTO: TBS, pH 7.0, 5% dry milk, 1% BSA.
3. Recombinant RII.
4. TBS.
5. Primary antibody (1:5000).
6. HRP-linked secondary antibody.
7. Chemiluminescent detection reagents.
8. Autoradiography film.

2.3. Peptide Overlay

1. Nitrocellulose filter.
2. TBS.
3. Slot-blot manifold.

4. RII proteins.
5. BLOTTO: TBS, pH 7.0, 5% dry milk, 1% BSA.
6. Biotinylated RII-binding peptide (0.4 m*M*).
7. TTBS.
8. 1:10,000 dilution of streptavidin-HRP.

2.4. Band-Shift Assay

1. Nondenaturing (ND) PAGE gels.
2. Binding buffer: 5 m*M* HEPES, 10 m*M* DTT, 1 m*M* benzamidine, 100 m*M* KCl, and 0.01% Tween.
3. ND sample buffer: 100 m*M* MOPS, 40% glycerol, 0.01% bromophenol blue.
4. Coomassie based stain.
5. Fresh acrylamide stock.
6. Fresh binding buffer.
7. Isobutanol.
8. Vertical electrophoresis apparatus.
9. Gel solutions (omitting SDS).

3. Methods

3.1. Protein Overlay Techniques

3.1.1. The RII-Overlay

Detailed study of PKA anchoring was made possible by the original observation of Lohmann and colleagues *(16)* that many, though most likely not all, AKAPs retain their ability to bind RII after transfer to nitrocellulose. As a result, an overlay technique has been developed that is essentially a modification of the Western blot procedure, in which the typical antibody probe is replaced by ^{32}P labeled RII protein *(14)*. The overlay technique (*see* **Subheading 3.1.1.1.**) is summarized in **Fig. 2**. Using this approach, we have been able to survey AKAPs from a variety of tissue sources (**Fig. 3A**). A routine control experiment that determines specificity uses an anchoring inhibitor peptide to block binding (**Fig. 3B**). For greater precision the basic overlay technique can be used after a two dimensional separation of proteins (**Fig. 3C**). Samples are initially separated by isoelectric focusing (IEF) in the first dimension, and by SDS-PAGE in the second dimension. After electrotransfer, the standard overlay procedure is performed. Another adaptation is the development of nonradioactive methods for detection of RII binding (*see* **Subheading 3.1.1.2.**). The use of chemiluminescence to detect RII–AKAP complexes increases the sensitivity of this technique 20- to 50-fold.

3.1.1.1. Radioactive (^{32}P) RII Overlay

1. Protein samples are separated by SDS-PAGE and transferred to immobilon or nitrocellulose by standard electrotransfer techniques (**ref.** ***28***; *see* **Note 1**).

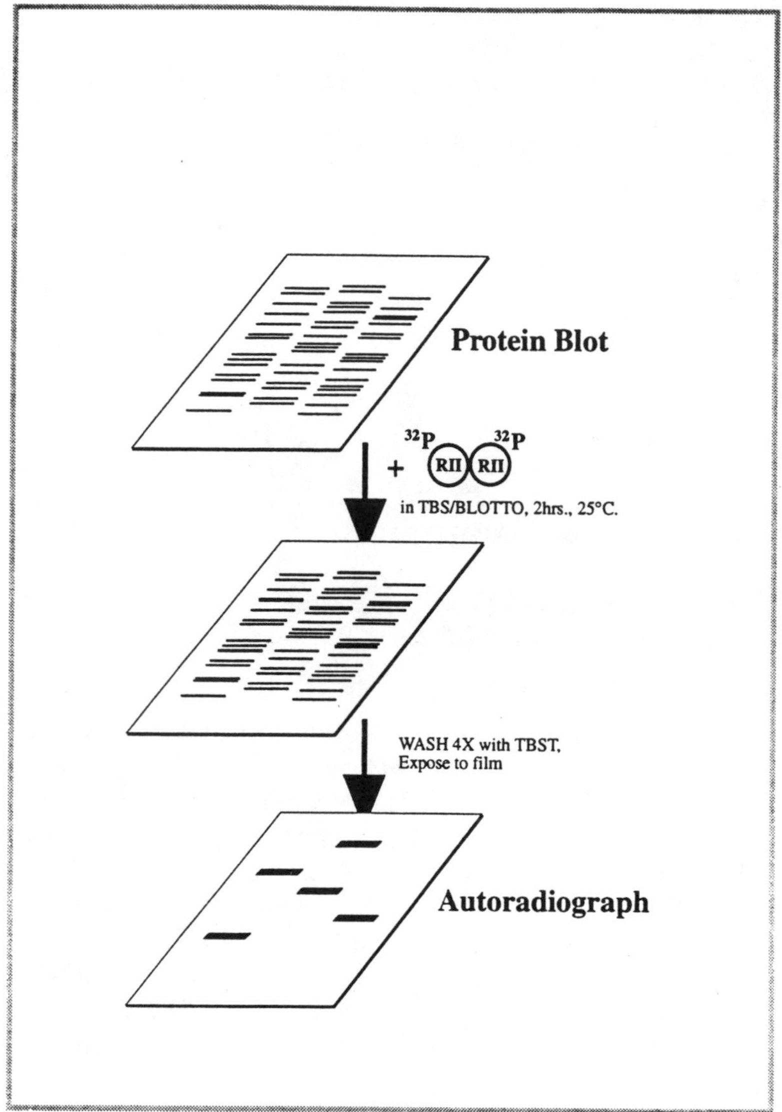

Fig. 2. The RII overlay. A schematic diagram of the RII overlay.

2. Stain bound proteins with Immobilon stain or Ponceau stain for nitrocellulose (*see* **Subheading 2.1.1., item 3**).
3. Destain the filter with Immobilon destain (*see* **Subheading 2.1.1., item 4**) or with water for the nitrocellulose (*see* **Note 2**).
4. The membrane is blocked by incubation in BLOTTO + BSA (TBS, pH 7.0), 5% dry milk, 1% BSA for 1 h.

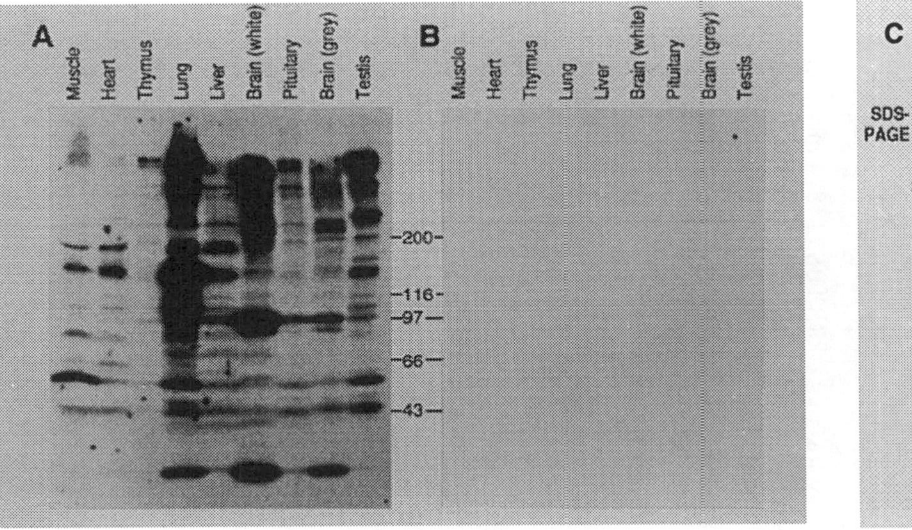

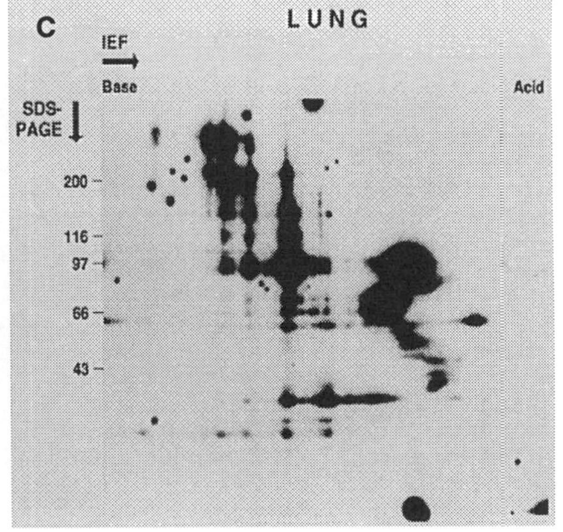

Fig. 3. Applications of the overlay. Crude protein extracts from nine bovine tissues were analyzed by RII overlay for anchoring proteins. Protein samples (50 μg) were separated by electrophoresis on a 4–12% SDS polyacrylamide gradient gel. After electrotransfer to immobilon, RII-binding proteins were detected, as described in the experimental methods. Two identical blots were incubated with either ^{32}P RIIα **(A)** or ^{32}P RIIa in the presence of 0.4 μ*M* Ht 31 (493–515) peptide **(B)**. Tissue sources are marked above each lane (Reproduced with permission from *J. Biol. Chem.*). **(C)** Protein extract from bovine lung was separated by isoelectric focusing in the first dimension and electrophoresis on 4–12% gradient SDS-PAGE gels before transfer to Immobilon. RII-anchoring proteins were detected by autoradiography after incubation of the blot with ^{32}P RIIα. The direction of IEF and mol-wt markers are indicated on the sides of each overlay. (Reproduced with permission of *Trends Biochem. Sci.*)

5. RII (2 μg) is radiolabeled by incubation with PKA catalytic subunit (0.1 μg) and [γ-^{32}P]-ATP (50 μCi), in 50 m*M* MOPs, pH 6.8, 50 m*M* NaCl, 2 m*M* $MgCl_2$, 1 m*M* DTT, 0.1 mg/mL BSA at 30°C for 15 min.
6. Radiolabeled protein is separated from free [^{32}P] ATP on a excellulose GF-5 desalting column (Pierce) equilibrated in TTBS.
7. Radiolabeled RII probe (specific activity 10^5 cpm/mL of BLOTTO) is incubated with the blocked membrane from step 4 for a minimum of 3 h, with light agitation. (*see* **Note 3**).
8. Wash with TTBS (3 × 15 min) to remove free ^{32}P RII.
9. Filter is dried by blotting on 3MM paper and RII-binding proteins are detected by autoradiography (*see* **Note 4**).

3.1.1.2. Nonradioactive RII Overlay

1. Follow **steps 1–4** of **Subheading 3.1.1.1.** (*see* **Note 5**).
2. Add RII protein to a concentration of 0.5 μg/mL of BLOTTO and incubate with the blocked membrane for a minimum of 3 h.
3. The filter is washed with TTBS (3 × 15 min), followed by incubation with RII antibodies (*see* **Note 6**).
4. Excess antibody is removed by washing with TTBS (3 × 15 min), followed by incubation with HRP-conjugated secondary antibody (1:10,000) in TTBS for 40 min.
5. Uncomplexed secondary antibody is removed by washing in excess TTBS (3 × 15 min), and the immune complex is detected using an enhanced chemiluminescence kit (Renaissance by New England Nuclear) (*see* **Notes 7** and **8**).

3.1.2. AKAP Overlay

The AKAP overlay is a modification of **Subheadings 3.1.1.1.** and **3.1.1.2.**, except that RII is immobilized and the AKAP is used as a probe. Using this technique, RII–AKAP complexes can be detected immunochemically with anti-AKAP antibodies or by radiolabeling the anchoring protein. One limitation of this technique seems to be that small fragments of RII, such as residues 1–50, which bind AKAPs in solution, are unable to interact with anchoring proteins when immobilized to the solid-phase support ***(19,20)***. An apparent explanation for this observation is that a larger percentage of the total surface area on small proteins is required for contact with the solid-phase membrane than in larger protein. Accordingly, this may decrease the number of active binding sites that are accessible to the AKAP. Nevertheless, the AKAP overlay is a simple technique that can be used to rapidly screen RII mutants for altered AKAP-binding properties ***(20)***.

3.1.3. Semiquantitative Overlays (Slot-Blot Analysis)

A valid criticism of the overlay procedures is that they are purely qualitative. Therefore, we have made an effort to adapt the basic technique into a semiquantitative overlay procedure that permits comparison of relative bind-

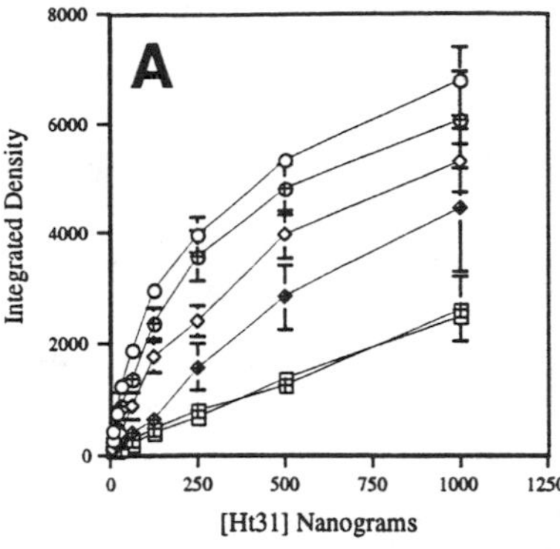

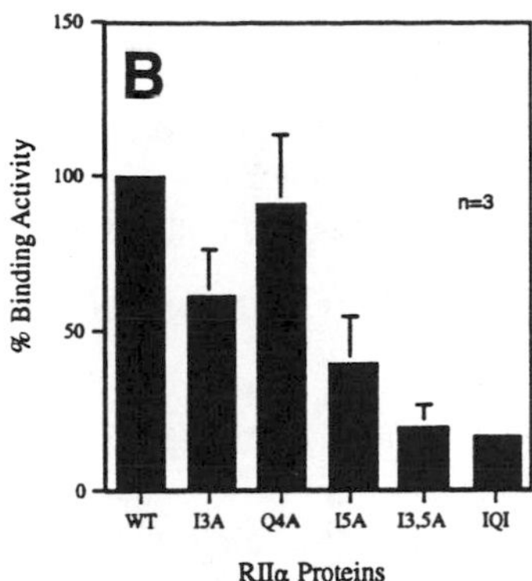

Fig. 4. Slot-blot overlay. Quantitation of AKAP binding to RIIα mutants. The binding of RIIα and mutants to a recombinant fragment of the human thyroid anchoring protein Ht31 was measured by a quantitative overlay procedure. **(A)** Binding curves for individual protein probes from three experiments are RIIα (o), RIIα I3A (◊), RIIα Q4A (⊕), RIIα I5A (♦), RIIα I3A I5A (□) and RIIα IQI, AAA (⊞). **(B)** The degree of Ht31 binding obtained at a single concentration of protein (25 ng) is presented as a percent binding compared with wild-type RIIα. Data are presented with permission from the *J. Biol. Chem.*

ing affinities for various RII–AKAP interactions. This was achieved by using a slot-blot manifold to immobilize the proteins on the surface of the membrane in a uniform manner. Accordingly, a filter of immobilized proteins (over a range of concentrations) is probed with a ligand of known specific activity. The linear range of the assay can be determined by monitoring the intensity of signal at each concentration of immobilized protein. This information is necessary for comparison of various binding affinities. One advantage of the slot-blot overlay is that a single filter can be used to compare the binding affinity of several RIIα mutants for an individual AKAP ***(19)***. Alternatively, a single RII mutant can be used to screen for altered binding properties with a variety of AKAPs (**Fig. 4**).

3.1.3.1. Slot-Blot Overlay

1. Soak a nitrocellulose filter with 0.2 mL of TBS using a slot-blot manifold (e.g., Hybri-slot, BRL) (*see* **Note 9**).
2. Target proteins (RII or AKAP) are immobilized onto nitrocellulose at various concentration over a range of 0.3 ng–100 ng, using the slot-blot manifold (*see* **Note 10**).
3. The membrane is blocked in BLOTTO for 1 h.
4. Probe membrane with bait protein. If using a radioactive protein probe continue following **steps 5–9** of **Subheading 3.1.1.1.** For a nonradioactive protein probe, continue following **steps 2–5** of **Subheading 3.1.1.2.** (*see* **Note 11**).

5. The relative intensity of binding is measured by densitometric analysis of the autoradiogram. This is achieved by digitally scanning images into a computer and analyzing the band density using the NIH image program (*see* **Note 12**).
6. Numeric values correlating to band intensity can now be plotted against concentration to obtain binding curves (*see* **Note 13**).

3.1.4. Alternate Detection Methods

The detection methods described above are useful if antibodies to the protein probe are available or if the protein probe can be radiolabeled. For example, RII is an excellent probe because it has a autophosphorylation site that allows incorporation of stoichiometric levels of ^{32}P into the protein. However, a number of alternative methods are available to detect the protein probe. One vector developed in our laboratory, called pET-kfc, produces chimeric recombinant proteins in *Escherichia coli* containing a phosphorylatable affinity ligand ***(29)***. The kfc tail is a 51 residue peptide that encodes a consensus PKA phosphorylation site LRRA<u>S</u>LG (<u>K</u>), a restriction proteinase site for Factor X (<u>F</u>), and a high-affinity calmodulin binding domain (<u>C</u>). Recombinant kfc-proteins can be purified in one step by affinity chromatography on calmodulin-Sepharose, and are phosphorylated to a stoichiometry of 1 by the C subunit of PKA. Furthermore, immobilized kfc proteins can be detected by a solid-phase overlay technique, using biotinylated calmodulin as a probe ***(29)***. Other affinity fusion tags are commercially available, such as glutathione-*S*-transferase (GST) and His T7 tag, which permit rapid one-step purification of recombinant proteins ***(30,31)***. Again, antibodies are available to both of these affinity tags, permitting detection of the immobilized fusion protein in overlay assays.

3.2. Overlay Cloning Strategies

The *in situ* overlay method is easily adapted to screening cDNA expression libraries for proteins that associate with the ligand or bait protein (e.g., RII). The technique is quite sensitive, since bacterial expressed products often adopt their native conformation. Two methods for overlay screening are described. The first method is a direct adaptation of the *in situ* overlay described in **Subheading 3.1.** using radiolabeled bait protein as a probe. Because radiolabeling is not always possible, or may interfere with binding, a second method of screening is described that uses unlabeled bait protein and antibody detection (similar to **Subheading 3.1.2.**) (**Fig. 5**).

3.2.1. Radioactive RII Interaction Screening

1. Plate bacteriophage λ (e.g., λgt11 or λZap) cDNA expression library at $1–5 \times 10^4$ PFU/150-mm plate and perform lifts with IPTG-soaked nitrocellulose filters, as described by Sambrook et al. ***(32)***. Save master plates at 4°C.

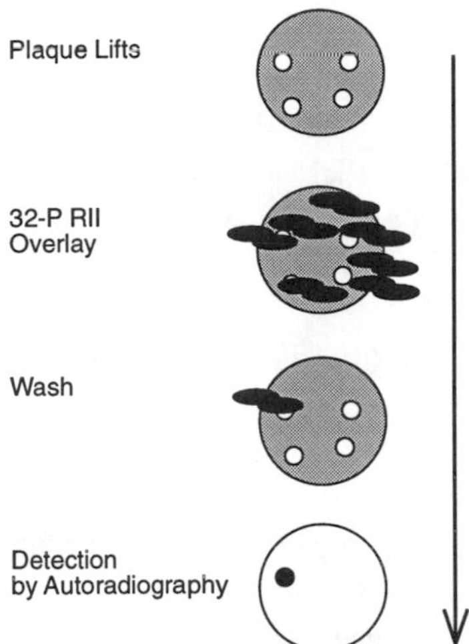

Fig. 5. An overlay expression cloning strategy. A schematic diagram of the an interaction cloning strategy that uses radioactive RII as a probe.

2. Block filters in BLOTTO for 2 h at room temperature.
3. Radiolabel bait protein, as described in **Subheading 3.1.1.1.** (**steps 5** and **6**) and incubate with filters at ~5×10^4 cpm/mL of BLOTTO or other binding media for 4–16 h at room temperature.
4. Decant incubation solution into radioactive liquid waste and wash filters in BLOTTO or TBST for 15 min. Repeat washes three times.
5. Blot dry filters, cover with plastic wrap, and expose to autoradiography film for 1–3 d.
6. Align film to master plates. Pick positive plaques, replate, and perform secondary screenings using **steps 2–5**.

3.2.2. Nonradioactive RII Interaction Screening

1. Follow **steps 1–2** in **Subheading 3.2.1.**
2. Incubate blocked filters with purified bait protein in BLOTTO or other binding buffer for 4 h at room temperature. For cloning of RII binding proteins, we use 0.5 μg of recombinant RII per mL of BLOTTO.
3. Wash filters with TBS for 15 min. Repeat washes three times.
4. Incubate the filters with primary antibody in TBS for 2 h at room temperature. We use our antibodies at dilutions similar to those used in Western blots (1:5000 for affinity-purified antibody against RII).
5. Wash filters as in **step 3**.
6. Incubate the filters with HRP-linked secondary antibody in TBS for 1 h at room temperature. Use the same dilution of antibody used in Western blots (e.g., 1:10,000).

7. Wash filters as in **step 3**.
8. Incubate with chemiluminescent detection reagents and expose to autoradiographic film. Exposure times are usually two to five times longer than for Western blots.
9. Align film to master plates. Pick positive plaques, replate, and perform secondary screenings, using **steps 2–8** (*see* **Notes 14–16**).

3.3. Peptide Overlay

Recent experiments with biotinylated anchoring inhibitor peptides have provided a nonradioactive assay for comparing RII-binding mutants. This technique has value for a number of systems in which the binding domains are small linear sequences (e.g., SH2 or SH3 recognition sequences, or small peptide hormone ligands). Peptides encompassing these binding regions can be purchased with a biotin conjugate to the α-amino group. Furthermore, the hydrophilic nature of the biotin moiety often increases the solubility of the peptide, as is the case for the HT31 peptide. This assay is a rapid nonradioactive technique that we have used to compare binding of different isoforms of RII, RII mutants, and truncations that affect AKAP binding.

1. Soak a nitrocellulose filter with 0.2 mL TBS, using a slot-blot manifold (e.g., Hybri-slot, BRL) (*see* **Note 17**).
2. RII proteins are immobilized by slot blotting the proteins in their native state onto nitrocellulose at a concentration range of 0.3–100 ng (*see* **Note 18**).
3. The membrane is blocked in TBS 5% dry milk, 1% BSA for 1 h.
4. A biotinylated RII-binding peptide (0.4 μ*M*) is added to the blocking solution.
5. Incubate for 1–3 h at room temperature with gentle agitation (*see* **Note 19**).
6. The filter is washed three times with TTBS then probed with a 1:10,000 dilution of streptavidin-HRP in TTBS for 40 min.
7. Excess peptide is removed by washing in TTBS (three times).
8. The peptide–protein complex is detected using standard chemiluminescence methods.
9. The relative intensity of binding is measured by densitometric analysis of the autoradiogram. This is achieved by digitally scanning images into a computer and analyzing the band density using the NIH image program (*see* **Note 20**).
10. Numeric values correlating to band intensity can now be plotted against concentration to obtain binding curves (*see* **Note 21**).

3.4. Band-Shift Analysis

In contrast to many overlay techniques, band-shift analysis examines protein–protein interactions under nondenaturing conditions ***(14,33)***. This method takes advantage of the observation that a protein complex migrates on a native polyacrylamide gel with a different mobility than its individual components (**Fig. 6**). Proteins are preincubated in binding buffer to allow complex forma-

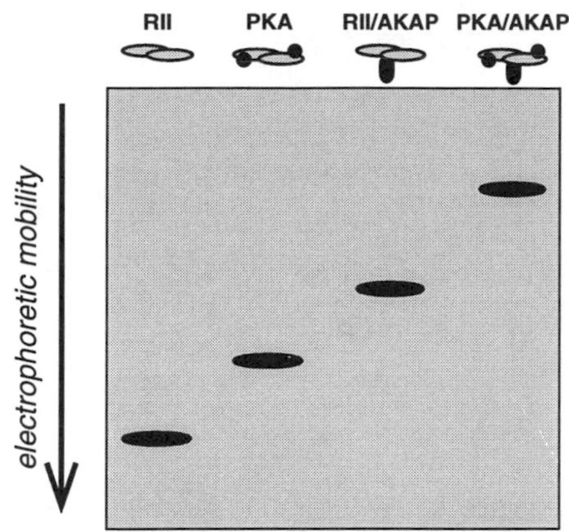

Fig. 6. The band shift. A schematic diagram of the band-shift analysis.

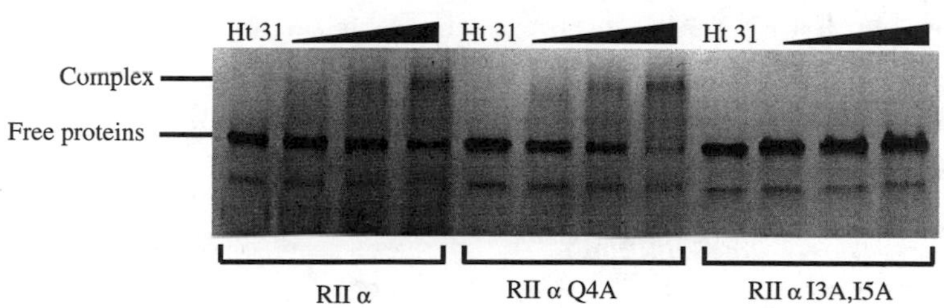

Fig. 7. Mutation of isoleucines 3 and 5 impairs AKAP-binding as assessed by band-shift analysis. AKAP binding in solution was analyzed by the band-shift analysis using Ht 31 as a probe. Selected RIIα mutants (1 μ*M*) were incubated with aliquots of Ht 31 over a range of concentrations (0.33–1 μ*M*). The free and complexed proteins were separated on a 6% polyacrylamide gel: RIIα (panel 1), RIIα Q4A (panel 2), and RIIα I3A, I5A (panel 3). Detection was by protein staining with Fast stain™ (Zion Research).

tion, and, after dilution with sample buffer, free and complexed proteins are separated by electrophoresis. The migrating bands are detected by Coomassie blue staining or autoradiography.

Data in **Fig. 7** demonstrate the use of the band-shift analysis to compare the binding affinities of several RII mutants that contain point mutations in the AKAP-binding domain. For example, wild-type RII binds a recombinant AKAP fragment more readily than the double mutant RIIα I3A, I5A; a control mutation (Q4A) has no obvious effect upon binding. The sensitivity of this technique is limited by the high concentrations of protein required for detection of complexes, and equilibrium conditions are not maintained during electrophoresis.

1. Nondenaturing (ND) PAGE gels. ND-PAGE gels are prepared by the methods of **ref.** ***34***, except with the omission of SDS (*see* **Note 22**).
2. RII and AKAP (approx 3 μg) are incubated in binding buffer (5 m*M* HEPES, 10 m*M* DTT, 1 m*M* benzamidine, 100 m*M* KCl, and 0.01% Tween) at room temperature for 1 h.
3. Samples are diluted 1:1 in ND sample buffer (100 m*M* MOPS, 40% glycerol, 0.01% bromophenol blue), and are separated by electrophoresis at 30–50 mV at 16°C for ~3 h.
4. Stain the gel with a Coomassie-based stain for detection of protein bands (*see* **Note 23**).

3.5. Conclusions

Although the techniques that are described in this chapter are tailored for use in the analysis of RII–AKAP interactions, the approaches should be applicable to study of a wide range of protein–protein interactions. The speed and simplicity of these methods often make them a first choice for investigating the components of certain multiprotein complexes. However, one important point that must not be overlooked is that the overlay and band-shift methods we have described are at best semiquantitative. Therefore, it will often be necessary to more rigorously define many protein–protein interactions by more quantitative methods such as equilibrium dialysis, equilibrium centrifugation, or surface plasmon resonance measurements.

4. Notes

1. Unless otherwise stated, all procedures are performed at room temperature.
2. This step is important for correlation of nonspecific binding to abundant proteins within the extract.
3. Blots are often incubated overnight.
4. Dimerization between the labeled RII probe and immobilized RII monomer is weakly detected by the overlay, giving a band at 52–55 kDa. Although the ^{32}P overlay procedure seems to be specific for the detection of many RII-binding proteins, the C subunit of PKA is not detected by this procedure.
5. Unless otherwise stated, all procedures are performed at room temperature.
6. Incubation time is dependent upon the affinity and specificity of the antibody. Generally, we incubate with anti-RII antibodies (1: 20,000) for 3 h.
7. Multiple exposures are advisable to ensure that the signal is within the linear sensitivity range of the X-ray film.
8. Depending on the source of the antibody, endogenous RII will be detected in protein extracts screened by the nonradioactive overlay. Therefore, control filters should be screened in the absence of added RII protein to detect any background signals and false positives generated by the primary and secondary antibodies alone.
9. Immobilon cannot be used for this procedure, because the vacuum manifold will dry the filter, thereby destroying its protein-binding properties.

10. Air bubbles on the surface of the membrane prevent uniform adherence of the protein to the nitrocellulose.
11. AKAPs containing an endogenous, or engineered (**Subheading 3.1.4.**), PKA phosphorylation site can be labeled as described in **Subheading 2.1.1., steps 5–6**.
12. A maximal and minimal intensity control band is included on each image to normalize the analyzed images.
13. We have observed that purified AKAPs or RII directly immobilized on nitrocellulose, as compared to SDS-PAGE-separated samples, increases the sensitivity of detection 10- or 100-fold, respectively.
14. The bait protein used in these screening methods can be native, recombinant, or an isolated fragment thereof. We have also had success using biotinylated peptides as bait with streptavidin-HRP and chemiluminescent detection (*see* **Subheading 3.3.**).
15. For some interactions, nonmilk-based binding media, supplemented with additional factors (activators, divalent cations, and so on) may be required. When high background is problematic, we employ TBS with detergent (e.g., 0.5% Triton-X100) and high salt (0.5*M* NaCl) as the binding and washing buffer.
16. When using the nonradioactive screen (**Subheading 3.2.2.**), all positive plaques must also be screened in the absence of bait protein (**Subheading 3.2.2., step 2** omitted) to eliminate false positives retrieved by the antibodies alone (e.g., clones expressing cDNAs encoding the bait protein itself). This control step is easily performed on duplicate filters.
17. Immobilon cannot be used for this procedure, because the vacuum manifold will dry the filter, thereby destroying its the protein-binding properties.
18. Make sure to prevent bubbles from forming on the surface of the membrane, because the protein solution is applied to the nitrocellulose.
19. The probing time can be as short as 1 h, but optimal binding needs to be empirically determined for each peptide.
20. A maximal and minimal intensity control band is included on each image to normalize the analyzed images.
21. The peptide overlay was found to be linear for interaction with AKAPs in a very narrow range (80–15 ng). RII proteins can also be separated by SDS-PAGE, transferred to a hydrophobic membrane, and probed with the biotinylated peptides. We have observed that the latter method has a decreased sensitivity of up to 100-fold.
22. The optimal gel concentration needs should be determined empirically for the proteins being used. For example, separation of RII/AKAP complexes is optimally achieved with 6% (w/v) polyacrylamide separating gels and a 4% (w/v) stacking gel.
23. Several factors contribute to good quality of protein bands. These are:
    a. Prepare fresh acrylamide stock.
    b. Freshly prepare binding buffer.
    c. Separating gel should be rinsed free of isobutanol, if used, thoroughly before pouring the stacking gel.
    d. Gel should be kept at 16°C during the separation.

Acknowledgments

The authors wish to thank other members of the Scott lab for their critical evaluation of this manuscript. This work was supported in part by NIH grants DK 48239 (to J. D. S.) and DK 09059 (to V. M. C.).

References

1. Harper, J. F., Haddox, M. K., Johanson, R., Hanley, R. M., and Steiner, A. L. (1985) Compartmentation of second messenger action: immunocytochemical and biochemical evidence. *Vitam. Horm.* **42,** 197–252.
2. Mochly-Rosen, D. (1995) Localization of protein kinases by anchoring proteins: a theme in signal transduction. *Science* **268,** 247–251.
3. Hubbard, M. and Cohen, P. (1993)On target with a mechanism for the regulation of protein phosphorylation. *TIBS* **18,** 172–177.
4. Pawson, T. and Gish, G. D. (1992) SH2 and SH3 domains: from structure to function. *Cell* **71,** 359–362.
5. Pawson, T. (1995) Protein modules and signaling networks. *Nature* **373,** 573–580.
6. Songyang, Z. and Cantley, L. C. (1995) Recognition and specificity in protein tyrosine kinase-mediated signaling. *Trends Biochem. Sci.* **20,** 470–475.
7. Cohen, P. and Cohen, T. W. (1989) Protein phosphatases come of age. *J. Biol. Chem.* **264,** 21,435–21,438.
8. Sontag, E., Numbhakdi-Craig, V., Bloom, G. S., and Mumby, M. C. (1995) A novel pool of protein phosphatase 2A is associated with microtubules and is regulated during the cell cycle. *J. Cell. Biol.* **128,** 1131–1144.
9. Coghlan, V., Perrino, B. A., Howard, M., Langeberg, L. K., Hicks, J. B., Gallatin, W. M., and Scott, J. D. (1995) Association of protein kinase A and protein phosphatase 2B with a common anchoring protein. *Science* **267,** 108–111.
10. Chapline, C., Ramsay, K., Klauck, T., and Jaken, S. (1993) Interaction cloning of PKC substrates. *J. Biol. Chem.* **268,** 6858–6861.
11. Mochly-Rosen, D., Khaner, H., and Lopez, J. (1991) Identification of intracellular receptor proteins for activated protein kinase C. *Proc. Natl. Acad. Sci. USA* **88,** 3997–4000.
12. Rubin, C. S. (1994) A kinase Anchor proteins and the intracellular targeting of signals carried by cAMP. *Biochemica et Biophysica Acta* **1224,** 467–479.
13. Scott, J. D. and McCartney, S. (1994) Localization of A-kinase through anchoring proteins. *Mol. Endocrinol.* **8,** 5–13.
14. Carr, D. W. and Scott, J. D. (1992) Blotting and band-shifting: techniques for studying protein-protein interactions. *TIBS* **17,** 246–249.
15. Skalhegg, B. S., Tasken, K., Hansson, V., Huitfeldt, H. S., Jahnsen, J., and Lea, T. (1994) Location of cAMP-dependent protein kinase type I with the TCR-CD3 complex. *Science* **263,** 84–87.
16. Lohmann, S. M., DeCamili, P., Enig, I., and Walter, U. (1984) High-affinity binding of the regulatory subunit (RII) of cAMP-dependent protein kinase to microtubule-associated and other cellular proteins. *Proc. Natl. Acad. Sci. USA* **81,** 6723–6727.

17. Leiser, M., Rubin, C. S., and Erlichman, J. (1986) Differential binding of the regulatory subunits (RII) of cAMP-dependent protein kinase II from bovine brain and muscle to RII-binding proteins. *J. Biol. Chem.* **261,** 1904–1908.
18. Scott, J. D., Stofko, R. E., McDonald, J. R., Comer, J. D., Vitalis, E. A., and Mangili, J. (1990) Type II regulatory subunit dimerization determines the subcellular localization of the cAMP-dependent protein kinase. *J. Biol. Chem.* **265,** 21,561–21,566.
19. Hausken, Z. E., Coghlan, V. M., Hasting, C. A. S., Reimann, E. M., and Scott, J. D. (1994) Type II regulatory subunit (RII) of the cAMP dependent protein kinase interaction with A-kinase anchor proteins requires isoleucines 3 and 5. *J. Biol. Chem.* **269,** 24,245–24,251.
20. Li, Y. and Rubin, C. S. (1995) Mutagenesis of the regulatory subunit (RIIb) of cAMP-dependent protein kinase IIb reveals hydrophobic amino acids that are essential for RIIb dimerization and/or anchoring RIIb to the cytoskeleton. *J. Biol. Chem.* **270,** 1935–1944.
21. Carr, D. W., Stofko-Hahan, R. E., Fraser, I. D. C., Bishop, S. M., Acott, T. S., Brennan, R. G., and Scott, J. D. (1991) Interaction of the regulatory subunit (RII) of cAMP-dependent protein kinase with RII-anchoring proteins occurs through an amphipathic helix binding motif. *J. Biol. Chem.* **266,** 14,188–14,192.
22. Carr, D. W., Stofko-Hahn, R. E., Fraser, I. D. C., Cone, R. D., and Scott, J. D. (1992) Localization of the cAMP-dependent protein kinase to the postsynaptic densities by A-kinase anchoring proteins. *J. Biol. Chem.* **24,** 16,816–16,823.
23. Coghlan, V. M., Langeberg, L. K., Fernandez, A., Lamb, N. J. C., and Scott, J. D. (1994) Cloning and characterization of AKAP95, a nuclear protein that associates with the regulatory subunit of type II cAMP-dependent protein kinase. *J. Biol. Chem.* **269,** 7658–7665.
24. McCartney, S., Little, B. M., Langeberg, L. K., and Scott, J. D. (1995) Cloning and characterization of A-Kinase Anchor Protein 100 (AKAP100): a protein that targets A-Kinase to the sarcoplasmic reticulum. *J. Biol. Chem.* **270,** 9327–9333.
25. Carr, D. W., Hausken, Z. E., Fraser, I. D. C., Stofko-Hahn, R. E., and Scott, J. D. (1992) Association of the type II cAMP-dependent protein kinase with a human thyroid RII-anchoring protein cloning and characterization of the RII-binding domain. *J. Biol. Chem.* **267,** 13,376–13,382.
26. Rosenmund, C., Carr, D. W., Bergeson, S. E., Nilaver, G., Scott, J. D., and Westbrook, G. L. (1994) Anchoring of protein kinase A is required for modulation of AMPA/kainate receptors on hippocampal neurons. *Nature* **368,** 853–856.
27. Johnson, B. D., Scheuer, T., and Caterall, W. A. (1994) Voltage-dependent potentiation of L-type Ca^{2+} channels in skeletal muscle cells requires anchored cAMP-dependent protein kinase. *Proc. Natl. Acad. Sci. USA* **91,** 11,492–11,496.
28. Towbin, H., Staehelin, T., and Gordon, J. (1979) Electrophoretic transfer of proteins from polyacrylamide gels to nitrocellulose sheets: Procedure and some applications. *Proc. Natl. Acad. Sci. USA* **76,** 4350–4354.
29. Stofko-Hahn, R. E., Carr, D. W., and Scott, J. D. (1992) A single step purification for recombinant proteins. Characterization of a microtubule associated protein

(MAP2) fragment which associates with type II cAMP-dependent protein kinase. *FEBS Lett.* **302,** 274–278.

30. Smith, D. B. and Johnson, K. S. (1988) Single-step purification of polypeptides expressed in *Escherichia coli* as fusions with glutathione S-transferase. *Gene* **67,** 31–40.
31. Sassenfeld, H. M., Brewer, A. H., and Marston, A. O. (1984) *Bio-Technology* **2,** 76–81.
32. Sambrook, J., Fritsch, E. F., and Maniatis, T. (1989) *Molecular Cloning: A Laboratory Manual* (Nolan, C., ed.), Cold Spring Harbor Laboratory, Cold Spring Harbor, NY.
33. Bollag, D. M. and Edelstein, S. J. (1991) *Protein Methods* Wiley-Liss, pp. 143–160.
34. Laemmli, U. K. (1970) Cleavage of structural proteins during the assembly of the head of bacteriophage T4. *Nature* **227,** 680–685.

6

Size-Exclusion Chromatography

Identification of Interacting Proteins

James Beattie

1. Introduction

Size-exclusion chromatography (gel filtration) is a widely used method for the estimation of protein mol wt (M_r). Although, strictly speaking, the technique measures not M_r as such, but a property known as hydrodynamic radius *(1)*, the correlation between the two is such that this distinction has all but disappeared from the literature. Gel filtration has the advantage over other methods for determining protein M_r, in that it is typically a nondenaturing methodology and therefore reports on native protein M_rs. In addition, the nondenaturing nature of the technique allows for the study of protein–protein interactions (e.g., enzyme–substrate, hormone–receptor, and protein subunits) that occur normally in vivo. Therefore, provided that an appropriate reporting assay is available, this technique can be employed to examine a wide range of protein interactions of biological significance. The widespread use and availability of high-performance liquid chromatography (HPLC) and fast-protein liquid chromatography (FPLC) systems allows for the rapid and reproducible generation and analysis of data.

Drawing on this laboratory's experience of high-performance size exclusion chromatographic analysis of growth hormone (GH) and insulin-like growth factor (IGF) binding proteins (BPs), this chapter reports a step-by-step procedure on the use of this technique for the analysis of GH and IGFBPs in serum and culture medium. It is intended that the procedures described would be generally applicable for examination of other protein–protein interactions by size-exclusion chromatography.

From: *Methods in Molecular Biology, Vol. 88: Protein Targeting Protocols*
Edited by: R. A. Clegg Humana Press Inc., Totowa, NJ

2. Materials

2.1. Equipment

1. HPLC system comprising pumps, autosampler, detector, and integrator (*see* **Note 1**).
2. Fraction collector (*see* **Note 2**).
3. Glass autosampler incubation vials.
4. Superose 12 FPLC column (Pharmacia, Herts, UK).
5. Helium line (*see* **Note 3**).
6. 1- to 2-mL Syringes, 0.22-μm filters (*see* **Note 4**).

2.2. Reagents

1. Phosphate buffered saline (PBS): Tween-20 (PBS-T): 0.15*M* NaCl, 10 m*M* Na phosphate, pH 7.4, 0.02% Na azide, 0.1% (v/v) Tween-20.
2. Mol-wt markers: Blue dextran (Vo), β-amylase (200 kDa), bovine serum albumin (BSA) (66 kDa), carbonic anhydrase (29 kDa), cytochrome-*c* (12.3 kDa), IGF-1 (7.5 kDa), tyrosine (Vt).
3. Recombinant human (rh) insulin-like growth factor I (IGF-1) (Bachem, UK).
4. ^{125}I-IGF-1 (~200 μCi/μg) (*see* **ref. 2** for iodination protocol).
5. Serum or conditioned medium containing IGFBP for analysis.

3. Methods

3.1. Column Equilibration and Calibration

1. Pump PBS-T through the Superose 12 column at a flow rate of 0.5 mL/min, until a steady baseline is achieved (*see* **Note 5**).
2. Zero the detector.
3. Dissolve mol-wt markers at 1 mg/mL in PBS-T and filter through 0.22-μm filters into glass autosampler incubation vials.
4. Inject 10 μL (10 μg protein) of standard.
5. Monitor column eluent at 280 nm to obtain retention times (Rt) for each standard.
6. Construct a plot of log M_r vs Rt to allow for determination of mol wt in sample (**Fig. 1**).

3.2. Sample Preparation, Incubation, and Analysis

1. Filter all biological fluids (serum, milk, and conditioned medium) to be examined through a 22-μm filter (*see* **Note 4**).
2. Retain the protein loading within the limits of the Superose 12 column by diluting serum and milk 1:5 and 1:10 in PBS-T (*see* **Note 6**).
3. Add 250 μL of sample to 250 μL PBS-T containing 5 × 10^5 cpm ^{125}I-IGF-1 (*see* **Notes 7–9**).
4. Incubate in a glass autosampler vial for 16 h at 4°C.
5. Inject 100 μL of the reaction mixture onto Superose 12 column.
6. Elute column with PBS-T at a flow rate of 0.5 mL/min.
7. Collect 1-min fractions directly into counting inserts compatible with counting facility (*see* **Note 10**).

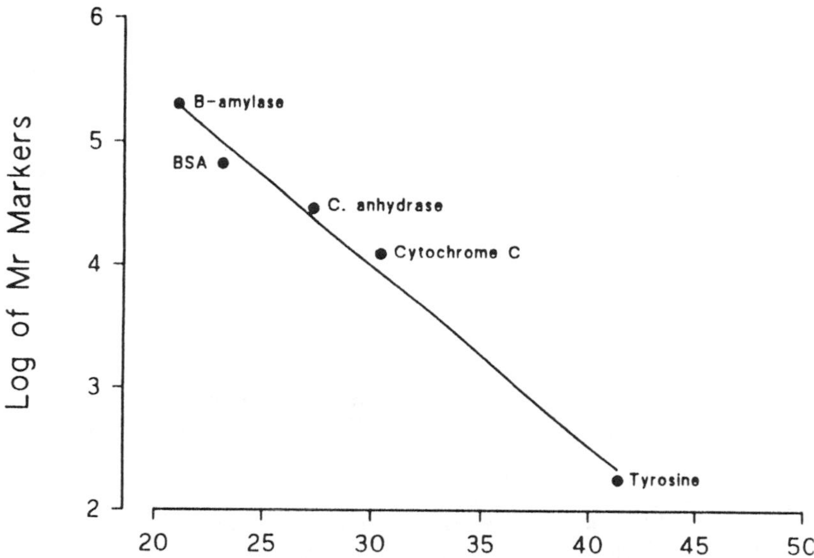

Fig. 1. Calibration for Superose 12 column. Mol-wt markers were analyzed separately in PBS-T buffer, as described in **Subheading 3.**

8. Plot radioactivity in each fraction against fraction number to obtain mol-wt profile for IGFBPs present in biological sample (*see* **Fig. 2** and **Note 11**).

3.3. Method Validation

1. Purify ^{125}I-IGF-1 on Superose 12 column prior to incubation with biological sample (*see* **Note 12**).
2. Test specificity of interaction between ^{125}I-IGF-1 and IGFBPs by including unlabeled IGF-1 incubation mixture (*see* **Note 13**).

4. Notes

1. Spectraphysics HPLC (supplied by Thermo Separation Labs, Staffs, UK) comprising P2000 pump, AS 3000 autosampler, UV 1000 detector, and Data Jet integrator.
2. LKB 2212 Helirac (Pharmacia).
3. FPLC buffers are degassed in a gentle stream of helium. In buffers containing detergent, excessive degassing is to be avoided.
4. Retention of protein by filters can cause large losses of sample. We typically use polyvinylidene difluoride (PVDF) 0.2 μm Acrodisc® filters (prod. no. 4455, Gelman Sciences, Northampton, UK).
5. This time will vary depending on eluent flow rate, column, and dead-space volume. The latter should be minimized by configuring HPLC components (including column) with the minimum lengths of tubing.

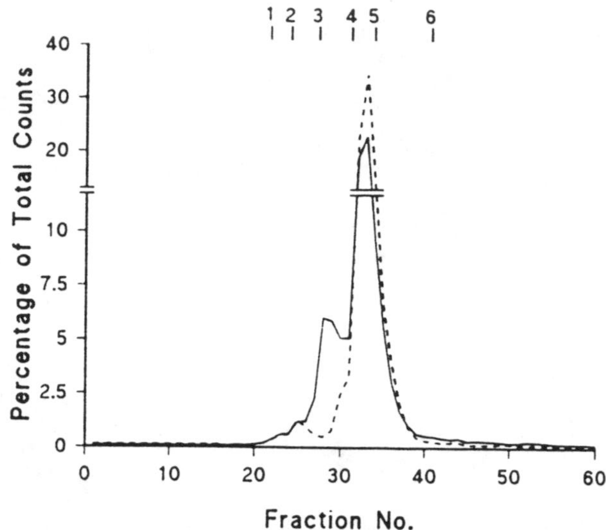

Fig. 2. High-performance size-exclusion chromatography of IGFBP activity in medium conditioned by sheep adipose tissue explants. Radioactive profiles for conditioned (—) and unconditioned (----) medium are indicated. Mol-wt markers are: 1, β-amylase (200 kDa); 2, BSA (66 kDa); 3, carbonic anhydrase (29 kDa); 4, cytochrome-*c* (12.3 kDa); 5, IGF-1 (7.5 kDa); 6, tyrosine (Vt). A peak of ^{125}I-IGF-1-BP complexes is seen eluting with an Rt similar to carbonic anhydrase. Subtraction of IGF–1 M_r (7.5 kDa) gives a mol wt for the IGFBP of approx 21.5 kDa. Further analysis of this IGFBP, by alternative methods, confirmed the presence of a single species of binding protein of M_r ~21 kDa (*see* **ref. *3***).

6. Protein loading limits vary according to which high-performance size-exclusion column is used. For the Pharmacia Superose 12 column, we work at 5–10 mg protein/mL and restrict injection volume to 200 μL.
7. Repeated chromatography of ^{125}I-labeled compounds may lead to a buildup of radioactivity on columns, filters, tubing, and so on. This can be avoided by periodic injection of 100 μL 2% KI (in PBS-T) into the FPLC system.
8. Continual analysis of serum samples will eventually lead to column blockage, typically at column inlet filters, leading to increased back pressures during operation. Precolumns and sample filtration will to some extent combat this, but it is recommended that manufacturer's column-cleaning instructions are closely adhered to.
9. Consideration should be given to the M_r of target molecule(s) during selection of gel filtration columns. Columns spanning several M_r ranges are available from many manufacturers. For example, for analysis of the IGFBPs in conditioned medium with M_r ~30 kDa, the Superose 12 column (range 1–100 kDa) is adequate. A major IGFBP component of serum, however, is a complex of 150 kDa ***(4)***. To ensure effective chromatography of this molecule, a column with an alternative separating range should be used (e.g., Superose 6, range = $10^4 - 2 \times 10^6$ Dalton).

10 A more sophisticated alternative for γ-radioactivity determination is the use of an in-line monitor fitted with an HPLC eluant flow splitter. In our laboratories, we use a Packard Series A-500 Radio-Chromatography detector. Such a system has the advantage of minimizing errors obtained in M_rs of radiolabeled substances, which are related to delay time between flow cell and fraction collector.
11. M_r for IGFBP(s) are obtained after deduction of 7.5 kDa as mol wt for IGF-1.
12. It is important to ensure that ^{125}I-IGF-1 is clearly separated from IGFBP/^{125}I-IGF-1 complexes. In this context, problems may arise with aging and aggregation of tracer. This material may elute with an Rt value similar to IGFBP/^{125}I-IGF-1 complexes, thus complicating identification of the latter. For this reason, it may be necessary to fractionate ^{125}I-IGF-1 label on the Superose 12 column, pooling material of authentic M_r for use in binding-protein analyses.
13. The binding of ^{125}I-IGF-1 to components of biological fluids is specifically to IGFBPs *(5–7)*. To establish this, binding should be displaceable with unlabeled IGF-1, returning the radioactive profile to that obtained with free ^{125}I-IGF-1. Under the incubation conditions described above (*see* **Subheading 3.2.**), we generally obtain complete tracer displacement with 1–10 μg per incubation of unlabeled IGF-1. When analyzing IGFBP profiles in conditioned medium, it is advisable also to run control incubations of ^{125}I-IGF-1 with unconditioned medium.

References

1. Hagel, L. (1989) Gel filtration, in *Protein Purification. Principles, High Resolution Methods and Applications* (Jamson, J. C. and Ryden, L., eds.), VCH, New York, pp. 63–106.
2. Fraker, P. J. and Speck, J. C., Jr. (1978) Protein and cell membrane iodinations with sparingly soluble chloramide 1, 3, 4, 6–tetrachloro–3a, 6a–diphenyl glycoluril. *Biochem. Biophys. Res. Comm.* **80,** 849–857.
3. Beattie, J. and Vernon, R. G. (1995) Glucocorticoids regulate the secretion of a 21 kDa-IGF-binding protein by sheep adipose tissue explants. *Mol. Cell. Biochem.* **145,** 151–157.
4. Baxter, R. C., Martin, J. L., and Beniac, V. A. (1989) High molecular weight insulin-like growth factor binding protein complex. *J. Biol. Chem.* **264,** 11,843–11,848.
5. Baxter, R. C. (1990) Circulating levels and molecular distribution of the acid-labile (α) subunit of the high molecular weight insulin-like growth factor-binding protein complex. *J. Clin. Endocrinol. Metab.* **70,** 1347–1353.
6. Park, J. H. Y., McCusker, R. H., Vanderhoof, J. A., Mohammadpour, H., Harty, R. F., and McDonald, R. G. (1992) Secretion of insulin-like growth factor II (IGF-II) and IGF-binding protein-2 by intestinal epithelial (IEC-6) cells: implications for autocrine growth regulation. *Endocrinology* **131,** 1359–1368.
7. Zumkeller, W., Schwander, J., Mitchell, C. D., Morrell, D. J., Schofield, P. N., and Preece, M. A. (1993) Insulin-like growth factor (IGF)-I, -II and IGF binding protein-2 (IGFBP-2) in the plasma of children with Wilms' tumour. *Eur. J. Cancer* **29A,** 1973–1977.

7

Overlay and Bead Assay

Determination of Calcium Channel Subunit Interaction Domains

Victoria E. S. Scott, Christina A. Gurnett, and Kevin P. Campbell

1. Introduction

Based on electrophysiological and pharmacological properties, voltage-dependent Ca^{2+} channels are classified as L-, N-, T-, and P/Q- type Ca^{2+} channels ***(1,2)***. The brain N-type Ca^{2+} channels ***(3)*** and the skeletal muscle L-type ***(4,5)*** have both been purified and shown to have a similar subunit composition (α_1-, α_2/δ-, and β-subunits).

Complementary DNA studies have identified six different genes encoding the α_1-subunits (S, A, B, C, D, and E) and four β-subunit genes, each of which can form multiple-splice variants (reviewed in **ref.** ***6***). Electrophysiological studies have shown that all of the α_1- and β-subunits cloned to date from different tissues can associate and yield Ca^{2+} channels with characteristic current amplitude, voltage dependencies of activation, and inactivation properties (reviewed in **ref.** ***7***). This suggests that these two proteins are directly interacting, possibly through a common binding domain. Several complementary approaches have recently been developed and used in our laboratory to examine these binding events in greater detail. The first approach that was taken to characterize the subunit–subunit interactions, and to determine the interaction motif on the α_1-subunit for the smaller β component in voltage-dependent Ca^{2+} channels, exploited the overlay binding assay ***(8)***. Radiolabeled in vitro-translated β-subunit probes were prepared and shown to bind to the α_{1S} of the purified dihydropyridine receptor after electrophoresis and transfer onto nitrocellulose membranes. The subsequent screening of an α_{1S} epitope expression library with similar radiolabeled β-subunit probes facilitated the identification of a conserved binding motif that is present on all of the α_1-subunits cloned to date,

From: *Methods in Molecular Biology, Vol. 88: Protein Targeting Protocols*
Edited by: R. A. Clegg Humana Press Inc., Totowa, NJ

namely, the α interaction domain (AID). Site-directed mutagenesis of residues within the AID consequently revealed precise amino acids that are essential for this association, in addition to being critical for β-subunit-induced current stimulation.

To investigate the complementary binding motif on the β-subunit or β interaction domain (BID), the strategy taken was quite different ***(9)***. Preliminary experiments showed that it was not possible to overlay in vitro-translated α_1-subunits onto the denatured β-subunits immobilized on nitrocellulose; thus, screening a β-subunit epitope library to identify the minimum sequence could not be performed. As an alternative approach, truncated [^{35}S]-labeled β-subunit fragments were generated and these were overlaid on the AID_A GST-fusion protein on nitrocellulose membrane. After narrowing the BID to approx 40 amino acids, the essential residues that were required for this interaction were also established by site-directed mutagenesis of amino acids within the BID motif. This interaction was characterized further by expression of truncated β-subunits in *Xenopus* oocytes, together with the full-length α_{1A} and $\alpha_2\delta$-subunits and the measurement of functional changes in the current stimulation, inactivation kinetics and voltage-dependence of the resultant current. Since the functional assays that were used to test the effects of the β-subunit and truncated mutants on the α_1-induced currents can only be applied to ion channel-subunit interactions, and have been previously well-described ***(10)***, these methods will not be described here. The aim of this chapter is to describe the different experimental approaches that were used to determine the interaction domains through which these two Ca^{2+} channel subunits associate (*see* **Note 1**).

2. Materials

2.1. Overlay Binding Assay

1. $\beta_{1\beta}$-subunit in pcDNA3 vector (construct of interest containing a T7, SP6, or T3 RNA polymerase recognition site).
2. [^{35}S]-Methionine (Amersham [Arlington Heights, IL]).
3. Rabbit reticulocyte TNT in vitro translation kit (Promega [Madison, WI]).
4. RNasin Ribonuclease inhibitor (BMB [Indianapolis, IN]).
5. Nuclease free H_2O.
6. Sodium dodecyl sulfate-polyacrylamide gel electrophoresis (SDS-PAGE) on 3–12% gradient gel ***(11)***.
7. Purified dihydropyridine receptor prepared as detailed elsewhere ***(5)***.
8. 30°C Heating block.
9. Cocktail of protease inhibitors: Pepstatin A, chymostatin, aprotinin, antipain, and leupeptin, each at a final concentration of 0.1 μg/mL (Sigma [St. Louis, MO]).
10. Calf liver tRNA, final concentration 40 μg/mL (Sigma).
11. PD 10 column (Pharmacia [Piscataway, NJ]) contains G-25 Sephadex.
12. G-50 Sephadex resin (Pharmacia).

13. Nitrocellulose membrane (Pharmacia).
14. Phosphate-buffered saline (PBS): 150 m*M* NaCl, 50 m*M* sodium phosphate, pH 7.5.
15. Blocking solution I: 5% nonfat dry milk prepared in PBS, pH 7.5.
16. Blocking solution II: 0.1% gelatin, 5% bovine serum albumin (BSA), 0.1% Tween-20 in PBS, pH 7.5.
17. Blocking solution III: 5% BSA, 0.5% nonfat dry milk in PBS, pH 7.5.
18. Overlay buffer I: same as blocking solution III.
19. Overlay buffer II: 150 m*M* NaCl, 20 m*M* HEPES, 2 m*M* $MgCl_2$, 2 m*M* dithiothreitol, and 5% BSA, pH 7.5.
20. X-ray film (Kodak).

2.2. Preparation and Use of an α_1 Epitope Library to Identify the AID

1. 10X DNase reaction buffer: 100 m*M* $MgCl_2$, 200 m*M* Tris-HCl, pH 7.5, 0.25 mg/mL BSA.
2. RNase free DNase (Promega).
3. Seakem LE agarose gel (FMC Bioproducts [Rockland, ME]).
4. 1-kb DNA markers (BRL).
5. Qiaex gel extraction kit (Qiagen).
6. Phosphorylated *Eco*RI linkers (8-mer) (NEB).
7. T4 DNA ligase (1 U/μL) (BMB).
8. *Eco*RI enzyme (20 U/μL) (NEB).
9. Phenol-chloroform-isoamyl alcohol (25:24:1) (U.S. Biochem).
10. Spectrophotometer.
11. λ-gt11/*Eco*RI/CIAP-treated vector and packaging kit (Gigapack II Gold; Stratagene).
12. Suspension media (SM): 5.8 g NaCl, 2 g $MgSO_4 \cdot 7H_2O$, 50 mL 1*M* Tris-HCl, pH 7.5, 5 mL 2% (w/v) gelatin, H_2O to 1 L. Sterilize.
13. Chloroform (Kodak).
14. Y1090 *E. coli* cells.

2.3. Expression, Growth, and Purification of GST-Fusion Proteins

1. 50 mL LB media containing 50 μg/mL ampicillin.
2. 300-500 mL LB media containing 50 μg/mL ampicillin.
3. 1*M* IPTG (isopropyl-β-D-thiogalactopyranoside) (Sigma).
4. JA 10 centrifuge bottles.
5. Stock protease inhibitors: 0.2*M* benzamidine and 0.1*M* phenylmethylsulfonylfluoride (PMSF) prepared in ethanol and stored in a brown bottle.
6. Ice-cold PBS: 150 m*M* NaCl, 50 m*M* sodium phosphate, pH 7.5, containing 0.83 m*M* benzamidine, 0.23 m*M* PMSF.
7. 10% (w/v) Triton X-100.
8. JA 17 centrifuge tubes.
9. 2 mL Glutathione–Sepharose (Pharmacia) in a 10-mL plastic syringe plugged with a glass fiber filter.

10. Ice-cold 1% Triton X-100 in PBS containing 0.83 m*M* benzamidine and 0.23 m*M* PMSF, pH 7.5.
11. Ice-cold 50 m*M* Tris-HCl, pH 8.0, containing 0.83 m*M* benzamidine and 0.23 m*M* PMSF, with and without 10 m*M* glutathione.
12. 3–12% SDS polyacrylamide gel ***(11)***.
13. 20% (w/v) sarcosyl in H_2O.

2.4. Identification of the BID, Using the Overlay Assay

1. β_{1b} plasmid ***(12)***.
2. In vitro-translated truncated β_{1b}-subunit in pGEM3 expression vector.
3. Qiaex DNA purification kit (Qiagen).
4. 3–12% SDS polyacrylamide gel ***(11)***.
5. Nitrocellulose membrane (Pharmacia).
6. X-ray film (Kodak).

2.5. Measurement of the Affinity of the Interaction Between the α_1- and β-Subunits

1. Glutathione–Sepharose (Pharmacia).
2. In vitro-translated [^{35}S]-labeled-β_{1b}-subunit.
3. Ice-cold PBS: 150 m*M* NaCl, 50 m*M* sodium phosphate, pH 7.5, containing protease inhibitors.
4. Grafit data-fitting program (Sigma).
5. Scintillation counter for quantifying [^{35}S]-β-subunit.

2.6. Purification of Native Ca^{2+} Channel β-Subunits with the AID

1. CNBr-activated Sepharose (Sigma).
2. Purified AID GST-fusion protein (purified as detailed in **Subheading 2.3.**).
3. Cocktail of protease inhibitors: 76.8 µ*M* aprotinin, 0.83 m*M* benzamidine, 1.1 µ*M* leupeptin, 0.7 µ*M* pepstatin, 0.23 m*M* PMSF.
4. 3–12% SDS polyacrylamide gel and nitrocellulose membrane.
5. β-subunit-specific antibodies ***(13)***.
6. Homogenization buffer: 10 m*M* HEPES buffer, pH 7.4, 1% 3-[(3-cholamidopropyl) dimethylammonio]-1-propane sulfonate (CHAPS), 1*M* NaCl containing cocktail of protease inhibitors.

3. Methods

3.1. Overlay Binding Assay

The principle of the overlay binding assay for determining subunit–subunit interactions requires that the binding conformation is maintained after separation of either one of the proteins in question by SDS-PAGE. The preparation of a radiolabeled derivative of the other subunit facilitates detection of the interaction following association. This section describes the development of an overlay binding assay to characterize the interaction of the α_1- and β-subunit of Ca^{2+} channels.

3.1.1. Synthesis of Labeled β-Subunit Probe

Although newer methods of protein biotinylation are being developed, we utilized [^{35}S]-methionine-labeled in vitro translation products. It is possible, however, to incorporate other radiolabeled amino acids during translation (i.e., [^{35}S]-cysteine), if the probe of interest does not contain any methionine residues.

3.1.1.1. Designing a Construct for In Vitro Translation

When designing a construct for efficient in vitro translation, it is of utmost importance that the cDNA sequence contains a strong translation-initiation site (i.e., Kozak consensus sequence *[14]*). In addition, a promotor/enhancer such as Alfalfa mosaic virus (AMV) or cytomegalovirus (CMV), is required for good synthesis. Often, the transcription of probes is from a T7 polymerase recognition site, although SP6 or T3 RNA polymerase-driven transcription is adequate.

3.1.1.2. In Vitro Translation Procedure

All the reagents for translation are thawed after storage at –70°C and immediately placed on ice. A typical reaction is performed as follows (*see* **Notes 2–5**):

TNT Rabbit reticulocyte lysate	25 µL
TNT Reaction buffer	2 µL
TNT RNA polymerase (SP6, T3, or T7)	1 µL
Amino acid mixture minus methionine, 1 m*M*	1 µL
[^{35}S]-methionine (1000 Ci/mmol) at 10 mCi/mL	4 µL
RNasin ribonuclease inhibitor 40U/µL	1 µL
DNA template (pGEM3-β_{1b})	1 µg
Nucl ease free H_2O	to a final volume of 50 µL

The success of the translation can readily be tested by analysis of the translated β-subunit by SDS-PAGE, followed by autoradiography **(Fig. 1A)**.

3.1.2. Determining the Interaction of the α_1–β-Subunits by the Overlay Assay

Assessing the interaction between the two Ca^{2+} channel proteins is achieved after separation of the components of the purified skeletal muscle dihydropyridine receptor on a 3–12% SDS gel, electrophoretically transferring the gel onto nitrocellulose membrane and incubating the resulting membrane with the in vitro-translated β-subunit **(Fig. 1B)**.

1. Resolve aliquots (5–10 µg) of the purified dihydropyrdine receptor on 3–12% SDS polyacrylamide gels under reduced conditions *(11)* and transfer electrophoretically onto nitrocellulose, as described in **ref. *5***.
2. Block by incubating the membrane with blocking solution I, II, or III for 1 h at room temperature.

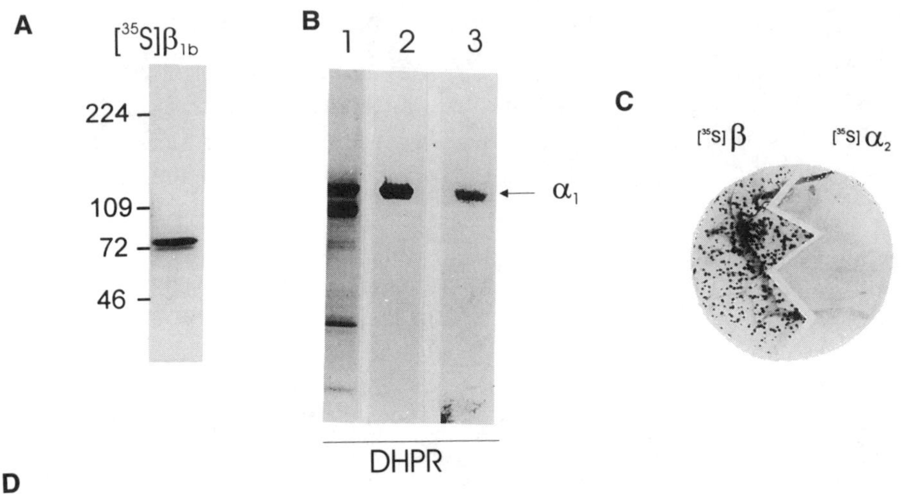

D

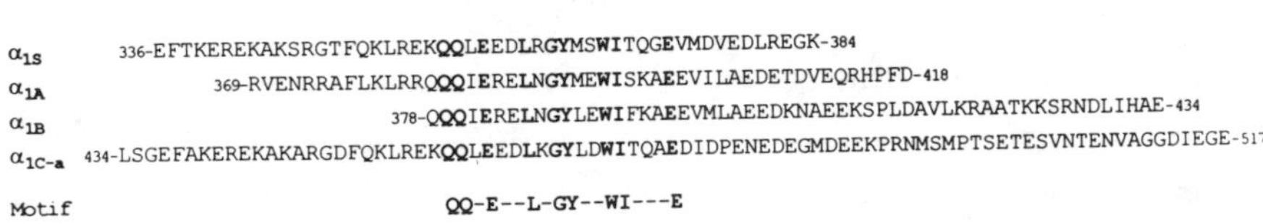

Fig. 1. Experimental approaches used to identify the interaction sites between the α_1- and β-subunits of the voltage dependent Ca^{2+} channel. **(A)** Autoradiogram of full-length in vitro-translated [^{35}S]-met labeled β_{1b}-subunit probe resolved using 3–12% SDS-PAGE. Mol wts are listed on the left. **(B)** Overlay technique demonstrates an interaction between the two proteins. Shown in lane 1 is Coomassie blue-stained gel of purified dihydropyridine receptor (DHPR) from skeletal muscle. Lane 2 shows an identical nitrocellulose blot stained with IIF7 monoclonal antibody to identify the α_1-subunit. Lane 3 is an autoradiogram of an identical nitrocellulose blot that has been incubated with the [^{35}S]-met labeled β_{1b} in vitro-translated probe, washed extensively, and exposed to film. Arrow indicates the binding of the β_{1b}-subunit probe to the α_1-subunit immobilized on nitrocellulose. **(C)** Demonstration of the specificity of the interaction of the β_{1b}-subunit probe with the plaque-purified α_1-subunit epitope clone. The voltage-dependent Ca^{2+} channel α_2-subunit probe was unable to bind the purified clone. **(D)** Sequence alignment of multiple α_1-subunit clones identified from screening four different α_1-subunit epitope libraries (α_{1A} ,α_{1B}, α_{1C}, α_{1D}) with the same β-subunit probe. Regions of overlap were then used to map and characterize the interaction motif between the α_1- and β-subunits. All parts of figure are modified from **ref. *8***.

3. Incubate the membrane in overlay buffer I for 1 h with the addition of the labeled probe (1 μL/mL overlay buffer), mixing gently for 12 h at 4°C.
4. Wash blots, subsequent to overlay incubations, for 1 h with 5% BSA in PBS at room temperature, dry in air (to complete dryness), and expose to X-ray film.

In the experiment illustrated in **Fig. 1B** autoradiography revealed that the β-subunit interacted with the α_1-subunit of the Ca^{2+} channel (**Fig. 1B**) and this was confirmed by comparison with Coomassie blue staining of the purified dihydropyridine receptor and immunoblot analysis with an α_1-specific antibody that migrated at the same position.

Notably, the overlay technique is limited in its usefulness, since large amounts of protein may be required to measure good interaction. For example, in the case of the calcium channel, relatively large quantities of the purified skeletal muscle dihydropyridine-sensitive receptors are required to detect the interaction between the [^{35}S]-labeled β-subunit and the α_{1S}-subunit. Another limitation of this technique is that the interaction site on the protein present on the blot must be relatively unaltered by treatment with SDS, or renatured after removal of SDS, once transferred onto nitrocellulose. The binding motif relies on the tertiary structure of the protein, but is more likely to be identified if it is in a linear sequence (*see* **Note 8**).

3.2. Preparation and Use of an α_1 Epitope Library to Identify the AID

To establish the precise location of the AID, we have generated α_1 epitope expression libraries and screened them with the in vitro-translated [^{35}S]-labeled β-subunit probe. Epitope library screening is particularly useful in identifying protein–protein interaction sites on large proteins (>5000 bp cDNA size) where production of individual fusion proteins for the entire protein would be extremely time- and cost-consuming. An outline of the protocols for making and screening an epitope library are shown in **Figs. 2** and **3**, respectively.

1. Digest approx 15 µg of purified α_1-subunit cDNA in DNase reaction buffer (1X final concentration) with 1 U DNase I. Remove aliquots (5 µg) at three time-points (i.e., 3, 6, and 9 min), in order to achieve differential digestions. Resolve digested DNA on a 1% agarose gel along with size markers. Excise the smear of digested DNA from the gel between 0 and 500 bases with a clean razorblade. Isolate the digested DNA from the gel using the Qiagen gel extraction kit.
2. Ligate the phosphorylated *Eco*RI linkers to the ends of the randomly digested α_1-subunit DNA fragments, using T4 DNA ligase (1 U) in 30 µL vol in T4 DNA ligase buffer overnight at 15°C. Inactivate the ligase enzyme by heating at 65°C for 10 min.
3. Digest the DNA with *Eco*RI for 3 h at 37°C. Purify the DNA by phenol-chloroform extraction (twice), followed by ethanol precipitation (*see* **Note 9**). DNA was quantified by determining $A_{260/280}$ ratio using spectrophotometer.
4. Ligate the purified digested DNA into λgt11 *Eco*RI-digested and CIAP-treated λ arms (1 µg) at a molar ratio of 5:1 insert to vector.
5. Package the ligated λgt11 arms using Gigapack Gold phage. Keep the packaging reagents at –80°C until use, then thaw the reagents rapidly. Add half the ligated

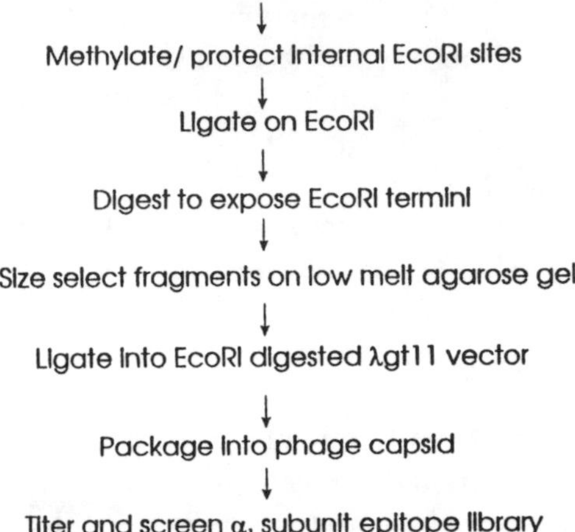

Fig. 2. Flow diagram for constructing an α_1-subunit epitope library. Epitope libraries of the α_1-subunit of the voltage dependent Ca^{2+} channel have been used for identification of protein interaction sites *(8)* and antibody recognition sites (Gurnett and Campbell, unpublished observations).

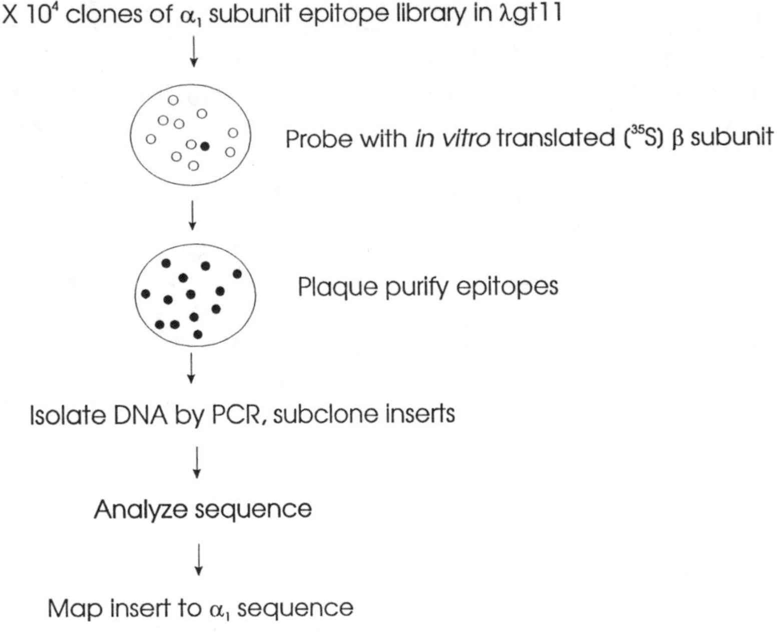

Fig. 3. Flow diagram for identification of protein–protein interaction sites using an epitope library. The α_1-subunit epitope library was screened with [^{35}S]-met labeled β-subunit. Purification and screening of positive clones has been used to map the site of interaction on the α_1-subunit *(8)*.

*Eco*RI-digested λ arms to the kit extract, then add 15 μL sonic extract from the packaging kit. Incubated the samples for 2 h at room temperature. After incubation, add 500 μL SM media and 20 μL chloroform. This yields the unamplified library stock.

6. Titer and amplify the library immediately (*see* **Note 10**).
7. Use the β-subunit probe to screen 2 × 10^4 clones of each α_1-subunit epitope library in Y1090 *E. coli* (**Fig. 1C**). Amplify inserts from pure phage positives by PCR, using primers directed to λgt11-phage arms. Subclone these directly into a T-vector (prepared from Bluescript SK-plasmid) for sequencing, or digest with *Eco*RI and ligate into pGEX-1 vector for GST fusion protein production. Sequence all inserts in both directions. Perform peptide sequence homology searches using the BLAST network service provided by the National Center for Biotechnology Information (**Fig. 1D**).

3.3. Expression, Growth, and Purification of GST-Fusion Proteins

To verify and subsequently test the interactions identified by the library screen, we have prepared GST-fusion proteins of the AID by subcloning each of the positive clones after epitope screening into pGEX plasmids, transforming these constructs into *E. coli* DH5α cells and inducing the fusion protein production.

1. Inoculate 50 μL of glycerol stock of the AID fusion protein into 50 mL LB media containing ampicillin, to a final concentration of 50 μg/mL.
2. Incubate overnight at 37°C in an orbital shaker at 300 rpm.
3. Dilute the culture 10-fold, i.e., 50 mL in 300–500 mL LB media, and incubate at 37°C in the orbital shaker again for a further 1–2 h.
4. Add isopropyl-β-D-thiogalactopyranoside (IPTG) to a final concentration of 1 m*M* (at mid-log phase of growth) and incubate for an additional 3 h at 37°C shaking at 300 rpm.
5. Transfer cultures to JA10 bottles and add protease inhibitors (benzamidine [0.83 m*M*] and PMSF [0.23 m*M*]); sediment the bacteria at 5000*g* for 10 min at 4°C.
6. Decant off the supernatant; resuspend the whole cell pellet in a final volume of 9 mL PBS containing two protease inhibitors (PMSF and benzamidine), and add 1 mL of 10% Triton X-100 (to a final concentration of 1%).
7. Lyse the cells by sonication of the resuspended bacteria for a maximum of 30 s in 3 × 10 s bursts, to minimize proteolysis.
8. Prepare the bacterial lysate by centrifugation of the lysed cells in a JA 17 rotor at 13,800*g* for 10 min at 4°C (*see* **Note 11**).
9. To purify the GST-fusion protein, first equilibrate a glutathione–Sepharose column (1–2 mL) prepared in a 10-mL syringe plugged with a glass filter, with three bed volumes of 1% Triton X-100 in PBS containing two protease inhibitors, then transfer the glutathione–Sepharose to a 50-mL falcon tube and incubate with the bacterial lysate for 30 min at 4°C.

10. Pour the resin back into the column and discard the void. Wash the column extensively with 7 bed vol of 1% Triton X-100 in PBS containing two protease inhibitors and then with 10 bed vol of PBS containing the protease inhibitors. Finally, wash the column with 50 m*M* Tris-HCl, pH 8.0, and elute fusion proteins in the same buffer containing 10 m*M* reduced glutathione by collecting 10 bed volume fractions. Use analysis of the fractions by SDS-PAGE to identify, for subsequent pooling, those containing the most protein.
11. Determine the protein content by the Lowry protein assay ***(16)***, using BSA as a standard, after removal of the glutathione by gel filtration or dialysis.

3.4. Identification of the BID Using the Overlay Assay

The AID GST-fusion proteins have been instrumental in determining the complementary interaction domain on the β-subunit (BID), using the following protocol:

1. Amplify truncated β-subunit constructs by PCR (**Fig. 4A**) from cDNA-encoding β_{1b}, using specific primers, purify DNA products using the Qiaex extraction kit (Qiagen) and subclone them into pGEM3 vector, modified to contain a 5' alfalfa mosaic virus enhancer region and a poly(A)$^+$ tail for enhanced expression.
2. Electrophorese aliquots (100 μL) of bacterial lysates containing a control GST-fusion protein and AID-GST-fusion proteins on 3–12% SDS gels (**Fig. 4B**).
3. Transfer proteins electrophoretically transferred onto nitrocellulose membrane and incubate in overlay buffer I with each of the in vitro-translated truncated β-subunits overnight at 4°C.
4. After extensive washing for 1 h at 22°C as described in **Subheading 3.1.2., step 4**, for the intact [^{35}S]-labeled β-subunit interaction, expose the membranes to X-ray film to enable detection of the specific interaction by autoradiography (**Fig. 4B**).

The specimen results illustrated in **Fig. 4B** reveal that a region that is present on the second conserved domain of the β-subunit, contained within amino acid residues 211–418, is required for maintaining this interaction (**Fig. 4B**). In further experiments, beyond the scope of this chapter, these interactions were further assayed electrophysiologically to identify a very small portion of the β-subunit encompassing residues 211–265 as being essential for α_1–β interaction. Furthermore, we have found that this truncated β-subunit is also capable of modulating the kinetics of the channels, thereby narrowing not only the α_1–β interaction domain, but also the region on the β-subunit responsible for Ca^{2+} current stimulation, down to approx 40 amino acids ***(9)***. Site-directed mutagenesis of residues within this motif has allowed us to identify those amino acids that are essential for this interaction ***(9)***.

3.5. Measurement of Affinity of the Interaction Between the α_1- and β-Subunits

Having identified both interaction domains on the two-subunits, additional properties of this interaction can now be examined. How strong is this inter-

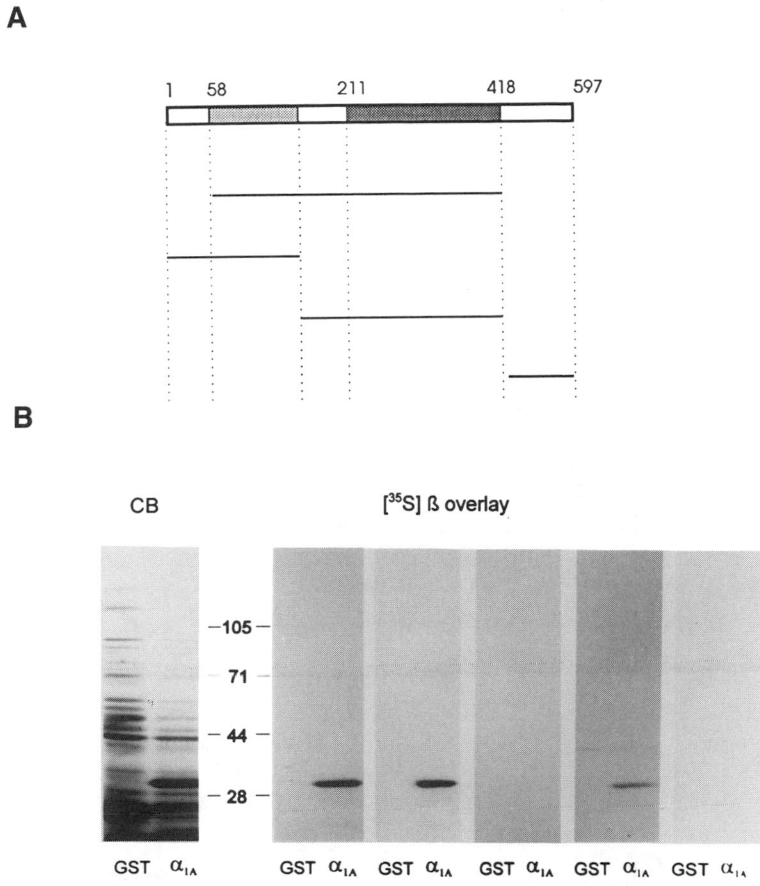

Fig. 4. Truncated probes can be used to identify the minimal sites required for protein interactions. **(A)** Truncated β-subunit constructs were generated for use as probes in the in the overlay assay *(9)*. Shaded areas of the full-length construct indicate two structurally conserved regions on all β-subunit genes. Amino acids are numbered above the full-length construct. **(B)** Coomassie blue stained gel of 3–12% SDS-PAGE resolved crude bacterial lysate containing GST fusion protein (lane 1) and GST-α_{1A} I-II cytoplasmic linker (AID) fusion protein (lane 2). To the right is an autoradiogram of an identical nitrocellulose blot demonstrating that the full-length [^{35}S]-β-subunit overlays only on the GST-α_{1A} AID fusion protein. Four truncated [^{35}S]-β-subunit probes were then tested for their ability to overlay on the immobilized GST-α_{1A} AID fusion protein. The region between amino acid residues 211–418 of the β-subunit, which consists of the highly conserved second domain, was shown to be the minimal region required for binding to the α_{1A} -AID. Mol-wt markers are indicated. Both parts of the figure are modified from **ref. *9***.

action? Is this association reversible? These questions may be addressed using GST-fusion proteins of the AID and in vitro-translated β-subunits, with the development of a GST-glutathione–Sepharose bead assay.

1. Incubate aliquot of [^{35}S]- labeled β-subunit (0.7–1.3 p*M*) overnight at 4°C in PBS (1 mL) with increasing concentrations (100 p*M*–1 m*M*) of an AID-GST-fusion protein noncovalently coupled to glutathione–Sepharose beads.
2. Sediment the beads at 13,000 rpm in a bench centrifuge for 2 min and wash them four times with ice-cold PBS.
3. Determine the quantified bound [^{35}S]- labeled β-subunit by scintillation counting.
4. Analyze the data using the data-fitting program Grafit (Sigma) and derive the K_D and B_{MAX} for the interaction.

Experiments of this type reveal that the interaction is indeed very strong, with a K_D of 5.8 n*M* for the AID_A GST-fusion protein and $β_{1b}$. However, the affinity of this interaction was 10 times greater than that of the $β_3$-subunit, suggesting that although certain conserved residues is required for interaction, other amino acids within and around these domains also determine the affinity of the association ***(17)***.

The association and dissociation kinetics of the interaction can also be tested using the AID_A-GST-fusion protein, by measuring the amount of [^{35}S]-labeled β-subunit bound to AID_A-GST at various time-points as the reaction approaches equilibrium (*see* **Note 12**).

1. Incubate an aliquot (~500 n*M*) of the AID_A-GST-fusion protein coupled to 40 µL of glutathione–Sepharose beads at 4°C for various times (0–300 min), with 0.32 p*M* of in vitro-translated [^{35}S]-labeled $β_{1b}$ probe in 1 mL PBS.
2. Wash the beads four times with ice-cold PBS and measure the relative association by scintillation counting.

The reversibility of this association may also be addressed in competition experiments using an 18-amino acid synthetic AID_A peptide. This shows that 100 µ*M* of this peptide is sufficient to completely prevent the association of [^{35}S]-labeled β with any of the AID GST-fusion proteins. Dissociation is measured by allowing the association to reach equilibrium by overnight incubation of the reactants, as described above, and then measuring the binding over a period of time (up to 8 h) at 4°C in the presence of 500 µ*M* AID_A peptide. At 4°C, the interaction between AID_A and $β_{1b}$ is almost irreversible, because no measurable decrease in the amount of $β_{1b}$ bound to the beads is observed within the time-period ***(9)***.

In conclusion, the GST-glutathione-bead assay using fusion proteins to specific interaction regions, together with the in vitro-translated probes, may be used to characterize certain properties of that association.

3.6. Purification of Native Ca^{2+} Channel β-Subunits with the AID

Because of the high affinity of this interaction, a GST-glutathione–Sepharose bead assay has been developed that has been used for identifying β-subunits that are free or not associated with α_1-subunits of voltage dependent Ca^{2+} channels from both skeletal muscle and brain tissue ***(18)***.

1. Covalently couple the purified AID_A-GST fusion proteins to CNBr-activated Sepharose at a concentration of 0.5 mg/mL resin, according to the manufacturer's instructions.
2. Prepare tissue extracts from homogenates in 50 m*M* HEPES, pH 7.4, containing 100 m*M* NaCl and no detergent in the presence of a cocktail of protease inhibitors: aprotinin (76.8 n*M*), benzamidine (0.83 m*M*), leupeptin (1.1 μ*M*), pepstatin A (0.7 μ*M*) and PMSF (0.23 m*M*) by incubation for 2 h at 4°C and centrifuged at 37,000 rpm (100,000*g*) for 35 min (*see* **Note 13**).
3. Incubate the resultant supernatant with the AID_A-covalently attached to Sepharose overnight at 4°C. Significant binding of free β-subunits can be detected by Western blot analysis ***(17)*** with subunit-specific antibodies ***(13)***.

The use of fusion proteins, coupled to GST-glutathione–Sepharose beads as an affinity matrix, clearly has very important implications for aiding in deciphering the association of these proteins with other unknown cellular components (i.e., cytoskeleton).

4. Notes

1. Subunit–subunit interactions may be investigated using both biochemical and molecular techniques alone or in concert with functional assays, as was the case for the identification of the AID and BID of Ca^{2+} channel subunits. These approaches have also recently been successfully applied to characterizing the protein–protein interactions among a number of the components of the dystrophin glycoprotein complex ***(19,20)***. Clearly these methodologies can readily be used for investigating the molecular interactions between a wide variety of different proteins.
2. Small-scale reactions may be performed by reducing volumes proportionately. Notably, multiple proteins can be expressed from the same or different promotors in the same reaction by adding appropriate TNT RNA polymerases.
3. In order to minimize proteolysis, translation should be performed in the presence of a cocktail of protease inhibitors: pepstatin A, chymostatin, aprotinin, antipain, and leupeptin, at a final concentration of 0.1 μg/mL. Calf liver tRNA may also be added, to a final concentration of 40 μg/mL to reduce background translation.
4. The advantage of using this kit over conventionally preparing RNA, and subsequently utilizing this RNA for protein translation in a rabbit reticulocyte lysate, is that the handling time is minimized (from 10 to 5 h) and the reaction occurs in a single tube. However, a disadvantage of this coupled system may be lower yields of translated material, although we have not performed direct comparisons of the two methodologies.
5. Free [^{35}S]-methionine may readily be removed from the labeled probe using a PD 10 column (Pharmacia, G-25 Sephadex), especially if binding assays are being performed using the radiolabeled probe. If dilution of the probe is a problem, the

[35S]-methionine removal can be accomplished by rapid gel filtration using G-50 Sephadex (Pharmacia) prepared in a 1-mL syringe column.

6. The blocking step for the proteins on the nitrocellulose is critical for reducing background and maximizing the interaction between the two proteins. Different blocking buffers can be used to reduce nonspecific binding of probe.
7. Overlay buffer II may be also be used for incubation with the radiolabeled probe overnight at 4°C with gentle agitation. Different blocking buffers and incubation conditions may be tested, since the interaction may be very sensitive to ionic strength, presence of cations, and reducing conditions.
8. In an attempt to alleviate this problem, the blot may be incubated with decreasing amounts of guanidine-HCl, which should renature the immobilized proteins somewhat, as described for the K^+ channel Shaker B α-subunit ***(15)***.
9. DNA was quantified by determining $A_{260}/_{280}$ ratio using a spectrophotometer.
10. The integrity of the library should be tested by direct immunoscreening with a monoclonal antibody directed toward the α_1-subunit.
11. Fusion proteins that contain hydrophobic domains are more difficult to purify, since their hydrophobicity causes them to be incorporated into inclusion bodies; they usually yield Triton X-100 insoluble preparations. These fusion proteins may be solubilized using 10% sarcosyl, after initial solubilization with 1% Triton X-100. After 30 min incubation and centrifugation to remove all insoluble material, followed by the addition of fivefold concentration Triton X-100, the fusion protein is purified on a glutathione–Sepharose column, as detailed above for the soluble fusion proteins. Transmembrane regions should be avoided when designing fusion proteins.
12. At a given AID_A-GST-fusion protein concentration, the association rate constant corresponds to a half-time of approx 20 min. The maximum association is not affected by changes in Ca^{2+} concentration (1 n*M*–1 m*M*), ionic strength (0–2*M* NaCl), or phosphorylation by protein kinase C. However, large variations in pH (4–10) could decrease the maximal association by ~40%, and the interaction was totally abolished at pH 12.0.
13. Treatment of tissue with homogenization buffer containing protease inhibitors induced some dissociation of the β-subunit from the channel complex and allowed purification of native, free β-subunits. This method of purifying the native Ca^{2+} channel β-subunits can be exploited in isolating large amounts of native protein that would be required for complex structural studies (i.e., NMR and X-ray crystallography).

References

1. Miller, R. J. (1992) Voltage-sensitive Ca^{2+} channels. *J Biol. Chem.* **267,** 1403–1406.
2. Mintz, I. M., Adams, M. E., and Bean, B. P. (1992) P type calcium channels in rat central and peripheral neurons. *Neuron* **9,** 85–95.
3. Witcher, D. R., De Waard, M., Sakamoto, J. Franzini-Armstrong, C., Pragnell, M., Kahl, S. D., and Campbell, K. P. (1993) Subunit identification and reconstitution of the N-type Ca^{2+} channel complex purified from brain. *Science* **261,** 486–489.
4. Curtis, B. M. and Catterall, W. A. (1984) Purification of the calcium antagonist receptor of the voltage sensitive calcium channel from skeletal muscle transverse tubules. *Biochemistry* **23,** 2113–2118.

5. Leung, A. T., Imagawa, T., and Campbell, K. P. (1987) Structural characterization of the 1,4-dihydropyridine receptor of the voltage-dependent Ca^{2+} channel from rabbit skeletal muscle. *J. Biol. Chem.* **262,** 7943–7946.
6. Birnbaumer, L., Campbell, K. P., Catterall, W. A., Harpold, M. M., Hofmann, F., Horne, W. A., Mori, Y., Schwartz, A., Snutch, T. P., Tanabe, T., and Tsien, R. W. (1994) The naming of voltage gated calcium channels. *Neuron* **13,** 505,506.
7. De Waard, M., Gurnett, C. A., and Campbell, K. P. (1996) Structural and functional diversity of voltage-activated calcium channels, in *Ion Channels*, vol. 4 (Narahashi, T., ed.), Plenum, New York, pp. 41–87.
8. Pragnell, M., De Waard, M., Mori, Y., Tanabe, T., Snutch, T. P., and Campbell, K. P. (1994) Calcium channel β subunit binds to a conserved motif in the I-II cytoplasmic linker of the α_1 subunit. *Nature* **368,** 67–70.
9. De Waard, M., Pragnell, M., and Campbell, K. P. (1994) Calcium channel regulation by a conserved β subunit domain. *Neuron* **13,** 495–503.
10. De Waard, M. and Campbell, K. P. (1995) Subunit regulation of the neuronal a1A Ca^{2+} channel expressed in *Xenopus* oocytes. *J. Physiol.* (London) **485.3,** 619–634.
11. Laemmli, U. K. (1970) Cleavage of structural protein during assembly of the head of bacteriophage T4. *Nature* **227,** 680–685.
12. Pragnell, M., Sakamoto, J., Jay, S. D., and Campbell. K. P. (1991) Cloning and tissue specific expression of the brain calcium channel β subunit. *FEBS Lett.* **291,** 253–258.
13. Scott, V. E. S., De Waard, M., Liu, H., Gurnett, C. A., Venzke, D. P., Lennon, V. A., and Campbell, K. P. (1996) β subunit heterogeneity in N-type Ca2+ channels. *J. Biol. Chem.* **271,** 3207–3212.
14. Kozak, M. (1986) Point mutations define a sequence flanking the AUG initiator codon that modulates translation by eukaryotic ribosomes. *Cell* **44,** 283–292.
15. Li, M., Jan, Y. N., and Jan, L. Y. (1992) Specification of subunit assembly by the hydrophilic amino-terminal domain of the Shaker potassium channel. *Science* **257,** 1225–1230.
16. Lowry, O. H., Rosebrough, N. J., Farr, A. L., and Randall, R. J. (1951) Protein measurement with the folin phenol reagent. *J. Biol. Chem.* **193,** 265–275.
17. De Waard, M., Witcher, D. R., Pragnell, M., Liu, H., and Campbell, K. P. (1995) Properties of the α_1-β anchoring site in voltage-dependent Ca^{2+} channels. *J. Biol. Chem.* **270,** 1–9.
18. Witcher, D. R., De Waard, M., Liu, H., and Campbell, K. P. (1995) Association of native Ca^{2+} channel β subunits with the α_1 subunit interaction domain. *J. Biol. Chem.* **270,** 1–6.
19. Jung, D., Yang, B., Meyer, J. Chamberlain, J. S., and Campbell, K. P. (1995) Identification and characterization of the dystrophin anchoring site on β dystroglycan. *J. Biol. Chem.* **270,** 27,305–27,310.
20. Yang, B., Jung, D., Motto, D., Meyer, J., Koretzky, G., and Campbell, K. P. (1995) SH3 domain-mediated interaction of dystroglycan and Grb2. *J. Biol. Chem.* **270,** 11,711–11,714.

8

Use of GST-Fusion and Related Constructs for the Identification of Interacting Proteins

Mark Harris

1. Introduction

Over the last 5 yr, the use of polypeptide affinity tags, in particular glutathione-*S*-transferase (GST), and to a lesser extent, six adjacent histidines (6-His), has become almost a compulsory techniquc in thc study of specific protein–protein interactions. For the most part these fusion proteins have been produced in *Escherichia coli* expression systems; their use has been well-documented. However, it is becoming increasingly clear that eukaryotic posttranslational modifications play an important role in protein–protein interactions, so this chapter will concentrate on the production and use of baculovirus-expressed GST- and 6-His fusion proteins, referring briefly, at the end, to aspects of *E. coli* expression that differ substantially from the methods described for baculovirus expression.

GST has a number of distinct properties that have facilitated its development as a fusion partner for affinity chromatography. First, it is an extremely stable and inert protein. Proteolytic degradation of *E. coli*-expressed GST is rarely (if ever) observed. In fact, GST-fusion proteins are often degraded down to GST alone. Second, the high affinity of GST for reduced glutathione means that fusion proteins can be rapidly purified from *E. coli* lysates in a one-step procedure, using glutathione immobilized on agarose or Sepharose. Finally, GST-fusion proteins are much more likely to be expressed in a soluble form in *E. coli*, compared to the expression of unfused foreign proteins that are more frequently found in insoluble inclusion bodies. For example, in the author's experience the HIV-1 Nef protein, when expressed in an unfused form in *E. coli*, is totally insoluble, but a GST-Nef fusion protein is predominantly soluble.

From: *Methods in Molecular Biology, Vol. 88: Protein Targeting Protocols*
Edited by: R. A. Clegg Humana Press Inc., Totowa, NJ

However, despite these advantages, there are also major disadvantages to *E. coli* expression of GST-fusion proteins. First, large or hydrophobic proteins tend to be poorly expressed and also are more likely to be insoluble. Being a prokaryotic system, the expressed proteins will lack any co- or posttranslational modifications, such as glycosylation or acylation. In the latter context, the universally popular (pGEX) expression vectors *(1)* produce a fusion protein in which the protein of interest is at the C-terminus; thus myristoylated proteins will not be modified, even when coexpressed with N-myristoyl transferase (NMT) *(2)*. In theory, this problem could be overcome by expressing GST as the C-terminal fusion partner; however, it is clear that the N-terminus of GST is an efficient translational initiation sequence in *E. coli*, but the majority of eucaryotic ATGs are in an unfavorable sequence context and thus initiate translation very poorly (George Reid, personal communication). For these reasons, a number of laboratories have developed the GST-fusion system for baculovirus expression. Two sets of vectors are available on request: Ian Jones (NERC Institute of Virology and Environmental Microbiology, Mansfield Road, Oxford OX1 3SR) has vectors to express proteins as C-terminal fusions either in cell-associated or secreted form *(3,4)*. In the latter vector, the signal sequence from the major baculovirus glycoprotein gp67 has been fused to the N-terminus of GST. Fusion proteins expressed from this vector will therefore be efficiently transported through the secretory pathway and glycosylated *(4)*. The author has a vector to express proteins as N-terminal fusions with GST, this is of particular use for myristoylated proteins *(5)*. The structure of these vectors is shown in **Fig. 1**. These baculovirus vectors offer a solution for the problems discussed at the beginning of this paragraph; this chapter discusses in detail the construction, production, and use of these fusion proteins.

Cloning of the coding sequences for foreign genes into these vectors is generally accomplished by polymerase chain reaction (PCR) in order to ensure that only the coding sequences are inserted and to maintain the open reading frame. It is worth stressing at this point that for C-terminal fusions the ATG should be omitted and the termination codon retained; for N-terminal fusions the converse is true. In the context of the N-terminal fusion, although most eucaryotic ATGs initiate translation efficiently in baculoviral systems, care should be taken when placing restriction sites directly adjacent to the initiator codon. The translatability of ATGs is clearly empirical, but when a *Bam*HI site is directly adjacent to the ATG, expression levels are extremely poor. I recommend placing a spacer of at least six nucleotides between the restriction site and the ATG; if there are concerns over the choice of sequence, TATAAG has been proved to work well for at least three proteins (HIV-1 Nef, CD4, and p56Lck) in the author's laboratory and may be a good starting point.

Detailed discussion of the generation of recombinant baculoviruses is beyond the scope of this chapter. This situation necessitates that the reader has a working knowledge of insect cell culture and baculovirus propagation. If this is not the case, the excellent volume by Possee and King ***(6)*** provides details of these methods. However, I will describe a rapid assay for the verification of expression of fusion proteins from early passage plaque isolates, which will save time and effort at later stages, particularly if several different proteins are being generated simultaneously.

2. Materials

Most materials will be standard components of the modern molecular biology laboratory, for example, L-broth, ampicillin, materials for SDS-PAGE analysis, and immunoblotting. This section therefore lists the materials that might be specifically required for the protocols listed in **Subheading 3.**

2.1. Growth of Insect Cells and 24-Well Assay for Expression

1. *Spodoptera frugiperda* (Sf9) cells (available from the American Type Culture Collection, accession number CRL-1711).
2. TC100 (Gibco-BRL Paisley, Scotland) medium supplemented with penicillin/streptomycin and 10% fetal calf serum.
3. Sterile plastic fine-tip "pastettes" (Alpha Laboratories, Eastleigh, Hampshire, UK) (optional, but more convenient than sterile Pasteur pipets).

2.2. Lysis of Infected Cells and Purification of Fusion Proteins

1. Cytoplasmic lysis buffer: phosphate buffered saline (PBS), 1% (v/v) Triton X-100.
2. Protease inhibitors: leupeptin, pepstatin A, aprotinin, benzamidine, phenylmethylsulfonyl fluoride (PMSF), EDTA.
3. Glutathione-agarose (Sigma [Poole, Dorset, UK] G4510).
4. 1 mL Disposable chromatography columns (Bio-Rad [Hertfordshire, UK] Polyprep).
5. Reduced glutathione (Sigma G6529).
6. Nuclear extraction buffer: 10 m*M* Tris-HCl, pH 7.5, 10% sucrose, 0.3*M* NaCl (optional, only required if working with nuclear proteins).

2.3. Materials Required for Binding Assays

Purified GST produced by recombinant baculovirus. A recombinant baculovirus expressing GST alone is available from the author upon request (*see* **Note 9**).

2.4. Detection of Interacting Proteins

The materials required will vary, depending on the detection method chosen (*see* **Subheading 3.4.**).

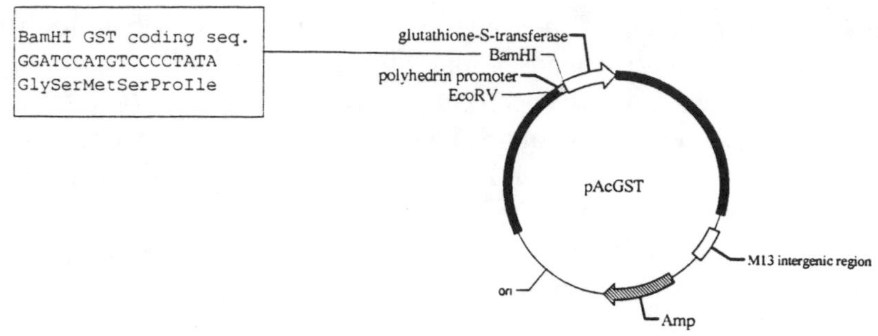

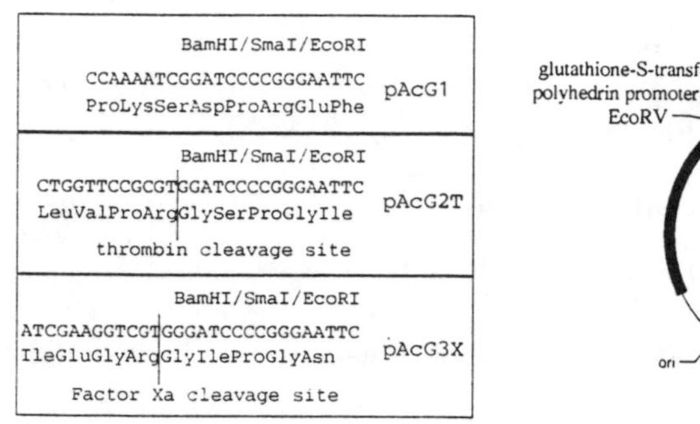

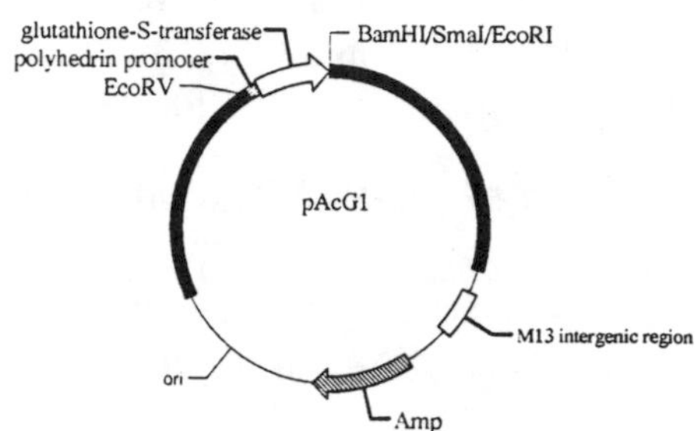

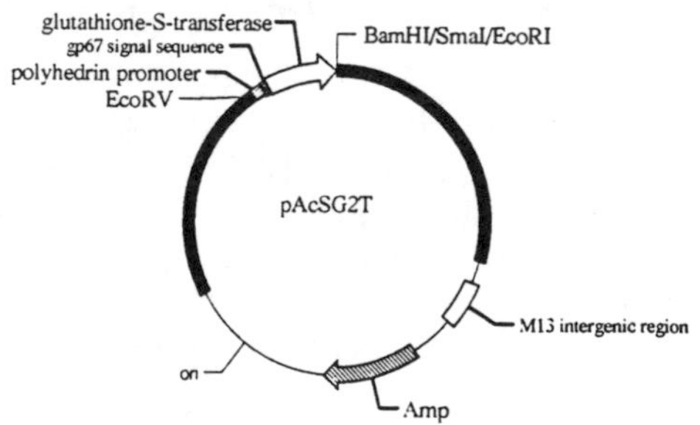

Fig. 1. Structure of baculovirus GST-fusion expression vectors. The structures of three plasmids that can be used to generate GST fusion constructs for expression by recombinant baculoviruses are shown. pAcGST is available from the author and is designed to generate fusions at the N-terminus of GST. A unique *Bam*HI site can be used for cloning. pAcG1 ***(3)*** is one of a series of baculo-GEX vectors that are equivalent to the pGEX series of bacterial vectors; thus, pAcG2T and pAcG3X are the equivalent of pGEX-2T and pGEX-3X ***(1)***, with thrombin or factor X_a cleavage sites following the GST coding sequence. pAcSG2T is a modification of pAcG1, which is the signal sequence from the major baculoviral structural protein gp67 was fused to the N-terminus of GST, thus providing for secretion of fusion proteins. pAcSG2T has

2.5. Coinfection Assay

1. Lysis buffer: 50 m*M* HEPES-KOH, pH 7.4, 150 m*M* NaCl, 10 m*M* EDTA, 1% Triton X-100 or Nonidet P-40 (NP40) (*see* **Note 1**).

2.6. Purification of Six-Histidine Tagged Proteins

1. Ni^{2+}-nitrilotriacetic acid-agarose (Ni-NTA agarose).
2. 50 m*M* $NiSO_4$.
3. 0.1*M* Sodium citrate buffer, pH 6.0 (11.5:88.5 [v/v] citric acid:trisodium citrate).
4. 20 m*M* Phosphate buffer, pH 7.2 (68.4:31.6 [v/v] Na_2HPO_4:NaH_2PO_4).
5. 250 m*M* Imidazole.

2.7. Purification of GST-Fusion Proteins Produced in E. coli

1. pGEX vector (Pharmacia [St. Albans, Herts, UK]).
2. Antifoam emulsion (BDH [Poole, Dorset, UK]).

3. Methods

3.1. The 24-Well Immunoblot Assay

1. Several hours before you intend to infect cells, seed 24-well multititer plates with 10^5 Sf9 cells in 1 mL of TC100 medium (Gibco-BRL) containing 10% fetal calf serum. Unless otherwise indicated, this medium will be used throughout the experiments described below.
2. Harvest individual white plaques obtained from plaque assay of transfection supernatant (first-round plaques) into 1 mL of medium using a sterile Pasteur pipet or plastic pastette.
3. Aspirate medium from the 24-well plate and add 500 µL of harvested plaque. Incubate at 28°C for 4–5 d, or until a good cytopathic effect is seen. Store the remaining plaque harvest at 4°C until the result of this assay is known.
4. Harvest medium and cells using a 1-mL Eppendorf pipet into a 1.5-mL microfuge tube.
5. Spin down the cells at low speed in a microfuge. If you are using a vector that generates cell-associated protein, aspirate the medium and lyse the cell pellet in 20 µL of lysis buffer containing protease inhibitors (*see* **Note 1**). If you are using a secreted vector, then save the medium for future analysis, but, since there should be substantial amounts of protein within the cytoplasm, proceed as for cytoplasmic proteins.

Fig. 1 (*continued*) been further modified by the addition of a monoclonal epitope tag downstream of the thrombin cleavage site to generate pAcSG2T-tag ***(4)***. The pAcG1 and pAcSG2T vectors are available from Ian Jones. All of these vectors are based on the baculovirus transfer vector pAcCL29 ***(8)***, which contains the M13 intergenic region, allowing the production of single-stranded DNA for mutagenesis purposes. The areas of the plasmids in black boxes represent baculovirus sequences for homologous recombination into the viral genome. Unique restriction enzyme sites have been indicated.

6. Analyze 10 μL of lysate by SDS-PAGE and immunoblotting, either using a previously characterized antibody to the protein of interest or an antibody to GST (*see* **Note 2**). Having identified positive plaques, return to the remaining plaque harvest and proceed with a second round of plaque purification.

3.2. Purification of Affinity Reagents

Having obtained a purified recombinant baculovirus expressing your protein of interest as a GST fusion, it is necessary to build up a large stock of virus for large-scale infections and subsequent purification of fusion protein. A convenient way to do this is to store the medium from the second-round 24-well assay and use 100 μL of this to infect a T75 flask seeded with 5×10^6 Sf9 cells. After 7 d incubation at 28°C the medium can be harvested, cell debris pelleted and the supernatant filtered through a 0.22-μm filter. This working virus stock should contain between 10^7 and 10^8 plaque-forming units per mL (verify by plaque assay), and should be aliquoted and stored at 4°C. This stock can then be used to bulk-up further by infecting larger amounts of cells (e.g., 1.5×10^7 in a T175 or spinner cultures at 5×10^5 cells per mL) at 0.1 PFU/cell. Again, virus should be harvested and titered after 7 d.

3.2.1. Large-Scale Infection for Protein Production

Generally, it is necessary to infect subconfluent cells at high multiplicity of infection (3–10 PFU/cell) for optimal protein expression.

1. Seed a number of T175 flasks with 2×10^7 Sf9 cells in 30 mL of medium several hours prior to infection (*see* **Note 3**).
2. Remove medium and add viral inoculum (3–10 PFU/cell, i.e., 6×10^7 to 2×10^8 PFU in total) in a final volume of 5 mL. Incubate at room temperature for 1 h on a rocking platform (*see* **Note 4**).
3. Remove inoculum and replace with 30 mL medium. Incubate at 28°C for 3 d.
4. Harvest cells by agitating the flasks vigorously (*see* **Note 5**). Pellet the cells (2K for 10 min at 4°C).

3.2.2. Lysis of Infected Cells and Purification of GST-Fusion Proteins

Clearly, for secreted proteins it is not necessary to lyse the infected cells. Protein can be purified directly from clarified culture supernatant (proceed to **step 4** below). However, for cell-associated proteins, the cells must be lysed under conditions that allow the binding of GST to glutathione-agarose (GA) beads (*see* **Note 12**).

1. Wash cell pellet twice with 10–20 mL PBS by gently resuspending with a 10 mL pipet (do not vortex) and pelleting (500*g* for 10 min at 4°C).
2. For cytoplasmic proteins, lyse the cells in PBS containing 1% Triton X-100 and protease inhibitors. Use 1 mL of lysis buffer per flask of cells. Incubate at 4°C for

30 min. For nuclear proteins, lysis can be accomplished by including 0.1% SDS in the lysis buffer; however, the concentration of SDS must be reduced to 0.03% prior to binding to GA beads, so a smaller starting volume is recommended. If preferred, nuclear proteins can be extracted as follows.

3. Pellet nuclei at 12,000*g* for 10 min at 4°C. Nuclear proteins can then be extracted by resuspending in nuclear extraction buffer containing protease inhibitors, incubating at 4°C for 60 min, and pelleting the nuclei again at 12,000*g* for 10 min at 4°C.
4. Transfer supernatant to a 15-mL polypropylene tube containing 0.5–1 mL preswollen GA beads. Beads should be preswollen in >10 vol of PBS for 30 min, with constant mixing on a rotating wheel, pelleted by centrifugation (500*g* for 5 min), and washed once with 10 vol of PBS prior to use. Incubate for 1 h at 4°C, with constant mixing on a rotating wheel.
5. Pellet beads (500*g* for 5 min), and wash twice with >10 vol of lysis buffer. Wash a further four times with >10 vol of 50 m*M* Tris-HCl, pH 8.0. During each wash, resuspend beads by gentle invertion. Do not vortex.
6. After the last wash resuspend the beads in 10 vol of 50 m*M* Tris-HCl, pH 8.0, and pour into a 1 mL disposable chromatography column. Allow to pack, but do not let the column dry out.
7. Elute fusion protein by adding 50 m*M* Tris-HCl, pH 8.0, containing 5 m*M* reduced glutathione. Collect 0.25-mL fractions and assay for protein content by Bradford assay or similar commercially available protein concentration assay kit.
8. Pool fractions containing protein and dialyze overnight against two changes of 50 m*M* Tris-HCl, pH 8.0. Verify integrity of protein by SDS-PAGE, followed by immunoblotting or Coomassie staining. An example of a typical purification is shown in **Fig. 2**.
9. Store aliquoted protein at –70°C (*see* **Note 6**).

3.3. Binding Assays

You are now in a position to use the purified protein to investigate interactions with cellular proteins (*see* **Note 7**).

1. Thaw an aliquot of protein on ice. Generally 100 μg will be sufficient for preliminary experiments. Add protein to GA beads to give a final ratio of 2 μg protein/μL packed beads (i.e., add 100 μg to 50 μL GA beads). The total volume of protein should not be less than the volume of beads, to ensure efficient mixing. Incubate on a rotating wheel at 4°C for 2 h.
2. Wash beads twice with 1 mL 50 m*M* Tris-HCl, pH 8.0. For immediate use, resuspend beads in lysis buffer (*see* **Note 1**). For storage at 4°C, resuspend in 50 m*M* Tris-HCl, pH 8.0, containing 0.1% sodium azide. It is convenient to resuspend beads in enough buffer to make a 20% slurry, this will facilitate accurate aliquoting of beads in subsequent steps. A small aliquot of beads (1–5 μL) can be analyzed by SDS-PAGE to verify efficient binding (*see* **Note 8**).
3. Prepare GA beads loaded with GST alone, according to **steps 1** and **2** above (*see* **Note 9**). These beads will be used both as negative controls and for preclearing of lysates (*see* **step 4**). Load GST at a ratio of 1 μg/μL packed beads.

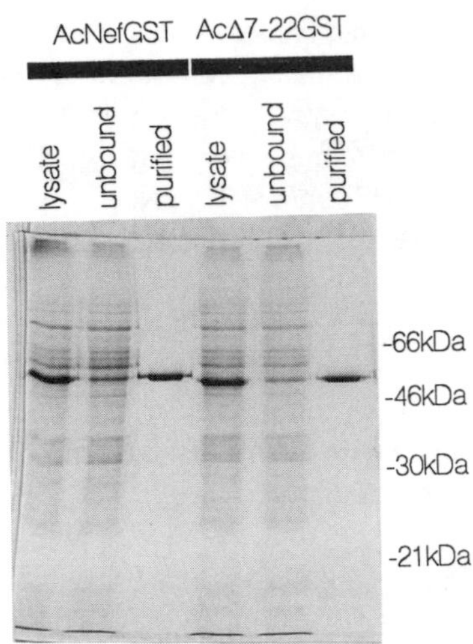

Fig. 2. Purification of baculovirus expressed GST-fusion proteins. This figure shows an example of the efficacy of single-step purification on GA beads. Sf9 cells infected with recombinant baculoviruses expressing either full-length Nef or an internal deletion (Δ7–22) as N-terminal fusions with GST were harvested and processed as described in the text (*see* **Subheadings 3.2.1.** and **3.2.2.**). Aliquots of the crude lysate (5 μL, equivalent to 10^5 cells), unbound fraction (5 μL, equivalent to 10^5 cells), and purified GST-fusion protein (1 μg) were separated by SDS-PAGE and visualized by Coomassie blue staining.

4. Preclear cell lysate (*see* **Note 7**) by adding to 1:10 vol of packed GA beads alone. Incubate at 4°C for 30 min on a rotating wheel. Pellet the beads in a microfuge at 3000*g* for 1 min and transfer supernatant to a second tube containing 1:10 vol of GST-loaded GA beads. Rotate at 4°C for 30 min.
5. Pellet the beads and transfer precleared lysate to a tube containing 1:10 vol of packed GA beads loaded with the protein of interest. Incubate at 4°C for 2 h on a rotating wheel.
6. Pellet the beads in a microfuge at 3000*g* for 1 min. Remove lysate and wash the beads five times with 0.5 mL lysis buffer (*see* **Note 10**). Transfer the beads to a new tube during the final wash.
7. Resuspend the beads in 20–50 μL of 1X SDS-PAGE sample buffer. Heat to 90°C for 3 min prior to gel electrophoresis.

3.4. Detection of Interacting Proteins

If the interacting proteins are previously identified, then samples of beads can simply be immunoblotted for the protein of interest. Alternatively, if you are looking for novel interactors, then it is necessary to use metabolically labeled cell extracts (*see* **Note 11**). Gels of bound proteins can then be autoradiographed to detect interacting proteins.

3.5. Coinfection Assay

The coinfection assay is useful if an interaction has been defined and clones are available for the two proteins. In addition, it may be useful if the interaction cannot be detected in vitro, for example, if one of the two proteins is a transmembrane protein and would thus undergo a conformational change when released from the membrane in detergent solution. One protein can be expressed as a GST- or 6-His-fusion protein, and the other as the native, unmodified protein. For example, the following procedure was used in the author's laboratory to identify a myristoylation-dependent interaction between human CD4 and a Nef-GST-fusion protein *(7)*.

1. Set up the required number of 25-cm^2 tissue culture flasks with 5×10^6 Sf9 cells in 5 mL TC100/10% FCS at least 1 h prior to infection.
2. Infect cells with 3–5 PFU/cell of each recombinant baculovirus. Rock for 1 h at room temperature.
3. Remove inoculum and replace with 5 mL TC100/10% FCS. Incubate at 28°C for 40–48 h.
4. By this time the cells should be easily dislodged by pipeting up and down. Pellet the cells in a 15-mL polypropylene tube at 500*g* for 5 min.
5. Wash cells in 1 mL ice-cold PBS and transfer to screw-cap Eppendorf tube.
6. Lyse pellet in 200 µL lysis buffer (*see* **Note 1**) containing protease inhibitors.
7. Clarify lysate (microfuge, 11,000*g*, 5 min). Store at –20°C.
8. Add 50 µL clarified lysate to 10 µL packed GA beads, prewashed in lysis buffer. Make up the vol to 100 µL with lysis buffer. Incubate at 4°C for 2 h on a rotating wheel.
9. Pellet the beads in a microfuge at 3000*g* for 30 s. Wash five times with 0.5 mL lysis buffer (*see* **Note 10**).
10. During the last wash, transfer the beads to a fresh tube. Resuspend the beads in 20–50 µL 1X SDS-PAGE sample buffer. Heat to 90°C for 3 min prior to gel electrophoresis.
11. Analyze by immunoblotting for the nonfused protein. Recovery of the tagged protein can be verified by subsequent stripping of blots and reprobing with antibodies to the fusion protein (or GST, *see* **Note 2**).

3.6. Purification of Six-Histidine Tagged Proteins

The purification of 6-His tagged proteins is more empirical than GST-fusion proteins, possibly because of the small nature of the affinity tag and the likelihood that it might be occluded within the tertiary structure of the protein. A purification strategy that works well for one protein might be unsuitable for another. Following is a detailed method, with possible alternative steps, that can be tried for their suitability for particular proteins.

1. Lyse infected cells as described in **Subheading 3.2.2.** (*see* **Note 12**).
2. Add clarified lysate to Ni-NTA agarose beads and incubate at 4°C for 1 h on a rotating wheel.

3. Wash beads twice with 10 vol PBS.
4. After the last wash, resuspend the beads in 10 vol of PBS and pour into a 1-mL disposable chromatography column. Allow to pack, but do not let the column dry out.
5. Elute the 6-His tagged protein with 0.1*M* citrate buffer, pH 6.0. Alternatively, elute fusion protein with 50 m*M* EDTA or 250 m*M* imidazole in PBS.
6. Collect 0.25-mL fractions and determine protein concentration by Bradford assay or similar commercially available protein concentration assay kit.
7. Pool protein-containing fractions and dialyze overnight against two changes of a suitable neutral buffer (*see* **Note 13**).
8. Ni-NTA agarose can be reused (*see* **Note 14**).

3.7. Modifications for Bacterial Expression

Expression of bacterial GST-fusion proteins can give very high levels of expression if the protein is expressed in a soluble and undegraded form. Yields as high as 15 mg/L of culture are possible. If the protein of interest is not post-translationally modified or if it is not large or hydrophobic, then an *E. coli* expression approach should be the first consideration. A number of pGEX vectors are now available commercially with a variety of cloning sites; however, it is still convenient in most cases to generate coding sequences by PCR. Positive clones for expression can be identified by immunoblotting of whole-cell lysates or immunodot blotting of cultures spotted onto nitrocellulose membranes as follows.

3.7.1. Identification of Positive Clones from Small-Scale Cultures by Immuno-Dot Blotting

1. Grow small-scale cultures (1–2 mL) overnight with shaking at 37°C in L-broth containing 100 μg/mL ampicillin.
2. Dilute 1:10 in L-broth (*see* **Note 15**) and grow for 2 h with shaking at 37°C.
3. Add IPTG from a stock of 50 m*M* (stored at 4°C) to a final concentration of 0.1 m*M*, and continue growth for 1 h.
4. For immunoblotting, pellet 250 μL of culture in a microfuge tube and resuspend in 20 μL of 1X SDS-PAGE sample buffer. Heat to 90°C for 3 min prior to gel electrophoresis (*see* **Note 16**).
5. Alternatively, for immuno-dot blotting, spot 5–10 μL of culture onto a nitrocellulose filter and place on a sheet of 3MM paper saturated in 1% SDS at 80°C for 30 min. Process the nitrocellulose as per standard Western blot procedure.

3.7.2. Large-Scale Purification of GST-Fusion Proteins from E. coli

For large scale purification of *E. coli*-expressed GST-fusion proteins, bacteria should be lysed by sonication to release the protein in a soluble and nondenatured form. The overriding considerations in the production of intact, undegraded protein are to work quickly and keep the samples at 4°C. With access to a large centrifuge rotor such as the Beckman JA10, up to 3 L of culture can be processed rapidly with only one spin.

1. Grow a 300-mL culture overnight, with shaking at 37°C in L-broth containing 100 µg/mL ampicillin.
2. Dilute 1:10 in L-broth (*see* **Note 15**) and grow for 2 h, with shaking at 37°C. L-broth used for dilution need not be sterilized, but should be prewarmed to room temperature, or, preferably, 37°C (*see* **Note 17**).
3. Add IPTG from a stock of 50 m*M* (stored at 4°C) to a final concentration of 0.1 m*M* and continue growth for 1–2 h.
4. Spin cells down in a prechilled centrifuge rotor (9000 rpm for 5 min). Rapidly resuspend the pellet in ice-cold PBS containing protease inhibitors (1 µg/mL leupeptin and pepstatin A, 2 µg/mL aprotinin, 0.2 m*M* PMSF, and 5 m*M* EDTA). Use 10 mL PBS per liter of starting culture.
5. Sonicate in glass universals for 3 × 30-s bursts. Chill on ice between bursts (*see* **Note 18**).
6. Spin sonicate at 20,000 rpm for 30 min at 4°C.
7. Add clarified lysate to 3 mL preswollen GA beads in a 50-mL polypropylene tube. Thereafter the samples can be processed as in **Subheading 3.2.2. (step 4** onward), with due allowance for the increased volume of beads during the washes and elution steps.

4. Notes

1. For proteins that are expected to be cytoplasmic, lyse in nonionic detergent, e.g., 1% Triton X100 or NP40; for expected nuclear proteins, lysis buffer should contain an ionic detergent, such as 0.1% SDS or sodium deoxycholate.
2. A suitable murine monoclonal specific for GST, designated vpg66, was produced by Tom Dunsford in the author's laboratory and is available from the author upon request.
3. A useful starting point is 10 flasks, which should yield up to 1 mg of purified GST-fusion protein.
4. If a rocking platform is not available, manually tilt the flasks every 15 min to distribute the inoculum evenly over the entire monolayer and to ensure that it does not dry out.
5. Cells can be dislodged either by vigorous shaking of the flasks, or bashing with the palm of your hand several times.
6. If required, protease inhibitors can be added prior to freezing stocks; however, proteolysis is most likely to be promoted by repeated cycles of freeze–thawing. It is more important to store protein in small aliquots so that each aliquot will only be frozen and thawed once.
7. A number of published studies have used protein purified from lysates directly to investigate interactions, rather than eluting the protein and rebinding to beads. However, in my experience, this leads to a greater-than-acceptable level of background, possibly caused by nonspecific binding of cellular proteins to GA beads. By specifically eluting GST-fusion proteins by competition with soluble reduced

glutathione, and subsequently rebinding to beads, these nonspecific contaminants can be eliminated.

8. Note that not all of the initial soluble protein will bind, the amount that does is determined by the initial concentration. Thus, if more that one protein sample is being loaded, it is important to ensure that the concentrations of each protein sample are normalized.
9. Baculovirus recombinants expressing either GST alone or a myristoylated GST species (with the HIV-1gag p17 myristoylation sequence at the N-terminus) are available from the author upon request. These recombinants express high levels of GST and can be used to prepare adequate stocks of purified control proteins.
10. To avoid loss of beads during washes, remove the tubes from the microfuge immediately when the spin has finished and place at an angle on ice so that the beads remain on the wall of the tube rather than settling to the bottom. Remove the wash by aspiration with a 1-mL syringe and 25-gage needle, keeping the needle point away from the beads.
11. At this stage, extracts from the target cells, i.e., those that the investigator believes contain proteins that may interact with the protein of interest are required. Initially, it will probably be necessary to prepare extracts from metabolically labeled cells to allow the detection of interacting proteins by autoradiography/fluorography. Details of such methods are beyond the scope of this chapter. Choice of lysis buffer and amounts of cells used in these assays are empirical; however, the author's experience in looking for proteins from Jurkat T-cells that interacted with the HIV-1 Nef protein may provide a useful starting point: Cells were labeled with (^{35}S)methionine for 4 h and lysed in a buffer containing 1% Triton X100 at a concentration of 5×10^7 cells/mL. 5×10^6 cell equivalents (100 μL) of lysate were used per assay ***(5)***.
12. Unlike GST-fusion proteins, which must be extracted under conditions that allow stable binding of GST to glutathione (nonionic detergents or less than 0.03% SDS), the 6-His tag will bind tightly to Ni-NTA under harsh denaturing conditions. Cells can therefore be lysed in ionic detergents if necessary.
13. In the author's laboratory, 20 m*M* sodium phosphate buffer at pH 7.2 was used.
14. This procedure strips the Ni^{2+} from the matrix. NTA-agarose can be regenerated by first washing in 3*M* NaCl to remove any residual protein and incubating in 50 m*M* $NiSO_4$, followed by washing in PBS. Store the matrix at 4°C in PBS, it is not necessary to add azide.
15. It is not necessary to add ampicillin at this stage.
16. Take care when loading the sample, it will be viscous because of the amount of chromosomal DNA. Viscosity can be reduced by passing the sample through a 25-gage needle several times, although, if this strategy is to be undertaken, larger volumes of lysate will need to be prepared (at least 200 μL from 2.5 mL of culture).
17. Growth will be optimized by the use of baffled flasks to increase aeration. Be sure to add antifoam emulsion and do not overfill the flasks, 1 L in a 2-L flask is sufficient.
18. It is convenient to divide the sample between three universals, so that one sample can be sonicated while the others are replaced on ice to cool down.

References

1. Smith, D. B. and Johnson, K. S. (1988) Single-step purification of polypeptides expressed in *Escherichia coli* as fusions with glutathione-S-transferase. *Gene* **67,** 31–40.
2. Duronio, R. J., Reed, S. I., and Gordon, J. I. (1992) Mutations of human myristoyl-CoA:protein N-myristoyltransferase cause temperature-sensitive myristic acid auxotrophy in Saccharomyces cerevisiae. *Proc. Natl. Acad. Sci. USA* **89,** 4129–4133.
3. Davies, A. H., Jowett, J. B. M., and Jones, I. M. (1993) Recombinant baculovirus vectors expressing glutathione-S-transferase fusion proteins. *Bio/Technology* **11,** 933–936.
4. Wang, Y., Davies, A. H., and Jones, I. M. (1995) Expression and purification of a glutathione-S-transferase tagged HIV-1 gp120: no evidence for an interaction with CD26. *Virology* **208,** 142–146.
5. Harris, M. and Coates, K. (1993) Identification of cellular proteins that bind to the human immunodeficiency virus type 1 *nef* gene product *in vitro*: a role for myristylation. *J. Gen. Virol.* **74,** 1581–1589.
6. King, L. A. and Possee, R. D. (1992) *The Baculovirus Expression System: A Laboratory Guide.* Chapman and Hall, London.
7. Harris, M. P. G. and Neil, J. C. (1994) Myristoylation-dependent binding of HIV-1 Nef to CD4. *J. Mol. Biol.* **241,** 136–142.
8. Livingstone, C. and Jones, I. (1989) Baculovirus expression vectors with single strand capability. *Nucleic Acids Res.* **17,** 2366.

9

Molecular Genetic Approaches I

Two-Hybrid Systems

Graeme B. Bolger

1. Introduction

The two-hybrid system is a powerful yeast-based genetic system for isolating cDNAs encoding proteins that interact with a protein of interest. First proposed by Fields and colleagues ***(1)***, the two-hybrid system has enabled investigators to isolate and characterize numerous protein–protein interactions, and to isolate novel interacting partners for many biologically important enzyme complexes, signaling proteins, and transcription factors. In some cases, the two-hybrid system has demonstrated interactions between proteins that were either too transient, or too unstable, to be detected by traditional biochemical analysis. However, the two-hybrid system can also generate numerous false-positive interactions that often complicate the analysis of results obtained with this method. This chapter will first describe the theoretical basis for the two-hybrid system, and provide a primer for understanding the yeast genetics needed for a full understanding of the method. It will then provide several detailed protocols for performing a two-hybrid screen. It will describe a battery of genetic tests required for confirming positives isolated by the method.

Finally, it will describe briefly the one-hybrid system, a variation on the two-hybrid system that has been described recently.

1.1. Understanding the Genetics Underlying the Two-Hybrid System

A basic knowledge of yeast genetics and molecular biology is necessary to understand how protein–protein interactions are identified by the two-hybrid system. The development of the two-hybrid system was based on research on

From: *Methods in Molecular Biology, Vol. 88: Protein Targeting Protocols*
Edited by: R. A. Clegg Humana Press Inc., Totowa, NJ

transcriptional activators performed in the 1980s by a number of groups, especially those of Ptashne and Struhl *(2–6)*. These groups demonstrated that a number of transcriptional regulatory proteins, including the bacterial LEXA protein and the yeast *GAL4* gene product, among many others, consisted of two independent protein domains: a DNA-binding domain, and an activation domain. The DNA-binding domain bound to a specific nucleotide sequence in the promoter of a gene, but was insufficient for activation of transcription. The activation domain could not bind to DNA, but could activate transcription when brought into close proximity with the DNA-binding domain. In the normal physiologic context, the DNA-binding and activation domains are part of the same polypeptide, but it is possible to activate the transcriptional machinery with DNA-binding domains and activation domains that are on separate polypeptides, provided that they are brought into close proximity with each other. The pairing of DNA-binding and activation domains need not be specific, in that a particular DNA-binding domain can be paired with a number of different activation domains, and vice versa.

Fields and colleagues *(1,7,8)* first demonstrated that the DNA-binding and acidic activation domains of the GAL4 protein *(9)* could be separated and that each of them could be fused to other proteins, yet retain their biological functions. Because two fusion proteins were generated in these experiments, the term "two hybrid" was used to describe these fusions. Next, Fields and colleagues demonstrated that the association between DNA-binding and activation-domain hybrids could be mediated by interactions between the regions of the hybrids that were derived from the other proteins in the hybrids, rather than directly between the DNA-binding and activation domains (**Fig. 1**). They then used the ability of the hybrids to interact and stimulate transcription, as an assay for interactions between the two other proteins incorporated in the fusions. Since hybrids incorporating any two proteins can be generated in this way, interactions between any two proteins could be tested. Furthermore, if a DNA-binding domain hybrid was generated with a particular protein of interest (i.e., to form a "bait"), cDNAs encoding proteins that interacted with this protein could be isolated from a library, if they were generated as fusions to the activation domain (the "prey"). In practice, baits are always created as fusions to the DNA-binding domain, and prey are generated as activation domain fusions.

1.2. Choice of Yeast Strains

The two-hybrid systems that are currently in use employ elements that are functionally equivalent to those developed by Fields and colleagues (**Tables 1–3**). Each of these systems was developed independently, and appear superficially to have little in common with each other. However, because the DNA-binding domains used in most of these systems can be activated by a variety of

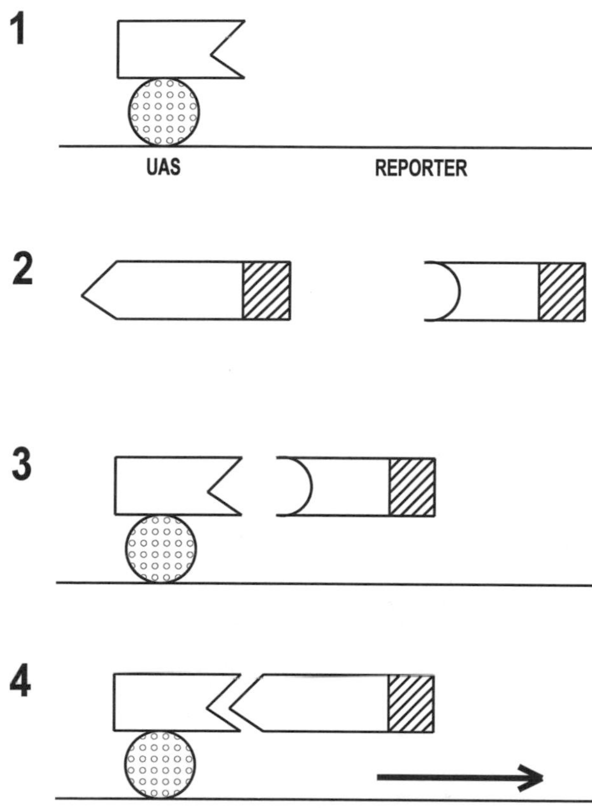

Fig. 1. The two-hybrid system. Schematic diagrams of various components of an *S. cerevisae* two-hybrid transcriptional system are shown. The heavy line indicates an upstream activating sequence acting as a promoter (UAS; e.g., *GAL1* or *LEXA*), and the reporter gene used to detect interactions (REPORTER; e.g., *LacZ* or *HIS3*). The DNA-binding domain is represented by a circle. The activation domain is represented by a cross-hatched box. The various proteins fused to either the DNA-binding domain, or to the activation domain, are represented by open figures. **(1)** A cell containing only the DNA-binding domain hybrid (the bait). The fusion protein binds to the promoter, but, in the absence of an activation domain, no transcription occurs. **(2)** Various DNA-binding domain fusions (prey) encoded by a two-hybrid cDNA library. Some of these fusions can potentially interact with the DNA-binding domain fusion in (1), whereas others cannot. **(3)** A cell as in (1), but also containing an activation-domain fusion protein. The activating domain functions when placed close to the DNA-binding domain, which occurs ONLY if the two proteins physically interact with each other. In this case, the prey does not interact with the bait, and no transcription occurs. **(4)** A cell as in (3), but containing a different prey, which interacts with the bait. In this cell, the DNA-binding and activation domains are brought into close proximity, and transcription of the reporter gene occurs. (Modified from **refs.** *1* and *7*.)

Table 1
Yeast Strains Commonly Used in the Two-Hybrid System

Name	Genotype[a]	Ref.
YPB2	*Mat***a** *ura3-52 his3-200 ade2-101 lys2-801 trp1-901 leu2-3,112 can*^{r} *gal4-542 gal80-538 LYS2::GAL1*$_{UAS}$*- LEU2*$_{TATA}$*- HIS3 URA3::GAL4*$_{17\text{-mers(3x)}}$ *-CYC1*$_{TATA}$*- lacZ*	***(14,45)***
YPB3	*Mat***a** *ura3-52 his3-200 ade2-101 lys2-801 trp1-901 leu2-3,112 can*^{r} *gal4-542 gal80-538 LYS2::GAL1*$_{UAS}$*- GAL1*$_{TATA}$*- HIS3*	***(15)***
Y153	*Mat***a** *leu2-3,112 ura3-52 trp1-901 his3-200 ade2-101 gal4 gal80 URA3::GAL-lacZ LYS2::Gal-HIS3*	***(12)***
L40	*Mat***a** *trp1-901 leu2-3,112 his3-200 ade2 GAL4 gal80? LYS2::(lexAop)*$_4$ *-HIS3 URA3::(lexAop)*$_8$ *-lacZ*	***(11)***
JC1	*Matα trp1 leu2 his3 lys2 ura3 ade2*	***(11)***
HF7c	*MAT***a** *ura3-52 his3-200 ade2-101 lys2-801 trp1-901 leu2-3,112 gal4-542 gal80-538 LYS2::GAL1*$_{UAS}$ *G-AL1*$_{TATA}$ *HIS3 URA3::GAL4*$_{17\text{-mers(3x)}}$ *-CYC1*$_{TATA}$*- lacZ*	***(15)***
EGY48	*Mat***a** *trp1 ura3 his3 LEU2::pLexAop6-LEU2*	***(18)***
PL3	*Matα ura3-1 his3-200 leu2-1 trp1::(ERE)*$_3$ *URA3*	***(19)***
AMR70	*Matα his3 lys2 trp1 leu2 GAL4 gal80? URA3::(lexAop)*$_8$ *lacZ*	

[a]The genotype is incomplete in many cases.

Table 2
Plasmids Encoding DNA-Binding Domain Fusions

Name	Domain	Selective markers[a]	Strain[b]	Ref.
pGBT9	*GAL4*	*TRP*	YPB2, YPB3	***(14,15,46)***
pBTM116 (pLEXA)	*LEXA*	*TRP*	L40	***(11)***
pAS1	*GAL4*	*TRP1*	Y153	***(12)***
pL202PL	*LEXA*	*HIS*	EGY48	***(18)***
pBL1	Estrogen receptor	*HIS*	PL3	***(19)***

[a]All plasmids also contain a gene encoding β-lactamase, for selection in *E. coli*.
[b]*S. cerevisiae* strain containing an appropriate reporter construct.

activation domains, the elements of many of the systems can be interchanged, as described in detail below (*see* **Subheading 1.2.3.**).

1.2.1. Introduction to Yeast Strain Nomenclature

A variety of strains of the yeast *Saccharomyces cerevisiae* have been developed for the two-hybrid system (**Table 1**). To understand the use of these strains, a brief introduction to yeast genetics and strain nomenclature is essen-

Table 3
Plasmids Encoding Activation Domain Fusions

Name	Domain	Selective markers	Compatible DNA binding domain	Ref.
pGAD, pGADGH	*GAL4*	*LEU*	(All)	***(7,14)***
pVP16	*VP-16*	*LEU*	(All)	***(11)***
pACT	*GAL4*	*LEU*	(All)	***(12)***[a]
pJG4-5	*B42*	*TRP*	*LEXA*, possibly others	***(18)***
pASV	*VP16*	*LEU*	(All)	***(19)***

[a]Also available as part of the lambda bacteriophage λACT.

tial. For further details, standard references should be consulted ***(10)***. Almost all the yeast mutations required for an understanding of the two-hybrid system are recessive and occur in genes encoding enzymes involved in the synthesis of amino acids. Strains with mutations in one or more of these genes will grow in rich medium (e.g., YPAD; *see* **Subheading 2.1.**), but will not grow in minimal medium lacking the appropriate amino acid(s). In the standard *S. cerevisiae* chromosomal genotyping nomenclature, recessive mutations are written in lower case, followed in most cases by the specific allele (e.g., *trp1-901* indicates a recessive mutation in the *TRP1* gene, in this case allele 901). Dominant mutations are written in upper case. Genes that have been disrupted by the insertion of a recombinant DNA construct are indicated by a double colon (e.g., *LYS2*::[lexAop]4 *HIS3* indicates a disruption of the *LYS2* gene by the insertion of a construct containing the *HIS3* gene, preceded by 4 copies of the lexA promoter). The complete genotype also includes the mating type (e.g., *MAT*α).

1.2.2. Recessive Chromosomal Mutations Can Be Complemented by Genes on Plasmids

A property of yeast that is essential to the two-hybrid system is that recessive chromosomal mutations can be complemented (i.e., their phenotype reversed) by the insertion of a plasmid containing the wild-type allele. For example, a yeast strain that contains a *trp1* mutation, which requires tryptophan for growth (i.e., is a tryptophan auxotroph), can grow on media lacking tryptophan if it contains a plasmid encoding the *TRP1* gene. The ability to grow in the absence of a certain amino acid (i.e., prototrophy) can be used to select for yeast cells that have taken up a certain plasmid. Multiple plasmids can be maintained in a yeast cell if they complement different yeast mutations, and when appropriate selective media is used. Plasmids can also be lost from a yeast cell if it is grown on nonselective medium (e.g., a cell that is chromosomally *trp1* and *leu2*, but containing two plasmids, one *LEU2* and the other *TRP1*, can be induced to lose selectively the *TRP1* plasmid by growing it in media containing tryptophan, but lacking leucine).

1.2.3. Strains Used in the Two-Hybrid System

The chief difference between the various yeast strains commonly used in two-hybrid screens is in the type of reporter gene construct that has been integrated in the yeast genome (**Table 1**). The first strains that were developed use a colorimetric assay to detect interactions. In these strains, a bacterial gene encoding β-galactosidase *(LacZ)* is placed downstream from the *GAL1* promoter. Activation of the *GAL1* promoter induces β-galactosidase activity, which can be detected by its ability to turn individual colonies blue (*see* **Subheading 3.7.**).

All the strains commonly in use today include two reporter constructs, which allow for interacting partners to be selected both by their ability to grow on media lacking various amino acids, as well as by a colorimetric assay (**Table 1**). The promoter construct for the colorimetric assay is similar to that described in the previous paragraph (i.e., it contains the *LacZ* gene downstream from the promoter used in the selective assay). Several different selective schemes have been developed. In the histidine selection scheme developed by Hollenberg and colleagues, the *HIS3* gene is placed downstream from a compound promoter generated from pieces of the yeast *GAL1* and *Escherichia coli LEXA* promoters, which allows interacting partners to be detected by growth in the absence of histidine ***(11)***. In the scheme of Elledge and colleagues, the *HIS3* gene is placed downstream of the *GAL1* promoter ***(12,13)***. Beach and colleagues have placed the *HIS3* gene downstream from the *GAL4* promoter ***(14–16)***. Brent and colleagues have placed the *LEU2* gene downstream from the *LEXA* promoter ***(17,18)***. LeDouarin and colleagues have placed the *URA3* gene downstream from the estrogen response element ***(19)***. Each of the above schemes can be further modified by additional engineering of the promoter sequences. It has now become common to use multiple copies of a core region of the promoter upstream of the reporter gene, which, at least in theory, increases the signal. Potentially, this increases the likelihood of detecting weak interactions, at the cost of some increase in background.

Two-hybrid screens that use histidine selection have the additional advantage that the histidine biosynthesis pathway can be inhibited, at least in part, by the addition of 3-aminotriazole (3-AT) to the culture medium ***(20)***. Addition of 3-AT increases the amount of *HIS3* activity required to produce a colony, and therefore can suppress background colonies that interfere with screening. The types of background that can be suppressed with the use of 3-AT include colonies that grow because of activity of the promoter in the absence of the activation domain ("leakiness"). The *GAL1* promoter in particular is quite leaky, and relatively high concentrations (25–50 m*M*) of 3-AT are necessary to reduce background when it is used. These high concentrations of 3-AT significantly increase the time needed for positive colonies to grow to detectable size, and also reduce the transformation efficiency. The *GAL4* and *LEXA* promoters have sufficiently low background that the use of 3-AT is frequently not necessary. However, in some situations, the use of low concentrations of 3-AT (1–5 m*M*) can reduce the number of colonies that grow as a result of weak interactions between the bait and prey. Many of these weak signals are unlikely to reflect physiologic interactions, and can greatly increase the labor involved in screening. Excessive use of 3-AT can obliterate all signals, including those generated by true positives.

The uracil selection scheme of LeDouarin and colleagues ***(19)*** provides a similar means for fine-tuning the strength of positives. In this scheme, 6-azauracil, an inhibitor of the *URA3* gene product, can be incorporated into the medium used to select positives.

Aside from the type of reporter construct, the yeast strains commonly used for the two-hybrid system may differ in other ways. The commonly used strains have different genetic backgrounds. In particular, each of the commonly used strains has a different (but overlapping) set of mutated genes encoding selectable markers (**Table 1**). This will in turn mean that each strain can be transformed only by a limited set of plasmids.

1.3. Choice of Vectors and Libraries

1.3.1. DNA-Binding Domain Plasmids Used in the Two-Hybrid System

A wide variety of plasmids that encode fusions between various DNA-binding domains and a protein of interest (i.e., baits) have been developed (**Table 2**). The pGBT... series, developed by Fields and colleagues ***(7)***, are the prototype DNA-binding fusion plasmids, and encode fusions with the DNA-binding domain (amino acids 1–147) of the yeast *GAL4* gene product ***(9)***. Other groups have also constructed plasmids using the *GAL4* DNA-binding domain ***(12,21)***. Several groups, including those of Fields and Brent, have developed plasmids encoding fusions with the DNA-binding and carboxyl-terminal oligomerization domains of the *LEXA* protein (amino acids 1–202 ***[22]***; e.g., pBTM116 ***[11]***, and pPL202PL ***[17,18]***). The DNA-binding domains of the yeast *ACE1* gene ***(23)***, and of the estrogen-response element ***(19)***, have also been used. The *GAL4* and *LEXA* DNA-binding domains are most commonly used at the present time.

Aside from the DNA-binding domain, the bait plasmids developed by various investigators can differ in other ways. Several different promoters have been used to initiate transcription of the DNA-binding domain fusion. The most commonly used promoter is the constitutive yeast *ADH1* promoter, and it is always paired with *ADH1* transcriptional termination sequences placed downstream of the fusion protein sequence. Other promoters have been used successfully (e.g., the yeast glyceraldehyde-3-phosphate dehydrogenase promoter *[23]*, the yeast phosphoglucokinase *[PGK]* promoter *[19]*, and the ADC1 promoter *[21]*). There is no clear advantage to choosing any one of these promoters over any other. However, the level of expression of the DNA-binding domain fusion may be important in some cases, because high-level expression of some baits may be toxic to the cell. Another factor that may influence the choice of DNA-binding domain vector is the selective marker that it encodes. Most frequently, this is *TRP1*, but others, e.g., *HIS3* ***(17–19)*** or *LEU2* ***(21)***, have been used.

1.3.2. Plasmids Encoding Activation-Domain Hybrid Proteins

Numerous plasmids that encode activation-domain hybrids (i.e., prey) have been developed (**Table 3**). The most important difference between these vectors is the particular activation domain that is used. The pGAD... series of plasmids employ the *GAL4* acidic-activation domain (amino acids 768–881 ***[9]***), and have been used by most groups ***(7,14,15)***. Other groups have also prepared *GAL4* activation-domain vectors ***(12,15,21)***. Other activation domains that have been employed include the VP16 acidic-activation domain ***(11,19)***, and the *ACE1* activation domain (in combination with the *ACE1* DNA-binding domain, ***[23]***). Most vectors express the activation–domain fusion off the *ADH1* promoter and terminator, but other promoters (e.g., ADC1 ***[12]***) have been used. Selection usually employs the *LEU2* gene ***(7,11,12,19,23)***, but other markers (e.g., *TRP1* ***[17,18,21]***) have also been employed.

Some of the activation-domain fusion vectors that have been described also contain other useful sequences of interest. Many contain f1 origins of replication (which can be used to generate single-stranded DNA for sequencing). Several groups have prepared two-hybrid λ-bacteriophage vectors, which can then be converted to activation-domain plasmids. These dual-function vectors are useful in the generation of two-hybrid libraries. For example, the λ-ACT system ***(12)*** allows activation–domain plasmid libraries to be generated from λ-bacteriophage libraries by the use of the cre/lox system, and the hybriZAP system (Stratagene, La Jolla, CA) allows activation domain plasmid libraries to be generated from lambda bacteriophage libraries by the use of single-stranded helper phage.

One important issue in the choice of an activation–domain vector is the use of a nuclear localization signal (NLS) on the fusion protein. Obviously, the two fusion proteins must migrate to the yeast nucleus to activate the promoter–reporter gene complex. In many cases, the two fusions may form a complex in the cytoplasm, which is then transferred to the nucleus. In others, the complex could be formed in the nucleus (e.g., after the DNA-binding fusion has already bound to the promoter). Most of the commonly used activation–domain fusion plasmids encode a NLS, which would enable complexes that form in the cytoplasm to migrate into the nucleus. Some DNA-binding fusion vectors have been designed to encode a NLS, but published experience with these vectors is limited *(19)*. In most cases, they increase signal, but at the cost of some increase in background. The *GAL4* gene product does not have a typical NLS, but has been shown to localize to the nucleus *(24)*.

1.3.3. Pairing of Bait and Prey Plasmids

Because almost all of the DNA-binding domains used in the two-hybrid system can be activated by a variety of activation domains, most of the commonly used bait/promoter–reporter systems can be paired with a variety of prey plasmids. This feature of the two-hybrid system allows many vectors to be used on more than one host, and is particularly useful when a cDNA library, originally designed for use with one host system, is used in a second host. The choice of selective markers encoded by both bait and prey plasmids must be compatible with the auxotrophic markers in the yeast strain that is used for the screen. If there is any doubt about the compatibility of any pair of bait and prey plasmids, pilot experiments should be performed, using plasmids encoding fusion proteins that are known to interact (**Table 3**) with the yeast strain that is to be employed in the screen.

2. Materials

2.1. Yeast Media

1. Standard microbiological media (*see* **Subheading 3.1.1.** for a complete list).
2. Amino acids, used preferably as base, without adjustment of pH, should be obtained from the highest quality supplier (Calbiochem, San Diego, CA, or Sigma, St. Louis, MO), and stored for a year or longer at 4°C. The other ingredients listed in **Subheading 3.1.2.** can also be purchased from the same suppliers.
3. Yeast nitrogen base (Difco, Detroit, MI).
4. Dextrose.
5. Standard microbiological plates.

2.2. Propagation and Storage of Strains and Libraries

1. Yeast media (*see* **Subheading 2.1.**).
2. Glycerol. Sterilize by autoclaving.

2.3. Amplification of Libraries

LB and TB media. *See* any standard molecular biology reference (e.g., **ref.** ***25***).

2.4. Preparation of the Bait

Standard reagents for preparation of plasmids *(25)*.

2.5. Transformation of Yeast

1. 3-Aminotriazole (3-AT) is available from Sigma. Prepare a 3*M* stock in water. Store at 4°C for up to 2 mo. Add to media, prior to autoclaving, to a final concentration of 1–50 m*M* (*see* **Subheading 1.2.3.**).
2. Yeast media (*see* **Subheading 2.1.**).
3. 100 m*M* Lithium acetate, 10 m*M* Tris-HCl, pH 8.0, 1 m*M* EDTA. Sterilize by autoclaving. Store at room temperature.
4. 40% Polyethylene glycol 4000, 100 m*M* lithium acetate, 10 m*M* Tris-HCl, pH 8.0, 1 m*M* EDTA. Sterilize by autoclaving. Store at room temperature.
5. Dimethyl sulfoxide. This should be of spectrophotometric grade.
6. Salmon testis DNA: Salmon testis DNA is available from Sigma. Resuspend to a concentration of 10 mg/mL in 10 m*M* Tris-HCl, pH 8.0, 1 m*M* EDTA by gentle agitation overnight. Shear to a fragment size of 500–2000 bp by passing through a 23-gage needle 10 times (or by briefly sonicating). Heat at 100°C for 10 min, and rapidly cool on ice. Aliquot into 1.5-mL tubes and store at –20°C (for up to 1 yr).

2.6. Testing of the Bait

1. Yeast media (*see* **Subheading 2.1.**).
2. Materials for β-galactosidase assays (*see* **Subheading 2.7.**).

2.7. β-Galactosidase Assays

1. Paper-filter circles suitable for colony or patch lifts (e.g., Whatman, Maidstone, UK, no. 50). Any nylon filter suitable for colony hybridizations can be used.
2. Thick paper filter circles of the same size as those use for colony lifts (e.g., Whatman no. 3).
3. Assay solution: 60 m*M*. Na_2HPO_4, 40 m*M* NaH_2PO_4, 10 m*M* KCl, 1 m*M* $MgSO_4$, 50 m*M* 2-mercaptoethanol (optional), 200 μL/filter Xgal stock. This solution, without the last two ingredients, should be made ahead of time, autoclaved, and stored at room temperature. Add the last two ingredients just prior to use. As Xgal is expensive, make up only the volume required for immediate use.
4. Xgal stock: 5-bromo-4-chloro-3-indolyl-β-D-galactopyanoside, dissolved in *N,N*-dimethyl formamide at a concentration of 20 mg/mL. Store for up to 1 mo at –20°C.
5. Liquid nitrogen.

2.8. Performing a Pilot Screen

Yeast media (*see* **Subheading 2.1.**).

2.9. Performing a Full-Scale Screen

Yeast media (*see* **Subheading 2.1.**).

2.10. Analysis of Positives Obtained from a Screen

1. Yeast media (*see* **Subheading 2.1.**).
2. Wooden toothpicks. These should be as flat as possible, and have blunt ends. Sterilize by autoclaving.
3. Materials for β-galactosidase assay (*see* **Subheading 2.7.**).
4. Materials for plasmid isolation from yeast (*see* **Subheading 2.11.**).
5. Materials for transformation of yeast (*see* **Subheading 2.5.**) and *E. coli* ***(25)***.

2.11. Plasmid Isolation from Yeast

1. Glass beads (0.45–0.50 mm diameter). They should be either purchased as prewashed, or washed with several volumes of concentrated nitric acid and rinsed thoroughly with double-distilled water prior to use.
2. "Smash and grab" mix: 2% Triton X-100 (optional), 1% lauryl sulfate (SDS), 100 m*M* NaCl, 10 m*M* Tris-HCl, pH 8.0, 1 m*M* EDTA. Store at room temperature.
3. Phenol/chloroform (1:1, v:v).
4. Standard reagents for transformation of *E. coli* ***(25)***.

2.12. Analysis of Positives That Have Survived Segregation Analysis

1. Yeast media (*see* **Subheading 2.1.**).
2. Materials for β-galactosidase assay (*see* **Subheading 2.7.**).
3. Materials for transformation of yeast (*see* **Subheading 2.5.**).

3. Methods

3.1. Preparation of Media

3.1.1. Rich Medium

The following recipe is for yeast peptone adenine dextrose (YPAD), a standard rich media for yeast. YPD (also called YPED) is the same medium, without adenine.

1. Combine the following:

Yeast extract	10 g
Peptone	20 g
Adenine (only if strains are *ade*)	4 mL of a 10 mg/mL stock (prepared in advance and stored at –20°C)
Dextrose	20 g
Agar (only for plates)	20 g
ddH_2O	to 1 L

2. Autoclave for 20 min.

3.1.2. Selective ("Drop-out") Medium

1. Prepare amino acid stocks by combining the following, in dry form, OMITTING any amino acid required for selection:

Adenine	0.5 g
Alanine	2.0 g
Arginine	2.0 g
Asparagine	2.0 g
Aspartic acid	2.0 g
Cysteine	2.0 g
Glutamine	2.0 g
Glutamic acid	2.0 g
Glycine	2.0 g
Histidine	2.0 g
Isoleucine	2.0 g
Leucine	4.0 g
Lysine	2.0 g
Methionine	2.0 g
myo-Inositol	2.0 g
para-Aminobenzoic acid	0.2 g
Phenylalanine	2.0 g
Proline	2.0 g
Serine	2.0 g
Threonine	2.0 g
Tryptophan	2.0 g
Tyrosine	2.0 g
Uracil	2.0 g
Valine	2.0 g

2. Grind the components thoroughly in a mortar, to assist blending. Pour into a 500-mL container, and mix the combination thoroughly by inverting the container up and down for at least 15 min (adding a few marbles is a good idea). This mixture is stable for at least 6 mo at room temperature (*see* **Note 1**).
3. Combine the following:

Yeast nitrogen base WITHOUT amino acids, WITH ammonium sulfate (Difco)	6.7 g
Amino acid mix, from above	2 g
Dextrose	20 g
Agar (only for plates)	20 g
ddH_2O	to 1 L

4. Autoclave for 15 min (longer autoclaving times often produce mushy plates).

3.2. Propagation and Storage of Yeast Strains

1. Store yeast strains as follows: For short-term storage (2–3 wk), streak out on plates (with selection as appropriate) and store at room temperature or at 4°C. For longer storage (a year or more), inoculate vials of solid media (with selection as appropriate) as stabs, and store at room temperature.
2. For secure long-term storage (many years), strains should be stored as glycerol stocks at –70°C. To prepare a stock for long-term storage, use a single colony to

inoculate a 1- to 5-mL liquid culture. Allow to grow overnight in appropriate medium (until grossly turbid). Add glycerol to a final concentration of 10–30%. Aliquot into 1.5-mL tubes and place at –70°C.

3. To grow up a strain that has been stored as a long-term stock, streak out the cells on selective plates, and allow to grow for 2–3 d. Use sterile wooden toothpicks to streak out large numbers of different strains. Grow the plates for 48–72 h at 30°C. Use a single colony from these plates to inoculate a culture intended for transformation. These cultures should be inoculated from plates that are not more than 7–10 d old.

3.3. Preparation and Amplification of Two-Hybrid Libraries

3.3.1. Preparation of Libraries

Detailed discussion of techniques for the preparation of cDNA libraries is outside the scope of this chapter. Almost any standard method for the production of cDNA libraries can be adapted to the two-hybrid system. Inserts derived directly from mRNA can usually be cloned into activating-domain vectors immediately after second-strand synthesis. Alternatively, the inserts of any standard cDNA library can be cut out of the bacterial-cloning vector and ligated into the activation-domain vector. The latter approach allows for an amplification step prior to cloning in the activation-domain vector. Several groups have prepared two-hybrid λ-bacteriophage vectors, which can then be converted to activation-domain plasmids in vivo. These vectors simplify the production of two-hybrid libraries (*see* **Subheading 1.2.5.**).

3.3.2. Amplifying a Two-Hybrid Library

Prior to performing a yeast transformation, all two-hybrid libraries require amplification. This step is particularly important because relatively large amounts of DNA (tens of micrograms to milligrams) are needed in a typical yeast transformation, even when high efficiency yeast transformation protocols are used. Two-hybrid libraries cloned initially into λ-vectors will be amplified when they are converted to plasmids in vivo. Libraries generated by cloning directly into a two-hybrid plasmid vector require amplification in an appropriate *E. coli* host (e.g., DH5α or HB101).

1. Libraries are usually stored as –70°C stocks, in *E. coli*.
2. Prepare 10 cultures of suitable bacterial medium (e.g., LB or TB broth), each 25 mL. Equilibrate at 37°C in a shaker.
3. Rapidly thaw the library aliquot by swirling in a 37°C water bath.
4. Aliquot the library equally into the 10 cultures. Allow to grow until late log phase (usually to an OD_{600} of approx 0.75). This will usually take 5–8 h.
5. Optional (but strongly recommended): Take a 1-mL aliquot from each of the 10 cultures. Pool the aliquots. Add 4 mL sterile glycerol, mix, aliquot, and store at –70°C. This will create backup amplifications of the library. Because these back-

ups have undergone a relatively small amount of amplification, they should retain almost all the complexity of the original library.

6. Use each of the 25-mL cultures to inoculate 200–400 mL of LB or TB broth, containing appropriate antibiotic (e.g., ampicillin). This will produce a total of 2–4 L of final culture. Grow for at least 12 h.
7. Purify the plasmid DNA from the cultures, using a standard plasmid purification protocol (e.g., alkaline lysis *[25]*).
8. Store plasmid libraries as DNA at 4°C (for weeks to months) or at –70°C (indefinitely). Store plasmid libraries that are maintained in *E. coli* as glycerol stocks at –70°C.

3.4. Generation of a Bait

1. Clone the cDNA that encodes the protein of interest into one of the DNA-binding domain plasmids discussed above (*see* **Subheading 1.3.1.**). This cDNA should contain the full open reading frame (ORF). The cDNA must be inserted in the correct reading frame, so that the resulting plasmid encodes a fusion protein between the protein of interest and the DNA-binding domain.
2. Transform this bait into an appropriate two-hybrid yeast host, as described in the next section. In parallel, transform the empty (i.e., without an insert) DNA-binding domain plasmid into the host strain. Select for transformants by growth on appropriate selective medium (e.g., if the DNA-binding domain plasmids encode *TRP1*, isolate transformants on medium lacking tryptophan).

3.5. Transformation of Yeast (High-Efficiency Method)

This protocol is a fusion of several "high efficiency" protocols that have been published previously *(26–29)*. It should generate approx 500,000 to >2,000,000 colonies per µg of DNA, depending on the yeast strain. It can be used for all yeast transformations in this chapter. The procedure is described here for a full-scale library transformation, and can be scaled down for many experiments.

1. Inoculate a 1- to 5-mL culture of liquid medium. Use selective medium if the yeast cells already contain a plasmid. Otherwise, grow yeast strains in YPD or YPAD. Use a single colony from a plate that is not more than 1 wk old. Do not use old plates, or inoculate directly from stabs or –70°C stocks. Grow at 30°C, with shaking overnight (8–12 h minimum). The culture should be grossly turbid prior to proceeding to **step 2**. Do not incubate longer than 24–36 h.
2. Place 200–500 mL of YPAD medium in a 2-L flask, and allow to equilibrate to 30°C in an incubator/shaker, then inoculate with 1/100 vol of the overnight culture prepared in **step 1**. Do not inoculate the culture at too high an initial density.
3. Grow the cells in a shaker at 30°C, to a density of $1–2 \times 10^7$/mL (*see* **Note 2**).
4. Pellet the cells by centrifuging at 2500*g* for 10–15 min at room temperature. A fixed-angle rotor gives better recovery. Discard the supernatant.
5. Gently resuspend the cell pellet in approx one-third the initial culture volume of sterile double distilled water. Centrifuge as in **step 4**, and discard the supernatant.

6. Resuspend the cell pellet in 1/100 the initial culture volume of 100 m*M* lithium acetate, 10 m*M* Tris-HCl, pH 8.0, 1 m*M* EDTA.
7. Thoroughly mix the library DNA (100–500 μg) in 0.5 to 2.5 mL of sheared, denatured salmon testis DNA, 10 mg/mL. Add this mix to the cells. Mix the cells and the DNA thoroughly by vortexing.
8. Add six times the volume of the resuspended cells (**step 6**) of 40% polyethylene glycol 4000, 100 m*M* lithium acetate, 10 m*M* Tris-HCl, pH 8.0, 1 m*M* EDTA. Mix thoroughly by inverting the tube. Incubate at 30°C for 1 h, with gentle shaking (the duration of this step can vary: For some strains, it can be omitted entirely).
9. Add dimethyl sulfoxide, to 0.7 times the volume of the resuspended cells (**step 6**). Mix thoroughly by inverting the tube.
10. Heat-pulse the cells by incubating the tube in a 42°C water bath for 15 min. The temperature (suggested range: 42–45°C) and time for this step may need to be optimized for the strain used, the volume of the sample, and the type of tube.
11. Rapidly cool the tube by incubating in a water bath at room temperature.
12. Pellet the cells by centrifuging at 1000*g* for 10 min. This centrifugation step needs to be less vigorous than that used previously. Gently resuspend the cells in approx 5 mL of selective medium by swirling the tube.
13. Plate the cells on selective media. As a minimum, the medium must lack the amino acids necessary for selection of cells containing the desired plasmids, and, in addition, selection for interacting positives (*see* **Subheadings 1.2.**, **3.8.**, **3.9.**, **Note 3**, and **step 14** for further experimental modifications). Grow at 30°C for 72–96 h.
14. Controls for transformation: In all transformations, the following controls are recommended.
    a. Treat an aliquot of cells from the culture as outlined above, but without the addition of plasmid DNA. This is an essential negative control.
    b. To assess transformation efficiency, plate various volumes (e.g., 1/10,000, 1/1000, and 1/100 of the initial culture) on medium that selects for cells containing the plasmid that is being transformed. This will provide a measure of transformation efficiency.
15. For a discussion of alternatives and refinements on this protocol, *see* **Notes 4–6**.

3.6. Testing the Bait

Generation of a correct bait is one of the keys to success in a two-hybrid screen. Unfortunately, there is no perfect way of predicting how well a particular bait will work in a two-hybrid screen. It is therefore necessary to test a bait in small-scale experiments prior to embarking on a large-scale screen. Often, several baits will need to be constructed and tested.

1. Take the transformants containing the bait and the empty DNA-binding domain plasmid (*see* **Subheadings 3.4.** and **3.5.**) and transform them a second time with the empty activation-domain vector. Use the protocol outlined in **Subheading 3.5.**, but select for transformants by their ability to contain BOTH plasmids (e.g.,

if the DNA-binding domain plasmid is *TRP1*, and the activation-domain plasmid is *LEU2*, plate the transformants on medium lacking both tryptophan and leucine).

2. Test the resulting transformants for interaction using the β-galactosidase assay (*see* **Subheading 3.7.**).
3. If the bait construct produces low background in this assay (i.e., has β-galactosidase activity that is as low as that produced by the empty DNA-binding plasmid), then it is likely to produce low background in a screen (*see* **Note 7** for a discussion of why some baits have high background, and possible strategies for reducing background).
4. On occasion, it may be useful to subject the bait to a number of tests to ensure that it is functional in a yeast cell (*see* **Note 8**).

3.7. Analysis of Interactions by β-Galactosidase Assay

The assay described here ***(30)*** uses filters and is only semiquantitative. A number of quantitative β-galactosidase assays have been developed ***(31,32)***, but are considerably more laborious than the filter assay.

1. Transfer the colonies to a filter. This is done by placing the filter onto the colonies on the surface of the plate, letting it stand for approx 10–30 s, and then removing it. Place the filter, colonies up, on a plate with medium that selects for the plasmids (e.g., lacking tryptophan and leucine). Allow to grow for 8–12 h at 30°C (if the colonies are very large, this step can sometimes be omitted). Proceed to **step 3**.
2. As an alternative approach (preferred by the author; *see* **Note 9**), the colonies can be analyzed as patches. Using sterile wooden toothpicks, transfer colonies from the screen plates onto a plate containing medium that selects for the plasmids (e.g., lacking tryptophan and leucine). Streak out each colony uniformly as a patch (0.5 × 1.0 cm). Approximately 50 patches can be placed on a single 160-mm plate. Also patch out two important controls: the yeast strain used in the screen, containing the empty DNA-binding and empty activation domain plasmids, as a negative control, and the yeast strain, containing bait and prey plasmids known to interact, as a positive control. The author uses the oncoproteins RAS and RAF as positive controls ***(11)***, but any pair of known positives can be used. Allow the plate to grow for 12–24 h, until the patches are confluent. Place a filter onto the patches, let stand for approx 10–30 s, and then remove. Place the filter, patches up, on a plate with medium that selects for the plasmids (e.g., lacking tryptophan and leucine). Allow both plates to grow for 8–12 h at 30°C.
3. Set up the following: For each plate, place two thick filter paper circles (e.g., Whatman no. 3) in the lid of a Petri plate, and wet thoroughly with X-gal solution (about 5–7 mL for a 160-mm filter).
4. Remove the filter paper containing the yeast cells from the plates, and place it in liquid nitrogen for 10 s to 2 min. This permeabilizes the cells.
5. Place the filter, cells up, onto the filter-paper circles prepared in **step 3**. Ensure that all bubbles between the filters are carefully removed. Place at 30°C. The

patches of cells containing interacting partners will gradually turn blue. The exact time required for the cells to change color will depend on the strength of the interactions, the age of the colonies/patches, and the freshness of the Xgal that is used. The positive controls on the filters usually change color in 20–40 min. When the positive controls turn blue, remove the filters from the plates, and allow them to dry at room temperature for 30–60 min. If the filters are not dried, they will continue to develop color over the next few days. Wrap the filters in plastic wrap, and store them flattened in a notebook.

3.8. Selection of the Prey Library, and Performing a Pilot Experiment

A critical component of a successful two-hybrid screen is the cDNA library. A large number of libraries encoding fusions between activation domains and members of a cDNA library have been constructed, and an increasing number are becoming commercially available (*see* **Subheading 3.3.1.**). Fortunately for the investigator, a cDNA library of prey that has been constructed as a fusion to a specific activation domain can frequently be used in a wide variety of strains, and with different DNA-binding domain fusion baits (*see* **Subheading 1.3.3.**). The investigator will also need to consider the tissue source of the library, especially if there is reason to suspect that the distribution of an interacting partner is highly tissue-specific. For additional comments about libraries, *see* **Note 10**.

Perform a pilot screen prior to a full-scale screen, particularly if the experimenter is a novice to the procedure. In this pilot, a small number of transformants (usually less than 500,000) is screened in a scaled-down procedure designed to test the plates, plasmids, strain, and transformation protocols, and to determine the background.

1. Take a single colony of cells containing the bait plasmid, and inoculate a 5-mL liquid overnight culture of selective medium (e.g., lacking tryptophan, for baits encoded by *TRP1* plasmids). Proceed through the transformation procedure (**Subheading 3.5., steps 1–12**), with the following modifications: Use 10–50 µg of the library DNA; and scale down the transformation procedure in proportion to the amount of DNA that is used.
2. Plate the final transformants on medium that selects for both the bait and library plasmids, and which also selects for interacting partners (e.g., in most cases, lacking both tryptophan and leucine [to select for the bait and library plasmids], and lacking histidine [to select for interacting partners]; any other component necessary for selection, such as 3-AT, should also be included in the plates). Plate progressively increasing amounts of the transformation per plate (e.g., 1/10,000, 1/1,000, 1/100, 1/10). Do not plate the entire transformation.
3. To assess the transformation efficiency, plate progressively increasing amounts of the transformation (as in **step 2**) on plates, selecting only for the plasmids (e.g., lacking only tryptophan and leucine).

4. If a prolonged incubation step is used to encourage the growth of interacting partners (*see* **Note 3**), repeat the platings on media, selecting only for plasmid growth (**step 3**) after the incubation.
5. Incubate the transformation efficiency plates for 72 h, and the screen plates for 72–96 h (or up to a week, if high concentrations of 3-AT are used).
6. Count the number of colonies on the transformation efficiency plates. Divide the number of colonies on each plate by the proportion of the transformation plated on that plate: This will give the total number of transformants. Divide this number by the amount of DNA used in the transformation: This will give the transformation efficiency. A transformation efficiency of at least 1,000,000 colonies/μg library DNA is highly desirable. If a prolonged incubation step is used (**step 4**), a 5- to 20-fold increase in colony number is usually seen, but this can vary widely.
7. Assess the screen plates for background. A thick mat of cells, which divided a few times and then stopped, is typical. The thickness of the mat will depend on the proportion of the transformation that is aliquotted per plate (**step 2**). True positives will be readily visible as 1- to 3-mm colonies that grow on top of the mat. Generally, true interacting partners should appear only at a rate of 1/100,000 colonies or less, unless they are present at unusually high proportions in the library. An extremely thick mat (i.e., one that obliterates individual colonies), or a large number of individual colonies/plate indicates high background.
8. Put low background baits into a full-scale screen (*see* **Subheading 3.9.**). Various solutions to the problem of high background baits are discussed in **Note 7**.

3.9. Performing a Full-Scale Library Screen

1. Transform the appropriate yeast strain with the bait plasmid, as in **Subheading 3.8., step 1**. It may be useful to put some transformants from this step into long-term storage.
2. Take a single colony from the selective plates, and proceed through the yeast transformation protocol exactly as written (*see* **Subheading 3.5., steps 1–12**).
3. Plate the final transformants on 160-mm plates of medium that selects for both the bait and library plasmids, and which also selects for interacting partners (e.g., in most cases, lacking both tryptophan and leucine [to select for the bait and library plasmids], and lacking histidine [to select for interacting partners]; any other component necessary for selection, such as 3-AT, should also be included in the plates). Plate the entire transformation. Use an amount of the transformation per plate (e.g., 1/100–1/10), depending on which proportion gave a mat of manageable thickness in the pilot study (**Subheading 3.8., step 7**). As many as 1,000,000 transformants can be plated on a 160-mm plate. The transformation can be spread fairly thickly on the plates (up to 500 μL/plate), and allowed to dry for 30–60 min before placing the plates into the incubator.
4. To assess transformation efficiency, remove aliquots (1/10,000, 1/1000, 1/100 of the mixture) and plate these on 100-cm plates containing medium that selects only for plasmid growth (e.g., lacking tryptophan and leucine).

5. If a prolonged incubation step is used to encourage the growth of interacting partners (*see* **Note 3**), repeat the platings on media selecting only for plasmid growth (**step 4**) after the incubation.
6. Incubate the transformation efficiency plates for 72 h, and the screen plates for 72–96 h (or up to 1 wk, if high concentrations of 3-AT are used).
7. Count the number of colonies on the transformation efficiency plates. Calculate the transformation efficiency, as described above for the pilot screen (*see* **Subheading 3.7.**). A transformation efficiency of at least 1,000,000 colonies/µg library DNA is highly desirable. If a prolonged incubation step is used (**step 5**), a 5- to 20-fold increase in colony number is usually seen, but this can vary widely. Most importantly, at least 10,000,000–50,000,000 transformants should have been plated on the screen plates. This number of transformants is required if the library is to be screened exhaustively.
8. Colonies that grow larger than 1–2 mm after 72–96 h of growth on fully selective media are suitable positives that can be put into the next step.

3.10. Analysis of Positives Obtained from a Screen

Analysis of the positives obtained from a typical two-hybrid screen is usually the most laborious aspect of performing the screen. Unfortunately, typically only a small proportion (often less than 20%) of the positives obtained in a screen actually reflect the isolation of true interacting partners, even with a low-backgound bait. The chief reasons for false positives are chromosomal mutations that mimic the phenotype generated by true interacting partners and library clones that interact with the bait in the environment of the yeast nucleus, but not physiologically.

Each of the positives obtained from a screen should be analyzed by a two-step process. In the first step, positives are assayed for β-galactosidase activity. In the second, segregation analysis is performed.

3.10.1. β-Galactosidase Assay on Screen Positives

Assay of positives for beta-galactosidase activity is a quick and reliable way to ensure that positives selected by amino acid prototrophy are in fact being generated by activation of the reporter construct.

1. Use the β-galactosidase assay (*see* **Subheading 3.7.**) to test the positives obtained in the screen. If there are numerous positives (>100), this is most easily done by placing filters directly on the screen plates. Alternatively, colonies can be patched onto filters.
2. Select for segregation analysis (*see* **Subheading 3.10.2.**) only those positives that have β-galactosidase activity that is equal to or higher than that of a positive control interaction (e.g., RAS/RAF, as described in **Subheading 3.7.**). Generally, approx 25–95% of screen positives (as selected by amino acid prototrophy) will also be *LacZ* (β-galactosidase) positive. Discard positives that are *LacZ* negative.

3.10.2. Segregation Analysis

Two different techniques for segregation analysis are presented here. They are conceptually identical. In either method, the prey or bait plasmid is in some way removed from the yeast cell, and the prey plasmid is analyzed for its ability to produce the phenotype of a true interacting partner. The term "segregation analysis" is used to describe this process because it has the objective of determining whether the desired phenotype segregates with either the prey plasmid or with the yeast chromosomal genome. The choice between the two methods described here will depend on the experience of the investigator with yeast genetics, and also on the markers on the particular bait and library plasmids that are used.

3.10.2.1. Segregation Analysis by Isolation and Subsequent Retesting of the Prey Plasmid

This method, although somewhat laborious, is recommended by the author for investigators unskilled in yeast genetics. It also requires no additional yeast strains beyond those used in the original screen. It also has the advantage that prey plasmids are isolated as DNA early on in the procedure, and can then be easily studied by a functional assay.

To isolate the prey plasmid, it is transferred to an *E. coli* strain containing a mutation that can be complemented by the selective marker encoded by the plasmid. The *E. coli* strains HB101 and KC8 have a mutation in the *leuB* gene. The *E. coli* strain MC1066 is *leuB*- and *trp*- ***(33)***. These strains can therefore be used to select for prey plasmids which encode either *LEU2* or *TRP1*, when grown on appropriate selective medium.

1. Use the smash and grab procedure (*see* **Subheading 3.11.**) to isolate the plasmid DNA from the yeast cells.
2. Use the plasmid DNA to transform KC8 or MC1066. Use any standard *E. coli* transformation protocol ***(25)***. Prior to plating the cells, wash them once in M9 medium. Plate the cells on LB_{Amp100}, and then replica-plate (*see* **Note 11**) on M9 plates containing ampicillin and proline, but lacking leucine ***(25)***. The resulting colonies, which may take 48 h to grow, will contain only the "prey" plasmid.
3. Isolate the prey plasmid DNA from the *E. coli*, using any one of several standard miniprep procedures ***(25)***.
4. Transform the prey plasmid back into the yeast strain used in the screen, along with the bait plasmid (*see* **Subheading 3.5.**). The yeast strain can be transformed sequentially with each of the two plasmids, or, in many cases, simultaneously. Select for transformants that contain both plasmids on the appropriate selective medium.
5. Take a single colony from the transformation, patch out on a plate selecting for the growth of both plasmids, and perform a filter β-galactosidase assay (*see* **Subheading 3.7.**).
6. Positives that are strongly positive in the β-galactosidase assay can then be tested in confirmatory tests (*see* **Subheading 3.12.**).

Table 4
Tester Strains Suitable for Mating Assays[a]

Name	Compatible Strains	Ref.
JC1	L40	*(11)*
AMR70	L40	
L40	PL3	*(11,19)*

[a]Genotypes for these strains are in **Table 1**.

3.10.2.2. Segregation Analysis by Mating

Many experienced yeast geneticists prefer this approach. One advantage of this method is that segregation analysis can often be combined with some of the confirmatory tests that are normally performed on positives (*see* **Subheading 3.12.**). In this method, cells from positive colonies are induced to selectively lose the bait plasmid. Cells that have lost the plasmid are then mated with a tester yeast strain containing the bait plasmid. They are also mated to a tester strain containing a different bait, as a control. As yeasts are normally haploid, the resulting cells are diploid. The diploids are then tested for β-galactosidase activity. Only cells that do have β-galactosidase activity upon mating with the tester/bait, but do not have activity on mating with the tester/control plasmid, are considered to be true positives.

A variety of tester strains (**Table 4**) have been used in this procedure ***(11,13,19)***; a similar approach is used in a commercially available kit (Clontech, Palo Alto, CA). The most important characteristic of the tester strain is that it must be of opposite mating type from the strain used in the original screen, and also have compatible auxotrophic markers. A wide variety of control plasmids have also been used. The most logical control plasmid would be the DNA-binding domain plasmid without an insert. However, because segregation analysis by mating is often combined with analysis of the specificity of the bait–prey interaction, a bait plasmid with an insert that is suspected not to interact with the prey, such as lamin ***(11)***, is often used (*see* **Subheading 3.12.**).

1. Inoculate a single positive colony or patch into 1–2 mL of selective medium that allows for the loss of the bait plasmid, but retains the prey plasmid. For example, if the bait plasmid is *TRP1*, and the prey plasmid is *LEU2*, grow the cells in medium lacking leucine, but containing tryptophan. Allow the cells to grow, shaking at 30°C, for 72–96 h.
2. Plate the culture onto media that selects for the prey plasmid (e.g., lacking leucine, if the prey plasmid is *LEU2*). It will be necessary to dilute the culture (1/100- or 1/10-fold usually works) prior to plating, to ensure that colonies are fully separated. A density of 75–300 colonies per 100-mm plate is ideal. Incubate the plate at 30°C until the colonies are approx 1 mm in diameter.

3. Transfer the colonies to plates that select for the bait plasmid (e.g., lacking tryptophan, with or without leucine). Transfer can be done either by patching out 20–30 colonies with a sterile toothpick, or by replica-plating (*see* **Note 11**).
4. Grow both the original and replica plates at 30°C until the colonies are fully grown (usually 1 d). Colonies that have lost the bait but retain the prey (e.g., that grow on leucine, but do not grow on tryptophan), can be put into the next step.
5. Mate the cells obtained from **step 4** with the tester strain. Using sterile toothpicks, mix each of the colonies with the tester strain on a small area of a plate containing rich medium (e.g., YPD). Grow for 4 h at 30°C. Then transfer to a plate that selects for diploids (e.g., lacking both leucine and tryptophan). Transfer can be done either by patching, or by replica plating. Grow for 2–3 d at 30°C. Diploids will grow to produce colonies 2–3 mm in diameter.
6. Analyze the diploids for β-galactosidase activity (*see* **Subheading 3.5.**).
7. Positives that are strongly positive in the β-galactosidase assay can then be tested in confirmatory tests (*see* **Subheading 3.12.**). Isolate the prey plasmid from the positives obtained in **step 4**, using the smash and grab method (**Subheading 3.11.**).

3.11. Isolation of Plasmid DNA from S. cerevisiae

This protocol is a modification of the smash and grab method ***(34)***. An alternative procedure uses a step with precipitation of the DNA with lithium chloride ***(35)***.

1. Inoculate 2 mL of selective medium with a single colony or patch. Grow by shaking at 30°C for 24 h, until obviously turbid.
2. Transfer to a 1.7-mL microfuge tube. Spin for 2 s at full speed and discard all but 100 μL of supernatant. Vortex the tube to thoroughly resuspend the cells.
3. Add 200 μL of smash and grab mix.
4. Add 200 μL of a mixture of phenol/chloroform (1:1 :: v:v).
5. Add approx 150 μL of glass beads.
6. Cap the tube firmly, and shake the tube as rapidly as possible for 10 min. The tube can be shaken by taping it onto the head of a vortex mixer. Commercially available shakers that can hold microcentrifuge tubes (e.g., the "Mini Beadbeater" [Biospec Products, Houston, TX]) can also be used.
7. Centrifuge the tube for 5 min at top speed. At the end of the centrifugation, two clear phases should be seen, separated by a white interface. A pellet, consisting of glass beads and cell debris, is also seen at the bottom of the tube.
8. Transfer the supernatant, which contains the plasmid DNA, to a fresh tube. The supernatant can be stored for at least several weeks at –20°C.
9. Use 5–10 μL of the supernatant to transform a standard recA- strain of *E. coli* (e.g., HB101 or DH5α). Use any standard *E. coli* transformation protocol ***(25)*** (*see* **Note 12**).

3.12. Analysis of Positives That Have Survived Segregation Analysis

After segregation analysis has been performed, a number of tests are necessary to demonstrate the specificity and strength of the bait–prey interaction.

Many clones isolated in two-hybrid screens are so-called false positives, i.e., they interact nonspecifically with many baits, or alternatively, cannot be demonstrated to interact with the bait in any way other than by a two-hybrid assay. In addition, prey can sometimes activate the reporter construct in the absence of a bait (e.g., by interacting with yeast proteins that normally bind to the promoter). In this section, several essential tests of two-hybrid positives are outlined.

3.12.1. Two-Hybrid Tests

To determine the specificity of the interaction, the prey plasmid is tested for its ability to interact with a variety of baits. This test can be particularly important in eliminating clones that are nonspecifically sticky, or activate the reporter construct in ways other than by interacting with the bait. It has the advantage of being extremely easy to perform, and in many cases, can be done in parallel with the segregation analysis.

1. Develop a panel of baits. The choice of baits can depend on various biological properties of the bait and the prey. Many investigators routinely test all prey with a preselected panel of baits. This panel includes the empty DNA-binding domain plasmid (an essential negative control), and various proteins predicted in advance not to bind to the prey (*see* **Note 13**).
2. Introduce each of the baits, with the prey plasmid, into a yeast cell containing a two-hybrid reporter construct. Either transformation or mating can be used (*see* **Subheadings 3.10.2.1.** and **3.10.2.2.**). Perform a filter β-galactosidase assay on the cells (*see* **Subheading 3.7.** and **Note 14**).

3.12.2. Tests Using an Independent Method

Eventually, novel positive clones isolated by the two-hybrid system will need to be tested for their ability to interact with the protein of interest, by a method other than yeast genetics. The exact methods that can be used to confirm these interactions are outside the scope of this chapter, although many are described in other chapters of this volume. A list of commonly used approaches is given below. Each of these methods has its own pitfalls and advantages.

1. Interactions can be tested between purified recombinant bait and prey proteins synthesized in *E. coli* or other hosts, and then studied by their ability to interact in vitro (e.g., by co-immunoprecipitation or similar approaches). Epitope tags (e.g., glutathione-*S*-transferase ***[36]***, maltose-binding protein ***[37]***, or influenza hemagglutinin ***[38]***) are commonly added to the proteins to facilitate these studies.
2. Interactions can also be studied by immunoprecipitation of recombinant proteins synthesized and allowed to interact within mammalian cells.
3. The interacting proteins can also be studied by immunolocalization experiments, to determine if they colocalize to similar cell structures.
4. Finally, if a functional test for one of the proteins is available, the effect of the second protein on the functional properties of the first can be assayed biochemically.

3.13. The One-Hybrid System

The one-hybrid system is an extension of the two-hybrid system, with the objective of cloning cDNAs encoding proteins that bind to specific DNA sequences of interest ***(39–41)***. The method has gained widespread interest among researchers studying the regulation of transcription and DNA replication. One great advantage of the one-hybrid system is that it allows the researcher to use any activation-domain fusion library that has been developed for the two-hybrid system. Because the one-hybrid system is in its infancy, only an outline of the procedure is given here (*see* **Note 15**).

1. Prepare the reporter plasmid. Multiple copies (at least three) of the DNA sequence of interest should be cloned upstream of a reporter construct on a plasmid. *HIS3* and *LacZ* are the two reporter constructs that are usually used.
2. Transform the reporter-construct plasmid into a suitable yeast host. Any standard laboratory strain of yeast can be used, provided that it has a recessive mutation in the auxotrophic marker used by the library (**step 3**). The reporter construct must integrate into a specific site in the yeast genome, usually one occupied by an auxotrophic marker, so that integrants can be selected by their inability to grow on selective media. For example, in the system of Li and Herskowitz ***(39)***, the *URA3* gene is disrupted by a plasmid containing a *LacZ* reporter construct. The high frequency of homologous recombination in yeast means that the integration of the reporter plasmid in a specific location in the yeast genome is a routine matter.
3. Transform the modified yeast strain with a typical two-hybrid activation-domain fusion library. Isolate transformants using selective media, as for the two-hybrid system.
4. Select for clones that have activated the reporter complex (e.g., by growth in the absence of histidine, for a *HIS3* reporter, or by β-galactosidase assay for a *LacZ* reporter). If a clone from the library encodes a protein binding to the DNA sequence of interest, the protein will bind to the DNA sequence of the reporter construct. As this protein is fused to an activation domain, transcription of the reporter complex will occur.
5. Isolate the library plasmid from the cell in a manner analogous to the two-hybrid system.

4. Notes

1. Premixed amino acids are available from several suppliers.
2. Harvesting the culture at the correct cell density is the single most important variable in achieving the maximum transformation efficiency. The best way to determine cell density is with a hemocytometer. The correct density usually corresponds to an OD_{600} of 0.3–0.5., but the OD/cell density will vary by strain. The usual doubling time for yeast in log-phase culture is 2–3 h, and the correct cell density is usually reached in 8–10 h.

3. Perform an extra incubation step if interacting partners are being isolated by selection in the absence of histidine. In this case, after finishing **Subheading 3.5., step 12**, resuspend the cells in the original culture volume of rich liquid medium, and grow at 30°C, with shaking for 1 h. This will allow the library plasmid to express its prototrophic marker. Then spin down as in **Subheading 3.5., step 12**, and resuspend in the original culture volume of liquid medium, with selection for both bait and prey plasmids (e.g., lacking tryptophan and leucine). Incubate with shaking at 30°C for 4–14 h. This will allow interacting partners to be expressed and activate the *HIS3* gene. Spin down and resuspend the culture as in **Subheading 3.5., step 12**, and then plate as in **Subheading 3.5., step 13**, on plates that select for histidine as well as the two plasmids (e.g., lacking tryptophan, leucine, and histidine, and, in some cases, with 3-AT). This step will increase the sensitivity of the screen, but may occasionally result in the preferential overgrowth of a transformant. For this reason, the incubation time should be kept to a minimum.
4. It is sometimes possible to transform a yeast cell simultaneously with two different plasmids, each containing a different selectable marker. The resulting double transformants can be selected on media selecting for both markers (e.g., lacking both tryptophan and leucine). Transformation efficiencies will obviously be much lower, as only cells that take up both plasmids will grow.
5. As an alternative transformation method, plasmid DNA can be introduced into yeast by electroporation ***(42)***. The efficiency will vary by the strain, and according to the voltage and other electroporation parameters.
6. Bendixen et al. ***(43,44)*** have used a yeast mating-selection approach to perform a two-hybrid screen. Conceptually, the screen is very similar to the classical approach described in detail in this chapter. However, their method replaces the necessity of performing a library transformation for each new screen. Two strains of *S. cerevisiae* are needed to perform a screen. The first strain is similar to those described previously by other groups, with both *HIS3* and *LacZ* under the control of the *GAL1* promoter, and *trp* and *leu* mutations. The second strain has the opposite mating type, but is otherwise genotypically identical. To perform a screen, a bait plasmid is constructed and transformed into one of the strains in the usual manner. The strain of opposite mating type is transformed with a library of prey, using high efficiency transformation protocol described above. To select for interacting partners, pools of cells containing the prey are mated with cells containing the bait, and positives are selected and studied by the usual HIS selection and β-galactosidase assays. The chief advantage of this approach is that there is no need to transform the library into yeast cells containing bait every time a new screen is performed. Published experience with this technique is relatively limited. Since most two-hybrid libraries are propagated and exchanged among researchers as plasmids in *E. coli*, it is not clear that this approach has any significant advantage for most researchers.
7. Baits may have a high background for a number of reasons, at least in theory. Unfortunately, it is often difficult to determine why a given bait produces a high

background signal. Possibilities include the following: the bait contains a region of amino acid sequence that acts as a built-in activation domain (regions of highly charged [either basic or acidic] amino acids may act in this manner) or the bait contains a region that is intrinsically sticky. A sticky bait tends to interact with other proteins that are naturally present in the yeast nucleus, in a way that activates the yeast transcriptional machinery. Other experimental variables will also influence the stickiness of a bait, in particular, the level of expression of the bait, and the amount that is targeted to the nucleus.

A number of maneuvers can be attempted to reduce the high background of a bait. The first is to subclone the bait into a number of smaller pieces and test each of these for background, as described above. This process can often remove regions of the bait that produce high background. This approach is particularly useful if the experimenter is already focused on a particular region of the protein that is being studied (e.g., one that has features homologous to those of proteins of known function). A potential problem with this approach is that small regions of a protein may fold differently when expressed alone, compared to when part of the native, intact protein. An alternative approach (which must be employed with caution) is to use the high-background bait in a screen, with the use of an alternative method to reduce background (e.g., the use of 3-AT, *see* **Subheading 1.2.3.**). The investigator may also wish to test different DNA-binding domain vectors and host strains for the background associated with a given bait, because it is often impossible to determine in advance which of the available systems is most compatible with a specific protein of interest.

8. A bait should be tested to determine if it is functional in a yeast cell, if it fails to yield any positives in a two-hybrid screen. The best positive control for a bait is a protein that is already known to interact with it. As an example, suppose the experimenter is interested in using as a bait a protein containing a SH3 domain. It may be useful to clone into an activation-domain vector various proteins known to interact with a variety of SH3 domains, and to test these against the bait.

   Frequently, however, there is no known interacting partner, and a definitive functional test of the bait is impossible. In this case, test the prey to ensure that it is synthesized in the yeast cell. In brief, prepare protein extracts from yeast cells that have been transformed with the bait plasmid, and immunoblot them with antisera to the protein of interest. Use the protocol of Field ***(38)*** as a guide (this protocol may require considerable modification, depending on the protein of interest and the strain used, but may be a useful starting point). If antisera to the protein of interest are not available, immunoblots can be performed with antisera to the DNA-binding domain. Antisera to the LEXA, GAL4, and UP-16 domains are commercially available (Clontech and Invitrogen, Carlsbad, CA). Immunoblotting is not a perfect substitute for a functional test, since it is possible that a DNA-binding fusion protein may be synthesized in adequate quantity in a yeast cell, but lack secondary modification, fold incorrectly, or be targeted to an inappropriate cellular compartment.
9. The advantage of patches is that they grow to a more uniform density than colonies transferred from the original screen plates. In addition, it is easier to incor-

porate controls onto plates with patches. Finally, the plate with the original patches can be stored at 4°C for several weeks, and can be used as a source of cells for subsequent segregation analysis.

10. One issue that is still being debated among two-hybrid users is whether the cDNAs that are used in activation-domain fusion libraries should be full-length. Most investigators prefer full-length cDNAs, because it is more likely that a full-length protein will fold correctly. Additionally, if an investigator isolates a partial cDNA in a two-hybrid screen, he or she will eventually need to clone a full-length cDNA and determine whether the properties of the full-length protein are compatible with those of the original, truncated, isolate. Most full-length two-hybrid cDNA libraries are now cloned directionally, which should increase the proportion of fusions generated from the sense strand of the mRNA (and thus increase the number of physiologic fusion partners in the library).

    A number of investigators have successfully used libraries of small insert size (350–700 nucleotides), most of which were generated by the polymerase chain reaction (PCR) ***(11)***. These libraries are easy to generate from small amounts of RNA, facilitate rapid sequence analysis of the insert, and minimize any bias towards carboxyl-terminal sequences. Thcy also have an interesting theoretical advantage in that they would encode separately any protein interaction domains that would normally be associated with inhibitory regions in the full-length polypeptide. The disadvantages of these libraries are clear: More clones must be screened, large interaction domains will be missed, and small fragments may fold in a manner different from that of the complete polypeptide, producing interactions that may not reflect the intact protein.
11. Replica-plating is performed as follows: Cut cotton velvet cloth into squares (approx 200 cm), and sterilize them by autoclaving. Place a velvet square, fuzzy side up, onto a replica plating tool (a cylinder approx 90 mm in diameter works well for a 100-mm plate). The velvet should be tightly secured onto the replica plating tool (e.g., by a circular clamp, or by a rubber band). Place the Petri plate, colonies down, onto the velvet, and press gently to transfer the colonies onto the velvet. Avoid smearing the colonies. Remove the plate. Place each of the selective plates onto the colonies on the velvet, and press gently to transfer the colonies. At least two transfers can be done from a single velvet.
12. As the supernatant obtained from the centrifugation step may contain inhibitors of transformation, use of excessive amounts of the supernatant in a transformation should be avoided. The supernatant can also be used to transform yeast cells, using a scaled-down version of the protocol in **Subheading 3.5.** The supernatant can also be used as a template for PCR amplification of the insert.
13. Lamin is commonly used as a test bait ***(11)***. Various transcription factors (e.g., several loop-helix-loop proteins, homeo-domain proteins, and so on) can be used if the bait is nuclear. Various cytoplasmic signaling factors (e.g., various protein kinases, protein phosphatases, RAS, and so on) are commonly used if cytoplasmic proteins are used as baits.
14. As the filter assay is only semiquantitative, the strength of any interaction detected by this assay can only be estimated approximately. However, any

detectable interaction of the prey with a member of the panel of baits is generally considered sufficient reason to discard the prey.

15. A number of features of the one-hybrid system have been designed to increase the possibility of obtaining cDNAs of interest. Integrating the reporter construct into the yeast chromosome allows precise regulation of the copy number of the reporter construct, and thus better control over its baseline level of transcription. In theory, this should improve the reproducibility of the system. If a *HIS3* reporter construct is used, the level of sensitivity of the system can be fine-tuned by the addition of various levels of 3-AT to the media used to select the positives. The cDNA libraries used in a one-hybrid screen must encode proteins with a nuclear localization signal.

    Many of the advantages and pitfalls of the two-hybrid system also apply to the one-hybrid system. In particular, both systems have the great advantage that a large number of cDNA clones can be screened in a relatively short period of time, and they provide a means for directly isolating a cDNA encoding the desired protein. There are several ways in which the one-hybrid system can generate false positives. For example, false positives can be generated when the hybrid proteins bind to the DNA sequence artifactually. The activation-domain hybrids can also activate transcription inappropriately by binding to protein(s) that are already bound to the DNA sequence. False negatives occur when proteins that normally would bind to DNA do not fold properly when they are encoded as a hybrid, or fail to initiate transcription when fused to the activation domain. As for the two-hybrid system, all positives isolated with the one-hybrid system need to be independently verified by a functional assay. Published experience with the one-hybrid system is limited to date, but seems likely to increase rapidly.

References

1. Fields, S. and Song, O. (1989) A novel genetic system to detect protein–protein interactions. *Nature* **340,** 245,246.
2. Keegan, L., Gill, G., and Ptashne, M. (1986) Separation of DNA-binding from the transcription-activating function of a eukaryotic regulatory protein. *Science* **231,** 699–704.
3. Hope, I. A. and Struhl, K. (1986) Functional dissection of a eukaryotic transcriptional activator protein, GCN4 of yeast. *Cell* **46,** 885–894.
4. Ma, J. and Ptashne, M. (1987) Deletion analysis of GAL4 defines two transcriptional activating segments. *Cell* **48,** 847–853.
5. Ma, J. and Ptashne, M. (1987) A new class of yeast transcriptional activators. *Cell* 51, 113–119.
6. Ma, J. and Ptashne, M. (1988) Converting a eukaryotic transcriptional inhibitor into an activator. *Cell* **55,** 443–446.
7. Chien, C. T., Bartel, P. L., Sternglanz, R., and Fields, S. (1991) The two-hybrid system: a method to identify and clone genes for proteins that interact with a protein of interest. *Proc. Natl. Acad. Sci. USA* **88,** 9578–9582.
8. Fields, S. and Sternglanz, R. (1994) The two-hybrid system: an assay for protein–protein interactions. *Trends Genet.* **10,** 286–292.

9. Laughon, A. and Gesteland, R. F. (1984) Primary structure of the *Saccharomyces cerevisiae* GAL4 gene. *Mol. Cell. Biol.* **4,** 260–267.
10. Rose, M. D., Winston, F., and Heiter, P. (1990) *Methods in Yeast Genetics: A Laboratory Course Manual.* Cold Spring Harbor Laboratory, Cold Spring Harbor, NY.
11. Vojtek, A. B., Hollenberg, S. M., and Cooper, J. (1993) A. Mammalian Ras interacts directly with the serine/threonine kinase Raf. *Cell* **74,** 205–214.
12. Durfee, T., Becherer, K., Chen, P. L., Yeh, S. H., Yang, Y., Kilburn, A. E., et al. (1993) The retinoblastoma protein associates with the protein phosphatase type 1 catalytic subunit. *Genes Dev.* **7,** 555–569.
13. Harper, J. W., Adami, G. R., Wei, N., Keyomarsi, K., and Elledge, S. J. (1993) The p21 Cdk-interacting protein Cip1 is a potent inhibitor of G1 cyclin-dependent kinases. *Cell* **75,** 805–816.
14. Hannon, G. J., Demetrick, D., and Beach, D. (1993) Isolation of the Rb-related p130 through its interaction with CDK2 and cyclins. *Genes Dev.* **7,** 2378–2391.
15. Feilotter, H. E., Hannon, G. J., Ruddell, C. J., and Beach, D. (1994) Construction of an improved host strain for two hybrid screening. *Nucleic Acids Res.* **22,** 1502–1503.
16. Hannon, G. J., Casso, D., and Beach, D. (1994) KAP: a dual specificity phosphatase that interacts with cyclin-dependent kinases. *Proc. Natl. Acad. Sci. USA* **91,** 1731–1735.
17. Gyuris, J., Golemis, E., Chertkov, H., and Brent, R. (1993) Cdi1, a human G1 and S phase protein phosphatase that associates with Cdk2. *Cell* **75,** 791–803.
18. Zervos, A. S., Gyuris, J., and Brent, R. (1993) Mxi1, a protein that specifically interacts with Max to bind Myc-Max recognition sites. *Cell* **72,** 223–232.
19. Le Douarin, B., Pierrat, B., vom Baur, E., Chambon, P., and Losson R. (1995) A new version of the two-hybrid assay for detection of protein–protein interactions. *Nucleic Acids Res.* **23,** 876–878.
20. Kishore, G. M. and Shah, D. M. (1988) Amino acid biosynthesis inhibitors as herbicides. *Annu. Rev. Biochem.* **57,** 627–663.
21. Chevray, P. M. and Nathans, D. (1992) Protein interaction cloning in yeast: identification of mammalian proteins that react with the leucine zipper of Jun. *Proc. Natl. Acad. Sci. USA* **89,** 5789–5793.
22. Ruden, D. M., Ma, J., Li, Y., Wood, K., and Ptashne, M. (1991) Generating yeast transcriptional activators containing no yeast protein sequences. *Nature* **350,** 250–252.
23. Munder, T. and Furst, P. (1992) The *Saccharomyces cerevisiae* CDC25 gene product binds specifically to catalytically inactive ras proteins in vivo. *Mol. Cell. Biol.* **12,** 2091–2099.
24. Silver, P. A., Keegan, L. P., and Ptashne, M. (1984) Amino terminus of the yeast *GAL4* gene product is sufficient for nuclear localization. *Proc. Natl. Acad. Sci. USA* **81,** 5951–5955.
25. Sambrook, J., Fritsch, E. F., and Maniatis, T. (1989) *Molecular Cloning: A Laboratory Manual,* 2nd ed. Cold Spring Harbor Laboratory, Cold Spring Harbor, NY.
26. Hill, J., Donald, K. A., and Griffiths, D. E. (1991) DMSO-enhanced whole cell yeast transformation [published erratum appears in *Nucleic Acids Res.* 1991 Dec 11; **19,** 6688]. *Nucleic Acids Res.* **19,** 5791.

27. Gietz, R. D. and Schiestl, R. H. (1991) Applications of high efficiency lithium acetate transformation of intact yeast cells using single-stranded nucleic acids as carrier. *Yeast* **7,** 253–263.
28. Gietz, D., St. Jean, A., Woods, R. A., and Schiestl, R. H. (1992) Improved method for high efficiency transformation of intact yeast cells. *Nucleic Acids Res.* **20,** 1425.
29. Gietz, R. D., Schiestl, R. H., Willems, A. R., and Woods, R. A. (1995) Studies on the transformation of intact yeast cells by the LiAc/SS-DNA/PEG procedure. *Yeast* **11,** 355–360.
30. Breeden, L. and Nasmyth, K. (1985) Regulation of the yeast HO gene. Cold Spring Harbor Symposium on Quantitative Biology **50,** 643–650.
31. Yocum, R. R., Hanley, S., West, R., and Ptashne, M. (1984) Use of LacZ fusions to delimit regulatory domains of the inducible divergent GAL1-GAL10 promoter in *Saccharomyces cerevisiae*. *Mol. Cell. Biol.* **4,** 1985–1998.
32. Guarente, L. (1983) Yeast promoters and LacZ fusions designed to study expression of cloned genes in yeast. *Methods Enzymol.* **101,** 181–191.
33. Gekakis, N., Saez, L., Delahaye-Brown, A.-M., Myers, M. P., Sehgal, A., Young, M. W., et al. (1995) Isolation of *timeless* by PER protein interaction: defective interaction between *timeless* protein and long-period mutant *PER-L*. *Science* **270,** 811–815.
34. Hoffman, C. S. and Winston, F. (1987) A ten-minute DNA preparation from yeast efficiently releases autonomous plasmids for transformation of *Escherichia coli*. *Gene* **57,** 267–272.
35. Ward, A. C. (1990) Single-step purification of shuttle vectors from yeast for high frequency back-transformation into *E. coli*. *Nucleic Acids Res.* **18,** 5319.
36. Smith, D. B. and Johnson, K. S. (1988) Single-step purification of polypeptides expressed in *Escherichia coli* as fusions with glutathione-S-transferase. *Gene* **67,** 31–40.
37. Maina, C. V., Riggs, P. D., Grandea, A. G., Slatko, E. E., Moran, L. S., Tagliamonte, J. A., et al. (1988) An *Escherichia coli* vector to express and purify foreign proteins by fusion to and separation from maltose-binding protein. *Gene* **74,** 365–373.
38. Field, J., Nikawa, J.-I., Broek, D., MacDonald, B., Rodgers, L., Wilson, I. A., et al. (1988) Purification of a RAS-responsive adenylyl cyclase complex from *Saccharomyces cerevisiae* by use of an epitope addition method. *Mol. Cell. Biol.* **8,** 2159–2165.
39. Li, J. J. and Herskowitz, I. (1993) Isolation of ORC6, a component of the yeast origin recognition complex by a one-hybrid system. *Science* **262,** 1870–1874.
40. Wang, M. M. and Reed, R. R. (1993) Molecular cloning of the olfactory neuronal transcription factor Olf–1 by genetic selection in yeast. *Nature* **364,** 121–126.
41. Wu, Y., Liu, Y., Lee, L., Miner, Z., and Kulesz Martin, M. (1994) Wild-type alternatively spliced p53: binding to DNA and interaction with the major p53 protein in vitro and in cells. *EMBO J.* **13,** 4823–4830.
42. Manivasakam, P. and Schiestl, R. H. (1993) High efficiency transformation of *Saccharomyces cerevisiae* by electroporation [published erratum appears in *Nucleic Acids Res.* 1993 Oct 11; **21,** 4856]. *Nucleic Acids Res.* **21,** 4414–4415.

43. Bendixen, C., Gangloff, S., and Rothstein, R. (1994) A yeast mating-selection scheme for detection of protein–protein interactions. *Nucleic Acids Res.* **22,** 1778–1779.
44. Gangloff, S., McDonald, J. P., Bendixen, C., Arthur, L., and Rothstein, R. (1994) The yeast type I topoisomerase Top3 interacts with Sgs1, a DNA helicase homolog: a potential eukaryotic reverse gyrase. *Mol. Cell. Biol.* **14,** 8391–8398.
45. van Aelst, L., Barr, M., Marcus, S., Polverino, A., and Wigler, M. (1993) Complex formation between RAS and RAF and other protein kinases. *Proc. Natl. Acad. Sci. USA* **90,** 6213–6217.
46. Cohen, G. B., Ren, R., and Baltimore, D. (1995) Modular binding domains in signal transduction proteins. *Cell* **80,** 237–248.

10

Molecular Genetic Approaches II

Expression–Interaction Cloning

Michael Csukai and Daria Mochly-Rosen

1. Introduction

Expression–interaction cloning provides a powerful tool for the identification of proteins that interact with each other. The method described here is based on the overlay procedure, which was originally developed to identify proteins that interact with protein kinase C (PKC) ***(1)***. A number of variations of this method have been developed ***(2,3)*** and used successfully to clone and identify proteins that interact with PKC by expression library screening ***(4,5)***. The principle of this method is the immobilizing of potential binding proteins on nitrocellulose and overlaying PKC in the presence or absence of PKC activators, and the detection of any interaction using anti-PKC antibodies in immunological detection assays. This procedure can identify receptors for activated C kinase (RACKs) and/or PKC substrates. The method could easily be adapted to allow interaction cloning using a protein of interest other than PKC, provided a good source of purified protein or epitope tagged peptides and antibodies (as a means of detection) are available.

2. Materials

2.1. Expression Libraries

A number of λ-phage or phagemid cDNA expression libraries are suitable for this technique; libraries in which protein expression is under the control of the *LacZ* promoter are convenient and widely used. Many libraries are now commercially available (e.g., from Stratagene [La Jolla, CA], Gibco-BRL [Gaithersburg, MD], New England Biolabs [Beverly, MA]). Alternatively,

From: *Methods in Molecular Biology, Vol. 88: Protein Targeting Protocols*
Edited by: R. A. Clegg Humana Press Inc., Totowa, NJ

λ-phage cDNA expression libraries can be constructed using standard molecular biological techniques *(6)*.

2.2. Phage Propagation and Filter Lifts

1. Correct bacterial strain for λ-phage library used.
2. Luria broth (LB): 1% (w/v) tryptone, 0.5% (w/v) yeast extract, 0.5% (w/v) NaCl, pH 7.0.
3. Luria agar (LA): as LB, with 1.5% (w/v) agar.
4. Top layer agar (TLA): as LB, with 0.7% (w/v) agar.
5. Suspension medium (SM): 5 g NaCl, 2 g $MgSO_4 \cdot 7H_2O$, 50 mL 1*M* Tris-HCl, pH 7.5, 5 mL molten 2% (w/v) gelatin, make up to 1 L with H_2O, sterilize by autoclaving, and store at room temperature.
6. Maltose: 20% (w/v) stock filter-sterilized, store at 4°C.
7. Magnesium sulfate: 1*M* stock autoclaved.
8. Nitrocellulose filters.
9. Isopropyl β-D-thiogalactopyranoside (IPTG): 100 m*M* stock filter-sterilized.
10. Chloroform.

2.3. Overlay Procedure

2.3.1. Overlaying Proteins

1. Overlay block: 0.2*M* NaCl, 50 m*M* Tris-HCl pH 7.5, 3% (w/v) bovine serum albumin (BSA), 0.1% polyethylene glycol 15,000–20,000 (PEG).
2. Overlay buffer: 0.2*M* NaCl, 50 m*M* Tris-HCl, pH 7.5, 12 m*M* 2-mercaptoethanol, 0.1% BSA, 1% (w/v) PEG, 20 μg/mL soybean trypsin inhibitor (SBTI), 20 μg/mL leupeptin, 1.7 μg/mL phenylmethylsulfonylflouride (PMSF). SBTI and leupeptin stocks are 20 mg/mL in 20 m*M* Tris-HCl, pH 7.5, PMSF stock is 17 mg/mL in isopropanol. Protease inhibitor stocks are stored at –20°C and added to overlay buffer immediately prior to use.
3. Overlay wash: 0.2*M* NaCl, 50 m*M* Tris-HCl, pH 7.5, 12 m*M* 2-mercaptoethanol, 0.1% (w/v) PEG.
4. Phospholipids (PLx2): 240 μg/mL phosphatidylserine (PSer), 8 μg/mL diacylglycerol (DG) in 20 m*M* Tris-HCl, pH 7.5. PSer and DG are supplied in chloroform (Avanti Polar Lipids, Alabaster, AL), which is evaporated under a flow of nitrogen gas. The phospholipids are resuspended in 20 m*M* Tris-HCl, pH 7.5 and sonicated for 30 s, then placed on ice for 1 min, sonication is repeated three times. PLx2 can be stored at 4°C for up to 14 d.
5. Purified PKC *(7)* or recombinant PKC fragments.

2.3.2. Overlaying Recombinant PKC Fragments or Peptides

1. Overlay block: 150 m*M* NaCl, 20 m*M* HEPES, pH 7.4, 5% (w/v) BSA.
2. Overlay buffer: 150 m*M* NaCl, 20 m*M* HEPES, pH 7.4, 1 % (w/v) BSA.
3. Overlay wash: 150 m*M* NaCl, 20 m*M* HEPES, pH 7.4, 0.3 % (w/v) BSA, 0.05% (v/v) Tween-20.
4. Purified recombinant PKC fragments or peptides.

2.4. Detection Procedure

1. Primary antibody, raised against overlaid protein or epitope tag.
2. Secondary antibody (alkaline phosphatase-conjugated).
3. 5-bromo-4-chloro-3-indolyl phosphate *p*-toluidine salt (BCIP): 25 mg/mL (w/v) stock solution in dimethylformamide.
4. p-Nitro-tetrazolium blue (NBT): 50 mg/mL (w/v) stock solution in 70% (v/v) dimethylformamide.
5. AP buffer: 100 m*M* Tris-HCl, pH 9.5, 100 m*M* NaCl, 5 m*M* $MgCl_2$.
6. Stop solution: 20 m*M* Tris-HCl, pH 2.9, 1 m*M* EDTA.

3. Methods

3.1. Plating Phage and Filter Lifts

This section describes a standard method for plating λ-phage.

1. Set up an overnight culture of a suitable *Escherichia coli* strain in 50 mL LB containing 10 m*M* $MgSO_4$ and 0.2% maltose.
2. Spin down cells for 10 min at 1000*g*.
3. Gently resuspend pellet in 10 m*M* $MgSO_4$ to give OD_{600} = 0.5; this should give approx 15 mL of culture and cells can be stored for 2–3 d at 4°C.
4. In a sterile test-tube incubate 200 μL cells with 1 × 10^4 phage for 90 mm plate (600 μL cells with 2.5 × 10^4 phage for 150 mm plate), at 37°C for 20 min (*see* **Note 1**).
5. Add 3 mL of molten (48°C) TLA containing 10 m*M* $MgSO_4$ and 0.2% maltose to each test tube for 90-mm plates (9 mL for 150-mm plates) and plate on a dry LA plate (*see* **Note 2**).
6. Incubate plates for 3–4 h at 42°C or until plaques are just visible (*see* **Note 3**).
7. Soak nitrocellulose filter disks in 10 m*M* IPTG and air-dry on filter paper (*see* **Note 4**).
8. Number nitrocellulose filters with a soft pencil.
9. Number plates and place corresponding nitrocellulose filter onto agar (avoid trapping air bubbles; *see* **Note 5**).
10. Incubate for 4 h at 37°C. Remove lids from plates for final 20 min (*see* **Note 6**).
11. Mark the position of the filters on the plate with a needle and waterproof ink (to aid later alignment marks should be asymmetrical, i.e., three marks at one side of the filter and two marks at the other).
12. Remove filters and wash in overlay wash to remove any TLA still attached (*see* **Note 7**).
13. Wrap and store plates at 4°C.

3.2. Overlay Procedure

The composition of overlay buffers is dependent on whether intact enzyme or enzyme fragments are used for screening purposes. This method has been used successfully with fragments of PKC containing a FLAG epitope tag

(Kodak, New Haven, CT) for detection. All incubations are carried out on an orbital shaker (*see* **Note 8**).

1. Incubate nitrocellulose filters from IPTG-induced cDNA library plates in overlay block for 2 h at room temperature.
2. Remove filters and place directly into overlay buffer (approx 5 mL per 82 mm filter; 10 mL per 138 mm filter) containing protein of interest with or without PKC activators (PLx2 at 10 μL/mL) as appropriate. Incubate at room temperature for 1 h or overnight at 4°C.
3. Wash in overlay wash three times for 15 min (*see* **Note 9**).

3.3. Detection

A number of different immunodetection systems can be used that utilize radiochemical or chromogenic reagents of your choice. Immunodetection using alkaline phosphatase has been successful in our hands. All incubations are carried out on an orbital shaker.

1. Incubate filters in overlay block solution in the presence of primary antibody for 2 h at room temperature (*see* **Note 10**).
2. Wash filters in overlay wash four times for 5 min.
3. Incubate filters in overlay block containing alkaline phosphatase-conjugated secondary antibodies for 1 h at room temperature (*see* **Note 11**).
4. Wash filters in overlay block four times for 5 min.
5. Rinse filters in water.
6. Incubate filters in AP buffer containing 100 μg/mL NBT and 50 μg/mL BCIP, purple color is visible in minutes.
7. Stop color reaction by washing briefly in stop solution and dry on filter paper. Store filters protected from light.
8. Positive plaques should produce a blue dot or donut-shaped mark.
9. The filters are used to locate the putative positive plaque on the plates using the needle holes as reference. As plaques are closely packed in a primary screen, the area containing the putative positive plaques is picked as a plug of agar using the wide end of a sterile Pasteur pipet. Add the plug to 0.5 mL SM and 10–20 μL chloroform and agitate vigorously; store at 4°C.

3.4. Secondary Screening

Plaques that give a purple color after overlaying with PKC and anti-PKC antibodies could be PKC-binding proteins (RACKs), PKC substrates, or PKC isozymes themselves. In order to differentiate between these possibilities, secondary screening must be carried out.

1. Plate a number of different dilutions of putative positive phage from the SM buffer containing the agar plugs (*see* **Note 12**).
2. Chose a dilution that will allow single plaques to be picked and induce protein production as described in **Subheading 3.1.**

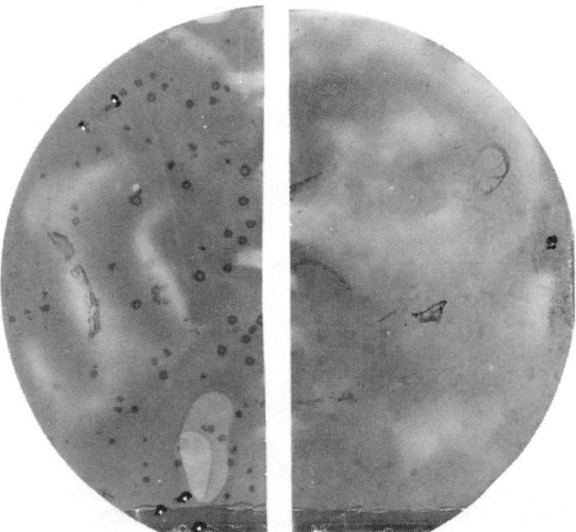

Fig. 1. Isolation of a potential RACK–cDNA clone by the overlay assays rescreening of a single isolate. Putative positive clones are rescreened for anti-PKC binding after overlaying in the presence of PKC activators with or without PKC. Shown is a single isolate that reacted with anti-PKC antibodies when overlaid with PKC (left), but not when overlaid with buffer without PKC (right).

3. Nitrocellulose filters are cut in half.
4. One-half is incubated with PL and calcium (PKC activators) in the presence of PKC, whereas the other half is incubated in buffer in the absence of PKC (*see* **Fig. 1**).
5. Positive plaques are identified (*see* **Note 13**), using anti-PKC antibodies, and picked using the tip of a Pasteur pipet (*see* **Note 14**).
6. The secondary screen is repeated to ensure that a pure population is obtained.
7. Phage DNA is isolated, sequenced and the encoded protein identified using standard molecular biological techniques (*see* **ref. *6*** and **Note 15**).

4. Note s

4.1. Plating Phage and Filter Lifts

1. The required plaque titer is obtained by serial dilution in SM. Care should be taken with dilutions; if plaques are too crowded, expressed protein will be difficult to detect. Phage dilutions can be stored at 4°C for later use with the addition of 10–20 μL of chloroform.
2. When plating out phage, use LA plates that have been thoroughly dried at 37°C for 1–2 h with lids slightly open, or plates left to dry on bench for 24 h . If plates are not dry, the top layer agar often sticks to the nitrocellulose filters when removed. If sticking of top layer agar to the nitrocellulose filters continues to be a problem, agarose can be substituted for agar in the top-layer recipe, resulting in a slightly stiffer media.

3. In order to get a large number of plaques per plate and good protein production, IPTG induction should be started when plaques are just visible (pin-prick plaques).
4. Nitrocellulose filters should be handled with blunt-ended forceps.
5. To avoid trapping air bubbles when placing on plates, hold the nitrocellulose filter at edges, bend and touch middle of filter down first, then lower and release edges.
6. Removing lids from plates for final 20 min of the 37°C incubation helps to prevent top layer from sticking to filter.
7. Once the filters are removed from the plates, they must not be allowed to dry during any of the subsequent steps.

4.2. Overlay Procedure

8. To prevent filters from sticking to each other and to ensure access of solutions to filters in both overlay and detection procedures, all incubations should be carried out in small batches in Petri dishes or sealable bags. All washes should be carried out in large volumes.
9. Fixation of overlaid protein to its binding protein has been used ***(5)***. This procedure follows overlay washes: incubate nitrocellulose filters in PBS containing 0.3% (v/v) formaldehyde for 20 min, neutralize excess formaldehyde groups by incubation in PBS containing 2% (w/v) glycine for 20 min. Wash filters three times in PBS, 5 min each wash then proceed with normal detection procedure. We find this step unnecessary when the affinity between the binding protein and overlay proteins is high ***(4)***.

4.3. Detection

10. Use primary antibody at a dilution that detects 50 pg and gives acceptable background. Primary antibody milk solution contains sodium azide and can therefore be stored at 4°C for 4–8 wk, and can normally be used more than once.
11. Alkaline phosphatase-conjugated secondary antibody that reacts with species-specific determinants are commercially available and are used at the dilution recommended by the manufacturer.

4.4. Secondary Screening

12. Because of the time taken for phage to diffuse out of agar plugs containing the picked phage plaque, phage titer in SM containing the plug does not reach a maximum until plugs have been stored overnight.
13. Criteria for positive clones from the secondary screen: If positive plaques are observed only after incubation in the presence of PKC, but not in the absence of PKC, this clone expresses a PKC-binding protein, a putative RACK or PKC substrate. If a particular isolate gives rise to positive plaques on both halves, this clone expresses a PKC isozyme. If both halves are negative, the clone was a false positive in the primary screen.
14. Phage diffuse relatively large distances in top layer agar so when single plaques are picked well isolated plaques should be chosen.

15. Methods to determine if the proteins are RACKs and/or substrates are outside the immediate scope of this procedure (*see* **refs.** *2* and *4* for dctails).

Acknowledgments

We wish to thank Che-Hong Chen for his help in preparing this protocol.

References

1. Wolf, M. and Sahyoun, N. (1986) Protein Kinase C and phosphatidylserine bind to Mr 110,000/115,000 polypeptides enriched in cytoskeletal and postsynaptic density preparations. *J. Biol. Chem.* **261,** 13,327–13,332.
2. Mochly-Rosen, D., Khaner, H., and Lopez, J. (1991) Identification of intracellular receptor proteins for activated protein kinase C. *Proc. Natl. Acad. Sci. USA* **88,** 3997–4000.
3. Hyatt, S. L., Klauck, T., and Jaken, S. (1990) Protein kinase C is localized in focal contacts of normal but not transformed fibroblasts. *Mol. Carcinog.* **3,** 45–53.
4. Ron, D., et al. (1994) Cloning of an intracellular receptor for protein kinase C: a homolog of the beta subunit of G proteins. *Proc. Natl. Acad. Sci. USA* **91,** 839–843.
5. Chapline, C., Ramsay, K., Klauck, T., and Jaken, S. (1993) Interaction cloning of protein kinase C substrates. *J. Biol. Chem.* **268,** 6858–6861.
6. Sambrook, J., Fritsch, E. F., and Maniatis, T. (1989) *Molecular Cloning: A Laboratory Manual.* Cold Spring Harbor Laboratory, Cold Sping Harbor, NY.
7. Mochly-Rosen, D. and Koshland, D. E., Jr. (1987) Domain structure and phosphorylation of protein kinase C. *J. Biol. Chem.* **262,** 2291–2297.

11

Molecular Genetic Approaches III

Determination of Protein Sequence Motifs Involved in Protein Targeting by Use of Coupled Transcription–Translation Systems

Grant Scotland and Miles D. Houslay

1. Introduction

For many years it has been possible to express proteins in the absence of their cells or tissues by virtue of in vitro translation of purified polyadenylated mRNAs *(1)*. This was largely because of an observation made in 1976 by Pelham and Jackson *(2)* that endogenous mRNAs could be removed from rabbit reticulocyte lysates by treatment with Ca^{2+}-dependent micrococcal nuclease, which, in turn, could be inactivated by addition of the chelating agent ethylene glycol-*bis* (β-aminoethyl ether)-*N,N,N',N'*-tetra-acetic acid (EGTA). By this method they were able to develop a very efficient and sensitive cell-free protein synthesizing system that had the ability to readily translate a variety of exogenous mRNAs in vitro. This methodology continues to be utilized at the present time by, for example, molecular biologists checking the biological activity and integrity of mRNA before constructing cDNA libraries. As such, several biochemical suppliers provide off the shelf kits for this function. Until recently, cell-free protein synthesis was only achievable by means of separate transcription and subsequent translation reactions. As a result of developments in recent years, however, it is now possible to combine both transcription and translation, thereby circumventing the need to isolate mRNA. Thus, the gene for the protein, or fragment of protein, of interest can be cloned into plasmid vectors and used to generate protein in a single reaction *(3)*. These single tube systems also have the advantage that they can yield two- to sixfold more protein than the more conventional transcription and subsequent translation reac-

From: *Methods in Molecular Biology, Vol. 88: Protein Targeting Protocols*
Edited by: R. A. Clegg Humana Press Inc., Totowa, NJ

tions *(4)*. This can be an asset in cases in which the protein has proven difficult to purify by conventional methods.

One aspect of the ability to synthesize protein in a cell-free environment has been exploited by researchers in the field of subcellular localization. George and Blackshear *(5)*, for example, demonstrated that, when the myristoylated, alanine-rich, protein kinase C substrate MARCKS was myristoylated in a cell-free translation system, it was able to bind to membranes in a manner identical to that observed in intact cells. In contrast, the nonmyristoylated mutant did not show this ability. A similar strategy was adopted by Resh *(6)* to investigate plasma membrane association of the tyrosyl protein kinase pp60$^{v\text{-}src}$ encoded by the RNA enveloped Rous sarcoma virus.

However, one potential drawback that can be encountered when using such overexpression systems is the possibility that multiple transcripts may be generated that take the form of N-terminal truncated protein species *(4)*. This, in many instances, is undesirable, because species may provide a false interpretation of results, especially if an inherent protein property, such as enzyme activity, is being monitored. Indeed, failure to assess protein products of in vitro transcription and translation systems can lead to serious errors. Thus, analysis of protein products should be *de rigeur* in all experiments. These multiple transcripts have been attributed to the presence of suboptimal Kozak sequences around the initiating AUG start codon *(7)* and, in general, can only be eliminated during the cloning stages by deletion of the downstream ATG codons if they are found to reside within a suboptimal Kozak sequence. This, however, may in itself cause problems by generating a mutant protein product. More recently, it has been suggested that this promiscuity could be exploited in experimental strategies evolved so as to elucidate peptides or amino acids suspected of involvement in the subcellular localization (targeting) of proteins *(8)*. For example, it has been demonstrated that certain cyclic AMP phosphodiesterase (PDE) isoforms are membrane-associated *(9–11)*, despite observations that they contained no obvious membrane targeting signals or significant stretches of hydrophobic amino acids able to form transmembrane α-helices. Shakur et al. *(10)*, however, were able to prove conclusively that the cDNA for the cAMP specific (PDE4) phosphodiesterase, RD1, when transfected into COS cells, became membrane-associated because of information contained within the N-terminal 25 amino acids of this protein. This observation was confirmed by exploiting the aforementioned promiscuity of coupled transcription–translation systems. Such analyses were done using a specially constructed fusion protein expression vector that generated in-frame chimeric species formed between various RD1 fragments and the N-terminus of the soluble bacterial enzyme, chloramphenicol acteyltransferase (CAT). The generation of N-terminal truncated chimeric species in the in vitro transcription and translation system has allowed the identification of specific regions in the N-terminal splice region of RD1 that confer membrane association upon this enzyme.

2. Materials

1. Thermal cycler.
2. Agarose gel apparatus.
3. Power pack.
4. UV transilluminator (312-nm wavelength).
5. 10X reaction buffer: 1500 m*M* NaCl, 60 m*M* Tris-HCl, pH 7.9, 60 m*M* $MgCl_2$, 10 m*M* dithiothreitol (DTT) (*see* **Note 1**).
6. *Xba*I.
7. *Xho*I.
8. 10X *Taq* buffer: 500 m*M* KCl, 100 m*M* Tris-HCl, pH 9.0, 1.0% Triton X-100.
9. 25 m*M* $MgCl_2$ solution.
10. *Taq* polymerase.
11. 2 m*M* dNTPs.
12. SP6 Coupled transcription–translation kit.
13. TEN buffer: 40 m*M* Tris-HCl, pH 7.8, 10 m*M* ethylenediamine-tetra-acetic acid (EDTA), 120 m*M* NaCl.
14. Plasmid pGS7.

The eukaryotic expression vector pGS7 (**Fig. 1**) was constructed ***(8)*** to investigate membrane association elements of the type IV phosphodiesterase RD1 ***(12)***. This was generated so as to contain a fragment of this gene encoding the N-terminal first 100 amino acids as an in-frame fusion at the 5' end of the bacterial CAT gene. CAT is a bacterial enzyme that is normally found in the soluble cytosol fraction, both in bacteria and when transfected into mammalian cells ***(13)***. This, combined with the fact that CAT is not endogenously expressed in mammalian cells, provides the basis of a useful reporter system. The vector contains an SP6 promoter upstream of the polyclonal linker to facilitate expression in cell-free coupled transcription–translation systems, as well as the SV40 early promoter, to drive expression in mammalian COS cells ***(14)***. The RD1 fragment of this construct can be removed by digestion with the restriction enzymes *Xba*I and *Xho*I and replaced with DNA fragments containing any putative membrane association element. Thus, such a system has general applicability for investigating not only membrane-association domains, but also protein–protein interactions. Synthetic oligonucleotide primers must be designed that allow generation of the fragment of interest as an in-frame fusion with the CAT gene of pGS7 by use of the polymerase chain reaction (PCR). Fragments can be subcloned into pGS7 by inclusion of restriction enzyme recognition sites for *Xba*I and *Xho*I in the sense and antisense primers, respectively.

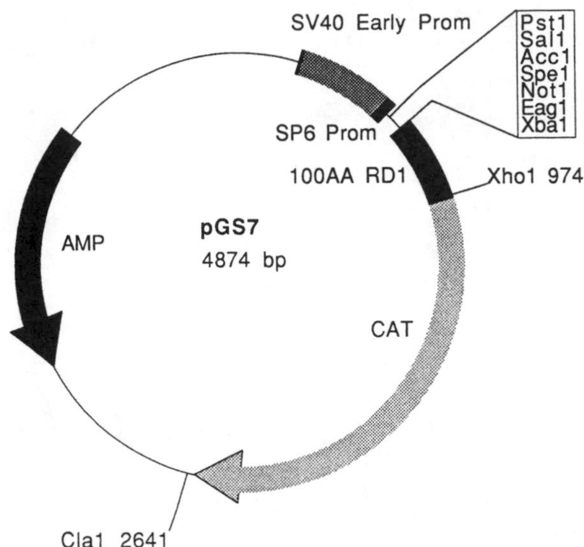

Fig. 1. The SP6 promoter containing eukaryotic expression vector pGS7. The tk promoter region from pBLCAT2 ***(15)*** was replaced with the first 100 amino acids of RD1 by digestion of the plasmid with *Xba*I and *Xho*I, followed by gel purification of the major digestion product, to generate the plasmid pGS4. The RD1 fragment was generated by polymerase chain reaction (PCR) using the primers 5'-GCGAGGGAATTCTAGAATGCCTCTGGTT-3' (sense) and 5'-GGCTCCTCGAGCTTCCAGTGTGT-3' (antisense) containing restriction sites for *Xba*I and *Xho*I, respectively (underlined). The SV40 early promoter and SP6 promoter were obtained by *Cla*I/*Xba*I digestion of pSV.SPORT1, followed by gel purification of the promoter-containing fragment, and subcloned into *Nar*I/*Xba*I digested pGS4. Both the *Nar*I and *Cla*I sites were lost because of the cloning strategy. (Reproduced with permission from **ref. *8***.)

3. Methods

3.1. Generation of *Xba*I/*Xho*I Digested pGS7

1. Assemble the following in a 0.5-mL microfuge tube: 10 µg DNA, 5 µL 10X reaction buffer, 10 U *Xba*I, 10 U *Xho*I, and distilled water to 50 µL.
2. Incubate at 37°C for 4 h.
3. Add 10 µL loading dye to the reaction mixture (*see* **Note 2**).
4. Run on a 1.0% low melting point (LMP) agarose gel (*see* **Note 3**) against *Hin*dIII-digested λ DNA mol-wt markers.
5. Identify and excise the 4.8-kb band by UV transilluminator and excise with a sharp scalpel (*see* **Note 4**).
6. Purify the DNA fragment by the preferred method, e.g., Promega (Southampton, UK) Wizard PCR system (*see* **Note 5**).

3.2. PCR

3.2.1. Reaction Conditions

Assemble the following components in a 0.5-mL microtube: 1 μg template DNA, 25 pmol 5'-primer, 25 pmol 3'-primer, 5 μL 10X *Taq* Buffer, 5 μL 2 m*M* dNTPs, 3 μL 25 m*M* $MgCl_2$ (*see* **Note 6**), 0.5 μL *Taq* polymerase (5 U/μL), and distilled water to 50 μL.

Overlay the reaction mix with 40 μL mineral oil. The first cycle of PCR was designed when the addition of restriction enzyme recognition sites to a DNA fragment is required for subcloning.

3.2.2. PCR Conditions

Denaturation	94°C	1 min
Annealing (*see* **Note 7**)	37°C	2 min
Extension	72°C	3 min
For 1 cycle (*see* **Note 8**), followed by		
Denaturation	94°C	1 min
Annealing	50°C	2 min
Extension	72°C	3 min
for 30 cycles		

3.2.3. Purification of PCR Fragments

1. Remove the mineral oil.
2. Add 50 μL chloroform.
3. Vortex for 30 s to remove any remaining oil.
4. Spin the sample in a microfuge for 30 s to separate the phases.
5. Remove the aqueous (top) phase containing the PCR fragment (approx 40 μL).
6. Add 10 μL loading dye.
7. Run on 1.75% LMP agarose gel against *Hae*III digested ΦX174 mol-wt markers and undigested PCR product.
8. Identify the band of interest by UV transilluminator and excise with a sharp scalpel.
9. Purify the PCR fragment by the preferred method (e.g., Promega Wizard PCR system, Qaiex II Gel Extraction kit [Qiagen]).
10. Ligate into *Xba*I/*Xho*I digested pGS7.

3.3. Coupled Transcription–Translation Reactions

As mentioned in **Subheading 1.**, cell-free coupled transcription–translation systems are commercially available from at least two biochemical suppliers (Promega, Amersham). The method outlined here makes use of the TnT™ kit obtained from Promega.

1. Assemble the following components in a 0.5-mL microtube: 25 μL lysate, 2 μL TnT™ buffer, 1 μL SP6 polymerase, 1 μL amino acid mix (minus methionine), 4 μL [^{35}S] methionine (1000 Ci/mmol), 0.5–2 μg plasmid DNA, and distilled water to 50 μL.

2. Incubate the reaction at 30°C for 60–120 min (*see* **Note 9**).
3. Proceed with the membrane association step, or store the reaction mix at –20°C.

3.4. Membrane Association Assay

Set up the following:

1. Pipet duplicate 10-µL aliquots of the above reaction mixture into 0.5-mL microtubes and label (–) and (+) membranes.
2. Add 10 µL TEN buffer (*see* **Note 10**) to the tube labeled (–).
3. Add 10 µL TEN buffer containing membranes to the tube labeled (+) (*see* **Note 10**).
4. Incubate at 37°C for 30 min.
5. Transfer the samples to 200-µL centrifuge tubes.
6. Spin at 28 psi (150,000*g*) in a Beckman Airfuge for 20 min.
7. Remove the supernatant fractions to 0.5-mL microtubes.
8. Resuspend the pellets with 20 µL TEN buffer.
9. Repeat the centrifugation as above.
10. Remove and combine the supernatants from the first and second spins.
11. Finally, resuspend the pellets with 40 µL TEN buffer containing 0.5% Triton X-100 (this ensures complete recovery of the pellet).
12. Adjust the supernatant fractions to 0.5% Triton X-100 (final concentration).
13. Run the pellet and supernatant fractions on sodium dodecyl sulfate-polyacrylamide gel electrophoresis (SDS-PAGE) against a sample of the original reaction mixture.
14. Visualize the results by phosphorimager or by autoradiography.

3.5. Discussion

Coupled transcription–translation systems can be susceptible to multiple initiation events that give rise to a mixture of full-length and truncated proteins in the same reaction mixture *(3,4)*. This feature has been attributed to the presence of suboptimal Kozak sequences within the DNA sequence under investigation *(3,7)*. It is possible to exploit this promiscuity in the investigation of membrane association and an example is demonstrated in **Fig. 2**. Using the plasmid pGS7, which contains the first 100 amino acids of the type IV phosphodiesterase RD1, it was noted that three major protein species were generated with mol wt ~38, ~35, and ~33 kDa (**Fig. 2**, lanes 4–6). These corresponded to proteins initiated from Met 1, Met 26, and Met 37, all of which were found to be located within suboptimal Kozak sequences (**Table 1**). However, only the full-length 38-kDa fusion protein became associated with the membrane pellet fraction (lane 5). In contrast, the 35- and 33-kDa species remained in the supernatant fraction (lane 6). The identical intensity of the 35- and 33-kDa species in lane 4 (the sample to which no membranes were added) and lane 6 demonstrate how these two truncated species served as internal controls for membrane association, i.e., when membranes are offered a choice of the full-length and the N-terminally truncated chimeras, then only the full-length species will

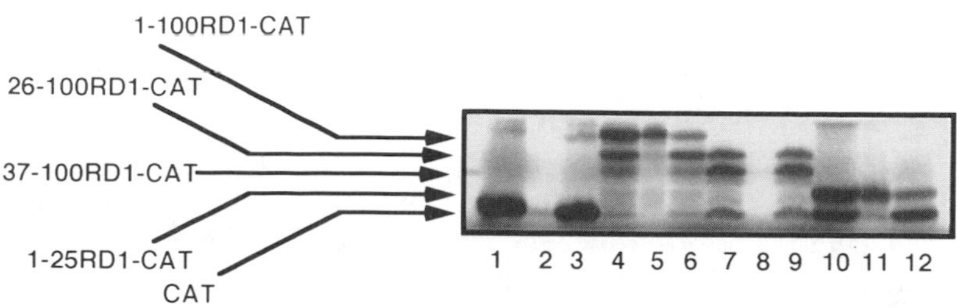

Fig. 2. Cell-free expression of various RD1-CAT chimeras generated by variants of pGS7. Lanes 1–3 represent native CAT provided by the plasmid pGS8; lanes 4-6 represent 1–100RD1-CAT provided by the plasmid pGS7; lanes 7–9 represent 26–100RD1-CAT provided by the plasmid pGS11; lanes 10–12 represent 1–25RD1-CAT provided by the plasmid pGS13. The lanes are in sets of three, where the first track shows the original products of the transcription/translation reaction, the second, the membrane (high speed pellet) fraction, and the third, the soluble (high-speed supernatant) fraction. Thus, lanes 1, 4, 7, and 10 show the original material emanating from the transcription/translation experiment; lanes 2, 5, 8, and 11 show the high speed pellets after incubation in the presence of COS membranes (0.27 mg/mL protein) and lanes 3, 6, 9, and 12 the high speed supernatants obtained after centrifugation of the incubation mixture done in the presence of COS membranes. Shown are the predicted products, with initiation beginning at the indicated met residues. Sizes of these species are given in the text. Reproduced with permission from **ref. *8***.

Table 1
Kozak Sequences Required for Initiation of Transcription

Optimal Kozak sequence	ACCATGG
Met 1 Start sequence	AGAATGC
Met 26 sequence	AGGATGC
Met 37 sequence	GAAATGA

Kozak *(7)* determined the optimal sequence for the initiation of transcription and discovered that suboptimal sequences existed that contained a purine at position –3 from the initiating AUG codon and could initiate transcription in the absence of the optimal sequence. Shown here are the Met codons in the N-terminus of RD1 and their suboptimal Kozak sequences.

become membrane-associated. The degree of association can be readily quantified using the internal controls, as an indicator of recovery and separation. In this instance, the generation of N-terminal truncated species not only provides internal controls but also helps to identify the region of the RD1 fragment that contains information relating to membrane targeting. This shows that it is feasible to use coupled transcription–translation systems to identify protein-domain sequences responsible for membrane (or protein–protein) association. In this particular instance, the soluble species were generated spontaneously to give internal controls. However, in other instances, this may not be the case, for example, in situations in which the initiating AUG codon does not lie within an optimal Kozak sequence *(7)*. This is easily remedied, however, by adding the plasmid encoding the chimeric protein to the in vitro transcription–translation kit, a plasmid encoding the native CAT gene only, such as pGS8 *(8)*, is added. This vector encodes a soluble CAT that will then be produced to yield an internal control.

The particular observations *(10)* that information contained within the extreme N-terminus of RD1 was essential for membrane association was further confirmed by a similar experiment in which the plasmid pGS13 was substituted for pGS7. In this construct, amino acids 1–25 of RD1 replaced the 1–100 amino acid fragment in pGS7. Upon translation, in the coupled transcription–translation system, two protein species were generated of mol wt ~30 and ~25 kDa. These correspond to 1–25RD-CAT and native CAT, respectively. As before, only the species with the 1–25 amino acid fragment of RD1 was found associated with the membrane pellet fraction (**Fig. 2**, lane 11); native CAT remained entirely soluble (**Fig. 2**, lane 12). This result was reflected in the data acquired when pGS7 and pGS13 were transfected into COS 7 cells *(8)*. In this instance, expression was driven by the presence of the SV40 early promoter cloned into the plasmid constructs specifically for this reason.

Such experiments also highlight the need for using a detection system for the protein itself, and not enzyme assays for CAT. Although such a system does indeed generate enzymatically active CAT, interpretation of the distribution of this activity would not be meaningful, because of the mixture of products formed. This is also likely to happen in transfected cells, and provides a cautionary note for the use of such chimeric species (*see* **ref. *8***).

4. Notes

1. 10X Buffer. Buffer composition will vary according to the source from which the enzymes were purchased. Most suppliers will provide a tube of 10X buffer.
2. 0.2% Bromophenol blue, 0.2% xylene cyanol, 15% Ficoll 400 (Ficoll 400 is a high-mol-wt synthetic glucose homopolymer, which, when mixed with a DNA sample ensures that the DNA sinks to the bottom of the well).
3. 1.0% LMP agarose gel, dissolve 1.0 g low melting point agarose (1.75 g for 1.75% gel, *see* **Subheading 3.2.3., step 7**) in 100 mL 1X TBE (0.089 m*M* Tris, 0.89 m*M* boric acid, 0.02 m*M* EDTA) by heating until the solution becomes clear. When the agarose has cooled to 45°C, pour into the assembled gel tank and allow to set (the gel will set quicker if cast at 4°C). Once set, fill the gel tank with

enough 1X TBE to cover the surface of the gel and remove the comb. It is advisable to run the gel at 4°C to prevent melting, and it is recommended at a constant voltage not exceeding 4V/cm (this distance is determined by measuring the distance between the electrodes of the gel tank).

4. Take as small a slice from the gel as possible, because excess agarose can impair recovery of the DNA. If necessary, cut large slices into smaller pieces and recover the DNA by treating each piece separately.
5. Postpurification, the DNA should be pooled and concentrated by precipitation upon the addition of one-tenth volume of 3*M* sodium acetate pH 5.2 (CH_3COONa) and 3X volumes of absolute ethanol followed by incubation in a dry ice/methanol bath for 15 min then centrifuged at 12,000 rpm for 15 min at 4°C; aspirate off the supernatant and wash the pellet with 1 mL 70% ethanol and spin as before. When the pellet has been allowed to dry for 15 min at room temperature re suspend in the desired volume.
6. This gives a working concentration of 1.5 m*M* $MgCl_2$ in the reaction mixture which is sufficient for most PCR reactions.
7. Annealing temperatures should be 5°C below the true melting temperature of the primer as determined from the base composition. Generally, this should be between 50 and 60°C.
8. Most thermal cyclers have the ability to link programs together. For specific details of how to do this, the manufacturer's instruction manual should be consulted.
9. Maximal protein expression as measured by autoradiography occurs between 30 and 60 min and remains unchanged for at least 4 h postincubation.
10. The amount of membranes required to completely bind the protein of interest, but prevent nonspecific binding of the truncated species, may vary for types in a concentration-dependent manner, and should be determined for each membrane used by incubating the reaction mixture with a range of membrane concentrations.

References

1. Merrick, W. C. (1983) Translation of exogenous mRNAs in reticulocyte lysates. *Methods Enzymol.* **182,** 606–615.
2. Pelham, H. R. B. and Jackson, R. J. (1976) An efficient mRNA dependent translation system from reticulocyte lysates. *Eur. J. Biochem.* **67,** 247–256.
3. Craig, D., et al. (1992) Plasmid cDNA-directed protein synthesis in a coupled eukaryotic in vitro transcription-transcription system. *Nucleic Acids Res.* **20,** 4987–4995.
4. Promega (1993) Protein Guide: Tips and Techniques. Promega Corporation, Madison, WI.
5. George, D. J. and Blackshear, P. J. (1992) Membrane association of the myristoylated alanine-rich C kinase substrate (MARCKS) protein appears to involve myristate-dependent binding in the absence of a myristoyl protein receptor. *J. Biol. Chem.* **267,** 24,879–24,885.
6. Resh, M. D. (1989) Specific and saturable binding of $pp60^{v\text{-}src}$ to plasma membranes: evidence for a myristyl-src receptor. *Cell* **58,** 281–286.

7. Kozak, M. (1986) Point Mutations define a sequence flanking the AUG initiator codon that modulates translation by eukaryotic ribosomes. *Cell* **44,** 283–292.
8. Scotland, G. and Houslay, M. D. (1995) Chimeric constructs show that the unique N-terminal domain of the cyclic AMP phosphodiesterase RD1 (RNPDE4A1A; rPDE-IV_{A1}) can confer membrane association upon the normally cytosolic protein chloramphenicol acteyltransferase. *Biochem. J.* **308,** 673–681.
9. Pyne, N. J., Cooper, M. E., and Houslay, M. D. (1986) Identification and characterisation of both the cytosolic and particulate forms of cyclic GMP-stimulated cyclic AMP phosphodiesterase from rat liver. *Biochem. J.* **234,** 325–334.
10. Shakur, Y., Pryde, J. G., and Houslay, M. D. (1993) Engineered deletion of the unique N-terminal domain of the cyclic AMP-specific phosphodiesterase RD1 prevents plasma membrane association and the attainment of enhanced thermostability without altering its sensitivity to inhibition to rolipram. *Biochem. J.* **292,** 677–686.
11. Shakur, Y., et al. (1994) Identification and characterisation of the type-IV cyclic AMP specific phosphodiesterase RD1 as a membrane-bound protein expressed in cerebellum. *Biochem. J.* **308,** 801–809.
12. Davis, R. L., et al. (1989) Cloning and Characterisation of Mammalian Homologs of the Drosophila Dunce+ Gene. *Proc. Natl. Acad. Sci. USA* **86,** 3604–3608.
13. Gorman, C. M., Moffat, L. F., and Howard, B. H. (1982) Recombinant genomes which express chloramphenicol acetyl transferase in mammalian cells. *Mol. Cell. Biol.* **2,** 1044–1051.
14. Gluzman, Y. (1981) SV40-transformed simian cells support the replication of early SV40 mutants. *Cell* **23,** 175–182.
15. Luckow, B. and Schutz, G. (1987) CAT Constructions with multiple unique restriction sites for the functional analysis of eukaryotic promoters and regulatory elements. *Nucleic Acids Res.* **15,** 5490.

12

Molecular Genetic Approaches IV

Recombinant Expression of Wild-Type and Acylation-Resistant G-Protein α-Subunits Using Transient Transfection Systems

Morag A. Grassie and Graeme Milligan

1. Introduction

The ability to express recombinant proteins in eukaryotic systems by transiently expressing cloned cDNAs in cell lines, such as COS-1, COS-7 *(1)*, or human embryonic kidney HEK293 cells *(2)*, has enabled rapid analysis of a variety of wild-type and mutant signal transduction polypeptides. These have included receptors, G proteins (α-, β-, and γ-subunits), and effector molecules. This chapter aims to outline the techniques used in such experiments and to highlight potential problems, which, unless specifically investigated, may not normally be appreciated.

This chapter will concentrate particularly on the transient expression of G-protein α-subunits and illustrate how transient systems have helped to elucidate the role that the lipid modifications myristoylation and palmitoylation play in targeting the α-subunit to the membrane.

A number of α-subunit mutants have now been created with modified N-terminal regions such that either glycine at amino acid position 2 and/or cysteine at position 3 in $G_{i1\alpha}$ *(3)*, $G_{o\alpha}$ *(4,5)*, and $G_{z\alpha}$ *(6,7)*, or the cysteine at position 9 and/or 10 in $G_{q\alpha}$ *(8)*, and $G_{11\alpha}$ *(9)*, have been altered so that myristoylation at the glycine and/or palmitoylation at cysteine does not occur. By transiently expressing these mutants, the relative contribution that each modification makes, either in isolation or in combination with the other, has been assessed.

From: *Methods in Molecular Biology, Vol. 88: Protein Targeting Protocols*
Edited by: R. A. Clegg Humana Press Inc., Totowa, NJ

Cos cells are monkey kidney cells that have been transformed with SV40 large T antigen, resulting in the stable expression of this polypeptide. The large T antigen then functions as a transcription factor; any transfected cDNA that is under the control of an SV40 early promoter is transcribed at high levels in the cytoplasm. Two different clones of COS cells are generally used, either COS-1 or COS-7 cells. We currently find that higher levels of expression can be obtained with COS-7 cells.

In order for transcription of the transfected cDNA to occur, the cDNA must be expressed in a suitable vector that is capable of episomal replication in the COS cell cytoplasm (by virtue of an SV40 origin of replication present in the vector). A number of such eukaryotic vectors are commercially available, one of which is pSV SPORT (BRL, Life Technologies, Paisley, Scotland). This vector is specifically designed for use in transient transfection systems to give a high yield of recombinant protein. Other eukaryotic vectors that do not contain the SV40 early promoter can also be used successfully in this system. Such vectors include pEXV-3 ***(10)***, pCMV ***(11)***, and pcDNA (Invitrogen), all of which express the subcloned cDNA under the control of an cytomegalovirus (CMV) promoter. These vectors also have the advantage that they can be used in the generation of stable cell lines, since, in addition to the eukaryotic promoter upstream and the polyadenylation signal downstream of the multiple cloning site, they also express a eukaryotic antibiotic-resistance marker gene. To generate stable cell lines, the cells are transfected under conditions that allow the transfected cDNA and the antibiotic resistance marker encoded by the vector to become permanently incorporated into the host genome. Because recombination of the transfected cDNA and vector into the host genome is a very rare event, a large number of cells are usually transfected, and successfully transfected cells are selected in the presence of the appropriate antibiotic that will kill all untransfected cells, i.e., those lacking vector.

We have found the vector pcDNA3 to be particularly useful for both stable and transient transfections. pcDNA3 not only gives high levels of expression of transfected cDNAs in COS cells, but also contains a large number of potential cloning sites and, because of its high copy number, very easily generates large amounts of DNA. This vector also expresses resistance to neomycin, which can be used, as indicated previously, in stable cell line generation. Additionally, we have found pcDNA3 to be very efficient in expressing transfected cDNAs in HEK293 cells, a second cell line of human derivation used for transient experiments. HEK293 cells differ from COS cells because they are adenovirus-transformed (compared to COS cells, which were originally transformed by SV40). We have only been able to get good levels of expression of transfected cDNAs in such cells when the vector pcDNA3 has been used.

2. Materials

2.1. Equipment

1. Tissue culture facilities.
2. Tight-fitting teflon on glass homogenizer.
3. Sodium dodecyl sulfate polyacrylamide gel electrophoresis (SDS-PAGE) gel apparatus and power pack.
4. Microcentrifuge and refrigerated ultracentrifuge (capable of 200,000*g*).
5. Spectrophotometer and far UV cuvet.
6. Western blotting apparatus.
7. Scanning densitometer.

2.2. Reagents

1. Cos/HEK293 cell growth medium: DMEM containing 10% newborn calf serum (NCS), 20 m*M* glutamine, 100 U/mL penicillin, and 100 μg/mL streptomycin (BRL Life Technologies, Paisley, Scotland).
2. Transfection medium: DMEM containing 10% nuserum original (Stratech Scientific, Lutton, UK; *see* **Note 1**), 20 m*M* glutamine, 100 U/mL penicillin, and 100 μg/mL streptomycin.
3. Serum-free medium: DMEM containing 20 m*M* glutamine, 100 U/mL penicillin, and 100 μg/mL streptomycin.
4. Sterile TE: 10 m*M* Tris-HCl, pH 7.5, 1 m*M* EDTA.
5. Phosphate-buffered saline (PBS): 0.2 g KCl, 0.2 g KH_2PO_4, 8 g NaCl, 1.14 g Na_2HPO_4 (anhydrous) to 1000 mL with H_2O (pH should be in the range of 7.0–7.4).
6. DEAE-dextran 10 mg/mL in PBS, filter-sterilized.
7. Chloroquine: 100 m*M* in PBS, filter-sterilized.
8. 10% DMSO (v/v) in PBS.
9. Lipofectin Reagent (BRL Life Technologies).
10. Lowry stock solutions: 1% (w/v) copper sulfate, 2% (w/v) sodium potassium tartrate, 2% (w/v) sodium carbonate in 0.1*M* sodium hydroxide, Folins reagent (BDH Laboratory Supplies, UK) diluted 1:1 with H_2O, 1 mg/mL bovine serum albumin (BSA).
11. Solubilization buffer: 1% (w/v) sodium cholate in 10 m*M* Tris-HCl, 0.1 m*M* EDTA pH 7.4.
12. SDS-PAGE solutions for 10% gels as follows—acrylamide: 30 g acrylamide, 0.8 g *bis*-acrylamide to 100 mL with H_2O; buffer 1: 18.17 g Tris, 4 mL 10% SDS, pH 8.8, to 100 mL with H_2O; buffer 2: 6 g Tris, 4 mL 10% SDS, pH 6.8, to 100 mL with H_2O; 50% glycerol in H_2O; 10% (w/v) ammonium persulfate (APS) in H_2O; TEMED; 0.1% SDS; Laemmli sample buffer: 3 g urea, 0.5 g SDS 0.6 g DTT, 0.5 mL 1*M* Tris-HCl, pH 8.0, bromophenol blue (make to 10 mL with H_2O); running buffer: 28.9 g glycine, 6 g Tris, 2 g SDS (make to 2 L with H_2O).
13. Western blotting buffer: 72 g glycine, 15 g Tris, 1 L methanol, to a final volume of 5 L with H_2O.
14. Ponceau S stain: 0.1% (w/v) Ponceau S in 3% (w/v) trichloroacetic acid (TCA).
15. 5% (w/v) Gelatin in PBS containing 0.004% (w/v) thimerosal.

16. 1% (w/v) Gelatin in PBS containing 0.2% (v/v) Nonidet P-40 (NP40) + 0.004% (w/v) thimerosal.
17. 0.2% (v/v) NP40 in PBS.
18. Developing buffer: 40 mL PBS, 1 mL 1% (w/v) orthodiansidine in H_2O.
19. 1% (w/v) Sodium azide in H_2O.

3. Methods

3.1. Subcloning cDNA into Eukaryotic Vector

Unlike the expression of subcloned cDNAs in prokaryotic vectors, the exact distance of a cDNA downstream of its promoter in eukaryotic vectors is not crucial. In order to achieve successful transcription of a subcloned cDNA in a vector such as pcDNA3 or pSVSPORT, the cDNA simply should be cloned into the vector downstream of the promoter, at the multiple cloning site, in a 5'–3' orientation (*see* **Note 2**).

3.2. Preparation of DNA for Transfection

DNA for transfections can be prepared by classical methods, such as alkaline lysis or CsCl gradient purification, or by column kit methods, such as the Promega Wizard Maxi/Mini Preps, as per the manufacturers' instructions, depending on the amount of DNA required, as dictated by the number of transfections to be carried out (*see* **Note 3**).

The DNA should be accurately quantitated by measuring its optical density (OD) at 260 nm, using a far UV quartz cuvet. An OD reading of 1 at 260 nm corresponds to 50 µg/mL. The purity of the DNA can also be assessed by comparing the OD 260/280 nm ratio. This should be between 1.8 and 2.

3.3. DEAE-Dextran Transfection Method

1. Grow COS/HEK293 cells on 100 mm tissue culture plates in 8–10 mL of growth medium until the cells are 60% confluent.
2. For each 100-mm plate to be transfected take 5 µg of DNA and make to a final volume of 250 µL with sterile TE.
3. Make DEAE-dextran to a final volume of 200 mL with sterile TE.
4. Combine the DNA and DEAE-dextran solutions slowly in a 10-mL polypropylene tube and leave at room temperature for 30 min (*see* **Note 4**).
5. Prepare transfection medium by adding chloroquine to a final concentration of 100 µ*M* (10 µL stock solution to 10 mL of transfection medium) and warm to 37°C.
6. Add 10 mL of transfection medium containing chloroquine to each tube and mix.
7. Remove growth medium from cells to be transfected and carefully add the transfection medium, containing the DNA–DEAE-dextran complexes, dropwise, with a gentle swirling motion to each plate.
8. Incubate at 37°C for 3 h.
9. Remove medium and shock each plate of transfected cells by adding 4 mL of 10% DMSO-PBS for exactly 2 min (*see* **Note 5**).

10. Remove DMSO-PBS and wash cells carefully with PBS alone (twice).
11. Add 10 mL of fresh growth medium and incubate at 37°C for 48–72 h.

3.4. Lipofectin Transfection Method

Lipofectin reagent can be used as an alternative to the DEAE-dextran transfection method if the cell line being transfected is found to be sensitive to **steps 7–10** in **Subheading 3.3.** This has been found to be a problem with HEK293 cells on some occasions, when a number of the cells were found to wash off the plate. Using the DEAE-dextran transfection protocol exactly as detailed in **Subheading 3.3.** this cell loss can be minimized, however, if cells are still found to be washed from the plate by the PBS washes, the following protocol may be preferable.

1. Grow COS/HEK293 cells on 100-mm tissue culture plates in 8–10 mL of growth medium, until the cells are 60% confluent.
2. For each 100-mm plate to be transfected take 5 μg of DNA and make to a final volume of 250 μL with serum-free medium (sterile H_2O can also be used).
3. Take 50 mL Lipofectin™ reagent (*see* **Note 6**) and make to a final volume of 250 mL with serum-free medium.
4. Combine the DNA and Lipofectin solutions slowly in a 10-mL polypropylene tube and leave at room temperature for 15 min (*see* **Note 4**).
5. While the Lipofectin-DNA complexes are forming wash the cells twice with 5 mL of serum free medium to remove all traces of serum.
6. Add 6 mL of serum-free medium to the Lipofectin-DNA, mix gently, and add to the cells, swirling the plates carefully to ensure an even distribution of DNA over the entire plate.
7. Incubate at 37°C for 6–8 h (*see* **Note 7**).
8. Remove Lipofectin-DNA-containing medium and replace with 8–10 mL of growth medium.
9. Incubate at 37°C for 48–72 h.

3.5. Cell Harvesting and Fractionation

1. Remove medium and scrape cells into 5 mL of ice-cold PBS. Add a further 5 mL to the plate to collect any remaining cells, then centrifuge for 10 min at 1000*g* to collect the cell pellet.
2. Discard the supernatant, and resuspend the cell pellet in a further 10 mL of PBS and repeat centrifugation step.
3. Discard supernatant and freeze cell pellet at –80°C until required.
4. Thaw cell pellet and resuspend in 400 μL of ice-cold TE buffer.
5. Homogenize cells on ice with 25 slow strokes of a tight fitting teflon on glass homogenizer.
6. Centrifuge the samples at 200,000*g* for 30 min at 4°C to generate a soluble fraction containing cytoplasmic material (supernatant) and a particulate fraction containing the cell membranes (pellet).

7. Remove and retain the supernatant. If the membrane sample is to be detergent-solubilized, proceed to **Subheading 3.6., step 1**; otherwise, continue to **step 8**.
8. Add 400 µL of ice-cold TE buffer to the particulate fraction and resuspend by passing the sample through a wide- then fine-gage needle until the membranes are evenly resuspended.
9. Aliquot the samples into suitable volumes retaining enough to quantitate the protein by a Lowry assay, then store samples at –80°C until required.

3.6. Membrane Protein Solubilization

We have found during our analysis of various G-protein α-subunit mutants by transient transfections that a larger proportion of the expressed α-subunit than expected can sometimes be found in the particulate fraction. In order to ascertain that this protein was membrane-associated in a suitably folded conformation and not merely being isolated together with the cell membranes because of the high levels of protein expression resulting in polypeptide aggregation, we now routinely solubilize our particulate fractions. After detergent solubilization, as detailed below, if the transfected polypeptide has formed a nonfunctional aggregated mass, these polypeptides are found in the particulate fraction; G-protein α-subunits, which were membrane-associated, are released into the solubilized supernatant fraction. This allows a more accurate estimation of the relative distribution of transfected α-subunits between the membrane and the cytoplasm.

1. Add 400 µL of solubilization buffer directly to the particulate cell fraction and, using a 200-µL pipet tip, resuspend the pellet (*see* **Note 8**).
2. By using the smallest size of magnetic stirrer/bar possible (approx 4 mm), stir constantly in an iced water bath for 1 h.
3. Remove the magnetic stirrer bar and centrifuge the samples at 200,000*g* for 30 min at 4°C to generate a solubilized fraction and a particulate fraction containing insoluble material, including overexpressed transfected protein, which has formed aggregated masses.
4. Retain the solubilized supernatant fraction and resuspend the insoluble pellet directly in a known volume of Laemmli buffer (so that exactly equivalent amounts of solubilized and nonsolubilized material can be analyzed by Western blotting).

3.7. Lowry Analysis

Protein levels in membrane and cytoplasmic preparations can be determined using the following method (*see* **Note 9**).

1. The following reagents are adequate for 20 samples (these should be mixed and left at room temperature for 10 min).

   Lowry mix:

   200 µL 1% (w/v) copper sulfate
   200 µL 2% (w/v) sodium potassium tartrate
   20 µL 2% sodium carbonate in 0.1*M* sodium hydroxide

2. Prepare BSA samples for a standard calibration curve. Using a stock solution of 1 mg/mL BSA, aliquot a range of protein amounts (0–25 µg) in duplicate, and make to a final volume of 25 µL with H_2O.
3. Aliquot samples to be analyzed in duplicate. Ensure that the protein concentration of the sample analyzed will fall within the calibration curve, by using several different quantities of each sample, making the final volumes up to 25 µL with H_2O.
4. Add 1 mL of Lowry mix to each sample, and vortex.
5. Incubate at room temperature for 10 min.
6. Add 100 mL of Folins reagent, and vortex.
7. Incubate at room temperature for 30 min.
8. Read the optical density of the samples at 750 nm and plot the OD_{750} of the BSA standards against their known protein levels (in µg).
9. Using this graph, the protein levels of a given volume of the unknown samples can be determined by direct comparison of their OD readings.

3.8. Western Blotting Analysis

3.8.1. Sample Preparation

In order to analyze the relative distribution of protein in the cytoplasmic and membrane-associated fraction, equivalent volumes of each fraction should be loaded on the polyacrylamide gel. It is therefore important to always note the initial volume of the cytoplasmic fraction, so that exactly equivalent amounts of material can be analyzed. The actual amount of protein loaded per track will vary between approx 20 and 100 µg, depending on the protein being investigated and the antibody being used. For samples that have been solubilized, a proportion of each transfected plate should be loaded on the gel (10% of a 100-mm transfected tissue culture plate is a good starting point).

1. Take the required volume of each membrane sample (as determined by a Lowry assay) to give a specified protein level.
2. TCA-precipitate the membrane sample and the equivalent volume of cytoplasmic material by making the samples to 750 µL with H_2O. Add 6.5 µL 2% (w/v) sodium deoxycholate, followed by 250 µL 24% TCA, and vortex.
3. Precipitate on ice for a minimum of 10 min then centrifuge at full speed for 10 min in a microcentrifuge.
4. Discard the supernatant and neutralize samples with 20 µL of 1*M* Tris base.
5. Add 30 µL of Laemmli buffer, mix samples thoroughly and heat to 100°C for 10 min.
6. Pulse in a microcentrifuge to collect samples at the base of the tube and load on gel.

3.8.2. SDS-PAGE Analysis

The recipes for a single 16 × 18 cm 10% acrylamide gel are detailed in **Table 1**.

Table 1
10% Acrylamide Gel Recipe

Resolving gel (lower)		Stacker gel (upper)	
H_2O	8.2 mL	H_2O	9.75 mL
Buffer 1	6 mL	Buffer 2	3.75 mL
Acrylamide	8 mL	Acrylamide	1.50 mL
50% Glycerol	1.6 mL	10% APS	150 μL
10% APS	90 μL	TEMED	8 μL
TEMED	8 μL		

1. Add the resolving gel reagents in the order given and mixed thoroughly. Carefully pour into prepared gel plates.
2. Very carefully overlay gel mixture with approx 1 mL of 0.1% SDS and leave gel to polymerize.
3. Once gel has polymerized pour off SDS.
4. Prepare stacker gel using the above recipe and mix thoroughly.
5. Pour stacker gel on top of resolving gel and place the well-forming comb in top of gel, ensuring no air bubbles are trapped under the comb. Leave to polymerize.
6. Once gel has polymerized, remove the comb and place the gel in the gel tank, containing enough running buffer in the base to cover the bottom edge of the gel, and add the remaining running buffer to the top.
7. Load the prepared samples in the preformed wells using a Hamilton syringe.
8. Run the gel overnight (approx 16 h) at 12 mA and 60 V, until the dye front reaches the bottom of the gel plates. Disconnect the power.

3.8.3. Electroblotting

1. Cut two pieces of 3-mm blotting paper and one piece of nitrocellulose membrane (for each gel to be blotted) slightly larger than the gel to be blotted. Pre-equilibrate these together with electroblotting sponges in the blotting buffer.
2. Remove the gel from the gel plates (noting where position 1 on the gel lies).
3. Make a gel sandwich in the blotting apparatus holders in the following order: sponge, blotting paper, gel, nitrocellulose, blotting paper, sponge. Smooth out all air bubbles, which may have been trapped between the nitrocellulose and gel, to the side of the gel. Place the sandwich in the blotting tank filled with blotting buffer, ensuring that the nitrocellulose is positioned between the positive electrode and the gel.
4. Electrophorese at 1 A for 90–120 min.
5. Disconnect the power supply and disassemble the sandwich.
6. The nitrocellulose membrane can be Ponceau S-stained at this stage, to confirm equal loading of samples in each lane, and also to check that the transfer has been successful. Add enough stain to cover the gel and leave for 5 min.
7. Remove stain (this can be reused), washing off excess stain with distilled water. The protein bands should be visible on the nitrocellulose.

8. Remove all traces of Ponceau S stain by washing with several changes of PBS.
9. Block nitrocellulose for a minimum of 1 h in 5% gelatin at 37°C.
10. Remove gelatin and wash nitrocellulose with distilled water (at least three times)
11. Add primary antibody at the appropriate dilution in 1% gelatin in PBS + 0.2% NP40 (v/v) and incubate at 37°C for a minimum of 1 h.
12. Remove primary antibody and wash the nitrocellulose with 2 quick changes of PBS + 0.2% NP40 buffer, followed by 3 × 5-min washes.
13. Add second antibody (e.g., HRP conjugated goat antirabbit, if primary antibody was raised in rabbit) and incubate at 37°C for a minimum of 1 h.
14. Remove second antibody and wash the nitrocellulose with 2 quick changes of PBS + 0.2% NP40 buffer, followed by 3 × 5-min washes with PBS + 0.2% NP40 buffer.
15. Wash the nitrocellulose with at least six changes of PBS buffer to remove all traces of NP40.
16. Develop blot by adding developing buffer + 5 μL hydrogen peroxide.
17. Stop reaction by placing nitrocellulose in 1% (w/v) sodium azide in H_2O.
18. Wash off traces of sodium azide with distilled water then allow nitrocellulose to air-dry.
19. The relative amounts of G protein α-subunit in the particulate and cytoplasmic fractions or cytoplasmic, solubilized, and particulate fraction, may now be quantitated by scanning the blot using a scanning densitometer.

4. Notes

1. Nuserum Original is a low-protein, serum supplement, with added growth factors especially designed for transfections.
2. Problems may be encountered with low levels of expression of the transfected cDNA, if a large amount of untranslated DNA is present upstream of the initiation (start) codon of the cDNA. Such large untranslated regions should be avoided.
3. Care should be taken at the last stages of the DNA preparation, to ensure that DNA is resuspended in sterile TE. If the DNA is not sterile, it can be ethanol-precipitated, then resuspended in sterile TE, and quantitated.
4. DNA and DEAE-dextran should be combined dropwise, to avoid samples precipitating out of solution. This can be a considerable problem if higher concentrations of DNA than stated are used.
5. Care must be taken when shocking cells not to disturb the cell monolayer. HEK293 cells are very sensitive to the DMSO-PBS and PBS washes. These should be carried out with particular care in order to minimize the number of cells that are washed off the plate.
6. An alternative product, LipofectAMINE (BRL, Life Technologies), is now available, which is claimed to give greater efficiencies of transfection.
7. Because the Lipofectin transfection method requires serum-free medium, it is essential to establish if the cell line being used can tolerate the absence of serum for the stated incubation period. If a cell line is intolerant of serum free medium, the 6- to 8-h incubation period this time should be shortened accordingly. However, this may reduce the transfection efficiency.

8. To solubilize the particulate fraction, add the solubilization buffer directly to the centrifuge tube to avoid any loss of material. It should be noted that total resuspension of the particulate pellet at this stage can be very difficult; however, if a small proportion of the pellet remains intact, the membrane proteins are still efficiently solubilized.
9. The Lowry method of protein quantitation should not be used to determine protein levels in detergent-solubilized samples because detergent will interfere with this assay.

Acknowledgments

Studies in our laboratory in this area are supported by The Medical Research Council, The Biotechnology and Biological Sciences Research Council and The Wellcome Trust.

References

1. Cullen, B. R. (1987) Use of eukaryotic expression technology in the functional analysis of cloned genes. *Methods Enzymol.* **152,** 684–704.
2. Didsbury, J. R., Uhing, R. J., Tomhave, E., Gerard, C., Gerard, N., and Synderman, R. (1991) Receptor class desensitization of leukocyte chemoattractant receptors. *Proc. Natl. Acad. Sci. USA* **88,** 11,564–11,568.
3. Galbiati, F., Guzzi, F., Magee, A. I., Milligan, G., and Parenti, M. (1994) N-terminal fatty acylation of the G-protein G_i1: only the myristoylated protein is a substrate for palmitoylation. *Biochem. J.* **303,** 697–700.
4. Parenti, M., Vigano, M. A., Newman, C. M. H., Milligan, G., and Magee, A. I. (1993) A novel N-terminal motif for palmitoylation of G protein α subunits. *Biochem. J.* **291,** 349–353.
5. Grassie, M. A., McCallum, J. F., Guzzi, F., Magee, A. I., Milligan, G., and Parenti, M. (1994) The palmitoylation status of the G-protein $G_o1\alpha$ regulates its avidity of interaction with the plasma membrane. *Biochem. J.* **302,** 913–920.
6. Hallak, H., Brass, L. F., and Manning, D. R. (1994) Failure to myristoylate the α subunit of G_z is correlated with an inhibition of palmitoylation and membrane attachment, but has no affect on phosphorylation by protein kinase C. *J. Biol. Chem.* **269,** 4571–4576.
7. Wilson, P. T. and Bourne, H. R. (1995) Fatty acylation of α_z. *J. Biol. Chem.* **270,** 9667–9675.
8. Wedegaertner, P. B., Chu, D. H., Wilson, P. T., Levis, M. J., and Bourne, H. R. (1993) Palmitoylation is required for signaling functions and membrane attachment of $G_{q\alpha}$ and $G_{s\alpha}$. *J. Biol. Chem.* **268,** 25,001–25,008.
9. McCallum, J. F., Wise, A., Grassie, M. A., Magee, A. I., Guzzi, F., Parenti, M., and Milligan, G. (1995) The role of palmitoylation of the guanine nucleotide binding protein $G_{11}\alpha$ in defining interaction with the plasma membrane. *Biochem. J.* **310,** 1021–1027.
10. Miller, J. and Germain, R. N. (1986) Efficient cell surface expression of class II MHC molecules in the absence of associated invariant chain. *J. Exp. Med.* **164,** 1478–1489.
11. Andersson, S., Davis, D. N., Dahlback, H., Jornvall, H., and Russel, D. W. (1989) Cloning, structure and expression of the mitochondrial cytochrome P–450 sterol 26-hydroxylase, a bile acid biosynthetic enzyme. *J. Biol. Chem.* **264,** 8222–8229.

13

Use of Synthetic Peptides in the Dissection of Protein-Targeting Interactions

John D. Scott and Maree C. Faux

1. Introduction

Phosphorylation of protein substrates by kinases and phosphatases is a major process in the control of cellular function *(1)*. The mechanisms involved in the regulation of kinase and phosphatase activity have been thc subject of intense investigation since glycogen phosphorylase was first recognized to be regulated by phosphorylation *(2,3)*. The use of synthetic peptides has featured extensively in structure and function studies, establishing regions that are important for the control of substrate phosphorylation. The regulation of kinases and phosphatases is achieved at many levels. One level of regulation involves the subcellular localization of kinases and phosphatases through interactions with targeting proteins. This chapter will focus on the use of synthetic peptides in the identification of functional domains on targeting proteins, the characterization of bioactive peptides in vitro, and the use of peptides to disrupt enzyme localization in cells.

1.1. Kinase Substrates and Inhibitors

Knowledge of the substrate specificity of protein kinases has enabled an understanding of substrate and inhibitor recognition, which has shed some light on the way in which protein kinases are regulated *(4)*. Synthetic peptide studies have proved to be very useful in determining specific side-chain determinants in a phosphorylation consensus sequence. These studies have demonstrated that synthetic peptides modeled on the phosphorylation site sequence of substrate proteins could be phosphorylated with kinetic constants comparable to natural substrates. For example, the cAMP-dependent protein kinase (PKA) phosphorylates the sequence LRRASLG (Kemptide) from the liver pyruvate

From: *Methods in Molecular Biology, Vol. 88: Protein Targeting Protocols*
Edited by: R. A. Clegg Humana Press Inc., Totowa, NJ

kinase with kinetic parameters similar to the native protein *(5)*. The development of synthetic peptide substrates, such as Kemptide, has enabled selective and specific measurement of protein kinase activity in cell extracts, using the filter-paper assay of Corbin and Riemann *(6)* (*see* **Subheading 3.3.2.1.**). Since the introduction of Kemptide as the preferred commercial reagent to detect PKA activity, several peptide analogs have been developed to circumvent the need for radioactivity. In particular, fluorescent Kemptide analogs have been designed, and phosphorylation can be detected spectrophotometrically.

Many protein kinases exist in latent, inactive forms, because part of their structure blocks access to the active site. The pioneering work on this aspect of kinase regulation came from the laboratory of Corbin et al., where the autoinhibitory region of the type II regulatory (RII) subunit PKA was called a pseudosubstrate, because it has features that resemble the substrate and it binds in the active site *(7)*. This hypothesis was largely confirmed by synthetic peptide studies performed in the laboratories of Kemp, Walsh, and Krebs, where pseudosubstrate sequences were shown to be potent competitive inhibitors of PKA activity *(8–10)*. The type I regulatory (RI) subunit, as well as the heat-stable protein kinase inhibitor (PKI), was shown to inhibit PKA competitively with substrate *(8,9,11)*. Structure–function studies with synthetic peptides of PKI(5–24) have demonstrated potent inhibition (2.3 n*M*) and identified the residues important for inhibition *(8,9,11)*. Inhibitor peptides for other autoregulated protein kinases have also been identified and are listed in **Table 1**. The pseudosubstrate sequence of protein kinase C (PKC) is also a potent substrate antagonist that inhibits competitively, with respect to peptide substrate, and noncompetitively with ATP *(12)*. Modification of peptides has enabled their use inside cells. For example, *N*-myristoylation of the peptide $F^{20}ARKGALRQ^{28}$, derived from the pseudosubstrate sequence of PKC, allows the peptide to permeate the cells and to specifically inhibit PKC *(13)*. This method has recently been used to powerful effect in human breast cancer MCF7-MDR cells, in which the *N*-myristoylated peptide to the pseudosubstrate region of PKC-α has been shown to partially reverse multidrug resistance through inhibition of PKC-α *(30)*. In addition, antipeptide antibodies raised against the pseudosubstrate sequence (residues 19–36) have been shown to activate PKC in the absence of external activators *(31)*. The studies illustrate the many ways in which synthetic peptides have been used to understand aspects of structure and regulation of these enzymes, as well as their use as probes for biological function.

1.2. The Targeting Hypothesis

It is becoming apparent that the subcellular location of signaling enzymes represents an important means to control the actions of multifunctional protein kinases and phosphatases. A flurry of recent advances from a variety of labora-

Table 1
Protein Kinase Pseudosubstrate Peptide Inhibitors

Protein kinase	Pseudosubstrate sequence	K_i/IC_{50} μM
cAMP-dependent PK		
PKI(5–24)	TTYADFIASGRTGRRNAIHD	0.0023
cGMP-dependent PK(α_2)		
cGMP PKα(54–69)	GPRTTRAQGISAEP	2100
Protein kinase C		
PKCβ(19–31)	RFARKGALRQKNV	0.13
smMLCK		
smMLCK(787–808)	SKDRMKKYMARRKWQKTGHAV	0.0012
smMLCK(774–807)	LQKDTKNMEAKKLSKDRMKKYMARRKWQKTGHAV	0.0003
CaM-II PK (α_2)		
CaM-II PK(281-309)	MHRQET*VDCLKKFNARRKLKGAILTTMLA	2.7
(290–309)	LKKFNARRKLKGAILTTMLA	24
Phosphorylase β kinase ($\alpha\beta\gamma\delta$)		
α(332–353)	VIRDPYALRPLRRLIDAYAFRI^{353}	
β(420–436)	KRNPGSQKRFPSNCGRD^{436}	921

Based on substrate and pseudosubstrate sequences described in **ref. *35***.

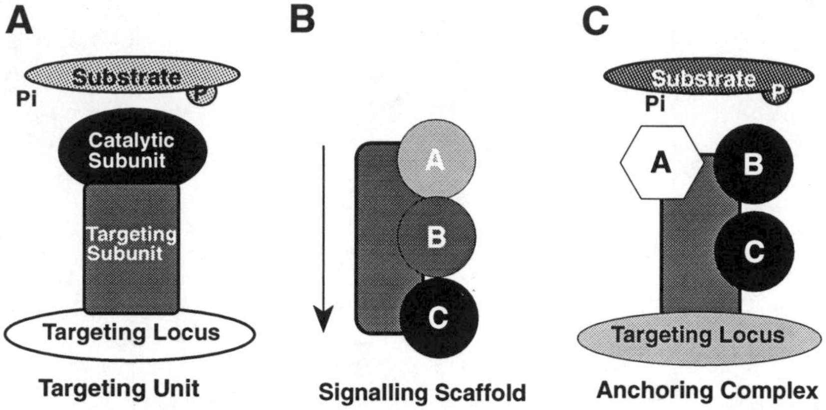

A B C

Substrate
Pi
Catalytic Subunit
Targeting Subunit
Targeting Locus
Targeting Unit

A
B
C
Signalling Scaffold

Substrate
Pi
A
B
C
Targeting Locus
Anchoring Complex

Fig. 1. Subcellular targeting of protein kinases and phosphatases. **(A)** Schematic diagram depicting the catalytic subunit of a kinase or phosphatase positioned close to substrate proteins through a targeting subunit. **(B)** Schematic diagram of a kinase signaling scaffold, where A, B, and C represent several kinases in a pathway bound to a scaffold protein. **(C)** Schematic diagram of an anchored kinase/phosphatase signaling complex, where A, B, and C represent kinases or phosphatases anchored close to substrate proteins.

tories indicates that the subcellular location of these enzymes is maintained by association with specific targeting proteins. For example, PKA, PKC, and the Ca^{2+}/calmodulin-dependent protein kinase II (CaM kinase II) are localized by specific binding proteins *(17,23,25)*. Likewise, protein phosphatases (PP-) 1, 2A, and 2B are positioned through association with phosphatase targeting subunits. The "targeting hypothesis" proposes that targeting subunits or proteins specify the location and catalytic and regulatory properties of protein kinases and phosphatases *(14)*. The targeting subunit is defined as that part of a kinase or phosphatase that directs the catalytic subunit to a subcellular location (**Fig. 1A**). An additional level of complexity in the subcellular targeting of signaling enzymes involves the formation of kinase–phosphatase signaling complexes, in which more than one enzyme may be targeted through one molecule. This allows the coordination of phosphorylation events through multivalent targeting proteins, providing an efficient means to regulate signal transduction events *(15,32)*. Two related, but distinct, classes of targeting protein mediate this process. Scaffold proteins simultaneously associate with several kinases of a pathway, allowing signals to pass from one enzyme to the next (**Fig. 1B**); anchoring proteins are tethered to targeting loci and maintain their complement of enzymes close to their site of action (**Fig. 1C**). The following sections describe the use of peptides in defining the regions of A-kinase anchor proteins (AKAPs) involved in the subcellular targeting of PKA, and their use as reagents to probe the function of anchored enzymes (*see* **Subheading 3.1.**). Chapter 5 describes methods used to study kinase anchoring using AKAPs as a model; this chapter will concentrate on our analysis of a neuronal anchoring protein, AKAP79, which has been shown to act as a scaffold for three signaling enzymes, PKA, PKC (*see* **Subheading 3.3.**), and PP-2B, calcineurin (CaN) (*see* **Subheading 3.2.**) *(15)*.

2. Materials

2.1. Dissection of PKA–AKAP Interactions

2.1.1. Peptide Block of RII–AKAP Interaction in RII Overlay

1. Sodium dodecyl sulfate-polyacrylamide gel electrophoresis (SDS-PAGE) apparatus and solutions.
2. Immobilon (Millipore, Bedford, MA) or nitrocellulose membrane (Protran, Schleicher & Schnell, Keene, NH).
3. BLOTTO: Tris-buffered saline, pH 7.0 (TBS), 5% dry milk, 1% bovine serum albumin (BSA).
4. RII (recombinant protein).
5. [γ-^{32}P]-ATP (10 mCi/mL) *NEN* Dupont (Boston, MA).
6. PKA catalytic subunit (purified from bovine brain).
7. Reaction buffer: 50 m*M* MOPS, pH 6.8, 50 m*M* NaCl, 2 m*M* $MgCl_2$, 1 m*M* dithiothreitol (DTT), 0.1 mg/mL BSA.
8. Excellulose GF-5 desalting column (Pierce) (Rockford, IL).
9. Tris-buffered saline (TBS)/0.05% Tween-20 (TTBS).
10. Anchoring inhibitor peptides: Ht31 (493–509); control Ht31 (494–509Pro^{502}), stock solutions stored at –20°C.
11. 3MM paper (Whatman) (Maidstone, UK).

2.1.2. Peptide Elution of AKAPs Following Copurification with RII

1. Bovine brain tissue.
2. Hypotonic buffer: 10 m*M* HEPES, pH 7.9, containing 1.5 m*M* $MgCl_2$, 10 m*M* KCl, 10 μ*M* IBMX, 0.5 m*M* DTT, and protease inhibitors: 1 m*M* AEBSF, 2 μg/mL pepstatin/leupeptin, 1 m*M* benzamidine.
3. cAMP-agarose (Sigma, St. Louis, MO).
4. Anchoring inhibitor peptide and control (*see* **Subheading 2.1.1., step 10**).
5. 75 m*M* cAMP (Sigma).
6. 6% TCA.
7. SDS sample buffer: 80 m*M* Tris-HCl, pH 6.8, 100 m*M* DTT, 2% SDS, 10% glycerol, 0.0012% bromophenol blue.
8. SDS-PAGE apparatus and solutions.
9. ^{32}P-RII (prepared as described **Subheading 3.1.1.**).
10. Antibodies to RII.

2.1.3. PKA-Anchoring Inhibitor Peptides in vivo

1. Cultured rat hippocampal neurons (5–12 d).
2. Intracellular medium under recording conditions: 10 m*M* HEPES, pH 7.2, 65 m*M* NaCl, 2.4 m*M* KCl, 2 m*M* $CaCl_2$, 1 m*M* $MgCl_2$, 10 m*M* glucose, 1 μ*M* tetrodotoxin, 100 μ*M* picrotoxin.
3. Recording pipets containing: 10 m*M* HEPES, pH 7.3, 155 m*M* caesium gluconate, 10 m*M* BAPTA, 5 m*M* Mg-ATP, 2 m*M* $MgCl_2$.
4. Peptides: PKI (5–24), anchoring inhibitor peptides: Ht31(493-509) and AKAP79(394–409), control anchoring inhibitor proline peptide Ht31(493–509Pro^{502}).
5. PKA catalytic subunit.

2.1.4. Delivery of Cell Soluble Peptide

1. *N*-myristoylated anchoring inhibitor peptide.
2. Nonmyristoylated anchoring inhibitor peptide.
3. Cultured rat hippocampal neurons.
4. 0.1% DMSO/phosphate-buffered saline (PBS).
5. PBS.
6. 3.7% Formaldehyde in PBS.
7. 100% Acetone stored at –20°C; PBS containing 0.1% BSA stored at 4°C.
8. Peptide antibody to anchoring inhibitor peptide (stored at 4°C).
9. Fluorescent secondary antibody (Molecular Probes, Eugene, OR).

2.2. Dissection of Calcineurin–AKAP Interactions

2.2.1. CaN Activity Assay

2.2.1.1. Preparation of ^{32}P-RII Peptide Substrate

1. [γ-^{32}P]-ATP; radioactive concentration 10 mCi/mL (*NEN* Dupont).
2. "Cold" ATP 10 m*M* stock, pH 7.0 (stock aliquoted and stored at –20°C).
3. pH 1.9 buffer: 2% formic acid, 8% acetic acid, 90% H_2O.
4. RII peptide.
5. PKA catalytic subunit (2 μg/mL).
6. [γ-^{32}P]-ATP stock (1000 cpm/pmol).
7. Reaction buffer: 20 m*M* MOPS, pH 7.0, 2 m*M* MgAcetate, 5 m*M* β-mercaptoethanol.
8. Acetic acid.
9. AG1X8 resin (Bio-Rad [Hercules, CA]).
10. C-18 Sep Pak cartridge (Pierce).
11. 0.1% TFA.
12. 50% CH_3CN, 49.9% H_2O, 0.1% TFA.
13. 1*M* $(NH_4)_2CO_3$.
14. pH paper.

2.2.1.2. CaN Assay

1. 5X concentrate assay buffer: 200 μ*M* Tris-HCl, pH 7.5, 0.5*M* KCl, 0.5 m*M* $CaCl_2$, 30 m*M* MgAcetate, 2.5 m*M* DTT, and 0.5 mg/mL BSA, stored at 4°C; DTT added freshly from 1*M* stock stored at –20°C.

2. Calmodulin 5 mg/mL stock.
3. CaN (recombinant protein expressed in baculovirus).
4. CaN diluting buffer: 40 μ*M* Tris-HCl, pH 7.5, 0.1*M* KCl and 0.5 m*M* DTT, stored at –20°C.
5. ^{32}P-RII peptide (prepared as described in **Subheading 3.2.1.1.**)
6. 75 m*M* phosphoric acid.
7. AG50W-X8 resin (Bio-Rad).
8. Glass Pasteur pipets with glass bead placed at base to make a column or polyprep plastic columns (Bio-Rad).
9. Aqueous-compatible scintillant.

2.2.2. Inhibition of CaN

As for CaN assays (*see* **Subheading 2.2.1.2.**); CaN inhibitor peptide AKAP79(88–102).

2.3. Dissection of PKC–AKAP Interactions

2.3.1. Peptide Block of PKC–AKAP Interaction in PKC Overlay

1. SDS-PAGE apparatus and solutions.
2. Immobilon or nitrocellulose membrane.
3. BLOTTO: TBS, pH 7.0, 5% dry milk, 1% BSA.
4. TBS, pH 7.0.
5. Phosphatidyserine (PS) 20 μg/mL: Brain extract Type III from Sigma.
6. 1.4 m*M* PS/0.04 m*M* diacylglycerol (DG) in 20 m*M* HEPES, pH 7.5 (*see* **Note 23**), from Avanti Polar Lipids (Alabaster, AL).
7. PKC: Partially purified from rabbit brain.
8. PKC assay buffer: TBS, 1% albumin, 1.2 m*M* Ca^{2+}, 1 m*M* EGTA, 10 μg/mL leupeptin, 10 μg/mL pepstatin.
9. PBS wash buffer: PBS, pH 7.0, 1.2 m*M* Ca^{2+}, 1 m*M* EGTA, 20 μg/mL PS.
10. 3.7% Paraformaldehyde/PBS stock.
11. PBS + 2% glycine.
12. AKAP peptides (residues 31–52 from AKAP79 to block PKC binding; AKAP79 388–409 as control RII binding peptide).
13. Chemiluminescence reagents (Pierce).

2.3.2. Peptide Inhibition of PKC Activity

2.3.2.1. PKC Activity Assays

1. 4X concentrate assay buffer stock: 80 m*M* HEPES, pH 7.5, 40 m*M* $MgCl_2$, 4 m*M* DTT.
2. 10X stocks of the following effectors: 3 m*M* Ca^{2+} (or 5 m*M* EGTA); 1.4 m*M* PS/ 0.04 m*M* DG in 20 m*M* HEPES, pH 7.5 (*see* **Note 23**) (or 20 m*M* HEPES, pH 7.5).
3. 1 m*M* [γ-^{32}P]-ATP (200 cpm-pmol).
4. EGF-Receptor peptide substrate (Sigma), stock concentration 5 mg/mL (~4.175 m*M*), diluted to 10 μ*M* in assay.
5. PKCβII (expressed in baculovirus), diluted to 5 n*M* (final) in assay.

6. PKC diluting buffer: 20 m*M* Tris-HCl, pH 7.9, 1 mg/mL BSA, 1 m*M* DTT.
7. Phosphocellulose P81 paper (2 × 2-cm squares).
8. Wire cage that fits inside 500-mL beaker.
9. 75 m*M* Phosphoric acid.
10. Hair dryer used to dry P81 papers.

2.3.2.2. Inhibition of PKC

1. As for PKC assay (*see* **Subheading 2.3.2.1.**).
2. Peptide inhibitor AKAP79 (residues 31–52).

3. Methods: Dissection of Signaling Complexes with Bioactive Peptides

3.1. Dissection of PKA–AKAP interactions

Since several AKAPs apparently bind to the same or overlapping sites on RIIα, it seemed likely that these molecules share a common RII-binding domain. However, comparison of these sequences revealed no striking homology (**Fig. 2A**), leading us to examine the RII-binding site in each anchoring protein for a conserved secondary structure binding motif. Computer-aided secondary structure predictions of each putative RII-binding site showed a high probability for amphipathic helix formation. The distinction between the hydrophobic and hydrophilic faces can be clearly seen when the sequences are drawn in a helical-wheel configuration (**Fig. 2B**). In each RII-anchoring protein there was a similar alignment of acidic residues throughout the hydrophilic face of each putative helix.

Analysis of Ht 31, a novel human thyroid RII-anchoring protein of 1035 amino acids, identified a potential amphipathic helix between residues 494 and 509 ***(16)***. This sequence (Leu-Ile-Glu-Glu-Ala-Ala-Ser-Arg-Ile-Val-Asp-Ala-Val-Ile-Glu-Gln) was 43% identical to region within the RII-binding site of MAP 2 (**Fig. 2A**). A peptide that spans the putative amphipathic helix region of Ht 31 binds RIIα with an affinity of approx 4 n*M* ***(18)***, and circular dichroism analysis suggests it can adopt an α-helical conformation. This anchoring-inhibitor peptide has been used extensively as a tool to probe for AKAP-RII interaction in solid-phase RII overlays (*see* **Subheading 3.1.1.**) and to specifically elute AKAPs following copurification with RII (*see* **Subheading 3.1.2.**). An additional method for dissecting PKA–AKAP interactions has involved the use of biotinylated anchoring inhibitor peptides in a peptide overlay technique. This method is described in detail in Chapter 5 of this volume. The anchoring-inhibitor peptide has recently been used to disrupt the interaction between RII and AKAPs in neurons, which affects the modulation of glutamate receptor channels (*see* **Subheading 3.1.3.**). Finally, *N*-myristoylation of this peptide allows it to be permeable to cells (*see* **Subheading 3.1.4.**).

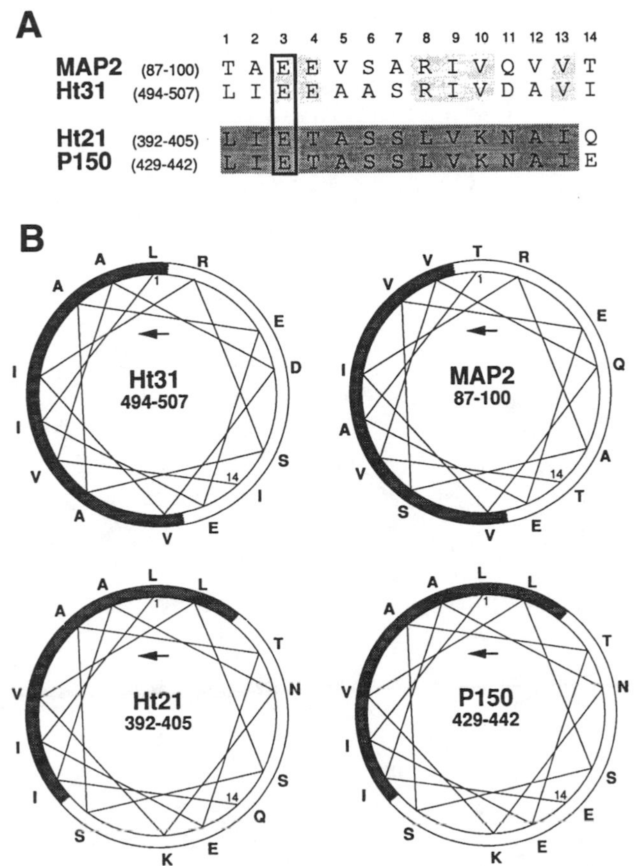

Fig. 2. The RII-binding region of AKAPs. **(A)** Primary sequence comparison of the RII binding region of 4 AKAPs, MAP2, Ht31, Ht21 (AKAP79), and P150 (AKAP150). **(B)** Helical wheel representation of the four AKAPs in (A) drawn as an amphipathic helix. The shaded area indicates hydrophobic residues and the open area indicates hydrophilic residues. Amino acids are indicated in the single letter code. The arrow indicates the direction of the helix.

3.1.1. Peptide Block of RII–AKAP Interaction in RII Overlay

The RII overlay is an established method for detection of RII-binding proteins (such as AKAPs) *(17)*. The anchoring-inhibitor peptide is incubated with radiolabeled RII and specifically blocks interaction of the protein immobilized on the blot and the radiolabeled RII. A control peptide for the Ht31 peptide (residues 493–509) has been designed that has a single proline substituted for isoleucine at 502, which disrupts the amphipathic helix and can no longer bind RII.

1. Separate protein samples by SDS-PAGE and transfer to Immobilon or nitrocellulose membranes by standard electrotransfer techniques (**ref. *33***; *see* **Note 1**).
2. Block membrane by incubation with BLOTTO + 1% BSA (TBS, pH 7.0, 5% dry milk, 1% BSA) for 1 h at room temperature (*see* **Note 2**).
3. RII protein (2 µg) is radiolabeled by incubation with PKA catalytic subunit (0.1 µg) and [γ-^{32}P]-ATP (50 µCi) in a reaction buffer containing 50 m*M* MOPS, pH 6.8, 50 m*M* NaCl, 2 m*M* $MgCl_2$, 1 m*M* DTT, and 0.1 mg/mL BSA at 30°C for 15 min.
4. Separate radiolabeled protein from free ^{32}P-ATP on a excellulose GF-5 desalting column equilibrated in TBS/0/05% Tween-20 (TTBS) (*see* **Note 3**).
5. Incubate anchoring inhibitor peptide (e.g., Ht31 [residues 493–509] peptide or control proline peptide Ht31 peptide [residues 493–509 Pro^{50}2] [0.4–1.0 µ*M*] and radiolabeled RII (specific activity 10^5 cpm/mL) in BLOTTO with blocked-protein blot, for a minimum of 4 h at room temperature, with agitation (*see* **Notes 4** and **5**).
6. Wash blot extensively with TTBS (4 × 15 min) to remove free ^{32}P-RII.
7. Expose to film overnight at –70°C and develop autoradiograph.

3.1.2. Peptide Elution of AKAPs Following Copurification with RII

A common method to demonstrate that a complex between an AKAP and RII exists inside cells is to copurify the complex using an affinity matrix, such as cAMP agarose. A cell lysate is passed over cAMP-agarose and nonspecific binding proteins removed before specific elution with cAMP. A variation on this technique is to elute the AKAP from RII using the anchoring-inhibitor peptide (**Fig. 3B**), followed by the cAMP elution to remove the RII from the cAMP agarose (**Fig. 3C**). Thus, the interaction of the AKAP with RII is shown to specifically occur through an amphipathic helix on the AKAP, which is disrupted in the presence of the anchoring-inhibitor peptide. CaN also copurified with RII and the AKAP, and was shown to be displaced with the AKAP from RII (**Fig. 3A**) (*see* **Subheading 3.2.**).

1. Prepare cell lysate from tissue or cultured cells. For example, for copurification of RII and AKAP75 (the bovine homolog of AKAP79), a bovine brain extract was prepared from flash-frozen bovine cortex. Chunks (approx 3 g) of frozen brain cortex were ground to a fine powder in liquid nitrogen with a mortar and pestle. The frozen powder was added to 6 mL ice-cold hypotonic buffer (10 m*M* HEPES, pH 7.9 containing 1.5 m*M* Mg Cl_2, 10 m*M* KCl, 10 µ*M* IBMX, 0.5 m*M* DTT, 0.1% NP40, and protease inhibitors: 1 m*M* AEBSF, 2 µg/mL pepstatin/leupeptin, 1 m*M* benzamidine). The frozen slurry was homogenized until uniform in consistency in several batches with an ice-cold dounce homogenizer. The homogenate was centrifuged at 25,000*g* for 30 min at 4°C and the lysate supernatant retained.
2. Incubate lysate supernatant (2 mL) with cAMP-agarose (1 mL packed beads) overnight at 4°C on a horizontal rotator.
3. Centrifuge at 3000*g* for 5 min at 4°C and decant supernatant.

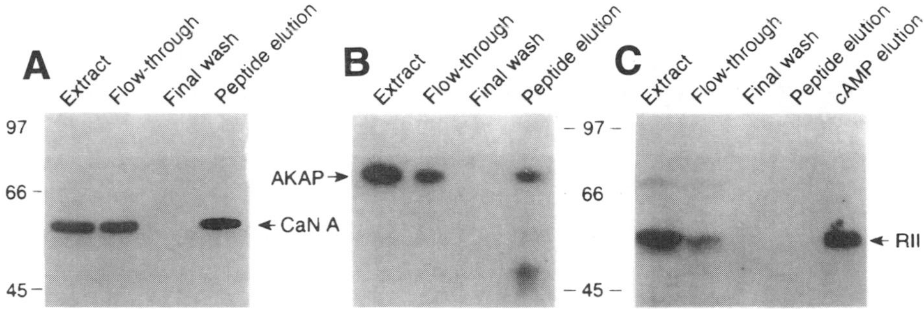

Fig. 3. Copurification of CaN and PKA from bovine brain by affinity chromatography on cAMP-agarose. The Ht31 (493–515) peptide was used to specifically displace AKAPs from the cAMP-affinity column. Protein blots were probed with antibodies to CaN **(A)**, ^{32}P-RII to detect AKAPs **(B)**, or antibodies to RII **(C)**. The latter shows that RII was still bound to the cAMP-agarose following peptide elution, but was specifically eluted with cAMP. Positions of mol-wt markers are indicated in kDa *(23)*.

4. Resuspend the cAMP-agarose beads in hypotonic buffer and transfer to a 2-mL column (Bio-Rad).
5. Wash column with 5 column volumes hypotonic buffer, containing 1*M* NaCl, and 20–30 column volumes hypotonic buffer (*see* **Note 6**).
6. Elute the AKAP from RII with 1 ml 0.5 m*M* anchoring-inhibitor peptide or the control proline peptide (*see* **Subheading 3.1.1.**) by incubating with cAMP-agarose beads at room temperature for 1 h.
7. Elute RII from the cAMP-agarose with 1 mL 75 m*M* cAMP by incubation at room temperature for 1 h (*see* **Notes 7** and **8**).
8. Concentrate the 1*M* NaCl wash, low-salt wash, peptide, and cAMP elutions by TCA precipitation in order to load all of the sample on a SDS-gel. Add ice-cold TCA to 6% to each sample and incubate on ice for 20–30 min. Centrifuge at 16,000*g* for 5 min and remove supernatant. Wash protein pellet with ether/ethanol (80:20), vortex vigorously, and centrifuge at 16,000*g*. Remove supernatant. Allow pellet to dry before adding SDS-sample buffer, boil for 5 min, and load on SDS-gel (*see* **Note 9**).
9. Detect proteins by RII overlay and/or Western blot (*see* **Fig. 3**).

Comment: This technique can also be used for immunoprecipitation experiments, in which an antibody to an AKAP is used to precipitate the AKAP and the proteins that are associated with it. To demonstrate that RII is specifically associated, the anchoring inhibitor peptide is used to displace RII from the AKAP. This technique has tremendous advantages over the more general SDS-sample buffer elution.

3.1.3. PKA-Anchoring Inhibitor Peptides In Vivo

The majority of RII/AKAP interactions have been studied in vitro and under nonphysiological conditions. However, the high affinity of the amphipathic

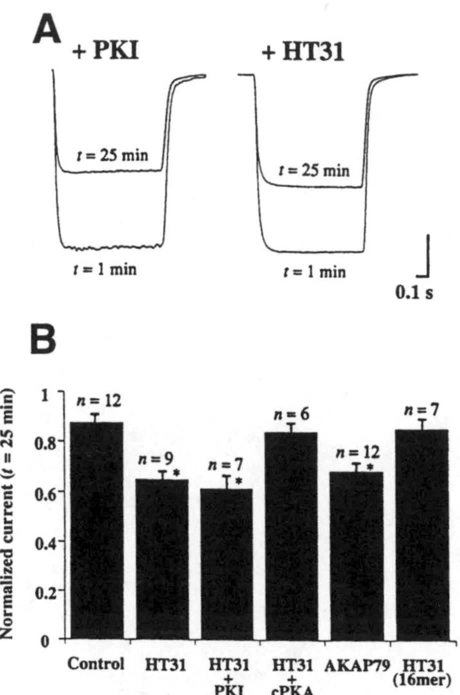

Fig. 4. Displacement of RII by anchoring inhibitor peptides blocks the regulation of AMPA/kainate channels by PKA. **(A)** Inward currents evoked by kainate (20 μ*M*) at 1 and 25 min after the start of whole cell recordings are superimposed. Left, in presence of PKI(5–24) (1 μ*M*) in the recording pipet. Right, in presence of the Ht31 anchoring-inhibitor peptide. **(B)** Amplitude of AMPA/kainate currents after 25 min of recording in the presence of ATP in the patch pipet. Histogram bars show mean current amplitudes ***(20)***.

helix peptides for RII made them ideal antagonists of PKA anchoring in vivo. The test system for these studies was the compartmentalization of PKA to the postsynaptic densities in hippocampal neurons, in which the kinase has easy access to the ionotrophic glutamate receptors. These receptors are central to the process of signal transduction across the synaptic membranes; PKA-dependent phosphorylation is required to maintain the activity of AMPA/kainate responsive glutamate receptor channels ***(19,20)***.

Bioactive peptides were introduced into the neurons via a microdialysis technique that took advantage of the patch pipet as a delivery system. The role of PKA in maintaining channel activity was confirmed by a gradual decline in whole-cell currents evoked by kainate (20 μ*M*), recorded in the presence of ATP (20 μ*M*) and 1 μ*M* PKI (5–24) peptide, a potent and specific inhibitor of the catalytic subunit of PKA (61.8 ± 3.2% *n* = 11) (**Fig. 4A**). To test the role of AKAPs in localizing the kinase near the channel, the anchoring-inhibitor peptides (1 μ*M*) were added to the whole-cell pipet. The anchoring-inhibitor peptide derived from two AKAPs, Ht 31 or AKAP79, inhibited AMPA/kainate currents to the same extent as the PKI peptide (64.9 ± 3.2% $n = 12$ and 68.8 ± 3.3% $n = 12$) (**Fig. 4B**). The effects of PKI and the anchoring inhibitor peptides were not additive. However, the action of the Ht 31 peptide could be overcome by the C subunit of PKA (0.3 μ*M*) suggesting that the anchoring inhibitor peptide interfered with PKA-dependent phosphorylation, but did not directly inhibit the kinase. In addition, the control peptide unable to block RII/AKAP interaction had no effect on kainate currents (85 ± 4.1% $n = 7$). Finally, currents evoked by AMPA (1 μ*M* $n = 6$) behaved in the same manner as those evoked by application of kainate. These results indicate that PKA localization is required for modulation of AMPA/kainate currents. These studies represented the first physiological evidence of the importance of PKA anchoring in the modulation of a specific cAMP-responsive event ***(20)***. Recently, Catterall and colleagues have used these peptides to demonstrate that disruption of PKA anchoring close to the L-type Ca^{2+} channel is required to maintain the channel in the active state ***(21)***. The functional effect of phosphorylation of the receptors appears to be desensitization for their agonist.

3.1.4. Delivery of Cell-Soluble Peptides

In order to perform the biochemical experiments, it is often necessary to introduce bioactive peptides into cells. Recently, covalently modified forms of peptides have been introduced into fibroblasts and neurons. A myristoylated peptide based on the Ht31(493–515) anchoring inhibitor peptide was synthesized according to the methods of Eichholtz et al. ***(13)***. This technique demonstrates that myristoylation is a viable means to introduce these peptides into living cells.

1. Dissolve myristoylated peptide and nonmyristoylated peptide 10 m*M* (anchoring-inhibitor peptide) in 100% DMSO and dilute to a final concentration of 500 μ*M* in 5% DMSO/PBS (*see* **Note 10**).
2. Incubate myristoylated and nonmyristoylated control peptide with living cultures of rat hippocampal neurons for 1 h at 37°C (*see* **Note 11**).
3. Wash cultures extensively in PBS.
4. Fix cultures with 3.7% formaldehyde for 5 min at room temperature, wash in 100% acetone at –20°C for 1 min and incubate in a blocking solution of PBS containing 0.1% BSA for 30 min at room temperature.
5. Stain individual cover slips for uptake of myristoylated peptide with an antibody to the Ht31 (493–509) peptide followed with fluorescently labeled goat antirabbit IgG secondary antibody (*see* **Note 12**). Alternatively, the myristoylated peptide can be labeled with a fluorescent tag and intracellular uptake visualized directly by fluorescence.

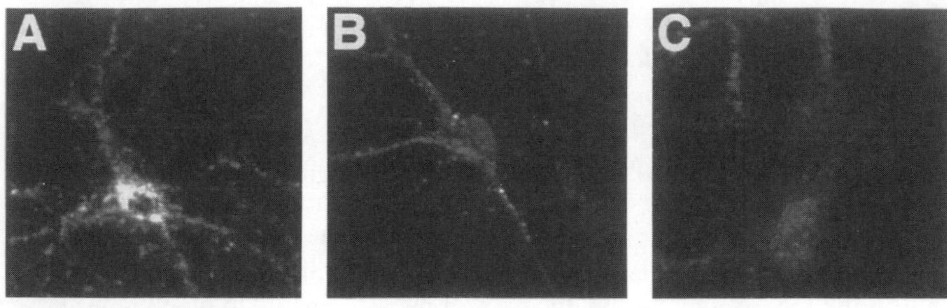

Fig. 5. Confocal immunomicroscopy of cultured rat hippocampal neurons incubated with myristoylated anchoring inhibitor peptide **(A)**, nonmyristoylated anchoring inhibitor peptide **(B)**, or absence of peptide **(C)**.

6. Indirect immunofluorescent detection of intracellular uptake of peptide visualized using a confocal microscope. The uptake of the myristoylated anchoring-inhibitor peptide is shown in **Fig. 5A**. Confocal analysis of individual neurons was performed on nine focal planes (0.5 µm) to confirm that detection of immunofluorescence was predominantly intracellular. Increased amounts of the myristoylated Ht31 (493–515) peptide were detected inside neurons (**Fig. 5A**) when compared to cells incubated with the non-myristoylated form (**Fig. 5B**). Control experiments incubated in the absence of peptide demonstrate the background level of staining (**Fig. 5C**).

3.2. Dissection of Calcineurin–AKAP Interactions

Bioactive peptides have also been used as reagents to decipher the complex web of protein–protein interactions that participate in the formation of the AKAP79 signaling complex. This section outlines studies that utilized synthetic peptides to map binding sites on AKAP79 for the protein phosphatase-2B, calcineurin (CaN). Our model for colocalization of PKA and CaN through AKAP79 implies that the AKAP contains distinct sites for kinase and phosphatase binding *(23)*. Residues 88–102 of AKAP79 (Arg-Arg-Lys-Arg-Ser-Glu-Ser-Ser-Lys-Gln-Gln-Lys-Pro-Phe-Lys) were considered likely to comprise the CaN binding site because of homology with a region of the immunophilin FKBP-12 that contains determinants for CaN association (**Fig. 6A**). As CaN was inactive when isolated as a complex with the AKAP, we examined the effects of a synthetic peptide, corresponding to AKAP79 residues 81–102, on CaN activity. The peptide inhibited both CaN forms, but the Ht31 (493–515) peptide did not inhibit CaN (Fig. 6B). In addition, the observed inhibition was specific for calcineurin; the peptide did not significantly affect the activity of protein phosphatases 1 or 2A, at peptide concentrations as high as 0.4 m*M*. The following outlines the methods used to assay CaN and measure the inhibition caused by the AKAP79 peptide (residues 81–802).

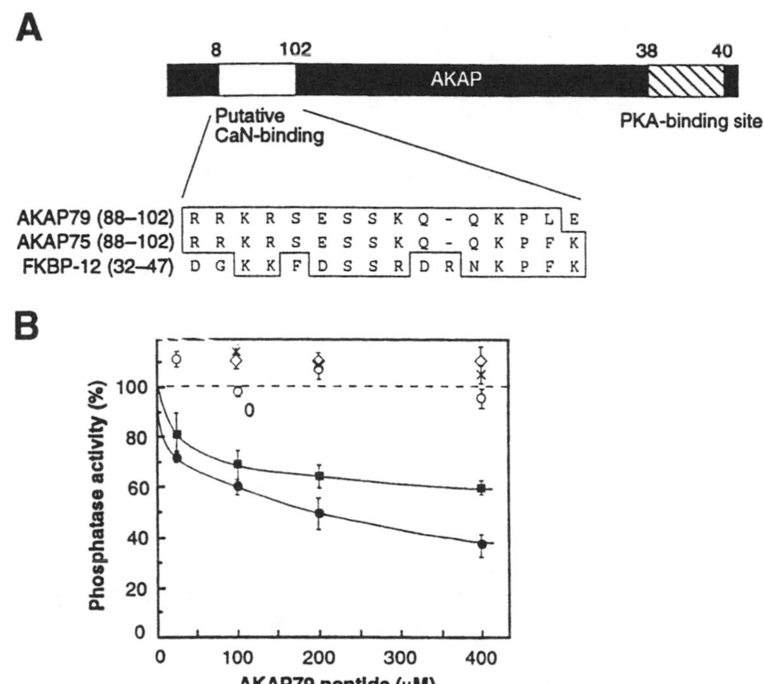

Fig. 6. Inhibition of CaN by AKAP79(88–102) peptide. **(A)** Schematic representation of AKAP79, indicating the PKA- and CaN-binding sites. Also shown is the sequence comparison of sites within AKAP79, AKAP75, and bovine FKBP12. Amino acid numbers are indicated and residues are indicated by the single letter code. **(B)** Dose–response curves of CaN (filled circles) and the Ca^{2+}-calmodulin independent fragment of CaN ($CaN_{42}0$) (filled squares) activity in the presence of the AKAP79(88–102) peptide. A control peptide corresponding to the RII-binding site of Ht31 did not inhibit CaN activity (open circles). The AKAP79 peptide did not inhibit protein phosphatase 1 (open diamonds) or 2A (crosses). Values are mean ± SD ***(23)***.

3.2.1. CaN Activity Assay

The substrate used to assay CaN activity is a phosphorylated peptide derived from RII (Asp-Leu-Asp-Val-Pro-Ile-Pro-Gly-Arg-Phe-Asp-Arg-Arg-Val-Ser-Val-Ala-Ala-Glu).

3.2.1.1. Preparation of ^{32}P-RII Peptide Substrate

1. To make [γ-^{32}P]-ATP stock ***(34)***:
   a. Calculate the amount of [γ-^{32}P]-ATP required: (for a 1-mL final volume)

desired specific activity (cpm/pmol) × conc. (mmol/L) × 10^6/
[radioactive concentration of material as supplied (mCi/mL) × 2.2 × 10^6]
= volume [γ-^{32}P]-ATP (μL) to be added

b. Calculate the amount of cold ATP required:

$$\text{volume cold ATP} = \text{desired conc. ATP} \times \text{total volume (e.g., 1 mL)}/\text{conc. ATP stock}$$

c. Add calculated volume of [γ-^{32}P]-ATP, cold ATP and adjust to 1 mL with H_2O. (*see* **Note 13**).

d. Measure specific activity of [γ-^{32}P]-ATP stock: Take an aliquot of [γ-^{32}P]-ATP stock (10 μL) and dilute to 1 mL with pH 1.9 buffer (2% formic acid: 8% acetic acid:90% H_2O). The extinction coefficient of a 1 mmol/L stock of ATP at pH 1.9 at 257 nm is 14.7. Measure absorbance at 257 nm of diluted solution and count 10-μL aliquots. Specific activity (SA) of the stock can be calculated:

$$\text{SA (cpm/pmol)} = \text{cpm} \times \text{dilution factor}/[\text{conc. (μmol/L)} \times 10^6]$$

2. RII peptide (1 m*M*) is radiolabeled by incubation with PKA catalytic subunit (2 μg/mL) and [γ-^{32}P]-ATP (1000 cpm/pmol) in 20 m*M* MOPS, pH 7.0, 2 m*M* MgAcetate, 5 m*M* β-mercaptoethanol at 30°C for 15 min in 400 μL. Stop reaction by adding 120 μL glacial acetic acid (30% final concentration) (*see* **Note 14**).
3. Apply reaction mix to AG1X8 resin equilibrated in 30% acetic acid (*see* **Note 15**).
4. Wash the AG1X8 resin with 4 × 1 mL 30% acetic acid and collect each aliquot in microfuge tubes.
5. Dry down samples eluted from AG1X8 resin in Speedvac (Sorvell).
6. Resuspend dried samples in 0.1% TFA (500 μL) and apply to activated C-18 Sep Pak cartridge (*see* **Note 16**).
7. Apply radiolabeled RII peptide to cartridge and collect flow through. Wash with 0.1% TFA (10 mL) and collect flow through. Elute ^{32}P-RII peptide with 50% CH_3CN, 0.1% TFA (5 × 1 mL) and collect in microfuge tubes (5 × 1 mL). Count Cerenkov radiation for sample, flow through and each 1 mL elution (*see* **Note 17**).
8. Dry down eluted ^{32}P-RII peptide and resuspend in 500 μL H_2O. Add 1*M* NH_4CO_3 to neutralize (check with pH paper).
9. Dry down sample and resuspend ^{32}P-RII peptide in 200 μL H_2O. Count Cerenkov radiation (2 μL) (*see* **Notes 18** and **19**).

3.2.1.2. CaN Assay

Protein phosphatase assay using AG50W-X8 resin to separate ^{32}P-RII from free phosphate. The AG50W-X8 is a cation-exchange resin that binds the phosphopeptide; the released $^{32}P_i$ passes through directly into the scintillation vial. This involves pouring 1-mL AG50W-X8 columns for each reaction tube.

1. Make a stock containing 5X concentrate assay buffer. The final concentration in the assay should be: 40 μ*M* Tris-HCl, pH 7.5, 0.1*M* KCl, 0.1 m*M* $CaCl_2$, 6 m*M* MgAcetate, 0.5 m*M* DTT, and 0.1 mg/mL BSA.
2. In a 20-μL reaction volume, add 5X assay buffer, 1.5 μ*M* calmodulin (final conc.) and 1 μ*M* CaN (final conc.) diluted in ice cold buffer containing 40 μ*M* Tris-HCl, pH 7.5, 0.1*M* KCl, and 0.5 m*M* DTT, to each tube. Preincubate tubes at 30°C (*see* **Note 20**).

3. At 20-s intervals, start reaction with addition of ^{32}P-RII peptide (30 μ*M*), and vortex (*see* **Note 21**).
4. Stop reaction with 75 m*M* phosphoric acid (100 μL) at 20-s intervals.
5. When all time-points have been taken, add the 120-μL reaction volume to 1-mL AG50W-X8 columns, equilibrated in H_2O, and placed in scintillation counting vials. This allows direct collection of the free phosphate released following dephosphorylation of the ^{32}P-RII peptide by the phosphatase (*see* **Note 22**).
6. Wash AG50W-X8 columns with 4 × 250 μL H_2O, add aqueous scintillant, and count by liquid scintillation counting.

3.2.2. Inhibition of CaN

To determine the half-maximal inhibitor constant for a peptide, assay CaN as described above, but in the presence of increasing amounts of inhibitor peptide. It is important to assay CaN activity at K_m for the ^{32}P-RII peptide. The K_m can be determined by assaying CaN over a range of substrate (^{32}P-RII) concentrations and plotting a double-reciprocal plot of 1/v (μmol/min/mg) vs 1/substrate conc. (μ*M*) (Lineweaver-Burk plot). The K_m is then determined from the *x*-intercept. The half-maximal inhibition of a peptide inhibitor is determined by plotting the percent CaN activity vs inhibitor concentration. 100% CaN activity is the amount of dephosphorylation of the substrate in the absence of inhibitor.

3.3. Dissection of PKC–AKAP Interactions

PKC, a family of ser-thr kinases, is tethered to the postsynaptic density (PSD) through association with binding proteins *(26)*. We used a solid-phase binding assay (overlays) (*see* **Subheading 3.3.1.**) to demonstrate recombinant AKAP79 bound to PKC in the presence of Ca^{2+} and phosphatidylserine. Fragments encompassing the first 75 residues of AKAP79 bound PKC, but COOH-terminal fragments containing the RII and CaN-binding regions did not, which implies that PKC binds to AKAP79 at a site that is distinct from those bound by RII and CaN *(27,28)*. Basic and hydrophobic regions are determinants for binding of certain proteins to PKC *(15)*, which drew our attention to a region located between residues 31 and 52 of AKAP79 (**Fig. 7A**). A peptide encompassing this region (Lys-Ala-Ser-Met-Leu-Cys-Phe-Lys-Arg-Arg-Ly-Lys-Ala-Ala-Lys-Ala-Pro-Lys-Ala-Gly) specifically blocked the interaction of AKAP79 with PKC in the overlay assay (**Fig. 7B**) (*see* **Subheading 3.3.1.**), but did not affect RII binding to the AKAP (**Fig. 7C**). Conversely, the RII anchoring inhibitor peptide (AKAP79 390–411) did not affect PKC-binding (**Fig. 7B**), but did block interaction with RII (**Fig. 7C**). We had observed previously that many kinases or phosphatases bind to anchoring proteins in an inactive state *(22,23)*. Accordingly, recombinant AKAP79 protein inhibited PKC activity (IC_{50} = 0.35 ± 0.06 μ*M*, *n* = 3) (**Fig. 7D**). In addition, the AKAP79 peptide (residues 31–52) and a recombinant AKAP79 fragment (residues 1–75) inhib-

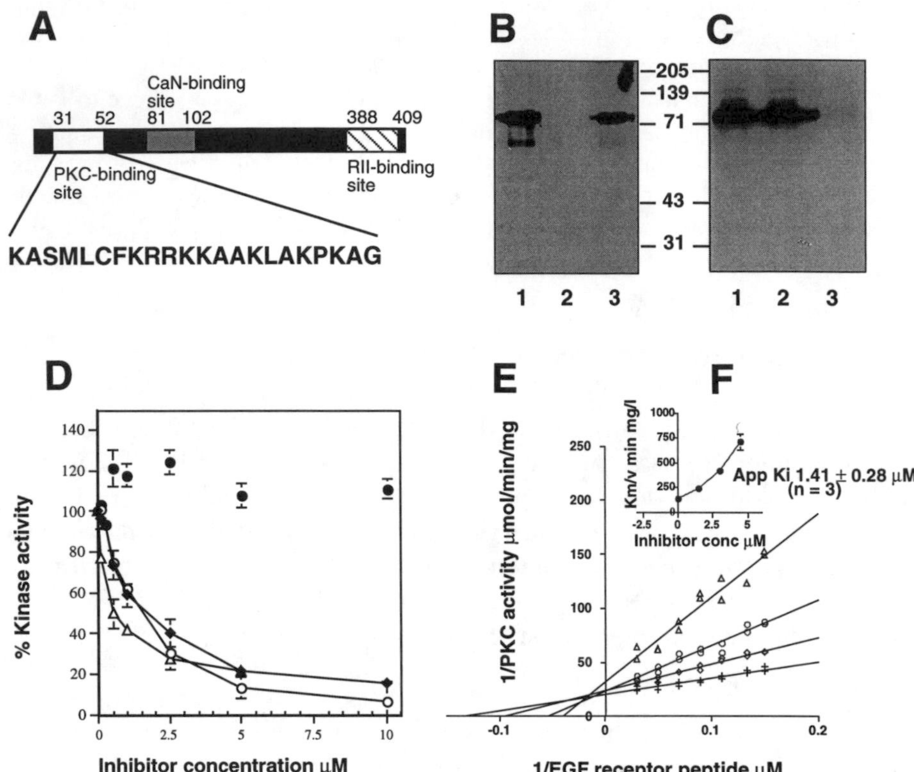

Fig. 7. Mapping the PKC-binding site on AKAP79. **(A)** Schematic diagram of AKAP79 showing binding sites for PKA, CaN, and PKC. The amino acid sequence for residues 31–52 is indicated. **(B)** Recombinant AKAP79 was blotted and PKC overlays were performed in the absence (lane 1) and presence of either 1.5 μ*M* AKAP79(31–52) (lane 2) or 1.5 μ*M* RII-anchoring inhibitor peptide AKAP79(390–412) (lane 3) with ~12.5 n*M* PKC. **(C)** ^{32}P-RII overlays were performed under the same conditions as in B. **(D)** Dose–response curve of PKC activity in the presence of recombinant AKAP79 (open triangles), AKAP79(31–52) (closed diamonds), and residues 1–75 recombinant fragment of AKAP79 (open circles). AKAP79(31–52) did not inhibit PKA activity (closed circles). **(E)** Lineweaver-Burk plot of PKC phosphorylation in the absence of inhibitor peptide (crosses) and in the presence of 1.5 μ*M* (open diamonds), 3 μ*M* (open circles) and 4.5 μ*M* (open triangles) AKAP79 (31–52) peptide. Inset **(F)** shows the secondary plot of K_m/V_{max} as a function of AKAP79(31–52) concentration and the apparent K_i value. Values given are as mean ± SEM ***(15)***.

ited PKC ($IC_{50} = 2.0 \pm 0.6$ μ*M*, *n* = 4) and ($IC_{50} = 1.6 \pm 0.3$ μ*M*, *n* = 4) (**Fig. 7D** ***[18]***; *see* **Subheading 3.3.2.**). In contrast, the 31–52 peptide did not inhibit the activity of the catalytic subunit of PKA (**Fig. 7D**; **ref.** ***18***). Inhibition of PKC activity by the 31–52 peptide was mixed with an apparent inhibition constant (K_i) of 1.41 ± 0.28 μ*M* (*n* = 3) (**Fig. 7E**). The secondary plot of the Michaelis constant divided by the maximal velocity (K_m/V_{max}) as a function of inhibitor concentration, was nonlinear, suggesting binding at more than one site (**Fig. 7F**). These peptide studies were powerful, in that they allowed us to map a site of contact to residues 31–52 on the AKAP.

3.3.1. Peptide Block of PKC-AKAP Interaction in PKC Overlay

The PKC overlay is similar to the RII overlay (*see* **Subheading 3.1.1.**) except that an antibody to PKC is used to detect the PKC bound to PKC-binding proteins ***(24)***.

1. Separate protein samples by SDS-PAGE and transfer to nitrocellulose membrane by standard electrotransfer techniques (**ref.** ***33***; *see* **Note 1**).
2. Wash 3 × 5 min with TBS and block membrane by incubation with BLOTTO + 1% BSA for 30 min at room temperature (*see* **Note 2**).
3. Wash 3 × 5 min with TBS.
4. Incubate blot for 1 h with PKC (approx 10 μg/mL, but this should be titrated for each prep) ± anchoring peptides (1.5 μ*M*) and 20 μg/mL phosphatidylserine (PS) or 1.4 m*M* PS/0.04 m*M* diacylglycerol (DG) vesicles (*see* **Notes 23** and **26**) in PKC assay buffer (TBS, 1% albumin, 1.2 m*M* Ca^{2+}, 1 m*M* EGTA, and protease inhibitors [leupeptin and pepstatin {2 μg/mL}]).
5. Wash blot with PBS wash buffer (PBS containing 1.2 m*M* Ca^{2+}, 1 m*M* EGTA, 10 μg/mL PS) for 2 × 3 min to remove excess PKC.
6. Fix blot with 0.5% paraformaldehyde in PBS wash buffer for 20 min at room temperature (*see* **Note 27**) (optional).
7. Incubate with PBS + 2% glycine, pH 7.4, for 20 min at room temperature to block free amine groups.
8. Wash 2 × 5-min with TBS.
9. Develop as for standard Western blot with primary antibody to PKC to detect PKC-binding proteins. Develop by chemiluminescence.

3.3.2. Peptide Inhibition of PKC Activity

3.3.2.1. PKC Activity Assays

Protein kinase assay using phosphocellulose cation exchange paper (P81 paper). This method relies on the basic nature of the substrate. Because many kinases have requirements for basic residues, and synthetic peptides have proved to be good substrates, this method is ideal for assaying kinase activity. There are many peptide substrates available commercially. We have routinely used a peptide to the EGF-receptor (VRKRTLRRL) available from Sigma.

1. Make stocks containing 4X concentrate assay buffer, 10X $CaCl_2$, 10X EGTA, and 10X PS/DG vesicles and the [γ-^{32}P]-ATP stock (200 cpm/pmol; 1 m*M* [*see* **Section 3.2.1.1.**). The final concentration in the assay should be: 20 m*M* HEPES,

pH 7.5, 10 m*M* $MgCl_2$, 1 m*M* DTT, 0.3 m*M* Ca^{2+} (or 0.5 m*M* EGTA), 0.14 m*M* PS/0.004 m*M* DG in 2 m*M* HEPES, pH 7.5 (*see* **Note 23**) (or 2 m*M* HEPES, pH 7.5), and 0.1 m*M* [γ-^{32}P]-ATP.
2. In a 40-µL reaction volume, add the appropriate volume of concentrated stocks (*see* **step 1**) with peptide substrate, vortex, and preincubate at 30°C.
3. Dilute PKC in ice-cold buffer (20 m*M* Tris, pH 7.9, containing 1 mg/mL BSA, 1 m*M* DTT) and start reaction by addition of diluted enzyme at 20-s intervals, vortex, and incubate at 30°C (*see* **Note 24**).
4. The reaction is stopped by taking 30-µL aliquots from each tube at 20-s intervals, spotting on to 2 × 2 cm P81 paper, and dropping into 75 m*M* phosphoric acid (*see* **Note 25**).
5. When all time-points have been taken, pour the first wash into radioactive waste and wash (2 × 3 min) with 500 mL 75 m*M* phosphoric acid. Wash once with ethanol and dry papers before counting by liquid scintillation.

3.3.2.2. Inhibition of PKC

To determine the half-maximal inhibitor constant, assay PKC as described above, in the presence of increasing amounts of inhibitor peptide. To assay for inhibition, it is important to assay enzyme activity at K_m for the substrate peptide. The K_m can be determined by assaying PKC over a range of substrate concentrations (as described in **Subheading 3.2.2.**). The half-maximal inhibition of the peptide inhibitor is determined by plotting the percentage of PKC activity vs inhibitor concentration. To determine the K_i and the mechanism of inhibition, the enzyme is assayed over a range of substrate concentrations at varying inhibitor concentrations (*see* **Fig. 7E,F**). The Lineweaver-Burk plots for each inhibitor concentration are plotted on the same axis. If inhibition is competitive with respect to peptide substrate, the Lineweaver-Burk plots intersect at the Y-axis at $1/V_{max}$. If inhibition is noncompetitive, they intersect at the X-axis at $1/K_m$. The K_i value is then determined from a secondary plot of K_m/V_{max} versus inhibitor concentration where the inhibitory constant intersects at the X-axis at $-K_i$.

3.4. Conclusions

The studies outlined in this chapter have highlighted the use of synthetic peptides as tools to evaluate the interactions between anchoring proteins and signaling enzymes. In particular, peptides have been used to map biologically important binding sites on specific AKAPs. The advantages of peptides over recombinant proteins is that a relatively short sequence (for example, 20 amino acids) can be custom-synthesized in large quantities and can be quickly used to define biologically important sites. Stoichiometric incorporation of myristoyl or phosphate moieties into the polypeptide often significantly enhances the action of certain peptides. For example, the esterification of aliphatic lipids can significantly enhance the versatility of peptide reagents by rendering them cell-soluble. No doubt the development of additional cell-soluble peptides for use in cell-based assays will be a topic of considerable interest to both researchers and commercial entities alike.

Although the generation of cell-soluble peptides increases the versatility of certain reagents, a major concern remains their susceptibility to proteolysis in vivo. For example, the radioiodinated PKA-inhibitor peptide, PKI 5-24, has a half-life of a few seconds when microinjected into *Xenopus* oocytes (M. F. Cicerelli and J. D. Scott, unpublished observation). Nevertheless, numerous studies have demonstrated that the PKI 5–24 peptide is very effective in broken cell extracts or when introduced at high concentrations. Another limitation of peptide fragments is that they often exhibit a diminished biological potency, compared to their parent protein. For example, the PKI 5-24 peptide has a K_i of 4–8 n*M*, and the parent protein inhibits the C subunit with a K_i of 0.23 n*M* ***(29)***. Likewise, the anchoring-inhibitor peptide Ht 31 493–515 binds RII or the type II PKA holoenzyme with a K_d of 3.8-4 n*M*; however, it is clear that a recombinant fragment of the Ht 31 protein binds with much higher affinity. Although bioactive peptides, such as PKI 5–24 and Ht 31 495–515, which act in the nanomolar range, may be suitable for certain cell based assays, it is less clear whether peptides that are active in the micromolar range will be active in cells. Despite these limitations, it is clear that synthetic peptides will continue to be valuable reagents in the dissecting protein-targeting interactions.

4. Notes

1. The transferred proteins on the membrane can be visualized by staining with Coomassie blue (46% methanol/9% acetic acid/0.05% Coomassie) for Immobilon or Ponceau stain (0.2% Ponceau in 1% acetic acid) for nitrocellulose. Stain for 1–2 min and then destain with 46% methanol/9% acetic acid for Immobilon, or with water for the nitrocellulose. This is very useful to correlate nonspecific binding to abundant proteins in an extract.
2. Blots are often incubated overnight.
3. Collect 200-µL fractions from column and count 1 µL by Cerenkov counting. Expect the radiolabeled protein to elute in fraction 4 or 5 with 100,000 cpm/µL.
4. It is important to incubate an identical blot with control peptide, or in the absence of peptide, to be sure that the RII-binding protein is present.
5. Blots are often incubated overnight.
6. This can be done at room temperature. This step is important for removing nonspecific proteins.
7. Either the sodium salt of cAMP or the free acid (SIGMA) can be used, but to use the free acid, it is necessary to adjust the pH of the solution.
8. It is very important that incubation occurs at room temperature for both the peptide elution and the cAMP elution.

9. The amounts of protein present in the elution are often very small, and so it is important to load all of the sample.
10. It was necessary to dilute the anchoring inhibitor peptide in DMSO, because it is very hydrophobic and not very soluble.
11. Rat hippocampal neurons were prepared from neonatal rats and cultured on rat astrocyte cultures for 2 wk.
12. For the myristoylated Ht31 peptide (493–509), an affinity-purified antibody to the peptide was used at a 1:200 dilution.
13. 1 μCi = 2.2×10^6 cpm. Decay tables are available to calculate the radioactive concentration and specific activity of the stock. When making the cold ATP stock, it is important to neutralize the solution to pH 7.0. This stock can be aliquoted and frozen at –20°C.
14. Take four 3-μL aliquots to count and spot on P81 paper. Wash two aliquots with 75 m*M* phosphoric acid (3 × 3 min washes), wash with ethanol (1 × 2 min), and dry. Count Cerenkov radiation for both washed ^{32}P-RII and unwashed (total counts).
15. AG1X8 resin is an anion exchange resin used to separate free [γ-^{32}P]-ATP from radiolabeled peptide. We pour the resin in a glass Pasteur pipet with a glass bead at the base.
16. Activate C-18 cartridge by washing with 100% CH_3 CN, 0.1% TFA (10 mL), followed by washing with 0.1% TFA (10 mL).
17. It is important to collect 1-mL aliquots of eluted ^{32}P-RII because >90% should elute in the first mL.
18. To calculate incorporation:

$$1 \text{ m}M \text{ RII}/10^{-3} \text{ mol/L} \times 4 \times 10^{-6}\text{L} = 400 \times 10^3 \text{ pmol}$$

$$400 \times 10^3 \text{ pmol}/520\ \mu\text{L} = \text{pmol}/\mu\text{L} \times 10\ \mu\text{L} = \text{pmol RII}$$
(reaction volume 400 μL, final vol 520 μL)

$$\text{pmol RII} \times \text{cpm/pmol [}\gamma\text{-}^{32}\text{P]-ATP} = \text{cpm expected for 1:1 incorporation}$$

19. To calculate concentration of ^{32}P-RII:

$$\text{cpm (of final 2-}\mu\text{L aliquot)/cpm/pmol [}\gamma\text{-}^{32}\text{P]-ATP} \times 2 = \text{pmol}/\mu\text{L}$$

20. Always include a background control, containing no enzyme.
21. The reaction should be carried out so that the rate of dephosphorylation is linear and less than 10% of the substrate is dephosphorylated. This will mean that the reaction time will vary, but is generally between 5 and 10 min.
22. We have used either glass Pasteur pipets with a glass bead placed at the bottom or BIORAD polyprep chromatography columns.
23. To prepare PS/DG vesicles: PS and DG are stored at –20°C in chloroform (Avanti Polar Lipids), and must be aliquoted using glass pipet tips or a Hamilton syringe, and stored in glass tubes. Aliquot the appropriate volume of PS and DG and dry under a constant stream of nitrogen gas. Resuspend in 20 m*M* HEPES, pH 7.5, sonicate for 30 s, and store at 4°C. It is a good idea to make fresh solutions every couple of weeks. The solution will be opaque, even following sonication.

24. For inhibition assays, enzyme can be preincubated with inhibitor and reaction started with reaction mix containing buffer, activators, and substrates, or the inhibitor can be added to the reaction mix and reaction initiated with enzyme.
25. A convenient way to do this is to place the spotted P81 papers into a wire cage inside a 500-mL beaker containing 75 m*M* phosphoric acid. The beaker is placed on a magnetic stir plate. The papers are kept in the wire cage until they are dried prior to counting.
26. PS/DG vesicles are sometimes used in preference to PS.
27. Make from 3.7% paraformaldehyde PBS stock.

Acknowledgments

The authors wish to thank their colleagues at the Vollum Institute for critical evaluation of this manuscript and Ruth Frank for her assistance in the preparation of this manuscript. M. F. and J. D. S. were supported in part by DK 44239.

References

1. Krebs, E. G. and Beavo, J. A. (1979) Phosphorylation-dephosphorylation of enzymes. *Annu. Rev. Biochem.* **43,** 923–959.
2. Fischer, E. H. and Krebs, E. G. (1955) Conversion of phosphorylase b to phosphorylase a in muscle extracts. *J. Biol. Chem.* **216,** 121–132.
3. Krebs, E. G., Graves, D. J., and Fischer, E. H. (1959) Factors affecting the activity of muscle phosphorylase b kinase. *J. Biol. Chem.* **234,** 2867–2873.
4. Kemp, B. E., Parker, M. W., Hu, S., Tiganis, T., and House, C. (1994) Substrate and pseudosubstrate interactions with protein kinases: determinants of specificity. *TIBS* **19,** 440–444.
5. Kemp, B. E., Graves, D. J., Benjamini, E., and Krebs, E. G. (1977) Role of multiple basic residues in determining the substrate specificity of cyclic AMP-dependent protein kinase. *J. Biol. Chem.* **252,** 4888–4894.
6. Corbin, J. D. and Reimann, E. M. (1974) A filter assay for determining protein kinase activity. *Methods Enzymol.* **38,** 287–294.
7. Corbin, J. D., Sugden, P. H., West, L., Flockhart, D. A., Lincoln, T. M., and McCarthy, D. (1978) Studies on the properties and mode of action of the purified regulatory subunit of bovine heart adenosine 3':5'-monophosphate-dependent protein kinase. *J. Biol. Chem.* **253,** 3997–4003.
8. Scott, J. D., Fischer, E. H., Takio, K., DeMaille, J. B., and Krebs, E. G. (1985) Amino acid sequence of the heat-stable inhibitor of the cAMP-dependent protein kinase from rabbit skeletal muscle. *Proc. Natl. Acad. Sci. USA* **82,** 5732–5736.
9. Scott, J. D., Glaccum, M. B., Fischer, E. H., and Krebs, E. G. (1986) Primary-structure requirements for inhibition by the heat-stable inhibitor of the cAMP-dependent protein kinase. *Proc. Natl. Acad. Sci. USA* **83,** 1613–1616.
10. Cheng, H.-C., Kemp, B. E., Pearson, R. B., Smith, A. J., Misconi, L., Van Patten, S. M., and Walsh, D. A. (1986) A potent synthetic peptide inhibitor of the cAMP-dependent protein kinase. *J. Biol. Chem.* **261,** 989–992.

11. Glass, D. B., Cheng, H.-C., Kemp, B. E., and Walsh, D. A. (1986) Differential and common recognition sites of the catalytic sites of the cGMP-dependent and cAMP-dependent protein kinases by the inhibitory peptides derived from the heat-stable inhibitor protein. *J. Biol. Chem.* **261,** 12,161–12,171.
12. House, C. and Kemp, B. E. (1987) Protein kinase C contains a pseudosubstrate prototope in its regulatory domain. *Science* **238,** 1726–1728.
13. Eichholtz, T., de Bont, D. B., de Widt, J., Liskamp, R. M., and Ploegh, H. L. (1993) A myristoylated pseudosubstrate peptide, a novel protein kinase C inhibitor. *J. Biol. Chem.* **268,** 1982–1986.
14. Hubbard, M. and Cohen, P. (1993) On target with a mechanism for the regulation of protein phosphorylation. *TIBS* **18,** 172–177.
15. Klauck, T. M., Faux, M. C., Labudda, K., Langeberg, L. K., Jaken, S., and Scott, J. D. (1996) Coordination of three signaling enzymes by AKAP79 a mammalian scaffold protein. *Science* **271,** 1589–1592.
16. Carr, D. W., Stofko-Hahn, R. E., Fraser, I. D. C., Bishop, S. M., Acott, T. S., Brennan, R. G., and Scott, J. D. (1991) Interaction of the regulatory subunit (RII) of cAMP-dependent protein kinase with RII-anchoring proteins occurs through an amphipathic helix binding motif. *J. Biol. Chem.* **266,** 14,188–14,192.
17. Carr, D. W. and Scott, J. D. (1992) Blotting and band-shifting: techniques for studying protein-protein interactions. *TIBS* **17,** 246–249.
18. Carr, D. W., Hausken, Z. E., I. Fraser, D. C., Stofko-Hahn, R. E., and Scott, J. D. (1992) Association of the type II cAMP-dependent protein kinase with a human thyroid RII-anchoring protein cloning and characterization of the RII-binding domain. *J. Biol. Chem.* **267,** 13,376–13,382.
19. Greengard, P., Jen, J., Nairn, A. C., and Stevens, C. F. (1991) Enhancement of glutamate response by cAMP-dependent protein kinase in hippocampal neurons. *Science* **253,** 1135–1138.
20. Rosenmund, C., Carr, D. W., Bergeson, S. E., Nilaver, G., Scott, J. D., and Westbrook, G. L. (1994) Anchoring of protein kinase A is required for modulation of AMPA/kainate receptors on hippocampal neurons. *Nature* **368,** 853–856.
21. Johnson, B. D., Scheuer, T., and Catterall, W. A. (1994) Voltage-dependent potentiation of L-type Ca2+ channels in skeletal muscle cells requires anchored cAMP-dependent protein kinase. *Proc. Natl. Acad. Sci. USA* **91,** 11,492–11,496.
22. Scott, J. D. and McCartney, S. (1994) Localization of A-kinase through anchoring proteins. *Mol. Endocrinol.* **8,** 5–13.
23. Coghlan, V., Perrino, B. A., Howard, M., Langeberg, L. K., Hicks, J. B., Gallatin, W. M., and Scott, J. D. (1995) Association of protein kinase A and protein phosphatase 2B with a common anchoring protein. *Science* **267,** 108–111.
24. Wolf, M. and Sahyoun, N. (1986) Protein kinase C and phosphatidylserine bind to Mr110,000/115,000 polypeptides enriched in cytoskeletal and postsynaptic density preparations. *J. Biol. Chem.* **261,** 13,327–13,332.
25. McNeill, R. B. and Colbran, R. J. (1995) Interaction of autophosphorylated Ca2+/calmodulin-dependent protein kinase II with neuronal cytoskeletal proteins: char-

acterization of binding to a 190 kDa postsynaptic density protein. *J. Biol. Chem.* **270,** 10,043–10,050.
26. Newton, A. C. (1995) Protein kinase C: structure, function and regulation. *J. Biol. Chem.* **270,** 28,495–28,498.
27. Carr, D. W., Stofko-Hahn, R. E., Fraser, I. D. C., Cone, R. D., and Scott, J. D. (1992) Localization of the cAMP-dependent protein kinase to the postsynaptic densities by A-kinase anchoring proteins. *J. Biol. Chem.* **24,** 16,816–16,823.
28. Coghlan, V. M., Hausken, Z. E., and Scott, J. D. (1995) Subcellular targeting of kinases and phosphatases by association with bifunctional anchoring proteins. *Biochem. Soc. Trans.* **23,** 592–596.
29. Glass, D. B., El-Maghrabi, M. R., and Pilkis, S. J. (1986) Synthetic peptides corresponding to the site phosphorylated in 6-phosphofructo–2-kinase/fructose–2, 6-bisphosphatase as substrates of cyclic nucleotide-dependent protein kinases. *J. Biol. Chem.* **261,** 2987–2993.
30. Gupta, K. P., Ward, N. E., Gravitt, K. R., Bergman, P. J., and O'Brian, C. A. (1996) Partial reversal of multidrug resistance in human breast cancer cells by an N-myristoylated protein kinase C-a pseudosubstrate peptide. *J. Biol. Chem.* **271,** 2102–2111.
31. Maskowske, M. and Rosen, D. M. (1989) Complete activation of protein kinase C by an antipeptide antibody directed against the pseudosubstrate peptide. *J. Biol. Chem.* **264,** 16,155–16,159.
32. Faux, M. C. and Scott, J. D. (1996) Molecular glue: kinase anchoring and scaffold proteins. *Cell* **85,** 9–12.
33. Towbin, H., Staehelin, T., and Gordon, J. (1979) Electrophoretic transfer of proteins from polyacrylamide gels to nitrocellulose sheets: procedure and some applications. *Proc. Natl. Acad. Sci. USA* **76,** 4350–4354.
34. Pearson, R. B., Mitchelhill, K. I., and Kemp, B. E. (1993) Studies of protein kinase/phosphatase specificity using synthetic peptides, in *Protein Phosphorylation: A Practical Approach* (Hardie, D. G., ed.), IRL, New York, pp. 265–291.
35. Kemp, B. E. and Pearson, R. B. (1991) Design and use of peptide substrates for protein kinases. *Methods Enzymol.* **200,** 121–135.

14

SH2 and SH3 Domains

Unraveling Signaling Networks with Peptide Antagonists

Rob Stein

1. Introduction

Regulated protein–protein interactions are central to cell signaling. Many proteins involved in the signaling process contain specialized noncatalytic modular domains whose function is to localize the protein or to allow interaction with other signaling molecules (reviewed in **ref. *1***).

The src homology domain type 2 (SH2) binds to phosphotyrosine residues such as are found in activated receptor- or cytoplasmic-tyrosine kinases. Specificity of binding is determined by the 3–5 residues immediately C-terminal to the phosphotyrosine. Consensus binding sequences may be defined for individual SH2 domains. For instance, the src SH2 domain binds to ptyr-glu-glu-ile; the consensus sequence for the N-terminal SH2 domain of the PI3-kinase p85 regulatory subunit is ptyr-met/val/ile/glu-xxx-met. Binding does not occur in the absence of phosphorylation of the tyrosine residue. The specificity of the more recently described and less common phosphotyrosine-binding domain (PTB) is determined by the three residues N-terminal to the phosphotyrosine.

SH3 domains, which bind to proline-rich sequences, are commonly found in signaling proteins and have also been identified in cytoskeletal proteins and in the neutrophil cytochrome oxidase. The core sequence recognized by the SH3 domain consists of seven fairly highly conserved residues, of which three are prolines. Two classes of peptides have been described that differ in the orientation in which they bind to the SH3 domain. Both classes adopt a pseudo-symmetrical, left-handed α-helical orientation. When optimum binding sequences for individual domains have been determined with the aid of ran-

From: *Methods in Molecular Biology, Vol. 88: Protein Targeting Protocols*
Edited by: R. A. Clegg Humana Press Inc., Totowa, NJ

dom peptide libraries, it is evident that specificity is determined by residues flanking the core peptide. SH3–peptide-binding affinities measured in vitro are substantially lower than those described for the PTB and SH2 domains but this may reflect inadequate definition of the flanking sequence *(2)*. The method of regulation of SH3 domain–peptide binding is not clear; it may well involve either conformational change in the domain, induced by events distant from the SH3 domain, or by relocation of one of the binding partners.

Since SH2 and SH3 domains are found in many proteins, identifying protein pairs that interact through these domains in vivo is a major problem in understanding signaling networks. The study of these domains is greatly facilitated by their modular structure, which means that isolated domains can readily be expressed in recombinant form and purified by affinity chromatography *(3)* or by virtue of tags, particularly glutathione-*S*-transferase (GST). Both SH2 and SH3 domains will readily bind to appropriate peptides in vitro; consequently, short synthetic peptides are a valuable tool in investigation of SH2 and SH3 domain–ligand interactions. For instance, random peptide libraries have been used to define the consensus binding sequence of particular SH2 or SH3 domains *(4,5)*. Another widely used technique has been to identify potential binding partners for a defined ligand by "fishing" in cell or organ lysates with a synthetic peptide, immobilized on beads by coupling through the amino terminus *(6)*.

Synthetic peptides may also be used to inhibit interactions between SH2 and SH3 domain-containing proteins and their binding partners. To date, little success has been achieved with this approach in vivo *(7)*. Large peptides are required for high-affinity interactions, particularly with SH3 domains, which creates problems in the delivery of the peptide to intracellular sites. Additionally, peptides are potentially vulnerable to degradation by intracellular endo- and exopeptidases and, particularly in the case of SH2 domain-binding peptides, tyrosine phosphatases. The development of nonhydrolyzable phosphotyrosine analogs offers a partial solution, and such peptides have been demonstrated to have activity in vivo when introduced into cells by microinjection *(8)*.

Peptide inhibitors have been more useful in in vitro studies. ELISA assays have a number of potential applications. In addition to their use as a screen for drug discovery, they can be used to give a measure of peptide–domain binding affinity in competition assays, and to compare the relative ability of different peptides to inhibit a particular protein–protein interaction *(7)*. Peptides may also be used to probe the interactions between signaling molecules using detection methods based on in vitro kinase assays or Western blotting, or in gel overlay assays. These techniques are potentially valuable in helping to determine whether interactions observed in vivo by immunoprecipitation are real and in mapping interaction sites *(9)*.

2. Materials

2.1. Equipment

2.1.1. ELISA

1. Multichannel (8 or 12) pipet, range 50–250 μL.
2. Plate washer (optional).
3. Plate reader with 490 nm filter.

2.1.2. Affinity Precipitation Assay

1. Shielding for working with ^{32}P isotopes.
2. Heat block.
3. SDS polyacrylamide gel apparatus.
4. Power pack.
5. Gel dryer.
6. Western blotting apparatus: wet transfer preferred (optional).
7. Film cassette and X-ray film, or phosphorimager and cassette.

2.2. Materials

2.2.1. ELISA

1. 96-Well flat-bottomed plates.
2. Coupling buffer: 2.25 mL 0.2*M* Na_2CO_3, 4.0 mL 0.2*M* $NaHCO_3$; to 25 mL with distilled water.
3. Phosphate buffered saline (PBS): 9 g NaCl, 0.726 g $Na_2HPO_4 \cdot 7H_2O$, 0.21 g KH_2PO_4; to 1 L with distilled water.
4. PBST: PBS + 0.05% Tween-20.
5. Citrate–phosphate (substrate) buffer: 6.25 mL 0.1*M* citric acid, 6.25 mL 0.2*M* Na_2HPO_4, distilled water to 25 mL; pH adjusted to ≤5.0.
6. Avidin or streptavidin for use with biotinylated reagents.
7. Protein A or protein G for immobilization of immunoprecipitated reagents.
8. Bovine serum albumin (BSA): fraction V is generally adequate.
9. *o*-Phenylendiamine tablets 10 mg (as free base).
10. Urea peroxide or 35% hydrogen peroxide.
11. 2*M* H_2SO_4.

2.2.2. Affinity Precipitation Assay

1. Glutathione-agarose or protein A-agarose or protein G-agarose.
2. Lysis buffer: 150 m*M* NaCl, 20 m*M* Tris-HCl, pH 7.5, 1% Triton-X100 or NP40, 10 m*M* NaF, 0.2-1.0 m*M* Na orthovanadate, 0.1% 2-mercaptoethanol, protease inhibitors (0.2–1.0 m*M* PMSF, 4 m*M* benzamidine, and so on).
3. Tyrosine kinase buffer: 100 m*M* NaCl, 20 m*M* HEPES, pH 7.5, 10 m*M* $MnCl_2$.
4. [γ-^{32}P]-ATP 37*M*Bq/mL.
5. Acrylamide and solutions required for pouring and running SDS-PAGE.
6. PVDF membrane and transfer buffer: 29 g glycine, 5.8 g Tris base, 1 g SDS, 20% methanol; to 1 L with distilled water.

3. Methods

3.1. ELISA

ELISA methods have generally worked better with the ligand immobilized and the SH2/SH3 domain protein applied in solution. In general, ELISA methods are well-suited to SH2 domain interactions, which have higher binding affinities in vitro to their ligands than SH3 domains. Concentrations of proteins and peptides to be used depend on the assay to be run and some optimization will be necessary in each case.

3.1.1. Immobilization of Ligand (see **Note 1**)

A variety of techniques can be used for immobilizing ligand. Concentrations to be used will vary according to the assay.

3.1.1.1. Peptides

Peptides are most easily immobilized when biotinylated.

1. Coat the plate with avidin or streptavidin (*see* **Notes 1** and **2**) at 10–20 μg/mL in coupling buffer for 1 h at 37°C, or overnight at 4°C. The ELISA plate should be placed in a plastic box containing moistened filter paper, or wrapped in cling film to prevent evaporation.
2. Wash three times with PBST.
3. Block with PBST + 1% BSA for 1 h at 37°C (*see* **Notes 2** and **3**).
4. Apply biotinylated ligand in the same volume as used for coating the plate (*see* **Note 4**); 30 min at room temperature will generally suffice.

3.1.1.2. Proteins in Cell Lysates

In general, immunoprecipitation of the protein of interest from cell lysates, followed by capture onto the ELISA plate coated with either an appropriate anti-immunoglobulin antibody or protein A/G, is far more efficient and cleaner than direct adsorption of protein in crude lysate onto the plate (*see* **Note 5**). It is important to ensure that antibodies used for immunoprecipitation and capture are from a different species than those used for detection of SH2/SH3 domain binding. The capturing antibody should preferably be polyclonal, e.g., goat antimouse immunoglobulin.

1. Coat the plate for 1 h at 37°C, or overnight at 4°C using the same precautions as for avidin coating. For antibody capture, a 1:500–1000 dilution of commercially available antibody preparations (i.e., to approx 2–4 μg/mL) is suggested.
2. Wash three times in PBST.
3. Lyse cells (*see* **Note 6**) and incubate for 1–2 h with an appropriate amount of immunoprecipitating antibody.
4. Block with PBST + 1% BSA for 30 min: 1 h (*see* **Note 3**).
5. Apply lysate to ELISA plate, typically for 1 h at room temperature.

3.1.1.3. Purified Protein Ligand

Where the protein ligand can be purified directly by nonantibody-dependent methods, it may be possible to coat the plate directly. Alternatively, antibody-based capture methods, as described in **Subheading 3.1.1.2.**, may be used.

3.1.2. ELISA Assay

1. Apply SH2/SH3 domain protein (*see* **Note 6**), together with test peptide in PBST ± 1% BSA (*see* **Note 3**). In general, premixing of peptide and protein is not necessary. The interaction between SH2-domain proteins and phosphopeptides is rapid; 15–30 min at room temperature is sufficient.
2. Wash three to four times with PBST.
3. Apply the first antibody diluted in PBST for 1 h at room temperature. This can be a specific antibody directed against the SH2/SH3 domain, or, if the domain is expressed as a GST protein, an anti-GST antibody.
4. Wash three to four times with PBST.
5. Apply enzyme (e.g., peroxidase)-conjugated second antibody diluted in PBST for 1 h at room temperature. A typical dilution would be 1:1000.
6. Wash three to four times with PBST.
7. Add substrate solution. For peroxidase-conjugated second enzyme, dissolve 10 mg *o*-phenylendiamine and either 25 mg urea peroxide or 15 µL 35% hydrogen peroxide in 25 mL citrate–phosphate buffer, pH 4.0, shortly before use.
8. Stop the reaction when sufficient color has developed (usually 10–60 min). For a peroxidase reaction, add 50 µL 2*M* H_2SO_4.
9. Read the plate at 490 nm (*see* **Note 7**).

3.1.3. Optimization

1. Some optimization is generally required for ELISA assays (*see* **Note 5**). The assay is particularly sensitive to the amounts of ligand immobilized on the plate and to the concentration of SH2/SH3 domain added (*see* **Note 4**). Test plates, in which these two parameters are varied systematically across rows and columns in checkerboard fashion, can be used to determine optimum concentrations. First and second antibodies and substrate should be present at, or close to, excess. An optical density of 1–1.5 in the readout gives a good "window" and is within the linear range of most plate readers.
2. Background, caused by nonspecific binding of components used in the assay to the plate, has the effect of reducing the sensitivity of the assay. This has been a particular problem with some SH2-domain ELISAs, especially with avidin-coated plates. Changing to streptavidin (*see* **Note 2**), and the addition of 1% BSA to the solution containing the SH2 domain (*see* **Note 3**), may help. Antibodies may also give rise to background; increasing the dilution may result in a substantial reduction in noise, with little effect on the signal. Since ELISA plates vary in their characteristics, experimenting with different plates may prove helpful.

3.2. Affinity Precipitation Assay

Many proteins containing or interacting with SH2/SH3 domains possess intrinsic tyrosine kinase activity. The principle of the assay is that, for a pair of interacting proteins, the protein without catalytic activity is immobilized onto beads and used to fish for the protein with catalytic activity. Test peptides are used to inhibit binding. The presence of enzymatic activity in the complex is detected by in vitro kinase assay, in which one or both interacting proteins become phosphorylated, followed by SDS-PAGE to separate the proteins from unincorporated radioactivity. In the case of an SH2 domain-based interaction, e.g., binding of an immobilized isolated SH2 domain to a receptor tyrosine kinase, prior tyrosine phosphorylation of the receptor is necessary for an interaction to take place. Nevertheless, sufficient additional autophosphorylation is generated by the in vitro kinase assay that binding can, in general, be readily detected.

Far less optimization is required for this assay than for an ELISA, but the assay suffers from the disadvantages that it is more technically difficult to perform and that limited numbers of samples can be processed.

3.2.1. Assay

The example given here is for the interaction of an isolated SH2 domain, expressed as a GST-fusion protein with a receptor tyrosine kinase present in cell lysates. Other possible variations are discussed below.

1. Incubate GST–SH2 protein with glutathione-agarose beads in lysis buffer on a wheel at 4°C for 1–2 h (*see* **Note 8**). The fusion protein may be presented either in the form of a crude cell lysate or (preferably for reasons of reproducibility) as purified protein from a previously prepared stock. A bed volume of 10–15 µL glutathione-agarose beads per Eppendorf tube is optimal.
2. Obtain tyrosine-phosphorylated receptor by stimulating serum-starved cells with the appropriate growth factor for 5–10 min, followed by washing in cold PBS and lysis, or by using recombinant protein expressed in baculovirus-Sf9 cell system (*see* **Note 6**).
3. Incubate crude lysate and test peptide with immobilized GST–SH2 protein on a wheel at 4°C for 30 min. Preincubation of enzyme and test peptide is unnecessary.
4. Wash beads three to four times with lysis buffer, followed by two times with tyrosine kinase buffer.
5. Perform kinase assay in approx 25 µL tyrosine kinase buffer with 0.185–0.37 MBq [γ-^{32}P]-ATP per tube for 20 min at room temperature.
6. Terminate the reaction by the addition of 25 µL 2X Laemmli sample buffer.
7. Boil sample for 5 min (taking precautions to prevent the Eppendorf lid from blowing off), and then cool and briefly spin down.
8. Load sample onto an SDS-polyacrylamide gel and electrophorese (*see* **Note 9**).
9. The gel may now be fixed. Washing the fixed gel may serve to reduce background a little (*see also* **Note 9**). If it is desired to visualize bands on the gel, then

staining with either silver or Coomassie blue, followed by destaining, may be undertaken at this point. The gel is then dried and radioactivity detected by exposure to X-ray film or phosphorimager cassette.

3.2.2. Variations

A number of variations in the basic assay described above are possible. In particular, the kinase assay may be combined with or replaced by Western blotting. When both assays are combined, the ^{32}P-labeled proteins are transferred from gel to a PVDF membrane using a Western blotting apparatus (*see* **Note 10**). This allows proteins to be detected by Western blotting, using nonradioactive detection in addition to the detection of radioactivity. Additionally, non-GST-fusion proteins may be immunoprecipitated and immobilized onto protein A or protein G-agarose beads in a manner analogous to that described for the ELISA assay (*see* **Subheading 3.1.1.2.**).

3.2.3. Optimization

As in the case of the ELISA assay, the principal variables for optimization are the amounts of the two interacting proteins used in the assay (*see* **Note 8**). In general, however, this seems to be less critical for this assay. When one of the proteins used in the assay is obtained from crude cell lysates, it may be possible to improve reproducibility by making a large batch of lysate and storing it frozen in aliquots, with the addition of 10% glycerol, rather than using fresh lysate for each assay.

3.3. Gel Overlay Assay

Gel overlay assays may also be used to probe SH2/SH3-ligand interactions. In this assay, the protein ligand of the SH2/SH3 domain is immobilized onto a nitrocellulose membrane by SDS-PAGE, followed by electrophoretic transfer. The membrane is then exposed to the SH2/SH3-domain protein and test peptide. Binding may be detected by antibody-based techniques, or through the use of biotinylated or radiolabeled SH2/SH3-domain proteins. Detailed descriptions of gel overlay techniques are given in Chapters 5 and 7 of this volume.

4. Notes

1. The discussion of the ELISA assumes that assays are run in 96-well (flat bottomed) plate format and that coating and all subsequent steps are performed with 100 µL solution per well, except blocking, for which 150 µL is used.
2. Streptavidin is significantly more expensive than avidin, but its use may substantially reduce background.
3. Extensive blocking has been found to be necessary to reduce background with some SH2-domain assays, especially when avidin is used to coat the plate. It may

be possible to achieve satisfactory results using shorter blocking periods or lower concentrations of BSA.

4. For an ELISA assay of the interaction of full length GRB2 (as a GST-fusion protein) with a 17-amino acid biotinylated phosphopeptide based on Y1139 of c-*erb*B2, approx 1 ng/well was applied to an avidin-coated plate. Satisfactory readings were obtained with GST–GRB2 concentrations in the range of 5–50 ng/mL. Broadly similar quantities of biotinylated peptide (± one order of magnitude) have been immobilized for other SH2 domain-based ELISA assays. For an SH3 domain binding ELISA using the interaction of full-length GRB2 with a 19-amino acid biotinylated peptide derived from mSOS, coating was performed with approx 10 ng/well. Satisfactory OD readings were obtained with GST-GRB2 concentrations in the of range 10–100 ng/mL.
5. Some of the ELISA methods described here are very complex, especially those requiring capture of the immobilized ligand onto the plate using an antibody-based method. In the event of difficulties in getting such assays to work, satisfactory capture of the immunoprecipitating antibody and ligand can be checked by ELISA. To check capture of immunoprecipitating antibody, simply use a second antibody raised against the appropriate species of immunoglobulin; immobilization of the ligand may be monitored using specific antibodies, followed by an appropriate noncrossreacting second antibody, if these are available. Because of the extreme sensitivity of the ELISA method, small signals obtained in this context probably represent inadequate ligand immobilization.
6. Where crude cell lysates are used in assays that depend on phosphotyrosine motifs, it is essential to add 0.1–1.0 m*M* sodium orthovanadate to all buffers used in steps in which the phosphotyrosine peptide/protein comes into contact with the lysate to block any tyrosine phosphatases that may be present.
7. In the event of the substrate reaction being allowed to proceed too far, so that the OD lies outside the linear range of the plate reader, linearity may be restored simply by rereading the plate at a sub optimal wavelength. Try approx 50 nm to either side of the absorption maximum in the first instance.
8. For example, an assay was developed for the interaction of GST-PI3kinase p85α with baculovirus/Sf9 cell expressed PDGFRβ in which approx 250 ng GST-p85α was immobilized onto glutathione-agarose and incubated with 1.2 μg crude Sf9 cell lysate. PDGFR concentration in the cell lysate was unknown, but is likely to constitute a small percentage of the total cellular protein.
9. Only a small fraction of the [γ-^{32}P]-ATP is incorporated into protein by the in vitro kinase reaction. Unincorporated radioactivity runs close to the dye front during electrophoresis. This will therefore pass into the lower buffer chamber, if electrophoresis is continued long enough to run the dye front off the bottom of the gel. Alternatively, to keep noise levels down to acceptable levels, the bottom of the gel containing the dye front should be removed and discarded before the gel is fixed.
10. More complete transfer of proteins from polyacrylamide gel to membrane is generally achieved by the use of wet rather than semidry Western blotting apparatus.

Incomplete transfer with semidry apparatus may be exploited to split the sample between gel (for autoradiography) and membrane, both being processed separately thereafter. However, the results obtained with this technique are difficult to predict and to quantify.

References

1. Pawson, T. (1995) Protein modules and signalling networks. *Nature* **373,** 573–580.
2. Feng, S., Kasahara, C., Rickles, R. J., and Schreiber, S. L. (1995) Specific interactions outside the proline-rich core of two classes of Src homology 3 ligands. *Proc. Natl. Acad Sci. USA* **92,** 12,408–12,415.
3. Koegl, M., Kypta, R. M., Bergman, M., Alitalo, K., and Courtneidge, S. A. (1994) Rapid and efficient purification of Src homology 2 domain-containing proteins: Fyn, Csk and phosphatidylinositol 3-kinase p85. *Biochem. J.* **302,** 737–744.
4. Yu, H., Chen, J. K., Feng, S., Dalgarno, D. C., Brauer, A. W., and Schreiber, S. L. (1994) Structural basis for the binding of proline-rich peptides to SH3 domains. *Cell* **76,** 933–945.
5. Songyang, Z., Shoelson, S. E., McGlade, J., Olivier, P., Pawson, T., Bustelo, X. R., Barbacid, M., Sabe, H., Hanafusa, H., Yi, T., Ren, R., Baltimore, D., Ratnofsky, S., Feldman, R. A., and Cantley, L. C. (1994) Specific motifs recognized by the SH2 domains of Csk, 3BP2, fps. fes, GRB-2, HCP, SHC, Syk and Vav. *Mol. Cell. Biol.* **14,** 2777–2785.
6. Gout, I., Dhand R., Hiles, I. D., Fry, M. J., Panayotou, G., Das, P., Truong, O., Totty, N. F., Hsuan, J., Booker G. W., Campbell, I. D., and Waterfield, M. D. (1994) The GTPase dynamin binds to and is activated by a subset of SH3 domains. *Cell* **75,** 25–36.
7. Gilmer, T., Rodriguez, M., Jordan, S., Crossby, R., Alligood, K., Green, M., Kimmery, M., Wagner, C., Kinder, D., et al. (1994) Peptide inhibitors of src SH3-SH2-phosphoprotein interactions. *J. Biol. Chem.* **269,** 31,711–31,719.
8. Wange, R. L., Isakov, N., Burke, T. R., Jr., Otaka, A., Roller, P. P., Watts, J. D., Aebersold, R., and Samelson, L. E. (1995) F2(Pmp)2-Tamξ3, a novel competitive inhibitor of the binding of ZAP-70 to the T cell antigen receptor, blocks early T cell signalling. *J. Biol. Chem.* **270,** 944–948.
9. Arvidsson, A.-K., Rupp, E., Nånberg, E., Downward, J., Rönnstrand, L., Wennström, S., Schlessinger, J., Heldin, C.-H., and Claesson-Welsh, L. (1994) Tyr-716 in the platelet-derived growth factor β-receptor kinase insert is involved in GRB2 binding and ras activation. *Mol. Cell. Biol.* **14,** 6715–6726.

15

PH Domain of Serine–Threonine Protein Kinase B (RAC–PKB)

Expression and Binding Assay for Phosphoinositides and Inositol Phosphates

Matthias Frech and Brian A. Hemmings

1. Introduction

The Pleckstrin homology (PH) domain, as a recent newcomer to the family of protein modules involved in signal transduction, has attracted great interest *(1–3)*. The PH domain was first recognized as an internal repeat in pleckstrin, the major substrate of protein kinase C in activated platelets *(4)*. Initially overlooked because of the very low sequence similarity between the different PH domains, presently over 90 proteins are known to possess PH domains *(5–9)*. This domain is often found in proteins involved in signal transduction or cytoskeletal function and forms an independent folding domain of about 100 amino acids. Despite of the very low similarity, their three-dimensional structures are highly related. Several structures of isolated PH domains derived from different proteins are known: pleckstrin *(10)*, dynamin *(11–14)*, β-spectrin *(15–17)*, and phospholipaseCδ-1 *(18)*.

In all structures, the N- and C-terminal residues are in close proximity, so that the PH domain forms an independent module that can be built into proteins, possibly without affecting their overall topology. The core of the protein module is composed of an antiparallel β-sandwich structure containing 7 β-strands and a C-terminal α-helix. The β-sheets form a scaffold made of a four-stranded antiparallel sheet that packs almost orthogonally against a second sheet of three strands. The C-terminal amphipathic α-helix closes off one side of the β-sandwich structure. Additional short stretches of α-helix and β-strands, as seen in

From: *Methods in Molecular Biology, Vol. 88: Protein Targeting Protocols*
Edited by: R. A. Clegg Humana Press Inc., Totowa, NJ

the structures of dynamin and β-spectrin, are located in loops without altering the basic structure.

How the PH domain functions in the context of a protein and in a signal transduction pathway still remains to be elucidated. Regardless of this consideration, the PH domain appears to play an essential function in several molecules involved in signal transduction pathways. The cytoplasmic Bruton tyrosine kinase (Btk) is implicated as the defective gene in human and murine B-cell deficiencies ***(19–22)***. In the X-linked agammaglobulinemia (XLA) syndrome and X-linked immunodeficiency (XID), mutations in the PH domain of Btk probably influence its interaction with phospholipids ***(21,22)***. Results obtained with the insulin receptor substrate-1 (IRS-1), where deletion of its PH domain led to a reduction of the tyrosine phosphorylation in vivo, but not to a total abolition of the subsequent downstream signaling, support the idea that the PH domain may be a membrane-targeting module ***(23,24)***. The PH domain of RAC–PKB (*R*elated to *A* and *C* kinase/*P*rotein *K*inase *B*) is necessary for full stimulation of its kinase activity and is a mediator of phosphatidylinositol 3-kinase (PI3-K) signaling ***(26,28)***. Besides membrane targeting, it is possible that the kinase activity of RAC–PKB can be regulated by the phospholipid products of PI3-K via the PH domain ***(25–28)***. Further, the PH domain of the nucleotide exchange factor Sos seems to be important for an effective activation of the Ras protein ***(29)***.

Molecules, such as inositol phosphates and phospholipids, and proteins, such as the βγ-subunits of G proteins, are now known to interact with PH domains. The β-adrenergic receptor kinase (βARK) and Btk have provided some insight into this interaction. The N-terminal PH domain of Btk binds βγ-subunits in vitro ***(30)***, which increases its kinase activity ***(31)***. βARK has also been shown to interact with βγ-subunits ***(32)***. The region involved in the binding is located in the C-terminus of the receptor kinase, which contains a PH domain ***(33)***. PH domains of other proteins were also shown to bind to βγ-subunits; however, their binding affinities were found to differ greatly.

The best-characterized ligands for PH domains are phosphatidyl-inositol phosphates and inositol phosphates. ***(34–38)***. It has been suggested that phospholipid- and/or inositol phosphate-binding is a characteristic of all PH domains. Phospholipid or inositol-phosphate binding has been demonstrated for every PH domain so far tested.

Unequal charge distribution, another conserved feature of PH domains, leads to a strongly polarized molecule. The side of the protein where the α-helix is located is negatively charged. The three loops are located on the positively charged side of the molecule. They show considerable variation in amino acid sequence and length, and are involved in the binding of phospholipids and inositol phosphates. The structures of complexes between PH domains and inositol (1,4,5)-trisphosphate delivers valuable information regarding the interaction between certain amino acid residues of the PH domain and this ligand ***(16,18)***. For β-spectrin, the amino acids Lys^8, Arg^{21}, Ser^{22}, Trp^{23}, and Tyr^{69} can be seen to be in the binding site and in close contact with oxygen atoms of the phosphate groups attached to the inositol ring. The hydroxyl group of Ser^{22} is hydrogen-bonded to the oxygen of the phosphate group at the position 1 of the inositol ring. Tyr^{69} and Trp^{23} are hydrogen bonded to the phosphate group at position 4. The ε-amino group of Lys^8 is involved in a salt bridge with the phosphate groups at positions 4 and 5. Finally, the guanidinium group of Arg^{21} makes a salt bridge with the phosphate group attached at position 5 of the inositol ring.

In light of the high variation in primary structure, this arrangement for the binding of inositol (1,4,5)-trisphosphate may not necessarily apply in detail to all other PH domains. This could lead to an altered set of interactions for other PH domains and to differential binding behavior toward inositol phosphates or phospholipids. A possible example of this is the phospholipaseCδ-1 PH domain, which binds certain inositol phosphates with a higher affinity than the β-spectrin PH domain ***(18,38)***. This can be explained structurally, by additional hydrogen bonds and salt bridges between the protein and the inositol (1,4,5)-trisphosphate; moreover, the location of the binding site is different between these two PH domains.

In summary, the known characteristics of the PH domain are its interaction with phospholipids, inositol phosphates, and βγ-subunits of heterotrimeric G proteins. Both phospholipids and βγ-subunits are membrane-bound species, supporting the view that the PH domain may fulfill its functions at the membrane. Here, it could act as a targeting module for the protein, or as a transmitter receiving and integrating signals from phospholipids and/or βγ-subunits. This could lead to changes in the interactions of the PH domain-containing protein with other molecules.

Our studies on the interaction of inositol phosphates and phosphoinositides with RAC-PKB have recently been published ***(40)***.

2. Materials

2.1. Expression of RAC–PKB Pleckstrin Homology Domain as a GST-Fusion Protein

1. Bacterial strain: JM109.
2. Expression plasmid: pGEX-2T (Pharmacia, Sollentuna, Sweden) containing a *Bam*HI–*Eco*RI fragment encompassing amino acids 1–131 of RAC–PKBα.
3. 100 mg/mL Ampicillin (Sigma, St. Louis, MO).
4. 50 m*M* $CaCl_2$.
5. 2xYT Medium: 16 g/L bacto-tryptone, 10 g/L bacto-yeast extract (Difco, Paisley, Scotland), and 5 g/L NaCl, pH 7.0.

6. 100 m*M* Isopropyl-thiogalactopyranoside (IPTG; Promega, Madison, WI), in distilled water, kept at –20°C.
7. Phosphate buffered saline (PBS) solution: 8 g/L NaCl, 0.2 g/L KCl, 1.44 g/L Na_2HPO_4, 0.24 g/L KH_2PO_4, pH 7.4.
8. Culture flasks: 250 mL, 2000 mL.
9. Incubator at 37°C.
10. Falcon tubes.

2.2. Purification of RAC–PKB Pleckstrin Homology Domain

1. Bacterial cell paste after induction.
2. 100 m*M* phenylmethylsulfonyl fluorid (PMSF; Sigma) solution in isopropanol kept at –20°C.
3. 10 mg/mL lysozyme solution (Sigma), freshly made prior to use in 50 m*M* Tris-HCl, pH 8.0, 1 m*M* dithiothreitol (DTT), 1 m*M* EDTA.
4. 4% Sodium deoxycholate solution.
5. 1*M* $MgCl_2$.
6. DNaseI (Boehringer Mannheim, Mannheim, Germany), freshly made prior to use as a 1 mg/mL solution in 50 m*M* Tris-HCl, pH 8.0.
7. Glutathione coupled to agarose (Sigma).
8. 10 m*M* reduced glutathione (Sigma) in 50 m*M* Tris-HCl, pH 8.0, 1 m*M* EDTA, kept at –20°C.
9. Thrombin from human plasma (Sigma, St. Louis, MO). The lyophylisate is dissolved in 50 m*M* Tris-HCl, pH 8.0, 1 m*M* EDTA, to a concentration of 1 U/µL, shock-frozen in liquid nitrogen, and kept in aliquots at –70°C.
10. Lysis buffer: 50 m*M* Tris-HCl, pH 8.0, 1 m*M* DTT, 1 m*M* EDTA, 1 m*M* PMSF.
11. Buffer A for FPLC: 50 m*M* Tris-HCl, pH 8.0, 1 m*M* EDTA (0.45-µm filtered).
12. Buffer B for FPLC: 50 m*M* Tris-HCl, pH 8.0, 1 m*M* EDTA, 0.05*M* NaCl (0.45-µm filtered).
13. Anion exchange column MonoQ HR 5/5 (Pharmacia).
14. Centricon-10 (Amicon, Beverly, MA).

2.3. Solubilization of Phospholipids

1. Phosphatidylinositol (4,5)-*bis*-phosphate (Fluka, Buchs, Switzerland).
2. 20 m*M* HEPES-NaOH, pH 7.0, 0.22-µm filtered.
3. Solution of CH_3OH:CH_3Cl:H_2O:1*M* HCl in the ratio 20:9:1:0.01 by volume.
4. Desiccator.

2.4. Protein Concentration Determination

1. Bio-Rad Protein Assay (Bio-Rad, Hercules, CA).
2. Plastic cuvets.
3. Spectrometer.

2.5. Fluorescence Assay

1. Spectrometer (Perkin-Elmer Luminescence Spectrometer LS 50 B).
2. Fluorescence cuvets.

3. 70% Ethanol.
4. Isopropanol.
5. 500 m*M* HEPES-NaOH, pH 7.0, 0.22-μm filtered.
6. 1*M* $MgCl_2$, 0.22-μm filtered.
7. Double-distilled water, 0.22-μm filtered.
8. Inositol phosphates (Fluka) dissolved at a concentration of 1 m*M* in 20 m*M* HEPES-NaOH, pH 7.0, and stored at –70°C.
9. Phosphatidylinositol (4,5)-*bis*-phosphate (Fluka).
10. Recombinant PH domain: PH131; concentration 1–2 mg/mL in 50 m*M* Tris-HCl, pH 8.0, 1 m*M* EDTA, 450 m*M* NaCl.
11. Data analysis and graphics program (GraFit, Robin J. Leatherbarrow, Erithacus Software).

3. Methods

3.1. Expression of the Pleckstrin Homology Domain of RAC–PKB as a GST-Fusion Protein

For the expression of the PH domain, we used the GST-fusion protein system (Pharmacia). This expression system has several advantages: the IPTG-inducible *tac* promoter leads to an overexpression of the fusion protein; the purification is easy and rapid, the highly soluble GST helps to keep the fusion partner in solution, so that the biochemical characterization is also possible with the fusion protein, and a thrombin cleavage site can be used to release the fusion partner from the GST (*see* **Note 1**). Because the pGEX vectors carry the *lacI^q^* gene, no specific host is required. This easily makes it possible to test different strains for highest expression of soluble protein.

The RAC–PKB PH domain composed of amino acids 1–131 was generated by PCR. The resulting 5' *Bam*HI–3' *Eco*RI fragment was cloned into the expression vector pGEX-2T. For expression, we used the bacterial strain JM109 transformed with the expression plasmid, using the $CaCl_2$ method. We found that a short induction time of 2–3 h is sufficient to express the protein and that low temperature increases the yield of soluble protein. From 5 L of culture we obtain, under these conditions, about 15–20 mg of GST-PH131.

1. Inoculate 50 mL of 2xYT medium containing 100 μg/mL ampicillin, with a single colony, in a 250-mL flask, in a shaker at 150 rpm at 37°C overnight.
2. Dilute the bacterial culture 50 times in 2xYT and grow at 37°C to an OD_{600} of 0.6.
3. After lowering the temperature to 25°C, induce the cells at an OD_{600} of 0.8–0.9 with 0.1 m*M* IPTG for 3 h on the shaker with 150 rpm at 25°C.
4. Harvest the cells by centrifugation (20 min, 4°C, 5000*g*), wash twice with PBS, transfer to a 50-mL Falcon tube, freeze in liquid nitrogen and store at –70°C.

3.2. Purification of the RAC–PKB PH Domain

The purification of recombinant PH domain consists of the following steps: binding of the GST-fusion protein to glutathione-agarose, elution of the fusion protein, subsequent thrombin cleavage; and further purification on a MonoQ column (*see* **Note 1**). All steps of the purification are done at 4°C, unless stated otherwise. This purification scheme gives some freedom to change and adapt the conditions according to the protein of interest. The buffer can easily be exchanged during the washing steps, while the fusion protein is still bound to the glutathione matrix. If desired, the thrombin cleavage can be performed directly on the beads to simplify further steps of the purification.

1. Thaw the frozen bacterial cells in a total volume of fivefold the bacterial pellet in 50 m*M* Tris-HCl, pH 8.0, 1 m*M* EDTA, 1 m*M* DTT, and 1 m*M* PMSF.
2. After thawing and resuspending the cells, add lysozyme to a final concentration of 0.5–1.0 mg/mL, and stir for 30 min at 4°C.
3. To promote lysis add sodium deoxycholate to a final concentration of 0.1 % and stir the suspension for 30 min at 4°C.
4. To the now highly viscous solution, add $MgCl_2$ to a final concentration of 10 m*M*. Then add DNaseI (final concentration 20 µg/mL) and continue stirring the solution at 4°C, until the viscosity decreases. This normally takes about 10 min.
5. Centrifuge at 20,000*g* for 45 min at 4°C. This is normally sufficient to clear the extract.
6. Add glutathione-agarose to the clear supernatant, according to the description of the manufacturer. The agarose is first preswollen for 2 h in 50 m*M* Tris-HCl, pH 8.0, 1 m*M* EDTA.
7. After 1 h incubation on a roller at 4°C, gently spin down the glutathione-agarose at 100*g* for 5 min; decant and keep the supernatant for further analysis to check whether the binding was complete. Wash the pelleted agarose five times with 50 mL PBS, followed by three washes with 50 m*M* Tris-HCl, pH 8.0, 1 m*M* EDTA gently centrifuging the agarose (as above), between the washing steps.
8. For elution of the fusion protein, resuspend the agarose in 5 mL of 50 m*M* Tris-HCl, pH 8.0, 1 m*M* EDTA, 10 m*M* reduced glutathione, and incubate for 2 h at room temperature on a roller shaker.
9. After centrifugation subject the agarose to a wash step: Resuspend in 5 mL of 50 m*M* Tris-HCl, pH 8.0, 1 m*M* EDTA, 10 m*M* reduced glutathione, and re-spin. Combine the supernatant with that from **step 8**.
10. Thrombin cleavage: 2.5 U is sufficient to cleave 1 mg of recombinant GST-PH131 in 2 h at room temperature. If necessary, the reaction can be stopped by adding 1.0 m*M* PMSF (*see* **Note 1**).
11. Load the solution, after cleavage, onto a MonoQ HR5/5 (Pharmacia) at a flow rate of 1 mL/min at room temperature. After loading, wash the column with buffer A until the absorption reaches the starting value.
12. Elute the protein from the column with a 20-mL linear gradient from 0 to 100% (by volume) buffer B in buffer A, at a flow rate of 1 mL/min. The PH domain elutes at about 450 m*M* NaCl. The column is run at room temperature.
13. Examine peak fractions by 15% SDS-PAGE (**Fig. 1**). Pool pure fractions and concentrate, using a Centricon-10 spin concentrator (Amicon, Beverly, MA).

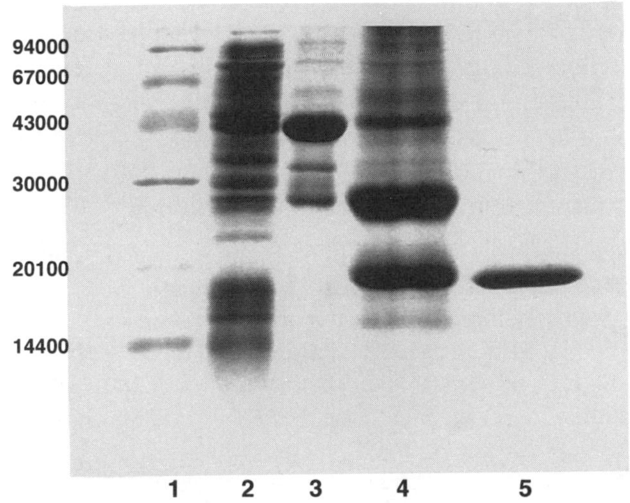

Fig. 1. Purification of the RAC–PKB PH131 domain as a GST fusion protein. Lane 1, mol-wt markers (Bio-Rad); lane 2, soluble extract of JM109 expressing the fusion protein GST-PH131; lane 3, GST-PH131 after elution from the glutathione-agarose; lane 4, GST and PH131 after thrombin cleavage; lane 5, pooled fractions after MonoQ chromatography. Molecular weights are shown at the left of the gel in Daltons.

14. For storage of the protein, shock-freeze in liquid nitrogen and keep aliquots at –70°C.

3.3. Solubilization of Phospholipids

The phospholipids used in our assay are phosphatidylinositol (4,5)-*bis*-phosphate, phosphatidylinositol (3,4)-*bis*-phosphate, and phosphatidyl-inositol (3,4,5)-trisphosphate, the latter ones as dioctanoyl derivatives ***(39)***. The solubility of these compounds in aqueous solution increases with the number of phosphate groups attached to the inositol ring, and decreases with the length of the fatty acids bound to the glycerol moiety of the molecule. The dioctanoyl derivatives of phosphatidylinositol (3,4)-*bis*-phosphate and phosphatidylinositol (3,4,5)-trisphosphate, which are water-soluble to a much larger extent than the natural compounds, are much more suitable for our assay, and do not give rise to difficulties, even at high concentrations. The measurement of the interaction with phosphatidylinositol (4)-monophosphate or phosphatidylinositol by this method is not possible, because their affinities are too weak, and therefore the concentrations necessary for the titration are too high to be used in aqueous solutions. High concentrations of lipids nonspecifically interact with the PH domain, which can be, in our case, monitored as an increase of the fluorescence intensity. This interaction is not observed with inositol phosphates, and this nonspecific binding cannot be competed by an excess of inositol phosphates. The interaction of these poorly soluble phospholipids with the PH domain should be assessed by a vesicle-binding assay. If possible, it is far better to switch to the soluble inositol phosphate derivatives or the glycero-inositolphosphate to study the interaction in solution.

1. Solubilize phosphatidylinositol (4,5)-*bis*-phosphate is solubilized in CH_3OH:CH_3Cl:H_2O:1*M* HCl (ratio 20:9:1:0.01 by volume).
2. Dry the lipid solution in a desiccator under vacuum.
3. Add 20 m*M* HEPES-NaOH, pH 7.0 to the dried lipids to obtain a final concentration of 50 µ*M*, and sonicate the solution in a water bath. This should result in a clear solution.

3.4. Protein Concentration

Protein concentrations are determined by the method of Bradford using the manufacturer's protocol (Bio-Rad), with BSA as standard.

3.5. Binding of Phospholipids and Inositol Phosphates to the RAC–PKB PH Domain Monitored with a Fluorescence Assay

The fluorescence of tryptophan residues is particularly sensitive to polarity changes in their environment. Protein–ligand interactions can therefore be monitored by changes in fluorescence intensity, if the environment of a tryptophan is influenced. This can either be the result of a direct interaction of the ligand with the tryptophan, or can be caused by a conformational change in the protein. The crystallographic structures of PH domains complexed with inositol (1,4,5)-trisphosphate show that in both cases a tryptophan residue is hydrogen-bonded to an oxygen of a phosphate group of the inositol ring. Indeed, it should be possible to study any PH domain containing a tryptophan at this position, using this kind of assay. Furthermore, the low sequence conservation of PH domains may make it possible to introduce a tryptophan residue in the inositol phosphate binding site. Amino acid substitutions in this solvent-exposed area of the protein probably do not disturb the overall structure. Fluorescence techniques offer an extensive range of possibilities for examining the protein itself, as well as its interaction with other molecules. Stability, structural information, conformation of the protein, time-resolved studies, and, especially, presteady state measurements could be used to investigate binding mechanisms and subsequent conformational changes.

Based on data obtained with phospholipase Cδ1 and β-spectrin ***(16,37)***, probably the tryptophan 22 of the RAC–PKB PH domain will also interact with phospholipids or inositol phosphates. In agreement with this suggestion,

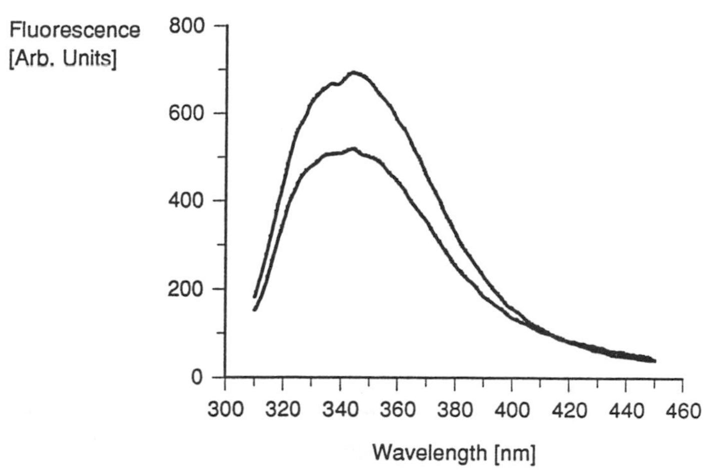

Fig. 2. Fluorescence spectrum of RAC/PKB PH domain, measured using 0.16 µ*M* PH131 in 20 m*M* HEPES/NaOH, pH 7.0, 10 m*M* $MgCl_2$, at 25°C, λ_{EXC} 290 nm, excitation slit 5 nm bandwidth, emission slit 15 nm bandwith. Upper curve, emission spectrum of the PH domain alone; lower curve, emission spectrum of the PH domain in the presence of 2 µ*M* phosphatidylinositol (3,4,5) trisphosphate.

addition of inositol phosphates or phospholipids in low concentrations to the RAC–PKB PH domain results in the quenching of the tryptophan fluorescence (**Fig. 2**). The maximal decrease in the fluorescence was found to be about 30% for all the substances we used. This signal can be used to determine affinity constants.

Fluorescence-quenching experiments are recorded with a Perkin-Elmer Luminescence Spectrometer LS 50 B. at 25°C in 20 m*M* HEPES-NaOH, pH 7.0, 10 m*M* $MgCl_2$, typically with a protein concentration of 0.1 µ*M* (determined by the Bradford assay) in a reaction volume of 1 mL. Tryptophan residues are excited at a wavelength of 290 nm, in order to keep excitation of tyrosine residues to a minimum, and to minimize energy transfer to tryptophan residues. The maximum of emitted light is found at 345 nm.

1. Rinse the fluorescence cuvet carefully several times with 70% ethanol and with isopropanol. Then blow out all dust particles and dry the cuvet under a stream of nitrogen.
2. Filter all solution used (0.22 µm) to avoid scattering by dust particles.
3. From emission spectra, conditions are determined empirically to obtain the optimal signal. Set the excitation slit width and the emission slit width to give the best signal and the best signal-to-noise ratio.
4. Set the excitation wavelength to 290 nm; the maximum of the emitted fluorescence is at 345 nm, as shown in **Fig. 2** (*see* **Note 3**).

5. Premix 40 µL 500 m*M* HEPES-NaOH, pH 7.0, 10 µL 1*M* $MgCl_2$; add PH131 and double-distilled water to obtain a final concentration of PH131 of 0.1–0.2 µ*M* in a 1 mL volume (*see* **Note 4**). Mix by pipeting up and down, fill the fluorescence cuvet, and place it in the spectrometer.
6. Record an emission spectrum and watch the fluorescence signal for 30 min for stability and constancy.
7. Add the ligands to the cuvet in increasing amounts and record the change in the fluorescence (*see* **Note 5**).
8. A plot of the change in the fluorescence (ΔF) against the concentration of the added ligand ([L]), resulting in a graph that can be fitted to the hyperbolic function $\Delta F = \Delta F_{MAX} \cdot [L]/(K_D + [L])$, to give the values for the maximal change of the fluorescence ΔF_{MAX} and the dissociation constant K_D for the protein–ligand complex (**Fig. 3**). Robust weighting is used during the fitting procedure (*see* **Notes 4** and **6**).

4. Notes

1. The use of GST fusions for the assay is possible. We found that the fluorescence of GST fusion protein responds in the same way to inositol phosphates as the untagged recombinant protein. In cases in which there are problems with the stability of the cleaved proteins, this could be a convenient solution.
2. High phospholipid concentrations are not compatible with this assay. In particular, phospholipids acylated with C18 or C16 fatty acids bind nonspecifically to the PH domain. In our case, such binding could not be competed for with an excess of inositol phosphates.
3. Fluorescence can also be used to check whether the protein is denatured. The tryptophan located in the C-terminal α-helix is the only highly conserved residue in every PH domain. In all structures now solved, this residue points into the hydrophobic interior of the PH domain, making contacts to the β-strand 1. This can be used to monitor the denaturation of the protein. We see a shift of the emission maximum toward longer wavelengths, upon denaturation of the PH domain.
4. It is best to work under the classical conditions for the titrations: Concentration of the protein should be far below the ligand concentration. As an upper limit, the protein concentration should not exceed 0.2-fold the value of the dissociation constant. Otherwise, the simple hyperbolic function cannot be used, because changes in the free ligand concentration are not negligible. Further, under these classical conditions the determination of the dissociation constant is independent of the protein concentration.
5. The volume of the added ligand should be sufficiently small that the total change in volume and concentration of the sample does not exceed 5%. Since the fluorescence is measured as a function of the concentration of the protein, the dilution caused by the added volumes leads to a reduction of the fluorescence, and should be corrected for.
6. The low sequence homology of PH domains will probably allow the insertion or exchange of tryptophan residues, to enable this fluorescence assay to be widely used.

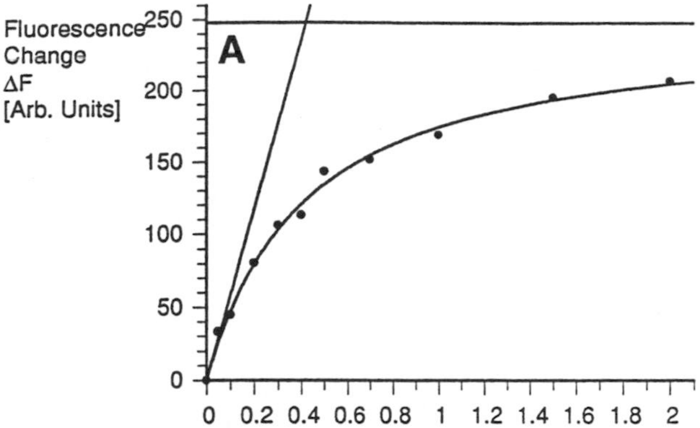

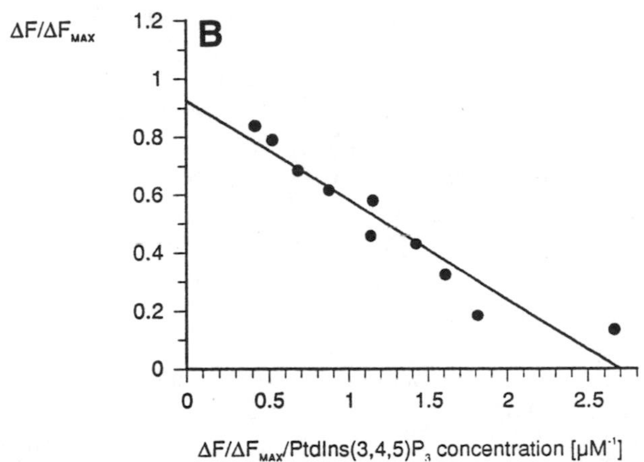

Fig. 3. Titration of RAC–PKB PH domain with increasing concentrations of phosphatidylinositol (3,4,5) trisphosphate: PH131 was used at 0.16 μ*M* in 20 m*M* HEPES-NaOH, pH 7.0, 10 m*M* $MgCl_2$, at 25°C, λ_{EXC} 290 nm, excitation slit 5 nm bandwidth, emission slit 15 nm bandwidth. **(A)** Titration and nonlinear fit to a hyperbolic function resulting in a ΔF_{MAX} of 250 arbitrary units and a dissociation constant of 400 n*M*. **(B)** Scatchard plot of the data from panel A, indicating a stoichiometry of 1:1 for the PH domain phosphatidylinositol (3,4,5) trisphosphate complex.

Acknowledgments

We thank T. Millward, M. Andjelkovic, R. Meier, and J. Hofsteenge for comments.

References

1. Haslam, R. J., Koide, H. B., and Hemmings, B. A. (1993) Pleckstrin domain homology. *Nature* **363,** 310,311.

2. Mayer, B. J., Ren, R., Clark, K. L., and Baltimore, D. (1993) A putative modular domain present in diverse signaling proteins. *Cell* **73,** 629,630.
3. Musacchio, A., Gibson, T., Rice, P., Thompsen, J., and Saraste, M. (1993) The PH domain: a common piece in the structural patchwork of signalling proteins. *Trends Biochem. Sci.* **18,** 343–348.
4. Tyers, M., Rachubinski, R. A., Stewart, M. I., Varrichio, A. M., Shorr, R. G. L., Haslam, R. J., and Harley, C. B. (1988) Molecular cloning and expression of the major protein kinase C substrate of platelets. *Nature* **333,** 470–473.
5. Shaw, G. (1993) Identification of novel Pleckstrin homology (PH) domains provides a hypothesis for PH domain function. *Biochem. Biophys. Res. Commun.* **195,** 1145–1151.
6. Gibson, T. J., Hyvönen, M., Musachio, A., Saraste, M., and Birney, E. (1994) PH domain: the first anniversary. *Trend Biochem. Sci.* **19,** 349–353.
7. Ingley, E. and Hemmings, B. A. (1994) Pleckstrin homology (PH) domains in signal transduction. *J. Cell. Biochem.* **58,** 1–8.
8. Saraste, M. and Hyvönen, M. (1995) PH domains: a fact file. *Curr. Opin. Struct. Biol.* **5,** 403–408.
9. Parker, P. J., Hemmings, B. A., and Gierschik, P. (1994) PH domains and phospholipases—a meaning relationship? *Trends Biochem. Sci.* **19,** 54,55.
10. Yoon, H. S., Hajduk, P. J., Petros, A. M., Olejniczak, E. T., Meadows, R. P., and Fesik, S. W. (1994) Solution structure of a pleckstrin-homology domain. *Nature* **369,** 672–675.
11. Downing, A. K., Driscoll, P. C., Gout, I., Salim, K., Zvelebil, M. J., and Waterfield, M. D. (1994) Three-dimensional solution structure of the pleckstrin homology domain from dynamin. *Curr. Biol.* **4,** 884–891.
12. Ferguson, K. M., Lemmon, M. A., Schlessinger, J., and Sigler, P. B. (1994) Crystal structure at 2. 2 Å resolution of the pleckstrin homology domain from human dynamin. *Cell* **79,** 199–209.
13. Fushman, D., Cahill, S., Lemmon, M. A., Schlessinger, J., and Cowburn, D. (1994) Solution structure of pleckstrin homology domain of dynamin by heteronuclear NMR spectroscopy. *Proc. Natl. Acad. Sci. USA* **92,** 816–820.
14. Timm, D., Salim, K., Gout, I., Guruprasad, L., Waterfield, M., and Blundell, T. (1994) Crystal structure of the pleckstrin homology domain from dynamin. *Structural Biol.* **1,** 782–788.
15. Macias, M. J., Musacchio, A., Ponstingl, H., Nilges, M., Saraste, M., and Oschkinat, H. (1994) Structure of the pleckstrin homology domain of β-spectrin. *Nature* **369,** 675–677.
16. Hyvönen, M, Macias, J. M., Nilges, M., Oschkinat, H., Saraste, M., and Wilmans, M. (1995) Structure of the binding site for inositol phosphates in a PH domain. *EMBO* **14,** 4676–4685.
17. Zhang, P., Talluri, S., Deng, H., Branton, D., and Wagner, G. (1995) Solution structure of the pleckstrin homology domain of Drosophila β-spectrin. *Structure* **3,** 1185–1195.
18. Ferguson, K. M., Lemmon, M. A., Schlessinger, J., and Sigler, P. B. (1995) Structure of the high affinity complex of inositol trisphosphate with a Phospholipase C pleckstrin homology domain. *Cell* **83,** 1037–1046.

19. Tsukada, S., Saffran, D. C., Rawlings, D. J., Parolini, O., Allen, R. C., Klisak, I., Sparkes, R. S., Kubagawa, H. Mohandas, T., Quan, S., Belmont, J. W., Cooper, M. D., Conley, M. E., and Witte, O. N. (1993) Deficient expression of a B cell cytoplasmic tyrosine kinase in human X-linked agammaglobulinemia. *Cell* **72,** 279–290.
20. Vetrie, D., Vorechovsky, I., Sideras, P., Holland, J., Davies, A., Flinter, F. Hammarstrom, L. Kinnon, C., Levinsky, R., Bobrow, M., Smith, C. I. E., and Bentley, D. R. (1993) The gene involved in X-linked agammaglobulinaemia is a member of the src familiy of protein-tyrosine kinases. *Nature* **361,** 226–233.
21. Rawlings, D. J., Saffran, D. C., Tsukada, S., Largaespada, D. A., Grimaldi, J. C., Cohen, L., Mohr, R. N., Bazan, J. F., Howard, M., Copeland, N. G., Jenkins, N. A., and Witte, O. N. (1993) Mutation of unique region of Bruton's tyrosine kinase in immunodeficient XID mice. *Science* **261,** 358–361.
22. Thomas, J. D., Sideras, P., Smith, C. I. E., Vorechovsky, I., Chapman, V., and Paul, W. E. (1993) Colocalization of X-linked agammaglobulinemia and X-linked immunodeficiency genes. *Science* **261,** 355–358.
23. Myers, M. G., Grammer, T. C., Brooks, J., Glasheen, E. M., Wang, L.-M., Sun, X. J., Blenis, J., Pierce, J. H., and White, M. F. (1995) The pleckstrin homology domain in insulin receptor substrate-1 sensitizes insulin signaling. *J. Biol. Chem.* **270,** 11,715–11,718.
24. Voliovitch, H., Schindler, D. G., Hadari, Y. R., Taylor, S. I., Accili, D., and Zick, Y. (1995) Tyrosine phosphorylation of insulin receptor substrate-1 in vivo depends upon the presence of its pleckstrin homology region. *J. Biol. Chem.* **270,** 18,083–18,087.
25. Datta, K., Franke, T. F., Chan, T. O., Makris, A., Yang, S.-I., Kaplan, D. R., Morrison, D. K., Golemis, E. A., and Tsichlis, P. N. (1995) AH/PH domain-mediated interaction between Akt molecules and its potential role in Akt regulation. *Mol. Cell. Biol.* **15,** 2304–2310.
26. Franke, T. F., Yang, S.-I., Chan, T. O., Datta, K., Kazlaukas, A., Morrison, D. K., Kaplan, D. R., and Tsichlis, P. N. (1995) The protein kinase encoded by the Akt proto-oncogene is a target of the PDGF-activated phosphatidylinositol 3-Kinase. *Cell* **81,** 727–736.
27. Kohn, A. D., Kovacina, K. S., and Roth, R. A. (1995) Insulin stimulates the kinase activity of RAC-PK, a pleckstrin homology domain containing ser/thr kinase. *EMBO J.* **14,** 4288–4295.
28. Andjelkovic, M., Jakubowicz, T., Cron, P., Ming. X.-F., Han, J.-W., and Hemmings, B. A. (1996) Activation and phosphorylation of a PH domain containig protein Kinase (RAC-PK/PKB) by serum and protein phosphatase Inhibitors. *Proc. Natl. Acad. Sci. USA* **93,** 5699–5704.
29. McCollam, L., Bonfini, L., Karlovich, C. A., Conway, B. R., Kozma, L. M., Banerjee, U., and Czech, M. P. (1995) Functional roles for the pleckstrin and Dbl homology regions in the Ras exchange factor Son-of-sevenless. *J. Biol. Chem.* **270,** 15,954–15,957.
30. Tsukada, S., Simon, M. I., Witte, O. N., and Katz, A. (1994) Binding of βγ-subunits of heterotrimeric G proteins to the PH domain of Bruton tyrosine kinase. *Proc. Natl. Acad. Sci. USA* **91,** 11,256–11,260.

31. Langhans-Rajasekaran, S. A., Wan, Y., and Huang, X.-Y. (1995) Activation of Tsk and Btk tyrosine kinases by G protein βγ-subunits. *Proc. Natl. Acad. Sci. USA* **92,** 8601–8605.
32. Koch, W. J., Inglese, J., Stone, W. C., and Lefkowitz, R. J. (1993) The binding site for the βγ-subunits of heterotrimeric G proteins on the β-adrenergic receptor kinase. *J. Biol. Chem.* **268,** 8256–8260.
33. Touhara, K., Inglese, J., Pitscher, J. A., Shaw, G., and Lefkowitz, R. J. (1994) Binding of βγ-subunits to pleckstrin homology domains. *J. Biol. Chem.* **269,** 10,217–10,220.
34. Rebecchi, M., Peterson, A., and McLaughlin, S. (1992) Phosphoinositide-specific phospholipase C-d1 binds with high affinity to phospholipid vesicles containing phosphatidylinositol 4,5-bisphosphate. *Biochemistry* **31,** 12,742–12,747.
35. Garcia, P., Gupta, R., Shah, S., Morris, A. J., Rudge, S. A., Scarlata, S., Petrova, V. McLaughlin, S., and Rebecchi, M. (1995) The pleckstrin homology domain of Phospholipase c-δ_1 binds with high affinity to phosphatidylinositol 4,5-bisphosphate in bilayer membranes. *Biochemistry* **34,** 16,228–16,234.
36. Harlan, J. E., Hajduk, P. J., Yoon, H. S., and Fesik, S. W. (1994) Pleckstrin homology domains bind to phosphatidylinositol–4,5-bisphosphate. *Nature* **371,** 168–170.
37. Lemmon, M. A., Ferguson, K. M., O'Brien, R., Sigler, P. B., and Schlessinger, J. (1995) Specific and high- affinity binding of inositol phosphates to an isolated pleckstrin homology domain. *Proc. Natl. Acad. Sci. USA* **92,** 10,472–10,476.
38. Zheng, J., Cahill, S., Lemmon, M. A., Fushman, D., Schlessinger, J., and Cowburn, D. (1996) Identification of the binding site for acidic phospholipids on the PH domain of dynamin: implications for stimulation of GTPase activity. *J. Mol. Biol.* **255,** 14–21.
39. Reddy, K. K., Saady, M., Whited, G., and Falck, J. R. (1995) Intracellular mediators: synthesis of L-α-phosphatidyl-D-myo-inositol 3,4,5-trisphosphate and glyceryl ether analogs. *J. Org. Chem.* **60,** 3385–3390.
40. Fech, M., Andjelkovic, M., Ingley, E., Reddy, K. K., Falck, J. R., and Hemmings, B. A. (1997) High affinity binding of inositol phosphates and phosphoinositides to the pleckstrin homology domain of RAC/protein kinase B and their influence on kinase activity. *J. Biol. Chem.* **272,** 8474–8481.

16

Membrane Targeting via Protein *N*-Myristoylation

R. A. Jeffrey McIlhinney

1. Introduction

1.1. Enzymology

The covalent modification of cell proteins by the attachment of myristic acid, a 14 carbon saturated fatty acid, to their N-terminal amino acid is now recognized to be a widespread phenomenon ***(1–5)***. The enzyme responsible for the attachment of myristic acid to these proteins is myristoyl-CoA: Protein *N*-myristoyltransferase (NMT; EC 2.3.1.97). This enzyme catalyzes the transfer of myristic acid from myristoyl-CoA to the N-terminal amino acid of the target protein and results in the fatty acid being amide-bonded to the α-amino group of the amino acid. Because this transfer is susceptible to protein synthesis inhibitors, it must take place as the protein is synthesized ***(6,7)***. Data from the studies on both the sequence of known myristoylated proteins, and from those on the sequence requirements for NMT, suggests that the N-terminal amino acid is always a glycine residue ***(5)***. However the other sequence requirements for protein N-myristoylation are less certain and the resulting vague general consensus sequence is summarized in **Fig. 1**. Although the majority of proteins that are substrates for NMT are myristoylated, the enzyme can make use of a limited range of other fatty acids, including shorter-chain and unsaturated fatty acids. In general, this occurs when these fatty acids form the majority of the acyl-CoA pool in a cell or tissue, for example, in the retina ***(8)***. For most practical purposes, however, NMT can be regarded as essentially specific for myristic acid.

The best-characterized NMT is that of yeast, which is a single chain polypeptide with an apparent mol wt of about 50,000 kDa on sodium dodecyl sulfate (SDS) polyacrylamide gels ***(3)***. The human enzyme has also been cloned and an active form of this identified, which has a similar mol wt ***(9)***. The transfer of

From: *Methods in Molecular Biology, Vol. 88: Protein Targeting Protocols*
Edited by: R. A. Clegg Humana Press Inc., Totowa, NJ

$$NH_2\text{-}G_1X_2X_3X_4S_5X_6X_7X_8$$

X_2 = C,A,L,N,Q,V,S,G X_3 = T,Y,F,Q,V,A,L
X_4 = X_3+P X_6 = X_2+X_3+R,K
X_7 and X_8 = K,S,L,E,V,G,P,N,F,D, Q,T

Fig. 1. Permitted sequences for N-terminal myristoylation by mammalian NMT. The single-letter nomenclature for the amino acids has been used, and the permitted residues are based on the sequences of known myristoyl-proteins, as described by Rudnick et al. ***(5)***. The glycine at position 1 is obligatory. Serine is the most common amino acid found at position 5, and increases the affinity of yeast NMT for substrate peptides, but other amino acids are found here in mammalian myristoyl-proteins. Proline has not yet been found at position 6, nor have tryptophan or tyrosine been found at positions 7 and 8. Generally, acidic residues are not found at position 4.

the myristic acid from the acyl-CoA to the substrate protein takes place via an ordered Bi-Bi mechanism ***(10)***. This involves the formation of complex between the myristoyl-CoA and NMT, followed by binding of the substrate, accompanied by release of CoA, and, finally, release of the myristoylated substrate.

1.2. Function of the Myristic Acid

Many myristoylated proteins are found associated with intracellular membranes, or the inner surface of the plasma membrane. However, although many studies show that myristate is necessary for the membrane attachment of these proteins, it now seems unlikely that myristate is acting as a simple hydrophobic anchor. First, a number of myristoylated proteins, such as the catalytic subunit of protein kinase A and calcineurin B, are cytosolic. Second, recent thermodynamic calculations suggest that the addition of myristic acid to a protein would result in a dissociation constant of $10^{-4}M$ for the complex, which would be insufficient to give a stable interaction with the lipid bilayer ***(11,12)***. Third, a number of studies on the α-subunits of the heterotrimeric G proteins ***(13)***, some members of the src-related family of tyrosine kinases ***(14)***, and the ADP-ribosylation factors ***(15,16)*** have suggested that the addition of myristate alone is not sufficient to guarantee their membrane association. Other features of these proteins, including N-terminal polybasic sequences and adjacent protein domains or palmitoylation sites, have been implicated in their membrane binding. The role of myristate may therefore be to provide an initial interaction with the lipid bilayer, which is then stabilized by other interactions with phospholipids or other membrane proteins.

Alternatively, the fatty acid could be facilitating the interaction of the protein with a specific membrane myristoyl-protein receptor. Myristate can stabilize protein–protein interactions, as evidenced in the X-ray crystallographic studies on polio virus *(17)*, and could act in a similar way with a membrane protein. Indeed, using affinity columns of the myristoylated HIV protein Nef, Harris et al. *(18)* were able to identify proteins from cell extracts which specifically bound only to the myristoylated protein, suggesting that there are indeed myristate-mediated protein–protein interactions. Evidence for a membrane myristoyl-protein receptor has been provided by experiments demonstrating the saturable, high-affinity binding of p60*src*-based myristyol-peptides, but not nonmyristoylated peptides, to cell membranes *(19)*. The later identification of the protein responsible for this specific binding of myristoyl-peptides to membranes as a mitochondrial protein, the adenine nucleotide translocator *(20)*, does not, however, preclude the existence of other membrane myristoyl-protein receptors.

The precise role or roles of the N-terminal myristic acid in acylated proteins may be unclear, but it is clear that the fatty acid is essential for the proper functioning of these proteins. The identification of new substrates for NMT is consequently of some importance.

1.3. Identification of Myristoyl-Proteins

Since the consensus sequence for myristoylation defined in **Fig. 1** is not particularly stringent, it is difficult from inspection of a given protein sequence to determine if that protein is myristoylated. The absence of an N-terminal glycine in a protein precludes it from being myristoylated, but variations in amino acid sequence at other positions are harder to predict. The purpose of this chapter is to provide investigators with the methods to identify if their protein of interest is myristoylated or not. The discussion and methods will be based on the assumption that the protein is not available in sufficient quantities or purity for direct determination of the acylation status of the protein. If the protein is available in reasonable quantities (e.g., 100 pmol), then a variety of methods exist to determine its acylation status. However, these methods nearly all depend on mass spectrometric analyses and need the availability of the appropriate instrumentation *(21–24)*.

In the past, the general strategy for identifying myristoylated proteins has been to label cells, containing the protein of interest, with radioactive myristic acid and to immunoprecipitate the protein. The immunoprecipitate is then analyzed on SDS polyacrylamide gels, followed by autoradiography, to determine if the protein incorporated the labeled myristic acid. Because of the possibility of interconversion of the fatty acids, it is necessary to show that the incorporated label is indeed myristic acid; this can be done by identifying the labeled material released following acid hydrolysis of the protein. Alternatively, the presence of myristoyl-glycine in the protein can be determined following exhaustive proteolytic digestion of the protein. Protocols for these analyses follow.

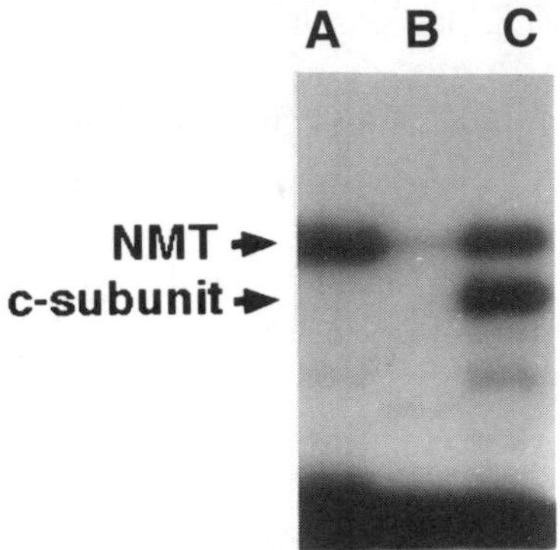

Fig. 2. Coexpression of the catalytic subunit of protein kinase A (encoded in the plasmid pLWS-3) with NMT (encoded in pET-NMT) in the *E. coli* strain BL21(DE3). The plasmids were transfected into the bacteria and expressed in the presence of ^{3}H-myristic acid, as described in **Subheading 3.9.**, and the labeled products, analyzed on a 10% polyacrylamide gel. The tracks are **(A)** pET-NMT, **(B)** pLWS -3 alone, and **(C)** pLWS-3 + pET-NMT. The autoradiograph was exposed for 24 h at –70°C. The upper radioactive band at 50 kDa is the complex formed between myristoyl-CoA and NMT. The lower 45-kDa band is the myristoylated catalytic subunit, with the free fatty acids giving the intense band at the bottom of the gel.

More recently, it has become possible to exploit the coexpression of NMT and the protein of interest in *Escherichia coli* (which does not contain NMT) to determine if a protein is myristoylated. This approach does not depend on the availability of an antiserum to the protein of interest since few proteins are labeled following labeling of *E. coli* with radioactive myristic acid, even in bacteria expressing NMT. Therefore any labeled myristoyl-protein is clearly visible, following autoradiography, on an SDS-polyacrylamide gel of the *E. coli* lysate **(Fig. 2)**. However this approach does depend on the availability of a suitably cloned form of the target protein. The absence of NMT from *E. coli* makes this coexpression system more attractive than the alternatives of expressing the protein in yeast or baculovirus which contain their own NMT and consequently contain endogenous myristoylated proteins. However it should not be forgotten that the *E. coli* coexpression system makes use of an artificial system in which there is a very high level of expression of both the enzyme and the substrate protein. Consequently there may be a risk that a protein, normally a poor substrate for NMT, may appear to be myristoylated under these conditions.

2. Materials

1. [9, 10 ^{3}H]-myristic, palmitic, and stearic acids with a specific activity of at least 30 Ci/mmol. These can be obtained from Amersham (England), and New England Nuclear (Boston, MA).

2. Dialyzed fetal calf serum: This is produced by dialyzing fetal calf serum against phosphate-buffered saline (PBS), three changes of 100 vol, at 4°C over 24 h. The dialyzed serum is then filter-sterilized and stored at –20°C in 10-mL samples.
3. 100 m*M* sterile sodium pyruvate (Gibco-BRL [Paisley, Scotland]). This is used to supplement the cell-growth medium during myristate labeling, in order to minimize catabolism of the fatty acid.
4. Radioimmunoprecipitation analysis (RIPA) buffer: 50 m*M* Tris-HCl, pH 7.4 containing 150 m*M* NaCl, 0.5% Nonidet NP40 (v/v), 0.5% sodium deoxycholate (w/v), 0.1% SDS (w/v), 1 m*M* EGTA and 1 m*M* $MgCl_2$.
5. Pronase (Sigma) at 2 mg/mL in 50 m*M* Tris-HCl, pH 7.2.
6. 6*N* HCl.
7. 2,5-Diphenyloxazole (PPO) (22% w/v) in dimethylsulfoxide (DMSO) (*see* **Note 1**).
8. 1*M* Sodium salicylate in water, with the pH adjusted to 6.8 with HCl (*see* **Note 1**).
9. C-18 reverse-phase thin-layer chromatography (TLC) plates (e.g., KC-18, Whatman; RP 18, Merck [Dorset, UK]).
10. C-18 reverse-phase HPLC column (e.g., 5 μm Apex Octadecyl 25 cm × 4.6 mm, Jones Chromatography).
11. A fixed suspension of *Straphylococcus aureus* insoluble protein A (Sigma) at 1:1 in (RIPA) buffer. This is produced by washing the commercially obtained fixed bacteria three times with 5 vol of RIPA buffer by repeated centrifugation and resuspension. The final pellet is resuspended in an equal volume of RIPA buffer (*see* **Note 2**).
12. Gel sample buffer: 62.5 m*M* Tris-HCl, pH 6.8 containing 2% (w/v) SDS, 2% (v/v) 2-mercaptoethanol, 10% (v/v) glycerol and 0.001% bromophenol blue (*see* **Note 3**).
13. Fatty acid standards for TLC and HPLC can be obtained from Sigma. Myristoylglycine can be easily prepared by reaction of glycine with the *N*-hydroxysuccinimide ester of myristic acid or myristoylchloride ***(25)***.
14. *O*-phenanthroline (OP; Sigma) 2 mg/mL in DMSO (*see* **Note 4**).
15. Dichloroisocoumarin (DCI; Sigma) 2.2 mg/mL in DMSO (*see* **Note 4**).
16. E-64 (1.8 mg/mL; Boehringer-Mannheim) in distilled water (*see* **Note 4**).
17. Luria broth: 10 g/L bacto-tryptone, 5 g/L bacto-yeast extract, 10 g/L NaCl.
18. Isopropylthiogalactoside (IPTG) 100 m*M* in distilled water and filter-sterilized. Aliquots of this can be stored frozen at –20°C.
19. Plasmids containing NMT in a prokaryotic expression vector. Two of these containing yeast NMT are available from Prof. Jeffrey Gordon (Department of Molecular Biology and Pharmacology, Washington University School of Medicine, Washington University Medical centre, 660 south Euclid Avenue, St. Louis, Missouri 63110). One pBB125 has the enzyme under the control of an IPTG-inducible *tac* promoter and is kanamycin-resistant, the other pBB131 is under the control of a nalidixic acid inducible recA promoter and is ampicillin-resistant ***(26)***. Gordon has also produced human NMT in similar vectors ***(27)***. A plasmid-containing human NMT as a fusion protein, tagged with an N-terminal polyhistidine tag (pTrc-NMT), has been produced in both an ampicillin- ***(28)*** and

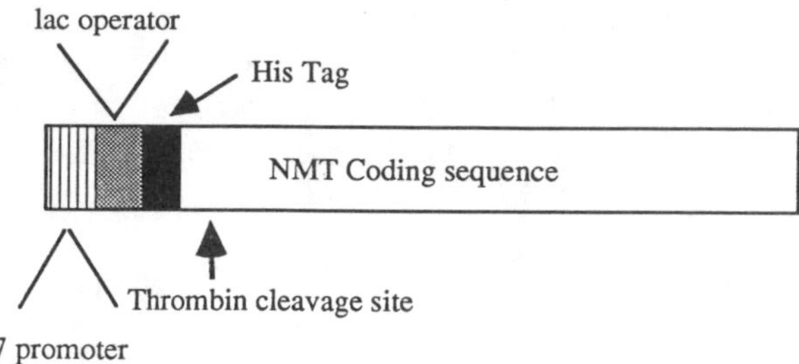


```
1            5                10               15
MetGlySerSerHisHisHisHisHisHisSerSerGlyLeuValProArgGlySer
20               25               30               35
HisMetAlaSerMetThrGlyGlyGlnGlnMetGlyArgGlySerIleGlnGluIle
                                MetAsnSerLeuProAlaGluArgIleGlnGluIle
```

Fig. 3. Construction of pET-NMT plasmid fusion protein. This was derived from the pTRC-NMT plasmid ***(28)*** by cutting the human NMT cDNA with *Bam*HI and *Hin*dIII and inserting the purified fragment into the cloning site of pET-28c (Novagen, Madison, WI). The resulting protein is missing the first eight amino acids of the human NMT sequence, which are replaced by the fusion sequence illustrated above. The N-terminal polyhistidine tag facilitates the purification of the enzyme on metal chelate columns and does not interfere with the activity of the enzyme (*see* **ref.** ***28***). The pET plasmid confers kanamycin resistance. The underlined sequence is the correct N-terminal sequence for the cloned human NMT ***(9)***; the residues highlighted in bold type indicate where the pET-NMT and human sequences start to correspond.

kanamycin-resistant form (pET-NMT; **Fig. 3**). The former is IPTG inducible and is under the control of the Trc promoter. The latter is cloned into a pET vector under the control of the T7 polymerase promoter. In the bacterial strain BL21(DE3) following IPTG induction this plasmid produces very high levels of enzyme.

20. Plasmid containing the protein of interest in an inducible prokaryotic expression vector with a different antibiotic resistance from that of the vector containing NMT.

3. Methods

3.1. Labeling Cells with ^{3}H-Myristic Acid

1. Dry the radioactive myristic acid under nitrogen in a fume cupboard and redissolve the fatty acid in ethanol, to give a final concentration of 10 mCi/mL (*see* **Note 5**).
2. Grow at least 3×10^6 cells to near confluence in an appropriate flask or culture vessel using the appropriate growth medium. For most adherent cells 1×25 cm^2 flask of cells is sufficient.
3. Remove the growth medium from the cells and replace it with prewarmed (37°C) medium supplemented with 5% dialyzed fetal calf serum and 5 m*M* sodium pyru-

vate. Add ^{3}H-myristic acid to give a final concentration of 200 µCi/mL and incubate for 4 h at 37°C.

3.2. Immunoprecipitation of Labeled Proteins

1. Remove the growth medium and wash the labeled cells with Tris saline three times (10 mL per wash). Dispose of the radioactive washes according to the local regulations.
2. Lyse the cells in RIPA buffer (1 mL), which has been precooled to 4°C. At this stage, 10 µL of each of the protease inhibitors OPd, DCI, and E64 should be added (*see* **Notes 4** and **6**).
3. Transfer the lysate to an Eppendorf microfuge tube and centrifuge (14,000*g*) for 15 min at 4°C.
4. Transfer the supernatant to a clean Eppendorf tube. Avoid transferring the DNA, which will form part of the pellet.
5. Split the lysate into two equal aliquots.
6. Add an appropriate amount of the specific antiserum to one aliquot. This should be determined empirically in a separate series of experiments, but, as a rule 2–5 µL works well. Add an equal amount of the control serum (usually a preimmune serum from the same rabbit that produced the antiserum) (*see* **Note 7**).
7. Mix the lysate with the serum by rotation at 4°C. The time of this incubation can vary with each serum, but overnight is practical and fits in with the running of the gels (*see* **Note 8**).
8. The next day, add 50 µL of the *S. aureus* insoluble protein A suspension to each lysate, and continue the rotation for 1 h at 4°C (*see* **Note 2**).
9. Centrifuge the fixed bacteria and wash them three times with 1 mL RIPA buffer by resuspension and centrifugation. Following each resuspension, the bacteria should be mixed by rotation at 4°C for 10 min.
10. Finally, wash the bacteria with 50 m*M* Tris, pH 7.5, and pellet them once more.
11. The precipitated proteins can now be eluted by heating the pellet with 50 µL of SDS-polyacrylamide gel sample buffer at 100°C for 2 min. The eluates can be analyzed on SDS-polyacrylamide gels immediately, or frozen at –20°C.

3.3. SDS-Polyacrylamide Gel Analysis of Labeled Proteins

1. The samples are prepared as described above, or as needed for the gel system being used, and the gel loaded (*see* **Note 3**).
2. When the electrophoresis of the gel is finished, remove any mol wt marker tracks for staining and impregnate the remainder of the gel with fluor, in order to determine the position of the labeled proteins. Either:
   a. Place the gel into 100 mL of 1*M* sodium salicylate pH 6.8 and shake gently for 1 h at room temperature. Then dry the gel at 80°C under a vacuum (*see* **Note 1** and proceed to **step 7**); or
   b. Place the gel into 100 mL of dimethyl sulfoxide (DMSO) and shake for 30 min at room temperature.
3. Repeat the DMSO treatment.

4. Place the gel, which should have shrunk in size significantly, into 100 mL of the 22% PPO solution and shake for 1 h.
5. Place the gel into 200 mL of distilled water and shake for a further hour. This precipitates the PPO and turns the gel white.
6. Following this dry the gel as above.
7. Place the dried gels against Kodak XOMAT AR5 film in a cassette and place at –70°C. The period of time needed for a good exposure will depend on the level of expression of the protein and could range from 24 h to several weeks.

3.4. Release of the Attached Fatty Acid

1. Following exposure of the gels and development of the film, use the autoradiograph to locate the band of interest. Excise this and rehydrate it with distilled water.
2. Remove the blotting paper backing and wash the gel slice(s) several times for 10 min at room temperature with distilled water (or with DMSO, if water-insoluble fluors were used in **step 2** of **Subheading 3.3.**, followed by distilled water), until all the fluor is removed and the gel is clear.
3. Cut the slice(s) into roughly 2–3 mm^2 pieces and dry under a vacuum.
4. Add 0.7 mL of 6*M* HCl to the gel slice(s) and incubate in a sealed **glass** tube at 100°C for 4 h (*see* **Note 5**).
5. Allow the hydrolysate to cool and add 0.3 mL 10*M* NaOH.
6. Add 3.7 mL of chloroform:methanol 1:1 (v/v) and vortex mix several times over 5 min. Centrifuge the tube for 10 min at 800–1000*g* to separate the phases.
7. Remove the lower layer using a Pasteur pipet. The gel slices should remain at the interface.
8. Extract the upper phase with a further 2 mL of chloroform, as before.
9. Pool the two chloroform phases and dry under nitrogen.
10. Redissolve the extract in a small volume (200–300 μL) of chloroform and add 20–40 μg of unlabeled myristic acid as a standard. This material can be stored at –20°C under nitrogen before analysis.

3.5. Release of Myristoyl-Glycine

1. Proceed as in **Subheading 3.4., steps 1** and **2.**
2. Rehydrate the gel pieces in 0.7 mL of 50 m*M* Tris-HCl, pH 7.2.
3. Add 100 μL of the 2 mg/mL pronase solution and add a drop of toluene as a bacteriostat. Incubate in a sealed glass tube at 37°C for 24 h.
4. Repeat **step 3** twice.
5. Acidify the digest with 6*M* HCl (50 μL) and extract as described in **steps 6–9** in **Subheading 3.4.**
6. Dry the combined extracts and redissolve in 200 μL chloroform. This also can be stored at –20°C under nitrogen before analysis.

3.6. Identification of the Released Fatty Acid by TLC

1. Spot the extracted fatty acid onto a C-18 TLC plate.
2. In adjacent positions, spot the radioactive fatty acid standards (50,000 dpm).

3. Develop the plate with acetonitrile:acetic acid (90:10 v/v).
4. Dry the platc. This can be done in 2 min at 90°C in an oven, if one is available, or the plate can be left in a fume cupboard for 30 min.
5. Then either spray the plate with EN^{3}HANCE (Dupont NEN), or scrape 0.5- to 1-cm lengths of the different tracks and determine their radioactivity in a scintillation counter. If the plate is sprayed it must be dried and then exposed to X-ray film, as described in **Subheading 3.3.**

3.7. HPLC Analysis of Released Fatty Acids

1. Pre-equilibrate the C-18 reverse-phase column with 90% acetonitrile containing 10% distilled water and 0.1% trifluoroacetic acid.
2. Calibrate the column by running samples of radioactive fatty acid standards at 1 mL/min with the same solvent. Collect 60 0.5-min fractions and determine their radioactivity by scintillation counting.
3. Wash the column for a further 30 min.
4. Load the released fatty acids and elute the column in exactly the same way (*see* **Note 9**).

3.8. Identification of Myristoyl-Glycine

1. Pre-equilibrate the C-18 reverse phase column with distilled water containing 0.1% trifluoroacetic acid.
2. Calibrate the column by loading myristoyl-glycine and ^{3}H-myristic acid. Myristoyl-glycine may be synthesized as a radioactive standard, or not. In the latter case, its elution position can be monitored at 214 nm.
3. Elute the column with a 30-mL gradient from 0 to 90% acetonitrile in the presence of 0.1% trifluoroacctic acid at a flow rate of 1 mL/min. Collect 1-mL fractions and determine their radioactivity by scintillation counting. This system will readily separate myristoyl-glycine from myristic acid (**Fig. 4**; *see* **Note 10**).
4. Run a gradient from 90 to 0% acetonitrile containing 0.1% trifluroacetic acid to re-equilibrate the column.
5. Load the digest sample; repeat elution **step 3** again.

3.9. Coexpression of NMT and Other Proteins in E. coli

1. Transfect the two plasmids containing NMT and the protein of interest into a suitable strain of *E. coli*. For the plasmid pET-NMT, this is BL21(DE3). These two plasmids must confer different antibiotic resistances. Freshly prepared, competent *E. coli* work best (*see* **Notes 11–13**).
2. Plate the transfected cells onto agar plates containing both antibiotics. For pET-NMT, we use 30 μg/mL kanamycin and, for pTrc-NMT, ampicillin at 100 μg/mL (*see* **Note 12**).
3. Once colonies are visible, several should be picked and plasmid DNA prepared. Analyze this by restriction analysis to confirm the presence and integrity of the two plasmids. A suitable clone should then be chosen and expanded.

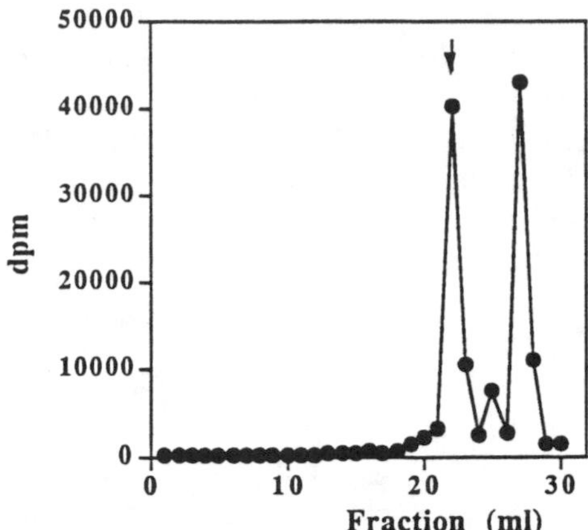

Fig. 4. HPLC analysis of myristoyl-glycine and myristic acid on a PEPRPC HR 5/5 column (Pharmacia). The radioactive samples were loaded and eluted as described in **Subheading 3.8.** The arrow indicates the position of myristoyl-glycine, the later peak being myristic acid.

4. Inoculate 5 mL of Luria broth, containing both antibiotics, with the chosen *E. coli* clone, and grow overnight at 37°C in a shaking incubator (*see* **Note 13**).
5. Inoculate 5 mL of Luria broth with 50 µL of the overnight culture. Grow this culture at 30°C until the OD 600 nm becomes 0.5–0.7.
6. Remove 1 mL of this culture and place in a clean culture tube. Add IPTG to give a final concentration of 1 m*M* and add 100–200 µCi/mL ^{3}H-myristic acid.
7. Continue the incubation at 30°C for a further 2 h.
8. Centrifuge the bacteria and dispose of the radioactive culture supernatants according to the local regulations.
9. Resuspend the bacterial pellet in SDS-polyacrylamide gel sample buffer (200 µL) and heat to 100°C for 5 min. This sample may be stored for later analysis, but should be heated again before being used.
10. Analyze the lysate (10–20 µL) by SDS-PAGE and impregnate the gel, as described in **Subheading 3.3.** (*see* **Note 14**).

4. Notes

1. The SDS-polyacrylamide gels used to analyze ^{3}H-myristate-labeled proteins require to be impregnated with a fluor in order to detect the labeled bands by autoradiography. There are a number of commercial fluors available, including EN^{3}HANCE, Enlightening and Entisfy, from Dupont-NEN, which can be used to detect labeled bands on SDS-polyacrylamide gels. In addition, sodium salicylate impregnation can be used for the same purpose ***(29)***. However, the PPO/DMSO system originally described by Bonner and Laskey ***(30)*** is the most sensitive. The times given for the incubations are for 20 × 20-cm gels, 1 mm thick. These times

can be reduced by half for the most minigel systems. The PPO/DMSO can also be used several times. The salicylate impregnation method must be used when analysis of the radioactivity contained in the protein is to be carried out. Should quantitation of the autoradiograph be wanted, then the film should be preflashed, as described by Laskey and Mills ***(31)***. This also increases the sensitivity of the film.
2. The use of insoluble Protein A assumes that the antiserum being used is derived from an animal that produces IgG, which binds to Protein-A (rabbit, mouse, rat). In the event of this not being the case it may be necessary to pre-incubate the insoluble Protein A with a rabbit antiserum raised against the IgG being used, before proceeding with the precipitation. Alternatively, the IgG from the antiserum can be coupled directly to one of the commercially available affinity supports and used directly to precipitate the antigen. In this case, **step 8** in **Subheading 3.2.** can be omitted. Protein A coupled to an affinity support, which is commercially available from a number of companies, can be substituted for the fixed *S. aureus*, and may give a lower background precipitation of nonspecific proteins. However these supports are expensive.
3. The sample buffer given is for the Laemmli discontinuous SDS-polyacrylamide gel system ***(32)***, which is a commonly used gel system. The appropriate sample buffer for the gel system in the reader's laboratory can be substituted.
4. These solutions are used at 1:100 dilutions to inhibit proteases and can be stored at –20°C. We have found that this cocktail of protease inhibitors is generally satisfactory, is cheaper, and is as effective as the often more complex peptide cocktails described in the literature. However, the use of other, or more complex, mixtures of protease inhibitors may be required if the protein of interest is susceptible to proteolytic degradation.
5. Under no circumstances should the fatty acid be dried in a polypropylene tube or container. Fatty acids have a high affinity for plastic and much of the radioactivity will remain on the walls of the tube. This should be borne in mind when processing the proteins in subsequent methods.
6. The use of RIPA buffer is generally applicable to most situations, and will solubilize most proteins. However, RIPA can lead to relatively high nonspecific immunoprecipitation of cell proteins, since all the proteins are solubilized and DNA is released during the lysis. This problem can be overcome by first lysing the cells in Tris saline containing 1% Triton X-100, then removing the nuclei by centrifugation, and adding SDS to the lysate, to give a final concentration of 0.1%. This protocol will solubilize most membrane and cytosolic proteins, but not cytoskeletal-associated proteins or nuclear membrane proteins. Should the protein of interest be resistant to solubilization with RIPA, then an alternative lysis protocol is to lyse the cells by scraping them into 200 µL of 5% 2-mercaptoethanol and 2% SDS in distilled water. The total lysate is then heated to 100°C for 5 min and centrifuged at 14,000 rpm in a microcentrifuge for 5 min. The supernatant is then either frozen or used immediately. For immunoprecipitation, the lysate is diluted 10 times with RIPA and aliquots processed as described. This method obviates the need for the addition of protease inhibitors, and may

have advantages when using antipeptide antibodies, since the proteins are denatured and may expose otherwise hidden epitopes. However, these same arguments may prevent this method for working for some sera.

7. Usually, when immunoprecipitation is being performed with whole serum, the control used is to include a precipitation performed, using an equal volume of the preimmune serum. The volumes of serum to be used for both the specific and nonspecific immunoprecipitations should be determined empirically, using cells labeled with ^{35}S-methionine, before attempting the ^{3}H-myristic acid labeling. The protocols described here can be used by substituting methionine-free medium for the incubation and using 100 μCi/mL of ^{35}S-methionine. If antipeptide sera are being used, then the best control is to include an immunoprecipitation in which the lysate is spiked with the peptide (10-20 μg) to which the serum was made.
8. The time of incubation with the primary serum can be shortened and depends on the antiserum being used. This should be empirically determined using ^{35}S-methionine-labeled cells prior to the ^{3}H-myristic acid labeling.
9. This isocratic elution system for the fatty acids is robust and causes the elution of the fatty acids in order of their chain length (i.e., myristate before palmitate, followed by stearate). However, the precise elution position for each fatty acid will depend on the accuracy of the preparation of the acetonitrile:water eluant. Therefore, it is important to run the calibration and analytic columns in the same batch of eluant, in order to ensure coincident elution of the peaks. This problem can be overcome if ^{14}C-fatty acid standards are coapplied with the sample for analysis. Then double counting can be used to determine the position of the ^{3}H-analytic sample relative to the ^{14}C-standards.
10. There is often a peak of myristic acid in the extract from the pronase hydrolysate caused by either contamination with myristic acid from the gel, or nonspecific amidases in the pronase. Consequently, the elution position of myristic acid must be determined.
11. In the bacterial coexpression system established by Duronio et al. ***(33)*** two different expression systems, induced by different compounds, are used to express the NMT and target proteins. This allows the two proteins to be expressed at different times. This is generally done by inducing the NMT first ***(26)***. Since the myristoylation of cell proteins is generally cotranslational, one might assume that it would be better for some NMT to be synthesized before inducing the expression of the substrate protein. For full details of this system and the plasmids used, the reader is referred to **ref.** ***26***. However, when the pET-NMT plasmid is coexpressed with the catalytic subunit of PKA (pLWS-3) as illustrated in **Fig. 4**, both proteins are induced simultaneously by the addition of IPTG. As shown in **Fig. 2** this does not seem to prevent the extensive myristoylation of the PK-A catalytic subunit. The methodology described in this section applies to the pET-NMT system, specifically.
12. The availability of pET-NMT and pTrc-NMT, which both produce a polyhistidine-tagged human NMT, allows for the rapid purification of this protein to a level at which it can be used to label proteins in vitro, in the presence of

myristoyl-CoA *(28)*. Although this process is variable in its efficiency and does not always produce stoichiometric myristoylation of proteins (McIlhinney, unpublished), this system provides a means of testing the myristoylation of a target protein without having to coexpress it with NMT. In addition, because myristoyl-CoA can be produced at very high specific activities, the labeled product could be used in binding assays to determine membrane targeting.

13. It should be noted that yeast and human NMT have similar but not identical patterns of protein substrates. Consequently the choice of system for use in the testing of a target protein should be given some thought.
14. To control for nonspecific incorporation of myristic acid into the target protein, cultures of bacteria expressing this alone, and NMT alone, should be included in this experiment. These should be the same *E. coli* strain as used for the coexpression experiment.
15. Relatively few bacterial proteins are labeled with myristic acid, even when NMT is expressed (**Fig. 2**). However Rudnick et al. *(26)* have reported two such proteins at 45 and 55 kDa, using yeast NMT; as can be seen in **Fig. 2** with human NMT, a band at 50 kDa appears in the NMT alone track. This represents the formation of a myristoyl-CoA/NMT complex in this system (McIlhinney, unpublished). If the protein of interest has a similar mol wt to these bands, then immunoprecipitation will be needed to confirm the myristoylation of the target protein. In the event of the target protein being myristoylated in the *E. coli* coexpression system, the presence of amide-linked myristic acid and/or myristoyl-glycine should be confirmed, as described in **Subheadings 3.4.** and **3.5.** Ideally, the N-terminal glycine of the protein should be mutated to alanine or another amino acid and the effects of this on myristoylation should be examined. Such mutations should prevent myristoylation.

Acknowledgments

The author would like to thank J. I. Gordon for supplying pBB201 containing the human cDNA coding for NMT, Zoya Katarova for her invaluable help in subcloning pTrc-NMT into pET 28c, and Kate McGlone for her technical help in establishing these methods.

References

1. Towler, D. A., Gordon, J. I., Adams, S. P., and Glaser, L. (1988) The biology and enzymology of eukaryotic protein acylation. *Ann. Rev. Biochem.* **57,** 69–99.
2. McIlhinney, R. A. J. (1990) The fats of life: the importance and function of protein acylation. *TIBS* **15,** 387–390.
3. Rudnick, D. A., McWherter, C. A., Gokel, G. W., and Gordon, J. I. (1993) Myristoyl-CoA: protein N-myristoyltransferase. *Adv. Enzymol.* **67,** 375–435.
4. Schmidt, M. F. G. and Burns, G. R. (1989) Hydrophobic modifications of membrane proteins by palmitoylation in vitro. *Biochem. Soc. Trans.* **17,** 625,626.
5. Gordon, J. I., Duronio, R. J., Rudnick, D. A., Adams, S. P., and Gokel, G. W. (1991) Protein N-myristoylation. *J. Biol. Chem.* **266,** 8647–8650.

6. McIlhinney, R. A. J., Pelly, S. J., Chadwick, J. K., and Cowley, G. P. (1985) Studies on the attachment of myristic and palmitic acid to cell proteins on human squamous carcinoma cell lines: evidence for two pathways. *EMBO J.* **4,** 1145–1152.
7. Magee, A. I. and Courtneidge, S. A. (1985) Two classes of fatty acid acylated proteins exist in eukaryotic cells. *EMBO J.* **4,** 1137–1144.
8. Dizhoor, A. M., Ericksson, L. H., Johnson, R. S., Kumar, S., Olshevsakya, E., Zozulya, S., Neubert, T. A., Stryer, L., Hurley, J. B., and Walsh, K. A. (1992) The NH2 terminus of retinal recoverin is acylated by a small family of fatty acids. *J. Biol. Chem.* **267,** 16,033–16,036.
9. Duronio, R. J., Reed, S. I., and Gordon, J. I. (1992) Mutations of human myristoyl-CoA-protein N-myristoyltransferase cause temperature-sensitive myristic acid auxotrophy in *saccharomyces-cerevisiae. Natl. Acad. Sci. USA* **89,** 4129–4133.
10. Rudnick, D. A., McWherter, C. A., Roegue, W. J., Lennon, P. J., Getman, D. P., and Gordon, J. I. (1991) Kinetic and structural evidence for a sequential ordered bi-bi mechanism of catalysis by *saccharomyces cerevisiae* myristoyl-CoA: protein N-myristoyltransferase. *J. Biol. Chem.* **266,** 9732–9739.
11. Peitzch, R. M. and McLaughlin, S. (1993) Binding of acylated peptides and fatty acids to phospholipid vesicles: pertinence to myristoylated proteins. *Biochemistry* **32,** 10,436–10,443.
12. Buser, C. A., Sigal, C. T., Resh, M. D., and Mclaughlin, S. (1994) Membrane binding of myristylated peptides corresponding to the NH2 terminus of Src. *Biochemistry* **33,** 13,093–13,101.
13. Milligan, G., Parenti, M., and Magee, A. I. (1995) The dynamic role of palmitoylation in signal transduction. *Trends Biochem. Sci.* **20,** 181–186.
14. Resh, M. D. (1994) Myristylation and Palmitylation of SRC family members–the fats of the matter. *Cell* **76,** 411–413.
15. Randazzo, P. A., Terui, T., Sturch, S., Fales, H. M., Ferrige, A. G., and Kahn, R. A. (1995) The myristoylated amino terminus of ADP-ribosylation factor 1 is a phospholipid- and GTP-sensitive switch. *J. Biol. Chem.* **270,** 14,809–14,815.
16. Franco, M., Chardin, P., Chabre, M., and Paris, S. (1995) Myristoylation of ADP-ribosylation factor 1 facilitates nucleotide exchange at physiological Mg^{2+} levels. *J. Biol. Chem.* **270,** 1337–1341.
17. Chow, M., Newman, J. F. E., Filman, D., Hogler, J. M., Rowlands, D. J., and Brown, F. (1987) Myristoylation of picornavirus capsid protein VP4 and its structural significance. *Nature* **327,** 482–486.
18. Harris, M. and Coates, K. (1993) Identification of cellular proteins that bind to the human immunodeficiency virus type–1 nef gene product in vitro—a role for myristylation. *J. Gen. Virol.* **74,** 1581–1589.
19. Resh, M. D. (1989) Specific and saturable binding of Pp60V-Src to plasma membranes—evidence for a myristyl-Src receptor. *Cell* **58,** 281–286.
20. Sigal, C. T. and Resh, M. D. (1993) The ADP/ATP carrier is the 32-kilodalton receptor for an NH2-terminally myristylated Src peptide but not for pp60(src) polypeptide. *Mol. Cell. Biol.* **13,** 3084–3092.

21. Goddard, C. and Felsted, R. L. (1988) Identification of N-myristoylated proteins by reverse phase high pressure liquid chromatography of an azlactone derivative of N-myristoylglycine. *Biochem. J.* **253,** 839–843.
22. Aitken, A. (1991) Structure determination of acylated proteins, in *Lipid Modification of Proteins* (Hooper, N. M. and Turner, A. J., eds.), IRL, Oxford, pp. 63–88.
23. Neubert, T. A. and Johnson, R. S. (1995) High resolution structural determination of protein-linked acy groups, in *Methods in Enzymology, vol. 250: Lipid Modifications of Proteins* (Casey, P. J. and Buss, J. E., eds.), Academic, New York, pp. 487–495.
24. McIlhinney, R. A. J. and Harvey, D. J. (1995) Determination of N-terminal myristoylation of proteins using a combined gas chromatographic/mass spectrometric assay of derived myristoylglycine: electron impact-induced fragmentation of acylglycine derivatives. *J. Mass Spectrom.* **30,** 900–910.
25. McIlhinney, R. A. J. (1992) Labelling of cells with radioactive fatty acids and methods for studying palmitoyl-acyl transferase, in *Lipid Modifications of Proteins: A Practical Approach* (Hooper, N. M. and Turner, A. J., eds.), IRL, Oxford, pp. 15–35.
26. Rudnick, D. A., Duronio, R. J., and Gordon, J. I. (1992) Methods for studying myristoyl-C0A: protein N-myristoyltransferase, in *Lipid Modifications of Proteins: A Practical Approach* (Hooper, N. M. and Turner, A. J., eds.), IRL, Oxford, pp. 37–59.
27. Knoll, L. J., Johnson, D. R., Bryant, M. L., and Gordon, J. I. (1995) Functional significance of myristoyl moeity, in *Methods in Enzymology, vol. 250: Lipid Modifications of Proteins* (Casey, P. J. and Buss, J. E., eds.), Academic, New York, pp. 405–435.
28. McIlhinney, R. A. J., Patel, P. B., and McGlone, K. (1994) Characterization of a polyhistidine-tagged form of human myristoyl-CoA:protein N-myristoyltransferase produced in Eschcrichia coli. *Eur. J. Biochem.* **222,** 137–146.
29. Chamberlain, J. P. (1979) Fluorographic detection of radioactivity in polyacrylamide gels with the water soluble fluor, sodium salicylate. *Anal. Biochem.* **98**, 132.
30. Bonner, W. M., and Laskey, R. A. (1974) A film detection method for tritium-labelled proteins and nucleic acids in polyacrylamide gels. *Eur. J. Biochem.* **46,** 83–88.
31. Laskey, R. A. and Mills, A. D. (1975) Quantitative film detection of 3H and 14C in polyacrylamide gels by fluorography. *Eur. J. Biochem.* **56,** 335–341.
32. Laemmli, U. K. (1970) Cleavage of structural proteins during the assembly of the bacteriophage T4. *Nature* (London) **227,** 680–685.
33. Durino, R. J., Jackson-Machelski, E., Heuckeroth, R. O., Olins, P. O., Devine, C. S., Yonemoto, W., Slice, L. W., Taylor, S. S., and Gordon, J. I. (1990) Protein N-myristoylation in Escherichia Coli: reconstitution of a eukaryotic potein modification in bacteria. *Proc. Natl. Acad. Sci. USA* **87,** 1506–1510.

17

Membrane Targeting via Protein Palmitoylation

Michael Veit and Michael F. G. Schmidt

1. Introduction

Palmitoylation (*S*-acylation) is the posttranslational attachment of fatty acids to cysteine residues and is common among integral and peripheral-membrane proteins. Palmitoylated proteins have been found in every eukaryotic cell type examined (yeast, insect, and vertebrate cells), as well as in viruses grown in these cells. Integral membrane proteins are palmitoylated at cysteine residues located at the boundary between the transmembrane segment and the cytoplasmic tail. Peripheral membrane proteins are often acylated at a N-terminal MGCXXS motif, which provides a dual signal for amide-myristoylation, as well as *S*-palmitoylation. However, comparison of the amino acids in the vicinity of all known palmitoylated cysteine residues reveals no obvious consensus signal for palmitoylation. Thus, palmitoylation of a protein cannot be predicted from its amino acid sequence. An enzyme responsible for the transfer of fatty acids (PAT) has not yet been purified, but several in vitro systems suggest that it is membrane-bound ***(1–5)***.

The slow progress in this field is partially because of technical difficulties in the detection of palmitoylated proteins by metabolic labeling with ^{3}H-palmitic acid. Palmitic acid is a major fatty acid of cellular lipids. Thus, the vast majority (>99.5%) of the radioactivity is incorporated into lipids and only a tiny amount remains for the labeling of proteins. **Subheading 3.1.1., step 3** describes our standard protocol for metabolic labeling of palmitoylated proteins, and also for the procedures to prove a covalent and ester-type linkage of the fatty acids. A protein must be fairly abundant in the cell type analyzed to detect palmitoylation. It is advisable to overexpress the protein using viral-expression vectors, if a cDNA of the protein is available. A description of viral-expression systems is beyond the scope of this chapter (**ref.** ***6***; *see also* Chapters 8 and 12).

From: *Methods in Molecular Biology, Vol. 88: Protein Targeting Protocols*
Edited by: R. A. Clegg Humana Press Inc., Totowa, NJ

Palmitate is usually found as the predominant fatty acid in *S*-acylated proteins, but other fatty acid species (myristic, stearic, oleic, and arachidonic acid) are often minor and sometimes even main components. In accordance, many *S*-acylated proteins can be labeled with more than one fatty acid, and the palmitoyl-transferase shows no strict preference for palmitate in vitro ***(7–9)***. The functional significance of protein acylation with more than one fatty acid is not known. **Subheading 3.1.4.** describes a simple method to analyze the fatty acid content of *S*-acylated proteins.

Palmitoylation is unique among hydrophobic modifications because the fatty acids may be subject to cycles of de- and reacylation. The turnover of the fatty acids is often enhanced upon treatment of cells with physiologically active substances. It is supposed that reversible palmitoylation plays a role for the function of these proteins by controlling their membrane-binding and/or their protein–protein interactions ***(10,11)***. A palmitoyl-thioesterase has recently been purified and the encoding cDNA has been cloned ***(12)***. However, for reasons that are not known, turnover of fatty acids does not occur on every palmitoylated protein. **Subheading 3.2.** describes two methods for analyzing possible dynamic palmitoylation for a given protein.

The function of palmitoylation in integral membrane proteins is still enigmatic. It is established that palmitoylation is neither required for their stable attachment to membranes nor for their intracellular targeting ***(13)***. By contrast, several peripheral membrane proteins require palmitoylation for membrane-anchoring, although other hydrophobic modifications (prenylation, myristoylation), often occurring simultaneously on the same protein, may also contribute to membrane targeting ***(14)***. **Subheading 3.3.** describes protocols to compare membrane binding of palmitoylated and fatty acid-free proteins. Because of space limitations, the basic methods to analyze palmitoylation (SDS-PAGE, fluorography) cannot be described in detail; the reader is referred to a recent volume of this series ***(15)***. Additional information about methods to analyze lipid modifications can be found in Chapter 12, 16, 18, and 19 of this volume, as well as elsewhere ***(15,16)***.

2. Materials

1. Tritiated fatty acids, [9, 10-^{3}H (N)]-palmitic acid and [9, 10-^{3}H (N)]-myristic acid, both at a specific activity of 30–60 Ci/mmol, are available from Amersham (Arlington Heights, IL), NEN-DuPont (Boston, MA), or ARC (St. Louis, MO). [9, 10-^{3}H]-stearic acid, 10–30 Ci/mmol, is delivered by ARC only.
2. Protein A Sepharose CL-4B is available from Sigma (St. Louis, MO). Wash the beads three times with PBS. The packed beads are then resuspended in an equal volume of PBS and stored at 4°C.
3. HPTLC RP 18 thin-layer plates and hydroxylamine are available from Merck (Darmstadt, Germany). Glass ampules for hydrolysis (e.g., Wheaton micro product V Vial, 3.0 mL with solid screw cap) are available from Aldrich (Milwaukee,

WI). Scintillators for fluorography are available from Amersham (Amplify) or DuPont (Enlightening, En3Hance). En3Hance is also available as spray for fluorography of thin-layer plates.

4. Phosphate-buffered saline (PBS): 0.14*M* NaCl, 27 m*M* KCl, 1.5 m*M* KH_2PO_4, 8.1 m*M* Na_2HPO_4.
5. Buffer A: 20 m*M* HEPES/NaOH, pH 7.4, 50 m*M* NaCl, 1 m*M* EDTA, 1 m*M* PMSF, 1 μg/mL leupeptin, 1 μg/mL pepstatin. The protease inhibitors are stored as stock solutions at –20°C (pepstatin: 10 mg/mL in ethanol, leupeptin: 1 mg/mL in distilled water). Phenylmethyl sulfonyl fluoride (PMSF) is made as a 100-m*M* stock solution in 2-propanol and stored at room temperature.
6. RIPA-buffer: 0.1% SDS, 1% Triton-X-100, 1% deoxycholate. 0.15*M* NaCl, 20 m*M* Tris, 10 m*M* EDTA, 10 m*M* Iodacetamide, 1 m*M* PMSF.
7. Triton-lysis buffer: SDS and deoxycholate are omitted from the RIPA-buffer.
8. SDS-PAGE sample buffer (nonreducing, 4X concentrated): 0.1*M* Tris-HCl, pH 6.8, 4% SDS, 20% glycerol, 0.005% (w/v) bromphenol blue. 10% mercaptoethanol is present in 4X concentrated, reducing sample buffer.
9. Gel-fixing solution: 20% methanol, 10% glacial acetic acid.

3. Methods

3.1. Detection of Palmitoylated Proteins

3.1.1. Metabolic Labeling of Cells with ^3H-Palmitate

The quantities given in this paragraph are for labeling of one cell monolayer grown in a plastic dish with a diameter of 3.5 cm (approx 1×10^5–1×10^6 cells).

1. Transfer 500 μCi ^3H-palmitic acid to a polystyrene tube and evaporate the solvent (ethanol or toluene) in a speed vac or with a gentle stream of nitrogen (*see* **Note 1**).
2. Redissolve ^3H-palmitic acid in 2.5 μL ethanol by vortexing and pipeting the droplet several times along the wall of the tube. Collect the ethanol at the bottom of the tube with a brief spin.
3. Add ^3H-palmitic acid to 500 μL tissue culture medium (*see* **Note 2**), vortex, and add the labeling medium to the cell monolayer.
4. Label cells for 1–16 h (*see* **Note 3**) at 37°C in an incubator. During longer labeling times, a slowly rocking platform is helpful to distribute the medium equally over the cell monolayer.
5. Put dishes on ice, remove labeling medium, wash cell-monolayer once with ice-cold PBS (1 mL), and lyse cells in 800 μL RIPA buffer for 15 min on ice.
6. Transfer cell lysate to an Eppendorf tube and pellet insoluble material for 30 min at 14,000 rpm in an Eppendorf centrifuge (*see* **Note 4**).
7. Transfer supernatant to a fresh Eppendorf tube. Add antibody and protein-A-Sepharose (30 μL) and rotate overnight at 4°C (*see* **Note 5**).
8. Pellet antigen-antibody-Sepharose complex (5000 rpm, 5 min), remove supernatant, add RIPA-buffer (800 μL) and vortex.
9. Repeat washing **step 8**, at least twice.

10. Solubilize antigen-antibody-Sepharose complex in 20 μL of nonreducing 1X SDS-PAGE sample buffer (*see* **Note 6**). Heat samples 5 min at 95°C. Pellet Sepharose beads (5000 rpm, 5 min).
11. Load the supernatant on a discontinuous polyacrylamide-gel ***(15)***. SDS-PAGE should be stopped before the bromphenol blue has reached the bottom of the gel.
12. Agitate the gel for 30 min in fixing solution. Treat gel with scintillator, as described by the manufacturer. All the commercially available scintillators, as well as PPO/DMSO ***(15)***, are suitable for detection of palmitoylated proteins. We usually use the salicylate method. Agitate the fixed gel for 30 min in distilled water, and then 30 min in 1*M* sodium salicylate, adjusted to pH 7.0.
13. Dry the gel on Whatman 3MM filter paper and expose in a tightly fitting cassette to X-ray film at –70°C. (*see* **Note 7**). Kodak X-OMAT AR film (Rochester, NY) is supposed to be most sensitive.

3.1.2. Chloroform/Methanol Extraction of ^{3}H-Palmitic Acid Labeled Proteins

Denaturing SDS-PAGE is usually sufficient to separate proteins from lipids, which run just below the dye front and appear as a huge spot at the bottom of the fluorogram. Some proteins have a strong affinity for phospholipids or other fatty acid-containing lipids. If the binding of only a small amount of lipids were to resist SDS-PAGE, this would simulate palmitoylation. To exclude possible noncovalent lipid binding, immunoprecipitated samples should be extracted with chloroform/methanol ***(18)*** prior to SDS-PAGE and the amount of chloroform/methanol resistant labeling should be compared with a nonextracted control.

1. Label cells with ^{3}H-palmitate and immunoprecipitate protein, as described.
2. Solubilize antigen–antibody–Sepharose complex in 30 μL phosphate-buffer (10 m*M*, pH 7.4; supplemented with 0.1% SDS), pellet Sepharose beads and dispense 2 × 15 μL of the supernatant into two Eppendorf tubes.
3. Add 300 μL chloroform/methanol (2:1) to one tube. Vortex vigorously and extract lipids for 30 min on ice. The unextracted sample also remains on ice.
4. Pellet precipitated proteins for 30 min at 25,000*g* in an Eppendorf centrifuge precooled at 4°C. Carefully remove the supernatant, air-dry the (barely visible) pellet and resuspend it in 1X SDS-PAGE sample buffer. Add 5 μL 4X concentrated sample buffer to the unextracted sample.
5. Proceed with SDS-PAGE and fluorography, as described. If the fatty acids are noncovalently bound, the ^{3}H-palmitic acid labeling of the extracted sample should be drastically reduced, compared to the control sample.

3.1.3. Hydroxylamine and Mercaptoethanol Treatment

Two types of fatty acid linkages have been described in acylated proteins: an amide bond in myristoylated proteins and an ester-type linkage in palmitoylated proteins. Although amide-linked fatty acids are resistant to treatment with hydroxylamine, the esters are readily cleaved. Treatment with hydroxylamine, adjusted either to neutral or basic pH, can also be used to discriminate between thioesters to cysteine and oxygenesters to serine or threonine. Under alkaline conditions (pH 9.0–11.0) hydroxylamine cleaves both thio- and oxygenesters, whereas at neutral pH (pH 6.5–7.5), thioesters are selectively cleaved ***(19)***. A thioester-type linkage can be further verified by its susceptibility to reducing agents, especially at high concentrations and temperatures. However, not all thioesters are equally sensitive to reducing agents (*see* **Note 6**).

Hydroxylamine treatment is usually done on gels containing ^{3}H-palmitate-labeled samples.

1. Run an SDS-PAGE with four samples of the ^{3}H-palmitate-labeled and immunoprecipitated protein. Each sample should be separated by two empty slots from its neighbors.
2. Fix the gel; wash out the fixing solution with distilled water (2 × 30 min).
3. Cut gel into four parts.
4. Treat two parts of the gel overnight under gentle agitation with 1*M* hydroxylamine (pH 7.0 and pH 10.0, respectively). The remaining two gel parts are treated with 1*M* Tris, adjusted to the same pH values (*see* **Note 8**).
5. Wash out the salt solutions with distilled water (2 × 30 min). Remove cleaved fatty acids by washing with dimethylsulfoxide (DMSO, 2 × 30 min), and wash out DMSO with distilled water. Proceed with fluorography treatment. Reassemble the gel parts before drying and expose to X-ray film.

Treatment with reducing agents is done prior to SDS-PAGE.

1. Immunoprecipitate ^{3}H-palmitate-labeled protein.
2. Solubilize protein in 100 µL nonreducing sample buffer (2 min, 95°C).
3. Pellet Sepharose beads. Make five aliquots of the supernatant and add mercaptoethanol to a final concentration of 5, 10, 15, and 20% (v/v). Mercaptoethanol is omitted from one sample. Dithiothreitol (DTT) can also be used at concentrations of 50, 100, 150, and 200 m*M*.
4. Heat samples for 10 min at 95°C. Centrifuge for 15 min at 25,000*g*. Some proteins may precipitate after treatment with reducing agents and are pelleted. Analyze (e.g., by Western-blotting or ^{35}S-methionine labeling) that an decrease in the ^{3}H-palmitate labeling is not due to aggregation. In this case, treatment with reducing agents should be done at lower temperatures (1 h, 50°C).
5. Proceed with SDS-PAGE and fluorography, as described.

3.1.4. Analysis of Protein-Bound Fatty Acids

^{3}H-palmitic acid is often converted into other ^{3}H-fatty acid species and even into ^{3}H-amino acids before incorporation into proteins. Thus, labeling of a protein with ^{3}H-palmitic acid does not necessarily prove that palmitate is its only, or even its major, fatty acid constituent, and therefore its actual fatty acid content has to be analyzed. Furthermore, identification of the ^{3}H-palmitate-derived labeling as a fatty acid is additional proof for its acylation. We describe a simple protocol feasible in laboratories without expensive equipment for lipid analysis. The method uses acid hydrolysis of ^{3}H-palmitate labeled proteins, present in gel slices and extraction of the released fatty acid with hexane. The fatty acids are then separated by thin-layer chromatography (TLC; *see* **Subheading 3.1.4.1.**) or high-pressure liquid chromatography (HPLC; *see* **Subheading 3.1.4.2.**).

1. Label your protein with ^{3}H-palmitate or another ^{3}H-fatty acid as long as possible to allow its metabolism. Proceed with immunoprecipitation and SDS-PAGE as described.
2. Localize the protein by fluorography and cut out the band. Remove the scintillator by washing with distilled water (hydrophilic scintillators, e.g., salicylate, Enlightening) or DMSO (hydrophobic scintillators, e.g., En3Hance, PPO). 2 × 20 min are usually sufficient. Wash out the DMSO with distilled water.
3. Cut the gel into small pieces, transfer them into glass ampules, and dry them in a desiccator.
4. Add 500 µL HCl (6*N*) and let the gel swell. The gel pieces should be completely covered with HCl after swelling.
5. Tightly seal glass ampoules and incubate at 110°C for at least 16 h. Polyacrylamide and HCl form a viscous fluid at high temperatures.
6. Cool vessels to room temperature until polyacrylamide becomes solid. Add an equal amount of hexane and vortex vigorously. Separate the two phases by gentle centrifugation (5 min, 500*g*). Most of the polyacrylamide is sedimented to the bottom of the vessel.
7. Remove the upper organic phase containing the fatty acids with a Pasteur pipet and transfer it to conical glass vessels. Leave behind the traces of polyacrylamide that are present between the two phases. Repeat extraction of fatty acids with hexane, twice.
8. Dry pooled organic phases in a stream of nitrogen.

3.1.4.1. Thin-Layer Chromatography

1. Redissolve dried fatty acids in 20 µL hexane.
2. Draw a line with a soft pencil on the concentration zone of the TLC-plate (HPTLC RP 18), approx 1 cm from the bottom. Apply your sample carefully in a spot as small as possible. Apply reference ^{3}H-fatty acids (^{3}H-myristate, ^{3}H-palmitate, and ^{3}H-stearate) on a parallel spot (*see* **Note 9**).
3. Put TLC-plate in an appropriate glass chamber containing the solvent system (acetonitrile/glacial acetic acid, 1:1). Take care that the samples do not dip into the solvent.
4. Develop chromatogram until the solvent front has reached the top of the plate (approx 50 min).

5. Air-dry plate under a hood. Measure radioactivity on the plate with a radiochromatogram-scanner. Alternatively, spray plate with En^{3}hance, air-dry completely, and expose to X-ray film. Detection of ^{3}H-fatty acids by fluorography of the TLC-plate requires long exposure times and is only feasible with a band easily visible in the SDS-gel after 3–5 days of film exposure.

3.1.4.2. High-Pressure Liquid Chromatography

1. Redissolve dried fatty acids in 50 µL ethanol, supplemented with unlabeled reference fatty acids (myristic, palmitic, and stearic acid, 20 m*M* each) as internal standard.
2. Perform HPLC, using a Nova-Pak C 18 column (Waters, Eschborn, Germany) and 90% acetonitrile as eluant, at a flow rate of 1 mL/min.
3. Collect fractions every 30 s and analyze the ^{3}H-fatty acid content by liquid scintillation counting.
4. Identify fatty acid species by the retention times of the unlabeled standard fatty acid with an absorbance detector set at 214 nm. Usual retention times for the standard fatty acids are: myristic acid, 4 min; palmitic acid, 7 min; stearic acid, 13 min. There is also a peak at 1.5 min after injection which is caused by ethanol. HPLC analysis, in combination with liquid scintillation counting, is more sensitive than fluorography of TLC plates.

3.2. Determination of a Possible Turnover of the Protein Bound Fatty Acids

3.2.1. Pulse–Chase Experiments with ^{3}H-Palmitate

To show deacylation of a protein directly, pulse–chase experiments with ^{3}H-palmitic acid have to be performed. Deacylation is visible as a decrease in the ^{3}H-palmitate labeling with increasing chase time. The half-time of the fatty acid cleavage can also be determined from these experiments ***(20)***. However, ^{3}H-palmitate labeling cannot be chased completely. A huge amount is present in cellular lipids, which themselves show fatty acid turnover, and a substantial fraction also as palmitoyl-coenzyme A, the acyl donor for palmitoylation. The following protocol is designed to minimize these problems.

1. Label several cell monolayers for 1 h with ^{3}H-palmitic acid, as described.
2. Remove labeling medium. Wash monolayer twice with 1 mL medium containing fatty acid-free bovine serum albumin (0.1%). Albumin will extract some of the remaining unbound fatty acids.
3. Add 1 mL medium supplemented with 100 µ*M* unlabeled palmitic acid. Palmitic acid is stored as a 100-m*M* stock solution in ethanol and is diluted 1:1000 into the cell-culture medium. Unlabeled palmitate will compete with ^{3}H-palmitate for the incorporation into protein.
4. Lyse one cell monolayer immediately and chase remaining cells for different periods of time (e.g., 20, 40, 60 min, up to 4 h) at 37°C.
5. Wash and lyse cells and proceed with immunoprecipitation, as described.

3.2.2. Cycloheximide Treatment

Treatment of cells with cycloheximide prevents protein synthesis immediately and nearly quantitatively, but has no obvious effect on palmitoylation *per se*. Thus, strong ^{3}H-palmitate labeling of a protein in the absence of ongoing protein synthesis is taken as an indication for reacylation of a previously deacylated protein. However, this issue is more complicated than it seems at first glance. Palmitoylation is a posttranslational modification. Therefore, freshly synthesized proteins continue to incorporate ^{3}H-palmitate until all molecules have passed their intracellular site of palmitoylation. This takes approx 10–20 min for proteins transported at a fast rate along the exocytotic pathway, and their ^{3}H-palmitate incorporation decreases during this time ***(21,22)***. In contrast, ^{3}H-palmitate incorporation into a previously deacylated protein is not dependent on the labeling time after cycloheximide addition. It is therefore advisable to compare the ^{3}H-palmitate labeling of a protein at different time points after blocking protein synthesis.

1. Add 6 µL cycloheximide to 6 mL cell-culture medium from a 50-mg/mL stock in ethanol to reach a final concentration of 50 µg/mL. Add 1 mL medium to cell monolayers and incubate at 37°C. One monolayer should not be treated with cycloheximide.
2. Label cells with ^{3}H-palmitic acid for 1 h, either immediately or 5, 10, 20, 30, and 60 min after cycloheximide addition. The labeling medium should also contain cycloheximide (50 µg/mL).
3. Proceed with immunoprecipitation, SDS-PAGE, and fluorography, as described.

3.3. Membrane-Binding of Palmitoylated Proteins

3.3.1. Separation of Cells into Membranous and Soluble Fractions

Separation of cells into membranous and soluble fractions by high-speed centrifugation is the most satisfying method to analyze membrane binding of a protein ***(23)***. A first hint for a membrane-binding function of covalently bound palmitate can be obtained by comparing the subcellular distribution of the palmitoylated pool of a protein (represented by ^{3}H-palmitate labeling) with the entire pool (by long-term ^{35}S-methionine labeling). A membrane-binding function of the fatty acids is indicated by the exclusive appearance of the ^{3}H-palmitate labeled protein in the membrane fraction; the ^{35}S-methionine-labeled protein is also present in the cytosol. A superior approach would be to compare membrane binding of a palmitoylated protein with its fatty acid-free mutant. In this case, a nonpalmitoylated mutant of the respective protein has to be created by site-specific mutagenesis of palmitoylation sites in its cloned gene. Wild-type protein and the mutant are then expressed in eukaryotic cells with a suitable expression system. However, description of recombinant DNA methods is beyond the scope of this chapter (**ref.** ***24***; *see also* Chapters 8 and 12). This section describes a small-scale approach to prepare membrane and cytosolic fractions.

1. Label cell monolayer in parallel for 1–4 h with ^{3}H-palmitate or ^{35}S-methionine (100 µCi/mL medium without methionine).
2. Scrape cells into 1 mL ice-cold PBS with a rubber policeman and transfer to an Eppendorf tube. Pellet cells (3500*g*, 2 min) in an Eppendorf centrifuge.
3. Wash cells once with 1 mL of ice-cold buffer A. Resuspend cells in 500 µL of buffer A and incubate on ice for 15 min.
4. Homogenize cells on ice with a tightly fitting dounce homogenizer; 20–40 strokes are usually sufficient to homogenize >80% of the cells. Pellet unbroken cells by low-speed centrifugation (3500*g*, 2 min). Cells may also be broken by three cycles of freezing in liquid nitrogen and thawing at 37°C. However, this method may cause unphysiological aggregation of proteins, leading to possible artifacts (*see* **Subheading 3.3.1.1.**).
5. Transfer supernatant to a centrifuge tube. Centrifuge for 1 hat 100,000*g*.
6. Add 500 µL 2X RIPA-buffer to supernatant (= cytosolic fraction). Solubilize pellet (= membranes) in 1 mL of 1X RIPA-buffer for 20 min on ice.
7. Pellet insoluble material (20 min, 14,000 rpm, Eppendorf centrifuge)
8. Subject supernatant to immunoprecipitation, SDS-PAGE, and fluorography, as described.

3.3.1.1. Solubilization of Aggregated Acylprotein

By using the method described above, a protein may appear in the membrane fraction, although it is not membrane-bound in vivo. This is probably caused by the formation of large aggregates, which sediment at 100,000*g*. Such aggregates often resist treatment with nondenaturing detergents (e.g., Triton X-100) under conditions in which membranes are solubilized. The following protocol is helpful to exclude such artifacts.

1. Solubilize the membrane pellet from **step 5** in the preceding protocol with 500 µL Triton lysis buffer. Incubate for 30 min on ice.
2. Centrifuge the samples for 1 h at 100,000*g*.
3. Add 1 mL RIPA buffer to the pellet and 500 µL 2X RIPA-buffer to the supernatant and proceed with **step 7** in the preceding protocol.

3.3.1.2. High-Salt Treatment of Membrane Sediments

Proteins without a stretch of hydrophobic amino acids long enough to span a lipid bilayer are bound to membranes either by interactions with a integral membrane protein or via covalently linked lipids. Protein–protein interactions are often susceptible to high-salt treatment, but lipid–lipid interactions are resistant. Thus, salt-resistant membrane-binding of a protein is another indication that a lipid modification is involved and the following protocol describes the procedure.

1. The membrane pellet is completely resuspended in 200 µL buffer A, supplemented with 1*M* NaCl, and incubated on ice for 30 min. High-salt concentrations might interfere with immunoprecipitation. Therefore, only a small volume of the high-salt buffer is used here to allow subsequent dilution with RIPA buffer. Carbonate treatment, which is also a standard method to extract peripheral membrane proteins, should not be used, because the basic pH may cleave the fatty acids.
2. The samples are centrifuged for one hour at 100,000*g*.
3. 200 µL 2X RIPA buffer plus 600 µL 1X RIPA-buffer are added to the supernatant (= proteins released from the membrane) and the membrane pellet is solubilized in 1 mL 1X RIPA-buffer.

4. Notes

1. 100 µCi–1mCi ^{3}H-palmitic acid per mL cell-culture medium are usually used for the labeling of acylated proteins. Tritiated fatty acids are supplied as solutions in ethanol or toluene at concentrations too low to add directly to the medium. Because of its cytotoxicity, the final concentration of ethanol in the labeling medium should not exceed 0.5%. Concentration of ^{3}H-palmitic acid can be done in advance and the concentrated stock should be stored at –20°C in tightly sealed polystyrene tubes. Concentration and storage in polypropylene (e.g., Eppendorf tubes) should be avoided, because this can result in irreversible loss of much of the label on the tube.
2. Use standard tissue culture medium for the cell line to be labeled. Possible addition of serum to the medium requires some consideration. Serum contains albumin, a fatty acid-binding protein, which may delay ^{3}H-palmitate uptake of the cells. Thus, for short labeling periods (up to 4 h), we usually use medium without serum. However, serum does not prevent ^{3}H-palmitate labeling of proteins and can be added, if required. For long labeling periods, the presence of serum may even be beneficial, because reversible binding of fatty acids to albumin may help to distribute the ^{3}H-palmitate uptake of the cells more evenly. Serum contains several poorly characterized factors with biological activities, and deacylation of particular proteins upon serum treatment of cells has been reported ***(3)***. Obviously, in these cases, serum addition is detrimental.
3. The necessary time for optimal labeling of palmitoylated proteins is variable and has to be determined empirically for each protein. Proteins with a low, but steady, amount of synthesis and no turnover of their fatty acids, should be labeled as long as possible, e.g., at least 4 h, up to 24 h. The amount of ^{3}H-palmitate incorporation into these proteins increases with time until it reaches saturation. Reversibly palmitoylated proteins show an increase in their labeling intensity in the beginning, until a peak is reached. Because of deacylation, their ^{3}H-palmitic acid labeling then decreases with time. Proteins expressed from a viral expression vector should be labeled, as long as the peak period of their synthesis prevails.
4. Sedimentation of insoluble material at higher g-values (e.g., 30 min, 100,000*g*) sometimes causes a cleaner immunoprecipitation. Make sure that your protein does not precipitate under these conditions. Another possibility to improve the

specificity of the immunoprecipitation would be to preincubate the cell lysate with Sepharose beads, but without antibodies (1 h, 4°C). Pellet the beads and transfer the supernatant to a fresh Eppendorf tube and proceed with immunoprecipitation as described.

5. The amount of a monoclonal antibody or antiserum necessary to precipitate a protein quantitatively from a cell lysate depends on its affinity for the antigen and must be determined empirically, but 1–5 μL of an high-affinity antiserum is usually sufficient for the conditions described here. To control for complete precipitation of a protein, transfer the first supernatant from **step 8** in **Subheading 3.1.1.** to a fresh Eppendorf tube. Add antibody and protein-A-Sepharose and proceed with immunoprecipitation. Antibodies of special subtypes do not bind to protein A. This has to be considered when monoclonal antibodies are used. However, most of these antibodies bind to protein G-Sepharose ***(25)***.
6. The thioester-type linkage of fatty acids to cysteine residues is labile upon treatment with reducing agents. Cleavage of the fatty acids by these compounds is concentration-, time-, and temperature-dependent, therefore, mercaptoethanol and DTT should be omitted from the sample buffer. If the protein requires reducing agents for solubilization, heating should be as brief as possible (95°C, 2 min), or the temperature should be decreased (e.g., 15 min at 50°C). Ester-linked fatty acids are highly susceptible to basic pH values above 12. Under these conditions, the fatty acids are cleaved quantitatively and rapidly (<1 min), even at low temperatures; therefore, basic pH values should be avoided under all circumstances. In contrast, treatment with acid pH (e.g., pH 1.0) for time periods up to 1 h is tolerated by the fatty acid bond. Acetic acid containing gel-fixing solutions do not lead to an obvious loss of ^{3}H-palmitate labeling.
7. Tritium-derived radioactivity has a very short range, and is essentially undetectable by this form of autoradiography, unless the weak β-emissions are first converted into photons to enable fluorographic detection, as described in **Subheading 3.1.1., steps 12** and **13**. Dry the gel as thin as possible and make sure that the X-ray film is in close contact with the gel. The times to detect a signal on the film are highly variable. Endogenous cellular proteins with low rates of synthesis require exposure times from several days up to 3 mo. For highly overexpressed proteins with multiple palmitoylation sites, they can be as short as several hours.
8. Hydroxylamine sometimes degrades if the pH is adjusted too quickly. Dissolve hydroxylamine in ice-cold distilled water and put the solution in an ice bath. Add solid NaOH pellets one by one while continuously stirring the solution until the desired pH is reached. Rapid pH changes, and the appearance of a brown color in the normally colorless hydroxylamine solution, are indications that degradation of hydroxylamine has occurred. In this case, the solution has to be discarded.
9. This TLC-solvent system separates fatty acids according to their hydrophobicity, i.e., the number of carbon atoms and double bonds. Myristic acid (C 14) runs faster than palmitic acid (C 16), which runs faster than stearic acid (C 18). Unsaturated fatty acids are not separated from saturated ones. A fatty acid with one double bond runs to the same position as a saturated fatty acid with

two methyl groups less, i.e., oleic acid (18:1) comigrates with palmitic acid (C 16:0). ^{3}H-Arachidonic acid (20:4) is not to be expected as protein-bound fatty acid after labeling with ^{3}H-palmitate, because cells cannot metabolize palmitate into arachidonate.

References

1. Schmidt, M. F. G. and Burns, G. R. (1989) Solubilization of protein fatty acyltransferase from placental membranes and cell-free acyl transfer. *Biochem. Soc. Trans.* **17,** 859,860.
2. McIlhinney, R. A. J. (1990) The fats of life: the importance and function of protein acylation. *Trends Biochem. Sci.* **15,** 387–391.
3. James, G. and Olson, E. N. (1990) Fatty acylated proteins as components of intracellular signaling pathways. *Biochemistry* **29,** 2623–2634.
4. Schlesinger, M. J., Veit, M., and Schmidt, M. F. G. (1993) Palmitoylation of viral and cellular proteins, in *Lipid Modifications of Proteins* (Schlesinger, M. J., ed.), CRC, Boca Raton, FL, pp. 1–19.
5. Bouvier, M., Moffett, S., Loisel, T. P., Mouillac, B., Hebert, T., and Chidiac, P. (1995) Palmitoylation of G-protein-coupled receptors: a dynamic modification with functional consequences. *Biochem. Soc. Trans.* **23,** 116–120.
6. Davison, A. J. and Elliot, R. M., eds. (1993) *Molecular Virology: A Practical Approach.* IRL, Oxford, UK.
7. Berger, M. and Schmidt, M. F. G. (1984) Cell-free fatty acid acylation of Semliki Forest virus polypeptides with microsomal membranes from eukaryotic cells. *J. Biol. Chem.* **259,** 7245–7252.
8. Veit, M., Herrler, G., Schmidt, M. F. G., Rott, R., and Klenk, H.-D. (1990) The hemagglutinating glycoproteins of influenza B and C viruses are acylated with different fatty acids. *Virology* **177,** 807–811.
9. Muszbek, L. and Laposata, M. (1993) Covalent modification of proteins by arachidonate and eicosapentaenoate in platelets. *J. Biol. Chem.* **268,** 18,243–18,248.
10. Milligan, G., Parenti, M., and Magee, A. I. (1995) The dynamic role of palmitoylation in signal transduction. *Trends Biochem. Sci.* **20,** 181–187.
11. Wedegaertner, P. B., Wilson, P. T., and Bourne, H. R. (1995) Lipid modification of trimeric G-proteins. *J. Biol. Chem.* **270,** 503–506.
12. Camp, L. A., Verkruyse, L. A., Afendis, S. J., Slaughter, C. A., and Hofman, S. L. (1994) Molecular cloning of a palmitoyl-protein thioesterase. *J. Biol. Chem.* **269,** 23,212–23,219.
13. Veit, M., Kretzschmar, E., Kuroda, K., Garten, W., Schmidt, M. F. G., Klenk, H.-D., and Rott, R. (1991) Site-specific mutagenesis identifies three cysteine residues in the cytoplasmic tail as acylation sites of influenza virus hemagglutinin. *J. Virol.* **65,** 2491–2500.
14. Resh, M. D. (1994) Myristylation and palmitylation of Src-family members: The fats of the matter. Cell **76,** 411–413.
15. Walker, J. M., ed. (1984) *Methods in Molecular Biology, vol. 1: Proteins.* Humana, Clifton, NJ.

16. Casey, P. J. and Buss, J. E., eds. (1995) *Methods in Enzymology, vol. 250: Lipid Modification of Proteins.* Academic, San Diego.
17. Hooper, N. M. and Turner, A. J. eds. (1992) *Lipid Modification of Proteins: A Practical Approach.* IRL, Oxford, UK.
18. Kates, M., ed. (1986) *Laboratory Techniques in Biochemistry and Molecular Biology: Techniques in Lipidology.* Elsevier, Amsterdam.
19. Bizzozero, O. A. (1995) Chemical analysis of acylation sites and species, in *Methods in Enzymology, vol. 250* (Casey, P. J. and Buss, J. E., eds.), Academic, San Diego, pp. 361–379.
20. Magee, A. I., Gutierrez, L., McKay, I. A., Marshall, C. J., and Hall, A. (1987) Dynamic fatty acylation of p21N-ras. *EMBO J.* **6,** 3353–3357.
21. Schmidt, M. F. G. and Schlesinger, M. J. (1980) Relation of fatty acid attachment to the tranlation and maturation of vesicular stomatitis and Sindbis virus membrane glycoproteins. *J. Biol. Chem.* **255,** 3334–3339.
22. Veit, M. and Schmidt, M. F. G. (1993) Timing of palmitoylation of influenza virus hemagglutinin. *FEBS Lett.* **336,** 243–247.
23. Findlay, J. B. C. and Evans, W. H., eds. (1987) *Biological Membranes: A Practical Approach.* IRL, Oxford, UK.
24. McPherson, M. J., ed. (1991) *Directed Mutagenesis: A Practical Approach.* IRL, Oxford, UK.
25. Harlow, E. and Lane, D., eds. (1989) *Antibodies: A Laboratory Manual.* Cold Spring Harbor Laboratory, Cold Spring Harbor, NY.

18

Agonist-Mediated Turnover of G-Protein α-Subunit Palmitoyl Groups

Role in Membrane Insertion

Morag A. Grassie and Graeme Milligan

1. Introduction

Membrane associated proteins are classically thought of as proteins that are inserted into the membrane lipid bilayer by virtue of transmembrane-spanning regions. Although heterotrimeric G proteins are membrane-associated, they do not contain such transmembrane regions, but have been shown by recent work to be located at the inner surface of the plasma membrane by virtue of lipid modifications *(1)*. One of these lipid modifications, myristoylation, is an irreversible cotranslational lipid modification that involves the addition of a saturated 14 carbon acyl group at the NH_2-terminal glycine of a subset of heterotrimeric G-protein α-subunits. A second modification, palmitoylation, in comparison, is a dynamic, reversible posttranslational modification in which the addition of a 16 carbon saturated fatty acyl group occurs via a labile thioester bond on cysteine residues. This modification is present on all heterotrimeric G-protein α-subunits examined to date, with the exception of transducin (which is myristoylated and further modified by other less hydrophobic fatty acids).

Such dynamic lipid modification is now believed to be a potential candidate as a regulating mechanism of heterotrimeric G proteins by determining their location and hence their functional activity. This has been demonstrated in the case of Gs_{α} *(2,3)*, $G_{q\alpha}$ *(4)*, $G_{z\alpha}$ *(5)*, and also the G-protein-coupled β_2-adrenergic receptor *(6,7)*.

This chapter will describe methodology to determine if a protein is modified by the addition of a palmitoyl group, and how the half-life of this lipid modifi-

From: *Methods in Molecular Biology, Vol. 88: Protein Targeting Protocols*
Edited by: R. A. Clegg Humana Press Inc., Totowa, NJ

cation can be investigated, together with the effect that the lipid group has on protein localization.

2. Materials

2.1. Equipment

1. Tissue culture facilities.
2. Tight-fitting teflon on glass homogenizer.
3. Microcentrifuge and refrigerated ultracentrifuge (capable of 200,000*g*).
4. Sodium dodecyl sulfate polyacrylamide gel electrophoresis (SDS-PAGE) apparatus and power pack.
5. Gel drier.
6. Hyperfilm-MP film (Amersham, Buckinghamshire, UK) and X-ray film developing facilities.

2.2. Reagents

1. Growth medium: DMEM containing 5% newborn calf serum (NCS), 20 m*M* glutamine, 100 U/mL penicillin and 100 μg/mL streptomycin (BRL Life Technologies, Paisley, Scotland).
2. [^{3}H] Palmitate labeling medium: As for growth medium, with NCS replaced with 5% dialyzed NCS (*see* **Subheading 2.2., step 5**), 5 m*M* Na pyruvate and 150 μCi/mL [^{3}H] Palmitic acid. [^{3}H] Palmitic acid supplied as 1 mCi/mL in ethanol: Dry under N_2 in a glass tube to remove ethanol, then resuspended in labeling medium, to give a final concentration of 150 μCi/mL of medium (*see* **Note 1**).
3. [^{3}H] Palmitate chase medium: DMEM containing 5% dialyzed NCS, 20 m*M* glutamine, 100 U/mL penicillin, 100 μg/mL streptomycin, 5 m*M* Na Pyruvate, 100 m*M* cold palmitic acid (*see* **Note 2**).
4. [^{35}S] methionine/cysteine labeling medium: 1 part growth medium, 3 parts DMEM lacking methionine and cysteine (GIBCO, Paisley, Scotland), supplemented with 50 μCi/mL Trans ^{35}S-label (ICN Biomedicals, Oscon, UK). **Caution:** [^{35}S] is volatile, and therefore stocks should be opened in a fume hood.
5. Dialysis of NCS should be carried out in dialysis tubing that had been boiled in 10 m*M* EDTA for 10 min, then this procedure repeated. Dialysis tubing can be stored at this point in 20% ethanol until required. Dialyze 50 mL of NCS against 2 L of Earles salts (6.8 g NaCl, 0.1 g KCl, 0.2 g $MgSO_4 \cdot 7H_2O$, 0.14 g NaH_2PO_4, 1.0 g glucose) over a period of 12–36 h, with three changes of buffer. Remove serum from dialysis tubing and filter-sterilize before storing at –20°C in 2 mL aliquots until required.
6. Stock solution of agonist.
7. Phosphate buffer saline (PBS): 0.2 g KCl, 0.2 g KH_2PO_4, 8 g NaCl, 1.14 g $NaHPO_4$ (anhydrous) to 1000 mL with H_2O (pH should be in range of 7.0–7.4).
8. 1 and 1.33% (w/v) SDS.
9. TE buffer: 10 m*M* Tris-HCl, 0.1 m*M* EDTA, pH 7.5.
10. Solubilization buffer: 1% Triton X-100, 10 m*M* EDTA, 100 m*M* NaH_2PO_4, 10 m*M* NaF, 100 μ*M* Na_3VO_4, 50 m*M* HEPES, pH 7.2.

11. Immunoprecipitation wash buffer: 1% Triton X-100, 0.5% SDS, 100 m*M* NaCl, 100 m*M* NaF, 50 m*M* NaH_2PO_4, 50 m*M* HEPES, pH 7.2.
12. Gel solutions for 10% gels: acrylamide—30 g acrylamide, 0.8 g *bis*-acrylamide to 100 mL with H_2O; buffer 1—18.17 g Tris, 4 mL 10% SDS, pH 8.8, to 100 mL with H_2O; buffer 2—6 g Tris, 4 mL 10% SDS, pH 6.8, to 100 mL with H_2O; 50% glycerol; 10% ammonium persulfate (APS); TEMED; 0.1% SDS; Laemmli sample buffer—3 g urea, 0.5 g SDS 0.6 g DTT, 0.5 mL 1*M* Tris-HCl pH 8.0, bromophenol blue to 10 mL with H_2O; running buffer—28.9 g glycine, 6 g Tris, 2 g SDS to 2 L with H_2O.
13. Gel solutions for 6*M* urea 12.8% acrylamide gels (*see also* **Note 7**): Urea—10.81 g in 30 mL H_2O final volume; urea acrylamide—10.81 g urea, 9 g acrylamide, 0.045 g *bis*-acrylamide in 30 mL H_2O final volume; urea Buffer 1—10.81 g urea, 5.45 g Tris-HCl, 1.2 mL 10% SDS, pH 8.8, in 30 mL H_2O final volume.
14. Fixing solution: 25% isopropanol, 65% H_2O, 10% acetic acid.
15. Amplify (Amersham, UK).

3. Methods

3.1. Cell Culture and Metabolic Labeling

1. Seed equal numbers of cells to be analyzed into 6-well culture dishes, using 1.5–2 mL growth medium per well (or in 100-mm tissue-culture dishes with 10 mL of growth medium, if cell fractionation is to be carried out). Incubate at 37°C in an atmosphere of 5% CO_2, until cells are 90% confluent. Remove growth medium and replace with 1 mL of [^{3}H] palmitate-labeling medium ± agonist for 2 h at 37°C.
2. Parallel control experiments using Trans [^{35}S]-label can be carried out ± agonist; however, addition of [^{35}S] methionine/cysteine-labeling medium should occur when cells are 60–80% confluent (*see* **Note 3**), and the cells labeled over a period of 18 h.

3.2. Pulse–Chase Analysis

The half-life of the palmitoyl group can be investigated using pulse–chase studies.

1. Label cells metabolically, as described in **Subheading 3.1.** for 2 h with [^{3}H] palmitate-labeling medium.
2. Remove radiolabeling medium and wash the cell monolayers carefully with growth medium (twice).
3. Chase the radiolabel from the cells by growing for up to 3 h at 37°C in the presence of chase medium that contains 100 μ*M* cold palmitic acid. A number of time-points should be taken during this time by harvesting the cells directly in 1% SDS (*see* **Subheading 3.4.**) immunoprecipitated (*see* **Subheading 3.6.**) and analyzed by SDS-PAGE (*see* **Subheading 3.7.**), with most suitable time-points varying, depending on the protein under investigation.

   Parallel experiments can also be carried out to investigate the half-life of the protein, rather than the lipid modification, by metabolically labeling with [^{35}S] methionine/cysteine. It should be noted that the half-life of the protein will be considerably longer than that of the lipid group.

4. Label cells metabolically, as described previously, by the addition of [^{35}S]methionine/cysteine-labeling medium for 18 h.
5. Remove the radiolabeling medium and wash the cell monolayers carefully with growth medium (twice).
6. Grow the radiolabeled cells in the presence of fresh growth medium and harvest the cells directly into 1% SDS at different time points over the next 72 h, immunoprecipitate, and analyze by SDS-PAGE.

3.3. Agonist Driven Palmitoylation

To investigate whether receptor activation by agonist can regulate α-subunit palmitoylation, cells can be grown in [^{3}H] palmitate-labeling medium, in the presence or absence of a maximal concentration of agonist. In these experiments the labeling medium is added at time zero, and cells grown in the presence or absence of agonist are harvested at various time-points (e.g., 2, 5, 15, 30, and 120 min), immunoprecipitated, and analyzed by SDS-PAGE.

3.4. Cell Harvesting and Sample Solubilization Prior to Immunoprecipitation

1. At the end of the labeling period, remove the labeling medium, add 200 μL of 1% SDS per well, scrape the monolayer of cells into the SDS solution, and transfer to a 2 mL screw-top tube.
2. Heat to 100°C for 20 min in a heating block, to denature proteins. If the samples have a stringy consistency after this stage, pass through a 20- to 25-gage needle and reboil for 10 min.
3. Remove the samples from the heating block and allow to cool for 2 min at room temperature. Pulse each tube briefly at high speed in a microcentrifuge to bring the contents to the bottom of the tube. The samples can now be frozen at –20°C until required, or proceed to **Subheading 3.6., step 2**.

3.5. Cell Harvesting for Fractionation Studies

1. Using cells labeled in 100-mm tissue culture dishes in order to obtain enough material, remove the labeling medium at the appropriate time and scrape the cells into 5 mL of ice-cold PBS. Add a further 5 mL to the plate to collect any remaining cells, then centrifuge for 10 min at 1000*g* to collect the cells as a pellet. Discard the supernatant, and resuspend the cell pellet in a further 10 mL of PBS and repeat centrifugation step. Discard supernatant and freeze cell pellet at –80°C.
2. Thaw cell pellet and resuspend in 300 μL of ice cold TE buffer. Homogenize cells on ice with 25 slow strokes of a tight-fitting teflon-on-glass homogenizer. Centrifuge the samples at 200,000*g* for 30 min at 4°C to generate a soluble fraction containing cytoplasmic material (supernatant) and particulate fraction containing the cell membranes (pellet). Remove the supernatant and resuspend the pellet in 300 μL of ice-cold TE buffer. Pass the particulate fraction through a fine

gage needle until the membranes are evenly resuspended. Store samples at -80°C until required or proceed to **Subheading 3.6., step 1**.

3.6. Immunoprecipitation

1. To 50 μL each of the soluble and particulate fractions add 150 μL of 1.33% SDS (to give a final concentration of 1% SDS). Heat the samples in 2-mL screw-top tubes to 100°C for 20 min then place on ice to cool. Pulse the samples to the bottom of the tubes by briefly centrifuging the samples at top speed in a microcentrifuge.
2. Add 800 μL of ice-cold solubilization buffer to each tube and mix by inverting. Pulse the samples to collect contents at the bottom of the tubes.
3. Before immunoprecipitating the G-protein α-subunit, first preclear the sample (*see* **Note 4**) by adding 100 μL of protein A-Sepharose (Sigma) or 100 μL of Pansorbin (a cheaper alternative of bacterial membranes containing protein A [*see* **Note 5**, Calbiochem, Nottingham, UK]) and mix at 4°C for 1–2 h on a rotating wheel. (Ensure caps are firmly closed before rotating.)
4. Spin samples for 2 min at maximum speed in a microcentrifuge to pellet the protein A-Sepharose/Pansorbin. Transfer the precleared supernatants to fresh screw top tubes.
5. To the precleared samples, add 5–15 mL of G-protein α-subunit specific antibody (volume will vary, depending on the antibody used) and 100 mL of protein A-Sepharose. Ensure caps are firmly closed and rotate at 4°C, as before, for 2–5 h (*see* **Note 6**).
6. Spin samples for 2 min at maximum speed in a microcentrifuge to pellet the immunocomplex. Remove the supernatant and resuspend the pellet in 1 mL of immunoprecipitation wash buffer. Invert the tube 10 times—do not vortex. The supernatant can be retained to analyze the efficiency of immunoprecipitation, if required.
7. Repeat **step 6**.
8. Spin samples for 2 min at maximum speed in a microcentrifuge and discard supernatant. Resuspend agarose immunocomplex pellet in 40 mL of Laemmli sample buffer.
9. Heat samples to 100°C for 5 min, then spin for 2 min at maximum speed in microcentrifuge. Analyze the samples by SDS-PAGE by loading an equal volume of each sample on a 10% acrylamide gel (*see* **Subheading 3.7.**).

3.7. SDS-PAGE Analysis

1. Recipes given below are for one 16 × 18 cm 10% acrylamide gel.

Resolving gel (lower)

H_2O	8.2 mL
Buffer 1	6.0 mL
Acrylamide	8.0 mL
50% Glycerol	1.6 mL
10% APS	90 μL
TEMED	8 μL

2. Add all reagents in order given and mixed thoroughly. Carefully pour into prepared gel plates.
3. Very carefully overlay gel mixture with approx 1 mL of 0.1% SDS and leave gel to polymerize.
4. Once gel has polymerized, pour off SDS.
5. Prepare stacker gel as indicated below and mix thoroughly.

Stacker gel

H_2O	9.75 mL
Buffer 2	3.75 mL
Acrylamide	1.50 mL
10% APS	150 µL
TEMED	8 µL

6. Pour stacker gel on top of resolving gel and place well-forming comb in top of gel, ensuring no air bubbles are trapped under the comb. Leave to polymerize.
7. Once gel has polymerized, remove the comb and place the gel in the gel tank, containing enough running buffer in the base to cover the bottom edge of the gel, and add the remaining running buffer to the top.
8. Load the prepared samples in the preformed wells, using a Hamilton syringe.
9. Run the gel overnight (approx 16 h) at 12 mA and a constant 60 V, until the dye front reaches the bottom of the gel plates.

3.8. SDS-PAGE Analysis Using 6M Urea Acrylamide Gels

In order to separate closely related G protein α-subunits, such as $G_{q\alpha}/G_{11\alpha}$ and $G_{o1\alpha}/G_{o2\alpha}$ 6*M* urea gels are used. These are run using freshly prepared solutions (*see* **Note 7**) and large gel plates.

Recipes given below are for one 20 × 20 cm 6*M* urea gel.

Resolving gel (lower)

Urea	12.2 mL
Urea Buffer 1	9.6 mL
Urea Acrylamide	16.2 mL
10% APS	30 µL
TEMED	8 µL

Mix all reagents as detailed for 10% acrylamide gels, pour gel, and gently overlay with 0.1% SDS. Allow to set for at least 2–3 h. Once set, add stacker gel, using recipe described in **Subheading 3.7.**

3.9. Enhancement of Radioactive Signal from Gel

In order to increase the weak signal emitted by [^{3}H]palmitic acid, the gel is treated with Amplify (Amersham), according to the manufacturer's instructions.

1. Fix proteins in gel, using fixing solution for 30 min.
2. Pour off fixing solution (**Caution:** This may contain radioactivity) and soak gel in Amplify, with agitation for 15–30 min.

3. Remove gel from solution and dry under vacuum for 2 h at 60–80°C.
4. Expose the gel to X-ray film (Hyperfilm-MP, Amersham) at –70°C for a minimum of 5 wk before developing.

4. Notes

1. When preparing [^{3}H]palmitic acid: Ensure radiolabel is dried in a glass tube to minimize loss of material by adsorption; and, when resuspending [^{3}H]palmitic acid, take great care to ensure all material is recovered from the sides of the glass tube and fully resuspended in the labeling medium. This can be confirmed by counting the amount of radioactivity present in a small proportion of the labeling medium and comparing it to the amount of radioactivity added originally.
2. Cold, nonradioactive palmitic acid can be prepared as a 1*M* stock in propanol. Because palmitic acid is difficult to solubilize warm propanol should be used to prepare the stock solution.
3. The confluency of cells required for ^{35}S labeling will varying, depending on the speed of growth of the cell line used. For rapidly growing cells, such as fibroblasts, add radiolabel at 60% confluency, for slow-growing cells, e.g., of neuronal derivation, add radiolabel when cells are approaching 80–85% confluency.
4. Preclearing samples before immunoprecipitation removes material that binds nonspecifically to protein A thus reducing the background levels in the final sample. This is especially useful for ^{35}S radiolabeled material in which it may be advisable to preclear for the maximum 2 h.
5. We have found Pansorbin (Calbiochem) to be a good, cheap alternative to protein A-Sepharose, especially for preclearing; however, the use of protein A-Sepharose is recommended for the immunoprecipitation reaction itself, because the use of Pansorbin has been found to give increased nonspecific background for some antibodies.
6. The length of time of immunoprecipitation should be determined empirically for each antibody used, in order to minimize the amount of nonspecific material present in the final sample. For most antibodies with high titer, the shorter the incubation, the less nonspecific material immunoprecipitated.
7. The solutions for 6*M* urea gels should be made just prior to casting the gel. Note that, in order to dissolve the urea, the solutions may require stirring in a bath of warm water and should be made up in a volume as near to the final volume as possible.

Acknowledgments

Studies in our laboratory in this area are supported by the Medical Research Council, the Biotechnology and Biological Sciences Research Council, and the Wellcome Trust.

References

1. Milligan, G., Parenti, M., and Magee, A. I. (1995) The dynamic role of palmitoylation in signal transduction. *TIBS* **20,** 181–186.

2. Degtyarev, M. Y., Spiegel, A. M., and Jones, T. L. Z. (1993) Increased palmitoylation of the G_s protein α subunit after activation by the β-adrenergic receptor or cholera toxin. *J. Biol. Chem.* **268,** 23,769–23,772.
3. Wedegaertner, P. B. and Bourne, H. R. (1994) Activation and depalmitoylation of $G_{s\alpha}$. *Cell* **77,** 1063–1070.
4. Wedegaertner, P. B., Chu, D. H., Wilson, P. T., Levis, M. J., and Bourne, H. R. (1993) Palmitoylation is required for signaling functions and membrane attachment of $G_{q\alpha}$ and $G_{s\alpha}$. *J. Biol. Chem.* **268,** 25,001–25,008.
5. Wilson, P. T. and Bourne, H. R. (1995) Fatty acylation of α_z. *J. Biol. Chem.* **270,** 9667–9675.
6. Mouillac, B., Caron, M., Bonin, H., Dennis, M., and Bouvier, M. (1992) Agonist-modulated palmitoylation of β_2-adrenergic receptor in Sf9 cells. *J. Biol. Chem.* **267,** 21,733–21,737.
7. Moffat, S., Mouillac, B., Bonin, H., and Bouvier, M. (1993) Altered phosphorylation and desensitization patterns of a human β_2-adrenergic receptor lacking the palmitoylated Cys 341. *EMBO J.* **12,** 349–356.

19

Membrane Targeting via Protein Prenylation

Jean H. Overmeyer, Robert A. Erdman, and William A. Maltese

1. Introduction

1.1. Biological Significance of Protein Prenylation

Posttranslational prenylation of proteins in mammalian cells involves the formation of a thioether linkage between a 15-carbon farnesyl or a 20-carbon geranylgeranyl moiety and one or more cysteine residues, at or near the carboxyl terminus of the polypeptide. The prenyl groups are donated by farnesyl pyrophosphate or geranylgeranyl pyrophosphate, which, in turn, are derived from a common precursor, mevalonate ***(1,2)***. Prenylation ranks among the most common lipid modifications of proteins in mammalian cells, with one estimate suggesting that 2% (by mass) of all cellular proteins may be modified in this way ***(3)***. A few of the known farnesylated or geranylgeranylated proteins include nuclear lamin B ***(4)***, H-, and K-Ras proteins ***(5,6)***, the γ-subunits of heterotrimeric G proteins ***(7,8)***, and Ras-related GTP-binding proteins belonging to the Rac ***(9)***, Rap ***(2,10)***, Ral ***(9)***, Rho ***(11,12)***, and Rab ***(13–15)*** families. The characterization of several protein:prenyltransferases ***(16–19)*** has led to rapid advances in knowledge concerning the enzymology of protein prenylation. However, much remains to be learned about the significance of the prenyl modification for the function of individual proteins in living cells.

Silvius and l'Heureux ***(20)*** have demonstrated that the hydrophobicity conferred on proteins by their prenylation can be sufficient to mediate reversible attachment to membrane lipid bilayers. In addition, accumulating evidence points to a role for the isoprenoid moieties in mediating the interactions of a variety of prenylated proteins with accessory proteins in the cytosol ***(21)***. These findings are consistent with the documented subcellular distribution of prenylated proteins in both the membrane and soluble compartments ***(22,23)***.

From: *Methods in Molecular Biology, Vol. 88: Protein Targeting Protocols*
Edited by: R. A. Clegg Humana Press Inc., Totowa, NJ

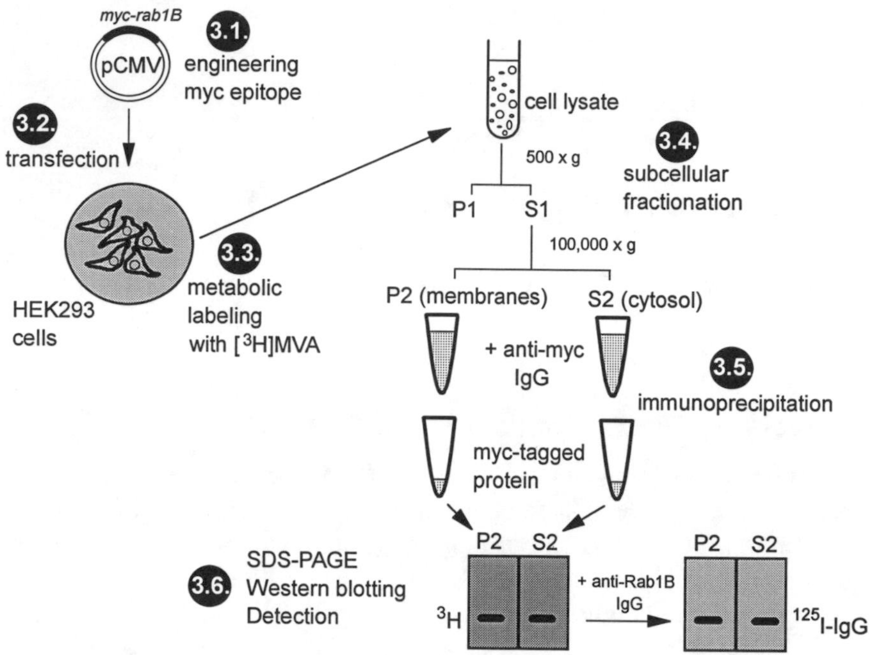

Fig. 1. Schematic diagram of the procedure for tracing the fate of prenylated proteins in intact cells. The numbered steps refer to the appropriate section in **Subheading 3.**

The molecular mechanisms that govern the cycling of prenylated proteins on and off intracellular membranes are poorly understood. In particular, there is a need for assays that can trace the fate of these proteins in intact cells. We describe here such a method, using the digeranylgeranylated GTP-binding protein, Rab1B, as a model prenylated protein. Key features of the method (*see* **Fig. 1**) are the molecular engineering of a c-Myc epitope tag at the amino terminus of the prenylated protein and the transient expression of the protein in transfected mammalian cells incubated in medium containing a radiolabeled isoprenoid precursor (i.e., [^{3}H]mevalonate). The fate of the labeled prenylated protein is then determined by immunoprecipitating it from subcellular fractions, using a commercially available antibody that specifically recognizes the Myc epitope tag. Because the Myc epitope tag can be attached to any protein for which the cDNA sequence is known, this approach should be generally applicable to the study of membrane targeting and recycling of a broad range of prenylated proteins.

1.2. Background Information about Rab1B

The particular protein that we have chosen to use as an example herein (i.e., Rab1B) is but one member of a large family of Rab proteins ***(24)***. These proteins play important roles in vesicular transport along the exocytic and endocytic pathways in mammalian cells. Each Rab protein probably functions in a unique transport step. For example, disruption of the function of Rab1B impairs the flow of glycoproteins between the endoplasmic reticulum (ER) and the Golgi apparatus ***(25,26)***. Consistent with this role, Rab1B is found in membranes of the ER, *cis*-Golgi, and intermediate vesicles ***(27)***. The precise mechanism through which Rab1B and other Rabs interact with the vesicular transport machinery has not been fully defined. However, it is generally believed that Rabs act as molecular switches, cycling on and off donor and acceptor membranes, depending on their guanine nucleotide-binding state ***(28–30)***. Geranylgeranylation of Rab proteins is critical for their participation in this cycle. Nonprenylated Rabs fail to associate with intracellular membranes ***(14,15,31,32)*** and are incapable of binding to a class of soluble proteins termed guanine nucleotide-dissociation inhibitors (GDIs) ***(33,34)***. The latter proteins appear to be involved in returning GDP-bound Rabs to the cytosol, where they remain until they are recruited to budding vesicles and are activated by exchange of GDP for GTP.

2. Materials

2.1. Epitope Tagging of Rab1B

1. Template DNA. We used the vector pGEM3Zrab1B ***(35)***, which encodes full-length Rab1B ***(36)***.
2. Oligonucleotide primers. To attach restriction sites and the *myc* tag to the *rab1B* template, we used the following 5' and 3' oligonucleotides: 5'-GCCAGCGAATT-CCATATGGAGCAGAAGCTGATCAGCGAGGAGGACCTGAACCCCGAAATGAC-TAC and 5'-ACGTCTAGAGGATCCTATCTAACAGCAGCCACCACTAGCAGA (*see* **Note 1**).
3. Reagents for polymerase chain reaction (PCR), contained in the GeneAmp PCR Core Reagent Kit from Perkin-Elmer (Foster City, CA).
4. Wax beads (Ampliwax PCR Gems, Perkin-Elmer).
5. DNA thermocycler (Perkin-Elmer or equivalent).
6. Equipment and supplies for agarose gel electrophoresis of DNA ***(37)***.
7. Reagents for purifying DNA from agarose gels ***(38)*** (e.g., Qiaex Gel Extraction Kit, Qiagen, Chatsworth, CA).
8. An expression vector that can be used for transient expression of proteins in cultured mammalian cells. We have used pCMV5 ***(39)***, in which the gene of interest is under the control of the cytomegalovirus (CMV) promoter. Similar vectors (pcDNA I and pCDM8) are commercially available from Invitrogen, San Diego, CA.
9. Standard restriction endonucleases, ligase, and reagents for subcloning the PCR product encoding the Myc-tagged Rab1B into the expression vector ***(40,41)***.
10. Reagents for transformation of *Escherichia coli* (e.g., strain HB101) with plasmid DNA ***(42)***.

11. Equipment and supplies for extraction and large-scale purification of plasmid DNA from *E. coli*. Purity of the DNA must be suitable for sequencing and transfection of mammalian cells. We use Qiagen maxiprep kits (Qiagen, Chatsworth, CA) to isolate plasmid DNA from *E. coli* expressing the pCMV*(myc-rab1B)* construct.
12. Supplies and equipment for dideoxy sequencing of DNA. We use the Sequenase Version 2.0 kit from United States Biochemical, Cleveland, OH.

2.2. Transfection of Human 293 Cells and Transient Expression of Myc-Tagged Rab1B

1. Human embryonal kidney (HEK) 293 cells (American Type Culture Collection, Rockville, MD).
2. Dulbecco's modified Eagle medium (DMEM; Gibco-BRL, Grand Island, NY).
3. Fetal bovine serum (FBS) (Sigma, St. Louis, MO). Serum should be heat-inactivated by incubation at 50°C for 30 min.
4. Transfection-quality plasmid DNA, i.e., pCMV*(myc-rab1B)* (*see* **Subheading 2.1.**).
5. 2.5*M* $CaCl_2$.
6. 0.1X TE: 1.0 m*M* Tris-HCl, pH 8.0, 0.1 m*M* EDTA.
7. 2X HBS: 280 m*M* NaCl, 2*M* HEPES, 2.8 m*M* Na_2HPO_4. Adjust the pH to 7.1 with approx 6 mL of 1*N* NaOH.
8. PBS: 2.7 m*M* KCl, 1.5 m*M* KH_2PO_4, 8.0 m*M* Na_2HPO_4, 137 m*M* NaCl.
9. 15% (v/v) glycerol in PBS.

2.3. Metabolic Labeling of Prenylated Proteins in Cultured 293 Cells

1. The isoprenoid precursor, [5-^{3}H]mevalonolactone (MVA) (20–40 Ci/mmol, DuPont/NEN, Boston, MA, or American Radiolabeled Chemicals, St. Louis, MO) (*see* **Note 2**).
2. Mevalonolactone (Sigma, St. Louis, MO). Dissolve in water to make a 0.5*M* solution, filter sterilize and store at –20°C.
3. (Optional) An inhibitor of cellular mevalonate synthesis, such as lovastatin *(43)* (*see* **Note 3**). We have obtained lovastatin from Merck Sharp and Dohme Research Laboratories, Rahway, NJ.

2.4. Subcellular Fractionation of Transfected Cells

1. Hanks balanced salt solution (HBSS) (Gibco-BRL).
2. Homogenization buffer (HB): 100 m*M* Tris-HCl, pH 7.4, 0.1 m*M* GDP, 1 m*M* $MgCl_2$, 50 m*M* NaF, 1 m*M* phenylmethylsulfonyl fluoride (PMSF).

2.5. Immunoprecipitation of [^{3}H]MVA-Labeled, Epitope-Tagged Rab Proteins from Membrane and Cytosolic Fractions

1. RIPA buffer: 100 m*M* Tris-HCl, pH 7.4, 2 m*M* EDTA, 0.1% (w/v) sodium dodecyl sulfate (SDS), 0.5% (w/v) sodium deoxycholate, 0.5% (v/v) Nonidet P-40. Dilute this stock with 100 m*M* Tris-HCl, pH 7.4, to obtain 1:5 RIPA buffer.

2. Monoclonal antibody 9E10 directed against the c-Myc epitope *(44)*. The antibody is available as c-Myc Ab-1 from Oncogene Science, Cambridge, MA. Alternatively, the antibody-secreting hybridoma cell line may be purchased from the American Type Culture Collection (ATCC CRL 1729).
3. Goat antimouse (GAM) IgG (Organon Teknika, Durham, NC).
4. Protein A-Sepharose CL-4B (Pierce, Rockford, IL).
5. PBS (*see* **Subheading 2.2.**).
6. SDS-sample buffer: 50 m*M* Tris-HCl, pH 6.8, 10% (v/v) β-mercaptoethanol, 2% (w/v) SDS, 30% (v/v) glycerol, 0.025% (w/v) bromophenol blue.

2.6. SDS Polyacrylamide Gel Electrophoresis (SDS-PAGE), Western Blotting, Fluorography and Immunodetection of Myc-Tagged Rab1B

1. Standard components for SDS-PAGE (e.g., acrylamide mix, SDS, vertical slab gel apparatus for running 1- to 1.5-mm-thick gels).
2. Polyvinylidene difluoride (PVDF) blotting membrane (Millipore, Bedford, MA).
3. Protein blotting equipment: We use the Trans-Blot cell from Bio-Rad (Hercules, CA).
4. Transfer buffer: 10 m*M* $NaHCO_3$, 3 m*M* Na_2CO_3, pH 9.8.
5. Methanol.
6. Buffer A: 50 m*M* Tris-HCl, pH 8.0, 2 m*M* $CaCl_2$, 80 m*M* NaCl.
7. Low-detergent blotto: Buffer A with 5% (w/v) nonfat dry milk and 0.2% v/v Nonidet P-40.
8. High-detergent blotto: Buffer A with 5% (w/v) nonfat dry milk, 2.0% (v/v) Nonidet P-40, and 0.2% (w/v) SDS.
9. Affinity-purified Rab1B polyclonal antibody (Zymed Laboratories, South San Francisco, CA).
10. ^{125}I-Labeled goat antirabbit IgG (2–10 μCi/μg, DuPont NEN).
11. A phosphorimager equipped with ImageQuant software (Molecular Dynamics, Sunnyvale, CA). Alternatively, quantitation of ^{3}H and ^{125}I may be accomplished with a scanning densitometer or a combination of a liquid scintillation counter (for ^{3}H) and γ-counter (for ^{125}I).

3. Methods

3.1. Epitope Tagging of Rab1B or Other Prenylated Proteins

We have found that many of the available polyclonal antibodies against prenylated GTP-binding proteins give variable results when applied in immunoprecipitation assays. By engineering a short Myc-epitope tag at the amino terminus of Rab1B or other prenylated proteins, it is possible to circumvent this problem by utilizing a commercially available anti-Myc monoclonal antibody to immunoprecipitate the tagged protein. Addition of the Myc epitope (MEQKLISEEDL) is easily accomplished by modifying the 5' end of the cDNA sequence encoding the protein of interest, using appropriate oligonucleotide primers (*see* **Subheading 2.1.**) and standard PCR techniques *(45)*. The Myc epitope tag does not interfere with the ability of Rab proteins to undergo geranylgeranylation in vitro or in vivo (Overmeyer, Wilson, Erdman, and Maltese, submitted). Moreover, addition of the Myc sequence is not known to alter the subcellular distribution of Rab proteins ***(46–48)*** or other Ras-related GTP-binding proteins ***(49)***.

The following protocol describes the engineering of the *rab1B* cDNA sequence to encode a Myc-tagged version of Rab1B. With minimal modifications, the same general approach could be used to tag other prenylated proteins for which cDNAs may be available.

1. Set up the following PCR reaction mix in a sterile 500-µL tube: 10 m*M* Tris-HCl, pH 8.3, 50 m*M* KCl, 10 m*M* $MgCl_2$, 0.8 m*M* dATP, 0.8 m*M* dCTP, 0.8 m*M* dGTP, 0.8 m*M* dTTP, and the 5' and 3' oligonucleotide primers (0.5 µg each), in a final volume of 25 µL.
2. Add one wax bead to the reaction mix, using sterile technique. Heat 5 min at 75°C to melt the wax. Cool to room temperature to allow the wax to harden.
3. On top of the wax layer add: 2.5 U *Taq* polymerase and 10 ng template DNA (pGEM3Z*rab1B*) in 13 m*M* Tris-HCl, pH 8.3, 67 m*M* KCl, in a total volume of 75 µL.
4. Amplify the DNA with a 1-min, 94°C melt; a 1-min, 55°C anneal; and a 1-min, 72°C extension, for 15–25 cycles, followed by a single final extension at 72°C 10 min.
5. Purify the resulting PCR product on an agarose gel ***(50)***.
6. Digest the PCR product with the appropriate restriction enzymes (in our case, *Eco*RI and *Xba*I) and insert the fragment into the pCMV vector, following standard cloning protocols ***(40,41)***.
7. Transform *E. coli* HB101 (or similar strain) with the resulting pCMV*(myc-rab1B)* plasmid ***(42)***.
8. Perform large-scale (maxiprep) isolation and purification of the pCMV*(myc-rab1B)* DNA, using standard protocols ***(50)*** or a commercially available kit (*see* **Subheading 2.1.**).
9. Confirm that PCR has not introduced changes into the DNA sequence encoding myc-Rab1B, using standard dideoxy-chain termination sequencing procedures ***(51,52)***.

3.2. Transfection of Human 293 Cells and Transient Expression of Myc-Tagged Rab1B

We have found that HEK293 cells efficiently and reproducibly overexpress Rab proteins when transfections are performed using the calcium phosphate precipitation procedure described by Gorman et al. ***(53)***.

1. The day before transfection, seed the HEK293 cells at 1.4×10^6 cells per 100-mm diameter tissue-culture dish in 10 mL DMEM with 10% (v/v) heat-inactivated FBS (*see* **Note 4**).

2. Three hours before transfection, feed the cells with 10 mL fresh medium with serum.
3. For each dish of cells, combine the following in a sterile, polypropylene tube: 550 µL 0.1X TE, 15 µg pCMV*(myc-rab1B)*, and 60 µL 2.5*M* $CaCl_2$.
4. Add 600 µL 2X HBSS to the tube and mix immediately by pipeting the solution in and out of a 1-mL sterile plastic pipet 5–10 times. The solution should appear turbid, but should not contain large clumps of precipitated material.
5. Add the entire volume of the DNA suspension to a 100-mm dish of HEK293 cells and mix immediately by gently swirling the medium.
6. Incubate the cells at 37°C in a humidified CO_2 incubator (10% CO_2) for 3 h.
7. Remove the medium and add 1.5 mL 15% glycerol in PBS. Incubate at room temperature for 30 s.
8. Remove the glycerol and wash the dish one time with 5 mL PBS.
9. Add 10 mL fresh medium with serum and return the culture to the incubator for 1 h prior to initiating the metabolic labeling step.

3.3. Metabolic Labeling of Prenylated Proteins in Cultured HEK293 Cells

1. Preparation of [^{3}H]MVA working stock: Allow 3 mL labeling medium per 100-mm dish, at 200 µCi [^{3}H]mevalonolactone (MVA) per mL (*see* **Note 2**). Place the appropriate amount of radiolabeled MVA (20–40 Ci/mmol) in a clean glass tube and evaporate any organic solvent under a gentle stream of N_2 under a vented fume hood. Immediately add sufficient unlabeled MVA (in a small volume of water), so that the final specific radioactivity of the [^{3}H]MVA is diluted to 2 Ci/mmol (*see* **Note 5**). Add 1 mL DMEM and filter-sterilize the solution by passing it through a 0.2-µ membrane. This constitutes the [^{3}H]MVA working stock. It can be refrigerated for several hours, but should not be stored for longer periods.
2. Remove the medium from each transfected culture 1 h after the glycerol shock. To each culture, add 3 mL of labeling medium: DMEM with 10% (v/v) FBS, 10 µ*M* lovastatin (optional; *see* **Notes 3** and **6**), and a total of 600 µCi [^{3}H]MVA, added from the working stock.
3. Incubate the transfected cells for 12–24 h (*see* **Note 7**) at 37°C with 10% CO_2.

3.4. Subcellular Fractionation of Transfected Cells

Prenylated Rab1B is localized in membranes of the ER and Golgi complex. The following procedure was developed to study the distribution of this protein between the cytosol and the total intracellular membrane fraction. Depending on the known or suspected distribution of other prenylated proteins, alternate fractionation procedures may be used to isolate specific membrane components or organelles.

1. Carefully remove the medium containing the [^{3}H]MVA. Particular care should be taken not to shake cultures that have been treated with lovastatin, since these cells tend to be easily dislodged from the surface of the dish. Gently scrape the cells into 5 mL HBSS with a rubber policeman, and transfer the suspension into

a 15-mL polystyrene conical tube. If necessary, cells from multiple dishes may be pooled (*see* **Note 4**).

2. Centrifuge the cells at 400*g* for 5 min and wash them at least two times with HBSS (5–10 mL) by sequential resuspension and centrifugation. The final cell pellet should be suspended in 525 μL HB and transferred to a 1.5-mL conical microfuge tube.
3. Gently homogenize the cells, while keeping the tube in an ice bath. We use a battery-operated, hand-held homogenizer with a pestle designed to fit into 1.5-mL microfuge tubes (available from VWR Scientific, Bridgeport, NJ). Remove 25 μL of the homogenate to assay for total expressed Myc-Rab1B protein. Add 225 μL sample buffer to this aliquot and store at –20°C.
4. Centrifuge the cell homogenate for 5 min at 500*g*, 4°C, to remove nuclei and unbroken cells (P1). This fraction may also contain cell membranes and organelles.
5. Transfer the low-speed supernatant (S1) to a Beckman polycarbonate 11 × 34 mm tube and centrifuge the sample for 30 min at 100,000*g*, 4°C, in a Beckman TLA 100 centrifuge, using the 100.2 rotor. The resulting cytosolic fraction (S2) and high-speed membrane pellet (P2) are used to analyze the distribution of prenylated Myc-tagged Rab1B, as described in **Subheadings 3.5.** and **3.6.**

3.5. Immunoprecipitation of [^{3}H]MVA-Labeled, Epitope-Tagged Rab Proteins from Membrane and Cytosolic Fractions

1. In a 1.5-mL microfuge tube, add 300 μL HB and 200 μL RIPA buffer to the cytosolic fraction (approx 500 μL).
2. Add 200 μL RIPA buffer to the P2 membrane fraction and homogenize the membrane pellet as described (*see* **Subheading 3.4., step 3**). Dilute the membrane suspension with 800 μL HB.
3. To immunoprecipitate the expressed Myc-Rab1B from the foregoing cytosolic and membrane fractions, add 5 μg of c-*myc* antibody to each fraction. Incubate for 2 h at 4°C with gentle mixing (we use an end-over-end rotator). To collect the immune complexes, add 50 μL protein A-Sepharose/GAM IgG slurry (*see* **Note 8**) to each tube and continue the incubation for 1 h.
4. Collect the Sepharose beads by centrifuging the samples 5 min at 3000*g*. Wash each pellet once with 500 μL RIPA buffer, twice with 1:5 RIPA buffer, and once with PBS.
5. Add 100 μL SDS sample buffer to each washed pellet and elute the immune complex containing the Myc-tagged Rab1B protein by boiling for 5 min. Centrifuge at 3,000*g* and remove the supernatant solution. At this point, the samples maybe stored at –20°C overnight, if desired.

3.6. Detection and Quantitation of Prenylated Rab1B Proteins

1. Resolve the samples containing the immunoprecipitated Myc-tagged Rab1B proteins (*see* **Subheading 3.5., step 5**) on a 12% SDS-polyacrylamide gel, using standard electrophoresis techniques ***(54)***. On a separate gel, run the samples that were removed from cell homogenates (*see* **Subheading 3.4., step 3**) to confirm

that the Myc-tagged proteins were expressed in each culture. Transfer the proteins from the gels to a PVDF membrane using standard techniques *(55)*. We keep the blotting apparatus at 4°C and transfer the proteins overnight at a constant current of 100 mA, using the transfer buffer described in **Subheading 2.6., step 4**.

2. The PVDF membrane is air-dried for several hours and the [^{3}H]MVA-labeled (i.e., prenylated) Myc-Rab1B proteins are detected by exposing the membrane to the tritium screen supplied with the Molecular Dynamics phosphorimager for 4–5 d. The screen is scanned with the phosphorimager and the tritium signal is quantitated with the ImageQuant software. Alternative approaches for detecting and quantitating the tritium-labeled protein are discussed in **Note 9**. Appropriate controls to correct for nonspecific background recovery of tritium in the immunoprecipitates are discussed in **Note 10**.
3. To correct for possible variations in recovery of Myc-tagged Rab1B in the immunoprecipitates, the same membrane that was scanned for tritium in **step 2** can be immunoblotted with a polyclonal antibody against Rab1B (*see* **Note 11**). Each tritium value can then be normalized to the amount of immunodetectable Rab1B (bound ^{125}I-labeled secondary IgG) in the corresponding region of the blot.
   a. Wet the membrane by briefly dipping it in methanol. Rinse thoroughly in buffer A.
   b. Block the membrane in low-detergent blotto for 1 h.
   c. Dilute the polyclonal antibody to Rab1B 1:1000 (v/v) in high-detergent blotto and incubate with the membrane for 2 h.
   d. Wash the membrane three times with high-detergent blotto (10 min per wash), then incubate the membrane for 1 h with ^{125}I-labeled goat antirabbit IgG, diluted to 0.45 μCi/mL in high-detergent blotto.
   e. Wash the membrane as in **step d**. Rinse two times briefly with buffer A. Wash two times for 5 min with buffer A. Air-dry the membrane for several hours and quantitate the amount of bound ^{125}I-IgG in the region of Myc-Rab1B (27–28 kDa) by phosphorimager analysis. Alternatively, the blot may be exposed to preflashed X-ray film (e.g., Kodak X-Omat AR) and the ^{125}I signal quantitated, either by scanning the film with a densitometer or excising the segment of the blot containing the Rab protein and counting it in a γ-counter.
4. The [^{3}H]MVA incorporation values obtained in **step 2** are corrected for any nonspecific radioactivity recovered in the immunoprecipitates by subtracting appropriate background values (*see* **Note 10**). A ratio can then be formed between each corrected [^{3}H]MVA incorporation value and the corresponding value for immunodetectable Rab1B in the same sample (bound ^{125}I-IgG, determined in **step 3**). This ratio provides an indication of the relative amount of prenylated Myc-Rab1B versus total Myc-Rab1B in each sample (*see* **Note 12**).

4. Notes

1. The 5' oligonucleotide primer described in **Subheading 2.1., step 2**, was designed with a 5' cap consisting of six bp, followed sequentially by *Eco*RI and *Nde*I restriction sites, the sequence encoding the *myc* epitope tag, and six codons

homologous to the 5' end of the *rab1B* cDNA sequence (minus the initial ATG). The ATG in the *Nde*I site is also the first codon of the *myc* tag and serves to encode the initiator methionine for the tagged protein. The 3' primer complements the last eight codons of the *rab1B* cDNA sequence, and incorporates additional sequence containing *Bam*HI and *Xba*I restriction sites. The restriction sites in both of the primers were designed to facilitate cloning of the *myc-rab1B* DNA construct into the mammalian expression vector, pCMV5, as well as other vectors.

2. Mevalonic acid rapidly reverts to the lactone form in neutral or mildly acidic aqueous solutions and is readily internalized by living cells. Hence, for metabolic labeling studies, mevalonolactone is customarily used instead of mevalonic acid.
3. Lovastatin is a competitive inhibitor of 3-hydroxy-3-methylglutaryl-CoA reductase ***(43)***, the enzyme that catalyzes the biosynthesis of mevalonate. When lovastatin is used to block mevalonate synthesis in cultured cells, the specific radioactivity of the intracellular pool of mevalonate (and its farnesyl-PP and geranylgeranyl-PP derivatives) is increased, since the exogenously supplied [^{3}H]MVA then constitutes the primary carbon source for isoprenoid biogenesis. This greatly facilitates subsequent detection of prenylated proteins. However, in transfected cells in which specific proteins are transiently overexpressed for 12–48 h, incorporation of [^{3}H]MVA into the expressed protein usually can be detected without blocking cellular MVA synthesis. Hence, we list the addition of lovastatin during the metabolic labeling procedure as an optional step.
4. We have found that some point mutations in *rab1B* (for example, mutations that alter guanine–nucleotide binding properties) may result in lower levels of protein expression in HEK293 cells. Therefore, to ensure that readily detectable amounts of [^{3}H]MVA-labeled Myc-tagged protein are immunoprecipitated from cells transfected with these constructs, we have found it useful to perform the transfection and [^{3}H]MVA-labeling in triplicate and then pool the cells from three parallel cultures prior to the subcellular fractionation.
5. Because isoprenoid biosynthesis is required for cell viability, it should be noted that when lovastatin is used, sufficient extracellular [^{3}H]MVA (50–100 μ*M*) must be provided to support the continued production of essential isoprenoids. This is why the high specific activity commercial preparations of [^{3}H]mevalonolactone must be diluted with unlabeled mevalonolactone prior to addition to the medium (*see* **Subheading 3.3., step 1**).
6. To prepare a 10.8 m*M* stock solution of lovastatin, suspend 30 mg in 0.6 mL of absolute ethanol and warm in a 50°C water bath until the solution is clear. Add 0.3 mL 0.6*N* NaOH and 6.0 mL PBS. Incubate at room temperature for 30 min. Adjust the pH to 7.5 by addition of a few microliters of 5*N* HCl. Filter-sterilize the solution by passage through a 0.2-μ membrane and store in 1.0-mL aliquots at –20°C.
7. Optimal times for transient expression of proteins in transfected HEK293 cells will vary. For the Myc-tagged Rab1B, we have seen the highest rates of protein accumulation during the interval between 12 and 24 h after transfection.
8. To prepare the protein A-Sepharose beads, suspend 0.5 g of dry beads in 10 mL 1 m*M* HCl and incubate 15 min at room temperature. Wash the beads in a funnel

with a sintered glass filter, first with 100 mL 1 m*M* HCl, then four times with 25 mL 1 m*M* HCl. Wash one time with 50 mL PBS. Suspend the beads in 1.0 mL PBS. Add 1 mg GAM IgG in 0.5 mL PBS, to bring the total volume to 1.5 mL PBS. Incubate 2 h, 4°C, with gentle mixing. Wash the Sepharose beads three times with PBS. Resuspend the pellet in 1.5 mL PBS, 0.02% (w/v) sodium azide.

9. If a phosphorimager is not available, an alternate protocol may be followed: Subject nine-tenths of the sample (90 µL) to SDS-PAGE, permeate the gel with fluorography reagent (e.g., Amplify, Amersham), dry the gel, and expose the dried gel to preflashed X-ray film in a cassette, with an intensifying screen (e.g., DuPont Quanta III), for 10 d or longer. The tritium bands on the resulting fluorogram can be quantitated with a scanning densitometer. The fluorogram can also be used to localize the prenylated protein in the dried gel. The appropriate sections of the dried gel may then be excised, solubilized by overnight incubation in 30% H_2O_2 (0.5 mL/cm^2 of gel), mixed with scintillation fluid, and counted in a liquid scintillation spectrometer. The remaining one-tenth of the sample (10 µL) should be electrophoresed on a separate gel and the proteins transferred to PVDF membrane, followed by immunodetection and quantitation of bound ^{125}I-IgG as described in **Subheading 3.6., step 3**.
10. [^{3}H]MVA will be incorporated into many prenylated proteins besides the Myc-tagged protein of interest. Although immunoprecipitation with the anti-Myc monoclonal antibody effectively isolates the prenylated Myc-tagged protein from other endogenous proteins in HEK293 cells, it is important to control for any nonspecific tritium that may be collected in the immunoprecipitates. An ideal control is a parallel culture transfected with the same expression vector (pCMV5) encoding a mutant Myc-tagged protein that lacks the carboxyl-terminal cysteines, which normally serve as acceptors for the prenyl groups (e.g., Myc-Rab1B$^{\Delta CC}$). Alternatively, if such a construct is not available, a parallel culture transfected with expression vector without an insert can be used. The control culture should be labeled with [^{3}H]MVA and the cells subjected to all of the fractionation, immunoprecipitation, electrophoresis, and blotting procedures. Any tritium detected in the region of the blot (or gel) where Myc-Rab1B (or other Myc-tagged protein of interest) would be found should be considered as background.
11. We use a rabbit polyclonal antibody against Rab1B for this step, because the immunoprecipitated Myc-Rab1B sample contains significant quantities of the mouse anti-Myc monoclonal antibody and GAM IgG (from the Sepharose beads). Thus, using the anti-Myc monoclonal antibody (or any other mouse antibody) and ^{125}I-labeled GAM IgG for this immunoblotting step would result in a high background in the 25–30 kDa region of the blot, because of the presence of the crossreacting mouse IgG light chains.
12. We have found that the relative amount of [^{3}H]MVA incorporated per unit of immunodetectable Myc-Rab1B is substantially higher in samples derived from the membrane fraction, compared to those derived from the cytosol. This is because much of the expressed Myc-Rab1B in the cytosol from transfected HEK293 cells is not posttranslationally modified. Thus, it is important to empha-

size that this procedure does not provide an accurate indication of the stoichiometry of protein prenylation. Rather, the value of the approach lies principally in its ability to track the partitioning of the prenylated (i.e., [^{3}H]MVA-labeled) pool of expressed protein between membrane and soluble compartments, in response to structural alterations or physiological manipulations that may affect its interactions with accessory proteins or membranes.

References

1. Glomset, J. A., Gelb, M. H., and Farnsworth, C. C. (1990) Prenyl proteins ineukaryotic cells: a new type of membrane anchor. *Trends Biochem. Sci.* **15,** 139–142.
2. Buss, J. E., Quilliam, L. A., Kato, K. ,Casey, P.J., S., P.A., Wong, G., Clark, R., McCormick, F., Bokoch, G. M., and Der, C. J. (1991) The COOH-terminal domain of the rap1A(Krev-1) protein is isoprenylated and supports transformation by an Hras:rap1A chimeric protein. *Mol. Cell Biol.* **11,** 1523–1530.
3. Epstein, W. W., Lever, D., Leining, L. M., Bruenger, E., and Rilling, H. C. (1991) Quantitation of prenylcysteines by a selective cleavage reaction. *Proc. Natl. Acad. Sci. USA* **88,** 9668–9670.
4. Farnsworth, C. C., Wolda, S. L., Gelb, M. H., and Glomset, J. A. (1989) Human lamin B contains a farnesylated cysteine residue. *J. Biol. Chem.* **64,** 20,422–20,429.
5. Hancock, J. F., Magee, A. I., Childs, J. E., and Marshall, C. J. (1989) All ras proteins are polyisoprenylated but only some are palmitoylated. *Cell* **57,** 1167–1177.
6. Casey, P., Solski, P. A., Der, C. J., and Buss, J. E. (1989) p21ras is modified by a farnesyl isoprenoid. *Proc. Natl. Acad. Sci. USA* **86,** 8323–8327.
7. Yamane, H. K., Farnsworth, C. C., Xie, H., Howald, W., Fung, B. K. K., Clarke, S., Gelb, M. H., and Glomset, J. A. (1990) Brain G-protein (gamma) subunits contain an all-trans-geranylgeranyl-cysteine methylester at their carboxyl termini. *Proc. Natl. Acad. Sci. USA* **87,** 5868–5872.
8. Mumby, S. M., Casey, P. J., Gilman, A. G., Gutawoski, S., and Sternweis, P. C. (1990) G-protein (gamma) subunits contain a twenty-carbon isoprenoid. *Proc. Natl. Acad. Sci. USA* **87,** 5873–5877.
9. Kinsella, B. T., Erdman, R. A., and Maltese, W. A. (1991) Carboxyl-terminalisoprenylation of ras-related GTP-binding proteins encoded by rac1, rac2, and ralA. *J. Biol. Chem.* **266,** 9786–9794.
10. Kawata, M., Farnsworth, C. C., Yoshida, Y., Gelb, M. H., Glomset, J. A., and Takai, Y. (1990) Posttranslationally processed structure of the human platelet protein smg p21B: evidence for geranylgeranylation and carboxyl methylation of the C-terminal cysteine. *Proc. Natl. Acad. Sci. USA* **87,** 8960–8964.
11. Hori, Y., Kikuchi, A., Isomura, M., Katayama, M., Miura, Y., Fujioka, H., Kaibuchi, K., and Takai, Y. (1991) Posttranslational modifications of the C-terminal region of the rho protein are important for its interaction with membranes and the stimulatory and inhibitory GDP/GTP exchange proteins. *Oncogene* **6,** 515–522.

12. Adamson, P., Marshall, C. J., Hall, A., and Tilbrook, P. A. (1992) Post-translational modifications of p21^{rho} proteins. *J. Biol. Chem.* **267,** 20,033–20,038.
13. Kinsella, B. T. and Maltese, W. A. (1991) rab GTP-binding proteins implicated in vesicular transport are isoprenylated in vitro at cysteines within a novel carboxyl-terminal motif. *J. Biol. Chem.* **266,** 8540–8544.
14. Khosravi-Far, R., Lutz, R. J., Cox, A. D., Conroy, L., Bourne, J. R., Sinensky, M., Balch, W. E., Buss, J. E., and Der, C. J. (1991) Isoprenoid modification of rab proteins terminating in CC or CXC motifs. *Proc. Natl. Acad. Sci. USA* **88,** 6264–6268.
15. Kinsella, B. T. and Maltese, W. A. (1992) rab GTP-binding proteins with three different carboxyl-terminal cysteine motifs are modified in vivo by 20-carbon isoprenoids. *J. Biol. Chem.* **267,** 3940–3945.
16. Reiss, Y., Goldstein, J. L., Seabra, M. C., Casey, P. J., and Brown, M. S. (1990) Inhibition of purified p21^{ras} farnesyl:protein transferase by Cys-AAX tetrapeptides. *Cell* **62,** 81–88.
17. Moomaw, J. F. and Casey, P. J. (1992) Mammalian protein geranylgeranyltransferase. *J. Biol. Chem.* **267,** 17,438–17,443.
18. Armstrong, S. A., Seabra, M. C., Sudhof, T. C., Goldstein, J. L., and Brown, M. S. (1993) cDNA cloning and expression of the alpha and beta subunits of rat Rab geranylgeranyl transferase. *J. Biol. Chem.* **268,** 12,221–12,229.
19. Andres, D. A., Seabra, M. C., Brown, M. S., Armstrong, S. A., Smeland, T. E., Cremers, F. P. M., and Goldstein, J. L. (1993) cDNA cloning of component A of rab geranylgeranyl transferase and demonstration of its role as a rab escort protein. *Cell* **73,** 1091–1099.
20. Silvius, J. R. and l'Heureux, F. (1994) Fluorimetric evaluation of the affinities of isoprenylated peptides for lipid bilayers. *Biochemistry* **33,** 3014–3022.
21. Marshall, C. J. (1993) Protein prenylation: A mediator of protein-protein interactions. *Science* **259,** 1865–1866.
22. Maltese, W. A. and Sheridan, K. M. (1987) Isoprenylated proteins in cultured cells: subcellular distribution and changes related to altered morphology and growth arrest induced by mevalonate deprivation. *J. Cell Physiol.* **133,** 471–481.
23. Maltese, W. A., Sheridan, K. M., Repko, E. M., and Erdman, R. A. (1990) Post-translational modification of low molecular mass GTP-binding proteins by isoprenoid. *J. Biol. Chem.* **265,** 2148–2155.
24. Simons, K. and Zerial, M. (1993) Rab proteins and the road maps for intracellular transport. *Neuron* **11,** 789–799.
25. Tisdale, E. J., Bourne, J. R., Khosravi-Far, R., Der, C. J., and Balch, W. E. (1992) GTP-binding mutants of rab1 and rab2 are potent inhibitors of vesicular transport from the endoplasmic reticulum to the Golgi complex. *J. Cell Biol.* **119,** 749–761.
26. Dugan, J. M., deWit, C., McConlogue, L., and Maltese, W. A. (1995) The ras-related GTP binding protein, Rab1B, regulates early steps in exocytic transport and processing of β-amyloid precursor protein. *J. Biol. Chem.* **270,** 10,982–10,989.
27. Plutner, H., Cox, A. D., Pind, S., Khosravi-Far, R., Bourne, J., Schwaninger, R., Der, C. J., and Balch, W. E. (1991) Rab1b regulates vesicular transport between the endoplasmic reticulum and successive Golgi compartments. *J. Cell Biol.* **115,** 31–43.

28. Pfeffer, S. R. (1994) Rab GTPases: master regulators of membrane trafficking. *Curr. Opin. Cell Biol.* **6,** 522–526.
29. Ferro-Novick, S. and Novick, P. (1993) The role of GTP-binding proteins in transport along the exocytic pathway. *Annu. Rev. Cell Biol.* **9,** 575–599.
30. Nuoffer, C. and Balch, W. E. (1994) GTPases: Multifunctional molecular switches regulating vesicular traffic. *Annu. Rev. Biochem.* **63,** 949–990.
31. Overmeyer, J. H. and Maltese, W. A. (1992) Isoprenoid requirement for intracellular transport and processing of murine leukemia virus envelope protein. *J. Biol. Chem.* **267,** 22,686–22,692.
32. Peter, M., Chavrier, P., Nigg, E. A., and Zerial, M. (1992) Isoprenylation of rab proteins on structurally distinct cysteine motifs. *J. Cell Sci.* **102,** 857–865.
33. Musha, T., Kawata, M., and Takai, Y. (1992) The geranylgeranyl moiety but not the methyl moiety of the smg25A/rab3A protein is essential for the interactions with membrane and its inhibitory GDP/GTP exchange protein. *J. Biol. Chem.* **267,** 9821–9825.
34. Soldati, T., Riederer, M. A., and Pfeffer, S. R. (1993) Rab GDI: A solubilizing and recycling factor for rab9 protein. *Mol. Biol. Cell* **4,** 425–434.
35. Wilson, A. L. and Maltese, W. A. (1993) Isoprenylation of rab1B is impaired by mutations in its effector domain. *J. Biol. Chem.* **268,** 14,561–14,564.
36. Vielh, E., Touchot, N., Zahraoui, A., and Tavitian, A. (1989) Nucleotide sequence of a rat cDNA: Rab1B, encoding a Rab1-YPT related protein. *Nucleic Acids Res.* **17,** 1770.
37. Voytas, D. (1989) in *Current Protocols in Molecular Biology* (Ausubel, F. M., Brent, R., Kingston, R. E., Moore, D. D., Seidman, J. G., Smith, J. A., and Struhl, K., eds.), Greene Publishing Associates and Wiley-Interscience, New York, pp. 2.5.1–2.5.9.
38. Selden, R. F. and Chory, J. (1989) in *Current Protocols in Molecular Biology* (Ausubel, F. M., Brent, R., Kingston, R. E., Moore, D. D., Seidman, J. G., Smith, J. A., and Struhl, K., eds.), Greene Publishing Associates and Wiley-Interscience, New York, pp. 2.6.1–2.6.8.
39. Andersson, S., Davis, D. L., Dahlback, H., Jornvall, H., and Russell, D. W. (1989) Cloning, structure, and expression of the mitochondrial cytochrome P-450 sterol 26-hydroxylase, a bile acid biosynthetic enzyme. *J. Biol. Chem.* **264,** 8222–8229.
40. Bloch, K. D. and Bartos, B. (1989) in *Current Protocols in Molecular Biology* (Ausubel, F. M., Brent, R., Kingston, R. E., Moore, D. D., Seidman, J. G., Smith, J. A., and Struhl, K., eds.), Greene Publishing Associates and Wiley-Interscience, New York, pp. 3.1.1–3.1.9.
41. Struhl, K. (1989) in *Current Protocols in Molecular Biology* (Ausubel, F. M., Brent, R., Kingston, R. E., Moore, D. D., Seidman, J. G., Smith, J. A., and Struhl, K., eds.), Greene Publishing Associates and Wiley-Interscience, New York, pp. 3.16.1–3.16.11.
42. Seidman, C. E., Struhl, K., and Sheen, J. (1989) in *Current Protocols in Molecular Biology* (Ausubel, F. M., Brent, R., Kingston, R. E., Moore, D. D., Seidman, J. G., Smith, J. A., and Struhl, K., eds.), Greene Publishing Associates and Wiley-Interscience, New York, pp. 1.8.1–1.8.8.

43. Alberts, A. W., Chen, J., Kuron, G., Hunt, V., Huff, J., Hoffman, C., Rothrock, J., Lopez, M., Joshua, H., Harris, E., Patchett, A., Monoghan, R., Currie, S., Stapley, E., Albers-Schonberg, G., Hensens, O., Hirshfield, J., Hoogsteen, K., Liesch, J., and Springer, J. (1980) Mevinolin: a highly potent competitive inhibitor of 3-hydroxy-3-methylglutaryl coenzyme A reductase and a cholesterol-lowering agent. *Proc. Natl. Acad. Sci. USA* **77,** 3957–3961.
44. Evan, G. I., Lewis, G. K., Ramsay, G., and Bishop, J. M. (1985) Isolation of monoclonal antibodies specific for the human c-myc proto-oncogene product. *Mol. Cell. Biol.* **5,** 3610–3616.
45. Delidow, B. C., Lynch, J. P., Peluso, J. J., and White, B. A. (1993) in *PCR Protocols: Current Methods and Applications* (White, B. A., ed.), Humana, Totowa, NJ pp. 1–29.
46. Chen, Y. T., Holcomb, C., and Moor, H. P. H. (1993) Expression and localization of two low molecular weight GTP-binding proteins, Rab8 and Rab10, by epitope tag. *Proc. Natl. Acad. Sci. USA* **90,** 6508–6512.
47. Beranger, F., Cadwallader, K., Profiri, E., Powers, S., Evans, T., de Gunzberg, J., and Hancock, J. F. (1994) Determination of structural requirements for the interaction of Rab6 with RabGDI and Rab geranylgeranyltransferase. *J. Biol. Chem.* **269,** 13,637–13,643.
48. Brondyk, W. H., McKiernan, C. J., Burstein, E. S., and Macara, I. G. (1993) Mutants of rab3A analogous to oncogenic ras mutants. *J. Biol. Chem.* **268,** 9410–9415.
49. Adamson, P., Paterson, H. F., and Hall, A. (1992) Intracellular localization of P21rho proteins. *J. Cell Biol.* **119,** 617–627.
50. Wilson, K. (1989) in *Current Protocols in Molecular Biology* (Ausubel, F. M., Brent, R., Kinston, R. E., Moore, D. D., Seidman, J. G., Smith, J. A., and Struhl, K., eds.), Greene Publishing Associates and Wiley-Interscience, New York, pp. 2.4.1–2.4.5.
51. Sanger, F., Niklen, S., and Coulson, A. R. (1977) DNA Sequencing with Chain-Terminating Inhibitors. *Proc. Natl. Acad. Sci. USA* **74,** 5463–5467.
52. Slatko, B. E., Albright, L. M., and Tabor, S. (1989) in *Current Protocols in Molecular Biology* (Ausubel, F. M., Brent, R., Kingston, R. E., Moore, D. D., Seidman, J. G., Smith, J. A., and Struhl, K., eds.), Greene Publishing Associates and Wiley-Interscience, New York, pp. 7.4.1–7.4.27.
53. Gorman, C. M., Gies, D. R., and McCray, G. (1990) Transient production of proteins using an adenovirus transformed cell line. *DNA Protein Eng. Techniques* **2,** 3–10.
54. Laemmli, U. K. (1970) Cleavage of structural proteins during the assembly of the head of bacteriophage T4. *Nature* **227,** 680–685.
55. Towbin, H., Staehlin, T., and Gordon, J. (1979) Electrophoretic transfer of proteins from polyacrylamide gels to nitrocellulose sheets: procedure and some applications. *Proc. Natl. Acad. Sci. USA* **76,** 4350–4354.

20

Nuclear Protein Import in a Permeabilized Cell Assay

Frauke Melchior

1. Introduction

An in vitro nuclear import assay, using digitonin-permeabilized cells, grown on cover slips, and supplemented with exogenous cytosol and fluorescent-transport ligand, was developed in our laboratory several years ago *(1)*. For a general introduction into this technique and references for alternative assays developed by other laboratories, *see* **refs.** *2* and *3*. Although the original assay faithfully reproduces transport, quantitation by methods such as densitometry on photographic negatives or ACAS (anchored cell analysis and sorting) interactive laser cytometry is a rather time-consuming process. Another disadvantage of the original assay involving attached cells is that the number of cells per assay cannot easily be controlled. Both problems are circumvented by using a modification of the import assay recently developed by Paschal and Gerace *(4)*, and described in detail below. Here, suspension cells are used as the source for permeable cells, and relative transport rates are determined rapidly by flow cytometry (an ELISA-based quantitative assay that allows determination of molar transport rates is described in **ref.** *5*).

A general outline of the assay described in this chapter is given below. Although we use HeLa cells and an artificial ligand containing the simian virus 40 (SV40) large T antigen nuclear localization signal (NLS) *(6)*, this protocol can easily be adapted for other cell types, different cytosol sources, or different artificial or natural transport ligands.

HeLa cells, grown in suspension, are treated with digitonin that selectively permeabilizes the plasma membrane *(7)*. Because the cells lose many of their cytosolic components during this treatment and the following washing steps, they are unable to support nuclear-protein import in this assay, unless exog-

From: *Methods in Molecular Biology, Vol. 88: Protein Targeting Protocols*
Edited by: R. A. Clegg Humana Press Inc., Totowa, NJ

enous cytosol and an ATP regenerating system are added. The transport ligand is FITC-labeled bovine serum albumin (BSA) that is conjugated to synthetic peptides containing the SV40 large T antigen NLS (CGGGPKKKRKVED). During the transport reaction, a fraction of this ligand accumulates in the nuclei of the cells. After transport, the cells are washed once in a large volume and the remaining intranuclear fluorescence is measured by flow cytometry (FACS) for 10^4 cells per sample.

2. Materials

2.1. HeLa Suspension Cells

1. HeLa cells adapted for continuous growth in suspension, e.g., HeLaS3.
2. HeLa medium: Joklik's modified minimal essential medium (Gibco-BRL, Gaithersburg, MD), 10% newborn calf serum, 20 m*M* HEPES, pH 7.2, penicillin/streptomycin.
3. Several Micro carrier flasks (Bellco Glass, Vineland, NJ), e.g., 2 × 300-mL, 1 × 1-L and 3 × 3-L flasks.

2.2. Preparation of Cytosol

1. PBS: 10 m*M* Na_2HPO_4/NaH_2PO_4, pH 7.4, 140 m*M* NaCl.
2. Washing buffer: 10 m*M* HEPES, pH 7.3, 110 m*M* KOAc, 2 m*M* $Mg(OAc)_2$, 2 m*M* dithiothreitol (DTT).
3. Lysis buffer: 5 m*M* HEPES, pH 7.3, 10 m*M* KOAc, 2 m*M* $Mg(OAc)_2$, 2 m*M* DTT, 1 m*M* PMSF, 1 μg/mL each of aprotinin, leupeptin, and pepstatin.
4. Transport buffer (TB): 110 m*M* KOAc, 20 m*M* HEPES, pH 7.3, 2 m*M* $Mg(OAc)_2$, 1 m*M* EGTA, 2 m*M* DTT, 1 m*M* PMSF, 1 μg/mL of each leupeptin, pepstatin, and aprotinin.
5. 40-mL tight-fitting stainless steel dounce homogenizer (Wheaton Industries, Millville, NJ).
6. Collodion membrane apparatus and Colloidon membranes, 8 mL vol, mol wt cutoff 10,000 (Schleicher and Schuell, Keene, NH).

2.3. Preparation of FITC-Labeled Transport Ligand

1. NLS peptide: Synthetic peptide containing the SV40 large T antigen wild-type nuclear localization signal (CGGGPKKKRKVED).
2. 1% Acetic acid.
3. Sephadex G10 column (10-mL bed vol, 1-cm diameter).
4. 50 m*M* HEPES, pH 7.0.
5. DTT.
6. Ellmann buffer: 0.1*M* sodium phosphate buffer, pH 7.4, 5 m*M* EDTA.
7. Ellmann's reagent: 1 m*M* dithiobisnitrobenzoic acid in methanol.
8. BSA: BSA (fatty acid free; Boehringer Mannheim, Indianapolis, IN).
9. FITC: 10 mg/mL FITC isomer I (Molecular Probes, Eugene, OR) in DMF, prepare directly before use.
10. Coupling buffer: 0.1*M* $NaHCO_3$, pH 9.0.

11. PBS: 10 mM Na_2HPO_4/NaH_2PO_4, pH 7.4, 140 mM NaCl.
12. SMCC: 20 mM Sulfo-SMCC (Pierce, Rockford, IL) in DMSO, prepare directly before use.
13. PD10 column (prepacked G25 column [10-mL bed vol], Pharmacia Biotech, Piscataway, NJ).

2.4. Transport Assay

1. HeLa cells: 1–2 mL Hela suspension cells per sample at a density of 4–6 × 10^5 cells/mL (*see* **Subheading 3.1.**).
2. Cytosol: 10 mg/mL cytosol in transport buffer (*see* **Subheading 3.2.**).
3. Fluorescent transport ligand: 1 mg/mL FITC conjugated, NLS containing BSA in transport buffer (*see* **Subheading 3.3.**).
4. Transport buffer (TB): 20 mM HEPES, pH 7.3, 110 mM KOAc, 2 mM $Mg(OAc)_2$, 1 mM EGTA, 2 mM DTT, 1 µg/mL of each leupeptin, pepstatin, and aprotinin.
5. Digitonin aliquots: 10% stock of high purity digitonin (Calbiochem-Behring, San Diego, CA) in DMSO; stored at –20°C.
6. Trypan blue (vital stain; Sigma, St. Louis, MO).
7. Creatine phosphate (CP): 80 mg/mL stock in water; stored at –20°C.
8. ATP aliquots: 100 mM stock in 20 mM HEPES, pH 7.4, 100 mM $Mg(OAc)_2$, pH titrated with NaOH; stored at –20°C.
9. Creatine phosphate kinase (CPK): 2000 U/mL in 50% glycerol, 20 mM HEPES, pH 7.4; stored at –20°C.
10. ATP regenerating system: a freshly prepared mixture of ATP:CP:CPK at a ratio of 2:2:1.
11. Clear 6-mL reaction tubes, 12 × 75 mm (Falcon tubes; Becton Dickinson, Lincoln Park, NJ).
12. 37% Formaldehyde.

3. Methods

3.1. HeLa Suspension Cells

1. For nuclear protein import assays (*see* **Subheading 3.4.**), maintain a continuously growing culture of Suspension HeLa cells that has a density of approx 4–7 × 10^5 cells/mL during the day. For this, grow cells in HeLa medium at 37°C in closed micro carrier flasks, with mixing at 30–50 rpm (*see* **Note 1**). Dilute cells every night with approx 1.5 vol HeLa medium to a density of 2–3 × 10^5 cells/mL (for counting of cells, use Hemocytometer).
2. For preparation of cytosol (*see* **Subheading 3.2.**), grow up 8 L HeLa cells to a density of 5–8 × 10^5 cells/mL (starting with 100 mL culture at 5 × 10^5 cells/mL this should take approx 6 d).

3.2. Preparation of HeLa Cytosol

We routinely prepare cytosol from 8-L HeLa suspension cells, which normally yield 25–30 mL cytosol with a protein concentration of ~10 mg/mL. However, this protocol can easily be adjusted for 1- to 16-L suspension cells.

Unless stated otherwise, all buffers are ice cold and procedures are carried out on ice or at 4°C. Protease inhibitor peptides, DTT, and PMSF are added to the buffers directly before use.

1. Harvest cells from 8 L HeLa culture at a density of 5–8 × 10^5 cells/mL by centrifugation at 250*g* for 10 min at 4°C in a Beckman JS5.2 rotor.
2. Wash the cells twice in ice-cold PBS, and once in ice-cold washing buffer by resuspension and centrifugation.
3. Resuspend the cell pellet in an equal volume of the hypotonic lysis buffer and let the cells swell on ice for 10 min.
4. Lyse the cells by five strokes in a 40-mL, tight-fitting, stainless steel dounce homogenizer (*see* **Note 2**).
5. Centrifuge the resulting homogenate at 1500*g* for 15 min at 4°C to remove cell debris and nuclei.
6. Centrifuge the supernatant first at 15,000*g* for 20 min in a Beckman JA20 rotor and subsequently at 100,000*g* for 1 h in a Beckman 70.1 Ti rotor.
7. Dialyze the final supernatant for 3 h with a collodion membrane apparatus (*see* **Note 3**) against three changes of transport buffer; if necessary, concentrate in the same apparatus to a final concentration of 10 mg/mL, and freeze in 200 μL aliquots in liquid nitrogen prior to storage at –80°C (*see* **Note 4**).

3.3. Preparation of FITC-Labeled Transport Ligand

Ligand is prepared in two steps: First BSA is conjugated with FITC (*see* **Subheading 3.3.2.**); subsequently peptides containing the wild-type SV40 nuclear localization sequence are coupled to FITC-BSA via their N-terminal cysteine (*see* **Subheading 3.3.3.**). Since the sulfhydryl group in the peptide tends to get oxidized, it might be necessary to pretreat the peptide with DTT prior to coupling (*see* **Subheading 3.3.1.**).

3.3.1. Reduction of Synthetic Peptide with DTT

1. Equilibrate a Sephadex G10 column (10-mL bed vol, 1-cm diameter) with 25 mL 1% acetic acid.
2. In the meantime, dissolve 10 mg NLS peptide in 1 mL 50 m*M* HEPES, pH 7.0, add 10 mg DTT, and incubate for 1 h at RT.
3. Separate peptide from free DTT by gel filtration on the equilibrated G10 column with 1% acetic acid. Collect 0.5-mL fractions.
4. Analyze the fractions using Ellman's reagents: For that, add 10-μL fraction to a test tube containing 900 μL Ellman buffer and 100 μL Ellman's reagent; fractions containing free sulfhydryl residues yield a bright yellow color. The first yellow peak contains the peptide, the second peak contains DTT.
5. Combine peptide-containing fractions, lyophilize eight aliquots in preweighed Eppendorf tubes to complete dryness, weigh again (should be approx 1 mg peptide per aliquot), and store at –70°C (*see* **Note 5**).

3.3.2. Preparation of FITC-BSA

1. Dissolve 20 mg fatty, acid-free BSA in 2 mL coupling buffer.
2. Add 200 µL freshly prepared FITC solution to the BSA and incubate at RT for 1 h.
3. In the meantime, wash a PD-10 column with 25 mL PBS.
4. Apply the FITC-BSA conjugate to the column, let the sample run into the column, and discard the eluent.
5. Elute the FITC-BSA conjugate with 3.5 mL PBS.
6. Dilute the eluate twofold with PBS; assuming a recovery yield of 80%, the final concentration of BSA should be approx 2.5 mg/mL.
7. Freeze 1 mL aliquots (2.5 mg) in liquid N_2 and store at –70°C.

3.3.3. Conjugation of NLS Peptides to FITC-BSA (see **Note 6**)

1. Thaw 1 mL (~2.5 mg) of FITC-BSA (from **Subheading 3.3.2.**), add 50 µL of freshly prepared SMCC, and incubate for 30 min at RT.
2. In the meantime, wash a PD-10 column with 25 mL PBS.
3. To remove unbound crosslinker, apply the mixture to the PD10-column, let the sample run into the column, wash with 1.5 mL PBS, and elute with 3.5 mL PBS. Collect only the bright yellow band, which should elute within this volume.
4. Dissolve 1 mg lyophilized peptide (from **Subheading 3.3.1.**) in the column eluate and incubate overnight at 4°C.
5. Equilibrate a PD-10 column with 25 mL transport buffer.
6. To remove free peptide from the transport ligand, apply the mixture to the PD10-column, let the sample run into the column, and elute with transport buffer. Collect only the bright yellow band (~2–3 mL, ~1.0 mg/mL)
7. Freeze 200-µL aliquots of the transport ligand in liquid N_2 and store at –70°C.
8. After thawing, keep aliquots at 4°C in the dark; they can be used for several months without significant loss of activity.

3.4. Transport Assay

The following protocol is designed for simultaneous testing of 20–40 individual transport assays. For the complete assay including quantitation by flow cytometry approx 3 h are required. We always use freshly permeabilized cells. For that, permeabilization of cells (*see* **Subheading 3.4.1.**) and set up of transport mixes (described under **Subheading 3.4.2.**) are carried out in parallel. Alternative protocols utilizing permeabilized cells that have been frozen in the presence of 5% DMSO have been described (e.g., **ref. *8***).

3.4.1. Permeabilization of HeLa Cells

The following protocol is designed for permeabilization of cells for up to 50 individual transport assays. This protocol can easily be scaled up or down, as long as all concentrations are kept constant.

1. Collect 50 mL HeLa suspension cells (at a density of 4–6 × 10^5 cells/mL) in a 50-mL falcon tube by centrifugation at 200*g* in a swing-out rotor, and wash once in 50 mL transport buffer by resuspension and centrifugation.
2. Resuspend the cells in 5 mL transport buffer (at an density of approx 5 × 10^6 cells/mL), add 4 μL digitonin (final concentration of 80 μg/mL [*see* **Note 7**]), and incubate the cells on ice for 6 min.
3. Dilute with 45 mL transport buffer (10-fold dilution) and harvest cells by centrifugation, as before.
4. Resuspend cells in 400 μL and keep them on ice until use in the transport reaction (*see* **Note 8**).
5. To determine the cell density, dilute 20 μL cell suspension with transport buffer to 1 mL and measure the OD_{550}. Use a standard curve (OD_{550} vs cell number, as determined with a hemocytometer) to calculate the cell concentration and adjust it with transport buffer to a density of 3 × 10^5 cells/10 μL (*see* **Note 9**).
6. Routinely check the degree of permeabilization prior to setting up transport reactions. For that, simply mix 5 μL cell suspension with 5 μL of the vital stain trypan blue on a glass slide, carefully cover the cells with a cover slip and observe the cells under a light microscope at ×20 magnification. Ideally, 90–95% of the cells should have accumulated the blue dye (*see* **Note 10**).

3.4.2. Import Reactions

1. For each 40-μL reaction, mix the following components on ice (premix):
   a. Cytosol: for maximal transport rates, 10–15 μL (2–3 mg/mL final concentration; *see* **Note 11**).
   b. ATP regenerating system: 1 μL (final concentrations 1 m*M* ATP, 5 m*M* creatine phosphate, and 10 U/mL creatine phosphate kinase).
   c. Transport ligand: 0.3–1.5 μL (*see* **Note 12**).
   d. Transport buffer and any other additions (such as 200 μ*M* of the import inhibitor GTPγS, or 16 U hexokinase/5 m*M* glucose) added to bring the volume up to 30 μL per assay.
2. For each reaction, combine 30 μL premix and 10 μL permeabilized cells in a 6-mL reaction tube on ice.
3. Keep one of the transport mixes in ice water (*see* **Note 13**) as a no-transport control.
4. Start the transport reaction in the remaining samples by transfer of the tubes into a 30°C water bath.
5. Allow transport to occur for up to 30 min, than stop reaction by following the protocols in either **Subheading 3.4.3.1.**, for microscopic analysis, or **Subheading 3.4.3.2.**, for quantitative analysis.

3.4.3. Analysis of Nuclear Protein Import

Two alternatives are described below for analysis of the import reactions, visual analysis by microscopy and quantitative analysis by flow cytometry (*see* **Fig. 1**). Since flow cytometry measures all cell-associated fluorescence, i.e.,

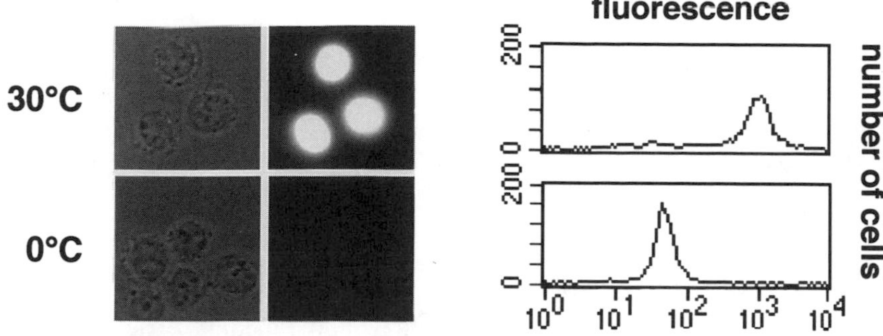

Fig. 1. Standard transport mixes were incubated for 30 min at 30°C or on ice (0°C). Left, after transport, the cells were fixed with 3.7% formaldehyde in transport buffer, mounted onto glass slides, and observed by phase contrast and epifluorescence (FITC channel). Right, after transport, the cells were washed once with 4 mL transport buffer and analyzed by flow cytometry. The mean fluorescent units per cell are 898 (transport at 30°C) and 56 (0°C), respectively.

nonspecific cytoplasmic staining (*see* **Note 14**), as well as specific intranuclear staining, it is essential to verify by light microscopy results obtained by FACS.

3.4.3.1. Analysis of Import by Microscopy

1. Immediately after transport, add 4 mL 3.7% formaldehyde in transport buffer (without protease inhibitors) and incubate samples at RT for 10 min.
2. Centrifuge samples for 5 min at 200*g*, 4°C, in a swing out rotor.
3. Aspirate all but approx 100 µL buffer, dilute with 4 mL transport buffer, and centrifuge again, as before.
4. Carefully aspirate all but approx 50 µL buffer, resuspend cells by flicking the tube manually, and keep samples on ice.
5. Place 10 µL cell suspension on a glass slide, carefully cover with cover slip, and seal with nail polish.
6. Observe cells by phase-contrast and epifluorescence microscopy on FITC channel.

3.4.3.2. Quantitation of Import Reactions by Flow Cytometry

For flow cytometric detection, we use a FACSort or FACScan and CellQuest™ or Lysis II software (Becton Dickinson). Fluorescein fluorescence is excited with the 488-nm line from an argon laser, and the emission is detected with the recommended standard filter, i.e., a bandpass filter (DF530), with optimum transmission at 530 nm. Instrument settings are chosen so that transport under optimal conditions yields approx 1000 fluorescent units. Under those conditions, background, i.e., cells after transport on ice, should give signals not higher than 50–100 U. Once determined, the instrument settings do not have to be changed again until a very different batch of ligand is used, or other instrument parameters have been changed.

1. Immediately after transport, add 4 mL ice-cold transport buffer and centrifuge samples for 5 min at 200*g* in a swing-out rotor.
2. Aspirate all but 300 µL buffer, and place the samples in ice water.
3. Carefully resuspend cells by flicking the tube manually and measure cell-associated fluorescence by flow cytometry for 10^4 cells per sample (this should take not more than 1 min per sample). Determine mean fluorescence per cell for each individual experiment.

4. Notes

1. No CO_2 is required for growth of the suspension cells, the pH in the medium remains stable because of the HEPES buffer in the medium. The cells are very sturdy and should be stirred fast to avoid clumping.
2. For optimal transport activity, homogenization is stopped when most cells are permeabilized, but not fragmented; the percentage of permeabilized cells can be visualized under the microscope after mixing the cell lysate 1:1 with the vital stain trypan blue.
3. Dialysis of cytosol serves two purposes: Buffer exchange and removal of free nucleotides. If a collodion apparatus is not available, dialysis can also be carried out in standard dialysis bags (cutoff 10,000). In this case, dialyze overnight against three changes of buffer.
4. Transport activity in cytosol is quite stable, storage over night on ice does not lead to a significant loss of activity, moreover, aliquots can be refrozen and used again, if necessary.
5. The concentration of peptide can be calculated from the absorption below 230 nm, which is caused by the peptide bond. Several different formulas can be found in the textbooks, one of which is: $[\text{peptide}]_{\text{mg/mL}} = 0.144 \times [A_{215} - A_{225}]$. Alternatively, the exact concentration of free sulfhydryl groups, equivalent with the concentration of reduced peptide, can be calculated using Ellman's reagent in combination with a standard curve of glutathione. However, for the purpose of ligand preparation, the approximate weight is sufficient.
6. We try not to exceed a ratio of 5–10 peptides per protein, since ligands with a higher ratio are very sticky, presumably as a result of their high positive charge, and tend to accumulate in nucleoli. They also give a higher background in the transport assay. The ratio is mainly influenced by the concentration of crosslinker used in the protocol. The coupling efficiency can be estimated by mobility shift on SDS-PAGE; for that, compare mobility of the BSA-SMCC conjugate with the final ligand. Please note that some higher mol wt bands can also be observed after crosslinking (probably BSA–BSA crosslinks), this does not pose any problem.
7. The amount of digitonin necessary for permeabilization varies among different batches of detergent and needs to be titrated for each new stock. The degree of permeabilization of the cells can be monitored by staining with the dye trypan blue, and the digitonin concentration should be adjusted to the minimum required to give ~95% permeable cells. An excess of digitonin can lead to permeabilization of the nuclear envelope. The integrity of the nuclear envelope is essential for the

success of the import assays. Several ways to test for nuclear integrity have been described. Anti-DNA antibodies, as well as large FITC dextrans (150 kDa), are excluded from intact nuclei, but small FITC dextrans (e.g., 9 kDa) have access ***(2,9)***.

8. The time between permeabilization of the cells and their use in the import reaction at least in part determines the proportion of cytosolic proteins that remain inside the cells. This strongly influences the requirement for exogenous cytosolic components, so it should be kept as constant as possible.
9. The OD measurement is faster than counting cells with the hemocytometer.
10. Even with a permeabilization of only 70% of the cells, transport reactions can still be carried out as long as the particular experiment is not sensitive to the ratio of cell associated vs soluble components. The FACS analysis (*see* **Subheading 3.4.2.1.**) allows for distinguishing between permeabilized and nonpermeabilized cells, because of the very low fluorescence associated with intact cells. More critical is an overpermeabilization of the cells that can lead to broken nuclei. In addition, over permeabilized cells are more fragile. As long as the plasma membranes of the permeabilized, trypan blue-stained cells appear to be intact by light microscopy, they are suitable for the assay.
11. Each cytosol has to be titrated to determine the saturation concentration. With 3–4 × 10^5 cells per assay, saturation should be reached at approx 2.5 mg/mL. Much higher concentrations of cytosol have an inhibitory effect on transport.
12. Every batch of ligand should be titrated to determine the optimal ratio between transport and background (ice control). It should be noted that, at the recommended ligand concentration, the transport system is not saturated with ligand; therefore, the amount of ligand in the assay strongly influences the level of intranuclear ligand accumulation.
13. Transport is detectable already after 2 min at 30°C, and low levels of transport can be observed even at 10°C. A true background control should therefore be kept in ice water all the time, until dilution with buffer. Under optimal transport conditions, the signal-to-background ratio, i.e., the intranuclear fluorescence in cells after 30 min transport at 30°C, compared with the fluorescence in cells after 30 min incubation on ice, should be between 10 and 20 (1000 vs 50–100 fluorescent units).
14. Nonspecific background tends to be a problem under the following conditions: low cytosol concentrations (below 1 mg/mL); when recombinant factors are used instead of cytosol; with ligands that contain a high mol fraction of peptide. We have also observed high cytoplasmic staining upon addition of a particular recombinant protein or a synthetic peptide. Although the significance of this staining is unclear, it certainly leads to misleading results in the flow cytometry analysis.
15. The transport assays must fulfill the following criteria: cytosol dependence (saturation at approx 2.5 mg/mL); energy dependence (depletion of ATP by addition of 16 U hexokinase and 5 m*M* glucose strongly inhibits protein import); time dependence (linear transport for at least 20–30 min); temperature dependence (no detectable transport on ice), inhibition by NEM, WGA, and nonhydrolyzable analogs of GTP such as GMP-PNP (reviewed in **refs.** ***2***, ***5***, and ***10***; examples in **refs.** ***4***, ***9***, and ***11***).

21

Clathrin-Coated Vesicles and Targeting

Preparation of Adaptor Proteins

Alain Pauloin

1. Introduction

In eukaryotic cells, receptor-mediated endocytosis and exit of specific trans-Golgi network cargo proteins (newly synthesized lysosome enzymes and secretory proteins) occur by way of clathrin-coated pits and clathrin-coated vesicles (CCVs). The major structural proteins of the coat are the heavy and light chains of clathrin. Along with clathrin, CCVs contain clathrin-associated proteins called assembly polypeptides (AP), because of their apparent ability to promote the polymerization of clathrin triskelions into polyhedral coat structures under physiological conditions. They have been renamed adaptors, since it was shown that they selectively bind cell-membrane receptors carrying endocytosis signals on their cytoplasmic tails. Pulled by the clathrin coat, membrane invaginates and pinches off, forming CCVs. The clathrin coat and parts of the adaptors are rapidly shed from the vesicle, which will be recycled for repeated rounds of coated pits assembly, invagination, and budding. Then the decoated vesicle carrying receptor-ligand complexes is suited to fuse with the acceptor compartment (for review, *see* **refs.** ***1*** and ***2***).

Two main types of adaptors have been identified and localized to distinct regions of the cell: one to the Golgi (AP-1) and the other to the plasma membrane (AP-2) ***(3,4)***. Both have been shown to contain a heterodimer of proteins from the 100- to 110-kDa group named adaptins ***(5)***, and two smaller associated proteins. Thus, AP-1 is made up of β1 (formerly β') and γ-adaptins allied to 47- and 20-kDa proteins (AP47 and AP20). Similarly, AP-2 is composed of α- (either α_{α} or α_{χ}) and β2 (formerly β)-adaptins associated with

From: *Methods in Molecular Biology, Vol. 88: Protein Targeting Protocols*
Edited by: R. A. Clegg Humana Press Inc., Totowa, NJ

50- and 17-kDa subunits (AP50 and AP17) ***(3,6)***. Monomeric adaptors, such as AP-3/auxilin, will not be considered in this chapter.

Since most of the reports on adaptors published so far use material purified from bovine brain, in part for historical reasons and also because brain is rich in CCVs, this source will be used. Purification of CCVs from others organs, such as liver, pancreas, and adrenal gland, will need some adjustments, since vesicle size and density depend on the tissue origin. However, the purification procedure described here for brain could be applied in a first approach, in any cases.

The first objective in the strategy for purifying adaptors is to obtain reasonably clean CCVs with a minimum of purification steps. The next stage requires the efficient extraction of the coat proteins from the vesicles and their separation from each other. Finally, fractions containing adaptors are submitted to various chromatographic steps to separate them further.

2. Materials

2.1. Equipment Required

1. Centrifuge and ultracentrifuge (Bekman, Gagny, France).
2. Low-pressure chromatography system (Bio-Rad, Ivry-sur-Seine, France).
3. FPLC chromatography system (Pharmacia, Orsay, France).
4. Spectrophotometer.
5. Waring blender, pH meter, Potter glass homogenizer and motor-driven pestle, SDS-PAGE gel apparatus.

2.2. Buffers

1. MES buffer: Dissolve 39.04 g 2-[*N*-Morpholino]ethane sulfonic acid (MES) and 5 g NaOH pellets in 1.9 L water (Milli-Q grade). Add 0.8 g ethylene glycol-*bis*(β-aminoethyl ether) *N,N,N',N'*-tetraacetic acid (EGTA), 0.8 g $MgCl_2 \cdot 6\,H_2O$, 0.4 g NaN_3, adjust the pH to 6.5 with a saturated NaOH solution, add 140 μL 2-mercaptoethanol, and complete the volume to 2 L with water. Final concentrations: 100 m*M* MES, 1 m*M* EGTA, 2 m*M* $MgCl_2$, 0.02% NaN_3, 1 m*M* 2-mercaptoethanol.
2. ^2H_2O-8% Sucrose MES buffer: Dissolve 1.95 g MES in 60 mL ^2H_2O and adjust the pH to 6.5 with a saturated NaOH solution in ^2H_2O. Add 8 g sucrose and then 40 mg EGTA, 40 mg $MgCl_2 \cdot 6H_2O$, 20 mg NaN_3, 7 μL 2-mercaptoethanol. Complete the volume to 100 mL with ^2H_2O. Final concentrations: 100 m*M* MES, 8% sucrose, 1 m*M* EGTA, 2 m*M* $MgCl_2$, 0.02% NaN_3, 1 m*M* 2-mercaptoethanol.
3. Tris buffer I: 1*M* Tris[hydroxymethyl]amino methane (Tris)-HCl, pH 7.2.
4. Tris buffer II: 0.5*M* Tris-HCl, pH 7.2.
5. 1*M* Na_2HPO_4/NaH_2PO_4, pH 7.2, phosphate buffer.
6. Buffer A: 20 m*M* Tris-HCl, pH 7.2, 1 m*M* Na_2HPO_4/NaH_2PO_4, pH 7.2, 2 m*M* 2-mercaptoethanol, 0.02% NaN_3.
7. Buffer B: 20 m*M* Tris-HCl, pH 7.2, 500 m*M* Na_2HPO_4/NaH_2PO_4, pH 7.2, 2 m*M* 2-mercaptoethanol, 0.02% NaN_3.
8. Buffer C: 20 m*M* Tris-HCl, pH 8.0, 1 m*M* EDTA, 0.02% NaN_3.

9. Buffer D: 20 m*M* Tris-HCl, pH 8.0, 1*M* NaCl, 1 m*M* EDTA, 0.02% NaN_3.
10. Antiprotease cocktail: aprotinin, antipain, and leupeptin (5 mg each) are solubilized together in 9 mL water. Pepstatin A and chymostatin (5 mg each) are jointly solubilized in 1 mL DMSO. The two solutions are joined, 10 µL NaOH 2*N* are added (to keep soluble pepstatin A and chymostatin) and the mixture is vortexed vigorously. Distribute in 200-µL aliquots and store at –20°C. Use 200 µL antiprotease cocktail per 100-mL sample.
11. Peterson's reagent A: Mix equal parts of stock copper-tartrate-carbonate (CTC), 10% SDS, 0.8*N* NaOH and water. CTC stock solution preparation: 100-mL solution of 20% (w/v) of $NaCO_3$ in water is added slowly while stirring to a 100 mL solution containing 0.2% cupric sulfate, $5H_2O$ and 0.4% sodium potassium tartrate, $4H_2O$. This solution is stable 2 mo at room temperature.
12. Peterson's reagent B: Dilute 1 vol Folin-Ciocalteu phenol reagent (2*N*) in 5 vol water. Solution stable in amber bottle at room temperature.

3. Methods

3.1. Preparation of Clathrin-Coated Vesicles

The essential features of the purification scheme are outlined in **Fig. 1**.

1. Cleanse the bovine brain of meninges with forceps and rinse it quickly under fresh water (*see* **Note 1**).
2. Scrape off the grey matter (coarsely corresponding to cortex convolutions and cerebellum) with a spatula. One brain gives 220–250 g of grey matter.
3. Homogenize grey matter in 2 vol (w/v) of MES buffer for two 15-s bursts at full speed in a 1-L Waring blender (*see* **Note 2**).
4. Centrifuge at 17,700*g* for 30 min at 4°C, in a Beckman JA-10 rotor (low-speed centrifugation). Save the pink, turbid supernatant and resuspend the resulting pellet in 1 vol of MES buffer. Centrifuge and resuspend pellet twice further in the same conditions.
5. Pool the three supernatants, decant through cheesecloth to remove the most part of floating lipids, and clarify by a 30-min low-speed centrifugation.
6. Discard the pellet and centrifuge the supernatant at 110,000*g*, for 1 h at 4°C in a Beckman 50.2 Ti rotor (high-speed centrifugation).
7. Discard the supernatants and resuspend the resulting pelleted material in MES buffer with a Potter glass homogenizer (type A, 30 mL size) and a motor-driven Teflon pestle (10 up-and-downs).
8. Treat with another round of low-speed (17,700*g* for 30 min)/high-speed (110,000*g* for 1 h) centrifugations. Resuspend the pelleted crude CCVs in 25 mL MES buffer with the Potter glass/Teflon homogenizer (10 up-and-downs), add 50 µL antiprotease cocktail and complete to 36 mL with MES buffer.
9. Layer on 6 × 6 mL ^2H_2O–8% sucrose (v/w) cushion and centrifuge 2 h at 28,000 rpm, 4°C (SW41 Beckman rotor, brake on) *(7)*. Discard membrane debris remaining at interfaces and ^2H_2O–8% sucrose cushion. CCVs are found as pellets (~3.6-g wet pellets, which correspond to ~90-mg proteins) (*see* **Note 3**).
10. Resuspend CCVs pellets in 20 mL MES buffer with the Potter glass/Teflon homogenizer and load (5-mL sample) onto a 2.5 × 95-cm Sephacryl S-1000 col-

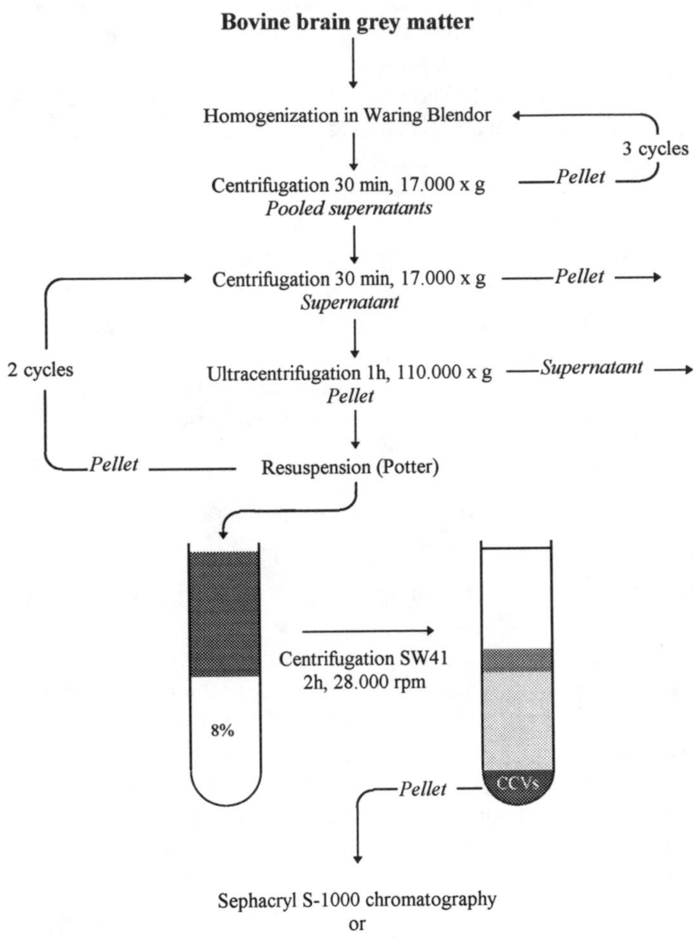

umn pre-equilibrated in MES buffer at 4°C and connected to a chromatography Bio-Rad Econo-System. Fractions (5 mL) are eluted at 1.2 mL/min. The 280-nm absorbance profile of the eluate showed two peaks. The second peak, smaller than the first, contained CCVs ***(8,9)*** (**Fig. 2**).

11. Pool the S-1000 fractions containing CCVs and centrifuge at 110,000*g*, 4°C for 1 h in a Beckman 50.2 Ti rotor. Purified CCVs are found as pellets (~10-mg proteins) (*see* **Note 4**).

3.2. Tris Dissociation of CCVs

1. Solubilize the CCVs pellet in 20 mL of Tris buffer I, using a Dounce glass homogenizer (7.5 mL size), and leave for 2 h at room temperature.

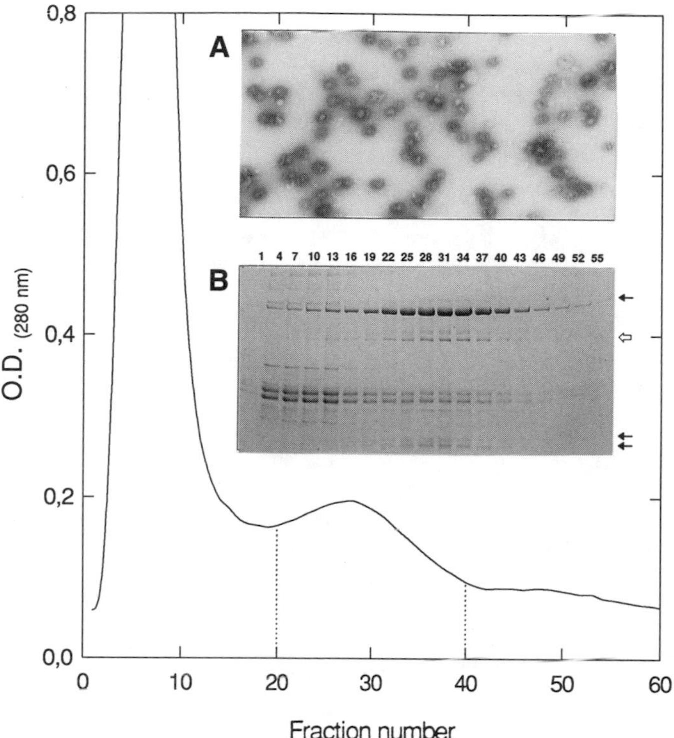

Fig. 2. Sephacryl S-1000 chromatography of CCVs. **(A)** Electron micrograph of CCVs (fraction 28) negatively stained with uranyl acetate (×50,000). **(B)** SDS-10% PAGE of fractions 1–55 (40 µL sample per well). Clathrin heavy chain (←), clathrin light chains (⇇), and adaptors (⇐) are indicated. Dotted lines indicate the boundaries of the CCVs pool.

2. Centrifuge the extract at 280,000*g* for 2 h at 4°C in a rotor SW55 Ti (brake on) to eliminate the stripped membranes. Discard the pellet.
3. Apply the resulting supernatant (sample vol = 5 mL) to a Sephacryl S-400 column (2.5 × 120 cm), pre-equilibrated in Tris buffer II at 4°C and connected to a low-pressure chromatography Bio-Rad Econo-System to separate the adaptors from clathrin. Collect 5-mL fractions at a flow rate of 1.2 mL/min. A typical S-400 chromatography profile is shown in **Fig. 3**. The first peak contains remaining stripped vesicles. Clathrin with both heavy and light chains is the main component of the second peak. The third peak contains the crude AP ***(10,11)*** (*see* **Note 5**).

3.3. Separation of AP-1 from AP-2 by Hydroxyapatite Chromatography

The AP-1/AP-2 separation is performed according to a modified version of the method of Ungewickell et al. ***(12)***.

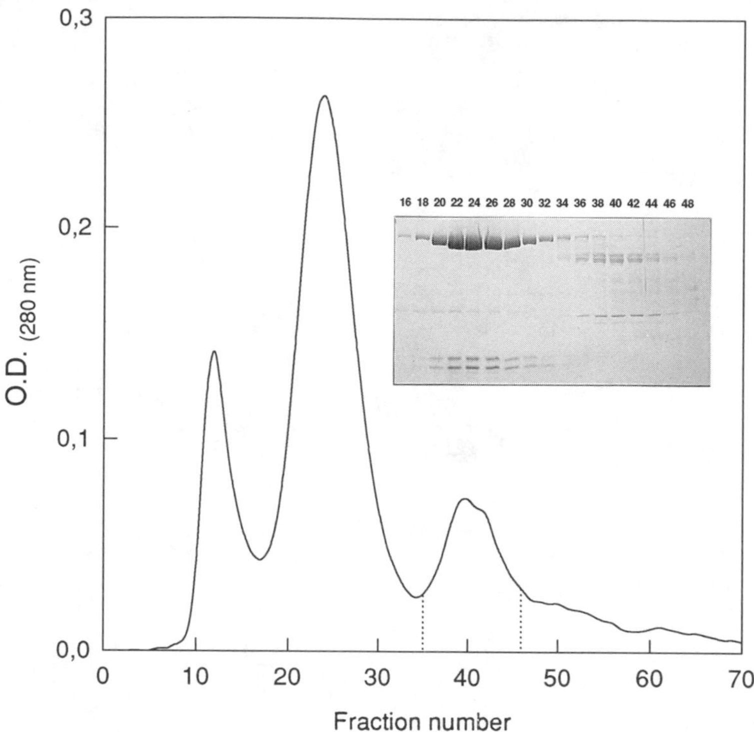

Fig. 3. Sephacryl S-400 chromatography of CCVs Tris extract. Insert panel: SDS-10% PAGE analysis of fractions 16–48 (40 μL sample per well). Dotted lines indicate the boundaries of the AP pool.

1. Pool the AP-containing fractions, add 1/500 vol of 1*M* Na_2HPO_4/NaH_2PO_4, pH 7.2, buffer (2 m*M* final concentration), and directly load the pool (1 mL/min) by means of a 50-mL Superloop (Pharmacia) onto a hydroxyapatite chromatography cartridge Econo-Pac CHT-II (Bio-Rad) connected to a FPLC system (Pharmacia) and previously equilibrated with the buffer A (*see* **Note 6**).
2. Wash the column with buffer A until the absorbance is returned to the baseline.
3. Develop the column with a 90-mL gradient ranging from 1 to 400 m*M* Na_2HPO_4/NaH_2PO_4. The column flow rate is 0.5 mL/min and 1-mL fractions are collected. AP-1 and AP-2 are eluted with ~150 and ~320 m*M* Na_2HPO_4/NaH_2PO_4 respectively (**Fig. 4**).

3.4. Purification of Adaptors by Mono-Q Chromatography

1. Pool individually AP-1- and AP-2-containing fractions and dialyze overnight at 4°C against 1 L buffer C.
2. Filter the dialysates on 0.22-μm filters and then separately apply onto a Mono Q HR 5/5 (Pharmacia) anion exchange column connected to the FPLC system and previously equilibrated with buffer C ***(12)***.

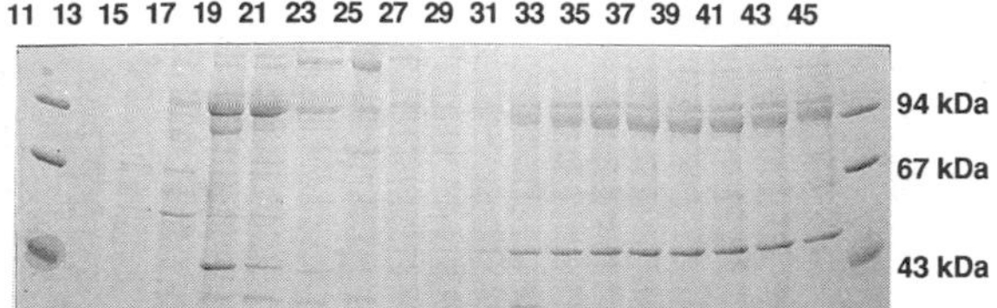

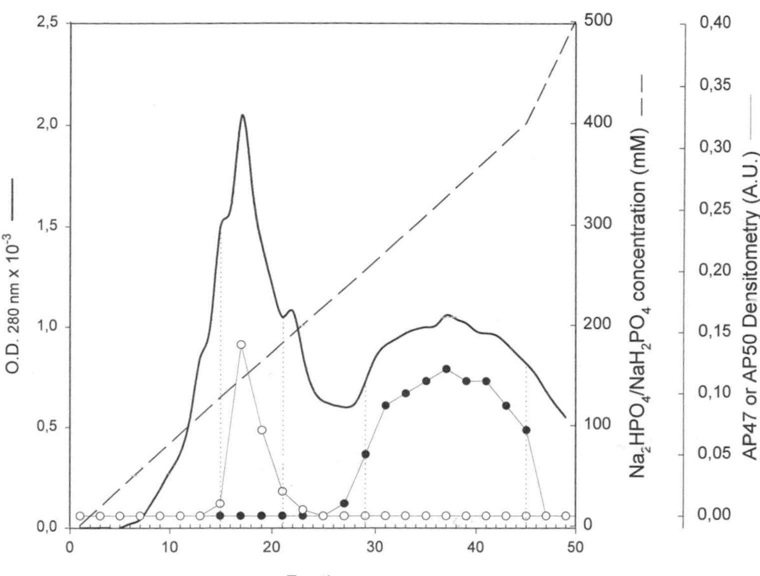

Fig. 4. Separation of bovine brain adaptors by hydroxyapatite adsorption chromatography. AP-1 and AP-2 peaks are localized by means of their respective accessory proteins (47 kDa, o—o, and 50 kDa, •—•, respectively) quantified by densitometry. Upper panel: SDS-10% PAGE analysis of fractions 11–45 (100 µL sample TCA precipitated per well). Dotted lines indicate the boundaries of the AP-1 and AP-2 pools. Na_2HPO_4/NaH_2PO_4 concentration gradient (-----).

3. Discarded the flowthrough and apply a 60-mL gradient of 0–500 m*M* NaCl when the absorbance is returned to the baseline. The column flow rate is 1 mL/min and 1-mL fractions are collected. AP-1 and AP-2 are eluted with 270 and 220 m*M* NaCl respectively. A typical preparation yields ~0.2 mg AP-1 and ~0.6 mg AP-2 (**Fig. 5**) (*see* **Note 7**).

3.5. SDS-PAGE and Protein Assay

Denaturing electrophoresis in sodium dodecyl sulfate (SDS) slab gels (10 and 15% acrylamide) (SDS-PAGE) are performed according to the method of Laemmli *(13)*. Coomassie blue-stained gels are analyzed by densitometry (ImageMaster, Pharmacia).

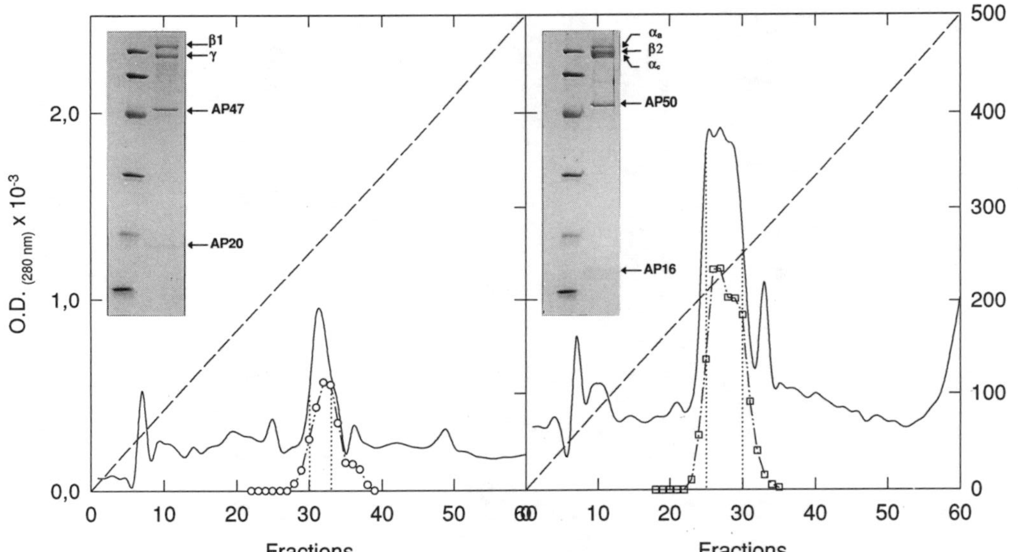

Fig. 5. Purification of AP-1 and AP-2 by FPLC Mono Q anion-exchange chromatography. Left panel, AP-1 Mono Q chromatography. Right panel, AP-2 Mono Q chromatography. AP-1 and AP-2 peaks are localized by means of their respective accessory proteins (47 kDa, o—o, and 50 kDa, •—•, respectively) quantified by densitometry. Dotted lines indicate the boundaries of the AP-1 and AP-2 pools. NaCl concentration gradient (-----). Insert in each panel displays SDS-15% PAGE analysis of each pool (60-μL sample per well). Molecular mass markers used: phosphorylase b, 94 kDa; bovine serum albumin, 67 kDa; ovalbumin, 43 kDa; carbonic anhydrase, 30 kDa; trypsin inhibitor, 20.1 kDa; α-lactalbumin, 14.4 kDa.

The Bradford method is not applicable, since it can quantify soluble proteins only. Rather, the Peterson method ***(14)***, which uses SDS and NaOH and therefore allows complete solubilization of membrane proteins, is performed.

1. Sample dilutions: serial dilutions are performed by mixing 111 µL of concentrated sample in 1 mL MES buffer, vortex, remove 111 µL, dilute in 1 mL MES buffer, and so on, until 1/1000 dilution.
2. Standard curve (5–50 µg/mL): Stock solution of bovine serum albumin (BSA) at 500 µg/mL is used. Aliquots of 10, 20, 30…100 µL are completed to 1 mL with MES buffer.
3. Add 1 mL of reagent A to 1 mL of sample or standard, vortex, and allow to stand for 10 min at room temperature.
4. Add 0.5 mL reagent B and vortex immediately. After 30 min, read absorbance at 750 nm within 2 h.
5. Draw the standardization curve and determine the sample protein concentration.

4. Notes

1. Bovine brain obtained from local slaughterhouse must be transported on ice and processed as soon as possible after death (within 2 h). All manipulations are executed on ice or at 4°C. One brain is sufficient for a preparation. **Caution:** In countries where the prion-induced neurodegenerative disease BSE may affect cattle brains, statutory restrictions may apply to the use of bovine brain tissue, and to the disposal of tissue residues. In any event, appropriate containment measures must be used in accordance with applicable biological safety protocols.
2. The stability of the coat is both pH- and buffer-dependent. Thus, mildly acidic pH and MES (or HEPES) buffer must be used all along the coated vesicle purification process.
3. ^2H_2O (99.8% deuterium) is from Euriso-Top (CEA, CEN-Saclay, France). You can use the cheapest form of ^2H_2O; NMR grade is unnecessary. The best way to layer samples onto the sucrose cushions is to use a peristaltic pump. Otherwise, it is preferable to use P-200 and P-1000 Pipetman, instead of glass pipet to have a better control of sample loading. The whole purification of CCVs can be performed in 2 d; if Sephacryl S-1000 CCVs purification step is included, the process time is extended to 3–4 d. This step may be avoided if the only goal is adaptor preparation.
4. Pellets of purified CCVs could be resuspended in MES buffer, supplemented with protease inhibitor cocktail, and stored at 4°C for weeks without detectable proteolysis. They could also be quick frozen in liquid nitrogen and stored at –80°C in 100-µL aliquots.
5. The best conservation medium for coat constituents is 0.5*M* Tris-HCl buffer, pH 7.5, at 4°C. Freezing methods must be avoided since thawing induces irreversible precipitation of adaptors.
6. Hydroxyapatite chromatography must be performed at room temperature, since phosphate buffer is vulnerable to crystallization at 4°C. The use of EDTA or

other calcium chelators must be avoided in buffers run with hydroxyapatite Econo-Pac CHT-II cartridge, because of chemical incompatibilities.

7. Mono Q purified adaptors must be quick-frozen in liquid nitrogen as 100-µL aliquots and then stored at –80°C as soon as they are obtained from the column.

References

1. Schmid, S. L. (1992) The mechanism of receptor-mediated endocytosis: more questions than answers. *Bioessays* **14,** 589–596.
2. Pley, U. and Parham, P. (1993) Clathrin: its role in receptor-mediated vesicular transport and specialized functions in neurons. *Crit. Rev. Biochem. Mol. Biol.* **28,** 431–464.
3. Ahle, S., Mann, A., Eichelsbacher, U., and Ungewickell, E. (1988) Structural relationships between clathrin assembly proteins from the Golgi and the plama membrane. *EMBO J.* **7,** 919–929.
4. Robinson, M. S. (1987) 100-kD coated vesicle proteins: molecular heterogeneity and intracellular distribution studied with monoclonal antibodies. *J. Cell Biol.* **104,** 887–895.
5. Pearse, B. M. F. (1988) Receptors compete for adaptors found in plama membrane coated pits. *EMBO J.* **7,** 3331–3336.
6. Robinson, M. S. (1989) Cloning of cDNAs encoding two related 100-kD coated vesicle proteins (a-adaptins). *J. Cell Biol.* **108,** 833–842.
7. Nandi, P. K., Irace, G., Van Jaarsveld, P. P., Lippold, R. E., and Edelhoch, H. (1982) Instability of coated vesicles in concentrated sucrose solution. *Proc. Natl. Acad. Sci. USA* **79,** 5881–5885.
8. Bar-Zvi, D. and Branton, D. (1986) Clathrin-coated vesicles contain two protein kinases activities. *J. Biol. Chem.* **261,** 9614–9621.
9. Pauloin, A. and Thurieau, C. (1993) The 50 kDa protein subunit of assembly polypeptide (AP) AP-2 adaptor from clathrin-coated vesicles is phosphorylated on threonine-156 by AP-1 and a soluble AP50 kinase which co-purifies with the assembly polypeptides. *Biochem. J.* **296,** 409–415.
10. Keen, J. H., Willingham, M. C., and Pastan, I. H. (1979) Clathrin-coated vesicles: isolation, dissociation and factor-dependent reassociation of clathrin baskets. *Cell* **16,** 303–312.
11. Pauloin, A. and Jollès, P. (1984) Internal control of the coated vesicle pp50-specific kinase complex. *Nature* **311,** 265–267.
12. Ungewickell, E., Plessmann, U., and Weber, K. (1994) Purification of Golgi adaptor protein 1 from bovine adrenal gland and characterization of its β1 (β') subunit by microsequencing. *Eur. J. Biochem.* **222,** 33–40.
13. Laemmli, U. K. (1970) Cleavage of structural proteins during the assembly of the head of bacteriophage T4. *Nature* **277,** 680–685.
14. Peterson, G. L. (1977) A simplification of the protein assay method of Lowry et al. which is more generally applicable. *Anal. Biochem.* **83,** 346–356.

22

Analysis of the Sorting of Secretory Proteins to the Regulated Secretory Pathway

A Subcellular Fractionation Approach

Eric Chanat, Andrea S. Dittié, and Sharon A. Tooze

1. Introduction

Protein secretion is a fundamental process common to all animal cells, whereby a subset of newly synthesized proteins is constitutively secreted into the external environment. In specialized cell types, such as those found in endocrine and neuronal tissues, protein secretion also occurs in a regulated fashion: A unique subset of newly synthesized proteins is stored in secretory granules within the cell and is only secreted after an external stimulus is received by the cell. To study these two pathways of secretion, the constitutive and the regulated, cell lines that are capable of both types of secretion have proved invaluable. We have been studying protein secretion in the neuroendocrine cell line PC12 (rat pheochromocytoma), with the aim of dissecting both the constitutive and regulated pathway at a molecular level. To characterize these two pathways in PC12 cells, the approaches we have adopted employ biosynthetic labeling of newly synthesized proteins (*see* **Subheading 3.2.**), treatment with well-characterized drugs (*see* **Subheading 3.3.**), and subcellular fractionation techniques (*see* **Subheading 3.5.**). To identify the molecules that are involved in the functioning of theses two pathways, we have used a variety of in vitro assays that faithfully reconstitute the cellular events (*see* **Subheadings 3.8.–3.9.**).

The PC12 cell provides an ideal model system for several reasons. First, in PC12 cells, there is a very efficient control of sorting into the regulated pathway. Several other cell lines, for example, AtT20 cells, do not exhibit such tight control. Although AtT20 cells possess a regulated pathway, a significant

From: *Methods in Molecular Biology, Vol. 88: Protein Targeting Protocols*
Edited by: R. A. Clegg Humana Press Inc., Totowa, NJ

percentage of the regulated secretory proteins are constitutively secreted *(1)*, which can make the results of experiments designed to look at features of the regulated pathway difficult to interpret. Second, PC12 cells synthesize a significant amount of two members of the granin family of proteins, namely, chromogranin B (CgB) and secretogranin II (SgII). The granin family of proteins are abundant, widespread markers for the regulated pathway *(2)*. The granins are particularly useful markers, because they are sulfated on tyrosine residues. Since sulfation is a *trans*-Golgi network (TGN; **ref.** *3*), specific posttranslational modification *(4)*, the granins can be labeled with radioactive sulfate (*see* **Subheading 3.2.2.**) selectively in the TGN, the compartment from which regulated and constitutive secretory vesicles (CSVs) form. In addition, the granins are acidic proteins that bind calcium (Ca^{2+}), a property that may be important in sorting to the regulated pathway. Finally, the granins are heat-stable, and therefore can be enriched in total cell extracts by boiling.

At the start of the experiments described below, the regulated pathway of secretion had been characterized in many morphological studies (*see*, for example, **ref.** *5*), including electron microscopic autoradiography of the newly synthesized proteins *(6)*. Briefly, it was known that regulated secretory proteins were segregated in the Golgi complex into dense-core aggregates, which eventually were enveloped by membrane and resided in the cytoplasm as secretory granules that later fused with the plasma membrane of the cell to release their content. Pioneering experiments by Gumbiner and Kelly led to the identification of the regulated and constitutive pathway within the same cell *(7)*. The purpose of this chapter is to present a series of techniques that have been used successfully to characterize elements of both constitutive and regulated secretion in the neuroendocrine cell line PC12. Only the transport and secretion of soluble proteins is addressed because little is known about the membrane proteins involved.

1.1. Sorting of Regulated Secretory Proteins in the TGN

Experiments such as those outlined above, and others (for review, *see* **ref.** *8*), suggested several possible models for sorting of newly synthesized proteins to the regulated pathway. Two models for the sorting have predominated: The first is based on the concept of a sorting domain within the regulated proteins, such as a linear sequence of amino acids (for example, *see* **ref.** *9*), and a receptor that would recognize the sorting domain; the second is based on the physicochemical properties of regulated proteins, which would result in coaggregation of the proteins in the TGN and segregation from constitutive secretory proteins (*see*, for example, **ref.** *10*). In fact, the most likely outcome of current experiments designed to test these hypotheses will be a hybrid of the two models, whereby aggregation occurs as the first step in the sorting process, followed by recognition and interaction of the aggregates with the TGN membrane.

The sorting of regulated secretory proteins in the TGN has been investigated by a wide variety of techniques. Here we describe and detail two approaches to investigate sorting of regulated secretory proteins that have provided important information. The first approach relies on the fact that CgB has a single disulfide loop in the amino-terminal domain ***(11)***. Treatment of cells with dithiothreitol (DTT) (*see* **Subheading 3.3.2.**), which is membrane permeable, results in the constitutive secretion of the newly synthesized, metabolically labeled (*see* **Subheading 3.2.1.**) or sulfate-labeled (*see* **Subheading 3.2.2.**) CgB, as assayed by secretion of CgB into the medium (*see* **Subheading 3.2.3.**). The single disulfide bond in CgB is reduced by DTT treatment (*see* **Subheading 3.12.4.**), suggesting that disruption of the loop directly causes missorting of the CgB. The second approach involves in vitro manipulation of isolated TGN membranes (*see* **Subheading 3.6.**), involving detergent permeabilization and incubation in medium at different pHs, with different Ca^{2+} concentrations. Using this system, it was demonstrated that aggregation of regulated secretory proteins required a low pH and high Ca^{2+} concentration similar to that believed to be present in the TGN ***(10)***.

1.2. Formation of Post-TGN Vesicles

After sorting of the regulated secretory proteins in the TGN, either by aggregation or interaction with a sorting receptor, or both, the secretory granules form by budding from the TGN. Concomitant with this budding process is the formation of CSVs from the TGN. To obtain information about these two budding events, we adopted two approaches: The first utilizes the different sedimentation behavior of the two classes of vesicles in medium containing sucrose. Using velocity-controlled sucrose gradient centrifugation, the precursor organelle, the TGN, can be resolved from the products, the post-TGN vesicles (*see* **Subheading 3.5.2.**). The second approach involves a cell-free assay to reconstitute the budding of the post-Golgi vesicles from the TGN. The separation of the precursor and product by the rapid velocity centrifugation step provided the basis to assay for cell-free budding (*see* **Subheading 3.8.**), and to dissect the requirements for budding from the TGN.

For the success of these experiments, sulfation on tyrosine residues was crucial: A short pulse of [^{35}S]-sulfate (*see* **Subheading 3.2.2.**) allows the exact timing of the sulfation in the TGN of markers for the regulated and constitutive pathways, SgII and the heparan sulfate proteoglycan (hsPG), respectively, and defines precisely the starting point for all the experiments. The identity of the isolated membranes as TGN was confirmed using an assay for a glycosyltranferase specific for the TGN, sialyltransferase (*see* **Subheading 3.10.1.**). After the 5-min pulse with sulfate, further incubation in the absence of label allows the sulfate-labeled proteins to be chased into post-TGN vesicles, indicating that budding has occurred. The chase can be performed either in vivo in intact cells, or in vitro, in a postnuclear supernatant (PNS) prepared from the labeled cells (*see* **Subheading 3.5.1.**; **ref.** *12*). Results from experiments in intact cells suggested that the $t_{1/2}$ of budding of CSVs and regulated secretory vesicles is identical—approx 5 min ***(12)***. Because the sulfate label is so specific in PC12 cells, manipulations and drug treatments can be performed on the intact cells to probe the requirements for vesicle formation from the TGN. Similar experiments can also be performed in vitro, the results of which have conclusively demonstrated that formation of both regulated and constitutive vesicles can occur from the TGN ***(12)***. Further work demonstrated that vesicle formation requires heterotrimeric GTP-binding proteins ***(13,14)***.

1.3. Characterization of Immature Secretory Granules

The regulated secretory vesicles and CSVs have distinct cargo molecules and properties. These different vesicles presumably have a distinct membrane composition. Although the composition and characteristics of the CSVs remain largely unknown, we have performed experiments, detailed below, to characterize the newly formed regulated secretory vesicles, called an immature secretory granule (ISG), in PC12 cells ***(15)***. Previous morphological observations suggested that several events occurred during secretory granule storage in the cell. We focused on two of these events by extending the techniques mentioned above.

The first characteristic of the ISG we focused on was the increase in size between the immature and the mature secretory granule. A two-step centrifugation protocol was employed, in which the immature and mature secretory granules are separated by velocity-controlled sucrose gradients, then further analyzed by equilibrium gradient centrifugation (*see* **Subheadings 3.5.2.–3.5.3.**). After this centrifugation protocol, enriched populations of immature and mature secretory granules were obtained, which were analyzed by electron microscopy. From these experiments, it was possible to conclude that the diameter of the dense core in ISGs was approx 80 nm; that of the mature secretory granule was approx 120 nm ***(15)***. Based on these data, the hypothesis has been made that during storage in the cell the ISGs increase to the size of a mature secretory granule through homotypic fusion.

The second characteristic of interest to us is the observation that ISGs have patches of clathrin on their surface ***(16,17)***. Clathrin has never been detected on mature secretory granules. Clathrin-coats are responsible for the formation of clathrin-coated vesicles from membranes, such as the plasma membrane and the TGN. The clathrin interacts with the membrane via a set of proteins called adaptors. The adaptors are thought to interact with transmembrane molecules, which then undergo vesicular transport within the cell (for review, *see*

ref. ***18***). The role of these clathrin patches on ISGs is still poorly understood. It has been proposed (for review, *see* **ref.** ***19***) that they could play a role in the granule maturation process, in which sorting would be achieved by removal of membrane. To investigate the formation of clathrin-coats on ISGs, and to identify the molecules that are interacting with the adaptors, we developed a cell-free assay to reconstitute the translocation, and binding of adaptors and clathrin from cytosol to ISGs (*see* **Subheading 3.9.**). Using this assay, we describe the binding of the AP-1 adaptor complex to isolated immature secretory granules and some of the properties of the AP-1 binding. AP-1 binding to ISGs has properties similar to those reported for AP-1 binding to TGN membranes ***(20)***.

2. Materials

All media and solutions described below are prepared with Milli-Q-purified water or equivalent. Chemicals are from Boehringer-Mannheim (Mannheim, Germany) and Sigma (St. Louis, MO).

2.1. Cell Culture of PC12 Cells

1. Rat pheochromocytoma PC12 cells (clone II-251; **ref.** ***21***).
2. Dulbecco's modified Eagle's medium (DMEM [Life Technologies, GmbH, Eggenstein, Germany]) containing 1 g/L glucose and 4 m*M* glutamine, supplemented with 10% (v/v) horse serum (Life Technologies) and 5% (v/v) fetal calf serum (growth medium).
3. Buffers and solutions of Dulbecco's phosphate-buffered saline (PBS) without Ca^{2+} and Mg^{2+} (PBS^-) and 0.05/0.02% trypsin/EDTA (ethylenediaminetetraacetic acid).
4. Cell culture facility. Inverted microscope and refrigerated low-speed centrifuge; sterile glass and plastic pipets; disposable plastic tubes and cell culture dishes.

2.2. Metabolic Labeling of PC12 Cells

2.2.1. Rough Endoplasmic Reticulum (RER) Labeling with [^{3}H]Tyrosine

1. Dishes of subconfluent cells.
2. DMEM without tyrosine and with 10% of the normal concentration of phenylalanine (tyrosine-free DMEM). Normal DMEM or DMEM containing twice the normal concentration of cold tyrosine (chase medium).
3. L-[2,3,5,6-^{3}H]tyrosine (TRK 530, Amersham Buchler, GmbH & CokG, Germany).

2.2.2. TGN Labeling with [^{35}S]Sulfate and Transport of [^{35}S]Sulfate-Labeled Proteins to Post-TGN Vesicles

2.2.2.1. Pulse Labeling of the TGN

1. Dishes of subconfluent cells.
2. DMEM containing $MgCl_2$ instead of $MgSO_4$ and 10% (w/v) of the normal concentration of methionine and cysteine (sulfate-free DMEM).
3. Carrier-free [^{35}S]sulfate (SJS1, Amersham).

2.2.2.2. In Vivo Transport of [^{35}S]Sulfate-Labeled Proteins to Post-TGN Vesicles

1. Materials as those described in **Subheading 2.2.2.1.**
2. Stock solution of 1*M* Na_2SO_4. Regular DMEM supplemented with Na_2SO_4 to reach twice the concentration (1.6 m*M*) of cold sulfate in normal DMEM (chase medium).

2.2.3. Kinetic Analysis of the In Vivo Transport and Release of [^{3}H]Tyrosine- or of [^{35}S]Sulfate-Labeled Proteins

Materials required are those described in **Subheadings 2.2.1.–2.2.2.**

2.2.4. Definition of Sulfated Marker Proteins of the Constitutive Secretory Pathway

1. Dishes of subconfluent cells.
2. Sulfate-free DMEM and DMEM supplemented with Na_2SO_4 (*see* **Subheading 2.2.2.**), both containing 20 m*M* HEPES-NaOH instead of bicarbonate.
3. Carrier-free [^{35}S]sulfate.

2.2.5. Definition of Sulfated Marker Proteins of the Regulated Secretory Pathway

1. Materials as those described in **Subheading 2.2.2.**
2. Horse and fetal calf serum, both dialyzed against PBS.

2.3. In Vivo Treatments of PC12 Cells

2.3.1. Xyloside Treatment of PC12 Cells

1. Materials as those described in **Subheading 2.2.2.**
2. Stock solution of 500 m*M* 4-methylumbelliferyl β-D-xyloside (xyloside) in dimethyl sulfoxide (DMSO). Store in aliquots at –20°C.

2.3.2. Dithiothreitol Treatment of PC12 Cells

1. Materials as those described in **Subheading 2.2.2.**
2. Freshly prepared stock solution of 100 m*M* DTT in H_2O.

2.4. Analysis of Intracellular and Secreted Proteins

2.4.1. Termination of Labeling and Intracellular Transport of Labeled Proteins

1. Stock solution of 1*M* Na_2SO_4 and of 250 m*M* phenylmethyl-sulfonylfluoride (PMSF) in 100% ethanol (store in aliquots at –20°C).
2. Tris-buffered saline (TBS): 25 m*M* Tris-HCl, 4.5 m*M* KCl, 137 m*M* NaCl, 0.7 m*M* Na_2HPO_4, pH 7.4.
3. TBS plus sulfate (TBSS): to TBS, add Na_2S0_4 to reach 1.6 m*M* (twice the concentration of Na_2S0_4 in DMEM).

2.4.2. Analysis of Protein Secretion After [^{3}H]Tyrosine or [^{35}S]Sulfate Labeling.

1. Tris-NaCl-Tween-EDTA (TNTE): 20 m*M* Tris-HCl, pH 7.4, 150 m*M* NaCl, 0.3% Tween-20, 5 m*M* EDTA (from 100 m*M* EDTA, pH 7.2).
2. Stock solutions: 100% (w/v) aqueous trichloroacetic acid (TCA); 250 m*M* PMSF in 100% ethanol.
3. Carrier proteins (e.g., bovine hemoglobin at 10 mg/mL in H_2O; store in aliquots at –20°C).
4. Ethanol/ether (50/50%: v/v).
5. Laemmli sample buffer and O'Farrell lysis buffer.
6. Equipment includes 4- to 5-mL polypropylene tubes; 1.5-mL microtubes; centrifuges.

2.5. Subcellular Fractionation of PC12 Cells

2.5.1. Preparation of PNS

1. Materials as those described in **Subheading 2.4.1.**
2. Stock solutions: 1*M* HEPES-KOH, pH 7.2; 2.3*M* sucrose.
3. Trypan blue.
4. Homogenization buffer (HB): 0.25*M* sucrose, 10 m*M* HEPES-KOH, pH 7.2, 1 m*M* EDTA (from 100 m*M* EDTA, pH 7.2), 0.5 m*M* PMSF, 1 m*M* $Mg(OAc)_2$.
5. Homogenization buffer plus sulfate (HBS): To HB, add Na_2SO_4 to reach 1.6 m*M*.
6. Equipment includes a rubber policeman made from one-quarter of a silicone stopper attached to a plastic pipet; 50- and 15-mL tubes; 22-gage needle and 1-mL syringe; cell cracker; inverted microscope; low-speed centrifuge.

2.5.2. Velocity Sucrose Gradient Centrifugation

1. Stock solutions as those described in **Subheading 2.5.1.**
2. Laemmli sample buffer.
3. Equipment includes 1.5-mL microtubes; Ultra-Clear™ ultracentrifuge tubes for a Beckman SW40 rotor; gradient forming device; a peristaltic pump.
4. Instruments: Beckman SW40 rotor; ultracentrifuges; refractometer.

2.5.3. Equilibrium Sucrose Gradient Centrifugation

Materials required are those described in **Subheading 2.5.2.**

2.6. Analysis of Regulated Secretory Proteins Aggregates in Compartments of the Secretory Pathway

1. Stock solutions: 10 m*M* HEPES-KOH, pH 7.2; 1*M* 4-morpholinoethanesulfonic acid (MES); 1*M* KCl; 1*M* $CaCl_2$; 5% (w/v) saponin in H_2O (stored in aliquots at –20°C); 5 mg/mL leupeptin in H_2O (stored in aliquots at –20°C);
2. Laemmli sample buffer.
3. Nonaggregative milieu: 10 m*M* MES-NaOH, 30 m*M* KCl, 1.2 m*M* leupeptin, pH 7.4.
4. Aggregative milieu: 10 m*M* MES-NaOH, 10 m*M* $CaCl_2$, 1.2 m*M* leupeptin, pH 6.4.

5. Equipment includes fixed-angle rotor (e.g., 70.1 TI with adaptors for microtubes or a Beckman TLA-45 to use in a Beckman TLA-100 tabletop ultracentrifuge); ultracentrifuge; appropriate tubes.

2.7. Analysis of the State of Reduction/Oxidation of Disulfide Bonds in Secretory Proteins After DTT-Treatment of the Cells

1. Materials as those described in **Subheadings 2.4.1.** and **2.5.**
2. Additional materials include sulfate-free DMEM; 10 m*M* HEPES-KOH, pH 7.2; 10 m*M* HEPES-KOH, pH 7.7; acetone stored at –20°C; [^{3}H]NEM (*N*-ethyl maleimide); liquid nitrogen; freshly prepared 100 m*M* DTT in H_2O.
3. Equipment includes low-speed centrifuge, fixed-angle rotor (e.g., 70.1 TI with adaptors for microtubes, or TLA-45 to use in a Beckman TLA-100 tabletop ultracentrifuge), ultracentrifuge, and appropriate tubes.

2.8. Cell-Free Formation of Immature Secretory Granules and Constitutive Secretory Vesicles

1. Materials as those described in **Subheadings 2.2.2.1.** and **2.5.**
2. ATP and an ATP regenerating system ***(22)***: 1:1:1 mix of 100 m*M* ATP (neutralize to pH 7.0 with NaOH or KOH), 800 m*M* creatine phosphate, 3200 U/mL (4 mg/mL) creatine phosphokinase in 50% (w/v) glycerol. Store stock solutions into aliquots at –20°C.
3. Stock solutions of 1 m*M* 3'-phosphoadenosine 5'-phosphosulfate (PAPS) and 10 m*M* Mg acetate.

2.9. Cell-Free Binding Assay to Reconstitute γ-Adaptin Binding to Immature Secretory Granules

2.9.1. Preparation of Bovine Brain Cytosol

1. One bovine brain obtained fresh from slaughterhouse and transported as rapidly as possible on ice.
2. Homogenization buffer (HB): 25 m*M* HEPES, 25 m*M* KCl, 2.5 m*M* magnesium acetate, pH 7.2. HB supplemented with protease inhibitors (PMSF as usual, 5 µg/µL leupeptin, 1 µg/µL pepstatin).
3. Equipment includes Waring blender, Sorvall centrifuges, ultracentrifuges, and appropriate tubes.

2.9.2. γ-Adaptin Binding Assay

1. For a total of 24 reactions, typically done as 12 conditions in duplicate, 3 mL of PC12 ISGs (pool of fractions 7–9 from one equilibrium gradient) prepared using methods in **Subheading 3.5.3.**, starting from six 15-cm^2 dishes, are used. The ISG pool will contain approx 0.5 mg/mL protein.
2. Bovine brain cytosol prepared as described in **Subheading 3.9.1.**
3. 10X Binding buffer (10X BB): 250 m*M* HEPES, 250 m*M* KCl, 25 m*M* magnesium acetate, pH 7.2, and 1X BB (25 m*M* HEPES, 25 m*M* KCl, 2.5 m*M* magnesium acetate, pH 7.2).

4. ATP and ATP regenerating system (*see* **Subheading 2.8.**).
5. 100 m*M* GTPγS in H_2O (stored in aliquots at –70°C).
6. Laemmli sample buffer.
7. TBS as described in **Subheading 2.4.1.**
8. Tween-20.
9. [^{125}I]-protein A.
10. Equipment includes 1.5-mL microtubes, Beckman TLA-45 rotor to use in a Beckman TL-100 tabletop ultracentrifuge and appropriate tubes, minigel vertical electrophoresis apparatus and gel solutions, nitrocellulose membrane, blotter unit, Kodak X-Omat AR-5 film and X-ray cassettes.

2.10. Analytical Methods

2.10.1. Sialyltransferase Assay

1. Materials as those described in **Subheading 2.5.**
2. Assay stock solutions: 20% (w/v) Triton X-100; 1*M* Na-cacodylate, pH 6.6; 50 mg/mL asialofetuin; cytidine 5'-monophosphate sialic acid (CMP-SA); [^{3}H]-CMP-SA.
3. 20% TCA with 1.0% phosphotungstic acid (PTA) in 0.5*M* HCl.
4. A tissue solubilizer such as Protosol.
5. Microtubes (1.5 mL).
6. Heating block.

2.10.2. Protease Protection Assays

1. Fractions containing intact vesicles or organelles in isotonic media, such as HB, or from sucrose gradients, e.g., ISGs, fractions 2–4 from velocity gradient (*see* **Subheading 3.5.2.**). For each fraction to be tested, four identical aliquots will be required.
2. Stock solutions of 100 m*M* dibucaine-HCl in 50% ethanol; 1 mg/mL proteinase K in H_2O; 20% Triton X-100 (w/v) in H_2O; 250 m*M* PMSF in 100% ethanol.
3. Laemmli sample buffer.

2.10.3. SDS-Polyacrylamide Gel Electrophoresis (SDS-PAGE), Two-Dimensional Polyacrylamide Gel Electrophoresis (2D-PAGE), and Immunoblotting

1. Ampholines, pH 3.5–5.0, 5.0–7.0, and 3.5–9.5.
2. [^{125}I]-protein A (IM144, Amersham).
3. Solutions for SDS-PAGE, 2D-PAGE, staining, and destaining of the gels.
4. PBS.
5. Low-fat milk powder.
6. Tween-20.
7. Equipment includes vertical electrophoresis apparatus, tube gel adaptator, and glass tubes for isoelectrofocusing, nitrocellulose membrane, blotter unit.

2.10.4. Fluorography and Drying

1. Stock solution of 1*M* sodium salicylate in H_2O.
2. 3MM Chromatography paper from Whatman, Saran wrap, Kodak X-Omat AR-5 film.
3. Equipment includes gel dryer and X-ray cassettes.

2.11. Quantifications

2.11.1. Pronase Elution of Proteins from Polyacrylamide Gels

1. Swelling solution: 10% (v/v) acetic acid, 30% (v/v) methanol in H_2O.
2. Pronase solution: Pronase (20 μg/mL) in 50 m*M* $(NH_4)HCO_3$. Add trace of phenol red.
3. Liquid scintillation cocktail.
4. Equipment includes 20-mL glass scintillation vials and a liquid scintillation counter.

2.11.2. Determination of the Efficiency of the Cell-Free Reaction

Materials are those described in **Subheading 2.11.1.**

3. Methods

3.1. Cell Culture of PC12 Cells (see Note 1)

In standard protocols, two 15-cm dishes are used per experimental condition when subcellular fractionation is performed. When kinetics of intracellular transport or of release of secretory proteins are analyzed, 3.5-cm diameter dishes are routinely used.

3.1.1. Standard Culture Conditions

Culture PC12 cells in growth medium in a humidified incubator at 37°C and 10% CO_2 (*see* **Note 1**).

3.1.2. Subculture

1. Use aseptic conditions. Warm all solutions to 37°C.
2. Remove growth medium and wash cells twice with 10 mL of PBS$^-$.
3. Replace wash by 5 mL of trypsin/EDTA solution and leave dishes in hood for ≈5 min, until patches of cells are rounded up or start to detach.
4. Hit the flask against the palm of your hand to help cells to detach from the plastic. Achieve detachment by pipeting up and down to the plastic support cell suspension with a 10-mL pipet.
5. Collect cell suspension in a 50-mL plastic tube and wash dish with 10 mL of growth medium. Collect and add wash to cell suspension.
6. Centrifuge cell suspension for 5 min at 200*g* and room temperature.
7. Aspirate supernatant and gently resuspend cells in ≈2 mL of growth medium with a flamed Pasteur pipet to get rid of clumps of cells (10–12 passes).
8. Dilute cells with growth medium to the required volume (50 mL per 175-cm^2 flask, 40 mL per 150-cm dish, and 2.5 mL for 3.5-cm dishes).
9. Seed dishes and put them in the incubator.

3.2. Metabolic Labeling of PC12 Cells (see Notes 2–10)

Although two 15-cm dishes are used per experimental conditions when subcellular fractionation is performed, typically only one is labeled. Volumes given below are for a 15-cm dish (*see* **Note 2**). For a 3.5-cm dish, only the volume of the labeling medium is reduced to 1 mL (*see* **Subheading 3.2.3.**). Use sterile conditions for incubations over 4 h. All solutions are prewarmed to 37°C.

3.2.1. RER Labeling with [^{3}H]Tyrosine

A short pulse (2–5 min) with radioactive amino acids labels newly synthesized proteins in the cell. In the case of the granins, tyrosine labeling has been chosen, since this amino acid is well represented and is the only one present in identical amounts in both mature CgB and SgII. Therefore, a direct comparison of the amount of these two proteins in PC12 cells is possible.

1. Remove growth medium and briefly wash cells twice with 10 mL of tyrosine-free DMEM.
2. Replace wash by 20 mL of tyrosine-free DMEM and preincubated for 30 min in incubator (*see* **Note 3**).
3. Aspirate preincubation medium and add 8 mL of fresh tyrosine-free DMEM containing 50 (5-min pulse) to 100 μCi/mL (2-min pulse) [^{3}H]tyrosine to the cells. Further incubate for 2 or 5 min in the incubator on a rocking platform (*see* **Note 4**).
4. Short chase (optional): Rapidly aspirate labeling medium, replace with 40 mL of chase medium and further incubate at 37°C for 2 min.
5. At the end of the pulse or chase, prepare a PNS from the cells (*see* **Subheading 3.5.1.**) and subject PNSs to subcellular fractionation (*see* **Subheading 3.5.2.**).

3.2.2. TGN Labeling with [^{35}S]Sulfate and Transport of [^{35}S]Sulfate-Labeled Proteins to Post-TGN Vesicles

3.2.2.1. Pulse Labeling of the TGN

Identical to standard protocol (*see* **Subheading 3.2.1.**), but using sulfate-free DMEM (*see* **Notes 3** and **5**), instead of tyrosine-free DMEM. Pulse-labeling of the cells is for 5 min (*see* **Note 6**), using 8 mL (*see* **Note 4**) of fresh sulfate-free DMEM containing 1 mCi/mL [^{35}S]sulfate.

3.2.2.2. In Vivo Transport of [^{35}S]Sulfate-Labeled Proteins to Post-TGN Vesicles

This specific transport step is routinely analyzed by comparing, after subcellular fractionation (*see* **Subheading 3.5.**), the distribution within the sucrose gradient of [^{35}S]sulfate-labeled proteins, prepared either from pulse-labeled cells or from cells pulse-labeled and chased.

1. Pulse-label PC12 cells as described in **Subheading 3.2.2.1.**
2. Following **step 4** of **Subheading 3.2.1.**, incubate a subset of PC12 cell dishes for 15 min in 40 mL of chase medium to chase [^{35}S]sulfate-labeled granins and hsPG from the TGN to ISGs and CSVs, respectively (*see* **Note 7**).
3. At the end of the pulse or chase, prepare a PNS from the cells (*see* **Subheading 3.5.1.**) and subject PNSs to subcellular fractionation (*see* **Subheading 3.5.2.**).

3.2.3. Kinetic Analysis of the In Vivo Transport and Release of [^{3}H]Tyrosine- or of [^{35}S]Sulfate-Labeled Proteins

1. Prepare multiple 3.5-cm dishes of subconfluent cells, one for each chase time-point, for example, 0, 10, 20, 30, and 60 min.
2. Preincubate for 30 min in 2.5 mL of the appropriate depletion medium.
3. Pulse-label cells (each dish separately, *see* **Note 8**) for 5 min with 1 mL of labeling medium, as described in **Subheading 3.2.1.** or **Subheading 3.2.2.1.**
4. Stop labeling of cells that will not be chased, as described in **Subheading 3.4.1.**
5. Chase other cells (*see* **Subheading 3.2.1., step 4**) for the desired time at 37°C using 2.5 mL of the appropriate chase medium.
6. Stop chase as described in **Subheading 3.4.1.** Process media and cells, as described in **Subheading 3.4.2.** for analysis.

3.2.4. Definition of Sulfated Marker Proteins of the Constitutive Secretory Pathway

Since constitutive secretion is inhibited at 20°C *(23)*, the pathway of secretion of the rapidly secreted sulfate-labeled proteins can be further characterized.

1. Following the standard protocol (*see* **Subheading 3.2.3.**), preincubate PC12 cells for 30 min, pulse-label cells for 10 min (*see* **Note 9**), and further incubate cells for 30 or 60 min in chase medium, but all at 20°C, in air and using sulfate-free DMEM and chase medium containing 20 m*M* HEPES-NaOH.
2. Further incubate a separate dish for 30 min at 37°C to resume the secretion of constitutive markers.
3. At the end of the chases, process media and cells, as described in **Subheading 3.4.** for analysis.

3.2.5. Definition of Sulfated Marker Proteins of the Regulated Secretory Pathway

To characterize further sulfated markers of the regulated secretory pathway and their sorting to the storage compartment, fusion of secretory granules with the plasma membrane will be triggered. In PC12 cells, regulated secretion can be induced by K^+ depolarization in the presence of Ca^{2+} (*see* **Note 10**).

1. Pulse-label PC12 for 6h or overnight and chase for 30 to 60 min (*see* **Note 7**).
2. Collect chase medium and replace with fresh chase medium containing either 5 m*M* KCl (control medium) or 55 m*M* KCl (depolarization medium). Further incubate for 15 to 30 min at 37°C.
3. At the end of the chases, process all media and cells as described in **Subheading 3.4.** for analysis.

3.3. In Vivo Treatments of PC12 Cells (see Notes 11–13)

3.3.1. Xyloside Treatment of PC12 Cells

The goal of the treatment with the xylose analog 4-methylumbelliferyl β-D-xyloside (xyloside) is to compensate for the lack of a soluble sulfated marker of the constitutive secretory pathway in a given cell system. Xyloside induces the synthesis of free-sulfated glycosaminoglycan (GAG) chains by the cells. Xyloside-induced free GAG chains have been demonstrated to be a constitutively secreted bulk-flow marker ***(10,24)***. Use xyloside at 1 m*M* final concentration. Add xyloside to growth medium 1.5 h before starting the preincubation step and in all subsequent media used for standard pulse or pulse–chase experiments with radioactive sulfate (*see* **Note 11**).

3.3.2. DTT Treatment of PC12 Cells

DTT is directly added to media (*see* **Note 12**). The standard final DTT concentration in media is 5 m*M*. Equivalent volume of sterile H_2O is added to control cells. When DTT is added a few min before the end of the preincubation period, the volume of the preincubation medium is reduced by one-twentieth, the volume of DTT stock solution or H_2O to be added to the cells. Five or 2.5 min before the end of the preincubation period, add DTT directly to the dish (can be done in the incubator) and further incubate for either 5 or 2.5 min. For pulse-labeling with either [^{3}H]tyrosine or [^{35}S]sulfate and chase, replace medium with appropriate DTT-containing labeling medium and DTT-containing chase medium, respectively (*see* **Note 13**).

3.4. Analysis of Intracellular and Secreted Proteins (see Notes 14–17)

3.4.1. Termination of Labeling and Intracellular Transport of Labeled Proteins

1. At the end of the pulse or the chase, remove dishes from the incubator and place them immediately on a ice-chilled sheet of aluminium.
2. Quickly aspirate medium (keep when appropriate) and add 2.5 mL ice-cold TBSS to the cells (*see* **Note 14**). Wash cells three times with 2.5 mL ice-cold TBSS, the last wash containing 0.5 m*M* PMSF.

3.4.2. Analysis of Protein Secretion After [^{3}H]Tyrosine or [^{35}S]Sulfate Labeling

1. Unless otherwise indicated, all steps will be performed on ice or at 4°C.
2. Centrifuge media for 5 min at 100*g* to remove detached cells and large cellular debris.
3. Collect supernatant in 4- to 5-mL polypropylene tubes and add 10 μg of carrier proteins per mL of medium.
4. Add 100% TCA to reach a final concentration of 10% and incubate 1 h on ice. Alternatively, proteins could be precipitated using acetone (*see* **Subheading 3.7., step 8**).
5. Centrifuge for 15 min at ≥6000*g* (full speed in Heraeus Megafuge, or equivalent).
6. Aspirate supernatant and add ice-cold ethanol/ether solution to protein pellet (at least, same volume as used during TCA precipitation). Vortex and centrifuge as above.

7. Remove supernatant and resuspend protein pellet in either 2 vol H_2O plus 1 vol 3 times concentrated Laemmli sample buffer and boil immediately for 5 min for analysis by SDS-PAGE or, for 2D-PAGE (*see* **Note 15**), in O'Farrell lysis buffer, and incubate 10–15 min at room temperature with agitation (*see* **Note 16**).
8. After washing of the cells with TBSS, add 1 mL of TNTE supplemented with 0.5 m*M* PMSF to the cells. Incubate on ice for 15–30 min.
9. Collect cell lysate in 1.5-mL microtubes.
10. Make a hole in tube caps and boil for 5 min.
11. Centrifuge for 15 min at top speed in an Eppendorf centrifuge.
12. Collect supernatant, referred to as heat-stable protein fraction (HSF), in 1.5-mL tubes. Freeze pellet.
13. Precipitate proteins from HSF using acetone (*see* **Subheading 2.7., step 8**) or TCA-precipitation, following **steps 4–7**, i.e., without addition of carrier protein, and with centrifugation as in **step 11** (*see* **Note 17**).
14. Analyze proteins from medium and HSF of the cells by SDS-PAGE and/or 2D-PAGE, followed by fluorography (*see* **Subheadings 3.10.3.–3.10.4.**).

3.5. Subcellular Fractionation of PC12 Cells (see Notes 18–30)

The following methods describe the preparation of a PNS from two 15-cm dishes (*see* **Note 18**).

3.5.1. Preparation of PNS

1. Unless otherwise indicated, all steps will be performed at 4°C.
2. Terminate labeling or chase of the cells, as described in **Subheading 3.4.1.**, using 10 mL of TBSS per wash.
3. Remove last wash and scrape cells from the dish in 10 mL TBSS containing 0.5 m*M* PMSF, using the flat edge from the silicone stopper of the rubber policeman (*see* **Note 19**).
4. Collect cells in a 50-mL tube and add cells scraped from the second dish.
5. Centrifuge for 5 min at ≈110*g*.
6. Aspirate supernatant and resuspend cells in 1 mL of HB or HBS (*see* **Note 20**) containing 0.5 m*M* PMSF.
7. Transfer cell suspension in a 15-mL tube (*see* **Note 21**) containing 5 mL of HB.
8. Centrifuge for 5 min at ≈550*g*.
9. Aspirate supernatant, estimate weight and volume (typically ≈ 0.2 g) of packed cells and resuspend cells in 1 mL of HB (4–6 passages in a blue tip). If necessary, further dilute cells with HB to reach a final volume equivalent to five times the volume of packed cells (*see* **Note 22**). Check the state of the cells using trypan blue exclusion and phase-contrast microscopy.
10. Pass the cell suspension through a 22-gage needle attached to a 1-mL syringe (usually five to six passes up and down) to obtain a single-cell suspension (*see* **Note 23**). Monitor using trypan blue exclusion and phase-contrast microscopy. Use 5- to 10-µL aliquots in 10- to 20-µL trypan blue.
11. Homogenize cells using a cell cracker *(25)* (*see* **Note 24**). Fill up ice-cold cell-cracker with HB using a 1-mL syringe attached to it (dead volume is ≈400 µL).

Aspirate cell suspension with a second 1-mL syringe and attach it to the cell cracker. Using both syringes, repeatedly force cell suspension through the cell cracker until quantitative breakage of the cells is obtained and nuclei appear free of debris. Usually, 5–6 passes back and forth are required. Monitor breakage every two passes, using trypan blue and phase-contrast microscopy. Collect homogenate and rinse the cell cracker with 1 mL of HB. Pool rinse with homogenate, typically yielding a total volume of 1.6 mL (*see* **Note 25**).

12. Centrifuge homogenate for 10 min at 1000*g* to pellet unbroken cells, large debris, and nuclei. Collect the resulting PNS (*see* **Note 26**) and keep on ice. PNS typically has a volume of 1.4 mL and contains 3–4 mg protein/mL.

3.5.2. Velocity Sucrose Gradient Centrifugation

In velocity sucrose gradient centrifugation, as in differential centrifugation by velocity, enrichment of organelles in a given part of the gradient is largely according to their size. The TGN structures obtained using the above conditions of homogenization are substantially larger than secretory granules and CSVs. Therefore, these different organelles of the secretory pathway can be separated from each other and fractions enriched with TGN vesicles can be prepared with this method. TGN vesicles obtained from PC12 cells pulse-labeled with [^{35}S]sulfate for 5 min were used for the study of granin aggregates in this compartment (*see* **Subheading 3.6.**) and cell-free formation of post-TGN secretory vesicles from the TGN (*see* **Subheading 3.8.**).

1. Prepare a 11.5-mL linear, 0.3–1.2*M*, sucrose gradient buffered with 10 m*M* HEPES-KOH, pH 7.2, in Beckman Ultra-Clear ultracentrifuge tube, using a gradient-forming device and a peristaltic pump. Place 5.5 mL of light sucrose solution in the back chamber of the gradient-forming device. Fill the connection between the two chambers by briefly opening the connection tap. Pour 6 mL of the heavy sucrose solution in the mixing chamber containing a stirring bar. Start to mix and to pump the sucrose into the tube. Open the connecting channel between the two chambers when the heavy sucrose solution has entered a few centimeters of the exit tube (*see* **Note 27**).
2. Carefully load PNS (typically 1.3 mL) on top of the gradient at 4°C (*see* **Note 28**). Balance tubes in pairs, adding a small amount of HB when appropriate.
3. Centrifuge in SW40 rotor for 15 min (*see* **Note 29**) at 4°C, counted from reaching the set speed of ≈110,000*g*, with brake at the end of the run.
4. Collect fractions (1 mL) in microtubes from the top to the bottom of the gradient (*see* **Note 27**).
5. After gentle mixing, withdraw an aliquot (typically 100 μL) from each fraction (*see* **Note 30**), add three times concentrated Laemmli sample buffer, and process samples for SDS-PAGE, followed by fluorography and quantification (*see* **Subheadings 3.10.3.–3.10.4.**, and **3.11.2.**).

3.5.3. Equilibrium Sucrose Gradient Centrifugation

Equilibrium sucrose gradient centrifugation separate organelles according their distinct buoyant density. Since secretory granules are known to have a greater buoyant density than CSVs, this technique provides an excellent follow-up to velocity sucrose gradient centrifugation, in which post-TGN vesicles have already been separated from their donor compartment, to separate CSVs, ISGs, and mature secretory granules from each other. This method was used to analyze the effects of DTT on the sorting of the granins in PC12 cells (*see* **Subheading 3.12.4.**) and is a crucial step in the cell-free assays described in **Subheadings 3.8.–3.9.**

1. Prepare a 9.5 mL linear, 0.5*M* (4.5 mL) to 2.0*M* (5.0 mL), sucrose gradient buffered with 10 m*M* HEPES-KOH (pH 7.2), as described in **Subheading 3.5.2.**
2. Pool from the velocity gradient the remainder of fractions 2 through 4 (*see* **Subheading 3.5.2., steps 4** and **5**), which contain the bulk of CSVs and ISGs. Load pooled material (≈2.7 mL) onto the gradient at 4°C.
3. Centrifuge in SW40 rotor for 5.5 h (minimum time, can be overnight) at ≈100,000*g* and 4°C; decelerate at end of run with brake on.
4. Process gradient as in **Subheading 3.5.2., steps 4–5**, to analyze the distribution of [^{35}S]sulfate-labeled proteins within the gradient by SDS-PAGE, followed by fluorography (*see* **Note 30**).

3.6. Analysis of Regulated Secretory Proteins Aggregates in Compartments of the Secretory Pathway (see Notes 31–35)

1. Prepare TGN vesicles (*see* **Note 31**) from PC12 cells pulse-labeled for 5 min with [^{35}S]sulfate (*see* **Subheading 3.2.2.**), using standard protocol (*see* **Subheading 3.5.1.**), followed by that in **Subheading 3.5.2.**
2. Pool fractions 8–10 of the velocity gradient, which contain the bulk of [^{35}S]sulfate-labeled TGN vesicles. Dilute sucrose slowly with an equal volume of 10 m*M* HEPES-KOH, pH 7.2.
3. Divide suspension into three equal aliquots per gradient and concentrate TGN vesicles by centrifugation at ≈110,000*g* for 15 min using a fixed-angle rotor.
4. Using a 200-μL tip for Pipetman, resuspend pellet in 100 μL of either nonaggregative milieu in the absence (control) or the presence of 0.5 mg/mL saponin (*see* **Note 32**) or aggregative milieu (*see* **Note 33**) containing 0.5 mg/mL saponin (*see* **Note 34**).
5. Incubate for 15 min on ice and centrifuge for 15 min at ≈110,000*g*.
6. Collect supernatant and resuspend pellets in 100 μL of either nonaggregative milieu or aggregative milieu (*see* **Note 35**). Add 50 μL of three times concentrated Laemmli sample buffer to pellet and supernatant samples. Boil immediately and analyze by SDS-PAGE, followed by fluorography (*see* **Subheadings 3.10.3.–3.10.4.**).

3.7. Analysis of the State of Reduction/Oxidation of Disulfide Bonds in Secretory Proteins After DTT Treatment of the Cells (see Note 36)

DTT treatment of PC12 cells induces missorting of the regulated secretory protein CgB to the constitutive pathway of secretion (*see* **Subheading 3.12.4.**). To confirm that modifications of the trafficking of a secretory protein in a given cell system upon DTT treatment is, most likely, caused by reduction of its disulfide bond(s), analysis of the state of the disulfide bond should be performed. Labeling with the alkylating agent NEM allows the detection of the proteins that contained free-sulfhydryl residues. To determine whether, in PC12 cells treated with DTT, the single disulfide bond of the missorted CgB molecules is reduced, NEM labeling was performed on post-TGN vesicles.

1. Incubate PC12 cells (15-cm dishes) for 22.5 min in serum-free DMEM, in the absence or presence of 5 m*M* DTT (*see* **Subheading 3.3.2.**).
2. Prepare PNS from the cells, as described in **Subheading 3.5.1.**
3. Fractionate PNS using velocity followed by equilibrium sucrose gradient centrifugation as described in **Subheadings 3.5.2.–3.5.3.**
4. Separately dilute sucrose in fractions 5–8 of the equilibrium gradient, slowly adding an equal volume of 10 m*M* HEPES-KOH, pH 7.2.
5. Centrifuge each diluted fraction for 30 min at 130,000*g* and 4°C to pellet organelles.
6. Resuspend each pellet in 200 μL of 10 m*M* HEPES-KOH, pH 7.7, and lyse organelles by three cycles of freezing (liquid nitrogen) and thawing.
7. Divide each fraction in two equal aliquots and incubate for 10 min at room temperature in the absence or presence of 5 m*M* DTT (*see* **Note 36**).
8. Remove DTT by precipitating proteins overnight using 80% (v/v) acetone (final concentration) at –20°C. Centrifuge for 15 min at ≥6000*g* and 4°C; discard supernatant.
9. Resuspend proteins by pipeting in 175 μL of 10 m*M* HEPES-KOH, pH 7.7, add 5 μCi of [^{3}H]NEM stock in pentane, and incubate for 15 min at 0°C.
10. Stop reaction by adding 20 μL of 100 m*M* DTT on ice.
11. Precipitate proteins as in **step 8** and subject samples to SDS- or 2D-PAGE analysis, followed by fluorography (*see* **Subheadings 3.10.3.–3.10.4.**).

3.8. Cell-Free Formation of Immature Secretory Granules and Constitutive Secretory Vesicles (see Notes 37–40)

To understand the molecular mechanisms underlying the formation of ISGs and CSVs from the TGN of PC12 cells, a cell-free system reconstituting this crucial step of the secretory pathway has been developed ***(12)***. Cell-free systems provide unique access to biochemical events controlling vesicular transfer between cellular compartments since transport assays can be done in a controlled manipulable environment. Parameters like time-, temperature-, energy-, and cytosol-dependence can easily be assessed. Moreover, addition of drugs and antibodies allows the molecular dissection of the process under study. Prerequisites for reconstitution of a given transport step are the following. First, functional organelles must be obtained in a more or less pure form. Second, specific markers should be available to monitor the transport between donor and acceptor, or "newborn," compartments, as is the case for post-TGN vesicles. Third, one should be able to follow the transport to the target organelle, i.e., to be able to discriminate marker molecules that are still in the donor compartment from those that have reached the downstream compartment after transport has occurred. This can be achieved using a biochemical modification of the transported molecule, which can only occur in the acceptor compartment. Alternatively, a physical separation of donor and target organelle can be used. In the following procedure, reconstitution of the budding of post-TGN vesicles is based on the ability to monitor by physical methods the transport of [^{35}S]sulfate-labeled SgII and hsPG from the TGN of PC12 cells to ISGs and CSVs, respectively, using the subcellular fractionation methods described in **Subheading 3.5.**

1. Pulse-label PC12 cells for 5 min with [^{35}S]sulfate to selectively label proteins in the TGN.
2. Prepare PNS from pulse-labeled cells (*see* **Subheading 3.5.1.**).
3. Supplement 1.25 mL of the PNS at 4°C with 25 μL of 1 m*M* PAPS (optional, *see* **Note 37**), 25 μL of 10 m*M* Mg acetate, and 50 μL of ATP and an ATP-regenerating system (*see* **Note 38**). Mix briefly by flicking with fingertip.
4. Incubate supplemented PNS at 37°C for 60 min without further agitation (keep control for the same time at 0°C; *see* **Note 39**).
5. Put sample on ice and fractionate PNS using velocity centrifugation (to separate TGN from ISGs and CSVs), followed by equilibrium centrifugation (to separate ISGs from CSVs), as described in **Subheadings 3.5.2.–3.5.3.**
6. Subject aliquot from each fraction to SDS-PAGE, followed by fluorography (*see* **Subheadings 3.10.3.–3.10.4.**), and determine efficiency of cell-free reaction, as described in **Subheading 3.11.2.** (*see* **Note 40**).

3.9. Cell-Free Binding Assay to Reconstitute γ-Adaptin Binding to Immature Secretory Granules (see Notes 41–45)

3.9.1. Preparation of Bovine Brain Cytosol

(Adapted from **ref.** ***26***.)
(*See* BSE "Caution" note on p. 283 [Note 1].)

1. Remove all meninges, blood vessels, and the cerebellum, while the brain is left on ice. Cut into large pieces. Estimate volume in beaker.
2. Add an equal volume of HB with protease inhibitors to brain.
3. Homogenize in Waring blender, with three 20-s bursts at maximum speed.
4. Centrifuge homogenate for 50 min at 20,000*g* and 4°C. Collect supernatant.
5. Centrifuge supernatant for 60 min at 100,000*g* and 4°C. Collect supernatant.
6. Dialyze supernatant overnight at 4°C against HB without protease inhibitors, with one change of buffer after 4 h.
7. Remove small aliquot (250 μL) for protein assay. Aliquot in 1-mL aliquots, freeze, and store in liquid nitrogen.

3.9.2. γ-Adaptin Binding Assay

1. Thaw rapidly three 1-mL aliquots of ISG stock (*see* **Note 41**) and transfer to ice.
2. Thaw rapidly one aliquot of bovine brain cytosol and transfer to ice. Pretreat as in **Note 42**.
3. Pipet 125 μL of ISGs into 1.5-mL microtube on ice for each reaction.

4. Add pretreated bovine brain cytosol to a final concentration of 2 mg/mL.
5. Add 8.3 µL of an ATP-regenerating system (*see* **Subheading 2.8.**) or H_2O.
6. Include additional reagents, such as GTPγS (final concentration of 100 µ*M*; *see* **Note 43**).
7. Add 10X BB to give 1X BB and adjust volume to 250 µL with H_2O.
8. Incubate for 30 min at 4°C on ice, or at 37°C.
9. Add 750 µL of ice-cold 1X BB to stop reaction and dilute sucrose.
10. Pellet ISGs by centrifugation for 60 min at 120,000*g* and 4°C in a TLA-45 rotor (45,000 rpm), using a TL-100 tabletop ultracentrifuge.
11. Pellets are resuspended in 20 µL of Laemmli sample buffer.
12. Solubilized proteins are electrophoresed in SDS-polyacrylamide minigels (7.5%), and then transferred to nitrocellulose membrane.
13. The exogenous γ-adaptin bound to ISGs is detected by incubation of the nitrocellulose filters with a primary antibody (*see* **Note 44**), followed by a rabbit-antimouse IgG serum for 1 h, and by incubation with 0.4 µCi [^{125}I]-protein A/mL in TBS/0.5% Tween-20 for 1 h, all at room temperature. The nitrocellulose filters are washed in TBS/0.2% Tween-20, air-dried, and exposed to film (Kodak XAR-5) at room temperature for 18 h.
14. Develop film and quantitate the γ-adaptin band (*see* **Note 45**).

3.10. Analytical Methods (see Notes 46–53)

3.10.1. Sialyltransferase Assay

1. Prepare Golgi membranes, or fractions containing Golgi membranes, isolated from sucrose gradient, as described in **Subheading 3.5.**, at a minimum concentration of 3.0 mg/mL (*see* **Note 46**).
2. Prepare substrate solution by mixing cold CMP-SA with [^{3}H]-CMP-SA, lyophilize, and resuspend in H_2O to allow for addition of 5 µL of 0.64 m*M* CMP-SA containing 0.1 µCi [^{3}H]-CMP-SA per assay.
3. Mix together stock solutions to obtain, in 50 µL, a final concentration per assay of: 0.5% Triton X-100, 50 m*M* Na-cacodylate, pH 6.6, 5 mg/mL asialofetuin, 5 µL [^{3}H]-CMP-SA solution, 100 µg of Golgi membranes. Adjust volume to 50 µL with H_2O.
4. Let sit on ice for 15 min, then transfer to 37°C for 30 min.
5. Add 500 µL 20% TCA, 1.0% PTA. Let sit for 30 min at 4°C.
6. Spin for 10 min at 14,000*g* and 4°C.
7. Wash pellet two times with 500 µL 20% TCA, 1.0% PTA, by resuspension with blue tip and centrifugation for 3 min at 14,000*g*.
8. Dissolve pellet in 500 µL tissue solubilizer by vigorous shaking at room temperature (*see* **Note 47**).
9. Quantitate [^{3}H]-CMP-sialic acid incorporation into asialofetuin by scintillation counting (*see* **Note 48**).

3.10.2. Protease Protection Assays

1. Mix together the vesicle suspension with dibucaine at a final concentration of 1 m*M* (*see* **Note 49**). Incubate for 5 min at 4°C. Divide into four aliquots.

2. Add 20% Triton X-100 to a final concentration of 0.3% to two samples (*see* **Note 50**). The other two receive the identical volume of H_2O. Vortex briefly.
3. Add 2 m*M* PMSF to one sample with Triton X-100 and one without Triton X-100 (*see* **Note 51**), mix briefly, then to all samples add a final concentration of 0.1 mg/mg proteinase K (*see* **Note 52**). Incubate 30 min at 4°C.
4. Add 2 m*M* PMSF to the samples that did not receive any PMSF in **step 3**; mix briefly.
5. Add three times concentrated Laemmli buffer to all samples, immediately boil for 5 min (*see* **Note 53**), then analyze the samples by SDS-PAGE.

3.10.3. SDS-PAGE, 2D-PAGE, and Immunoblotting

SDS-PAGE is performed according to Laemmli ***(27)***, using 18.50 × 21.50 × 0.15 cm size gel. For analysis of the granins we use 7.5% gels. This gel system gives a good separation of proteins in the M_r-range of 40–120 kDa. When analyzing samples containing [^{35}S]sulfate-labeled GAG chains, use 15% gels and omit staining and destaining steps. Fix gels for two periods of 10 min in 50% methanol, 10% acetic acid solution. For fluorography, replace **step 2** of **Subheading 3.10.4.** by a brief rinse in H_2O. Basically, 2D-PAGE is performed according to O'Farrell ***(28)***. For good resolution of the granins, we use a mixture of Ampholines, pH 3.5–5.0 (2.0% [v/v]), Ampholines, pH 5.0–7.0 (2.5% [v/v]), and Ampholines, pH 3.5–9.5 (2.5% [v/v]). For immunoblotting, we use the procedure of Burnette ***(29)***, except that blocking of the nitrocellulose sheet is in PBS containing 10% low-fat milk powder for 2 h. Immunoreactive proteins are revealed with ^{125}I-protein A and autoradiography using Kodak X-Omat AR-5 film at –80°C.

3.10.4. Fluorography and Drying

Impregnation of gel with enhancers dramatically reduces exposure time during autoradiography. Several commercial solutions are available. A cheap alternative, which we find as effective, involves incubation of the gel in a solution of 1*M* sodium salicylate ***(30)***.

1. Fix, stain, and destain gel.
2. Incubate the gel 2 × 15 min (can be reduced for thinner gels) in H_2O.
3. Soak gel for 30 min in ≈100 mL of 1*M* sodium salicylate, pH ≈7.0.
4. Transfer gel onto two layers of filter paper (3MM chromatography paper from Whatman). Cover gel with Saran wrap.
5. Dry the gel at ≈70–80°C under vacuum.
6. Expose dried gels to X-ray film (e.g., Kodak X-Omat AR-5) at –80°C in an X-ray cassette.
7. After exposure, develop the film.

3.11. Quantifications (see Note 54)

To quantitate the radioactivity present in [^{3}H]tyrosine-labeled CgB and SgII, or in [^{35}S]sulfate-labeled SgII and hsPG, the appropriate band from the polyacrylamide gel was quantified by liquid scintillation counting after pronase digestion (*see* **Subheading 3.11.1.**). In some experiments, [^{35}S]sulfate-labeled CgB, SgII, hsPG, and GAG chains were quantified by densitometric scanning of fluorograms. 2D-gel pieces were also treated with pronase to estimate the radioactivity present in [^{3}H]NEM-labeled CgB or in [^{35}S]sulfate-labeled CgB, SgII, and hsPG.

3.11.1. Pronase Elution of Proteins from Polyacrylamide Gels

Amount of a given protein in sample can be accurately quantified by counting the radioactivity contained in that protein after separation by SDS-PAGE or 2D-PAGE. The starting material is therefore protein contained in a single band or spot from fixed polyacrylamide gel. To avoid quenching by the gel itself during scintillation counting, the protein is eluted from the piece of gel prior to counting. Protease are allowed to diffuse into the gel and cleave the protein in peptides, which rapidly diffuse from the gel.

1. Locate the protein of interest according to the Coomassie blue staining or to the autoradiogram.
2. Excise the gel piece that contains the desired protein with a scalpel (try not to take too much paper) and place it in scintillation vial.
3. Swell gel pieces for 30 min in 2–5 mL 10% acetic acid, 30% methanol.
4. Wash three times (10 min each) with 5 mL H_2O.
5. Remove last wash and warm 10 min at 60–80°C to evaporate the remaining acetic acid and methanol.
6. Add 800 µL of pronase solution (*see* **Note 54**). Pronase solution must stay red, i.e., basic (pH 8.0) to be efficient. Incubate for ≈20 h at 37 °C with gentle shaking.
7. Add 10 mL of scintillation cocktail, shake vigorously for 1 h, and cool down to 4°C before counting.

3.11.2. Determination of Efficiency of Cell-Free Reaction

1. After SDS-PAGE followed by fluorography, and using either scintillation counting after pronase digestion of the band of interest or densitometric scanning of the fluorograms, determine the amount of [^{35}S]sulfate-labeled SgII and hsPG present in each fraction of the velocity gradient.
2. Calculate total radioactivity of [^{35}S]sulfate-labeled SgII contained in the TGN fractions by summing up [^{35}S]sulfate-labeled SgII contained in fractions 9–12, which contain the bulk of the TGN vesicles, from a control sample (kept at 0°C).
3. Calculate the sum of [^{35}S]sulfate-labeled SgII contained in fractions 1–4, which contain the bulk of post-TGN vesicles formed in the cell-free assay, from a sample incubated at 37°C.
4. Do the same calculation from a control sample, to subtract background.
5. Estimate cell-free-formed ISGs, expressing the amount (corrected for background) of [^{35}S]sulfate-labeled SgII in fractions 1–4 as percent of total [^{35}S]sulfate-labeled SgII present in the TGN fractions (budding efficiency). Pro-

ceed accordingly for the estimation of the efficiency of CSVs formation after quantitation of the hsPG.

3.12. Results (see Notes 55–57)

3.12.1. Identification of Sulfated Constitutive and Regulated Secretory Protein Markers

Typically, constitutively secreted proteins appear in the extracellular medium after a short chase incubation and are almost completely released during the first hour of chase. The kinetics of their release from the cells, and accumulation in the chase medium are represented by a sigmoid curve. When PC12 cells are pulse-labeled for 10 min with [^{35}S]sulfate and chased, a sulfated component with a diffuse electrophoretic mobility is rapidly released in the chase medium (*see* **ref. *12***, Fig. 1A). This component was shown to be an hsPG, which is sulfated on carbohydrate in the TGN ***(31)***. [^{35}S]sulfate-labeled hsPG is mostly released between 20 and 40 min of chase. Its secretion is reversibly inhibited by incubation at 20°C (*see* **ref. *12***, Fig. 1B). Based on these criteria, the hsPG can thus be considered a sulfated marker of the constitutive secretory pathway in PC12 cells.

Although the hsPG is almost completely secreted within 60 min of chase, virtually no SgII could be detected in the chase medium (*see* **ref. *12***, Fig. 1A). In fact, ≥95% of the granins, CgB and SgII, are retained in the cells over hours. When PC12 cells, labeled for several hours to accumulate [^{35}S]sulfate-labeled granins, are further incubated in chase medium containing 55 m*M* K^+ to induce the fusion of secretory granules with the plasma membrane, release of CgB and SgII is observed (*see* **ref. *12***, Fig. 1C). These results demonstrate that in PC12 cells the granins are sulfated protein markers of the regulated pathway of secretion (*see* **Note 55**).

3.12.2. Analysis of In Vivo Transport of [^{35}S]Sulfate-Labeled Protein Markers to Post-TGN Vesicles Using Subcellular Fractionation

Analysis of this particular transport step is based on the capacity to physically separate TGN and post-TGN vesicles using subcellular fractionation.

3.12.2.1. Analysis of In Vivo Transport of [^{35}S]Sulfate-Labeled Protein Markers to Post-TGN Vesicles: Separation of the TGN and Post-TGN Vesicles Using Velocity Sucrose Gradient Centrifugation

When PC12 cells are pulse-labeled for 5 min with [^{35}S]sulfate and subjected to subcellular fractionation using a velocity-controlled sucrose gradient, vesicles containing the [^{35}S]sulfate-labeled proteins are recovered in the bottom half of the gradient, with the peak in fractions 9 and 10 (*see* **ref. *12***,

Fig. 2A). Consistent with their presence in the TGN, the TGN enzyme marker sialyltransferase cosediments in the same fractions of the sucrose gradient, with the peak in fraction 10 (*see* **ref. *12***, Fig. 3D). When a PNS from PC12 cells, pulse-labeled for 5 min with [^{35}S]sulfate and chased for 15 min, is analyzed as above, vesicles containing the [^{35}S]sulfate-labeled proteins are found in fractions 1–5 of the gradient (*see* **ref. *12***, Fig. 2B). These results suggest that sulfated protein markers of the constitutive and regulated secretory pathway, which have left the TGN during this chase period, are packaged into post-TGN vesicles, the sedimentation of which is much slower than that of the TGN in the velocity gradient. This is supported by a morphological analysis of the TGN fractions and of the fractions present in the top of the gradient. Time-course analysis shows that, during a 5-min chase period, more than 50% of [^{35}S]sulfate-labeled (5-min pulse) SgII and hsPG exit from the TGN and are packaged into post-TGN vesicles (*see* **ref. *12***, Fig. 2C).

3.12.2.2. Analysis of In Vivo Transport of [^{35}S]Sulfate-Labeled Protein Markers to ISGs and CSVs: Separation of ISGs and CSVs by Sequential Velocity and Equilibrium Sucrose Gradient Centrifugation

When PC12 cells, pulse-labeled for 5 min with [^{35}S]sulfate, are chased for 15 min and subjected to velocity centrifugation, separation of vesicles containing [^{35}S]sulfate-labeled hsPG and SgII is often observed, with those containing SgII sedimenting slightly deeper (*see* **ref. *12***, Fig. 2B). Although suggestive, this small separation is not sufficient to prove that protein markers of the constitutive and regulated secretory pathway are packaged into distinct secretory vesicles, namely CSVs and ISGs, following their exit from the TGN. To test this hypothesis, the [^{35}S]sulfate-labeled post-TGN vesicles contained in fractions 2–4 of the velocity gradient are subjected to equilibrium sucrose gradient centrifugation. In this second gradient, separation of post-TGN vesicles into two overlapping populations is observed (*see* **ref. *12***, Fig. 5E). Vesicles containing [^{35}S]sulfate-labeled hsPG peak in fraction 6 (density 1.098 g/mL); those containing [^{35}S]sulfate-labeled SgII peak in fraction 9 (density 1.131 g/mL). Morphological analysis of the organelles present in the latter fraction by electron microscopy shows that they are highly enriched in membrane-bound organelles containing a dense-cored structure, which have the typical morphological appearance of secretory granules (*see* **ref. 12**, Fig.6D). In contrast, membranes obtained from the TGN fractions of the velocity gradient present a tubulovesicular structure characteristic of the TGN (*see* **ref. 12**, Fig 6A–C). These results indicate that upon exit from the TGN, the hsPG and SgII are sorted to, and packaged into, distinct post-TGN vesicles, the ISGs and CSVs, which can be separated from each other because of their different buoyant densities on sucrose gradients.

Thus, pulse-chase labeling of PC12 cells with [^{35}S]sulfate coupled to subcellular fractionation is a means of biochemically identifying and separating the TGN, ISGs, and CSVs from each other. This approach has also been successfully applied to investigate the effect of DTT on the sorting of the granins in PC12 cells (*see* **Subheading 3.12.4.**).

3.12.3. Analysis of Regulated Secretory Proteins Aggregates in the Compartments of the Secretory Pathway

The aims of this study were to determine the parameters involved in the formation of dense-cored aggregates in the TGN and the role of aggregation of regulated secretory proteins in their sorting to secretory granules. An obvious requirement for the analysis of the state of aggregation of a secretory protein in a given compartment is to distinguish, i.e., separate, the soluble and aggregated form of the protein contained in this compartment. A second requirement is to have access to the luminal side of the compartment in order to manipulate the luminal environment and thus identify the parameters involved in aggregation. With these aims, membranes were permeabilized with saponin (saponin-induced permeabilization of membranes is primarily caused by complex formation with membranous cholesterol), so that soluble, but not membrane-bound or aggregated, vesicular proteins can leak out in the incubation medium. Since saponin treatment, in contrast to many other detergents, does not solubilize membranes, organelles remain intact. Therefore, aggregated and soluble proteins can be physically separated using centrifugation. Proteins that are soluble in a given condition of incubation are then recovered from the supernatant; aggregated proteins, which do not leak from the permeabilized organelle, are recovered in the membranous pellet.

To develop such an assay, the first goal is to define conditions for permeabilization by saponin. To define the optimal concentration of saponin (lowest concentration allowing maximal release), one should test permeabilization in conditions in which granins are not aggregated. Since, upon release from the cells, granin aggregates are solubilized, the nonaggregative milieu mimics the conditions encountered in the extracellular space. [^{35}S]sulfate-labeled TGN, obtained by velocity centrifugation, is incubated for 15 min in nonaggregative milieu with increasing concentration of saponin (up to 1 mg/mL), centrifuged, and pellets and supernatant are analyzed by SDS-PAGE. The vast majority of [^{35}S]sulfate-labeled SgII is found in the supernatant upon incubation in the presence of 0.25 mg/mL saponin, and ≥90% of SgII is released when a concentration at ≥0.5 mg/mL is used (*see* **ref. *10***, Fig. 1; **ref. *32***, Fig. 2A). The conditions of permeabilization being defined, we investigated whether a low pH-, high-Ca^{2+} milieu (aggregative milieu), mimicking the conditions believed to exist in the TGN lumen, is sufficient to maintain the aggregation of the granins. When [^{35}S]sulfate-labeled TGN vesicles were permeabilized in aggregative milieu, ≥80% of SgII is recovered in the pellet (*see* **ref. *10***, Fig. 2A and Table I). To confirm that the retention of the granins in the permeabilized TGN incubated in aggregative milieu reflects their aggregated state, morphological analysis was performed using a fraction enriched in ISGs, prepared by differential sedimentation in isotonic sucrose ***(10)***. When ISGs are incubated in the absence of saponin, numerous dense-cored structures, which have the typical morphological appearance of ISGs, are observed (*see* **ref. *10***, Fig. 3, top panels; **ref. *12***, Fig. 6D). Upon incubation in the presence of saponin in the nonaggregative buffer, virtually no dense cores are found (*see* **ref. *10***, Fig. 3, middle panels). Although dense cores observed in samples permeabilized in aggregative buffer appear less electron-dense, they are found at a frequency that is 70% that of the control (*see* **ref. *10***, Fig. 3, bottom panels).

The hypothesis that aggregation of regulated secretory proteins is a sorting event was tested on TGN membranes prepared from PC12 cells treated with xyloside. Since the hsPG was found to be membrane-associated in the TGN (*see* **ref. *10***, Fig. 4A, left), this sulfated marker of the constitutive secretory pathway could not be used in our study. Instead, we investigated whether, xyloside-induced GAG chains, which are sulfated in the TGN ***(31)*** (*see* **ref. *10***, Fig. 4C) and secreted constitutively by PC12 cells (*see* **ref. *10***, Fig. 4B) as for other cells ***(24,33)***, were excluded from granins aggregates. If aggregation of the granins in the TGN, owing to the low pH-, high-Ca^{2+} milieu, is a sorting event, then markers of the constitutive pathway of secretion should be excluded from the aggregates. Consistent with this hypothesis, only a constant small percentage of xyloside-induced GAG chains is found in the pellet after permeabilization of [^{35}S]sulfate-labeled TGN vesicles in both nonaggregative and aggregative milieu (*see* **ref. *10***, Fig. 4D).

To prove that it is the low pH-, high-Ca^{2+} milieu of the TGN that induces aggregation of the granins in the TGN in vivo, we investigated whether the aggregative milieu induces aggregation of the granins in the endoplasmic reticulum (ER). When [^{3}H]tyrosine-labeled ER vesicles are incubated with 1% Triton X-100 in nonaggregative milieu, newly synthesized SgII and CgB (*see* **Note 56**) are found in the supernatant, but virtually all of both proteins are found in the pellet in aggregative milieu (*see* **ref. *10***, Fig 6). This behavior is in contrast to that of acidic resident proteins of the ER, such as the heavy-chain binding protein (grp 78 BiP) and protein disulfide isomerase, which leak out of saponin-permeabilized ER vesicles to the same extend in both conditions of incubation (*see* **ref. *10***, Fig. 5).

Concentration of the granins is an important additional parameter in their aggregation. No aggregation is observed when diluted granins, obtained from TGN fractions permeabilized at pH 7.4 (*see* **ref. *10***, Fig. 2B), are incubated in aggregative milieu. We also observed that, in hormone-treated GH_4Cl cells, the hormones increase the synthesis of the granins and thereby their concentration in the TGN; a greater proportion of SgII in the TGN was recovered in an aggregated state after permeabilization in aggregative milieu than in control cells (*see* **ref. *10***, Fig. 8).

3.12.4. Role of Tertiary Structure of Regulated Secretory Proteins in Their Sorting to the Regulated Secretory Pathway

The aim of this study was to investigate the role of the single, highly conserved disulfide bond of CgB, believed to form an exposed loop structure on its sorting to secretory granules. Although expression of mutated proteins is a very powerful approach to investigate mechanisms of protein sorting and to define sorting domains, this approach may not be ideal to the study of the sorting of endogenous regulated secretory proteins. Since granins are sorted to secretory granules as aggregates, and aggregation may be the first event in sorting, mutation of the disulfide-bonded loop of CgB will not induce missorting of the mutated protein, because it will coaggregate with endogenous normal CgB and be sorted correctly. Therefore, to test if the disulfide-bonded loop of CgB is required for its sorting, one must be able to interfere with its formation in the entire population of CgB molecules. Based on the observation that addition of membrane-permeable thiol-reducing agents to living cells perturbs the formation of disulfide bond in the ER ***(34–37)***, we have tested the effect of DTT on the sorting of CgB in PC12 cells. The presence of SgII in these cells, a granin that lacks cysteine residues and therefore cannot be directly affected by DTT, provides a means to evaluate any indirect effects of DTT on the regulated secretory pathway.

DTT treatment causes the missorting of reduced newly synthesized CgB to the constitutive pathway of secretion. When PC12 cells are preincubated for 2.5 min, pulse-labeled for 5 min with [^{35}S]sulfate, and chased for various times, all in the presence of 5 m*M* DTT, the kinetics of release of [^{35}S]sulfate-labeled CgB and hsPG are similar (*see* **ref. *38***, Fig. 4). Such an effect is not observed for SgII (*see* **ref. *38***, Fig. 4). These results suggest that, upon DTT treatment, newly synthesized CgB is selectively diverted to the constitutive pathway of secretion. To prove this, we investigated whether, in the presence of DTT, [^{35}S]sulfate-labeled CgB is packaged into CSVs at the exit of the TGN. PC12 cells are preincubated for 2.5 min, pulse-labeled with [^{35}S]sulfate for 5 min, and chased for 15 min, a sufficient time-period for sulfated secretory proteins to be packaged into post-TGN vesicles, all in the absence or presence of 5 m*M* DTT. The TGN, CSVs, and ISGs are then prepared from the PNSs using the sequential fractionation protocol. An aliquot of the CSVs and ISGs containing fractions from the equilibrium gradient is analyzed by 2D-PAGE, in order to separate and quantitate the hsPG and CgB. In the absencc of DTT, the hsPG and the granins (CgB and SgII) are resolved into the previously characterized distinct populations, reflecting their packaging into CSVs and ISGs, respectively. In contrast, the profile of the distribution of [^{35}S]sulfate-labeled CgB across the gradient superimposes that of hsPG when DTT is present during pulse and chase (*see* **ref. *38***, Fig. 5, panels D–F, compare open and closed circles). Consistent with these results, we proved that the effect of DTT on the sorting of newly synthesized CgB (*see* **Note 57**) takes place in the TGN (*see* **ref. *38***, Figs. 7 and 8).

To obtain evidence that missorting of CgB to CSVs upon DTT treatment was primarily caused by reduction of its single disulfide bond, labeling with NEM was undertaken. Unlabeled PC12 cells are treated with 5 m*M* DTT for 22.5 min and the proteins present in CSV and ISG fractions are labeled with [^{3}H]NEM, following **Subheading 3.7.** When PC12 cells have been treated with DTT in vivo, a large proportion of the missorted CgB in CSVs is labeled with [^{3}H]NEM before in vitro reduction (*see* **ref. *38***, Fig. 9, panels C and C'). In CSV-containing fraction obtained from control cells, virtually no [^{3}H]NEM-labeled CgB is found, although a small amount of CgB is present in this fraction, as revealed after in vitro reduction (*see* **ref. *38***, Fig. 9, panel A and A'). In contrast, in secretory granule fractions obtained either from control or DTT treated cells, only a minor proportion (compared to the total amount of CgB as revealed by [^{3}H]NEM-labeling after in vitro reduction of the sample) of [^{3}H]NEM-labeled CgB is found (*see* **ref. *38***, Fig. 9, fraction 8). These results show that the disulfide-bonded loop structure of these CgB molecules which are packaged in CSVs upon DTT treatment of PC12 cells, is reduced.

The observed missorting of CgB to the constitutive pathway of secretion could be explained in two ways. First, the reduced CgB molecules could escape the sorting mechanism, because they are not capable of undergoing aggregation in the TGN. Second, the CgB with a reduced disulfide bond does form aggregates upon arrival in the TGN; but this form is not capable of interacting with the membrane of the TGN in order to be sorted and packaged in ISGs. Using saponin permeabilization of TGN vesicles prepared from DTT-treated cells, we have shown that the reduced CgB undergoes low-pH-, high-calcium aggregation in the TGN to the same extent as in control cells (*see* **ref. *39***, Table 1). These results support the hypothesis that the missorting of reduced CgB is not caused by the incapability of CgB to aggregate, but rather suggests that the disulfide-bonded loop of CgB has a critical role in the sorting of the granin aggregates.

3.12.5. Cell-Free Formation of ISGs and CSVs

To investigate the mechanisms and molecules involved in the formation of post-TGN vesicles from the TGN, a cell-free assay reconstituting this step in vitro has been developed. The analysis of the post-TGN vesicles formed in vitro is based on the ability to monitor the transport of [^{35}S]sulfate-labeled hsPG and SgII from the TGN to CSVs and ISGs, respectively, using the fractionation methods described above.

A PNS is prepared from PC12 cells pulse-labeled for 5 min with [^{35}S]sulfate and supplemented with ATP, an ATP-regenerating system, and PAPS. When such a PNS is kept on ice for 60 min and subjected to velocity centrifugation, [^{35}S]sulfate-labeled hsPG and SgII are found in the TGN fractions (*see* **ref. *12***, Fig. 3A and C). Upon incubation at 37°C, the labeled proteins are found in the post-TGN vesicle fractions (*see* **ref. *12***, Fig. 3B and C). The efficiency of the in vitro reaction is in the 30–40% range. The shift of [^{35}S]sulfate-labeled proteins within the gradient is neither caused by fragmentation of the TGN nor by lysis of the TGN followed by release of soluble hsPG and SgII. After 60 min incubation at either 0 or 37°C, sialyltransferase remains in TGN fractions (*see* **ref. *12***, Fig. 3D), and [^{35}S]sulfate-labeled hsPG and SgII present in fractions 2–5 of the velocity gradient are resistant to proteinase K digestion in the absence of detergent (*see* **ref. *12***, Fig. 4, panel in vitro). Finally, after equilibrium centrifugation, the post-TGN vesicles formed in vitro are resolved into two distinct populations (*see* **ref. *12***, Fig. 5C and D) presenting a bell-shaped distribution very similar to that of ISGs and CSVs formed in vivo (*see* **ref. *12***, Fig. 5E). This indicates that sorting of secretory proteins upon exit from the TGN and formation of post-TGN vesicles, is reconstituted during the cell-free reaction.

Using this cell-free assay, it is possible to investigate the effect of different factors on the formation of post-TGN vesicles. Comparison of the efficiency of formation of the ISGs and CSVs, either in the presence of ATP and an ATP-regenerating system or in the presence of hexokinase and glucose to deplete ATP shows that formation of both classes of post-TGN vesicles is dependent on ATP (*see* **ref. *12***, Fig 7). Similarly, addition of GTPγS (1 μ*M*) to the cell-free reaction revealed the requirement for GTP in post-TGN vesicle formation ***(13)***. Consistent with this observation, it has been shown that both inhibitory and stimulatory heterotrimeric G proteins regulate the formation of CSVs and ISGs (for review, *see* **ref. *40***). Addition of $[AlF_4]^-$ ***(14)*** and mastoparan ***(41)***, a peptide that mimics an activated receptor and stimulates nucleotide exchange on αi/αo, inhibits cell-free vesicle formation. On the other hand, formation of CSVs and ISGs are stimulated by addition of purified G protein βγ-subunits from bovine brain to the cell-free reaction mixture ***(14)***.

3.12.6. Maturation of Secretory Granules in PC12 Cells

3.12.6.1. Density and Size Comparison of ISGs and Mature Secretory Granules

Pulse–chase labeling, coupled to subcellular fractionation of PC12 cells, has allowed the identification and characterization of the regulated secretory vesicles that bud from the TGN. These TGN-derived vesicles, referred to as ISGs, differ in several characteristics from mature secretory granules. Conversion of ISGs to mature secretory granules has been studied using subcellular fractionation.

When PC12 cells, pulse-labeled with [^{35}S]sulfate for 5 min are chased from 15 min to 2 h and subjected to velocity sucrose gradient centrifugation, [^{35}S]sulfate-labeled SgII gradually migrate more deeply into the sucrose gradient. When the distribution of [^{35}S]sulfate-labeled SgII across the gradient is compared after 15 min and 2 h chase, the peak of [^{35}S]sulfate-labeled SgII shifts by one fraction toward the bottom of the tube, ISGs peaking in fraction 3 and mature secretory granules peaking in fraction 4 (*see* **ref. *15***, Fig. 1). Confirming these results, when PC12 cells are labeled for 6 h and chased overnight, both SgII and CgB peak in fraction 4–5 (*see* **ref. *15***, Fig. 2B). Although, in the velocity sucrose gradient, separation of organelles is largely according to their size, the fact that mature secretory granules migrate more deeply in the velocity gradient than ISGs can also be explained by an increase in density, or both size and density. To discriminate between these possibilities, the sedimentation of ISGs and mature secretory granules was compared using sequential-velocity and equilibrium-gradient centrifugation. Following centrifugation, the peak of [^{35}S]sulfate-labeled ISGs is found in fraction 8, and the peak of mature secretory granules is found in fractions 9 and 10 (*see* **ref. *15***, Fig. 2D). The buoyant densities measured in the hypertonic sucrose gradient are 1.148 g/cm^3 and 1.178 g/cm^3 for ISGs and mature secretory granules, respectively. Since secretory granules approximate membrane-bonded spheres, the observed increase in density during maturation could reflect either an increase in the density of the material packaged in these spheres or an increase in their size, the density of the packaged material staying constant by unit of volume. To discriminate between these two possibilities, a morphological analysis of the organelles present in ISG-containing and mature secretory granule-containing fraction was undertaken. Relevant fractions were pooled and processed for thin section. EM observation revealed that both preparations were enriched in dense-cored vesicles, but of distinct mean diameters (*see* **ref. *15***, Fig. 2, panels E and F). Measurement of the size of the dense cores from micrographs of the secretory granules preparations gives a mean diameter of ≈80 nm for ISGs and ≈120 nm for mature secretory granules (*see* **ref. *15***, Table I). These results show that, during conversion of ISGs to mature secretory granules, the size of the regulated secretory vesicles increases. Although not proven, such an increase in size would correspond to the fusion of ≈4 ISGs during biogenesis of mature secretory granules. These results were confirmed using an independent approach based on sedimentation rates through isosmotic medium ***(15)***.

3.12.6.2. Cell-Free Assay for the Reconstitution of Adaptor Complexes Binding to ISGs

To demonstrate biochemically that ISGs can bind components of a clathrin-coat, a reconstitution assay was used. ISGs, isolated from PC12 cells using the sequential velocity and equilibrium sucrose gradients, were incubated at 37°C with cytosol from an exogenous source, bovine brain. The binding of the clathrin-coat components was monitored by detection of the AP-1 complex-specific component γ-adaptin. Binding of γ-adaptin to ISGs was shown to be ATP-independent, but increased by the addition of GTPγS. The addition of other nucleotides (GTP, ATPγS) had no effect on the binding. AP-1 is the adaptor complex that is believed to mediate the binding of clathrin to the TGN, and the binding of AP-1 to the TGN was known to have the same features as were identified for γ-adaptin binding to ISGs. Other experiments confirmed the specificity of the γ-adaptin binding to ISGs ***(20)***. Most importantly, mature secretory granules were found not to bind γ-adaptin, suggesting that the γ-adaptin binding protein is either inactive, or not present, on the mature secretory granule. With this assay, it has been possible to begin to dissect the components involved in the binding by the addition of fractions from cytosol and recombinant proteins. So far, ADP-ribosylation factor (ARF), a small mol-wt GTP-binding protein, has been shown to be required for γ-adaptin binding to ISGs. ARF is also required for γ-adaptin binding to TGN membranes. The data generated using this reconstitution system support the hypothesis that ISGs undergo membrane remodeling events during maturation that may be concomitant with ISG-ISG fusion.

3.12.7. Conclusions

From the above results, it is clear that [^{35}S]sulfate labeling, coupled to subcellular fractionation, is a very powerful approach to study multiple aspects of the sorting of secretory proteins to the regulated pathway of secretion and the biogenesis of secretory granules.

The final sorting step underlying the sorting of aggregated regulated secretory proteins to secretory granules, however, has yet to be established. In other words, the molecular basis for the recognition of aggregated proteins by the TGN membrane has to be elucidated. Further study of the association between regulated secretory proteins and membrane-associated proteins is needed to gain new insights into this sorting step. The question of the sorting of newly synthesized membrane proteins to secretory granules remains open. Full understanding of this specific sorting process has been delayed because of a very low protein content in secretory granule membranes, and because of the fact that none of the proteins studied so far have been shown to be unique to secretory granule membranes; each exhibits a distinct distribution also in nongranule membranes, such as those of the endocytic compartment.

Another black box concerns the mechanisms involved in the maturation of ISGs (or, in certain cell types, condensing vacuoles) to mature secretory granules. Depending on the cell type, mature secretory granules differ from ISGs, being either larger or smaller. In the former case, fusion between ISGs has been hypothesized. In the latter case, further condensation of the granular content has been implicated. In both cases, vesicular budding from the maturing secretory vesicles is needed during maturation. The study of the role of clathrin-coated patches on ISGs may provide new insights into this maturation process.

4. Notes

4.1. Cell Culture

1. Since PC12 cells grow in clumps that have the tendency to detach from the dish when they approach confluency, pass or use them when they reach ≈80% confluency. This is achieved by subculturing the cells (*see* **Subheading 3.1.2.**) once a week at ≈1:6 (surface area) dilution, e.g., six 15-cm diameter Petri dishes and one 175-cm^2 flask from one subconfluent 175-cm^2 flask, and using them 5–7 d after plating. Medium change during growth is not essential, although, if cell density is low, renewing the medium could help to reach the desired confluency on the planned day of experiment. It is not recommended to use PC12 cells beyond passage 18.

4.2. Metabolic Labeling

2. In order to save medium and radioactivity, in certain steps, the volume of incubation is reduced, compared to the volume of growth medium.
3. The rationale for the preincubation step in either tyrosine- or sulfate-free DMEM (*see* **Subheadings 2.2.1.** and **2.2.2.1.**) is to deplete the intracellular pool of tyrosine or inorganic sulfate, respectively. Reduced concentration of phenylalanine is used since this amino acid is the precursor of tyrosine. Reduced concentration of methionine and cysteine is necessary, since inorganic sulfate generated by their oxidation could partially compensate for the depletion of inorganic sulfate, decreasing the incorporation of radioactive sulfate in proteins *(42)*.
4. In order to use smaller amounts of radioactive tyrosine or sulfate, the volume of medium is reduced during the labeling step. Therefore, rocking of the dishes is required to expose the entire cell layer to labeling medium and to avoid drying of part of the cells.
5. Sulfate labeling of proteins is very efficient in DMEM. For unknown reasons, it does not work properly in certain other mediums; e.g., RPMI. Do not add penicillin-streptomycin because the antibiotic stock contains sulfate.
6. Sulfate uptake, synthesis of 3'-phosphoadenosine 5'-phosphosulfate (PAPS) in the cytosol, and PAPS translocation in the TGN are known to take ≈2 min *(4)*. The effective labeling time, therefore, is ≈3 min.
7. To chase, in vivo, [^{35}S]sulfate-labeled granins from the TGN to mature secretory granules, label PC12 cells with [^{35}S]sulfate (0.2–0.5 mCi/mL) for 6 h or over-

night in 2.5 mL (3.5-cm dish) or 20 mL (150-cm dish) sulfate-free DMEM supplemented with 1% (v/v) horse serum and 0.5% (v/v) fetal calf serum, both dialyzed against PBS to remove inorganic sulfate. Chase-label for 30–90 min in 2.5 mL (3.5-cm dish) or 40 mL (150-cm dish) of chase medium. During this chase period, [^{35}S]sulfate-labeled constitutive proteins are secreted in the extracellular medium.

8. It is convenient to start with the dish that will be chased longer.
9. Incorporation of radioactive sulfate in granins from PC12 cells is reduced by incubation at 20°C. Therefore, the length of the pulse needs to be extended in order to incorporate sufficient radioactivity for the analysis.
10. Depolarization-induced calcium-dependent exocytosis is also known to be inhibited by magnesium ions; e.g., 10 m*M* $MgCl_2$. It is worthwhile to control for the calcium dependence of the release of the various markers, since, at least in PC12, depolarization speeds up constitutive release, but in a calcium independent way. This phenomenon has been observed for the naturally occurring constitutive marker hsPG *(15)* and the xyloside-induced GAG chains (Chanat, unpublished results).

4.3. In Vivo Treatments of PC12 Cells

11. In our system, increased incorporation of [^{35}S]sulfate in GAG chains was observed during the first 30 min of chase, in the presence of both xyloside and twice the normal concentration of cold sulfate.
12. Serum proteins must be omitted during incubation in the presence of DTT, since the reducing agent will reduce disulfide bonds contained in some of these proteins, like serum albumin.
13. The effect of DTT on the exit of sulfated secretory proteins from the TGN to post-TGN vesicles of PC12 cells will be monitored by pulse–chase experiments with [^{35}S]sulfate (*see* **Subheading 3.2.2.2.**) coupled to subcellular fractionation (*see* **Subheading 3.5.**), except that cells will be preincubated for 2.5 min, pulse-labeled for 5 min with [^{35}S]sulfate, and chased for 15 min, all in the absence or presence of 5 m*M* DTT. To determine whether intramolecular disulfide bond(s) of regulated secretory proteins, missorted to CSVs, is reduced upon DTT treatment, NEM labeling of the proteins present in post-TGN vesicles will be performed (*see* **Subheading 3.7.**). In this case, incubate unlabeled PC12 cells in serum-free DMEM, in the absence or presence of 5 m*M* DTT for 22.5 min, during which time regulated secretory proteins reduced in the TGN reach post-TGN vesicles.

4.4. Analysis of Intracellular and Secreted Proteins

14. This rapid cooling of the cells is necessary to stop intracellular transport.
15. Since by SDS-PAGE, CgB cannot be quantitated because of the presence of a hsPG in the same region of the gel (cf. **ref. *10***, Fig. 1, left and **ref. *38***, Fig.1, control panel), samples from cells treated with DTT were analyzed by 2D-PAGE to separate CgB and the hsPG from each other.
16. To allow SDS-PAGE analysis of an aliquot of samples aimed to be analyzed by 2D-PAGE, proteins can be first dissolved in Laemmli sample buffer and boiled.

Proteins in Laemmli sample buffer can then be precipitated with 80% acetone at –20°C (*see* **Subheading 3.7., step 8**). Acetone-precipitated proteins are then redissolved in O'Farrell lysis buffer containing 5% NP40. This alternative protocol also improves solubilization of proteins.

17. An HSF can also be prepared from medium. After centrifugation, add carrier protein, Tween-20 (0.3% final), and EDTA (5 m*M* final) to the medium (note that the medium will become yellow; it turns back to red within a few min of incubation on ice) and process samples, as described for cells (**Subheading 3.4.2., steps 10–14**), except that, because of a higher volume, centrifugation will be at top speed (≥6000*g*) in an Heraeus Megafuge or equivalent.

4.5. Subcellular Fractionation of PC12 Cells

18. Since more than two dishes might be needed for multiple analysis of a single experimental condition, or more than one condition is being analyzed, multiple pools, each one containing the cells from appropriate dishes, should be prepared and separately subjected to homogenization. Note that there are only six buckets on the Beckman SW40 rotor, therefore limiting the number of samples that can be treated in one experiment.
19. Scraping of the cells from the dish leads to permeabilization of ≈20% of the cells as monitored by trypan blue exclusion. Higher damage to plasma membranes should be avoided, since it will result in loss of cytosol during subsequent washes.
20. Passage of the cells from high-salt (TBSS) to low-salt (HB) condition is crucial to avoid aggregation of organelles and therefore their pelleting during velocity sucrose gradient centrifugation. In HB, salts are replaced by sucrose. HB is slightly hyperosmotic and causes slight swelling of the cells, which facilitates homogenization.
21. Weigh tubes in order to estimate, after centrifugation, the recovery of cells from each condition.
22. In concentrated homogenates, organelles can aggregate. This will result in modified sedimentation properties. Therefore, concentration of the homogenate should be in the 10–20% (w/v) range, and should be standardized.
23. Single-cell suspension is a prerequisite for quantitative and reproducible homogenization in the cell cracker.
24. The stainless steel ball homogenizer, or cell cracker, we used is made by the European Molecular Biology Laboratory (EMBL) workshop, based on a design by Balch and Rothman *(43)*. Homogenization in cell cracker is based on the shear forces generated when repeatedly forcing cells between the wall of a small cylinder (diameter 8.02 mm) and a ball of known diameter. For PC12 cells, a clearance of 18 µm is used, when a ball of 8.002-mm diameter is introduced in the cylinder.
25. When PNSs from different experimental conditions have to be prepared, rinse cell cracker two to three times with HB between separate homogenizations.
26. When more than two dishes are used for a single experimental condition, pool the appropriate PNS from separate homogenizations at this step.

27. To form sucrose gradient, we use a Buchler Auto Densi-Flow IIC gradient collector to pump the mixed sucrose solution from the gradient-forming device and to deposit it in the tube. With this apparatus, the outlet of the tube automatically remains just above the level of the solution, while the tube is filled up. Alternatively, this can be done manually. This apparatus is also used to collect fractions after centrifugation. Gradients can be prepare in advance and kept at 4°C for a few hours before loading.
28. Do not decrease the volume of the gradients in order to load more sample. Rather use more gradients for a given condition. Overloading gradients promotes aggregation and causes a decrease in resolution and an increase in contamination of a given band by other organelles.
29. With shorter centrifugation period, the TGN has not yet sufficiently entered the gradient to be efficiently separated from post-TGN vesicles. If centrifugation is too long, post-TGN vesicles, especially mature secretory granules, enter the gradient more deeply, approaching the classical position of the TGN. On the other hand, when few gradients are centrifuged, e.g., two, the set speed is reached faster and therefore the overall centrifugal force applied to the sample is slightly reduced. In this case, centrifugation at nominal speed can be increased by 1–2 min. Although the primary function of the velocity gradient is to separate the TGN from post-TGN vesicles, small separation of CSVs, ISGs, and mature secretory granules in overlapping bands within the gradient is often observed.
30. Aliquots of the fractions can also be processed for protease-protection assays to determine membrane integrity (*see* **Subheading 3.10.2.**), sialyltransferase activity measurements to correlate sulfate labeling with a TGN-marker enzyme (*see* **Subheading 3.10.1.**), and any other types of assays or measurement of activities appropriate for the localization of the various organelles of interest within the gradient. Some assays may required a reduced sucrose content or a concentrated sample. If so, slowly dilute fraction two to three times with gradient buffer and pellet membranes. The morphology of the organelles and assessment of the contaminating structure can be determined by electron microscopy analysis of the fractions of interest. The density profile of the sucrose gradient can be determined after the run by measuring the refractive index of each fraction using a refractometer. Plot refractive index as sucrose concentration.

4.6. Analysis of Regulated Secretory Proteins Aggregates

31. This procedure can also be applied to other compartments of the secretory pathway, such as ER and secretory granules, after appropriate pulse–chase procedure, to study the state of aggregation of the granins and other markers, e.g., heavy-chain binding protein (grp 78/BiP) and protein disulfide isomerase for ER vesicles. In the latter case, prepare a PNS from PC12 cells pulse-labeled for 5 min with [^{3}H]-tyrosine. After fractionation on velocity sucrose gradient, pool fractions 4 and 5, which contain part of the peak of [^{3}H]-tyrosine-labeled granins, but less cytosolic proteins than fractions 2 and 3, and follow **Subheading 3.6., steps 3–6**, but using 1% (w/v) Triton X100 or 1 mg/mL saponin.

32. To define the optimal amount of saponin for quantitative permeabilization, various concentrations of saponin can be used. Depending of the cholesterol concentration of the membrane of the organelles under study (e.g., less in ER; *see* **Note 31**), the saponin concentration required for optimal permeabilization may have to be varied.
33. In the course of our study, we have also studied the effect of pH and Ca^{2+} concentration on aggregation of the granins. Any other ion or solute can be tested using the same procedure. In this case, keep the ionic strength constant using, for example, KCl. For better preservation of the structure of the organelles, 25 m*M* sucrose can be added to these buffers.
34. We add leupeptin at a concentration that is 10,000 times higher than in standard uses. Permeabilization of TGN-vesicles in the presence of high amounts of Ca^{2+} and at acidic pH (aggregative conditions), both factors known to induce proteolytic enzyme activity, lead to the complete digestion of the granins in the incubation medium. Such degradation was not observed in nonaggregative milieu. Therefore, degradation of the granins in our assay is probably caused by the induction of Ca^{2+}-dependent/low pH-induced proteolytic enzymes contained in the TGN-vesicles or in organelles contaminating the velocity gradient fractions we use. Although leupeptin was found to be the best inhibitor of these proteolytic enzymes, such high amounts of this compound was still necessary to efficiently protect the granins from degradation.
35. To analyze the state of aggregation of the granins and GAG chains in the TGN of xyloside-treated PC12 cells, the standard protocol was modified as follows. First, after permeabilization in either nonaggregative or aggregative milieu, a HSF fraction was prepared from pelleted TGN membranes. Second, after electrophoresis, staining and destaining of the gels was omitted to minimize the elution of GAG chains from the gel.

4.7. Analysis of the State of Reduction/Oxidation of Disulfide Bonds in Secretory Proteins After DTT Treatment of the Cells

36. This in vitro reduction allows for quantitation of the total amount of disulfide bound containing protein in the assay.

4.8. Cell-Free Formation of Post-TGN Vesicles

37. PNS could be supplemented with unlabeled PAPS to compete with radioactive PAPS contained in the PNS, following pulse-labeling with [^{35}S]sulfate, and to prevent further labeling of TGN proteins during incubation of the PNS.
38. Various compounds can be added to the reaction mixture in order to obtain more information on the molecular machinery involved in the budding of post-TGN vesicles from the TGN. In order to quantitate the full effect of these compounds, they should be added on ice just before warming the mixture to 37°C. As an example of this type of investigation, ATP and an ATP-regenerating system could be replaced by 50 µL of 10 mg/mL of hexokinase in 0.25*M* D-glucose to analyze the ATP requirements of the reaction. Similarly, the requirement for GTP-binding

proteins can be studied by adding guanine nucleotide and guanine nucleotide analogs like GTPγS. Incubation in the presence of compounds like pertussis and cholera toxin, aluminium fluoride $[AlF_4]^-$ and mastoparan or purified G-protein βγ-subunits from bovine brain has suggested that trimeric G proteins are involved in the regulation of the formation of secretory vesicles from the TGN ***(14,41)***. Finally, a role for protein phosphorylation in this step has also been demonstrated ***(44)***.

39. If multiple cell-free reactions are carried out, but for different periods of time, than at the end of each separate incubation samples are kept on ice until the last sample is stopped. All the samples will then be subjected to velocity centrifugation together.
40. The integrity of the vesicles formed in vitro can be assessed by protease protection assay (*see* **Subheading 3.10.2.**).

4.9. Cell-Free Binding Assay to Reconstitute γ-Adaptin Binding to ISGs

41. 18 mL of ISGs can be prepared from 36 15-cm^2 dishes, snap-frozen in 1-mL aliquots, and stored for up to 6 mo in liquid nitrogen.
42. Cytosol is incubated at 37°C for 30 min, then centrifuged for 60 min at 100,000*g* and 4°C in a TLA-45 rotor (45,000 rpm), using a TL-100 tabletop ultracentrifuge. This pretreatment removes nonspecific aggregates of protein, which may form during the assay incubation at 37°C and then sediment during the subsequent centrifugation step.
43. The amount of exogenous γ-adaptin bound to the ISG at 37°C can be increased by the addition of GTPγS.
44. Exogenous γ-adaptin can be detected using species-specific monoclonal antibody 100/3 ***(45)***. Incubation time (from 1 h to overnight) and temperature (either room temperature or 4°C) should be optimized for all antibodies used.
45. Quantitation of the nitrocellulose can be performed with a Molecular Dynamics phosphorimager.

4.10. Analytical Methods

46. If the membranes are not of sufficient concentration to use in the assay, dilute fraction to a maximum of 10% sucrose with 10 m*M* HEPES, pH 7.2, and centrifuge for 60 min at 100,000*g* and 4°C. Resuspend pellet in 50 m*M* Na-cacodylate, pH 6.6. Golgi membranes may be obtained using other methods.
47. It may require at least 1 h of shaking to dissolve the pellet in tissue solubilizer.
48. To calculate recoveries and specific activity of the membranes, an aliquot of the starting PNS should be saved and used at an appropriate concentration in the linear range of the assay.
49. Dibucaine-HCl, which is believed to act by intercalating in the lipid bilayer, increases the stability of the membrane, which, after the isolation, may be slightly perturbed ***(46)***. The effect of the addition of a solution of 50% ethanol should be controlled.
50. The addition of 0.3% Triton X-100 results in the complete solubilization of most membranes, and thus renders the molecules within the vesicles accessible to pro-

teinase K digestion. Molecules within intact vesicles without Triton X-100 should be resistant to proteinase K.

51. PMSF is added before the proteinase K to prevent any digestion of the molecules in the presence or absence of Triton X-100. This sample serves to ensure that all the samples are chemically identical and should be equivalent to an undigested sample.
52. Proteinase K is used for two reasons: First, it is a very efficient protease that can completely digest most proteins; second, it is very efficiently inhibited by PMSF.
53. Samples must be boiled in Laemmli sample buffer immediately to inactivate the proteinase K and any other protease, and to prevent any artifactual degradation of the samples before electrophoresis.

4.11. Quantifications

54. This method can also be used for estimation of radioactive phosphate in proteins. In the latter case, preincubate pronase solution for 30 min at 37°C to inhibit phosphatases possibly contaminating the pronase stock.

4.12. Results

55. In PC12 cells, storage of regulated secretory proteins is peculiarly efficient. In cells that present a less efficient storage capacity, regulated secretory proteins can still be defined, since their kinetics of appearance in the extracellular medium (basal release) are delayed, compared to kinetics of secretion of true constitutive secretory markers and externalization of the stored regulated secretory proteins does require secretagogs.
56. Since granins (the main secretory proteins in PC12 cells) are synthesized in high amounts, the main [^{3}H]tyrosine-labeled proteins observed after SDS-PAGE analysis of intracellular proteins, pulse-labeled with [^{3}H]tyrosine for 5 min, are CgB and SgII. Newly synthesized CgB has a M_r of ≈100,000. The mature form reaches a M_r of ≈113,000, because of sialylation in the TGN.
57. In contrast to influenza hemagglutinin, for which correct folding, oligomerization, and subsequent exit from the ER is dependent on disulfide bond formation, the tertiary structure of CgB is not critical for its exit from the ER.

Acknowledgments

We are grateful to W. B. Huttner for his support, contributions, unending enthusiasm, and stimulating discussions during the development of many of these methods in his laboratory. We wish to thank U. Weiss for her unsurpassed excellent technical assistance, which, combined with her ability to remain cheerful, made working together a pleasure. Finally, we thank John Tooze for his perseverance and care in reading the manuscript. Further work in this field is supported by the EU-TMR Research Netwoek ERB-FMRX-CT96-0023.

References

1. Moore, H.-P., Gumbiner, B., and Kelly, R. B. (1983) A subclass of proteins and sulfated macromolecules secreted by AtT20 (mouse pituitary tumor) cells is sorted with adrenocorticotropin into dense secretory granules. *J. Cell Biol.* **97,** 810–817.

2. Huttner, W. B., Gerdes, H.-H., and Rosa, P. (1991) Chromatogranins/secretogranins–widespread constituents of the secretory granule matrix in endocrine cells and neurons, in *Markers for Neural and Endocrine cells. Molecular and Cell Biology, Diagnostic Applications* (Gratzl, M. and Langley, K., eds.), VCH, Weinheim, pp. 93–131.
3. Griffiths, G. and Simons, K. (1986) The *trans* Golgi network: sorting at the exit site of the Golgi complex. *Science* **234,** 438–443.
4. Baeuerle, P. A. and Huttner, W. B. (1987) Tyrosine sulfation is a trans-Golgi-specific protein modification. *J. Cell Biol.* **105,** 2655–2664.
5. Farquhar, M. G. (1971) Processing of secretory products by cells of the anterior pituitary gland, in *Sub-Cellular Structure and Function in Endocrine Organs* (Heller, H. and Lederis, K., eds.), Cambridge University Press, Cambridge, pp. 79–122.
6. Farquhar, M. G., Reid, J. J., and Daniell, L. W. (1978) Intracellular transport and packaging of prolactin: a quantitative electron microscope autoradiographic study of mammotrophs dissociated from rat pituitaries. *Endocrinology* **102,** 296–311.
7. Gumbiner, B. and Kelly, R. B. (1982) Two distinct intracellular pathways transport secretory and membrane glycoproteins to the surface of pituitary tumor cells. *Cell* **28,** 51–59.
8. Burgess, T. L. and Kelly, R. B. (1987) Constitutive and regulated secretion of proteins. *Ann. Rev. Cell Biol.* **3,** 243–293.
9. Coll, D. R., Fenger, M., Snell, C. R., and Loh, Y. P. (1995) Identification of the sorting signal motif within pro-opiomelanocortin for the regulated secretory pathway. *J. Biol. Chem.* **270,** 8723–8729.
10. Chanat, E. and Huttner, W. B. (1991) Milieu-induced, selective aggregation of regulated secretory proteins in the *trans*-Golgi network. *J. Cell Biol.* **115,** 1505–1519.
11. Benedum, U. M., Lamouroux, A., Konecki, D. S., Rosa, P., Hille, A., Baeuerle, P. A., Frank, R., Lottspeich, F., Mallet, J., and Huttner, W. B. (1987) The primary structure of human secretogranin I (chromogranin B): comparison with chromogranin A reveals homologous terminal domains and a large intervening variable region. *EMBO J* **6,** 1203–1211.
12. Tooze, S. A. and Huttner, W. B. (1990) Cell-free protein sorting to the regulated and constitutive secretory pathways. *Cell* **60,** 837–847.
13. Tooze, S. A., Weiss, U., and Huttner, W. B. (1990) Requirement for GTP hydrolysis in the formation of secretory vesicles. *Nature* **347,** 207–208.
14. Barr, F. A., Leyte, A., Mollner, S., Pfeuffer, T., Tooze, S. A., and Huttner, W. B. (1991) Trimeric G-proteins of the *trans*-Golgi network are involved in the formation of constitutive secretory vesicles and immature secretory granules. *FEBS Lett.* **294,** 239–243.
15. Tooze, S. A., Flatmark, T., Tooze, J., and Huttner, W. B. (1991) Characterization of the immature secretory granule, an intermediate in granule biogenesis. *J. Cell Biol.* **115,** 1491–1503.
16. Orci, L., Ravazzola, M., Amherdt, M., Madsen, O., Perrelet, A., Vassalli, J.-D., and Anderson, R. G. W. (1986) Conversion of proinsulin to insulin occurs coordinately with acidification of maturing secretory vesicles. *J. Cell Biol.* **103,** 2273–2281.

17. Tooze, J. and Tooze, S. (1986) Clathrin-coated vesicular transport of secretory proteins during the formation of ACTH-containing secretory granules in AtT20 cells. *J. Cell Biol.* **103,** 839–850.
18. Pearse, B. M. F. and Robinson, M. S. (1990) Clathrin, adaptors, and sorting. *Ann. Rev. Cell Biol.* **6,** 151–171.
19. Arvan, P. and Castle, D. (1992) Protein sorting and secretion granule formation in regulated secretory cells. *Trends Cell Biol.* **2,** 327–331.
20. Dittié, A. S., Hajibagheri, N., and Tooze, S. A. (1996) The AP–1 adaptor complex binds to immature secretory granules from PC12 cells, and is regulated by ADP-ribosylation factor. *J. Cell. Biol.* **132,** 1–14.
21. Heumann, R., Kachel, V., and Thoenen, H. (1983) Relationship between NGF-mediated volume increase and "priming effect" in fast and slow reacting clones of PC12 pheochromocytoma cells. *Exp. Cell Res.* **145,** 179–190.
22. Davey, J., Hurtley, S. M., and Warren, G. (1985) Reconstitution of an endocytic fusion event in a cell-free system. *Cell* **43,** 643–652.
23. Matlin, K. S. and Simons, K. (1983) Reduced temperature prevents transfer of a membrane glycoprotein to the cell surface but does not prevent terminal glycosylation. *Cell* **34,** 233–243.
24. Burgess, T. L. and Kelly, R. B. (1984) Sorting and secretion of adrenocorticotropin in a pituitary tumor cell line after perturbation of the level of a secretory granule-specific proteoglycan. *J. Cell Biol.* **99,** 2223–2230.
25. Balch, W. E., Dunphy, W. G., Braell, W. A., and Rothman, J. E. (1984) Reconstitution of the transport of protein between successive compartments of the Golgi measured by the coupled incorporation of N-acetylglucosamine. *Cell* **39,** 405–416.
26. Malhotra, V., Serafini, T., Orci, L., Shepherd, J. C., and Rothman, J. E. (1989) Purification of a novel class of coated vesicles mediating biosynthetic protein transport through the Golgi stack. *Cell* **58,** 329–336.
27. Laemmli, U. K. (1970) Cleavage of structural proteins during the assembly of the head of bacteriophage T4. *Nature* **227,** 680–685.
28. O'Farrell, P. H. (1975) High resolution two-dimensional gel electrophoresis of proteins. *J. Biol. Chem.* **250,** 4007–4021.
29. Burnette, W. N. (1981) Western blotting: electrophoretic transfer of proteins from sodium dodecyl-polyacrylamide gels to unmodified nitrocellulose and radiographic detection with antibody and radioiodinated protein A. *Anal. Biochem.* **112,** 195–203.
30. Chamberlain, J. P. (1979) Fluorographic detection of radioactivity in polyacrylamide gels with the water-soluble fluor, sodium salicylate. *Anal. Biochem.* **98,** 132–135.
31. Kimura, J. H., Lohmander, L. S., and Hascall, V. C. (1984) Studies on the biosynthesis of cartilage proteoglycan in a model system of cultured chondrocytes from the swarm rat chondrosarcoma. *J. Cell Biochem.* **26,** 261–278.
32. Chanat, E. (1993) Mécanisme de tri des protéines sécrétoires et formation des granules de sécrétion dans les cellules neuroendocrines. *C. R. Soc. Biol.* **187,** 697–725.
33. Miller, S. G., Carnell, L., and Moore, H.-P. H. (1992) Post-Golgi membrane traffic: Brefeldin A inhibits export from distal Golgi compartment to the cell surface but not recycling. *J. Cell Biol.* **118,** 267–283.

34. Alberini, C. M., Bet, P., Milstein, C., and Sitia, R. (1990) Secretion of immunoglobulin M assembly intermediates in the presence of reducing agents. *Nature* **347,** 485–487.
35. Braakman, I., Helenius, J., and Helenius, A. (1992) Role of ATP and disulphide bonds during protein folding in the endoplasmic reticulum. *Nature* **356,** 260–262.
36. Braakman, I., Helenius, J., and Helenius, A. (1992) Manipulating disulfide bond formation and protein folding in the endoplasmic reticulum. *EMBO J.* **11,** 1717–1722.
37. Tatu, U., Braakman, I., and Helenius, A. (1993) Membrane glycoprotein folding, oligomerization and intracellular transport: effects of dithiothreitol in living cells. *EMBO J.* **12,** 2151–2157.
38. Chanat, E., Weiß, U., Huttner, W. B., and Tooze, S. A. (1993) Reduction of the disulfide bond of chromogranin B (secretogranin I) in the trans-Golgi network causes its missorting to the constitutive secretory pathway. *EMBO J.* **12,** 2159–2168.
39. Chanat, E., Weiß, U., and Huttner, W. B. (1994) The disulfide bond in chromogranin B which is essential for its sorting to secretory granules is not required for its aggregation in the trans-Golgi network. *FEBS Lett.* **351,** 225–230.
40. Barr, F. A., Leyte, A., and Huttner, W. B. (1992) Trimeric G proteins and vesicle formation. *Trends Cell Biol.* **2,** 91–93.
41. Leyte, A., Barr, F. A., Kehlenbach, R. H., and Huttner, W. B. (1992) Multiple trimeric G-proteins on the trans-Golgi network exert stimulatory and inhibitory effects on secretory vesicle formation. *EMBO J.* **11,** 4795–4804.
42. Baeuerle, P. A. and Huttner, W. B. (1986) Chlorate—a potent inhibitor of protein sulfation in intact cells. *Biochem. Biophys. Res. Commun.* **141,** 870–877.
43. Balch, W. E. and Rothman, J. E. (1985) Characterization of protein transport between successive compartments of the Golgi apparatus: asymmetric properties of donor and acceptor activities in a cell-free system. *Arch. Biochem. Biophys.* **240,** 413–425.
44. Ohashi, M. and Huttner, W. B. (1994) An elevation of cytosolic protein phosphorylation modulates trimeric G-protein regulation of secretory vesicle formation from the trans-Golgi network. *J. Biol. Chem.* **269,** 24,897–24,905.
45. Ahle, S., Mann, A., Eichelsbacher, U., and Ungewickell, E. (1988) Structural relationships between clathrin assembly proteins from the Golgi and the plasma membrane. *EMBO J.* **7,** 919–929.
46. Scheele, G., Jacoby, R., and Carne, T. (1980) Mechanism of compartmentation of secretory proteins: transport of exocrine pancreatic proteins across the microsomal membrane. *J. Cell Biol.* **87,** 611–628.

Index